Lecture Notes in Computer Science 4170

Commenced Publication in 1973
Founding and Former Series Editors:
Gerhard Goos, Juris Hartmanis, and Jan van Leeuwen

Jean Ponce   Martial Hebert
Cordelia Schmid   Andrew Zisserman (Eds.)

Toward Category-Level Object Recognition

Springer

Volume Editors

Jean Ponce
Ecole Normale Supérieure
Département d'Informatique
45 rue d'Ulm, 75230 Paris Cedex 05, France
E-mail: jean.ponce@ens.fr

Martial Hebert
Carnegie Mellon University
The Robotics Institute
Pittsburgh PA 15213, USA
E-mail: hebert@ri.cmu.edu

Cordelia Schmid
INRIA Rhône-Alpes
665, avenue de l'Europe, 38330 Montbonnot, France
E-mail: cordelia.schmid@inrialpes.fr

Andrew Zisserman
University of Oxford
Department of Engineering Science
Parks Road, Oxford OX1 3PJ, UK
E-mail: az@robots.ox.ac.uk

The cover illustration is a detail from the mosaic of Ulysses offering wine to Polyphemus, Villa Romana del Casale, Sicily. Permission to reproduce this detail was kindly granted by the J. Paul Getty Trust. © The J. Paul Getty Trust, 2006. All rights reserved.

Library of Congress Control Number: 2006938342

CR Subject Classification (1998): I.4, I.2.10, I.2.6, I.5.4, F.2.2

LNCS Sublibrary: SL 6 – Image Processing, Computer Vision, Pattern Recognition, and Graphics

ISSN   0302-9743
ISBN-10   3-540-68794-7 Springer Berlin Heidelberg New York
ISBN-13   978-3-540-68794-8 Springer Berlin Heidelberg New York

Springer is a part of Springer Science+Business Media

springer.com

© Springer-Verlag Berlin Heidelberg 2006
Printed in Germany

Typesetting: Camera-ready by author, data conversion by Scientific Publishing Services, Chennai, India
Printed on acid-free paper   SPIN: 11957959   06/3142   5 4 3 2 1 0

Preface

Object recognition —or, in a broader sense, scene understanding— is the ultimate scientific challenge of computer vision: After 40 years of research, robustly identifying the familiar objects (chair, person, pet), scene categories (beach, forest, office), and activity patterns (conversation, dance, picnic) depicted in family pictures, news segments, or feature films is still far beyond the capabilities of today's vision systems. On the other hand, truly successful object recognition and scene understanding technology will have a broad impact in application domains as varied as defense, entertainment, health care, human–computer interaction, image retrieval and data mining, industrial and personal robotics, manufacturing, scientific image analysis, surveillance and security, and transportation.

Although research in computer vision for recognizing 3D objects in photographs dates back to the 1960s, progress has been relatively slow and only now do we see the emergence of effective techniques for recognizing object categories with different appearances under large variations in the observation conditions. While much of the early work relied almost exclusively on geometric methods, modern recognition techniques are appearance-based, in which methods from standard statistical pattern recognition are applied to image descriptors. Tremendous progress has been achieved in the past five years, thanks in large part to the integration of new data representations, such as invariant semi-local features, developed in the computer vision community with the effective models of data distribution and classification procedures developed in the statistical machine-learning community.

This book exemplifies this progress. It is the outcome of two workshops that were held in Taormina in 2003 and 2004, and brought together about 40 prominent vision and machine-learning researchers interested in the fundamental and applicative aspects of object recognition, as well as representatives of industry. The main goals of these two workshops were (1) to promote the creation of an international object recognition community, with common datasets and evaluation procedures, (2) to map the state of the art and identify the main open problems and opportunities for synergistic research, and (3) to articulate the industrial and societal needs and opportunities for object recognition research worldwide.

These concerns are reflected in this book. Collecting all the workshops' contributions into a single book would have been impossible. We chose instead to select a relatively small number of papers that illustrate the breadth of today's object recognition research and the arsenal of techniques at its disposal and that discuss current achievements and outstanding challenges.

The book is divided into five parts. Each part includes a series of chapters written by contributors to the workshops. Most of the chapters are descriptions of technical approaches, intended to capture the current state of the art. Some of the chapters are of a tutorial nature. They cover fundamental building blocks for object recognition techniques.

Part I of the book introduces general background material on the state of object recognition research. We begin with a review of the history of the field, which sets the stage for the more recent developments reported later in the book. We then discuss the need for consistent evaluation procedures and common, challenging, datasets. This is a crucial aspect since, as the field matures, systematic evaluation of the different approaches becomes increasingly important. We conclude Part I with a discussion of the industrial needs and opportunities. As we shall see, the technology has matured to a point at which exciting applications are becoming possible.

Part II focuses on recognizing *specific* objects, an area where significant progress has occurred over the past five years. This is in part due to the advent of effective techniques for detecting and describing image patches with a controlled degree of invariance, together with efficient matching and indexing algorithms that exploit both local appearance models and powerful global geometric constraints arising from perspective imaging. As demonstrated by the five chapters making up this part of the book, reliable methods for localizing specific objects in photographs and video clips despite occlusion, clutter, and changes in viewpoint are now available.

Part III of the book attacks the difficult problem of category-level object recognition. In the methods described in these chapters, object categories are represented by collections of image patches (fixed image windows or invariant patches such as those used in Part II), potentially augmented with weak spatial layout constraints. The emphasis is on the generative or discriminative techniques used to learn the distribution of these features and their relationships, and subsequently used to classify the image instances.

Part IV investigates part-based object models that incorporate stronger structural components in the form of explicit geometric constraints, or tree-structured part assemblies, for example. The emphasis there is on the definition and identification of parts as well as on efficient algorithms for detecting object instances as part assemblies in images.

Finally, Part V of the book is concerned with classifying the image pixels into object foreground vs background (as opposed to simply detecting an object instance). As shown in the chapters making up this part, this process leads to a new, well-posed view of image segmentation incorporating both bottom-up and top-down interpretation processes.

This book is a testimony to the amazing progress achieved in object recognition research in the past five years. But much remains to be done: We can now recognize a limited number of categories in constrained settings (e.g., from particular viewpoints). However, *understanding* an image or video still remains an open problem. We must also improve current datasets and evaluation criteria to avoid toy problems and to allow meaningful comparisons (see the chapter on "Datasets" in Part I, for more on this issue). Further, category-level object recognition is today essentially viewed as a statistical pattern matching problem. The emphasis is in general on the features defining the patterns and the machine-learning techniques used to learn and recognize them, rather than on the representation of object, scene, and activity categories or the integrated interpretation of the various scene elements. Future progress will require explicitly addressing the representational issues involved in object recognition and, more generally, scene understanding. Contextual issues and hierarchical, incremental learning of a large number of categories must also be addressed. Exciting times lie ahead.

Acknowledgments. The two workshops were supported in part by the National Science Foundation under grant IIS-0335780, DARPA, the Institut National de la Recherche en Informatique et Automatique, the PASCAL European Network of Excellence IST-2002-506778, France Telecom, General Electric, Intel, Lockheed Martin, Microsoft Research, Toyota, and Xerox.

October 2006   Jean Ponce
                                                      Martial Hebert
                                                     Cordelia Schmid
                                                   Andrew Zisserman

Table of Contents

IV   Recognition of Object Categories with Geometric Relations

V   Joint Recognition and Segmentation

Part I
Introduction

Object Recognition in the Geometric Era: A Retrospective

Joseph L. Mundy

Division of Engineering,
Brown University
Providence, Rhode Island
mundy@lems.brown.edu

Abstract. Recent advances in object recognition have emphasized the integration of intensity-derived features such as affine patches with associated geometric constraints leading to impressive performance in complex scenes. Over the four previous decades, the central paradigm of recognition was based on formal geometric object descriptions with a focus on the properties of such descriptions under perspective image formation. This paper will review the key advances of the geometric era and investigate the underlying causes of the movement away from formal geometry and prior models towards the use of statistical learning methods based on appearance features.

1 Introduction

Object recognition by computer has been an active area of research for nearly five decades. For much of that time, the approach has been dominated by the discovery of analytic representations (models) of objects that can be used to predict the appearance of an object under any viewpoint and under any conditions of illumination and partial occlusion. The expectation is that ultimately a representation will be discovered that can model the appearance of broad object categories and in accordance with the human conceptual framework so that the computer can "tell" what it is seeing.

Advantages of Geometric Description. From the earliest attempts at recognition, geometric representations have dominated the development of the theory and resulting algorithms and systems. There are a number of reasons why geometry has played such a central role.

- Invariance to viewpoint - Geometric object descriptions allow the projected shape of an object to be accurately predicted under perspective projection.
- Invariance to illumination - recognizing geometric descriptions from images can be achieved using edge detection and geometric boundary segmentation. Such descriptions are reasonably invariant to illumination variations.
- Well developed theory - geometry has been under active investigation by mathematicians for thousands of years. The geometric framework has achieved a high degree of maturity and effective algorithms exist for analyzing and manipulating geometric structures.

J. Ponce et al. (Eds.): Toward Category-Level Object Recognition, LNCS 4170, pp. 3–28, 2006.

– Man-made objects - a large fraction of manufactured objects are designed
  using computer-aided design (CAD) models and therefore are naturally described by primitive geometric elements, such as planes and spheres. More
  complex shapes are also represented with simple geometric descriptions, such
  as a triangular mesh or polynomial patches.

There are, of course, deficiencies of the geometric approach to recognition, but
the discussion of such limitations will be postponed until after a review of the
broad sweep of geometric recognition research over the last four decades.

2   The Beginning

In the 1950s and early 1960s ideas from signal processing and detection theory, such as autocorrelation and template matching, were exploited to form the
first object recognition systems. Much of the research focus was on 2-d pattern
classification applications such as character recognition, fingerprint analysis and
microscopic cell classification. These early decades were dominated by methods
of statistical pattern recognition and perception classifiers based on parametric
learning. Even so, the features used in these classification schemes were often
derived from geometric descriptions. For example, an early approach [34] (1962)
to the definition of features for character recognition was based on geometric
invariance using moments. Geometric invariance will re-appear as a major research thrust in the early 1990s, three decades later. This example illustrates
that recognition ideas are continually re-visited as computational power and
feature segmentation methods advance.

2.1   The Blocks World

The dependence on statistics and signal methods rapidly gave way to the theme
of *artificial intelligence*, coined by Marvin Minsky and John McCarthy around
1956. The new approach focussed on establishing a theoretical framework for
cognitive tasks, such as vision, where computers could carry out the necessary
reasoning using formal logic and other mathematical tools. The plan was to
start with a simplification of the world so that the mathematical models can
apply rigorously and to solve the resulting recognition problem completely before
proceeding to more difficult situations.

For the computer vision problem, this simplification is called *the blocks world*
where objects are restricted to polyhedral shapes on a uniform background.
Polyhedra have simple and easily represented geometry and the projection of
polyhedra into images under perspective can be straightforwardly modeled with
a projective transformation. Under this projection, lines in 3-d map to lines in
2-d and polyhedral faces project to polygons. The goal is to be able to recognize general polyhedral shapes in an arbitrary spatial arrangement including
significant occlusion of one object by itself or others.

The blocks world framework dominated the vision research agenda for over
a decade before it was abandoned to tackle more realistic scenes. It is not that

all the problems of recognizing polyhedral objects and structures made up of polyhedra were definitively and completely solved. Instead it became clear that too many assumptions were being made in recognition strategies that could not be expected to hold in real world scenes. This tension between the desire for a sound theoretical basis for recognition and the ability to confront the complexities of recognizing complex objects such as trees and the human form, will re-immerge repeatedly during the geometric era.

2.2 Roberts and the Blocks World

Perhaps the most complete and powerful recognition system of the blocks world was that of L. G. Roberts [64]. Roberts' recognition algorithm exhibited most of

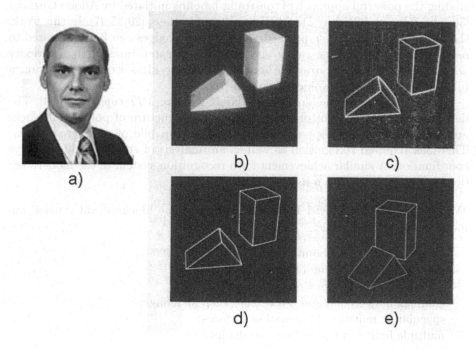

Fig. 1. A system for recognizing 3-d polyhedral scenes. a) L.G. Roberts. b)A blocks world scene. c)Detected edges using a 2x2 gradient operator. d) A 3-d polyhedral description of the scene, formed automatically from the single image. e) The 3-d scene displayed with a viewpoint different from the original image to demonstrate its accuracy and completeness. (b) - e) are taken from [64] with permission MIT Press.)

the steps that are still followed today, some four decades later. He carefully considered how polyhedra project into perspective images and established a generic library of polyhedral components that could be assembled into a composite structure. His philosophy towards recognition is defined by the quote, '... we shall assume that the objects seen could be constructed out of parts with which we are familiar. That is, either the whole object is a transformation (projection [1]) of a preconceived model, or else it can be broken into parts that are. ... The only requirement is that we have a complete description of the three-dimensional structure of each model.'

Roberts developed his own edge detector and line fitting algorithms along with feature grouping heuristics appropriate for polyhedral projections. The feature grouping formed hypotheses for 3-d polyhedral vertices and edges that were validated by solving for the associated projective camera model parameters. Interestingly, his linear resection algorithm is still used to initialize non-linear solvers in modern camera calibration methods. The result of these steps is shown in Figure 1 where the final extracted scene is displayed from a different viewpoint in order to demonstrate the accuracy and completeness of the recognition result.

The constraints of polyhedral scenes were exploited in many different ways including the powerful approach of constraint labeling initiated by Adolfo Guzmán [30] and fully exploited by David Waltz [81] and others [20,35,47]. In this work, the local constraints of the polyhedral vertices and edges can be propagated to neighboring vertices while ruling out multiple interpretations of the convexity and occluding state of projected boundaries. These ideas were later put on a fully algebraic basis by Kokichi Sugihara [76].

The culmination of the blocks world effort was the *MIT copy demo* [84]. The demo consisted of a robot observing a designed structure of polyhedral blocks and then recreating a copy of the structure from a pile of unordered blocks. This task required recognition as well as an analysis of stability and hand-eye coordination. A similar achievement for a recognition system of the modern era does not come readily to mind.

What the Blocks World Didn't Confront. The blocks world avoided numerous difficulties such as:

- curved surfaces and boundaries;
- articulated and moving objects;
- occlusion by unknown shapes;
- complex background and 3-d texture such as foliage;
- specular or mutually illuminating surfaces;
- multiple light sources and remote shadowing;
- transparent or translucent surfaces.

The blocks world was extended in various ways to begin coping with these conditions. An early exploration of the issues that arise in the recognition of generic curved objects was carried out by Guzmán [31]. His approach is illustrated in Figure 2. This work can be seen as an extension of the blocks world philosophy. By restricting the problem to line drawings, many of the difficult scene rendering issues can be avoided and research can focus on what happens when curved surfaces intersect and occlude and where generic objects categories can exhibit a wide range of composite parts. For example, in Figure 2 c) there can be

---

[1] Added for clarification within the quoted context.

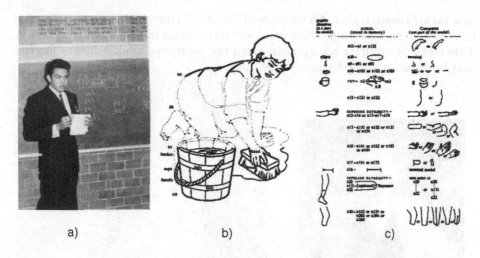

Fig. 2. A system for recognizing 2-d curved objects in line drawings. a) A. Guzmán in 1964. b) The feature analysis of a line drawing. c) A set of parts that can be used to describe generic curved objects. (b) and c) are taken from [31] with permission.)

many types of pants legs, with and without creases and highly variable geometric relations between such parts.

In spite of this innovative use of parts and constraint relations to enable the recognition of objects in more real-world scenes, the restriction to ideal line drawings seemed too far away from the real vision problem to build to a major focus of the recognition community. Instead, a new geometric representation was discovered that offered a way to extend the blocks world to composite curved shapes in 3-d - the generalized cylinder.

3 Binford and the World of Generalized Cylinders

The next major advance in representations for recognition was the generalized cylinder (GC) originated by Thomas Binford [8]. The key insight is that many curved shapes can be expressed as a sweep of a variable cross section along a curved axis. Issues such as self-intersection and surface singularities do arise but shapes like a coffee pot or cup are easily handled. An example of automatically extracting an object description using generalized cylinders is shown in Figure 3. This example was taken from the work of Gerald Agin [2], a Binford student at Stanford. Agin developed a structured light range camera and used generalized cylinders to model various curved shapes, such as dolls.

The recognition of simple curved 3-d objects, such as a hammer, based on the Agin range camera and generalized cylinder components was carried out at the same time by another Binford student, Ram Nevatia [56,57]. Nevatia has maintained a long-term commitment to the generalized cylinder representation and has pursued recovery and recognition of GC objects from intensity images as a major research goal. An example of Nevatia's later work some two decades later on GC part decomposition for object recognition is shown in Figure 4 [85]. This result is quite an achievement given the relatively weak evidence for GC part boundaries and interfaces in the image.

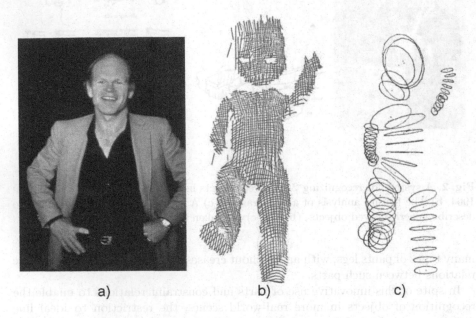

a)   b)   c)

Fig. 3. The representation of objects by assemblies of generalized cylinders. a) Thomas Binford. b) A range image of a doll. c) The resulting set of generalized cylinders. (b) and c) are taken from Agin [1] with permission.)

3.1 ACRONYM

Another Binford student, Rodney Brooks, developed a recognition system based on symbolic geometric constraints on objects composed of GC parts [13]. The system could essentially prove theorems concerning the existence of a parameterized GC configuration with associated tolerances. The system was called ACRONYM to avoid deriving a contrived name for the system, since ACRONYM is cleverly self-referential [2]. The Defense Advanced Projects Agency (DARPA) and the Central Intelligence Agency (CIA) established a classified project to use ACRONYM to recognize targets such as submarines as illustrated in Figure 5. The goal was to assist strategic intelligence analysts that monitor military installations using aerial photography. The project, called SCORPIUS, was designed to exploit various parallel computing architectures developed by DARPA in conjunction with the Strategic Computing Program (1983-1993) [65]. Since the SCORPIUS program was classified, it is not clear how effectively the ACRONYM recognition

---

[2] Binford's next generation system was called SUCCESSOR [9], thus eliminating the need for any future acronyms.

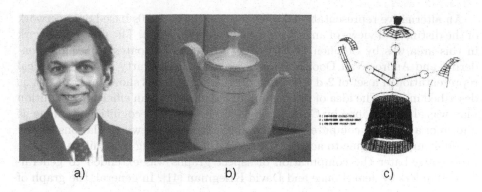

Fig. 4. Recognition by generalized cylinder parts. a) Ram Nevatia. b) An intensity image of a coffee pot. c) Automatically grouped and classified GC parts. (b) and c) are taken from [85] with permision.)

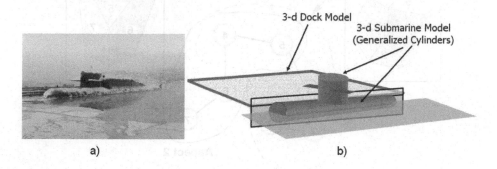

Fig. 5. The SCORPIUS project. a) A submarine at dock. b)An ACRONYM generalized cylinder model for the scene in a).

system performed. The results must have been encouraging enough since a new project, called RADIUS, was launched in 1993 with similar application goals [25]. However, the emphasis of RADIUS was on change detection and automated 3-d modeling from imagery rather than recognition.

4   Aspects

The early period of object recognition research was based solidly on the premise that objects live in 3-d space and the 3-d structure can account for all the changes in appearance that arise from viewpoint changes. There was not much interest in explaining image intensity variations except for the early work by Horn [33]. The rationale was that objects can be recognized from their outlines and interior intensity discontinuity boundaries and that these features can be reliably recovered without requiring an in-depth understanding of reflectance and image intensity formation. This framework is known as object-centered representation.

An alternative representational scheme arose in the 1970s based on a network of the distinct 2-d views of an object, called an *aspect graph*. The pioneering work in this area was by Stephen Underwood and Clarence Coates [80], Jan Koenderink and Andrea Van Doorn [39] and Indranil Chakravarty [17]. A graphical representation of a set of 2-d views of a polyhedral shape is shown in Figure 6, as described in [80]. The idea of pre-compiling 2-d views into an efficient recognition plan was also developed by Chris Goad [27], who viewed recognition planning as a form of automatic computer programming. Repeated view calculations should be pre-compiled off-line to achieve high performance during recognition runtime processing. Later the computation of aspect graphs was extended to generalized cylinders by Jean Ponce and David Kriegman [41]. In general, the graph of

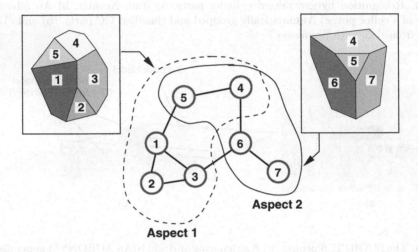

Fig. 6. Two views of a polyhedral solid. The adjacency of projected polygonal faces forms a graph. The view-based description is learned by associating new view structures with the existing graph. The figure is similar to one from [80].

related object views is called an *aspect* graph. The nodes of the graph represent object views that are adjacent to each other on the unit sphere of viewing directions but differ in some significant way. The most common view relationship in aspect graphs is based on the topological structure of the view, i.e., edges in the aspect graph arise from transitions in the graph structure relating vertices, edges and faces of the projected object.

The aspect graph representation gained a lot of momentum with resonance from the psycho-physics community where some researchers embraced the notion that human vision is view-based rather than object centered [77]. The hope was that visual aspects, compiled from 3-d models, or learned from example images could enable an efficient recognition strategy by guiding the search for image features. The family of deformable generalized cylinder parts called *geons* were introduced by Irving Biederman [7] who demonstrated that human object recognition can be characterized by the presence or absence of geons in the 3-d scene. Sven Dickinson, Sandy Pentland and Azriel Rosenfeld developed an aspect graph formulation of geon primitives for the recognition of 3-d objects [22].

The formal goal of precise computation of aspect graphs encountered some major difficulties in the 1990s. It was shown by Harry Plantinga and Charles Dyer [60] that under perspective viewing that the size of polyhedral aspect graphs can grow as rapidly as n^9. For curved surfaces, the complexity is dramatically greater. Sylvain Petitjean [59] found that the complexity of the aspect graph of algebraic surfaces is on the order of d^{18}, where d is the degree of the surface. This complexity arises since there are many small scale transitions that are topologically significant but may not be relevant for object recognition. Since the viewing distance is not known in advance, it is difficult to say what topological events are important and therefore the aspect graph enterprise becomes application specific.

The example of Figure 7 provides a clear illustration of this issue and was used in a debate heralding the end of substantial research on the formal aspect graph [23]. The dimples on the golf ball introduce intractable complexity to the graph representation but are not of individual significance in an effective description of the object class. More recently, Ben Kimia has formulated an

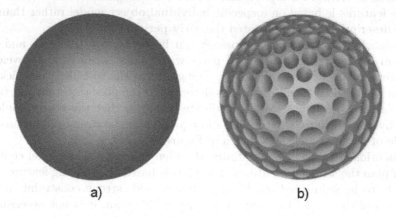

a)   b)

Fig. 7. The problem of scale for the aspect graph representation. a) A golf ball seen from a large viewing distance. b) The same ball from a close viewpoint. Each dimple generates a combinatorial explosion of occlusion events with respect to the other dimples.

aspect graph based on the geometric similarity of object views as measured by elastic deformation [21]. While this approach avoids the polynomial explosion of views based on topological details, the problem of scale still persists.

5 The Era of Pessimism

The early geometric period was founded on the notion that bottom-up boundary descriptions could be formed from single intensity views of an object. This process, later to be called *perceptual grouping* [48,45,69] presented some difficult problems such as:

- low contrast image intensity at boundaries;
- background clutter with high edge density;
- occlusion by objects with complex texture.

As an example of the first point, an image of a polyhedral edge will exhibit no intensity discontinuity at all if the illumination is directed along the direction of the mean surface normal of the intersecting planar faces (assuming Lambertian reflectance). This condition can be easily observed for polyhedral surfaces of modest complexity and thus reliable boundary detection cannot be practically achieved. The missing edges must be hypothesized based on reasoning about the object shape, which dictates that bottom-up grouping cannot be done in advance of considering a model hypothesis.

These difficulties generated a period of pessimism concerning the completeness and stability of bottom-up segmentation processes. Instead, a number of researchers implemented recognition systems based on fragmentary feature segmentations in terms of 2-d point and line or curve segments. The organization of these features is based on a specific individual object model rather than the generic descriptions that dominated the early period.

Some early examples of this approach can be seen in the 1970s [3] and [58]. A system for the recognition of 3-d parts with planar surfaces was developed by Walter Perkins at General Motors. The goal was the so-called "bin-picking" problem where the recognition process determined the pose (rotation and translation) of the object in a world coordinate frame so that the object could be placed by a robot into a fixture for subsequent manufacturing operations. An example of part recognition is shown in Figure 8.

As mentioned earlier, Goad initiated the idea that an object model could be used to plan the search for features. The plan is based on selecting features that are likely to be segmented reliably and that provide strong constraints on the projection of the model into the image. Given this plan, it is not necessary to carry out extensive feature grouping and linking in advance of the recognition stage. Instead the model constraints are imposed on the image during recognition and provide the required organization.

Perhaps the first research to carry out this approach in the implementation of a complete recognition system was David Lowe [45]. An example of his recognition system, called SCERPO [3], is shown in Figure 9. The basic approach is that a consistent interpretation of a set of image features will constrain the viewing hypotheses to a single perspective viewpoint of the model. This philosophy of minimal feature organization and strong model constraints quickly became a

---

[3] Spatial Correspondence, Evidential Reasoning, and Perceptual Organization.

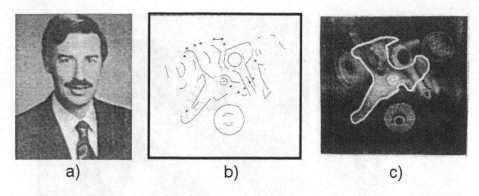

Fig. 8. Recognition of manufactured parts using a planar model. a) Walter Perkins. b) A set of point and curve features, extracted by bottom-up processing. c) The part model matched to the features in b).(From [58] with permission.)

compelling research focus during the early half of the 1980s [10,29,4]. An example of recognition with essentially ungrouped features is shown in Figure 10. This work by Eric Grimson and Tomas Lozano-Perez generated considerable enthusiasm for complete reliance on prior object models for the organization of features and the detection of objects under high degrees of occlusion and shadowing. Indeed, it became kind of an academic contest to see how occluded an object could be and still achieve successful recognition.

The emphasis in the early 1980s was mainly on 2-d planar shapes or 3-d objects as imaged by 3-d range cameras [11]. This restriction reduced the number of degrees of freedom for the image projection transformation relative to the number of constraints provided by each feature-to-model assignment. There was the sense that it is important to solve 2-d planar object recognition robustly and completely before re-attacking the harder problem of 3-d object recognition from a single intensity image.

The 2-d recognition approaches were driven by a search for model-to image-transformations based on the a small number of un-grouped features. Eric Grimson exploited the *interpretation tree* that is a pre-compiled search plan for matching features. This approach is similar to the recognition plan ideas of Goad [27]. Katsu Ikeuchi and Takeo Kanade also developed an extensive recognition planning system that took into account both projected 3-d shape and self-occlusion in a tree-like plan structure [37]. Their object representation included 3-d orientation constraints based on photometric stereo and so might be called a 2.5-d representation.

Another 2-d approach of the period is based on the data indexing method of hashing on a minimum number of features,e.g., three points or lines for planar affine matching [43]. The minimum feature set is used to retrieve from a hash table the set of confirming features that would be visible and placed in the image according to the transform computed from the search features. A match is declared if the hashed features are sufficiently confirmed in the image.

a)   b)

Fig. 9. Recognition based on viewpoint consistency. a) David Lowe. b)An example of recognizing plastic razors under conditions of high occlusion. (b) is taken from [42] with permission.)

It would be fair to say that the 2-d problem is now solved for many cases of practical interest such as industrial inspection and robotic placement. However, high background complexity along with expected significant occlusion can still confound existing 2-d methods by producing a large number of false hypotheses. These recognition error statistics were studied extensively by Grimson [28].

By the mid 1980s, attention refocused on the recognition of 3-d objects from 2-d intensity images. These approaches exploited viewpoint consistency (equivalent to object pose consistency) where the pose was computed from a minimal set of features. The constraint of full-perspective image formation was abandoned for the use of *affine* image projection models where the camera parameters can be determined from a small number of features such as three points or a point and two intersecting lines or two lines each with a fixed point. The affine camera model, called *weak perspective* has only six parameters: tip and tilt angles, image rotation, image x-y translation and scale. Unlike full perspective camera models, the weak perspective parameters can be determined uniquely without prior camera calibration.

Again, the feature grouping problem is avoided and model hypotheses are generated directly from a match of the minimal feature set. The hypotheses can be confirmed in various ways, such as projecting the model onto the image and checking that the expected features are present (the Goad philosophy). One of the first attacks on the 3-d problem in this era was by Dan Huttenlocher and Shimon Ullman [36]. They called the recognition process *alignment* since the image feature (in their case, a point triple) is sufficient to align the 3-d model with the image. The point triples are formed exhaustively so that the algorithm has a complexity of Mn^3, where M is the number of model triples

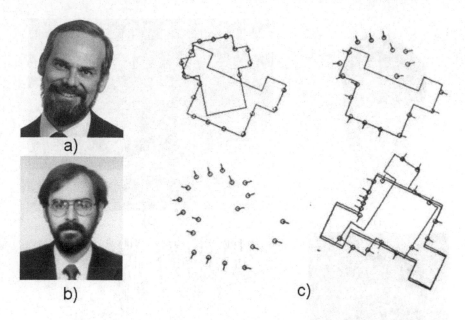

Fig. 10. The use of sparse, unorganized features for recognition. a) Eric Grimson. b) Tomas Lozano-Perez. c) Steps in forming a model recognition hypothesis based on oriented edge segments. (c) used by permission of Eric Grimson.)

and n is the number of feature points in the 2-d image. At the same time a similar approach was taken by the author and Dan Thompson[78]. In their system, the model hypothesis was determined by pose clustering. The idea is that a correct object hypothesis will have all features projected into the image with the same pose. The most consistent pose is found by voting into a space of affine transformations, similar to the generalized Hough transform [5,75]. They used a single image feature called a vertex-pair that required that two line segments be grouped around a common vertex. Two such vertices are sufficient to determine and over-constrain the object pose. In this approach, the complexity is Mn^2, where M is the number of model vertex-pairs and n is the number of vertex pairs in the 2-d image. Reduction in matching complexity is being traded off against modest feature grouping risk. Their system was applied to the problem of aerial surveillance and achieved a respectable recognition performance for the problem of detecting aircraft at airfields with 99% accuracy. The performance result was based on extensive testing and is reported in [52].

While these viewpoint consistency approaches can overcome the lack of feature grouping, there are still limitations fundamentally caused by the absence of object features resulting from the effects itemized at the beginning of this section. The vertex-pair system, shown in Figure 12 could hallucinate the presence of models when the number of features or the tolerance on viewpoint consistency is reduced. Figure 12 d) shows numerous false positive hypotheses where support for the model is found by accident. For example the bright sidewalk region in the

Fig. 11. Three-dimensional object recognition using alignment. a) Dan Huttenlocher. b) Shimon Ullman. c) A cluttered image. d) The aligned model, shown near the middle of the image. (c) and d) provided by Dan Huttenlocher, with permission.)

upper middle of the image provides strong support for the edges of the aircraft wings.

These approaches based on a manually constructed 3-d object model with extra attributes to express the reliability of segmented features can be quite successful under reasonably bland backgrounds and limited amounts of occlusion. The airfield problem is particularly well-suited to these limitations. However, the approach is encumbered with the need to construct a detailed 3-d model for each specific object. In spite of this drawback, there has been extensive use of detailed 3-d models to enable target recognition. Figure 13 has thousands of polygonal surface facets and is used to recognize this specific tank in synthetic aperture radar imagery (SAR). The rationale here is that there are only a finite number of military weapons and vehicles so that a concerted effort could "model the world" in this limited domain.

Fig. 12. The vertex-pair recognition system. a) The author. b) Dan Thompson. c) An example of aircraft recognition. d) Hallucination is possible. The same scene as c) with a relaxed tolerance to pose consistency.

Fig. 13. A highly detailed 3-d geometric model for a tank

6 The Era of Geometric Invariance

By the end of the 1980s there was a rising interest in the object recognition community to move beyond the manual modeling approach and to try to automate the acquisition of models for recognition. Ideally a single view or at worst a small number of views of the object would be sufficient to construct a recognition model. A promising avenue was the concept of geometric invariance where properties of an object are determined that do not vary with viewpoint. For example under affine viewing conditions the ratio of collinear segment lengths is independent of viewpoint. That is, the length ratio in the image will be the same as in the 3-d object, regardless of affine camera parameters.

The formation of recognition models is reduced to measuring the invariant values for feature constructions that have sufficient geometric constraints to enable the formation of invariants. Objects seen under perspective are described by projective invariants such as the cross ratio and the ratio of area ratios [54]. These constructions require four collinear points and five points or five lines respectively. The configurations must not be degenerate, so that no four of the five points are collinear, for example.

The research focus was initially on planar shapes because the theory of geometric invariance for perspective and affine image formation is complete. Plane to image mappings form a transformation group and the full machinery of group invariance developed by Felix Klein and other 19th century mathematicians can be brought to bear on the recognition task. The role of projective geometry was also elevated from a minor interest, mainly relevant to the field of graphics, to a central object of study and adaptation to computer vision. Again, the results of 18th and 19th century mathematics could be readily mined for ideas to solve the recognition task. Some of the main researchers in the geometric invariance movement are shown in Figure 14.

Fig. 14. A meeting of researchers central to the geometric invariance movement at Schenectady, New York during the month of July, 1992. Top row, left to right: Andrew Zisserman, Charles Rothwell, Luc VanGool, Joseph Mundy, Stephen Maybank and Daniel Huttenlocher. Bottom row, left to right: Thomas Binford, Richard Hartley, David Forsyth and Jon Kleinberg.

This hope of a complete theory for modeling and recognition created considerable interest in the late 1980s and early 1990s. However, the enthusiasm was tempered by two key drawbacks of representation by geometric invariance:

- it was proved independently by several researchers that no viewpoint invariants exist for general 3-d shapes [18,14,51];
- the grouping problem re-emerges; it is necessary to associate a rather large number of features (e.g. five lines) across views in order to check for consistent invariant values and thus a correct model hypothesis.

Nevertheless, keen interest in recognition based on invariants continued through the middle of the 1990s. It was felt that a sufficient number of classes of 3-d structures do possess invariants, such as surfaces of rotation and polyhedra, so that the lack of invariance in general does not pose a major defeat for the program. The grouping problem was sidestepped for the moment by focusing on the discovery of new invariants and integrating the representations into a complete recognition system [68,67]. Two systems for recognition by invariants are shown in Figure 15. The recognition systems were named after characters in the Oxford-based detective stories by Colin Dexter.

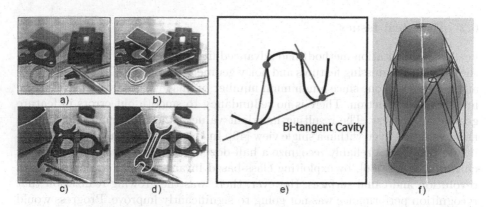

Fig. 15. Two recognition systems based on geometric invariance. a) A cluttered image with machine parts. b) Recognition of several objects by the LEWIS system using various invariant descriptions, such as five lines. c) A second image. d) Recognition by LEWIS using the invariant construction on bi-tangent cavities shown in f). Recognition of a surface of rotational symmetry by the MORSE system. The axis of rotation is recovered as well as invariants of the bi-tangent cavities.

6.1   Multiview Geometry

A complementary thread of research was intitated in 1992 by Richard Hartley and Oliver Faugueras with the goal to apply the theory of projective geometry to the relationship between multiple perspective views. An emphasis of this work was the reconstruction of 3-d geometry without the need for camera calibration. The resulting reconstruction was ambiguous up to a 3-d projective transformation and thus the central role of projective geometry in the analysis of camera configurations and reconstructed geometry.

It was quickly realized that the lack of general viewpoint invariants for a single view could be overcome if an object is seen in two or more views. Of course, one approach would be to reconstruct the 3-d geometry and then use direct 3-d recognition methods developed earlier for model-based recognition. A different approach, more in keeping with the invariance philosophy, is to derive invariants of a structure from correspondences across views. This approach is particularly attractive if the features can be easily tracked as would be the case in video image sequences. This concept was realized in recognition systems by Daphna Weinshall [82] and Stephan Carlsson [16].

From a slightly different approach one can take the position that invariants change with viewpoint but according to a set of 1-dimensional spaces. If there are sufficient constraints such as independent features on a model, it is possible to constraint the viewpoint and thus determine all the invariants for the object. In essence, the camera projection is being recovered in the invariant construction. This approach was initiated by David Jacobs [19] and extended to projective invariance by Isaac Weiss [83].

6.2 Practical Issues

Feature segmentation methods had advanced little since the early 1980s [15] and the problems of missing features and noisy geometry remained. Geometric invariants are noise-prone since a minimum number of image features are used for the invariant construction. There is no redundancy to smooth out errors in feature geometry recovery. The resulting invariant values can have significant random noise variance, even within a single view [49]. In spite of these limitations, by 1995 it was possible to reliably recognize a half-dozen or so 3-d objects in somewhat cluttered scenes [86], by exploiting class-based invariance such as of surfaces of revolution and canal surfaces. However, there was the growing realization that recognition performance was not going to significantly improve. Progress would depend on better image segmentation methods, not on extensions of the lexicon of invariant structures.

In retrospect, given recent advances in video feature tracking, it would have been a much better strategy for planar object recognition to compute the plane-to-plane projective transformation using all the features in a consistent statistical optimization strategy such as RANSAC [12,26]. With the transform known, all feature coordinates and parameters become, in effect, invariants. This same strategy could be employed for 3-d invariant calculations using mutual pose constraints among objects. This approach was not taken at the time since it was considered bad form for an invariance researcher to want to know anything about the transform parameters

7 The Rise of Appearance Methods

At the same time as the geometric invariance program was reaching the end of its active period, new recognition approaches strongly rooted in intensity appearance were discovered: appearance manifolds [55] and affine invariant intensity features[71]. Shree Nayar's system was based on SLAM [4] which is a C library of tools for processing images taken over a large number of viewpoints and lighting conditions. The input image set is compiled into a continuous eigen-space of the image intensity covariance, treating the entire image as a 1-d vector.

Recognition is achieved by finding the appearance space *closest* to the input image. In SLAM, distance is computed as Euclidean distance on a

---

[4] Software Library for Appearance Modeling.

low-dimensional subspace representing the largest eigenvalues. The SLAM algorithm produced very impressive results with high recognition rates on a large library of objects. Remarkably, no model assumptions or image segmentation is required and the recognition hypothesis carries with it an estimate of the object's 3-d pose. Nayar's work generated tremendous interest, overshadowing ongoing recognition research based on geometry. There was renewed interest in understanding intensity appearance phenomena [6] and in the development of invariance to illumination changes [72].

The geometry recognition community remained somewhat skeptical of the power of global appearance methods, such as SLAM, particularly with respect to the ability to withstand occlusion. In conjunction with a representation workshop in 1996 it was decided to carry out a comparison between SLAM and MORSE [53]. The experiments focused on surfaces of revolution (SOR). A set of images of SORs at different tilt angles was collected under varying degrees of occlusion. Recognition by SLAM was carried out using the standard nearest point algorithm while recognition in MORSE was based on invariants of the bi-tangent cavities formed on the outline of the SOR. The appearance manifold for example SORs and the MORSE results are shown in Figure 16. The result

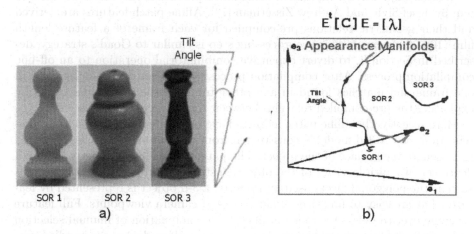

Fig. 16. SLAM vs MORSE. a)Example surfaces of revolution from the experiment. b) The SLAM appearance manifolds for the SORs.

of the comparison was very surprising – there was no clear winner. The presence of limited amounts of occlusion could be handled by SLAM as well as MORSE. Both systems faired badly under heavy occlusion. It is not well-understood why the global appearance manifold is somewhat immune to occlusion. Perhaps eliminating the higher order eigenvectors smears out the perturbations of occlusion so that the final manifold distance value is not much affected. In any case, the ability of SLAM to learn an effective 3-d recognition model for any object fully automatically without any explicit geometric representation was a compelling paradigm that set the stage for recognition research over the next decade.

The problem of occlusion in appearance methods can be solved by using more local intensity features such as planar regions about interest points. The successful application of this idea by Cordelia Schmid and Roger Mohr [72] inspired an intensive search for other intensity and affine projection invariant features [46,70,79,38,50]. The basic assumption is that intensity regions are derived from locally planar surface patches and viewed by an affine camera. Thus, local affine constructions such as ratios of areas can be used to determine consistent feature matches. A more global 3-d viewpoint consistency constraint can be invoked by deriving the fundamental matrix from hypothesized matches. Any correct match would be consistent with the epipolar geometry of the two views [32]. The recognition strategy is to generate hundreds of affine patch features and then sift them into object hypotheses by geometric match consistency.

In this approach object models are learned directly from a set of images without geometric segmentation, except for the detection of local corners or other interest operators. The models can be acquired at the video frame rate and recognition can also be carried out in real time [5].

Another impressive achievement using affine patches is the Video Google system by Josef Sivic and Andrew Zisserman [73]. Affine patch features are derived and their geometric relations pre-compiled for each frame of a feature length film (100,000 frames). This preprocessing step is similar to Goad's strategy, described in Section 4, to divert expensive combinatorial operation to an off-line compilation process. After compilation process, an object can be designated in one frame and matches found in any other frame of the movie in seconds by exploiting the pre-compiled relations between the extracted features.

More recently, the affine patch features have been integrated into a 3-d representation [66]. A 3-d model is constructed from a set of affine patches arranged to tessellate the surface of the object. The patch arrangement is derived from a dense set of multiple views of the object. Instead of purely geometric features such as the polygonal facets used by Roberts, a 3-d object is represented by features that are easy to find over a wide range of camera viewpoints. Full feature coverage over the viewsphere is obtained by a combination of manual selection and automated feature refinement. Issues such as self-occlusion are handled naturally by the 3-d structure as has always been the case for purely geometric methods. The constraint of viewpoint consistency is also exploited during the recognition process to rule out false matches.

Affine patches have also been exploited as *parts* in a new attack on the problem of generic object recognition [24,44]. The rationale is that invariant regions provide a stable description of objects and that a degree of flexibility in the geometric relationships between patches can account for in-class variations. One is guaranteed that parts defined in this way can be reliably segmented, an essential requirement for generic object recognition.

---

[5] The author viewed an impressive live demonstration of the SIFT recognition system by David Lowe in 2003 [61].

8   Coming Full Circle?

One way to look at the current state of object recognition research is that the four decade dependence on step edge detection for the construction of object features has been broken. Step edge boundaries are still useful in forming an object description where the object surface is bland and free of surface markings. But, for a large fraction of object surfaces and textures, affine patch features can be reliably detected without having to confront the difficult perceptual grouping problems that are required to form purely geometric boundary descriptions from edges.

Some revisiting of the earlier themes of geometry-based object recognition can be expected as the affine patch feature vocabulary is woven into the edge-based prior art. For example, one can envision affine-patch aspect graphs where the aspect cells are based on continuous measures of the variability of the affine properties of a patch. In this case, the cell boundary represents the removal and insertion of patches required to maintain good recognition performance. The problem of aspect scale is mitigated since the patch segmentation automatically adapts to the granularity of visible features [6]

The use of viewpoint consistency has been an integral part of the geometric recognition strategy since the beginning and is essential in filtering match hypotheses. General 3-d relations among patches are enforced by the epipolar constraint and local planarity relations can be tested by affine invariant relations among patches. However, if patches are treated as isolated features, it quickly becomes combinatorially impractical to rely on large degree n-ary patch relations to constrain match integrity. This combinatorial problem can be solved by re-introducing the classic role of generic shape models such as polyhedra and generalized cylinders.

The constraints that must exist between faces for a connected polyhedral surface [76] can be exploited to confirm feature matches and at the same time define the 3-d polyhedral shape [7]. A similar idea could be applied to generalized cylinder parts where the local "flow" of individual patch-to-image transforms can define the axis and boundaries of the cylinders. This extended representation can bridge the gap between the relatively local, but reliably detected, affine regions and more meaningful GC object components (parts) that are difficult to segment from step edge boundary information alone.

Global shape recovery from local estimates of affine properties was exploited by Jan Koenderink in his study of the capability of the human visual system to estimate surfaces from local orientation [40]. In this work, local surface normals were integrated to form a 3-d surface. The combination of local orientations from

---

[6] This kind of aspect graph was implemented for the vertex-pair matcher, based on the expected variance in the affine transformation computed from a given model vertex-pair as a function of viewpoint [52]. Also, the system by Art Pope and David Lowe [63] used a kind of aspect graph based on the probability of feature detection with respect to viewpoint.

[7] The polyhedral faces must have at least four sides to generate constraints, but for complex enough shapes, patch arrangements can be designed to satisfy Sugihara's constraint system.

affine patches could also be used to enable the recovery of surface geometry as a first step to recover generic shape descriptions.

In summary, it is certain that the role of geometric representations of objects in recognition will not be displaced for long. Beyond mere statistical dependence,there seem to be only two avenues to a theory of object class: geometry and function. Moreover, the characterization of function is itself largely couched in geometry along with the laws of physics [74]. Such models are essential to fuse statistical class correlations across scene contexts and to arrive at a formal understanding of categories. To quote Larry Roberts from four decades ago, 'The perception of solid objects is a process which can be based on the properties of three-dimensional transformations and the laws of nature.'

Acknowledgments

The author is honored to have been part of the geometric era and to have met and worked with many of the researchers that remain committed to understanding the mysteries of the recognition task. The author is particularly indebted to Thomas O. Binford for his thoughtful and determined effort to enlighten and inspire.

References

1. G. Agin and T. Binford. Computer description of curved objects. In *Proceedings 3rd International Conference on Artificial Intelligence*, pages 629–640, 1993.
2. G. J. Agin. *Representation and Description of Curved Objects*. PhD thesis, Stanford University, October 1972.
3. A. Ambler, H. Barrow, C. Brown, R. Burstall, and R. Popplestone. A Versatile Computer-Controlled Assembly System. In *International Joint Conference on Artificial Intelligence*, pages 298–307, 1973.
4. N. Ayache and O. Faugeras. HYPER: A New Approach for the Recognition and Positioning of Two-Dimensional Objects. *IEEE Transactions on Pattern Analysis and Machine Intelligence*, 8(1):44–54, January 1986.
5. D. Ballard. Generalizing the Hough Transform to Detect Arbitrary Shapes. *Pattern Recognition*, 13(2):111–122, 1981.
6. P. Belhumeur and D. Kriegman. Learning and recognizing objects using illumination subspaces. In *Proceedings of the IEEEConference on Computer Vision and Pattern Recognition*, pages 270–277, 1996.
7. I. Biederman. Human Image Understanding: Recent Research and a Theory. *Computer Vision, Graphics and Image Processing*, 32:29–73, 1985.
8. T. O. Binford. Visual Perception by Computer. *Proc. IEEE Conf. on Systems and Control*, December 1971.
9. T. O. Binford. Spatial understanding: the successor system. In *Proceedings of the ARPA Image Understanding Workshop*, pages 12–20. Defense Advanced Research Projects Agency, Morgan Kaufmann Publishers, Inc., 1992.
10. R. Bolles and R. Cain. Recognizing and locating partially visible objects: The local-feature-focus method. *International Journal of Robotics Research*, 1(3):57–82, 1982.

11. R. Bolles and R. Horaud. 3DPO: A Tree-dimensional Part Orientation System. *International Journal of Robotics Research*, 5(3):3–26, 1986.
12. R. C. Bolles and M. A. Fischler. A RANSAC-based approach to model fitting and its application to finding cylinders in range data. In *International Joint Conference on Artificial Intelligence*, pages 637–643, Vancouver, Canada, August 1981.
13. R. Brooks. Symbolic reasoning among 3D models and 2D images. *Artificial Intelligence Journal*, 17:285–348, 1982.
14. J. Burns, R. Weiss, and E. Riseman. *The Non-existence of General-case View-Invariants*, pages 120–131. MIT Press, 1992.
15. J. F. Canny. Finding edges and lines in images. Technical Report AI-TR-720, Massachusets Institute of Technology, Artificial Intelligence Laboratory, June 1983.
16. S. Carlsson. Multiple image invariance using the double algebra. In J. L. Mundy, A. Zissermann, and D. Forsyth, editors, *Applications of Invariance in Computer Vision*, volume 825 of *Lecture Notes in Computer Science*, pages 145–164. Springer-Verlag, 1994.
17. I. Chakravarty. The use of characteristic views as a basis for the recognition of three-dimensional objects. *Proc. Society for Photo-Optical Instrumentation Engineers conference on Robot Vision*, 336:37–45, May 1982.
18. D. Clemens and D. Jacobs. Space and time bounds on model indexing. *IEEE Transactions on Pattern Analysis and Machine Intelligence*, 13(10):1007–116, 1991.
19. D. T. Clemens and D. W. Jacobs. Model group indexing for recognition. In *Proceedings of the IEEEConference on Computer Vision and Pattern Recognition*, pages 4–9, Maui, HI, June 1991.
20. M. B. Clowes. On seeing things. *Artificial Intelligence Journal*, 2:79–116, 1971.
21. C. Cyr and B. Kimia. 3d object recognition using shape similiarity-based aspect graph. In *Proceedings of the International Conference on Computer Vision*, pages 254–261, Vancouver, Canada, July 2001.
22. S. Dickinson, A. Pentland, and A. Rosenfeld. 3-d shape recovery using distributed aspect matching. *IEEE Transactions on Pattern Analysis and Machine Intelligence, special issue on Interpretation of 3-D Scenes*, 14(2):174–198, 1992.
23. O. Faugeras, J. Mundy, N. Ahuja, C. Dyer, A. Pentland, R. Jain, K. Ikeuchi, and Bowyer K. Why aspect graphs are not (yet) practical for computer vision. In *IEEE Workshop on Directions in Automated CAD-Based Vision*, pages 98–104, 1991.
24. R. Fergus, P. Perona, and A. Zisserman. Object class recognition by unsupervised scale-invariant learning. In *Proceedings of the IEEE Conference on Computer Vision and Pattern Recognition*, volume 2, pages 264–271, June 2003.
25. O. Firschein, editor. *RADIUS: Image Understanding for Imagery Intelligence*. Morgan Kaufmann, San Francisco, 1997.
26. A. W. Fitzgibbon and A. Zisserman. Automatic 3D model acquisition and generation of new images from video sequences. In *Proceedings of European Signal Processing Conference (EUSIPCO '98), Rhodes, Greece*, pages 1261–1269, 1998.
27. C. Goad. Special purpose automatic programming for 3d model-based vision. In *Proc. DARPA Image Understanding Workshop*, pages 94–104, Arlington, VA, June 1983.
28. W. E. L. Grimson. *Object Recognition by Computer: The Role of Geometric Constraints*. The MIT Press, Cambridge, Massachusetts, London, England, 1990.
29. W. E. L. Grimson and T. Lozano-Pérez. Model-based recognition and localization from sparse range or tactile data. *International Journal of Robotics Research*, 3(3):3–35, 1984.
30. A. Guzman. Decomposition of a visual scene into three-dimensional bodies. In *Proceedings Fall Joint Computer Conference*, volume 33, pages 291–304, 1968.

31. A. Guzman. Analysis of curved line drawings using context and global information. In B. Meltzer and D. Michie, editors, *Machine Intelligence 6*, pages 325–375. John Wiley and Sons, Inc., New York, NY, 1971.

32. R. I. Hartley and A. Zisserman. *Multiple View Geometry in Computer Vision*. Cambridge University Press, ISBN: 0521623049, 2000.

33. B. K. P. Horn. Shape from shading: a method for obtaining the shape of a smooth opaque object from one view. Technical Report TR-79, MIT Project Mac, October 1970.

34. M. Hu. Visual pattern recognition by moment invariants. *IRE Transactions on Information Theory*, 8(2):179–187, February 1962.

35. D. A. Huffman. Impossible Objects as Nonsense Sentences. In B. Meltzer and D. Michie, editors, *Machine Intelligence 6*, pages 295–324. Edinburgh University Press, 1971.

36. D. P. Huttenlocher and S. Ullman. Object recognition using alignment. In *Proceedings of the First International Conference on Computer Vision, London*, pages 102–111, 1987.

37. K. Ikeuchi and T. Kanade. Applying sensor models to automatic generation of object recognition programs. In *Proc. Second Int'l Conf. Comput. Vision*, pages 228–237, Tampa, FL, December 1988.

38. T. Kadir, A. Zisserman, and M. Brady. An affine invariant salient region detector. In *Proceedings of the 8th European Conference on Computer Vision, Prague, Czech Republic*, May 2004.

39. J. J. Koenderink and A. J. van Doorn. The singularities of the visual mapping. *Biological Cybernetics*, 24:51–59, 1976.

40. J. J. Koenderink and Andrea J. van Doorn. Relief: pictorial and otherwise. *Image and Vision Computing.*, 13(5):321–334, 1995.

41. D. Kriegman and J. Ponce. Computing exact aspect graphs of curved objects:solids of revolution. *The International Journal of Computer Vision*, 5(2):119–136, November 1990.

42. R. Kurzweil. *The age of intelligent machines*. MIT Press, Cambridge, MA, 1990.

43. Y. Lamdan and H.J. Wolfson. Geometric Hashing: A General and Efficient Model-Based Recognition Scheme. In *Proceedings of the 2nd International Conference on Computer Vision, Tampa, Florida*, pages 238–249, December 1988.

44. S. Lazebnik, C. Schmid, and J. Ponce. Semi-local affine parts for object recognition. In *British Machine Vision Conference*, volume volume 2, pages 779–788, 2004.

45. D. Lowe. *Perceptual Organization and Visual Recognition*. Kluwer Academic Publishers, 1985.

46. D. G. Lowe. Object recognition from local scale-invariant features. In *ICCV '99: Proceedings of the International Conference on Computer Vision-Volume 2*, page 1150, Washington, DC, USA, 1999. IEEE Computer Society.

47. A. K. Mackworth. Interpreting pictures of polyhedral scenes. *Artificial Intelligence Journal*, 4:99–118, 1973.

48. D. Marr. *Vision*. W.H. Freeman and Co., 1982.

49. P. Meer, S. Ramakrishna, and R. Lenz. Correspondance of coplanar features through p^2-invariant representations. In J. L. Mundy, A. Zissermann, and D. Forsyth, editors, *Applications of Invariance in Computer Vision*, volume 825 of *Lecture Notes in Computer Science*, pages 437–492. Springer-Verlag, 1994.

50. K. Mikolajczyk, T. Tuytelaars, C. Schmid, J. Zisserman, A.and Matas, F. Schaffalitzky, T. Kadir, and Van Gool L. A comparison of affine region detectors. *Int. J. Comput. Vision*, To Appear, 1994.

51. Y. Moses and S. Ullman. Limitations of non model-based recognition systems. In G. Sandini, editor, *Proceedings of the 2nd European Conference on Computer Vision*, volume 588, pages 820–828, Santa Margherita Ligure, Italy, May 1992. Springer-Verlag.

52. J. L. Mundy and A. J. Heller. The evolution and testing of a model-based object recognition system. In *Proceedings of the 3rd International Conference on Computer Vision*, pages 268–282, Osaka, Japan, December 1990. IEEE Computer Society Press.

53. J. L. Mundy, A. Liu, N. Pillow, A. Zisserman, S. Abdallah, S. Utcke, S. K. Nayar, and C. Rothwell. An experimental comparison of appearance and geometric model based recognition. In *Object Representation in Computer Vision*, pages 247–269, 1996.

54. J. L. Mundy and A. Zisserman, editors. *Geometric Invariance in Computer Vision*. MIT Press, 1992.

55. H. Murase and S. Nayar. Learning and recognition of 3d objects from appearance. *The International Journal of Computer Vision*, 14(1):5–24, 1995.

56. R. Nevatia and T. O. Binford. Structured descriptions of complex obects. *Proc. 3rd International Joint Conference on Artificial Intelligence*, pages 641–647, 1973.

57. R. Nevatia and T. O. Binford. Description and Recognition of Curved Objects. *Artificial Intelligence Journal*, 8:77–98, 1977.

58. W. Perkins. A model-based vision system for industrial parts. *IEEE Transactions on Computers*, C-27(2):126–143, February 1978.

59. S. Petitjean. The complexity and enumerative geometry of aspect graphs of smooth surfaces. April 1994.

60. H. Plantinga and C. Dyer. Visibility, occlusion and the aspect graph. *The International Journal of Computer Vision*, 5(2):137–160, November 1990.

61. J. Ponce. Designing tomorrow's category-level 3D object recognition systems: an international workshop. Taormina, Sicily, September 2003.

62. J. Ponce, A. Zisserman, and M. Hebert, editors. *Object Represenation in Computer Vision II*, volume 1144 of *Lecture Notes in Computer Science*, Cambridge, UK, June 1996. Springer-Verlag.

63. A. Pope and D. Lowe. Learning Appearance Models for Object Recognition. In Ponce et al. [62], pages 201–219.

64. L. G. Roberts. Machine perception of three-dimensional solids. In Tippett, J. and Berkowitz, D. and Clapp, L. and Koester, C. and Vanderburgh, A., editor, *Optical and Electrooptical Information processing*, pages 159–197. MIT Press, 1965.

65. A. Roland and P. Shiman. *DARPA and the Quest for Machine Intelligence*. MIT Press, Cambridge, 2002.

66. F. Rothganger, S. Lazebnik, C. Schmid, and J. Ponce. 3d object modeling and recognition using affine-invariant patches and multi-view spatial constraints. In *CVPR*, pages 272–280, 2003.

67. C. Rothwell. *Object recognition through invariant indexing*. Oxford University Science Publications. Oxford University Press, February 1995.

68. C. A. Rothwell, D. A. Forsyth, A. Zisserman, and J.L. Mundy. Extracting projective structure from single perspective views of 3D point sets. In *Proceedings International Joint Conference on Computer Vision*, pages 573–582, Berlin, Germany, May 1993. IEEE Computer Society Press.

69. S. Sarkar and K. L. Boyer. Perceptual organization in computer vision: A review and a proposal for a classificatory structure. *IEEE Transactions on Systems, Man, and Cybernetics*, 23:382–399, 1993.

70. F. Schaffalitzky and A. Zisserman. Multi-view matching for unordered image sets, or "How do I organize my holiday snaps?". In *Proceedings of the 7th European Conference on Computer Vision, Copenhagen, Denmark*, volume 1, pages 414–431, 2002.

71. C. Schmid, P. Bobet, B. Lamiroy, and R. Mohr. An image-oriented cad approach. In Ponce et al. [62], pages 221–246.

72. C. Schmid and R. Mohr. Local greyvalue invariants for image retrieval. *IEEE Transactions on Pattern Analysis and Machine Intelligence*, 19(5):530–535, 1997.

73. J. Sivic and A. Zisserman. Video Google: A text retrieval approach to object matching in videos. In *Proceedings of the International Conference on Computer Vision*, October 2003.

74. L. Stark and K. Bowyer. Generalized Object Recognition through Reasoning About Association of Function to Structure. *IEEE Transactions on Pattern Analysis and Machine Intelligence*, 13:1097–1104, 1991.

75. G. Stockman. Object recognition and localization via pose clustering. *Computer Vision, Graphics, and Image Processing*, 40:361–387, 1987.

76. K. Sugihara. *Machine Interpretation of Line Drawings*. MIT Press, 1986.

77. M. J. Tarr and S. Pinker. When does human object recognition use a viewer-centered reference frame? *Psychological Science*, 1(42):253–256, 1990.

78. D. W. Thompson and J. L. Mundy. Three-dimensional model matching from an unconstrained viewpoint. In *Proceedings of the International Conference on Robotics and Automation, Raleigh, NC*, pages 208–220, 1987.

79. T. Tuytelaars and L. Van Gool. Matching widely separated views based on affine invariant regions. *Int. J. Comput. Vision*, 59(1):61–85, 2004.

80. S. A. Underwood and C. L. Coates. Visual Learning from Multiple Views. *IEEE Transactions on Computers*, C-24(6):651–661, 1975.

81. D. Waltz. Understanding line drawings of scenes with shadows. In Patrick H. Winston, editor, *The Psychology of Computer Vision*, pages 19–91. McGraw-Hill, 1975.

82. D. Weinshall and C. Tomasi. Linear and incremental acquisition of invariant shape models from image sequences. In *Proceedings International Joint Conference on Computer Vision*, pages 675–682, Berlin, Germany, 1993. IEEE Computer Society Press.

83. I. Weiss and M. Ray. Model-based recognition of 3d objects from single images. *PAMI*, 23(2):116–128, February 2001.

84. P. H. Winston. The MIT robot. In B. Meltzer and D. Michie, editors, *Machine Intelligence 7*, pages 431–463. Edinberg University Press, 1972.

85. M. Zerroug and R. Nevatia. From an intensity image to 3-d segmented descriptions. In J. Ponce, M. Hebert, and A. Zisserman, editors, *Object Representation in Computer Vision II*, pages 11–24, 1996.

86. A. Zisserman, J. Mundy, D. Forsyth, J. Liu, N. Pillow, C. Rothwell, and S. Utcke. Class-based grouping in perspective images. In *Proceedings of the 5th International Conference on Computer Vision*, pages 183–188, Boston, MA, June 1995. IEEE Computer Society Press.

Dataset Issues in Object Recognition

J. Ponce[1,2], T.L. Berg[3], M. Everingham[4], D.A. Forsyth[1], M. Hebert[5],
S. Lazebnik[1], M. Marszalek[6], C. Schmid[6], B.C. Russell[7], A. Torralba[7],
C.K.I. Williams[8], J. Zhang[6], and A. Zisserman[4]

[1] University of Illinois at Urbana-Champaign, USA
[2] Ecole Normale Supérieure, Paris, France
[3] University of California at Berkeley, USA
[4] Oxford University, UK
[5] Carnegie Mellon University, Pittsburgh, USA
[6] INRIA Rhône-Alpes, Grenoble, France
[7] MIT, Cambridge, USA
[8] University of Edinburgh, Edinburgh, UK

Abstract. Appropriate datasets are required at all stages of object recognition research, including learning visual models of object and scene categories, detecting and localizing instances of these models in images, and evaluating the performance of recognition algorithms. Current datasets are lacking in several respects, and this paper discusses some of the lessons learned from existing efforts, as well as innovative ways to obtain very large and diverse annotated datasets. It also suggests a few criteria for gathering future datasets.

1 Introduction

Image databases are an essential element of object recognition research. They are required for learning visual object models and for testing the performance of classification, detection, and localization algorithms. In fact, publicly available image collections such as UIUC [1], Caltech 4 [10], and Caltech 101 [9] have played a key role in the recent resurgence of category-level recognition research, driving the field by providing a common ground for algorithm development and evaluation. Current datasets, however, offer a somewhat limited range of image variability: Although the appearance (and to some extent, the shape) of objects does indeed vary within each class (e.g., among the airplanes, cars, faces, and motorbikes of Caltech 4), the viewpoints and orientations of different instances in each category tend to be similar (e.g., side views of cars taken by a horizontal camera in UIUC); their sizes and image positions are normalized (e.g., the objects of interest take up most of the image and are approximately centered in Caltech 101); there is only one instance of an object per image; finally, there is little or no occlusion and background clutter. This is illustrated by Figures 1 and 3 for the Caltech 101 database, but remains true of most datasets available today.

The problems with such restrictions are two fold: (i) some algorithms may exploit them (for example near-global descriptors with no scale or rotation invariance may perform well on such images), yet will fail when the restrictions

J. Ponce et al. (Eds.): Toward Category-Level Object Recognition, LNCS 4170, pp. 29–48, 2006.
© Springer-Verlag Berlin Heidelberg 2006

Fig. 1. Sample images from the Caltech 101 dataset [9], courtesy of Fei-Fei Li

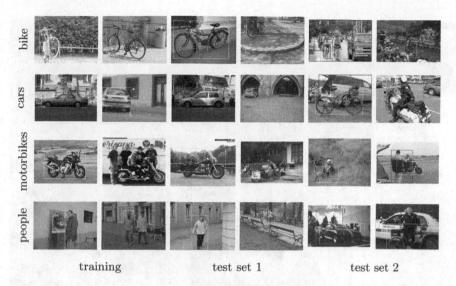

bike

cars

motorbikes

people

training   test set 1   test set 2

Fig. 2. Image examples with ground truth object annotation for different categories of the PASCAL 2005 challenge. The dataset may be obtained from http://www.pascal-network.org/challenges/VOC.

do not apply; and, related to this, (ii) the images are not sufficiently challenging for the benefits of more sophisticated algorithms (e.g., scale invariance) to make a difference. This means that progress in algorithm capability cannot be assessed. For example, multiple algorithms currently achieve close to 100% object vs. background classification accuracy on Caltech 4. There is a clear need for new datasets with more realistic and less restrictive image conditions: multiple object class instances within a single image, with partial occlusion (e.g., by other objects) and truncation (e.g., by the image edge), with size and orientation variations, etc. A first step in that direction has been taken with the datasets gathered for the PASCAL challenge, as illustrated by Figure 2. The rest of this chapter discusses some of the lessons learned from existing datasets such as Caltech 101 and those available under the PASCAL challenge. It also presents innovative ways to gather very large, annotated datasets from the World Wide Web, and concludes with some recommendations for future datasets, including a brief discussion of evaluation procedures.

2   Lessons Learned from Existing Datasets

2.1   The Caltech 101 Dataset

Most of the currently available datasets only contain a small number of classes, such as faces, pedestrians, and cars. A notable exception is the Caltech 101 database [9], with 101 object classes (Figure 1), which has become a de facto standard for evaluating algorithms for multi-class category-level recognition, and can be

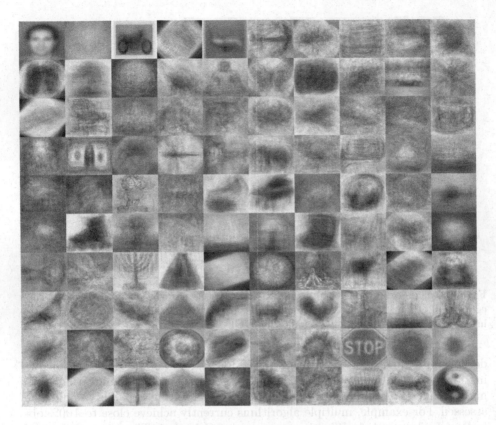

Fig. 3. The Caltech 101 average image

credited for a recent increase in efforts in this fundamental area of computer vision. Even though Caltech 101 is one of the most diverse datasets available today in terms of the amount of *inter-class* variability that it encompasses, it is unfortunately lacking in several important sources of *intra-class* variability. Namely, most Caltech 101 objects are of uniform size and orientation within their class, and lack rich backgrounds: This is demonstrated by the composite image shown in Figure 3, which was constructed by A. Torralba by averaging the RGB values of all the images for 100 of the object classes in the Caltech 101 dataset. The averaged images are computed by first resizing all the images to be 150×128 pixels and the intensity values of the final average are scaled to cover the range $[0, 255]$. They reveal regularities in the intensity patterns among all the images for each object category. If the images had a wide range of variations in object pose and object location, the resulting averages (before scaling the intensity values) would result in a (roughly) homogeneous field. This is clearly not the case, and many of the object classes are still easily recognizable by a human. Some of the characteristics of the dataset that are revealed by this experiment are that most images have little or no clutter, the objects tend to be centered in each image, and most objects are presented in a stereotypical pose.

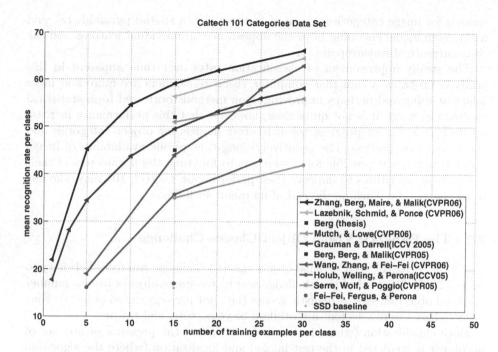

Fig. 4. A comparison of several algorithms on the Caltech 101 dataset [33], courtesy of H. Zhang

As noted earlier, despite its limitations, the Caltech 101 dataset has essentially become a de facto standard for multi-class recognition algorithms. Figure 4 shows the results of a comparative evaluation of several recent recognition algorithms on the Caltech 101 dataset [33], including those proposed by Fei-Fei *et al.* [9], Berg *et al.* [4], Grauman and Darrell [14], Holub *et al.* [17], Serre *et al.* [26] in 2005, and Berg [5], Lazebnik *et al.* [18], Mutch and Lowe [21], Ommer and Buhmann [22], Wang *et al.* [31], H. Zhang *et al.* [33] in 2006. The comparison also includes a baseline method comparing size-normalized greyscale images using correlation and nearest-neighbor classification [4].

We will not try to assess the merits of the different algorithms here. Instead, it is worth discussing what this comparison reveals about Caltech 101 as an evaluation tool. There are three clear trends: First, performance improves, as expected, with the number of training samples. Second, algorithms using SVMs as classifiers tend to do well, and include the two top performers [18,33]. Third, the classification rate steadily improves with time, from 17% in 2004 [9][1] to about 60% in 2006 [18,31,33]. None of these conclusions is very surprising, nor very telling about object recognition technology: The three methods achieving the best (and very close) performances for 30 training sample use totally different

---

[1] Very close to the 16% achieved by the baseline method — a reminder of the constant need for baseline comparisons.

models for image categories: a bag of features [33], a spatial pyramid [18], and a Bayesian model encoding both the appearance of individual features and the co-occurrence of feature pairs [31].

The steady improvement of classification rates over time apparent in this study is probably a sign that computer vision researchers are more and more adept at using and perhaps improving upon methods borrowed from statistical machine learning. It is not quite clear, however, that this performance increase *by itself* is a sign of progress toward better models for object categories and the recognition process. The (relatively) long-time public availability of image databases makes it possible for researchers to fine-tune the parameters of their recognition algorithms to improve their performance. Caltech 101 may, like any other dataset, be reaching the end of its useful shelf life.

2.2   The PASCAL Visual Object Classes Challenge

The first PASCAL[2] VOC (visual object classes) challenge ran from February to March 2005. The goal of the challenge was to recognize objects from a number of visual object classes in realistic scenes (i.e., not pre-segmented objects). Four object classes were selected: motorbikes, bicycles, cars, and people.

Both classification (where for each of the classes, the presence or absence of an object is predicted in the test image) and localization (where the algorithm must predict the bounding box and class of each object in the test image) were evaluated. A particular feature of the challenge was that two test sets were provided. For the first, images were assembled from a number of standard sources (e.g., the Caltech sets) and split randomly into training and test subsets with the same distribution of variability. Many algorithms already achieve very good performance on images of this difficulty; they have almost reached their peak performance. The second test set was designed to address this problem. It was assembled from new sources (Google image search, local photographs, etc.) with the intention of providing a harder test set with greater variability of scale, pose, background clutter and degree of occlusion, and assess the generalization ability of current algorithms. Needless to say, performance was inferior on the second test set. Twelve teams entered the challenge. Participants were provided with a development kit consisting of training and validation images, baseline algorithms, and evaluation software.[3] Figure 5 shows ROC curves for classification on the first and second test sets. The difference in performance is evident.

For the classification task, most participants used "global" methods in which a descriptor of the overall image content is extracted (such as a bag of words representation and a SVM classifier), which leaves the task of deciding which elements of the descriptor are relevant to the object of interest to the classifier.

---

[2] PASCAL stands for pattern analysis, statistical modelling and computational learning. It is the name of an EU Network of Excellence funded under the IST Program of the European Union.

[3] The development kit and test images are available from http://www.pascal-network.org/challenges/VOC/

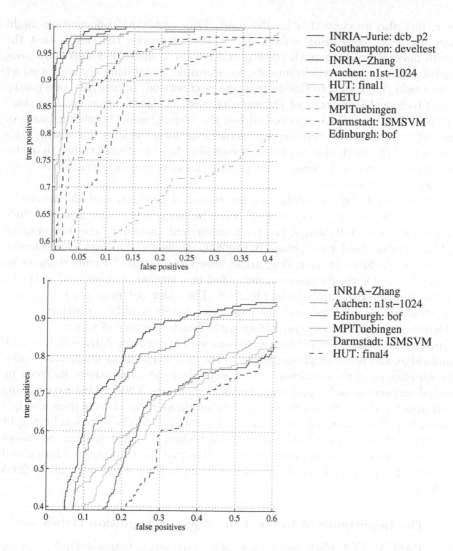

Fig. 5. PASCAL 2005 results. Top: ROC curves for classifying *motorbikes* images for test set 1 (where images taken from the same distribution of images as the training data). The best result in terms of EER (equal error rate) from each participant is shown, with curves ranked by decreasing EER. The axes cover a range equal to two times the maximum EER of the submitted results. Bottom: ROC curves for classifying *motorbikes* images for test set 2 (where images had more variability than the training data). The performance is inferior to that for test set 1.

All of these participants used only the class label attached to an image for training, ignoring additional annotation such as the bounding boxes of objects in the image. One possible advantage of "global" methods is that the image description captures information not only about the object of interest, e.g., a car, but also its context, e.g., the road. This contextual information might prove useful in recognizing some object classes; however, the risk is that the system may fail to distinguish the object from the context and thus show poor generalization to other environments, for example recognizing a car in a street vs. in a field. We return to this issue in the next section. In contrast, one participant (Technical University of Darmstadt) used a "classification by detection" approach which explicitly ignores all but the object, using bounding boxes or segmentation masks for training, and looking at local evidence for testing; this ensures that the method is modelling the object class of interest rather than statistical regularities in the image background, but may also fail to take advantage of contextual information.

Further details on the challenge, the tested algorithms, and the results of the evaluation can be found in [8].[4] The challenge is running again in 2006 with more classes (10) and a greater number and variability (in pose, partial occlusion) of images for each class. In the 2006 challenge, the classes are: bicycle, bus, car, motorbike cat, cow, dog, horse, sheep and people.[5] Figure 6 shows an average image for the 10 classes constructed in a similar manner to that shown for the Caltech 101 database in Figure 3. The color patterns are much more homogeneous in this case and the categories barely visible – providing some evidence of a greater image variability within each category of this set.

Images are obtained from three main sources: flickr.com, Microsoft Research Cambridge, and personal photographs. In the case of the flickr images the examples for each class are obtained by text search on the annotations, followed by manual inspection and annotation. In total there are 5,304 images, containing 9,507 annotated objects – each image may contain multiple objects from multiple classes, but all instances of the 10 classes are annotated. The data has been split into 50% for training/validation and 50% for testing. The distributions of images and objects by class are approximately equal across the training/validation and test sets. However, the level of difficulty is closer to that of test set 2 in the 2005 challenge.

2.3 The Importance of Context in Object Recognition Databases

In the PASCAL VOC challenge, several of the competing teams did quite well on full-image classification tasks. On the other hand, localization results were poor. As noted earlier, this suggests that background and contextual information may have played an important role in detection results. In other words, is it the object, or its background, which is recognized? J. Zhang *et al.* [34] have conducted a detailed study of this issue on the PASCAL dataset. We present in the rest of this section a summary of their findings.

A bag-of-features algorithm is used in the study. Like most modern approaches to category-level object detection, this algorithm does not attempt segmentation,

---

[4] Available at http://www.pascal-network.org/challenges/VOC/voc2005/chapter.pdf

[5] See http://www.pascal-network.org/challenges/VOC/voc2006/ for additional details.

Fig. 6. The PASCAL 2006 average image. Each cell is an average over all images containing a particular object category (of 10). Figure courtesy of T. Malisiewicz and A. Efros. Other averages are available at http://www.cs.cmu.edu/~tmalisie/pascal/means_trainval.html

and uses both foreground and background features as input in both training and testing tasks. Briefly, an image is characterized by its scale-invariant Harris and Laplacian regions, along with their SIFT descriptors. Clustering is used to construct the image's *signature* formed by the centers of its clusters and their relative sizes. Support vector machines (SVMs) using the Earth Mover's Distance [24] as a kernel are then trained on each object category, and used for image classification [34].

PASCAL images are annotated with ground truth object regions, as shown in Figure 2. Foreground features (FF) can thus be identified as those located within the object region, while background features (BF) are those located outside. Many object categories have fairly characteristic backgrounds. For example, most of the car images contain a street, a parking lot, or a building. To determine whether this information provides additional cues for classification, let us examine the change in classification performance when the original background features from an image are replaced by two specially constructed alternative sets: *random* and *constant natural scene* backgrounds (referred to as *BF-RAND* and *BF-CONST*, respectively). BF-RAND samples are obtained by randomly shuffling background features among all of the images in the PASCAL dataset. For example, the background of a face image may be replaced by the background of a car image. Note that the total number of features and the relative amount of clutter in an image may be altered as a result of this procedure. BF-CONST examples consist of background features extracted from images captured by a fixed camera observing a natural scene over an extended period of time, so they include continuous lighting changes and the movement of trees and clouds (Figure 7).

Figure 8 (a)–(b) shows ROC curves obtained by training and testing on only the background features (BF) for test sets 1 and 2. In the case of test 1, it is clear that background features alone are often sufficient to determine the category of the image. This is not quite the case for test set 2. For example, BF features perform close to chance level for bicycles. Thus, one of the reasons why test set 2 is considered more difficult than test set 1, is the fact that its background

Fig. 7. Image examples of the constant natural scene background. They are captured with lighting changes and the movement of clouds and trees.

features are much less correlated with the foreground. The performance of the BF-RAND and BF-CONST feature sets (not shown on the figure) is at chance level as one would expect, since they do not contain any information about the foreground object class by construction.

Figure 8 (c)–(e) evaluates combinations of foreground features with different types of background features. Due to space limitations only results for the people test set 1 are presented. Results for the other test sets are similar. AF denotes all the features extracted from the original image, AF-RAND denotes the combination of FF and BF-RAND and AF-CONST denotes the combination of FF and BF-CONST. Figure 8 (c) shows ROC curves for a situation where training and testing are performed on the same feature combination. FF gives the highest results, indicating that object features play the key role for recognition, and recognition with segmented images achieves better performance than without segmentation. Mixing background features with foreground features *does not* give higher recognition rates than FF alone. For images with roughly constant backgrounds (AF-CONST), the performance is almost the same as for images with foreground features only. It is intuitively obvious that classifying images with fixed backgrounds is as easy as classifying images with no background clutter at all. Finally, the ROC curves for AF-RAND are the lowest, which shows that objects with uncorrelated backgrounds are harder to recognize.

Figure 8 (d) shows ROC curves for a setup where the training set has different types of backgrounds and the test set has its original background (AF). We can observe that training on AF or AF-RAND while testing on AF gives the highest results. Thus, even under randomly changed training backgrounds, the SVM can find decision boundaries that generalize well to the original training set. Training on FF or AF-CONST and testing on AF gives lower results, most likely because the lack of clutter in FF set and the monotonous backgrounds in AF-CONST cause the SVM to overfit the training set. By contrast, varying the object background during training, even by random shuffling, tends to increase the robustness of the learned classifier.

Finally, Figure 8 (e) shows ROC curves for a situation where the training set has the original backgrounds and the test set has different types of backgrounds. When the test set is "easier" than the training one, performance improves, and when it is "harder," the performance drastically drops. This is consistent with the results of Figure 8 (d), where training on the "harder" sets AF or AF-RAND gave much better results than training on the "easier" sets FF and AF-CONST.

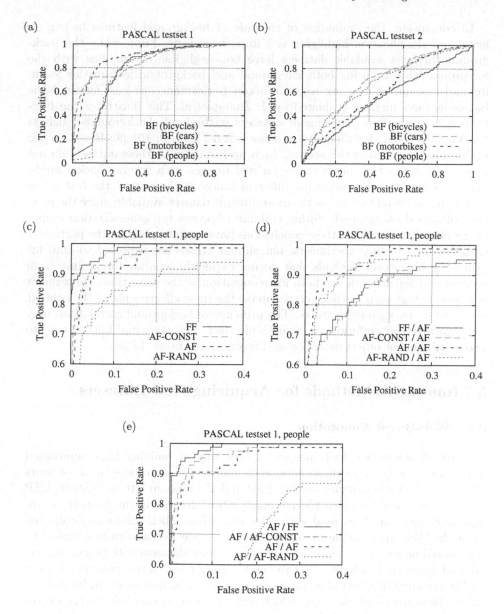

Fig. 8. ROC curves for the bag-of-features method of Zhang *et al.* [34] trained and tested on the PASCAL 2005 challenge dataset for different combinations of foreground and background features. (a)–(b): Training and testing on background features only. The left part of the figure corresponds to test set 1, and the right one to test set 2. (c)–(e): Training and testing using four combinations of foreground features with different types of background.

In conclusion, the evaluation of the role of background features in bag-of-keypoints classification highlights two important facts: First, while the backgrounds in most available datasets have non-negligible correlations with the foreground objects, using both foreground and background features for learning and recognition does not result in better performance, at least for the basic bag-of-features method evaluated by J. Zhang *et al.* This illustrates the limitations as evaluation platforms of datasets with simple backgrounds, such as CogVis [35], COIL-100 [36], and to some extent, Caltech 101 [9]: Based on the evaluation presented in this section, high performance on these datasets do not necessarily mean high performance on real images with varying backgrounds. Second, when the training set has different image statistics than the test set, it is usually beneficial to train on the most difficult dataset available, since the presence of varied backgrounds during training improves the generalization ability of the classifier. Note that these conclusions have been reached for the particular classifier used in the experiments, but similar trends are expected to hold for other bag-of-features methods that do not explicitly separate foreground from background features but use both for recognition at the same time. However, it is probable that such methods do not make the most effective use of the context provided by background features. The presence of background correlations may well improve the performance of methods that use contextual information to *prime* subsequent object detection and recognition stages [16,28].

3   Innovative Methods for Acquiring New Datasets

3.1   Web-Based Annotation

Web-based annotation tools provide a new way of building large annotated databases by relying on the collaborative effort of a large population of users [25,27,29,37]. Two examples are the ESP and Peekaboom internet games. ESP is an online game in which players enter labels describing the content of images [29]. ESP has been used with over 10 million labels for images collected from the Web. In a similar vein, the Internet game Peekaboom is designed to use "bored human intelligence" to label large image datasets with object, material, and geometry labels [30]. Peekaboom has been released to a general audience and it has already collected millions of data points. Its first task will be to label entire databases, such as Corel, which will be an enormous help to the object recognition community.

LabelMe is another online annotation tool that allows sharing of images and annotations [25]. The tool provides many functionalities such as drawing polygons, querying images, and browsing the database. Both the image database and all of the annotations are freely available. The tool runs on almost any Web browser, and includes a standard Javascript drawing interface that is easy to use (see Figure 9 for a screenshot). The resulting labels are stored in XML file format, which makes the annotations portable and easy to extend. A Matlab toolbox is available that provides functionalities for manipulating the database

Fig. 9. Screenshot from the LabelMe labeling tool in use [25]. The user is presented with an image, possibly with one or more existing annotations in the image. The user has the option of annotating a new object, by clicking around the boundary of the object, or editing an existing annotation. The user can annotate an arbitrary number of objects in the image. Once finished, the user then clicks the "Show New Image" button to see a new image.

(database queries, communication with the online tool, image transformations, etc.). The database is also searchable online.

Currently the database contains more than 36,000 objects labeled within 6,000 images covering a large range of environments and several hundred object categories (Figure 10, left). The images are high resolution and cover a wide field of view, providing rich contextual information. Pose information is also available for a large number of objects. Since the annotation tool has been made available online there has been a constant increase in the size of the database, with about 5,000 new labels added every month, on average.

One important concern when data is collected using Web-based tools is quality control. Currently quality control is provided by the users themselves. Polygons can be deleted and object names can be corrected using the annotation tool online. Despite the lack of a more direct mechanism of control, the annotations are of quite good quality (Figure 10). Another issue is the complexity of the polygons provided by the users – do users provide simple or complex polygon boundaries? Figure 10 (right) illustrates the average number of points used to define each polygon for four object classes that were introduced using the Web annotation tool. These object classes are among the most complicated. These polygons provide a good idea of the outline of the object, which is sufficient for most object detection and segmentation algorithms.

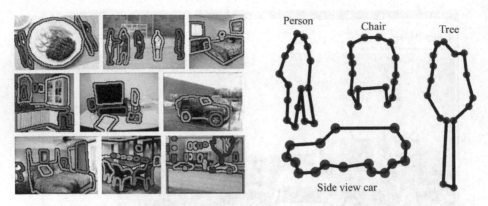

Fig. 10. Left: Examples of annotated images in the LabelMe database. The images cover a large range of scenes and object categories. Right: These polygons correspond to the average quality of the annotations for four object categories.

Another issue is what to label. For example, should you label a whole pedestrian, just the head, or just the face? What about a crowd of people – should you label all of them? Currently such decisions are left to each user, with the hope that the annotations will reflect what various people think are "natural" ways to segment an image. A third issue is the label itself. For example, should you call this object a "person", "pedestrian", or "man/woman"? An obvious solution is to provide a drop-down menu of standard object category names. Currently, however, people use their own descriptions, since these may capture some nuances that will be useful in the future. The Matlab toolbox allows querying the database using a list of possible synonyms.

3.2   Data Collection as Recognition

There is a plentiful supply of images available at the typing of a single word using Internet image search engines such as Google, and we discuss now two methods for obtaining object class images from this source. The first method uses Google image search as its source, the second uses web pages directly.

Starting from Image Search. Internet image search engines currently do not search directly on image visual content but instead use the image name and surrounding text. Consequently, this is not a source of pure images without filtering: for example, a Google image search for "monkey" yields only 30 actual monkey pictures in the first 100 results. Many of the returned images are visually unrelated to the intended category, perhaps arising from polysemes (e.g. "kite" can be kite-bird or kite-flying-toy). Even the small proportion of retrieved images that do correspond to the category are substantially more demanding than images in typical training sets (such as Caltech) – the number of objects in each image is unknown and variable, and the pose (visual aspect) and scale are uncontrolled.

Fergus *et al* [12] have proposed an unsupervised clustering method for extracting the "good" images from raw Google output. Each image is first described by a bag of keypoints/visual words. The clustering into visually coherent components is then achieved by applying probabilistic Latent Semantic Analysis (pLSA) [15] – a technique from the field of textual analysis originally developed for topic discovery in text corpus.

There then remains the problem of determining which of the clusters corresponds to the true object images. This problem could be solved by manual intervention, but Fergus *et al* [12] instead build a validation set automatically by noting that the first few images returned by Google tend to contain more good images than those returned later on. Using Google's automatic translation, the user's keyword is translated into a number of languages; the first few images are automatically downloaded, and combined to give a validation set of a reasonable size without degradation in quality.

In this manner, starting with Google image search, followed by clustering of visual words and automatic selection of the correct cluster using a generated validation set, image datasets can be generated using just the object's name. The main limitation of this approach is the effectiveness of the original image search engine. This limitation can be overcome by a semi-automatic method, as presented next.

Starting from Text Search. There are currently more than 8,168,684,336 Web pages on the Internet.[6] A search for the term "monkey" yields 36,800,000 results using Google text search. There must be a large number of images portraying "monkeys" within these pages, but retrieving them using Google image search is not successful, as described above. It has been known for a while that textual and visual information could effectively be combined in tasks such as clustering art [2], labeling images [3,13,19], or identifying faces in news photographs [6]. In these cases, an explicit relationship between words and pictures is given by image annotations, or photograph and video captions. On Web pages, however, the link between words and pictures is less clear. Berg and Forsyth consider in [7] the problem of combining the text and image information stored on Web pages to re-rank Google search results for a set of queries (see [11,32] for related work). They focus on *animal* categories because these provide rich and difficult data, often taking on a wide variety of appearances, depictions, and aspects, thus providing a good yardstick for demonstrating the benefits of exploiting the visual and textual information contained in Web pages.

In the method described in [7], a set of images is first obtained by text search. For example, 9,320 Web pages are collected using Google text search on 13 queries related to monkeys. From these pages, 12,866 distinct images of sufficiently large size (at least 120×120 pixels) are selected for further consideration. Of these images 2,569 are actual monkey images. The algorithm proceeds in two stages: first a set of visual exemplars (exemplars for short) is selected using only text-based information. Then, in the second stage, visual and textual cues are combined to rank the downloaded images, with monkey images being highly ranked.

---

[6] Google's last released number of indexed Web pages.

In the first stage Latent Dirichlet Allocation (LDA) is applied to the words contained in the Web pages to discover a set of latent topics for each category. These latent topics provide a distribution over words and are used to select highly likely words for each topic. Images are ranked according to their nearby word likelihoods and a set of 30 exemplars selected for each topic. As mentioned earlier, words and images can be ambiguous (e.g. "alligator" could refer to "alligator boots" or "alligator clips" as well as the animal). Currently there is no known method for breaking this polysemy-like phenomenon automatically. Therefore, at this point the user is asked to label each topic as relevant or background, depending on whether the associated images and words illustrate the category well. Using this labeling all selected topics are merged into a relevant topic and all unselected topics are merged into a background topic (and their exemplars and likely words are similarly pooled).

In the second stage, each image in the downloaded dataset is ranked according to a voting method using the knowledge base collected in the training stage. Voting uses image information in the form of shape, texture and color features as well as word information based on words on the associated pages that are located near the image.

Because exemplar-based voting incorporates multiple templates per category, it allows image retrieval across different poses, aspects, and even species. The top results returned by the composite classifier are in general quite good [7]: 81% of the top 500 images, and 69% of the top 1000 are correct (Figure 11). Most importantly, the images classified using both textual and visual features make up a very large, high-quality dataset for further object recognition research.

4   Recommendations

Research on object detection and recognition in cluttered scenes requires large image and video collections with ground truth labels. The labels should provide information about the object classes present in each image, as well as their shape and locations, and possibly other attributes such as pose. Such data is useful for testing, as well as for supervised learning. Even algorithms that require little supervision need large databases with ground truth to validate the results.[7] New algorithms that exploit context for object recognition [16,28] require databases with many labeled object classes embedded in complex scenes. Such databases should contain a wide variety of environments with annotated objects that co-occur in the same images. Future databases should exercise the ability of recognition systems to handle intra-class variability, varying size and pose, partial occlusion, and contextual cues. They should also display different levels of difficulty, including restricted viewpoints (e.g., cars will only be seen more or less from the side), reasonable levels of occlusion and viewpoint variation (e.g., cars from all viewing angles), a higher degree of intra-class variability (chairs,

---

[7] This is not to say that the annotations of future databases will be perfect: We expect that segmentations may be inaccurate, and labellings questionable, but scale will probably rescue us.

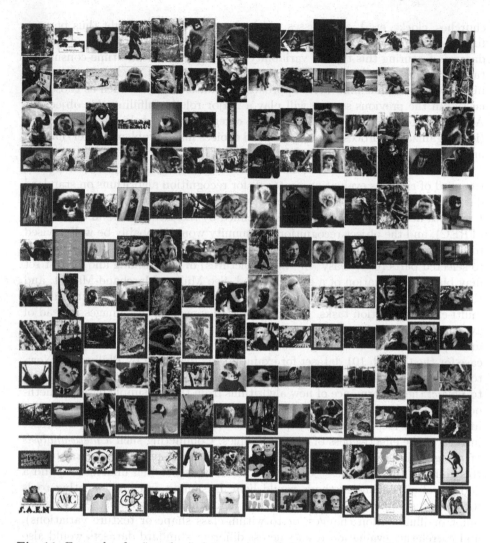

Fig. 11. Example of a "monkey" dataset generated semi-automatically, starting from a keyword search [7]. False positives are shown with a heavy border (dark red). The first 10 rows are sampled every 4th image from the top 560 results, while the last two rows are sampled every 250th image from the last 5,000-12,866 results. The dataset is quite accurate, with a precision of 81% for the top 500 images, and a precision of 69% for the top 1000 images. Deciding what images are relevant to a query doesn't have a single interpretation. Here, primates like apes, lemurs, chimps and gibbons have been included, but monkey figurines, people, monkey masks and monkey drawings have been excluded. The results include a huge range of aspects and poses as well as a depictions in different settings (e.g. trees, cages and indoor settings). The animal image classifiers inherently take advantage of the fact that objects are often correlated with their backgrounds ("monkeys" are often in trees and other greenery).

churches, clocks, etc.), and classes which share "parts" and might thus be confused (e.g., bikes/motorbikes, cars/lorries, etc.). Constructing large, annotated datasets featuring this type of variability will be a difficult and time-consuming task. It should also be one of the priorities of the object recognition community. We believe that innovative approaches to data collection such as those discussed in the previous section will play a major role in fulfilling this objective. A serious notion of object and/or scene category would help the data collection/organization process, since good/bad choices make problems easier/harder, and we do not know how to model this effect.

A very important issue that has not not been addressed in this chapter is the need of rigorous evaluation protocols for recognition algorithms on standard datasets. Standard performance measures for information retrieval, such as *interpolated average precision*, have been defined by the Text REtrieval Conference (TREC), and the object recognition community would probably be well advised to follow that example.[8] Further, the (rather typical) restriction of experiments to selected parts (e.g., "easy" or "hard" pictures) of the training and/or test set may bias the evaluation of a given method. See Müller, Marchand-Maillet, and Pun [20] for a discussion of this problem in the context of image retrieval.[9] In multi-class recognition tasks, gathering statistics over all test images instead of averaging them over categories may also bias the results when there are many more pictures for some "easy" classes than for some "hard" ones (this is the case for the Caltech 101 dataset for example). As discussed by Philips and Newton [23] in the face recognition domain, it is actually possible for some datasets to *predict* the performance of new algorithms from that of simple baseline methods (e.g., PCA plus nearest-neighbor classification, a.k.a. "eigenfaces"). This indicates that face recognition experiments often test the difficulty of a dataset instead of the effectiveness of new techniques. Conducting such a *meta-analysis* of category-level object recognition algorithms could prove to be fruitful. In this context, the "hardness" of different datasets is not well understood, and a good pool of baseline methods would help. Designing and implementing tools for testing specific aspects of recognition algorithms (e.g., robustness to viewpoint or illumination changes, or to within-class shape or texture variations), and correlating evaluation results across different standard datasets would also be extremely useful.

Acknowledgments. Many thanks to Fei-Fei Li for providing Figure 1, H. Zhang for providing Figure 4, and T. Malisiewicz and A. Efros for providing Figure 6. This work was supported in part by the National Science Foundation under grants IIS-0308087 and IIS-0535152; the IST Programme of the European Community, under the PASCAL Network of Excellence, IST-2002-506778; the French ACI project MoViStaR; the UIUC-CNRS-INRIA collaboration agreement; and

---

[8] Initial efforts are under way. See http://trec.nist.gov/pubs/trec10/appendices/measures.pdf and http://www-nlpir.nist.gov/projects/trecvid/.

[9] The discussion in this paper focuses on the Corel database, which is widely (and perhaps unwisely—see the comments in the article) used in the image retrieval community.

the Lava European project. M. Marszalek was supported by the INRIA student exchange program and a grant from the European Community under the Marie Curie Visitor project. Any opinions, findings, and conclusions or recommendations expressed in this publication are those of the authors and do not necessarily reflect the views of the National Science Foundation or European Community.

References

1. Agarwal, S., Roth, D.: Learning a sparse representation for object detection. In: Proc. European Conf. Comp. Vision. Volume LNCS 2353., Copenhagen, Denmark (2002) 113–127
2. Barnard, K., Duyguly, P., Forsyth, D.: Clustering art. In: Proc. IEEE Conf. Comp. Vision Patt. Recog. Vol. II (2001) 435–439
3. Barnard, K., Duygulu, P., Forsyth, D., de Freitas, N., Blei, D., Jordan, M.: Matching words and pictures. Journal of Machine Learning Research **3** (2003), 1107–1135
4. Berg, A., Berg, T.L., Malik, J.: Shape matching and object recognition using low distortion correspondence. In: Proc. IEEE Conf. Comp. Vision Patt. Recog. Vol. II (2005) 435–439
5. Berg, A.C.: Phd thesis. (To appear.)
6. Berg, T.L., Berg, A.C., Edwards, J., Forsyth, D.: Who's in the picture? In: Proc. Neural Inf. Proc. Syst. (2004)
7. Berg, T.L., Forsyth, D.: Animals on the Web. In: Proc. IEEE Conf. Comp. Vision Patt. Recog. (2006)
8. Everingham, M., Zisserman, A., Williams, C., Van Gool, L., Allan, M., Bishop, C., Chapelle, O., Dalal, N., Deselaers, T., Dorko, G., Duffner, S., Eichhorn, J., Farquhar, J., Fritz, M., Garcia, C., Griffiths, T., Jurie, F., Keysers, D., Koskela, M., Laaksonen, J., Larlus, D., Leibe, B., Meng, H., Ney, H., Schiele, B., Schmid, C., Seemann, E., Shawe-Taylor, J., Storkey, A., Szedmak, S., Triggs, B., Ulusoy, I., Viitaniemi, V., Zhang, J.: The 2005 PASCAL visual object classes challenge. In: Selected Proceedings of the First PASCAL Challenges Workshop. LNAI, Springer-Verlag (2006)
9. Fei-Fei, L., Fergus, R., Perona, P.: Learning generative visual models from few training examples: an incremental Bayesian approach tested on 101 object categories. In: Proc. IEEE Conf. Comp. Vision Patt. Recog Workshop on Generative-Model Based Vision. (2004)
10. Fergus, R., Perona, P., Zisserman, A.: Object class recognition by unsupervised scale-invariant learning. In: Proc. IEEE Conf. Comp. Vision Patt. Recog. Vol. II (2003) 264–271
11. Fergus, R., Perona, P., Zisserman, A.: A visual category filter for Google images. In: Proc. Europ. Conf. Comp. Vision. (2004)
12. Fergus, R., Fei-Fei, L., Perona, P., Zisserman, A.: Learning object categories from Google's image search. In: Proc. Int. Conf. Comp. Vision. (2005)
13. Giridharan, I., Duygulu, P., Feng, S., Ircing, P., Khudanpur, S., Klakow, D., Krause, M., Manmatha, R., Nock, H., Petkova, D., Pytlik, B., Virga, P.: Joint visual-text modeling for automatic retrieval of multimedia documents. In: Proc. ACM Multimedia Conference. (2005)
14. Grauman, K., Darrell, T.: The pyramid match kernel: Discriminative classification with sets of image features. MIT-CSAIL-TR-2006-020 (2006). Updated version of the ICCV'05 paper with the same title, featuring the improved results shown in Fig. 4.

15. Hofmann, T.: Unsupervised learning by probabilistic latent semantic analysis. Machine Learning **43** (2001) 177–196
16. Hoiem, D., Efros, A., Hebert, M.: Geometric context from a single image. In: Proc. Int. Conf. Comp. Vision. (2005)
17. Holub, A., Welling, M., Perona, P.: Combining generative models and fisher kernels for object class recognition. In: Proc. Int. Conf. Comp. Vision. (2005)
18. Lazebnik, S., Schmid, C., Ponce, J.: Beyond bags of features: Spatial pyramid matching for recognizing natural scene categories. In: Proc. IEEE Conf. Comp. Vision Patt. Recog. (2005)
19. Li, J., Wang, J.: Automatic linguistic indexing of pictures by a statistical modeling approach. PAMI (2003) **25**(9), 1075–1088
20. Müller, H., Marchand-Maillet, S., Pun, T.: The truth about Corel – Evaluation in image retrieval. In: The Challenge of Image and Video Retrieval (CIVR2002), London, UK (2002)
21. Mutch, J., Lowe, D.: Multiclass object recognition using sparse, localized features. In: Proc. IEEE Conf. Comp. Vision Patt. Recog. (2006)
22. Ommer, B., Buhmann, J.M.: Learning compositional categorization models. In: Proc. Europ. Conf. Comp. Vision. (2006)
23. Philips, P., Newton, E.: Meta-analysis of face recognition algorithms. In: Int. Conf. on Automatic Face and Gesture Recognition. (2002)
24. Rubner, Y., Tomasi, C., Guibas, L.: The Earth Mover's distance as a metric for image retrieval. International Journal of Computer Vision **40**(2) (2000) 99–121
25. B. C. Russell, A. Torralba, K.P.M., Freeman, W.T.: LabelMe: a database and web-based tool for image annotation. Technical report, MIT, AI Lab Memo AIM-2005-025 (2005)
26. Serre, T., Wolf, L., Poggio, T.: object recognition with features inspired by visual cortex. In: Proc. IEEE Conf. Comp. Vision Patt. Recog. (2005)
27. Stork, D.: The open mind initiative. IEEE Intelligent Systems and Their Applications **14**(3) (1999) 19–20
28. Torralba, A.: Contextual priming for object detection. International Journal of Computer Vision **53**(2) (2003) 153–167
29. von Ahn, L., Dabbish, L.: Labeling images with a computer game. In: Proc. ACM Conf. Hum. Factors Comp. Syst. (CHI). (2004)
30. von Ahn, L., Liu, R., Blum, M.: Peekaboom: A game for locating objects in images. In: Proc. ACM Conf. Hum. Factors Comp. Syst. (CHI). (2006)
31. Wang, G., Zhang, Y., Fei-Fei, L.: Using dependent regions for object categorization in a generative framework. In: Proc. IEEE Conf. Comp. Vision Patt. Recog. (2006)
32. Yanai, K., Barnard, K.: Probabilistic web image gathering. In: Workshop on MIR. (2005)
33. Zhang, H., Berg, A.C., Maire, M., Malik, J.: SVM-KNN: Discriminative nearest neighbor classification for visual category recognition. In: Proc. IEEE Conf. Comp. Vision Patt. Recog. (2006)
34. Zhang, J., Marszalek, M., Lazebnik, S., Schmid, C.: Local features and kernels for classification of texture and object categories: An in-depth study. Technical Report RR-5737, INRIA Rhône-Alpes (2005)
35. (http://www.vision.ethz.ch/projects/cogvis/CogVis-images/image-samples.html)
36. (http://www1.cs.columbia.edu/CAVE/research/softlib/coil-100.html)
37. (http://www.flickr.com)

Industry and Object Recognition: Applications, Applied Research and Challenges

Yutaka Hirano[1], Christophe Garcia[2], Rahul Sukthankar[3,4],
and Anthony Hoogs[5]

[1] Future Projects Division
Toyota Motor Corporation
Mishuku 1200, Susono-shi, Sizuoka-ken, 410-1193 Japan
yutaka@hirano.tec.toyota.co.jp
[2] France Telecom division R&D
4, rue du Clos Courtel
35512 Cesson Sevigne Cedex - France
christophe.garcia@francetelecom.com
http://perso.rd.francetelecom.fr/garcia/
[3] Intel Research Pittsburgh
4720 Forbes Ave. #410, Pittsburgh, PA 15213, USA
rahuls@cs.cmu.edu
[4] The Robotics Institute
Carnegie Mellon University, Pittsburgh, PA 15213, USA
[5] GE Global Research
One Research Circle
Niskayuna, NY 12309 USA
hoogs@research.ge.com

Abstract. Object recognition technology has matured to a point at which exciting applications are becoming possible. Indeed, industry has created a variety of computer vision products and services from the traditional area of machine inspection to more recent applications such as video surveillance, or face recognition. In this chapter, several representatives from industry present their views on the use of computer vision in industry. Current research conducted in industry is summarized and prospects for future applications and developments in industry are discussed.

1 Introduction

As visual recognition and computer vision in general have become more mature, industry has created an ever-increasing variety of computer vision products and services. From the traditional area of machine inspection, commercial vision applications have expanded into video surveillance, medical image analysis, face detection and recognition, and many others.

Significant challenges remain before generic, categorical object recognition can attain widespread commercial use. The major barriers include:

J. Ponce et al. (Eds.): Toward Category-Level Object Recognition, LNCS 4170, pp. 49–64, 2006.
© Springer-Verlag Berlin Heidelberg 2006

- Robustness w.r.t. variation in viewpoint, illumination, scale and imaging conditions.
- Scaling up to thousands of object classes. While some applications may only require class libraries of dozens of objects, many require much larger class diversity requiring human-level performance.

In this chapter, the visual recognition needs, challenges and current research of four industrial labs are described. These corporations – Intel, Toyota, General Electric, and France Telecom – are some of the largest technology and engineering firms in the world. Additional corporations and organizations sponsored the workshop, including Northup Grumman, Xerox, Lockheed Martin, Microsoft and DARPA.

2   Visual Recognition at France Telecom Research and Development

In the last decade, we have entered the digital era, with the convergence of telecommunication, video and informatics. Our society (press agencies, television channels, customers) is producing daily extremely large and increasing amounts of digital images and videos, making it more and more difficult to track and access this content via database search engines that rely mostly on manually annotated information. Content-based indexing via automatic object detection and recognition techniques has become one of most important and challenging issues for the years to come, in order to face the limitation of traditional information systems. Some expected applications include [34]: information and entertainment video production and distribution; professional video archive management including legacy footages; teaching, training, enterprise or institutional communication; TV program monitoring; self-produced content management; internet search engines; video surveillance and video conference archiving and management; and advanced object-based image coding.

There has been much research over the last decade to develop image and video content-based indexing systems [43,35]. Most existing commercial products rely on searching images "looking like" others, using global descriptions, by extracting feature vectors that summarize the content of the images in terms of luminance, color or texture. These feature vectors are traditionally statistical summaries of color distribution in different color spaces, textures in the form of histograms of gradient directions or Gabor coefficient statistics. These descriptors offer the advantage of being invariant to global image transformations such as warping or object motion. On the other hand, structural information in the image is not captured and different images can have very similar global feature descriptors. In order to take into account the heterogeneous nature of an image and somehow its structure, more advanced systems are based on the detection of patches or salient points (local contrast, edges, corners and junctions,etc.) where local signatures are computed around each patch to characterize the more visually discriminant parts of the image. Image comparison is then performed by matching patches.

Both approaches, using no a priori knowledge on the image content, allow treating images regardless of their specific semantic content. But, one can wonder what global similarity between images means, which is extremely subjective and application-dependent. For a large range of applications, accessing the semantic content and identifying high-level indices is a pre-requisite, regardless of the global context of the image. This is the goal of object detection and recognition techniques that aim at locating faces, human bodies, cars, buildings, etc. They can be successfully applied to adult content filtering in the web, traffic surveillance, security access control, visual geo-localization, visio-conferences or intelligent man-machine communication. More generally, key object detection in collections of images or video sequences may provide easy, accurate and more natural ways of indexing and retrieving information ("find my photos in front of the Eiffel tower", "find the photos of Barbara", etc.). Given the growing volume of personal digital pictures, and the rapid development of Peer-to-Peer applications, one of the key applications is the management of self-produced content, where collections of personal digital pictures have to be stored, shared, sorted and retrieved according to the presence of specific persons, of specific objects or buildings. They may be tagged with meta-data when recorded, or indexed a posteriori when users formulate a specific request, like finding photos of friends, family, etc.

If object detection and recognition methods have long been limited to the "world of cubes", using low-level image analysis and heuristics, new supervised learning-based appearance methods have appeared recently and proved to be very efficient for several specific applications. For instance, human face detection can be considered as a mature tool, even though progress must be made for full-profile view detection and accurate facial feature detection, for allowing efficient face recognition. The method proposed by Viola and Jones [44], relying on a boosted cascade of simple classifiers based on Haar low level features seems very appealing given its speed and its good detection rate. More recently, Garcia and Delakis [7] proposed a near-real time neural-based face detection scheme, named "Convolutional Face Finder" (CFF) that has been designed to precisely locate multiple faces of 20x20 pixel minimum size and variable appearance, rotated up to ±30 degrees in image plane and turned up to ±60 degrees, in complex real world images. As a generic object detection method, the proposed system automatically synthesizes simple problem specific feature extractors and classifiers from a training set of faces, without making any assumptions or using any hand-made design concerning the features to extract or the areas of the face pattern to analyze. Moreover, global constraints encoding the face model are automatically learnt and used implicitly and directly in the detection process. After training, the face detection procedure acts like a pipeline of simple convolution and subsampling modules that treat the raw input face image as a whole in order to locate faces, without requiring any local contrast preprocessing in the input image. Experiments have shown high detection rates with a particularly low number of false positives, on difficult test sets, without requiring the use of multiple networks for handling difficult cases. For instance, a good detection rate of 90.3% with 8 false positives have been reported on the CMU test set, which are the best results published so far on this test set (Figure 1).

Fig. 1. Some results of CFF on the CMU test set and a CFF-based face recognition system at France Telecom

One can notice that, for the time being, most approaches tackle detection of single objects with stable 2D appearances. There is still much to be done in the case of deformable 3D object detection. Moreover, most state-of-the-art successful methods rely on large training data sets, in order to infer the object class boundaries in discriminant feature space. Generative methods requiring fewer object examples must be investigated and combined with these discriminative methods, in order to ease the development of the pattern classifiers. More than single object detection, more general object category recognition techniques (like vehicles, buildings, etc.) have also to be considered in order to reduce the number of specific object detection methods and allow more powerful and natural user queries.

Beyond the development of specific algorithms, performance evaluation of object recognition techniques for content-based image and video indexing is still a critical issue. A few specific frameworks have been organized, for specific recognition tasks such as face recognition [1] or for more global video indexing [2], where measures such as good detection/false alarm rates, or accuracy/recall rates are estimated using test data with ground truth. Some challenges tend to be organized like the "Pascal Visual Object Classes Challenge" (VOCC), organized by Mark Everingham, Luc Van Gool, Chris Williams and Andrew Zisserman, in March 2005 [3]. The goal of this challenge was to assess different object recognition approaches for different visual object classes (motorbikes, bicycles, people and cars) in images of realistic scenes. A training set of labelled images and various test sets were provided to assess the generalization capabilities of supervised algorithms trained with a reduced and unique set of examples. Among the competing methods, a modified version of the CFF system [7] has been applied to the detection and localization of cars and motorbikes, showing good generalization capabilities, given the small number of examples and the variability of the objects to detect.

But, in general, given the very large number of possible applications and the very specific research projects, most approaches are tested on "home-made" reduced data sets, where the proposed techniques perform reasonably and that are not easily shared among the research groups. Evaluating each approach and comparing it with others is therefore difficult. Moreover, developers of industrial applications obviously require successful techniques, but also clearer insight regarding the limits of the approaches, i.e. when and why they fail, in order to offer reliable solutions.

3 Visual Recognition at Intel

Intel Research engages in a variety of research projects that address real-world problems using techniques from object recognition. In addition to conducting work that relates directly to its product roadmaps, Intel is also active in exploratory research, particularly in the context of open collaborative projects pursued with faculty and students in academia. These projects typically generate implementations that are released as open source. This section presents an overview of three selected projects: efficient sub-image retrieval using local descriptors; object-based image retrieval; and computational nanovision.

3.1 Efficient Sub-image Retrieval Using Local Descriptors

The goal of sub-image retrieval is to find all of the images in a database that have features in common with a query image. Applications include content-based image retrieval (CBIR), identifying copyright violations on the web and detecting image forgeries. However, unlike traditional CBIR, the query image cannot be matched against the database using global features. Our system [19] builds a parts-based representation of images using distinctive local descriptors which give high quality matches even under severe transformations. To cope with the large number of features extracted from the images, we employ locality-sensitive hashing [10] to index the local descriptors. This allows us to make approximate similarity queries that only examine a small fraction of the database. Although locality-sensitive hashing has excellent theoretical performance properties, a standard implementation would still be unacceptably slow for this application. By optimizing layout and access to the index data on disk, we can efficiently query indices containing millions of keypoints.

Figure 2 illustrates the system architecture. As images are added to the database, we perform feature extraction using the SIFT [25] detector and PCA-SIFT descriptor [20]. These keypoints are stored in a collection of LSH hashtables on disk. In typical experiments on a fine art collection, there are approximately 15 million keypoints for a set of 12,000 images. During retrieval, keypoints are extracted from the query image and the set of matching keypoints is efficiently retrieved from the database. The system employs a RANSAC-based geometric verification step (using an affine transform model) to eliminate false positives. Figure 3 shows a query generated by compositing patches from two images. The system correctly identifies both source images from a large collection of fine art images without finding any false positives. Our system achieves near-perfect accuracy (100% precision at 99.85% recall) on the tests presented in Meng *et al.* [28], and consistently strong results on our own, significantly more challenging experiments [19]. Query times are interactive even for collections of thousands of images.

3.2 Object-Based Image Retrieval

Object-based Image Retrieval is a collaborative effort between Intel Research Pittsburgh and Carnegie Mellon University, in the context of the Diamond project [13]. The goal is to create image retrieval systems based on the objects that appear in the images by learning the target concept *on-line* from a small set of examples provided by the user.

Unlike most existing systems that discriminate based on a histogram or clustering of color or texture features computed over the entire region, our system performs a windowed search over location and scale for each image in the database. This approach allows the retrieval of an image based on the presence of objects that may occupy only a small portion of the image. Also, we do not assume that a feature's value is independent of location within the window. This allows our system to retrieve images based on objects composed of colors and textures that are distinctive only when location within the window is considered, as is common with many man-made objects.

The system consists of two stages. An exhaustive windowed scan over scale and position generates a set of subimages. The first stage classifies and ranks

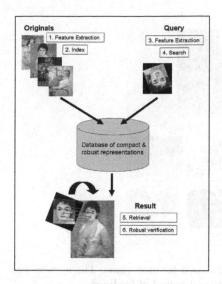

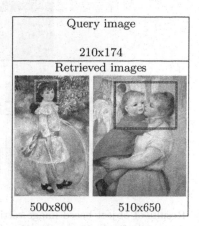

Fig. 2. System diagram: sub-image retrieval relies on efficient near-neighbor searches of PCA-SIFT descriptors

Fig. 3. Given a composite query, the system correctly retrieves the two source images, without false matches from a database containing over 6000 similar paintings

subimages using the posterior probability, computed from the estimated unconditional density and the object class conditional density. The second stage, trained using relevance feedback, reduces false positives by classifying subimages that are labeled as positive by the first stage. If a subimage passes both stages, the image is returned to the user.

3.3 Computational Nanovision

Silicon manufacturing technology is now able to shrink critical dimensions of structures down to scales well below 100 nm. These nanostructures are too small to see, even with the most sophisticated imaging equipment. This presents a challenge for Intel engineers who examine microprocessors to identify which nanostructures are defective, so repairs can be made. The Computational Nanovision research project addresses the challenge posed by the low resolution and the low signal-to-noise ratio of nano-imaging tools. Researchers apply computer vision techniques based on sophisticated mathematical models to measure and create visual representations of these structures, and to automate image and data analysis.

Computational nanovision exploits the availability of detailed models of microprocessor layouts and manufacturing processes. By integrating this information with knowledge of the physics underlying image formation, one can develop new model-based techniques for analyzing nanostructures in images. This has

Fig. 4. Results of object-based image retrieval search for stop signs. The system was trained on a total of only 12 stop sign images after 1 round of feedback.

led to tools for image reconstruction, feature detection and classification in noisy images.

Image and Surface Reconstruction. The smaller the structure, the noisier the image. Researchers have developed probabilistic techniques for real-time reconstruction of noisy images of nano-structures. This enables a user to observe features that are otherwise not visible through the noise, as shown in Figure 5.

To do this, researchers first create statistical models of the noise distribution of specific tools and incorporate them into a Bayesian de-noising framework. This allows them separate the real image structure from the noise, and provides the user with a significantly enhanced image. In some cases, users wish to see the real 3D structure of an object instead of a scanning beam image. To enable this, the research group has recently developed a novel technique for rapidly generating three-dimensional structures from two-dimensional images of scanning electron microscopes, which was computationally intractable in the past. Using this new technique, 3-D reconstructions of nano-structures visible in an SEM image can be obtained within minutes.

Nanofeature Detection and Classification. Some applications, such as nano-machining, require real-time capability to allow for fast visual feedback from manufacturing tools. Even if a nanostructure image can be perfectly reconstructed, currently the tool operator must make a decision, such as determining when a structure of interest is visible in the noisy image. Researchers use probabilistic techniques to automatically detect and classify nano-features, to assist users and reduce the risk of human error. The eventual goal is to fully automate the process, removing humans from the loop.

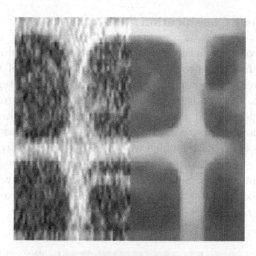

Fig. 5. Computational nanovision can perform image reconstruction on noisy input images (left), enable users to observe nanostructures through the noise (right)

4   Visual Recognition at General Electric Global Research

The Visualization and Computer Vision Lab within General Electric Global Research is currently engaged in the development of computer vision technology in video surveillance, medical image analysis, biological image analysis, industrial inspection, and broadcast media. In all of these applications, visual recognition is a critical enabling technology. For video surveillance, we are conducting research in a variety of areas, including: tracking people and vehicles [29,16,22]; segmenting moving crowds into individuals [32]; person re-identification [9]; detecting events and behaviors of interest [5,4]; camera calibration [21,41]; scene understanding [18,14]; and face analysis and recognition [24,40].

For broadcast video, we have developed methods for semantic object recognition using context established by the transcript [15,36,33]. For industrial inspection, we have focused on the problem of curved surfaces with complex reflectance [37]. In medical imaging, we have developed algorithms to automatically screen diagnostic images for early cancer detection [17,27]. We have also conducted research in recognizing partial or low-quality fingerprints [38,39], which has been used by the FBI.

In all of these areas, significant progress in visual recognition has been essential for developing prototypes and for transitioning algorithms into operations and products. As recognition technology improves, we envision significantly enhanced applications in many of the GE businesses.

Our recent efforts in scene content classification and person re-identification are perhaps the most relevant to this workshop, and are summarized briefly here.

4.1   Scene Content Classification

The goal of scene content classification is to label every pixel in an image with its category. We define this problem using a small number of broad categories, such that every pixel can be correctly classified into some category.

In our approach, we perform an initial, dense region segmentation on the image to form "superpixels", which are then attributed with a feature vector. We have explored and compared two formulations of this feature vector. First, following the work of [14,18,31], which we will call *perceptual features*, we include superpixel contrast, parallelism and continuity features derived from the region graph using adjacent regions. Second, following [42,?], which we will call *texton-based features*, a texture filter bank is computed at each pixel, quantized into textons, and histogrammed over the region.

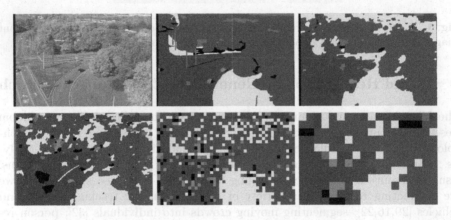

Fig. 6. Example results of our segmentation and classification methods, compared to image block classification. Top left: an image (not used in training); top middle: manual segmentation and labeling. The six classes are: dark gray=road, orange=vehicle, brown=building, dark green=tree, light green=grass, black=shadow. Four classification results from: perceptual features with AdaBoost.MV, with 75.2% pixel-wise correct classification (top right); texton features 66.0% (bottom left); 8x8 image blocks 62.6% (bottom middle); 20x20 image blocks 63.8% (bottom right).

Each attributed region is classified using a novel, generic extension of boosting for a multiclass problem, AdaBoost.MV. We treat the output of an ensemble of binary classifiers as a derived "vote" feature vector, performing MAP classification in this more discriminating space using a Gaussian distribution over classes.

Comparative results are shown in Figure 6. We compared our region-based methods to block-based methods, where each block is characterized by its texton histogram. On a set of 25 images, with 10 training and 15 test, AdaBoost.MV with perceptual features outperforms texton features 75.2% to 66% in pixel-wise classification accuracy. Textons on 20x20 image blocks scored 64%.

These scene classification methods have been applied to broadcast news content annotation [15] and tracking vehicles [16]. In the latter, knowledge of scene content is used to improve stabilization, moving object detection and track loss due to occlusion.

4.2 Person Re-identification Using Spatio-temporal Appearance

In many surveillance applications it is desirable to determine if a given individual has been previously observed over a network of cameras. This is the person

Fig. 7. Top ten person matches using the model-based algorithm. The query image is shown in the left column, and the remaining columns are the top matches ordered from left to right. The query and matching images are taken from different cameras. A box is used to highlight when a match corresponds to query. Third row shows an example where the correct match is not present in the top ten matches.

reidentification problem. Our approach focuses on reidentification algorithms that use the overall appearance of an individual as opposed to passive biometrics such as face and gait [9]. Person reidentification approaches have two aspects: (i) establish correspondence between parts, and (ii) generate signatures that are invariant to variations in illumination, pose, and the dynamic appearance of clothing. A novel spatiotemporal segmentation algorithm is employed to generate salient edgels that are robust to changes in appearance of clothing. The invariant signatures are generated by combining normalized color and salient edgel histograms. Two approaches are proposed to generate correspondences: (i) a model based approach that fits an articulated model to each individual to establish a correspondence map, and (ii) an interest point operator approach that nominates a large number of potential correspondences which are evaluated using a region growing scheme. These approaches were evaluated on a 44 person database across 3 disparate views.

5   Visual Recognition at Toyota

Recently the application of object recognition to real-world systems for cars and also to autonomous robots is rapidly growing. For cars, there already are some systems utilizing visual recognition as follows:

- A lane departure warning and lane-keeping assist system using white line detection.
- Detection of obstacles in front of the vehicle using stereo images.
- A pedestrian detection and warning system using infrared images.

Many more applications for future intelligent vehicles to prevent potential traffic accidents and also to assist driving are expected. For the realization of those future systems, recognition and prediction of the motion of pedestrians, other cars, other bikes etc. will be necessary. Also for autonomous and semi-autonomous driving, as well as for driving support, recognition of traffic signs, signals etc. and also segmentation and categorization of road area, sidewalks, guardrails, crosswalks, crossroads etc. will be necessary. Furthermore, to predict future possible dangers and prevent them, scene understanding considering the context of the scene will become important. However, there still are many difficulties for these tasks such as large occlusions, very large variations in weather, lighting conditions, shape of the objects, and so on.

One of the most challenging applications of visual recognition is pedestrian detection, because of 1) large appearance change with changes in posture and viewpoint; 2) large self occlusions and overlap between multiple people; 3) large variation of appearance due to clothes, age, gender, etc. By the recent development of many kinds of local feature descriptors and also combining those technologies with statistical learning technologies, some of these difficulties are gradually being addressed. [8] showed excellent performance of an Adaboost-based algorithm for this problem. [6] showed the potential of combining affine invariant local features and statistical learning. Recently [23] gave a more robust solution for pedestrian detection in cluttered scenes. But these methods still fall short of what is required for commercial systems.

On the other hand, for autonomous robots such as future service robots, object recognition in outdoor and indoor scenes is very important. One necessary capability of these robots is recognition of objects to be handled and also of obstacles and the 3D environment for autonomous navigation in cluttered scenes. Also categorization of floor, wall, furniture, moving human and so on is necessary for simultaneous localization and mapping. If shape and specific local descriptors for a 2D[30] or 3D[11] image are extracted, it is possible to detect and recognize objects by matching those descriptors between the input camera image and a database. It is also possible to estimate position and orientation of the known objects by the same way as camera pose estimation using corresponding feature points between the input image and the database image. For non-textured objects, a descriptor using the contour information can be used. On the other hand, if there is no such database but most of the objects can be fitted to simply shaped primitives, only separating each object and estimating the position and orientation make sense for grasping those objects by robot hand. We at first developed a technology based on 3D reconstruction of the object shape and then separate each object using 3D shape information [12]. For separating objects, an algorithm using graph-cut [26] was developed. And to fit the shape of the each object to primitives, clustering of normalized vectors of each surface is used. We plan to recognize objects with more complex shapes in cluttered environments by combining two approaches mentioned above.

There still are problems to be solved for these methods when applying them to operational systems. One is how to improve the accuracy of matching descriptors especially for low resolution images. Speedup and improvement of 3D reconstruction is also a big problem for the actual implementation. Sensor fusion of range sensor and multi-view vision is one possibility for addressing this problem.

Recently, thanks to the rapid growth of computation power and also to the development of mathematical theories, statistical methods are becoming more useful in all of the related engineering areas, including computer vision. Application of object classification as pedestrian detection owes much success to this trend. However there still are many unresolved problems such as error by over learning, how to construct a proper learning dataset, etc. On the other hand, the robustness and speed of local feature detectors and descriptors are still hot topics. Also for the matching problem, there still needs to be improvement in outlier rejection. There also remains the problem of how to speed up the matching for huge object databases. Now that computer vision is becoming useful for various real applications, the expectation of industry for academia to solve remaining problems is very strong. To accelerate this movement, frank and deep discussion about the matching of technical needs with academic research is becoming increasingly important.

Acknowledgments

Section 4 of this report was prepared by GE GRC as an account of work sponsored by Lockheed Martin Corporation. Information contained in this report constitutes technical information which is the property of Lockheed Martin Corporation. Neither GE nor Lockheed Martin Corporation, nor any person acting on behalf of either; a. Makes any warranty or representation, expressed or implied, with respect to the use of any information contained in this report, or that the use of any information, apparatus, method, or process disclosed in this report may not infringe privately owned rights; or b. Assume any liabilities with respect to the use of, or for damages resulting from the use of, any information, apparatus, method or process disclosed in this report.

References

1. The NIST humanid evaluation framework. www.frvt.org (2003)
2. The TREC video retrieval evaluation. www-nlpir.nist.gov/projects/trecvid (2003)
3. The Pascal visual object classes challenge.
   www.pascal-network.org/challenges/VOC (2005)
4. M. Chan, A. Hoogs, J. Schmiederer, M. Petersen. Detecting rare events in video using semantic primitives with HMM. In: Proc. ICPR. Volume 4. (2004) 150–154
5. M. Chan, A. Hoogs, A. Perera, R. Bhotika, J. Schmiederer, G. Doretto. Joint recognition of complex events and track matching. In: Proc. IEEE Conf. on Computer Vision and Pattern Recognition. (2006)
6. R. Fergus, A. Zisserman, and P. Perona. Object class recognition by unsupervised scale-invariant learning, in IEEE Conference on Computer Vision and Pattern Recognition (CVPR2003).
7. C. Garcia, M. Delakis. Convolutional face finder: A neural architecture for fast and robust face detection. IEEE Transactions on Pattern Analysis and Machine Intelligence 25 (2004) 1408–1423
8. D. Gavrila. Pedestrian detection from a moving vehicle, in Sixth European Conference on Computer Vision (ECCV2000), Springer, pp. 37-49.
9. N. Gheissari, T.B. Sebatian, P.H. Tu, J. Rittscher, R. Hartley. A novel approach to person reidentification. In: Proc. IEEE Conf. on Computer Vision and Pattern Recognition, 2006.
10. A. Gionis, P. Indyk, R. Motwani. Similarity search in high dimensions via hashing. In: Proc. Conference on Very Large Databases. (1999)
11. A. Johnson and M. Hebert: Using spin images for efficient object recognition in cluttered 3D scenes, IEEE Transactions on Pattern Analysis and Machine Intelligence, Vol. 21, No. 5, May, 1999, pp. 433 - 449.
12. Y. Hirano, K. Kitahama, and S. Yoshizawa. Image-based Object Recognition and Dexterous Hand/Arm Motion Planning Using RRTs for Grasping in Cluttered Scene, in IEEE/RSJ Conference on Intelligent Robots and Systems (IROS2005), Edmonton, Canada.
13. D. Hoiem, R. Sukthankar, H. Schneiderman, L. Huston. Object-based image retrieval using the statistics of images. In: Proc. Computer Vision and Pattern Recognition. (2004)

14. A. Hoogs, R. Collins, R. Kaucic, J. Mundy. A common set of perceptual observables for grouping, figure-ground discrimination and texture classification. T. PAMI **25** (2003) 458–475

15. A. Hoogs, J. Rittscher, G. Stein, J. Schmiederer. Video content annotation using visual analysis and large semantic knowledgebase. In: Proc. CVPR, IEEE (2003)

16. R. Kaucic, A.G.A. Perera, G. Brooksby, J. Kaufhold, A. Hoogs. A unified framework for tracking through occlusions and across sensor gaps. In: Proc. CVPR. (2005) 990–997

17. R.A. Kaucic, C.C. McCulloch, P.R.S. Mendonça, D.J. Walter, R.S. Avila, J.L. Mundy. Model-based detection of lung nodules in CT exams. In Lemke, H.U., Vannier, M.W., Inamura, K., Farman, A.G., Doi, K., Reiber, J.H.C., eds.: Computer Assisted Radiology and Surgery. Volume 1256 of International Congress Series., London, UK, Elsevier 990–997, 2003.

18. J. Kaufhold, A. Hoogs. Learning to segment images using region-based perceptual features. In: Proceedings of the Conference on Computer Vision and Pattern Recognition, IEEE (2004)

19. Y. Ke, R. Sukthankar, L. Huston. Efficient near-duplicate and sub-image retrieval. In: Proc. ACM Multimedia. (2004)

20. Y. Ke, R. Sukthankar. PCA-SIFT: A more distinctive representation for local image descriptors. In: Proc Computer Vision and Pattern Recognition. (2004)

21. N. Krahnstoever, P. Mendonca. Bayesian autocalibration for surveillance. In: Proc. ICCV, IEEE (2005)

22. N. Krahnstoever, T. Kelliher, J. Rittscher. Obtaining pareto optimal performance of visual surveillance algorithms. In: Proc. of IEEE International Workshop on Performance Evaluation of Tracking and Surveillance, 2005.

23. B. Leibe, E. Seemann, and B. Schiele. Pedestrian detection in crowded scenes, in IEEE Conference on Computer Vision and Pattern Recognition (CVPR2005), San Diego, CA.

24. X. Liu, T. Chen, J. Rittscher. Optimal pose for face recognition. In: Proc. IEEE Conf. on Computer Vision and Pattern Recognition, 2006.

25. D.G. Lowe. Distinctive image features from scale-invariant keypoints. International Journal of Computer Vision (2004)

26. J. Shi and J. Malik: Normalized Cuts and Image Segmentation, IEEE Transactions on Pattern Analysis and Machine Intelligence, 22(8), pp. 888-905, August 2000.

27. C.C. McCulloch, R.A. Kaucic, P.R.S. Mendonça, D.J. Walter, R.S. Avila. Model-based detection of lung nodules in computed tomography exams. Academic Radiology **11** (2004) 258–266

28. Y. Meng, E. Chang, B. Li. Enhancing DPF for near-replica image recognition. In: Proc. Computer Vision and Pattern Recognition. (2003)

29. A. Perera, C. Srinivas, A. Hoogs, G. Brooksby, W. Hu. Multi-object tracking through simultaneous long occlusions and split-merge conditions. In: Proc. IEEE Conf. on Computer Vision and Pattern Recognition, 2006.

30. F. Rothganger, S. Lazebnik, C. Schmid, and J. Ponce: 3D Object Modeling and Recognition Using Affine-Invariant Patches and Multi-View Spatial Constraints, Proceedings of the IEEE Conference on Computer Vision and Pattern Recognition (CVPR2003), Madison, WI, June 2003, Vol. II, pp. 272-277.

31. X. Ren, J. Malik. Learning a classification model for segmentation. In: Proc. IEEE International Conference on Computer Vision, 2003.

32. J. Rittscher, P. Tu, N. Krahnstoever. Simultaneous estimation of segmentation and shape. In: Proc. CVPR, IEEE, 2005.

33. J. Rittscher, A. Blake, A. Hoogs, G. Stein. Mathematical modeling of animate and intentional motion. Philosophical Transactions of the Royal Society of London: Biological Sciences **358** 475–490, 2003.
34. H. Sanson. Video indexing: Myth and reality. In: Fourth International Workshop on Content-Based Multimedia Indexing, Riga, Latvia (2005)
35. C. Snoek, M. Worring. Multimodal video indexing: A review of the state-of-the-art. Multimedia Tools and Applications **25** (2005) 5–35
36. G. Stein, J. Rittscher, A. Hoogs. Enabling video annotation using a semantic database extended with visual knowledge. In: Proceedings of the International Conference on Multimedia and Expo, IEEE, 2003.
37. P. Tu, P. Mendonca. Surface reconstruction via helmholtz reciprocity with a single image pair. In: Proc. CVPR. (2003)
38. P. Tu, J. Rittscher, T. Kelliher. In: Challenges to Fingerprints, 2005.
39. P. Tu, R. Hartley. Statistical significance as an aid to system performance evaluation. In: European Conference On Computer Vision. Volume II, 366–378, 2000.
40. P. Tu, R. Hartley, A. Allyassin, W. Lorensen, R. Gupta, L. Heier. Face reconstructions using flesh deformation modes. In: International Association for Craniofacial Identification, 2000.
41. P. Tu, J. Rittscher, T. Kelliher. Site calibration for large indoor scenes. In: Proceedings of the IEEE Conference on Advanced Video and Signal Based Surveillance, IEEE (2003)
42. M. Varma, A. Zisserman. Classifying images of materials: Achieving viewpoint and illumination independence. In: Proc. European Conference on Computer Vision. Volume 3, 255–271, 2002.
43. R.C. Veltkamp, M. Tanase. Content-based image retrieval systems: A survey. IEEE Image Processing **1** (2001) 100–148
44. P. Viola, M. Jones. Rapid object detection using a boosted cascade of simple features. In: Proceedings of IEEE Int. Conf. on Computer Vision and Patttern Recognition, Hawaii, US, 511–518, 2001.

Part II
Recognition of Specific Objects

What and Where: 3D Object Recognition with Accurate Pose

Iryna Gordon and David G. Lowe

Computer Science Department,
University of British Columbia
Vancouver, BC, Canada
lowe@cs.ubc.ca

Abstract. Many applications of 3D object recognition, such as augmented reality or robotic manipulation, require an accurate solution for the 3D pose of the recognized objects. This is best accomplished by building a metrically accurate 3D model of the object and all its feature locations, and then fitting this model to features detected in new images. In this chapter, we describe a system for constructing 3D metric models from multiple images taken with an uncalibrated handheld camera, recognizing these models in new images, and precisely solving for object pose. This is demonstrated in an augmented reality application where objects must be recognized, tracked, and superimposed on new images taken from arbitrary viewpoints without perceptible jitter. This approach not only provides for accurate pose, but also allows for integration of features from multiple training images into a single model that provides for more reliable recognition[1].

1   Introduction

Many existing approaches to object recognition match new images to a database of individual 2D training images, and thereby determine the best matching object without any precise notion of their 3D pose. However, some common applications, such as augmented reality or robotic manipulation, require that recognition also include a precise 3D pose solution. In this chapter, we address the problem of augmented reality, in which synthetic graphics must be superimposed on real images to a high degree of accuracy. Human vision is highly sensitive to misregistration errors, so the accuracy must be sub-pixel and minimize any jitter due to sensor noise.

Our solution is based on using invariant local features to obtain point matches between multiple 2D images of a rigid 3D object or scene. These are then used as input to bundle adjustment to obtain a metrically accurate 3D solution for the locations of the features and cameras. This follows a similar approach to building 3D models from local feature matches that was previously developed

---

[1] The research in this chapter was first presented at the International Symposium on Mixed and Augmented Reality, 2004 [8].

J. Ponce et al. (Eds.): Toward Category-Level Object Recognition, LNCS 4170, pp. 67–82, 2006.
© Springer-Verlag Berlin Heidelberg 2006

by Schaffalitzky and Zisserman [20]. In recent work, Rothganger *et al.* [18] have built 3D models from multiple affine-invariant feature correspondences and used these models for recognition. They demonstrate that the 3D models are particularly valuable for recognition as they integrate features from multiple views and are therefore more complete and robust than any single view representation. In this chapter we describe a number of improvements to previous methods that we have found useful, including a simple approach to initializing bundle adjustment, methods for filtering subsets of the most useful features, and a novel approach to jitter reduction in augmented reality. We are able to reliably build models of complex objects and scenes from multiple hand-held images using an uncalibrated camera. The models can then be recognized and tracked in long video sequences while maintaining minimal jitter.

1.1   System Overview

Our system operates in two stages. During the first, offline stage, SIFT features are extracted from the reference images and pair-wise correspondences are established. The process remains linear in the number of images by using fast approximate indexing and only linking image pairs forming a spanning tree. These correspondences are used to build a metric model of the real world to be augmented (which could be an individual object or a general scene). At the same time, camera calibration parameters and camera poses corresponding to image viewpoints are computed. Structure and motion recovery is performed with bundle adjustment using a simple initialization procedure.

Once the real world model has been obtained, the position, orientation and size of the virtual object must be specified relative to this model. For this purpose we provide an interactive procedure, which allows the user to determine the pose of the virtual object in the reference images.

Fig. 1. The coffee mug is recognized in each frame and its pose computed. The virtual teapot is superimposed to appear on top of the coffee mug. The last two frames demonstrate recognition of the partially occluded mug in cluttered scenes, without tracking from previous frames.

The second stage of the system involves recognition and accurate solution of the model pose for live video augmentation. Features detected in the current video frame are matched to those of the world model, and these matches are used to compute the current pose of the model. Jitter is minimized by regularizing the solution using the pose computed for the previous frame. The influence of the previous solution on the current one is weighted without imposing constraints on the overall camera motion. The tracker is very stable in practice (Figure 1 demonstrates some of its capabilities), and it performs online scene recognition and recovery from failure of tracking. Unlike previous systems for augmented reality, our method performs automatic recognition of any of a library of objects using natural features, making it suitable for a variety of mobile applications which involve augmentation of recognized scenes, such as computerized museum tour guides and augmentation of individual objects.

2   Related Research

In most previous research on marker-free systems for augmented reality, natural features are used only for establishing correspondences between consecutive frames in a video sequence. Some of the most common choices are the Harris corner detector [9], applied in [3,4], and the Kanade-Lucas-Tomasi (KLT) tracker [16], used in [23,7,19]. To automate the initialization and failure recovery of a tracker, reliable wide baseline matching is desired, which in turn imposes a demand for a higher degree of feature invariance.

A recent approach [5] proposes tracking of parallelogram-shaped and elliptical image regions, extracted in an affinely invariant way, which can be used for scene recognition. Impressive results are presented, but the tracker relies on the presence of planar structures in the viewed scene. In [13] viewpoint invariance is achieved by applying an eigen-image approach to a set of local image patches, which capture the appearance of a real-world point in several views. Their method relies on the pre-built CAD model of the object to be augmented, and requires manual matching of model points to their 2D projections in reference keyframes. In [11] edges of a CAD model are matched to detected image edges. Their visual tracking system is combined with rate gyroscopes in order to handle rapid movements of a head-mounted camera.

Various other techniques have been suggested in augmented reality for acquiring a reference representation of the real world. In [3] two or more reference views are used to compute current camera pose from epipolar geometry constraints on natural feature correspondences. Markers are still used to pre-calibrate the reference frames with standard calibration tools. The initial camera pose must be very close to one of the reference images, due to wide baseline matching limitations. A learning-based strategy is proposed in [7], where the scene is represented by a set of natural features, detected and calibrated during an initial marker-based tracking phase. The system presented in [12] uses fiducial detection to represent the environment and its virtual contents in an affine frame of reference, with an aim to avoid metric camera calibration. This innovative approach achieves comparable results with minimum initialization effort, however it does not allow the modeling of perspective projection effects at close camera distances. In [21] the coordinate frame of the real world is manually inserted into reference views, by specifying image locations of control points. Line intersections on fiducials are tracked to estimate the motion of the camera. Completely markerless and general techniques are presented in [4] and [19], where virtual object registration is achieved based on the results of a global bundle adjustment and self-calibration, leading to metric camera motion and scene structure recovery. Both of these methods perform offline batch processing of the entire video sequence, with no support for online scene recognition or tracking.

3   Learning Scene Geometry

The preliminary stage of the system takes as input an unordered set of images of the real world scene or object to modeled. The images are acquired from unknown, spatially separated viewpoints by a handheld camera, which does not need to be pre-calibrated. At least two snapshots are required; using more allows the capture of more scene features and thus enables a wider-range and more reliable tracking. In our experiments, we have used 5 to 20 images which were gathered from up to a full 360° range of viewpoints, separated by at most about 45°. The scene is assumed to be mostly rigid, with no special markers or known structures present. The system uses these input images to build a sparse 3D model of the viewed scene and to simultaneously recover camera poses and calibration parameters. The virtual object can then be inserted into the modeled environment. The problem is divided into the following steps:

1. Local invariant features are extracted from the input images.
2. A robust wide baseline matching technique is applied to find two-view feature correspondences, leading to the construction of multi-view matches.
3. A subset of multi-view matches is chosen as an input to an iterative algorithm for structure and motion recovery.
4. The remaining matches are triangulated using computed camera parameters, and outliers are removed.
5. The position, orientation and size of the virtual object are defined relative to the coordinate frame of the recovered model.

3.1   Feature Extraction and Matching

We extract SIFT features [14,15] from each input image for matching. The main attractions of SIFT features are their distinctiveness, invariance, and efficiency, resulting in a high probability of correct matches across a wide range of image variations. In addition, large numbers of these features can be found in a typical image (see Figure 2), making them suitable for recognition and tracking in the presence of occlusions, and generally increasing the robustness of recognition.

The best candidate match for a SIFT feature is its nearest neighbour, defined as the feature with the minimum Euclidean distance between descriptor vectors. The reliability of the nearest neighbour match can be tested by comparing its Euclidean distance to that of the second nearest neighbour from that image. If these distances are too similar, the nearest neighbour match is discarded

Fig. 2. SIFT keypoints extracted from a 640×480 image of a sneaker. The algorithm found 1533 features shown as white arrows, with size and direction corresponding to feature scale and orientation, respectively.

as unreliable. This simple method works well in practice, since incorrect matches are much more likely to have close neighbours with similar distances than correct ones, due in part to the high dimensionality of the feature space.

The large numbers of features generated from images, as well as the high dimensionality of their descriptors, make an exhaustive search for closest matches extremely inefficient. Therefore we employ an approximate Best-Bin-First (BBF) algorithm, based on a k-d tree search [2]. A k-d tree is constructed from all SIFT features which have been extracted from the reference images. The search examines tree leaves, each containing a feature, in the order of their closest distance from the current query location. Search order is determined with a heap-based priority queue. An approximate answer is returned after examining a predetermined number of nearest leaves. This technique finds the closest match with a high probability, and enables feature matching to run in real time.

For each feature in a reference image, the BBF search finds its nearest and second nearest neighbour pair in each of the remaining images. Putative two-view matches are then selected based on the nearest-to-second-nearest distance ratio (with the threshold value of 0.8). We improve this set of matches by applying an epipolar geometry constraint to remove remaining outliers. For each selected image pair, this constraint can be expressed as

$$\mathbf{x}_i^T F_{ij} \mathbf{x}_j = 0 \qquad (1)$$

where $\mathbf{x}_i = [u_i \ v_i \ 1]^T$ and $\mathbf{x}_j = [u_j \ v_j \ 1]^T$ are homogeneous image coordinates of the matched features in images i and j, respectively, and F_{ij} is a fundamental matrix of rank 2. The computation of F between each pair of N images has $\binom{N}{2}$ complexity, thus quickly becoming prohibitively expensive with increasing N. Therefore we apply a selective approach, similar to [20], which is linear in the number of images. Image pairs are selected based on a greedy algorithm, which constructs a spanning tree on the image set. Starting with the two images that have the most putative matches, we compute F consistent with the majority of matches using the RANSAC algorithm [6], discard outliers and join these images with an edge. This process is repeated for the image pair with the next highest

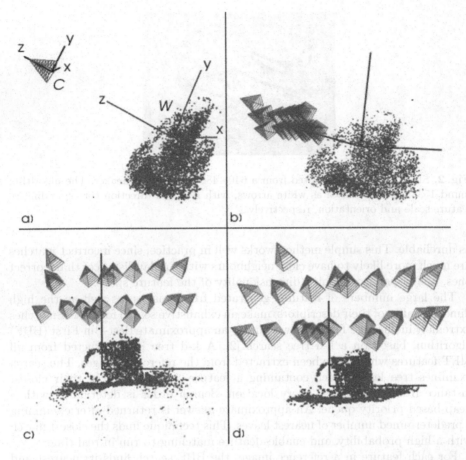

Fig. 3. Building a model of a coffee mug placed on top of a magazine from 20 reference images. Cameras are shown as wire cones and image features as points: (a) initialization places all cameras at the same location and all points at the same distance from the cameras (average reprojection error = 62.5 pixels); (b) results after 10 iterations (error = 4.2 pixels); (c) results after 20 iterations (error = 1.7 pixels); (d) final results after 50 iterations (error = 0.2 pixels).

number of matches, subject to the constraint that joining these images does not create a cycle. In this manner, the expensive cleanup operation is applied only to the more promising candidates.

The entire image set is considered processed when the addition of any remaining candidate image pair would create a cycle in the tree. At this point we establish multi-view 2D point correspondences by traversing the tree and stitching together two-view feature matches. Because the tree structure is free of cycles, the generation of multi-view matches is straightforward and unambiguous.

3.2   Motion and Structure Recovery

Once the multi-view matches have been established, we seek to compute world coordinates of the corresponding 3D points, calibration parameters and camera poses for each reference view. Formally, a 2D projection $\mathbf{x}_{ij} = [u_{ij}\ v_{ij}\ 1]^T$ of a 3D point $\mathbf{X}_j = [x_j\ y_j\ z_j\ 1]^T$ in an image i is expressed as

$$\mathbf{x}_{ij} \sim P_i \mathbf{X}_j \tag{2}$$

where $\sim$ denotes equality up to a scale factor, and P_i is a 3×4 camera matrix of the form

$$P_i = K[R_i\ \mathbf{t}_i] \tag{3}$$

In the above equation, matrix K contains camera calibration parameters, such as focal length, aspect ratio and principal point coordinates; R_i and $\mathbf{t}_i$ are the rotation and translation of the world frame relative to the camera frame for image i.

A classical approach to this problem begins with an algebraic initialization of projective structure and motion, using two- or three-view epipolar constraints. This is followed by an upgrade to a metric framework with self-calibration techniques, as well as a solution refinement via an iterative bundle adjustment optimization [10]. We employ an alternative technique suggested by Szeliski and Kang [22], which omits the linear initialization step and solves for all of the unknown parameters iteratively, using a general-purpose optimization algorithm, such as Levenberg-Marquardt [17]. The problem is formulated as the minimization of the reprojection errors over all camera parameters and world point coordinates, given image projections of the world points:

$$\min_{\mathbf{a}_{ij}} \sum_i \sum_j \|w_j(\Pi(\mathbf{a}_{ij}) - \mathbf{x}_{ij})\|^2 \tag{4}$$

where Π is the non-linear projection function and the vector $\mathbf{a}_{ij} = [\mathbf{X}_j^T\ \mathbf{p}_i^T\ \mathbf{c}^T]^T$ contains the unknown parameters: 3D coordinates $\mathbf{X}_j$ of a world point j, camera pose parameters $\mathbf{p}_i$ for an image i, and global calibration parameters $\mathbf{c}$ (or $\mathbf{c}_i$, in case of varying calibration parameters). After 15 iterations to establish an initial solution estimate, the confidence weight w_j associated with $\mathbf{X}_j$ is lowered for world points with high reprojection errors using the Huber norm, thus reducing the contribution of outliers to the final solution.

To initialize the algorithm, we back-project the 2D points from an arbitrary view to an xy-plane of the world frame, place all cameras at the same default distance along the z-axis directly facing the plane, and use default values for the calibration parameters. It is possible that bundle adjustment will converge to a false local minimum due to depth reversal (as illustrated in the Necker cube illusion). As suggested by [22], this can be avoided by reflecting the depth of the first model solution about the xy-plane, restarting the bundle adjustment, and selecting the solution with the best final reprojection error. This simple initialization allows us to achieve proper convergence with the cameras

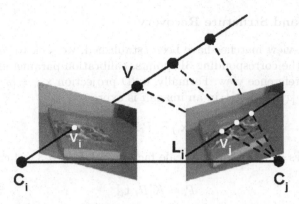

Fig. 4. The placement of the virtual frame origin **V** in 3D is achieved by anchoring its projection $\mathbf{v_i}$ in image i and adjusting its projection $\mathbf{v_j}$ in image j along the epipolar line $\mathbf{L_i}$.

as far as 90° apart, in a few dozen iterations. Figure 3 shows the sequence of convergence for even a large set of 20 images of a typical scene, although in practice, for efficiency, we only start with 5 images and then add others incrementally.

To reduce problem size, as an input to the Levenberg-Marquardt algorithm we select a limited number (at most 100) of the points with the most correspondences. Coordinates of the remaining points can be easily computed using standard triangulation techniques [10], once the camera parameters have been recovered. Lastly, we remove any model point outliers with large reprojection errors. The latter are usually a result of infrequent feature mismatches which have survived the epipolar constraint test.

3.3 Virtual Object Placement

For augmented reality, the insertion of the virtual object into the real world is achieved by adjusting its projection in the reference images until it appears correctly rendered. First, the 3D coordinates of the virtual frame origin V are established via triangulation, as follows. The projection of V is specified in one of the reference images with a click of a mouse button (the virtual frame is "anchored" in 2D). Afterwards, the relative depth of V is adjusted by switching to a different view and moving the corresponding projection of V along an epipolar line imposed by the anchoring view. This is equivalent to moving V along a line connecting the camera centre and the projection of V in the anchoring image (see Figure 4).

Next, the user is able to fine-tune the position, orientation and size of the virtual object in variable-size increments. Figure 5 shows an example of the virtual frame insertion and pose adjustment. The virtual object is rendered onto the reference images using previously recovered camera parameters. At any time the user can switch between the images to view the corresponding projection of the virtual contents. Note that the geometric relationships between the real world, its virtual contents and the cameras are defined in the same generic units, so that there is no need to recover the absolute scale of the real world model. If a metric object scale is required, this parameter can be provided by user input of a single known dimension or by presence of a calibrated object in one of the views.

4   Model Recognition and Camera Tracking

The online computations of the system are summarized in the following steps:

1. SIFT features are extracted from the current frame of the video sequence.
2. The new features are matched to the image features of the world model using the BBF algorithm, resulting in a set of 2D-to-3D correspondences.
3. The correspondences are used to compute the current camera pose, via a robust approach which combines RANSAC and Levenberg-Marquardt algorithms.

Fig. 5. Insertion of the virtual frame into a desk scene: a) initial placement into one of the reference images by specifying the desired location of the frame's origin; b) the frame's trajectory along the epipolar line in another image; c) subsequent orientation adjustment

To initialize the tracker, a k-d tree is constructed from the image features of the world model. Each image feature is a 2D projection with links to its 3D world coordinates, a reference image in which it was found and the corresponding recovered camera pose. During tracking, this structure is used to efficiently detect model point projections in each new frame. A nearest and a second nearest neighbour pair is found for each feature from the current frame via a BBF search, with the two neighbours belonging to different model points. As in Section 3.1, the reliability of the best match is tested by comparing its Euclidean distance to that of the second best match.

Tracking failure is assumed if the number of reliable best matches falls below a predefined threshold (set to 15 in our experiments, although a much lower threshold could be used with more careful verification). This occurs when all or most of the model disappears out of sight, or the frame contains too much motion blur. In such cases the rendering of virtual contents is postponed until enough model points are detected.

Given a set of putative 2D-to-3D matches $(\mathbf{x}_{tj}, \mathbf{X}_j)$ for the frame t, we can compute the corresponding camera pose parameters by minimizing the residual sum:

$$\min_{\mathbf{p}_t} \sum_j \|w_{tj}(\Pi(\mathbf{a}_{tj}) - \mathbf{x}_{tj})\|^2 \tag{5}$$

where the weight w_{tj} describes the confidence in the measurement $\mathbf{x}_{tj}$ and is set to the reciprocal of its estimated standard deviation in the image. Since SIFT features with larger scales are computed from more blurred versions of the image, they have lower location accuracy. Therefore, we set w_{tj} inversely proportional to the scale of each feature. This time the camera pose parameters $\mathbf{p}_t$ are the only unknowns in the vector $\mathbf{a}_{tj}$ (assuming unchanging calibration parameters). We initialize $\mathbf{p}_t$ to $\mathbf{p}_{t-1}$, computed for the previous frame. For the first frame of the video sequence or the one immediately after tracking failure, as an initial guess we use the camera pose of the reference image contributing the most 2D feature matches from the BBF search.

We apply RANSAC to compute the camera pose consistent with the most matches. The minimization given by (5) is performed for each RANSAC sample, and the final solution is computed using all of the inliers as input. Despite its iterative nature, this approach has proven to be sufficiently fast for online use. The small number of unknown parameters results in a rapid execution of Levenberg-Marquardt iterations. Very few RANSAC samples are needed, since the non-linear computation of 6 elements of $\mathbf{p}_t$, corresponding to the 6 degrees-of-freedom of the camera pose, requires the minimum of only 3 matches. Furthermore, the input set of matches usually contains a very small fraction of outliers due to the fact that ambiguous matches have already been removed by the distance ratio check.

4.1   Jitter Reduction

The solution to (5) provides a reasonable estimate of the camera pose, yet typically leads to a "jitter" of the virtual projection in the video sequence, particularly noticeable when the camera is fully or nearly stationary. This inaccuracy can be a result of image noise, as well as too few or unevenly distributed feature matches. In addition, the surface of the error function may be flat near its minimum, as it may be difficult to distinguish between slight changes in rotation and translation parameters for near-planar objects.

To stabilize the solution, we modify (5) by adding a regularization term which favours minimum camera motion between consecutive video frames:

$$\min_{\mathbf{p}_t} \sum_j \|w_{tj}(\Pi(\mathbf{a}_{tj}) - \mathbf{x}_{tj})\|^2 + \alpha^2 \|W(\mathbf{p}_t - \mathbf{p}_{t-1})\|^2 \tag{6}$$

where W is a 6×6 diagonal matrix of prior weights on the camera pose parameters, and α is a scalar which controls the tradeoff between the current measurements and the stable solution. Each diagonal entry of W is set to the inverse of the standard deviation of the corresponding parameter, reflecting the relative range of expected frame-to-frame change in the camera pose (e.g., a few degrees for a change in rotation).

feature extraction (SIFT algorithm)	150 ms
feature matching (BBF algorithm)	40 ms
camera pose computation	25 ms
frames per second	4

Fig. 6. Average computation times for a video sequence with 640×480 frame size. The real world model contains about 5000 3D points.

Instead of adopting the usual approach of setting α to a constant value, we adjust it separately for each video frame. We would like high levels of smoothing for slow motions while avoiding over-smoothing of large camera motions which would result in a virtual object "drifting" behind a faster moving scene. The amount of smoothing is determined by controlling its contribution to the total reprojection error: the contribution is required to be no higher than that of the image feature noise. This can be expressed by the inequality

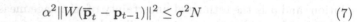

$$\alpha^2 \|W(\overline{\mathbf{p}}_t - \mathbf{p}_{t-1})\|^2 \le \sigma^2 N \tag{7}$$

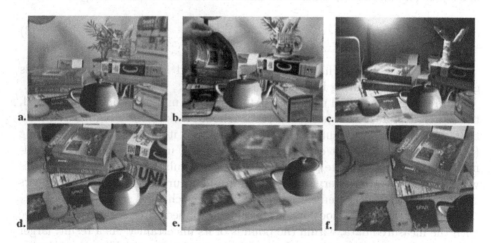

Fig. 7. Examples of tracking within a complex scene: a) a virtual teapot is placed in the modeled desk scene; b) the scene does not have to be fully static; c,d) recognition is robust to changes in lighting and viewpoint; e) moderate amounts of motion blur are acceptable; f) a partial view of the scene is correctly recognized

Fig. 8. The augmentation of the entrance to the university library with a new sign

Fig. 9. A virtual robotic dog in the modeled corner of the lab room. Successful results were achieved with people freely moving around the room.

where N is the number of matching image points, $\overline{\mathbf{p}}_t$ is the final new camera solution, and σ is the estimated uncertainty of an image measurement (e.g., 0.5 pixels). It follows that the maximum allowable amount of smoothing is

$$\alpha^2 = \frac{\sigma^2 N}{\|W(\overline{\mathbf{p}}_t - \mathbf{p}_{t-1})\|^2} \tag{8}$$

Because $\overline{\mathbf{p}}_t$ is unknown, α cannot be computed in advance; instead, it is gradually adjusted during LM iterations, as follows.

At first, $\mathbf{p}_t$ is computed using $\alpha = 0$. Once a local minimum has been reached, the search explores its immediate neighbourhood, looking for a regularized solution. This is done by executing a few additional LM iterations, this time solving (6) with α recomputed at each iteration as per (8), using the most recent estimate of $\mathbf{p}_t$ to approximate $\overline{\mathbf{p}}_t$. The search for a regularized solution terminates when $\mathbf{p}_t - \mathbf{p}_{t-1}$ becomes very small (which would occur for a camera that appears stationary within measurement noise) or no longer changes significantly.

Intuitively, as much smoothing as possible is applied while still trying to agree with the measured data, within the bounds of its uncertainty. As a result, larger values of α are used for slower frame-to-frame motions, significantly reducing jitter, while fast and abrupt camera motions are handled without drift. This method has worked very well in practice to almost eliminate perceived jitter, and experiments described below show that it leads to a large reduction in measured jitter (Figure 11).

5   Experiments

The system prototype has been implemented in C using OpenGL and GLUT libraries, on an IBM ThinkPad with a Pentium 4-M processor (1.8 GHz) and a Logitech QuickCam Pro 4000 video camera. An example of current computation times for the tracker is given in Figure 6. Current speed of recognition and tracking is about 4 frames/sec.

Fig. 10. ARToolkit marker in the scene (left). Virtual square, superimposed onto the marker during tracking (right).

To demonstrate the capabilities of the system, we have tested its performance on a variety of scenes and tracking scenarios. Some of the augmented video frames are shown in Figures 7 through 9. Video examples are available on the authors' web pages.

In order to test the accuracy of registration, we aligned a virtual square with an ARToolKit marker [1], which was present in a modeled scene (Figure 10).

While tracking the scene, the corners of the marker were detected using the ARToolKit library, and their image coordinates were used as the ground truth for the registration of the virtual square. Figures 11 and 12 compare the results for one of the corners.

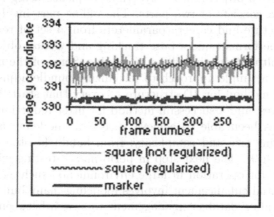

Fig. 11. Stationary camera results for 300 frames. Jitter of the virtual square is significantly reduced by camera pose regularization.

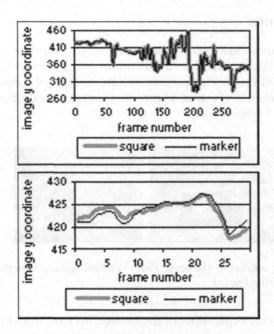

Fig. 12. Moving camera results for 300 frames (top) and the first 30 frames (bottom). The trajectories of the real and virtual corners are in close correspondence, with varying camera motion handled without noticeable drift.

6   Conclusions and Future Work

In this chapter we presented an approach to augmented reality that performs registration of virtual objects into a live video sequence using local image features. The system consists of two parts. The offline part involves recovery of metric scene structure and camera parameters from a set of reference images. The online part performs camera pose tracking and virtual object registration using models resulting from the offline processing. Some of the novel aspects of this work include a simple approach to initializing bundle adjustment, an efficient incremental method for 3D structure recovery that starts with subsets of images and features, and a successful method for jitter reduction.

Our system has been able to achieve successful modeling and recognition of scenes of varying size and complexity, from handheld objects to buildings (Figures 7 through 9). The next step in performance testing will focus on the system scalability for operation in large environments, such as a campus or a museum. A potential enhancement involves modeling many buildings, rooms or objects, and providing database management to switch between models as the user travels around his or her surroundings.

Acknowledgements

We would like to gratefully acknowledge the financial support of the Natural Sciences and Engineering Research Council of Canada (NSERC) and the Institute for Robotics and Intelligent Systems (IRIS).

References

1. ARToolKit: http://www.hitl.washington.edu/artoolkit/.
2. Jeffrey S. Beis and David G. Lowe. Shape indexing using approximate nearest-neighbour search in high-dimensional spaces. In *Proceedings of the IEEE Conference on Computer Vision and Pattern Recognition*, pages 1000–1006, 1997.
3. Kar Wee Chia, Adrian David Cheok, and Simon J.D. Prince. Online 6 DOF augmented reality registration from natural features. In *Proceedings of the International Symposium on Mixed and Augmented Reality*, pages 305–313, 2002.
4. Kurt Cornelis, Marc Pollefeys, Maarten Vergauwen, and Luc Van Gool. Augmented reality using uncalibrated video sequences. *Lecture Notes in Computer Science*, 2018:144–160, 2001.
5. V. Ferrari, T. Tuytelaars, and L. Van Gool. Markerless augmented reality with a real-time affine region tracker. In *Proceedings of the IEEE and ACM International Symposium on Augmented Reality*, pages 87–96, 2001.
6. M. Fischler and R. Bolles. RANdom SAmple Consensus: a paradigm for model fitting with application to image analysis and automated cartography. *Communications of the Association for Computing Machinery*, 24(6):381–395, 1981.
7. Y. Genc, S. Riedel, F. Souvannavong, C. Akinlar, and N. Navab. Marker-less tracking for AR: A learning-based approach. In *Proceedings of the International Symposium on Mixed and Augmented Reality*, pages 295–304, 2002.
8. Iryna Gordon and David G. Lowe, Scene modeling, recognition and tracking with invariant image features. *International Symposium on Mixed and Augmented Reality (ISMAR)*, Arlington, VA, pages 110–119, 2004.
9. C.J. Harris and M. Stephens. A combined corner and edge detector. In *Proceedings of the 4th Alvey Vision Conference*, pages 147–151, 1988.
10. R. Hartley and A. Zisserman. *Multiple View Geometry in Computer Vision*. Cambridge University Press, 2000.
11. Georg Klein and Tom Drummond. Robust visual tracking for non-instrumented augmented reality. In *Proceedings of the 2nd IEEE and ACM International Symposium on Mixed and Augmented Reality*, pages 113–122, 2003.
12. Kiriakos N. Kutulakos and James R. Vallino. Calibration-free augmented reality. *IEEE Transactions on Visualization and Computer Graphics*, 4(1):1–20, 1998.
13. Vincent Lepetit, Luca Vacchetti, Daniel Thalmann, and Pascal Fua. Fully automated and stable registration for augmented reality applications. In *Proceedings of the 2nd IEEE and ACM International Symposium on Mixed and Augmented Reality*, pages 93–102, 2003.
14. David G. Lowe. Object recognition from local scale-invariant features. *International Conference on Computer Vision*, pages 1150–1157, 1999.
15. David G. Lowe. Distinctive image features from scale-invariant keypoints. *International Journal of Computer Vision*, 60(2): 91-110, 2004.
16. B.D. Lucas and T. Kanade. An iterative image registration technique with an application to stereo vision. In *Proceedings of the International Joint Conference on Artificial Intelligence*, pages 674–679, 1981.

17. W.H. Press, S.A. Teukolsky, W.T. Vetterling, and B.P. Flannery. *Numerical Recipes in C: The Art of Scientific Computing.* Cambridge University Press, 1992.
18. Fred Rothganger, Svetlana Lazebnik, Cordelia Schmid, and Jean Ponce. 3D Object Modeling and Recognition Using Affine-Invariant Patches and Multi-View Spatial Constraints. *IEEE Conference on Computer Vision and Pattern Recognition,* Madison, WI, pages 272-277, 2003.
19. Harpreet S. Sawhney, Y. Guo, J. Asmuth, and Rakesh Kumar. Multi-view 3D estimation and applications to match move. In *Proceedings of the IEEE Workshop on Multi-View Modeling and Analysis of Visual Scenes,* pages 21–28, 1999.
20. F. Schaffalitzky and A. Zisserman. Multi-view matching for unordered image sets, or "How do I organize my holiday snaps?". In *Proceedings of the 7th European Conference on Computer Vision,* pages 414–431, 2002.
21. Yongduek Seo and Ki Sang Hong. Calibration-free augmented reality in perspective. *IEEE Transactions on Visualization and Computer Graphics,* 6(4), pages 346–359, 2000.
22. Richard Szeliski and Sing Bing Kang. Recovering 3D shape and motion from image streams using nonlinear least squares. *Journal of Visual Communication and Image Representation,* 5(1), pages 10–28, 1994
23. Annie Yao and Andrew Calway. Robust estimation of 3-D camera motion for uncalibrated augmented reality. Technical Report CSTR-02-001, Department of Computer Science, University of Bristol, March 2002.

Object Recognition Using Local Affine Frames on Maximally Stable Extremal Regions

Štěpán Obdržálek and Jiří Matas

Center for Machine Perception, Czech Technical University Prague

Abstract. Methods based on distinguished regions (transformation covariant detectable regions) have achieved considerable success in object recognition, retrieval and matching problems in both still images and videos. The chapter focuses on a method exploiting local coordinate systems (local affine frames) established on maximally stable extremal regions. We provide a taxonomy of affine-covariant constructions of local coordinate systems, prove their affine covariance and present algorithmic details on their computation. Exploiting processes proposed for computation of affine-invariant local frames of reference, tentative region-to-region correspondences are established. Object recognition is formulated as a problem of finding a maximal set of geometrically consistent matches.

State of the art results are reported on standard, publicly available, object recognition tests (COIL-100, ZuBuD, FOCUS). Change of scale, illumination conditions, out-of-plane rotation, occlusion, locally anisotropic scale change and 3D translation of the viewpoint are all present in the test problems.

1 Introduction

Viewpoint-independent recognition of objects is a fundamental problem in computer vision. Recently, considerable success in addressing the problem has been achieved by approaches based on matching of regions detected by processes that are quasi-invariant to viewpoint changes [16,20,19,30,28]. Such methods represent objects by sets of regions described by invariants computed from local measurements. The representation is learned from training images without manual intervention. During recognition, the same representation is built for the test image. The recognition problem is then formulated as a search for a geometrically consistent set of correspondences of regions in the test image and in one of the training (database) images. The search proceeds in two steps. First, a tentative set of correspondence is selected on the basis of similarity of local invariants. In a seconds step, a subset of the tentative correspondences that satisfies a certain geometric constraint, e.g. epipolar geometry, is sought. The confidence in the presence of an object is expressed as a function of the matched correspondences. Since it is not required that all local features match, the approaches are robust to occlusion and cluttered background. Since the framework is based on region-to-region correspondences, recognition also achieves localisation.

This chapter describes a method which represents objects by sets of measurements defined in local coordinate systems (*local affine frames*, LAFs) that are established on

J. Ponce et al. (Eds.): Toward Category-Level Object Recognition, LNCS 4170, pp. 83–104, 2006.
© Springer-Verlag Berlin Heidelberg 2006

affine-covariant regions [21]. The LAFs are constructed by exploiting multiple affine-covariant procedures that take the detected regions as an input. Assuming local planarity and adequacy of the affine approximation of the geometric changes induced by a movement of a perspective camera, any photometrically normalized image measurement expressed in local affine frame coordinates is viewpoint-invariant. Appearance of the objects is thus represented by local patches with shapes and locations given by the object-centred affine coordinate systems. The need for further processing of local image measurements to obtain invariant description, such as rotational or differential invariants, is eliminated. The structure of the proposed object recognition method is summarised in Algorithm 1 (the first four steps are visualised in Figure 1).

Affine coordinate systems cannot be constructed directly from interest points (e.g. [10,14,19]), or elliptical regions [29,20], since neither resolves all six degrees of freedom which an affine transformation possesses. A detector of more complex image regions is required. Such regions are e.g. obtained by various segmentation techniques [9,1] or the maximally stable extremal region (MSER) detector [18], which we exploit. MSER regions are of general, data-dependent shape, i.e. complex enough to provide sufficient constraints to define affine frames. They are connected, arbitrarily shaped, possibly nested, and do not cover the entire image, i.e. they do not form a partitioning. The formal definition of MSERs and a detailed description of the extraction algorithm is given in [18]. MSER performance evaluation and comparison to other detectors can be found in [21].

Algorithm 1. Structure of the proposed MSER-LAF method

---

1. For every database and query image, compute affine-covariant regions of data-dependent shape.
2. Construct local affine frames (LAFs) on the regions using several affine-covariant constructions.
3. Generate intensity representations of local image patches normalised according to the local affine frames. Photometrically normalise the patches.
4. Establish tentative correspondences between frames of query and database images. Compute similarity between the patches, select most similar pairs.
5. Find a globally consistent subset of the correspondences. Infer the presence and location of the objects.

The rest of the chapter is structured as follows. In Section 2, an overview and a taxonomy of affine-covariant constructions of local coordinate systems (frames) are presented, the affine covariance of the constructions is proven, and computation issues discussed. Section 3 describes the process of geometric and photometric normalisation of local appearance. A method for forming local region-to-region correspondences is described in Section 4. In Section 5, state of the art results are reported on publicly available object recognition tests (COIL-100, ZuBuD, FOCUS). Changes of scale and illumination conditions, out-of-plane rotation, occlusion, local anisotropic scaling, and 3D translation of the viewpoint are all present in the test problems.

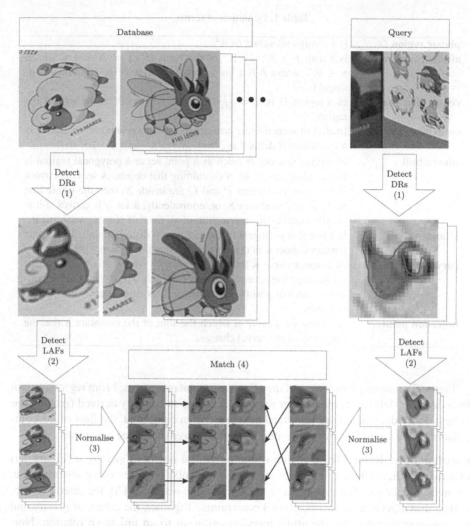

Fig. 1. Structure of the proposed MSER-LAF object recognition method

2   Local Affine Frames

2.1   Geometric Primitives Covariant with Affine Transformations

A two-dimensional affine transformation possesses six degrees of freedom. Thus, to determine an affine transformation, six independent constraints, e.g. given by a correspondence of three non-collinear points, have to be found. The constraints are derived from various affine-covariant geometric primitives detected on image regions of sufficiently complex shape. In particular, we use directions (providing a single constraint), 2D positions (providing two constraints), and the covariance matrix of a 2D shape (providing three constraints).

Table 1. Definition of terms

planar region Ω	is a contiguous subset of $\mathbb{R}^2$.
affine transformation	is a map $F : \mathbb{R}^n \to \mathbb{R}^n$ of the form $F(\mathbf{x}) = \mathsf{A}^\mathsf{T}\mathbf{x} + \mathbf{t}$, for all $\mathbf{x} \in \mathbb{R}^n$, where A is a linear transformation of $\mathbb{R}^n$, assumed non-singular.
centre of gravity μ	of a region Ω is $\mu = \frac{1}{|\Omega|} \int_\Omega \mathbf{x} d\Omega$, where $|\Omega|$ is the area of the region.
covariance matrix	(matrix of second-order central algebraic moments) of a region Ω is a 2×2 matrix defined as $\Sigma = \frac{1}{|\Omega|} \int_\Omega (\mathbf{x} - \mu)(\mathbf{x} - \mu)^\mathsf{T} d\Omega$.
convex hull	of a geometric object (such as a point set or a polygonal region) is the smallest convex set S containing that object. A set S is convex if whenever two points P and Q are inside S, then the whole line segment PQ is also in S, or, equivalently, a set S is convex if it is exactly equal to the intersection of all the half planes containing it.
bitangent	is a line that is tangent to a curve at two distinct points. Bitangents contain segments of the convex hull that bridge concavities.
curvature κ	of a planar curve is defined by $\kappa = \frac{d\Phi}{ds}$ where Φ is the tangential (or turning) angle, and s is segment length. The curve is called convex in areas of positive curvature and concave in areas of negative curvature.
inflection point	is a point on a curve at which the sign of the curvature κ (i.e. the convexity of the curve) changes.

Figure 2 presents an overview of the affine-covariant primitives. From regions output by a detector (left top corner), other regions are affine-invariantly derived (rectangular boxes). Individual primitives (elliptical boxes) are then computed, the flow of the computation is indicated by arrows. We divide the primitives into three categories:

Constructions derived from region shape only. The *centre of gravity* μ (Figure 2 i) of a region (the vector of first order algebraic moments) provides two constraints, i.e. resolves translation. The symmetric 2×2 *covariance matrix* Σ (ii), the matrix of second central algebraic moments, gives 3 constraints. Together, the centre of gravity and the covariance matrix fix the affine transformation up to an unknown rotation. Normalisation by the covariance matrix (see Figure 4) therefore allows for affine-invariant measurement of distances, angles and curvatures. From these we derive the points of *extremal distance* to the centre of gravity (iii) (2 constraints) and the points of *curvature extrema* (iv) (2 constraints).

Another group of shape-derived primitives is obtained on *concavities* (v) (4 constraints for the two tangent points). Given a bitangent, the point on the region boundary *farthest from the bitangent line* (vi) is defined affine-covariantly (2 constraints). A significant property of bitangents is their locality, i.e. they do not depend on correct detection of the whole region. If, for example, two regions get connected due to discretisation in one of the images, constructions based on integral characteristics, as is the centre of gravity or the covariance matrix, are incorrect, while concavities may be unaffected.

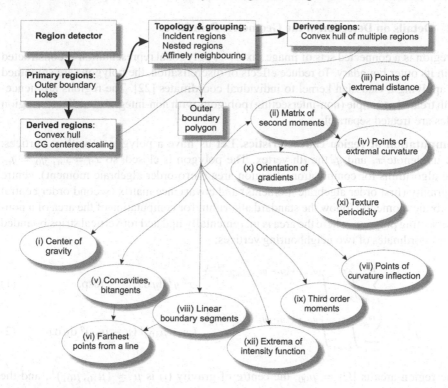

Fig. 2. Overview of affine-covariant primitives. Rectangular blocks represent regions, detected or derived, and elliptical blocks represent the primitives. The numbering refers to Sections 2.1, 2.2, and to Figure 3. Local affine frames are constructed by combining the primitives.

Finally, we exploit points of *curvature inflections* (vii), i.e. points where the shape changes from concave to convex or vice-versa (2 constraints), *straight line segments* (viii) of the region boundary, and *third order algebraic moments* [12] (ix).

Constructions derived from image intensities. Several constraints can be derived from pixel values inside a region or in its neighbourhood. After normalisation by the covariance matrix, directions based on *orientations of gradients* (x), obtained for example as peaks of gradient histogram [16], or the direction of *dominant texture periodicity* (xi), determine the unknown rotation. *Extrema of R, G, B components* (xii), or of any scalar function of RGB values provide 2 constraints.

Constructions derived from topology of regions. Finally, mutual configurations of regions are considered, i.e. *nested regions, neighbouring regions, holes* and *incident regions*. Region concavities and holes can be considered as distinguished regions of their own, and the computation of all of the constructions can be recursively applied. On the other hand, neither holes nor concavities have to be considered as part of the region, i.e. a convex hull can be substituted for the region, without loosing the affine invariance.

2.2 Details on Detection of the Geometric Primitives

A region is a connected sets of image pixels. A polygonal representation is constructed from its outer boundary. To reduce effects of discretisation, the polygons are smoothed by applying a Gaussian kernel to individual coordinates [22]. The regions are henceforth treated as simple (non-intersecting) polygons with non-integral coordinates, region holes are treated separately.

Computation of region characteristics. Let us have a polygon Ω with n vertices. Let us denote x_i and y_i the ith vertex. The polygon is closed, so $x_0 = x_n$, $y_0 = y_n$. The algorithms for computation of region area (zero order algebraic moment), centre of gravity (first order algebraic moments) and covariance matrix (second order central algebraic moments) follow the standard algorithm for computation of the area of a non-intersecting polygon, where the area is incrementally updated for vertical strips bounded by x coordinates of two neighbouring vertices:

$$\mu_{pq} = \sum_{i=1}^{n} \int_{x_{i-1}}^{x_i} \int_0^{y_{i-1}+(y_i-y_{i-1})\frac{x-x_{i-1}}{x_i-x_{i-1}}} x^p y^q \, dy \, dx, \qquad \text{resp.} \qquad (1)$$

$$\mu'_{pq} = \sum_{i=1}^{n} \int_{x_{i-1}}^{x_i} \int_0^{y_{i-1}+(y_i-y_{i-1})\frac{x-x_{i-1}}{x_i-x_{i-1}}} (x-\mu_{10})^p (y-\mu_{01})^q \, dy \, dx. \qquad (2)$$

The region area is $|\Omega| = \mu_{00}$, the centre of gravity (i) is $\mu = (\mu_{10}, \mu_{01})^\mathsf{T}$, and the covariance matrix (ii) is $\Sigma = \begin{pmatrix} \mu'_{20} & \mu'_{11} \\ \mu'_{11} & \mu'_{02} \end{pmatrix}$.

Once the covariance matrix is computed, the region shape is normalised so that the covariance matrix of the resulting shape equals to the identity matrix. This is achieved by transforming every polygon vertex by the inverse of Cholesky decomposition of the covariance matrix, i.e. by $\mathsf{A} = (\text{chol}(\Sigma))^{-1}$. The effect is illustrated in Figure 4, a detected region (a) is transformed into its normalised shape (b).

Shape normalisation, together with the position of the centre of gravity of the region, fixes the affine transformation up to an unknown rotation. The rotation is determined from local extrema of curvature (iv) or from contour points of extremal distance to the centre of gravity (iii). The computation of the curvature proceeds as follows: For each vertex X, two segments $l = \overline{XL}$ and $r = \overline{XR}$ of length a are spanned in opposite directions along the polygon boundary (see Figure 4 (c). The Cosine of the angle ϕ is $\cos\phi = \frac{l_x r_x + l_y r_y}{|l||r|}$, and the curvature κ is estimated as

$$\text{curvature } \kappa = s\frac{1+\cos\phi}{2}, \qquad \text{where } s = \begin{cases} 1 & \text{if } l_x r_y - l_y r_x > 0 \\ -1 & \text{otherwise} \end{cases} \qquad (3)$$

which ranges from -1 to 1, equals to 0 for straight segments, and is negative for concave and positive for convex curvatures. An example of the curvature values is shown in Figure 4 (d). The segment length a controls the scale at which is the curvature computed. Since the regions are shape and scale normalised, a is of a fixed value and need not be adapted to individual regions. Figure 4 (d) shows curvatures computed for two

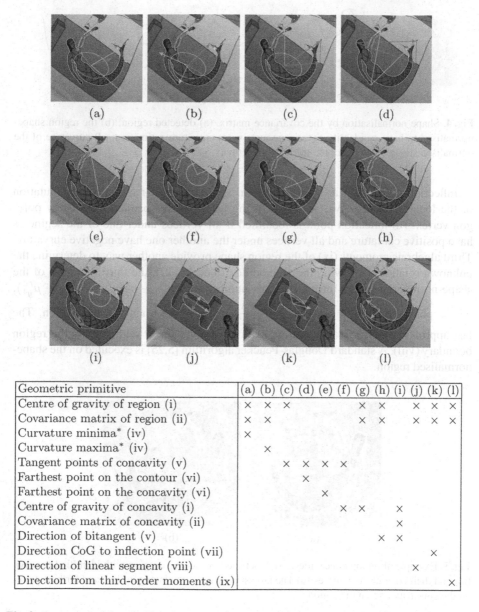

Geometric primitive	(a)	(b)	(c)	(d)	(e)	(f)	(g)	(h)	(i)	(j)	(k)	(l)
Centre of gravity of region (i)	×	×	×				×	×		×	×	×
Covariance matrix of region (ii)	×	×					×	×		×	×	×
Curvature minima* (iv)	×											
Curvature maxima* (iv)		×										
Tangent points of concavity (v)			×	×	×	×						
Farthest point on the contour (vi)				×								
Farthest point on the concavity (vi)					×							
Centre of gravity of concavity (i)							×	×		×		
Covariance matrix of concavity (ii)										×		
Direction of bitangent (v)									×	×		
Direction CoG to inflection point (vii)											×	
Direction of linear segment (viii)										×		
Direction from third-order moments (ix)												×

Fig. 3. Examples of local affine frames of different types. The table indicates which affine-covariant primitives were combined to obtain the frames.
* Affine-covariant localisation of curvature extrema requires prior shape normalisation by covariance matrix.

different values of a, $a = 0.5$ (thick line) and $a = 0.2$ (thin dashed line). In the experiments we use $a = 0.5$. Figure 4 (e) shows distances of vertices on the normalised contour to the centre of gravity of the region.

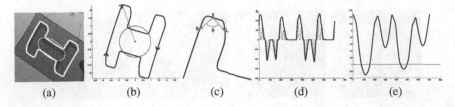

| (a) | (b) | (c) | (d) | (e) |

Fig. 4. Shape normalisation by the covariance matrix. (a) detected region, (b) the region shape-normalised to have an identity covariance matrix, (c) curvature estimation, (d) curvature of the normalised shape, (e) distances to the centre of gravity.

Inflection points (vii) are detected by an approach similar to that of computation of the local curvature. Two segments of the length a are spanned from every polygon vertex. An inflection point is identified if all vertices under one of the segments have positive curvature and all vertices under the another one have negative curvature. Third algebraic moments (ix) of the region shape provide another way to determine the unknown rotation. Following the method described in [12], the third moments of the shape-normalised region form a complex number $c = \mu'_{x^3} + \mu'_{xy^2} + i(\mu'_{x^2y} + \mu'_{y^3})$, whose phase angle $\alpha = \tan^{-1}(\frac{\mu'_{x^2y}+\mu'_{y^3}}{\mu'_{x^3}+\mu'_{xy^2}})$ changes covariantly with rotation. The last approach used to fix the rotation exploits straight linear segments on the region boundary (viii). A standard Douglas-Peucker algorithm [5,25] is executed on the shape-normalised region.

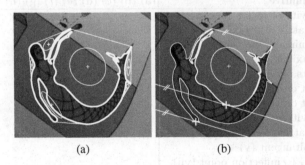

| (a) | (b) |

Fig. 5. Example of region concavities. (a) A detected non-convex region with identified concavities and their covariance matrices (b) The largest concavity: the bitangent line and farthest points on the concavity and on the region.

Concavities (v) are identified with segments of the region boundary that depart from the convex hull of the region. For each concavity, two points are found locally maximising distance to the corresponding bi-tangent line (vi). One of them is located on the contour segment that forms the concavity, the other one on the rest of the contour. Figure 5 illustrates a complex, non-convex region with six concavities. Figure 5 (a) shows the centre of gravity and the covariance matrix for each concavity. Figure 5 (b) demonstrates, for one of the concavities, the two points of locally maximal distance.

2.3 LAF Construction

A frame is constructed by combining affine-covariant primitives which, in correspondence, constrain all of the six degrees of freedom. The combinations we used in the experiments are illustrated in Figure 3. The images show basis vectors of the frames along with the primitives – points (e.g. inflection points), linear segments (e.g. bitangents), and ellipses representing covariance matrices. Figure 3 includes a table listing, for each of the frame types, the combination of primitives that define it.

3 Normalisation of Measurement Region

Object recognition from a single training view requires an object representation that does not change (is invariant) if the object is seen from different viewpoints and under different conditions, such as illumination. The previous section detailed constructions of local affine-covariant coordinate systems that are fully defined by image measurements. As such, they "stick" to the objects in the image if the viewpoint changes, and serve as object-centred frames of reference. Invariance of the object representation to geometric variations is thus achieved by normalising local appearance according to the detected frames. Image neighbourhood of every LAF is transformed into a canonical coordinate system, and a geometrically normalised patch is constructed. The patch is then normalised photometrically.

Geometric normalisation. The affine transformation between the canonical frame with origin $O = (0,0)^T$ and basis vectors $e_1 = (1,0)^T$ and $e_2 = (0,1)^T$ and a frame established in the image is described in homogenous coordinates by a 3 by 3 matrix

$$A = \begin{pmatrix} a_1 & a_2 & a_3 \\ a_4 & a_5 & a_6 \\ 0 & 0 & 1 \end{pmatrix}.$$

Measurement region (MR) is the part of the image, defined in terms of the affine frame, whose appearance, after appropriate encoding (see Section 4), is used to determine local correspondences. Each local affine frame is associated with one, or possibly multiple, MRs. The choice of MR shape and size is arbitrary. Larger MRs have higher discriminative potential, but are more likely to cover part of an object that is not locally planar. Based on experimental evaluation, our choice is to use a square MR centred around a detected LAF, specifically a region spanning $\langle -2, 3 \rangle \times \langle -2, 3 \rangle$ in the frame coordinate system. In image coordinate system, the measurement region of a frame A becomes a parallelogram with corners at (in homogenous coordinates):

$$c_1 = A \begin{pmatrix} -2 \\ -2 \\ 1 \end{pmatrix}, \quad c_2 = A \begin{pmatrix} -2 \\ 3 \\ 1 \end{pmatrix}, \quad c_3 = A \begin{pmatrix} 3 \\ -2 \\ 1 \end{pmatrix}, \quad c_4 = A \begin{pmatrix} 3 \\ 3 \\ 1 \end{pmatrix},$$

Photometric Normalisation. A linear camera (i.e. a camera without gamma-correction) is assumed and specular reflections and shadows are ignored. The combined effect of different scene illumination and camera and digitiser settings (gain, shutter speed, aperture) is modelled by affine transformations of individual colour channels, leading to the photometric transformation between two corresponding patches I and I' in the form:

$$\begin{pmatrix} r' \\ g' \\ b' \end{pmatrix} = \begin{pmatrix} m_r & 0 & 0 \\ 0 & m_g & 0 \\ 0 & 0 & m_b \end{pmatrix} \begin{pmatrix} r \\ g \\ b \end{pmatrix} + \begin{pmatrix} n_r \\ n_g \\ n_b \end{pmatrix}$$

The parameters m_r, n_r, m_g, n_g, m_b, n_b differ for individual correspondences. This model agrees with the monochromatic reflectance model [11] in the case of narrow-band sensor. It can be viewed as an affine extension of the diagonal model that has been shown by Finlayson to be sufficient in common circumstances [7], at least in conjunction with sensor sharpening [8]. To represent a patch invariantly to photometric transformations, intensities are transformed into a canonical form. The intensities of individual colour channels are affinely transformed to have zero mean and unit variance. The normalisation procedure of a local patch is summarised in algorithm 2.

Algorithm 2. Normalisation of a Local Representation

---

1. Establish a local affine frame, form the affine transformation $\mathbf{A}$ between a canonical coordinate system and the detected system.
2. Express the intensities of the $\mathbf{A}$'s measurement region in the canonical coordinate system $I'(\mathbf{x}) = I(\mathbf{A}\mathbf{x})$, $\mathbf{x} \in$ MR with some discretisation.
3. Apply the photometric normalisation $\hat{I}'(\mathbf{x}) = (I'(\mathbf{x}) - \mu)/\sigma$, $\mathbf{x} \in$ MR, where μ is the mean and σ is the standard deviation of I' over the MR.

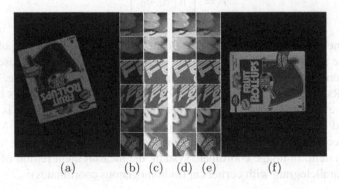

(a)   (b) (c) (d) (e)   (f)

Fig. 6. Normalised local image patches. (a), (f): Query and Database images, (b), (e): Examples of geometrically normalised MRs (measurement regions), (c), (d): Photometrically normalised MRs.

The twelve normalisation parameters ($a_1 \ldots a_6$ for geometric normalisation, m_r, n_r, m_g, n_g, m_b and n_b for photometric normalisation) are stored along with the descriptor of the normalised local patch. When considering a pair of patches for a correspondence,

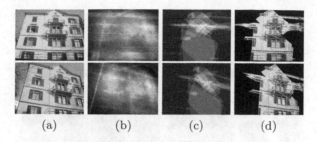

(a)   (b)   (c)   (d)

Fig. 7. Example of coverage of images by local patches. (a) original query and database images, (b) image coverage by local patches, whiter area – more overlapping patches, (c) image patches where correspondences between the images were found, (d) image area covered by the corresponding patches.

these twelve parameters are combined to provide the local transformations (both geometric and photometric) between the images. The transformations are exploited later during the matching step, as described in Section 4.1.

Figure 6 illustrates the normalisation procedure. On query (a) and database (f) images, MSERs are detected and LAFs constructed, independently on each image. Geometric normalisation according to the transformation between detected LAFs and the canonical coordinate system yields patches depicted in columns (b) and (e). Finally, the result of photometric normalisation of individual patches is shown in columns (c) and (d).

4 Descriptors of Local Appearance

A descriptor is a suitable data representation of a local image patch. It is associated with a similarity measure, often Euclidean distance. Because of the normalisation, any representation of the normalised patches (shown in Figure 6 (c) and (d)) is theoretically invariant to affine geometric and diagonal photometric transformations. There is therefore no need for e.g. rotation invariance of the representation. Obviously, directly the intensities of the normalised regions can be stored, but such a representation is sensitive to image noise and to imprecise alignment.

The following summarises the desirable properties of a descriptor. A descriptor has to be discriminative, to be able to distinguish between a large number of image regions. The similarity measure should well separate corresponding and not-corresponding regions. The ratio of similarities of matching and mismatched frames (discussed e.g. in Lowe's work [16]) should be maximised. The descriptor should be robust or invariant (i) to localisation errors of the detector, i.e. to misalignment of corresponding representations, and (ii) to image transformations not covered by the detector covariance. If the detector, for example, does not resolve rotation (as various feature point detectors do not) rotational invariants have to be used as descriptors. In our case, local affine frames provide covariance with affine transformations of the image. Our descriptor should thus be insensitive to small perspective distortion and to distortions caused by non-planarity of the surfaces. Finally, the descriptor should be efficient from the computational point of view. The data representation should be compact, to be memory efficient, and fast

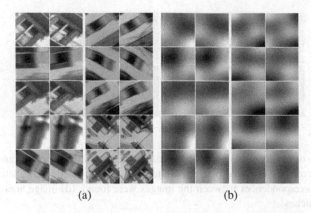

(a)   (b)

Fig. 8. Examples of correspondences established between frames of query (left columns) and database (right columns), for the image pair from Figure 7. (a) geometrically and photometrically normalised image patches, (b) the same patches reconstructed from 10 DCT coefficients per colour channel.

to construct. More importantly, efficient evaluation of similarity of two descriptors is required.

Discrete Cosine Transformation. We represent the local appearance by low-frequency coefficients of the discrete cosine transformation (DCT). For uniformly distributed data, the DCT approximates the Karhunen-Loeve transformation (KLT) [13], which is widely used in pattern recognition to reduce data dimensionality without significant deterioration of recognition rate. DCT has the desirable properties of a descriptor. It is computationally efficient, fast algorithms exist that computes DCT with $O(n \log n)$ time complexity. Hardware implementations of DCT are widely available due to its widespread use in image and video compression (JPEG, MPEG, etc.). Robustness to frame misalignment is achieved by storing only low-frequency coefficients, which are less sensitive to the misalignment than higher frequencies. Discriminativity of the DCT representation depends on the number of coefficients stored. In Section 5, it is experimentally shown how the number of coefficients affect the recognition performance, and that DCT representation outperforms descriptor composed of directly the normalised pixels. Our experiments showed that the DCT representation has about the same discriminative potential as the widely used SIFT descriptor [16].

In Figure 8 (b) an example is shown of what information is preserved if 10 DCT coefficients per colour channel are used. The image patches are the same as in Figure 8 (a).

4.1 Matching, Tentative Correspondences of Local Regions

Let us have a set $\mathcal{S}^D$ of frames F^D detected on a single database image, and a set $\mathcal{S}^Q$ of frames F^Q detected on a query image. Let each frame be associated with a descriptor of normalised local appearance. The set of tentative correspondences $\mathcal{T}$ is a subset of $\mathcal{S}^D \times \mathcal{S}^Q$ where $\times$ denotes the cartesian product. Frame pairs $\{F^D, F^Q\} \in \mathcal{T}$ iff

F^D and F^Q are considered potentially corresponding on the basis of local measurements (described later). The correspondences in T include many outliers as they are based solely on the properties of the two frames in question, regardless of other correspondences on the objects. At a later stage, the correspondences are verified and pruned according to consistency with a global model. Different strategies can be employed to obtain the set T:

Nearest match. This is the most commonly used strategy, used in all the experiments described in Section 5: For each frame $F^Q \in \mathcal{S}^Q$ find closest frame $F^D \in \mathcal{S}^D$: $F^D = \mathrm{argmin}_i(d(F^Q, \mathcal{S}_i^D))$. $\{F^Q, F^D\} \in T$ iff $d(F^Q, F^D) < \Theta_d$, where d is a "similarity" function discussed later.

Mutually nearest match. This strategy is suitable for symmetric matching problems, e.g. for wide-baseline stereo matching. The fraction of correct correspondences (inliers) in T is increased, causing the successive global consistency check execute faster. But the absolute number of inliers is typically reduced. For each frame $F^Q \in \mathcal{S}^Q$ find closest frame $F^D \in \mathcal{S}^D$: $F^D = \mathrm{argmin}_i(d(F^Q, \mathcal{S}_i^D))$: For the F^D find closest frame $\overline{F^Q} \in \mathcal{S}^Q$: $\overline{F^Q} = \mathrm{argmin}_i(d(F^D, \mathcal{S}_i^Q))$. $\{F^Q, F^D\} \in T$ iff $\overline{F^Q} = F^Q \wedge d(F^Q, F^D) < \Theta_d$.

All (or N most) similar. This strategy is used when repetitive structures are expected on the objects of interest. Repetitive structures induce ambiguous correspondences, which cannot be resolved at the time of forming of T. Here, each query frame is associated with a set of possibly corresponding frames – of which at most one is correct. The resolution about which of the correspondences is the correct one (if any) is left to the phase of verification of the global consistency. The drawback is in higher number of false correspondences (outliers), leading to increase of the computational load of the consistency check, or even to its failure due to small fraction of inliers: For each frame $F^Q \in \mathcal{S}^Q$ find all near frames (or N closest frames) $F^D \in \mathcal{S}^D$. $\{F^Q, \mathcal{S}_i^D\} \in T$ iff $d(F^Q, \mathcal{S}_i^D) < \Theta_d$.

The function d is a scalar function expressing similarity of two frames. Besides reflecting the similarity of the descriptors of the normalised patches, it might include terms related to the probability of the geometric and photometric transformations between the two frames.

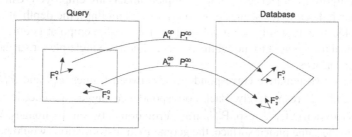

Fig. 9. Illustration of query to model transformations estimated from individual frame correspondences

Let F^D and F^Q denote the frames on query resp. database images. Let A^D and A^Q be the affine geometric transformations which transform the canonical coordinate system into image coordinates of the respective frames. Finally, let P^D and P^Q be the photometric transformations of the RGB values transforming the normalised intensities to the corresponding intensities in the images. Then the transformations $A^{QD} = A^D * (A^Q)^{-1}$ and $P^{QD} = P^D * (P^Q)^{-1}$ are the geometric resp. photometric transformations between the images – if the frames F^D and F^Q correspond. The situation is illustrated in Figure 9.

Generally, the probability distributions of the transformations A^{QD} and P^{QD} should be estimated from training scenes, and the frame similarity d should be penalised for unlikely transformations. In our experiments the probability distributions are approximated by a step function. If the transformations are out of allowed, problem-specific limits, the frame pair will not match, i.e. d evaluates to infinity. If they are within the limits, no penalty is imposed, and d evaluates directly to the similarity of the descriptors. It allows the function d to be implemented as a fast sequence of thresholdings.

4.2 Globally Consistent Subset of Tentative Correspondences

The process of obtaining tentative correspondences by pair-wise matching of local frames and their descriptors does not take into account the mutual relation between frames. It might for example happen that one of the tentative correspondences implies that the object is larger in the query image than in the model image, while another correspondence suggests that it is smaller and perhaps rotated. Such correspondences, although perfectly possible on their own, are not mutually consistent (assuming the object is rigid). A subset of the obtained tentative correspondences is therefore sought where all correspondences would be consistent with some global object model.

The first issue is the choice of the type of the global model. For general rigid 3D objects the obvious pick is a 3D model imposed through epipolar geometry. A method for estimating epipolar geometry from frame correspondences is described in [3]. The method takes advantage of the fact that a frame correspondence provides an affine transformation between the images, and consequently only three correspondences suffice to obtain the epipolar geometry. For deformable non-rigid (but not articulated) objects, an iterative method described in [6] can be used, although it is rather slow for practical exploitation.

For the purpose of object recognition, simpler models are employed. Unless we are recognising whole complex scenes (e.g. interior of a building), the depth of the visible part of an objects is typically too small to allow for reliable epipolar geometry estimation. We found it sufficient to model the object either as a single planar surface, or as a set of planar surfaces.

Let us have two tentative correspondences, between frames F_1^Q and F_1^D, and between F_2^Q and F_2^D respectively. Each correspondence suggest geometric A_1^{QD} resp. A_2^{QD} and photometric P_1^{QD} resp. P_2^{QD} transformation between the images. Would the frames lie on the same planar surface, the geometric transformations would be identical up to perspective distortion and an imprecision in frame localisation. Assuming light sources at infinity and no shadows nor specular reflections across the planar surface, the two photometric transformations would be also identical.

The set of tentative correspondences T is decomposed to subsets of consistent correspondences, i.e. subsets in which all correspondences imply identical image-to-image transformation. Each subset represents single plane in the scene. Subsets of low cardinalities are rejected as outliers, and the decision about the presence of an object in the scene relies only on the correspondences in subsets of high cardinality.

5 Experimental Validation

The performance of the proposed method was evaluated on several datasets. The COIL-100 dataset has been widely used in object recognition literature [31,24,15,2,32], and the experiment is included to compare the recognition rate with other state-of-the-art methods. The ZuBuD dataset represents a larger, real-world problem, with images taken outdoor, with occluded objects, varying background, and illumination changes. Finally, FOCUS database represents a retrieval problem, where product logos are sought in scanned advertising material. Typically, the logos occupy only a small portion (e.g. 1%) of the image.

(a)   (b)

Fig. 10. COIL-100: (a) Objects from the database, (b) Query images for the occlusion experiment

(a)   (b)

Fig. 11. ZuBuD dataset [27]: Examples of (a) query and (b) the corresponding database images

COIL-100. The Columbia Object Image Library (COIL-100)[1] is a database of colour images of 100 different objects; 72 images of each object placed on a turntable were acquired at pose intervals of 5°. Neither occlusion, background clutter, nor illumination changes are present. Several images from the database are shown in Figure 10(a). Two experiments were performed, differing in the number of images used for training. The achieved recognition rate was 98.2% for 4 training views per object (90° apart, 68 test views per object) and 99.7% for 8 training views (45° apart, 64 test views). Table 2 summarises the results and provides comparison to other published results.

---

[1] http://www.cs.columbia.edu/CAVE

In another experiment, occlusion of the objects was simulated by blanking one half of the test images (see Figure 10 (b)). Four full (unoccluded) training views per object were used in training. The recognition rate was 87%, which is comparable to published results on unoccluded images. Table 3 provides detailed information about the experiments.

Table 2. COIL-100 experiment: Comparison with published results

Method	Recognition rate	
	8 training views/object	4 training views/object
MSER+LAF	99.8%	98.2 %
Spectral representation [15]	96.3%	–
Kullback-Leibler SVM [31]	95.2%	84.3%
SNoW / edges [32]	89.2%	88.3%
Spin-Glass MRF [2]	88.2%	69.4%
SNoW / intensity [32]	85.1%	81.5%
Linear SVM [32]	84.8%	78.5%
Nearest Neighbour [32]	79.5%	74.6%

Table 3. Experimental results on COIL-100 and ZuBuD datasets

MSER+LAF	COIL-100			ZuBuD
1. Occluded queries	no	no	yes	n/a
2. Training view dist	90°	45°	90°	n/a
3. Number of DB images	400	800	400	1005
4. Number of DB frames	186346	385197	186346	251633
5. Number of query images	6800	6400	6800	115
6. Avg number of query frames	494	494	269	1594
7. avg time to build representation	520 ms	522 ms	251 ms	1255 ms
8. avg recall time	493 ms	3471 ms	277 ms	27234 ms
10. recognition rate	98.24%	99.77%	87.01%	100%

The ZuBuD dataset. The experiment was conducted on a set of images of 201 buildings in Zurich, Switzerland, which is publicly available [27]. The database consists of five photographs of the 201 buildings. A separate set of 115 query images is provided. For every query image, there are exactly five matching images of the same building in the database. Not all the database buildings have corresponding queries, the number of queries per building ranges from 0 to 5. Query and database images differ in viewpoint; variations in the illumination are present, but rare. Examples of corresponding query and database images are shown in Figure 11.

In the experiment, 115 query images were matched against 1005 database images, ie. 115575 matches were evaluated in total. For every query image, the R closest database images were retrieved. The recall rate r_R was evaluated, which is defined as $r_R = \frac{n_R}{N}$, where n_R is the number of correct answers in the first R retrieved images, and N the number of all possible correct answers. In our case, when every query has 5 corresponding images in the database, $N = \min(R, 5)$.

Two local patch representations (see Sect. 4) are compared, the directly stored intensities versus the DCT coefficients. The results are summarised in Table 4. For both methods, recall r_R is shown for $R = 1 \ldots 5$. The recall r_1 is equivalent to the percentage of correct images retrieved in rank 1. The last column shows the memory required to store the representation of the whole database of 1005 images. The last lines in Table 4 show other results.

The proposed retrieval system performed well, the retrieval performance was, or was close to, 100% in the first rank. The DCT representation performed slightly better than the direct intensity representation, due to the insensitivity to image noise and small frame misalignments. Regarding the memory requirements, the DCT representation is much more compact. The memory usage is reduced to circa 20–30% depending on the number of DCT coefficients stored.

Table 4. ZuBuD: Summary of experimental results

Method	Average recall r_R					Memory
	r_1	r_2	r_3	r_4	r_5	usage
direct intensity	98.3%	96.6%	93.6%	89.1%	81.9%	1300 MB
DCT 6 coeffs	99.1%	98.3%	95.7%	91.1%	84.0%	290 MB
DCT 10 coeffs	99.1%	98.7%	96.8%	92.2%	85.0%	370 MB
DCT 15 coeffs	100.0%	99.1%	97.4%	92.8%	85.4%	470 MB
HPAT [26]	86.1%					
Random subwindows [17]	95.7%					

The FOCUS database contains 360 colour high-resolution images of commercials scanned from miscellaneous magazines. Figure 13 illustrates example queries and identified commercials from the database. For comparison purposes, we run an experiment with an identical setup as the SEDL system introduced by Cohen [4]. The quality of the retrieval is assessed by the same two quantities as defined by Cohen, the recall rate r_R and the precision ρ_R:

$$r_R = \frac{n}{N} \qquad\qquad \rho_R = \frac{\sum_{i=1}^{n}(R + 1 - r_i)}{\sum_{i=1}^{n}(R + 1 - i)} \qquad (4)$$

where n is the number of correct answers in the first R retrieved images, N the number of all correct answers contained in the database, and r_i the rank of the i-th correctly retrieved answer.

In Table 5, average recall rate r_{20} and average precision ρ_{20} are given for the number of retrieved images $R = 20$. For each of the 25 queries used by Cohen, the database images were sorted according to the matching score (similarity measure) m, and the recall r_{20} and the precision ρ_{20} were computed according to formula (4). Each of the 25 queries has 2 to 9 correct answers in the database, with the total number of all correct answers equal to 90. The local affine frame (LAF) method achieves a 83% recall, which is approximately 5% better than results reported by Cohen. Note that the LAF method is not attempting to generalise the query (i.e. to categorise). Most database images missed

Fig. 12. FOCUS: Examples of query (left) and database images (right) not retrieved

Fig. 13. FOCUS: Query localisation examples. Query images, database images, and query localisations.

Table 5. FOCUS: Retrieval performance compared to the SEDL system

SEDL		LAFs	
recall r_{20}	avg precision ρ_{20}	recall r_{20}	avg precision ρ_{20}
70/90 = 77.8%	88%	75/90 = 83.3%	93.5%

depict *objects different from the query*. Figure 12 shows three such examples. The "failure" in such cases might be viewed as a strength, demonstrating the very high selectivity of the method, distinguishing items that superficially look identical, while being immune to severe affine deformations.

6 Conclusions

An object recognition method representing object appearance by a set of local measurements was described. Invariance to affine transformations is achieved by expressing local appearance in terms of affine-covariantly detected local coordinate systems.

An overview and classification of affine covariant constructions was presented, covariance of the constructions was proven, and computational issues were discussed. The choice of suitable representation of the local appearance, and the problem of formation of tentative region-to-region correspondences were investigated.

It was shown experimentally that the method achieves state-of-the-art results on publicly available object recognition tests (COIL-100, ZuBuD, FOCUS). Change of scale, illumination conditions, out-of-plane rotation, occlusion, locally anisotropic scale change and 3D translation of the viewpoint were all present in the test problems.

References

1. C. Ballester and M. Gonzalez. Affine invariant texture segmentation and shape from texture by variational methods. *Journal of Mathematical Imaging and Vision*, 9:141–171, 1998.
2. B. Caputo, J. Hornegger, D. Paulus, and H. Niemann. A spin-glass markov random field for 3-D object recognition. Technical Report LME-TR-2002-01, Lehrstuhl für Mustererkennung, Institut für Informatik, Universität Erlangen-Nürnberg, 2002.
3. O. Chum, J. Matas, and Š. Obdržálek. Enhancing RANSAC by generalized model optimization. In *Proc. of the Asian Conference on Computer Vision (ACCV)*, volume 2, pages 812–817, January 2004.
4. S. Cohen. Finding color and shape patterns in images. Technical Report STAN-CS-TR-99-1620, Stanford University, May 1999.
5. D. Douglas and T. Peucker. Algorithms for the reduction of the number of points required to represent a digitized line or its caricature. *Canadian Cartographer*, 10:112–122, 1973.
6. V. Ferrari, T. Tuytelaars, and L. Van Gool. Simultaneous object recognition and segmentation by image exploration. In *Proceedings of the European Conference on Computer Vision*, volume I, pages 40–54, May 2004.
7. G. Finlayson, M. Drew, and B.Funt. Color constancy: Generalized diagonal transforms suffice. *Journal of the Optical Society of America*, 11:3011–3019, 1994.
8. G. Finlayson, M. Drew, and B. Funt. Spectral sharpening: Sensor transformations for improved color constancy. *Journal of the Optical Society of America*, 11:1553–1563, 1994.
9. P.-E. Forssén and G. Granlund. Robust multi-scale extraction of blob features. In *Proceedings of the 13th Scandinavian Conference on Image Analysis*, LNCS 2749, pages 11–18, 2003.
10. C. Harris and M. Stephens. A combined corner and edge detector. In *Alvey Vision Conference*, pages 147–152, 1988.
11. G. Healey. Using color for geometry-insensitive segmentation. *Journal of the Optical Society of America*, 6:86–103, June 1989.
12. J. Heikkilä. Pattern matching with affine moment descriptors. *Pattern Recognition*, 37(9):1825–1834, 2004.
13. A. K. Jain. *Fundamentals of Digital Image Processing*. 1986.
14. T. Lindeberg. Feature detection with automatic scale selection. *International Journal on Computer Vision*, 30(2):79–116, 1998.
15. X. Liu and A. Srivastava. A spectral representation for appearance-based classification and recognition. In *Proceedings of the International Conference on Pattern Recognition*, pages 37–40, 2002.
16. D. G. Lowe. Distinctive image features from scale-invariant keypoints. *International Journal on Computer Vision*, 20(2):91–110, 2004.
17. R. Marée, P. Geurts, J. Piater, and L. Wehenkel. Random subwindows for robust image classification. In *Proceedings of the Conference on Computer Vision and Pattern Recognition*, 2005.
18. J. Matas, O. Chum, M. Urban, and T. Pajdla. Robust wide-baseline stereo from maximally stable extremal regions. *Image and Vision Computing*, 22(10):761–767, 2004.
19. K. Mikolajczyk and C. Schmid. Indexing based on scale invariant interest points. In *Proceedings of the International Conference on Computer Vision*, pages 525–531, 2001.

20. K. Mikolajczyk and C. Schmid. An affine invariant interest point detector. In *Proceedings of the European Conference on Computer Vision*, pages 128–142, 2002.

21. K. Mikolajczyk, T. Tuytelaars, C. Schmid, A. Zisserman, J. Matas, F. Schaffalitzky, T. Kadir, and L. van Gool. A comparison of affine region detectors. *International Journal of Computer Vision*, 65(7):43 – 72, November 2005.

22. F. Mokhtarian and A. K. Mackworth. A theory of multiscale, curvature-based shape representation for planar curves. *IEEE Transactions on Pattern Analysis and Machine Intelligence*, 14(8):789–805, 1992.

23. J. Mundy and A. Zisserman. *Geometric Invariance in Computer Vision*. 1992.

24. Š. Obdržálek and J. Matas. Object recognition using local affine frames on distinguished regions. In *Proceedings of the British Machine Vision Conference*, 2002.

25. U. Ramer. An iterative procedure for the polygonal approximation of plane curves. *Computer Graphics and Image Processing*, 1:244–259, 1972.

26. H. Shao, T. Svoboda, T. Tuytelaars, and L. Van Gool. HPAT indexing for fast object/scene recognition based on local appearance. In *International Conference on Image and Video Retrieval*, pages 71–80, 2003.

27. H. Shao, T. Svoboda, and L. Van Gool. ZuBuD — Zurich Buildings Database for Image Based Recognition. Technical Report 260, Computer Vision Laboratory, Swiss Federal Institute of Technology, March 2003. http://www.vision.ee.ethz.ch/showroom/zubud.

28. J. Sivic and A. Zisserman. Video Google: A text retrieval approach to object matching in videos. In *Proceedings of the International Conference on Computer Vision*, pages 1470–1477, 2003.

29. T. Tuytelaars and L. Van Gool. Content-based image retrieval based on local affinely invariant regions. In *Visual Information and Information Systems*, pages 493–500, 1999.

30. T. Tuytelaars and L. Van Gool. Wide baseline stereo matching based on local, affinely invariant regions. In *Proceedings of the British Machine Vision Conference*, 2000.

31. N. Vasconcelos, P. Ho, and P. J. Moreno. The Kullback-Leibler kernel as a framework for discriminant and localized representations for visual recognition. In *Proceedings of the European Conference on Computer Vision*, pages 430–441, 2004.

32. M. H. Yang, D. Roth, and N. Ahuja. Learning to Recognize 3D Objects with SNoW. In *Proceedings of the European Conference on Computer Vision*, pages 439–454, 2000.

Appendix A. Proofs of Affine Covariance of LAF Primitives

Bellow we show that the construction used to establish local affine frames are indeed covariant with affine transformation. In particular, we show how the area, centre of gravity, and covariance matrix of a region changes under affine transformations of the region, and that the properties of tangent points and of the farthest-from-a-line points are maintained.

Area. Consider a region Ω_1, and its transformed image $\Omega_2 = A\Omega_1$, i.e. $\Omega_2 = \{x_2 | x_2 = A^T x_1 + t; x_1 \in \Omega_1\}$ The area of Ω_2 is given as

$$|\Omega_2| = \int_{\Omega_2} d\Omega_2 = \int_{\Omega_1} |A| \, d\Omega_1 = |A||\Omega_1|, \qquad (5)$$

where $|A|$ is the determinant of A, and $|\Omega|$ is the area of region Ω. The area of a transformed region equals $|A|$ times the area of the original region.

Centre of gravity. The centre of gravity of region Ω is $\mu = \frac{1}{|\Omega|} \int_\Omega \mathbf{x} d\Omega$. The relation between the centres of gravity of transformed regions is:

$$\mu_2 = \frac{1}{|\Omega_2|} \int_{\Omega_2} \mathbf{x_2} \, d\Omega_2$$

$$= \frac{1}{|A||\Omega_1|} \int_{\Omega_1} (A^\mathsf{T} \mathbf{x_1} + \mathbf{t})|A| \, d\Omega_1$$

$$= A^\mathsf{T} \frac{1}{|\Omega_1|} \int_{\Omega_1} \mathbf{x_1} \, d\Omega_1 + \frac{1}{|\Omega_1|} \int_{\Omega_1} \mathbf{t} \, d\Omega_1$$

$$= A^\mathsf{T} \mu_1 + \mathbf{t}, \tag{6}$$

the centre of gravity changes covariantly with the affine transform.

Covariance matrix. The covariance matrix Σ of a region Ω is a 2x2 matrix defined as $\Sigma = \frac{1}{|\Omega|} \int_\Omega (\mathbf{x} - \mu)(\mathbf{x} - \mu)^\mathsf{T} \, d\Omega$. Covariance matrix of a transformed region Ω_2 is then:

$$\Sigma_2 = \frac{1}{|\Omega_2|} \int_{\Omega_2} (\mathbf{x_2} - \mu_2)(\mathbf{x_2} - \mu_2)^\mathsf{T} \, d\Omega_2$$

$$= \frac{1}{|A||\Omega_1|} \int_{\Omega_1} (A^\mathsf{T} \mathbf{x_1} + \mathbf{t} - (A^\mathsf{T} \mu_1 + \mathbf{t}))(A^\mathsf{T} \mathbf{x_1} + \mathbf{t} - (A^\mathsf{T} \mu_1 + \mathbf{t}))^\mathsf{T} |A| \, d\Omega_1$$

$$= \frac{1}{|\Omega_1|} \int_{\Omega_1} (A^\mathsf{T} (\mathbf{x_1} - \mu_1))(A^\mathsf{T} (\mathbf{x_1} - \mu_1))^\mathsf{T} \, d\Omega_1$$

$$= A^\mathsf{T} \left(\frac{1}{|\Omega_1|} \int_{\Omega_1} (\mathbf{x_1} - \mu_1)(\mathbf{x_1} - \mu_1)^\mathsf{T} \, d\Omega_1 \right) A$$

$$= A^\mathsf{T} \Sigma_1 A \tag{7}$$

Cholesky decomposition of a symmetric and positive-definite matrix Σ is a factorisation $\Sigma = U^\mathsf{T} U$, where U is an upper triangular matrix. Cholesky decomposition is defined up to a rotation, since $U^\mathsf{T} U = U^\mathsf{T} R^\mathsf{T} R U$ for any orthonormal R. For the decomposition of covariance matrix of a transformed region we write

$$\Sigma_2 = U_2^\mathsf{T} R_2^\mathsf{T} R_2 U_2 = A^\mathsf{T} U_1^\mathsf{T} R_1^\mathsf{T} R_1 U_1 A = A^\mathsf{T} \Sigma_1 A, \text{ thus} \qquad U_2^\mathsf{T} = A^\mathsf{T} U_1^\mathsf{T} R \tag{8}$$

Hence the triangular matrix U obtained as the Cholesky-decomposition of a covariance matrix Σ is covariant, up to an arbitrary orthonormal matrix R, with the affine transform applied to the region.

Line parallelism. Let us consider two lines, determined by points $\mathbf{p}$ and $\mathbf{q}$, and $\mathbf{r}$ and $\mathbf{s}$ respectively. The lines are parallel, iff

$$(\mathbf{p} - \mathbf{q}) = k(\mathbf{r} - \mathbf{s}), \, k \in \mathbb{R} \setminus \{0\}$$

Affinely transformed lines are then parallel iff

$$(A^\mathsf{T} \mathbf{p} + \mathbf{t} - A^\mathsf{T} \mathbf{q} - \mathbf{t}) = k(A^\mathsf{T} \mathbf{r} + \mathbf{t} - A^\mathsf{T} \mathbf{s} - \mathbf{t})$$
$$A^\mathsf{T} (\mathbf{p} - \mathbf{q}) = kA^\mathsf{T} (\mathbf{r} - \mathbf{s})$$
$$(\mathbf{p} - \mathbf{q}) = k(\mathbf{r} - \mathbf{s}) \tag{9}$$

which is true if and only if the lines were parallel before the transformation. Thus, affine transformation preserves line parallelism.

Ordering of distances to a line: Let us have a line determined by two points $\mathbf{p}$ and $\mathbf{q}$. For a point $\mathbf{x}$, its distance d_1 to the line $\mathbf{pq}$ is $d_1 = \frac{2S}{|\mathbf{p}-\mathbf{q}|}$, where S is the area of the $\mathbf{pqx}$ triangle. Using eq. 5, it follows that the transformed distance d_2 is given by

$$d_2 = \frac{2|A|S}{|A^\mathsf{T}\mathbf{p}+\mathbf{t}-A^\mathsf{T}\mathbf{q}-\mathbf{t}|} = \frac{|A||\mathbf{p}-\mathbf{q}|}{|A^\mathsf{T}\mathbf{p}-A^\mathsf{T}\mathbf{q}|}d_1 = kd_1$$

where k is a scalar constant for given line $\mathbf{pq}$ and transformation A. Affine transformation thus preserves ordering of distances of points from a line. It directly follows that a point $\mathbf{x} \in X$ with the property of being of all the points in X the one farthest from a line $\mathbf{pq}$, retains the property under affine transformations.

Incidence of points and lines: Under affine transformations, points incident with a line will remain on the line, and, vice-versa, distinct points will not be brought to the line unless the transformation is singular. The property is again easily shown exploiting the covariance of region area, from Equation. 5. Considering a line defined by two distinct points $\mathbf{p}$ and $\mathbf{q}$, and a point $\mathbf{x}$, the area S_1 of the $\mathbf{pqx}$ triangle equals to zero if $\mathbf{x}$ is on $\mathbf{pq}$ and nonzero otherwise. After affine transformation, the area of the triangle becomes $S_2 = |A|S_1$, where $|A|$ is the determinant of the transformation matrix (S_2 is the area of triangle given by points defining the transformed line, i.e. $A^\mathsf{T}\mathbf{p}+\mathbf{t}$ and $A^\mathsf{T}\mathbf{q}+\mathbf{t}$, and the transformed point $A^\mathsf{T}\mathbf{x}+\mathbf{t}$). Assuming nonsingular transformation, i.e. $|A| \neq 0$, the transformed triangle has area $S_2 = 0$ if and only if $S_1 = 0$. Thus the incidence is maintained.

Tangent and bitangent lines: Tangent line is a line incident with region boundary (in a tangent point $\mathbf{p}$), which does not pass through any of the region interior points. Since the incidence property between the tangent line and the boundary, respective interior points, is maintained, the line transformed by an affine transformation remains tangent to the transformed region, and the tangency occur in the transformed point $\mathbf{p}_2 = A^\mathsf{T}\mathbf{p}+\mathbf{t}$. An analogy holds for the bitangent lines, where both tangent points are maintained.

An affine transformation is either orientation-preserving or orientation-reversing, if determinant $|A|$ is positive or negative respectively [23]. Therefore the sign of the curvature $\kappa = \frac{d\Phi}{ds}$ of a transformed region is either reversed or preserved. It follows that **linear segments** of the contour (segments of zero curvature) and **inflection points** (points where the curvature changes its sign, without specifying whether from positive to negative or vice versa) are maintained.

3D Object Modeling and Recognition from Photographs and Image Sequences

Fred Rothganger[1], Svetlana Lazebnik[1], Cordelia Schmid[2], and Jean Ponce[1]

[1] Department of Computer Science and Beckman Institute
University of Illinois at Urbana-Champaign, Urbana, IL 61801, USA
{rothgang,slazebni,jponce}@uiuc.edu
[2] INRIA Rhône-Alpes
665, Avenue de l'Europe, 38330 Montbonnot, France
Cordelia.Schmid@inrialpes.fr

Abstract. This chapter proposes a representation of rigid three-dimensional (3D) objects in terms of local affine-invariant descriptors of their images and the spatial relationships between the corresponding surface patches. Geometric constraints associated with different views of the same patches under affine projection are combined with a normalized representation of their appearance to guide the matching process involved in object modeling and recognition tasks. The proposed approach is applied in two domains: (1) Photographs — models of rigid objects are constructed from small sets of images and recognized in highly cluttered shots taken from arbitrary viewpoints. (2) Video — dynamic scenes containing multiple moving objects are segmented into rigid components, and the resulting 3D models are directly matched to each other, giving a novel approach to video indexing and retrieval.

1 Introduction

Traditional feature-based geometric approaches to three-dimensional (3D) object recognition — such as alignment [13,19] or geometric hashing [15] — enumerate various subsets of geometric image features before using pose consistency constraints to confirm or discard competing match hypotheses. They largely ignore the rich source of information contained in the image brightness and/or color pattern, and thus typically lack an effective mechanism for selecting promising matches. Appearance-based methods, as originally proposed in the context of face recognition [43] and 3D object recognition [28], prefer a classical pattern recognition framework that exploits the discriminatory power of (relatively) low-dimensional, empirical models of global object appearance in classification tasks. However, they typically de-emphasize the combinatorial aspects of the search involved in any matching task, which limits their ability to handle occlusion and clutter.

Viewpoint and/or illumination invariants provide a natural indexing mechanism for object recognition tasks. Unfortunately, although planar objects and certain simple shapes—such as bilateral symmetries or various types of generalized cylinders—admit invariants, general 3D shapes do not [4], which is the

J. Ponce et al. (Eds.): Toward Category-Level Object Recognition, LNCS 4170, pp. 105–126, 2006.
© Springer-Verlag Berlin Heidelberg 2006

main reason why invariants have fallen out of favor after an intense flurry of activity in the early 1990s [26,27]. In this chapter, we revisit invariants as a *local* description of truly three-dimensional objects: Indeed, although smooth surfaces are almost never planar in the large, they are always planar in the small —that is, sufficiently small patches can be treated as being comprised of coplanar points. Concretely, we propose to capture the appearance of salient surface patches using local image descriptors that are invariant under affine transformations of the spatial domain [18,24] and of the brightness signal [20], and to capture their spatial relationships using multi-view geometric constraints related to those studied in the structure from motion literature [39]. This representation is directly related to a number of recent schemes for combining the local surface appearance at "interest points" [12] with geometric constraints in tasks such as wide-baseline stereo matching [44], image retrieval [36], and object recognition [20]. These methods normally either require storing a large number of views for each object, or limiting the range of admissible viewpoints. In contrast, our approach supports the automatic acquisition of explicit 3D object models from multiple unregistered images, and their recognition in photographs and videos taken from arbitrary viewpoints.

Section 2 presents the main elements of our object representation framework. It is applied in Sections 3 and 4 to the automated acquisition of 3D object models from small sets of unregistered images and to the identification and localization of these models in cluttered photographs taken from arbitrary and unknown viewpoints. Section 5 briefly discusses further applications to the video indexing and retrieval domain, including a method for segmenting dynamic scenes observed by a moving camera into rigid components and matching the 3D models recovered from different shots. We conclude in Section 6 with a short discussion of the promise and limitations of the proposed approach.

2 Approach

2.1 Affine Regions and Their Description

The construction of local invariant models of object appearance involves two steps, the detection of salient image regions, and their description. Ideally, the regions found in two images of the same object should be the projections of the same surface patches. Therefore, they must be *covariant*, with regions detected in the first picture mapping onto those found in the second one via the geometric and photometric transformations induced by the corresponding viewpoint and illumination changes. In turn, detection must be followed by a description stage that constructs a region representation *invariant* under these changes. For small patches of smooth Lambertian surfaces, the transformations are (to first order) affine, and we use the approach recently proposed by Mikolajczyk and Schmid to find the corresponding *affine regions*: Briefly, the algorithm iterates over steps where (1) an elliptical image region is deformed to maximize the isotropy of the corresponding brightness pattern (shape adaptation [10]); (2) its characteristic scale is determined as a local extremum of the normalized Laplacian in scale space (scale selection [17]); and (3) the Harris operator [12] is used to refine the position of the the ellipse's center (localization [24]). The scale-invariant interest point detector proposed in [23] provides an initial guess for this procedure, and the elliptical region obtained at convergence can be shown to be covariant under affine transformations. The affine region detection process used in this chapter implements both this algorithm and a variant where a difference-of-Gaussians (DoG) operator replaces the Harris interest point detector. Note that this operator tends to find corners and points where significant intensity changes occur, while the DoG detector is (in general) attracted to the centers of roughly uniform regions (blobs): Intuitively, the two operators provide complementary kinds of information (see Figure 1 for examples).

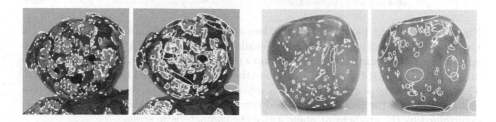

Fig. 1. Affine regions found by Harris-Laplacian (left) and DoG (right) detectors

The affine regions output by our detection process are ellipses that can be mapped onto a unit circle centered at the origin using a one-parameter family of affine transformations. This ambiguity can be resolved by determining the dominant gradient orientation of the image region, turning the corresponding ellipse into a parallelogram and the unit circle into a square (Figure 2). Thus, the output of the detection process is a set of image regions in the shape of parallelograms, together with affine *rectifying transformations* that map each parallelogram onto a "unit" square centered at the origin (Figure 3).

A rectified affine region is a normalized representation of the *local* surface appearance. For distant observers (affine projection), it is invariant under arbitrary viewpoint changes. For Lambertian patches and distant light sources, it can also be made invariant to changes in illumination (ignoring shadows) by subtracting the mean patch intensity from each pixel value and normalizing the Frobenius norm of the corresponding image array to one. The Euclidean distance between feature vectors associated with their pixel values can thus be used to compare rectified patches, irrespective of viewpoint and (affine) illumination changes. Other feature spaces may of course be used as well. As many others, we have found the Lowe's SIFT descriptor [20] —a histogram over both spatial dimensions and gradient orientations— to perform well in our experiments, along with a 10×10 color histogram drawn from the UV portion of YUV space when color is available.

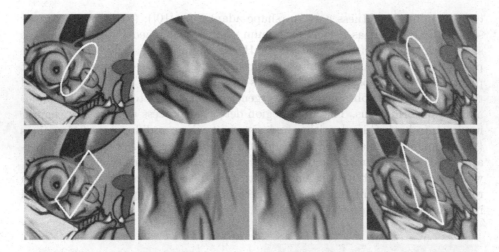

Fig. 2. Normalizing patches. The left two columns show a patch from image 1 of Krystian Mikolajczyk's graffiti dataset (available from the INRIA LEAR group's web page: http://lear.inrialpes.fr/software). The right two columns show the matching patch from image 4. The first row shows the ellipse determined by affine adaptation. This normalizes the shape, but leaves a rotation ambiguity, as illustrated by the normalized circles in the center. The second row shows the same patches with orientation determined by the gradient at about twice the characteristic scale.

2.2 Geometric Constraints

Given an affine region, let us denote by $\mathcal{R}$ the affine transformation from the image patch to its rectified (normalized) form, and by $\mathcal{S} = \mathcal{R}^{-1}$ the affine transformation from the rectified form back to the image patch (Figure 3). The 3×3 matrix $\mathcal{S}$ has the form

$$\mathcal{S} = \begin{bmatrix} \boldsymbol{h} & \boldsymbol{v} & \boldsymbol{c} \\ 0 & 0 & 1 \end{bmatrix},$$

and its columns enjoy the following geometric interpretation: The third column gives the homogeneous coordinates of the center c of the corresponding image parallelogram, while $\boldsymbol{h}$ and $\boldsymbol{v}$ are the vectors joining c to the midpoints of the parallelogram's sides (Figure 3). The matrix $\mathcal{S}$ effectively contains the locations of three points in the image, so a match between $m \geq 2$ images of the same patch contains exactly the same information as a match between m triples of points. It is thus clear that all the machinery of structure from motion [39] and pose estimation [13,19] from point matches can be exploited in modeling and object recognition tasks. Reasoning in terms of multi-view constraints associated with the matrix $\mathcal{S}$ provides a unified and convenient representation for all stages of both tasks.

Suppose there are n surface patches observed in m images, and that we are given a complete set of measurements $\mathcal{S}_{ij}$ as defined above for image indices

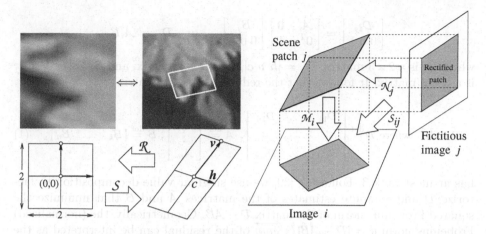

Fig. 3. Geometric structure. Top left: A rectified patch and the original image region. Bottom left: Interpretation of the rectification matrix $\mathcal{R}$ and its inverse $\mathcal{S}$. Right: Interpretation of the decomposition of the mapping $\mathcal{S}_{ij}$ into the product of a projection matrix $\mathcal{M}_i$ and an inverse projection matrix $\mathcal{N}_j$.

$i = 1, \ldots, m$ and patch indices $j = 1, \ldots, n$. (Later, we will show how to handle the "missing data" problem that results when not all patches are visible in all views.) A rectified patch can be thought of as a fictitious view of the original surface patch (Figure 3), and the mapping $\mathcal{S}_{ij}$ can thus be decomposed into an *inverse projection* $\mathcal{N}_j$ [5] that maps the rectified patch onto the corresponding surface patch, followed by a projection $\mathcal{M}_i$ that maps that patch onto its projection in image number i. In particular, we can write

$$\hat{\mathcal{S}} \overset{\text{def}}{=} \begin{bmatrix} \mathcal{S}_{11} & \ldots & \mathcal{S}_{1n} \\ \vdots & \ddots & \vdots \\ \mathcal{S}_{m1} & \ldots & \mathcal{S}_{mn} \end{bmatrix} = \begin{bmatrix} \mathcal{M}_1 \\ \vdots \\ \mathcal{M}_m \end{bmatrix} [\mathcal{N}_1 \ \ldots \ \mathcal{N}_n].$$

The inverse projection matrix can be written as

$$\mathcal{N}_j = \begin{bmatrix} \boldsymbol{H} & \boldsymbol{V} & \boldsymbol{C} \\ 0 & 0 & 1 \end{bmatrix}_j,$$

and its columns admit a geometric interpretation similar to that of $\mathcal{S}_{ij}$: the first two contain the "horizontal" and "vertical" axes of the surface patch, and the third one is the homogeneous coordinate vector of its center.

To extract the matrices $\mathcal{N}_j$ (and thus the corresponding patches' geometry) from a set of image measurements, we construct a reduced factorization of $\hat{\mathcal{S}}$ by picking, as in [39], the center of mass of the surface patches' centers as the origin of the world coordinate system, and the center of mass of these points' projections as the origin in each image. In this case, the projection equation $\mathcal{S}_{ij} = \mathcal{M}_i \mathcal{N}_j$ becomes

$$\begin{bmatrix} \mathcal{D}_{ij} \\ 0\ 0\ 1 \end{bmatrix} = \begin{bmatrix} \mathcal{A}_i & \mathbf{0} \\ \mathbf{0}^T & 1 \end{bmatrix} \begin{bmatrix} \mathcal{B}_j \\ 0\ 0\ 1 \end{bmatrix}, \quad \text{or} \quad \mathcal{D}_{ij} = \mathcal{A}_i \mathcal{B}_j,$$

where $\mathcal{A}_i$ is a 2×3 matrix, $\mathcal{D}_{ij} = [\boldsymbol{h}\ \boldsymbol{v}\ \boldsymbol{c}]_{ij}$ is a 2×3 matrix, and $\mathcal{B}_j = [\boldsymbol{H}\ \boldsymbol{V}\ \boldsymbol{C}]_j$ is a 3×3 matrix. It follows that the reduced $2m \times 3n$ matrix

$$\hat{\mathcal{D}} = \hat{\mathcal{A}}\hat{\mathcal{B}}, \text{ where } \hat{\mathcal{D}} \overset{\text{def}}{=} \begin{bmatrix} \mathcal{D}_{11} & \cdots & \mathcal{D}_{1n} \\ \vdots & \ddots & \vdots \\ \mathcal{D}_{m1} & \cdots & \mathcal{D}_{mn} \end{bmatrix}, \hat{\mathcal{A}} \overset{\text{def}}{=} \begin{bmatrix} \mathcal{A}_1 \\ \vdots \\ \mathcal{A}_m \end{bmatrix}, \hat{\mathcal{B}} \overset{\text{def}}{=} [\mathcal{B}_1\ \cdots\ \mathcal{B}_n], \quad (1)$$

has at most rank 3. Following [39] we use singular value decomposition to factorize $\hat{\mathcal{D}}$ and compute estimates of the matrices $\hat{\mathcal{A}}$ and $\hat{\mathcal{B}}$ that minimize the squared Frobenius norm of the matrix $\hat{\mathcal{D}} - \hat{\mathcal{A}}\hat{\mathcal{B}}$. Geometrically, the (normalized) Frobenius norm $d = |\hat{\mathcal{D}} - \hat{\mathcal{A}}\hat{\mathcal{B}}|/\sqrt{3mn}$ of the residual can be interpreted as the root-mean-squared reprojection error, that is, the distance (in pixels) between the center and side points of the patches observed in the image and those predicted from the recovered matrices $\hat{\mathcal{A}}$ and $\hat{\mathcal{B}}$. Given n matches established across m images (a match is an m-tuple of image patches), the residual error d can thus be used as a measure of inconsistency between the matches.

2.3   Matching

Matching is a fundamental process in both modeling and recognition. An image can be viewed as a collection of 2D patches, and likewise a 3D model is a collection of 3D patches. There are three steps in our general procedure for matching between two such patch sets A and B:

Step 1 – Appearance based selection of potential matches. For each patch in set A, this step selects one or more patches in set B with similar appearance, as measured by the descriptors presented in Section 2.1. Mismatches might occur due to measurement noise or confusion of similar (for example, repetitive) structures.

Step 2 – Robust estimation. Using RANSAC, alignment, or other related techniques, this step selects a geometrically consistent subset of the match hypotheses. Our assumption is that the largest consistent set will contain mostly true matches. This establishes the geometric relationship between the two sets of patches A and B.

Step 3 – Geometry-based addition of matches. This step seeks a fixed-point in the space $(A \times B)$ of matches by iteratively estimating a geometric model based on the current set of matches and then selecting all match hypotheses that are consistent with the model. At the same time it adds new match hypotheses guided by the model. Generally, the geometric model will not change significantly during this process. Rather, the resulting maximal set of matches benefits recognition, where the number of matches acts as a confidence measure, and modeling, where it produces better coverage of the object.

3   3D Object Modeling from Images

There are several combinatorial and geometric problems to solve in order to convert a set of images into a 3D model. The overall process is divided into four steps: (1) *matching*: match regions between pairs of images; (2) *chaining*: link matches across multiple images; (3) *stitching*: solve for the affine structure and motion while coping with missing data; (4) *Euclidean upgrade*: use constraints associated with the intrinsic parameters of the camera to turn the affine reconstruction into a Euclidean one. In the following we describe each of these steps. We will use a teddy bear to illustrate some of the steps of the modeling process. Additional modeling experiments will also be presented.

Matching. The first step is to match the regions found in a pair of images. This is an instance of the *wide-baseline stereo matching* problem which has been well studied in the literature [3,22,24,31,35,38,44]. Any technique that generates a set of matches between affine regions in a pair of images is appropriate, including the general matching procedure (Section 2.3). This algorithm appears in three different contexts in this work, so we have chosen to give the details of its application only in the object recognition case (Section 4). Here we give a very brief sketch of its application to 2D matching. For the appearance-based matching (Step 1) we compare SIFT descriptors. For robust estimation (Step 2) we take advantage of the normalized residual $d = |\hat{\mathcal{D}} - \hat{\mathcal{A}}\hat{\mathcal{B}}|/\sqrt{3mn}$ to measure the consistency of subsets of the matches. Finally, in Step 3 we use an estimate of the epipolar geometry between the two images to find additional hypothetical matches, which are again filtered using the consistency measure. For details on the 2D matching procedure, see [33].

Chaining. The matching process described in the previous section outputs affine regions matched across pairs of views. It is convenient to represent these matches by a single (sparse) *patch-view* matrix whose columns represent surface patches, and rows represent the images in which they appear (Figure 5).

There are two challenges to overcome in the chaining process. One is to ensure that the image measurements $\mathcal{S}_{ij}$ are self-consistent for all projections of a given patch j. To solve this, we choose one member of the corresponding column as reference patch, and refine the parameters of the other patches to maximize their texture correlation with it (Figure 6). The second challenge is to cope with mismatches, which can cause two patches in one image to be associated with the same column in the patch-view matrix. In order to properly construct the matrix, we choose the one patch in the image whose texture is closest to the reference patch mentioned above.

Stitching. The patch-view matrix is comparable to the data matrix used in factorization approaches to affine structure from motion [39]. If all patches appeared in all views, we could indeed factorize the matrix directly to recover the patches' 3D configurations as well as the camera positions. In general, however, the matrix is sparse. To cope with this, we find dense blocks (sub-matrices with complete data) to factorize and then register ("stitch") the resulting sub-models

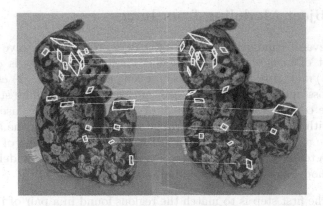

Fig. 4. Some of the matches found in two images of the bear (for readability, only 20 out of hundreds of matches are shown here). Note that the lines drawn in this diagram are *not* epipolar lines. Instead they indicate pairs of matched affine regions.

Fig. 5. A (subsampled) patch-view matrix for the teddy bear. The full patch-view matrix has 4,212 columns. Each black square indicates the presence of a given patch in a given image.

into a global one. The problem of finding maximal dense blocks within the patch-view matrix reduces to the NP-complete problem of finding maximal cliques in a graph. In our implementation, we use a simple heuristic strategy which, while not guaranteed to be optimal or complete, generally produces an adequate solution: Briefly, we find a dense block for each patch—that is, for each column in the patch-view matrix—by searching for all other patches that are visible in at least the same views. In practice, this strategy provides both a good coverage of the data by dense blocks and an adequate overlap between blocks.

The factorization technique described in Section 2.2 can of course be applied to each dense block to estimate the corresponding projection matrices and patch configurations in some local affine coordinate system. The next step is to combine the individual reconstructions into a coherent global model, or equivalently register them in a single coordinate system. With a proper set of constraints on the affine registration parameters, this can easily be expressed as an eigenvalue problem. In our experiments, however, we have found this linear approach to be numerically ill behaved (this is related to the inherent affine *gauge ambiguity* of our problem). Thus, in practice, we pick an arbitrary block as *root*,

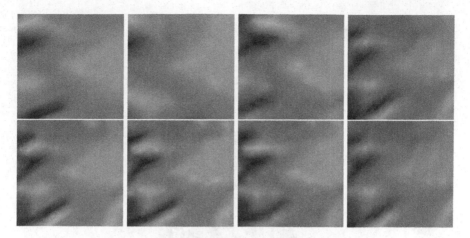

Fig. 6. Refining patch parameters across multiple views: rectified patches associated with a match in four views before (top) and after (bottom) applying the refinement process. The patch in the rightmost column is used as a reference for the other three patches. The errors shown in the top row are exaggerated for the sake of illustration.

and iteratively register all others with this one using linear least squares, before using a non-linear *bundle adjustment* method to refine the global registration parameters.

Euclidean Upgrade. It is not possible to go from affine to Euclidean structure and motion from two views only [14]. When three or more views are available, on the other hand, it is a simple matter to compute the corresponding Euclidean weak-perspective projection matrices (assuming zero skew and known aspect ratios) and recover the Euclidean structure [39,30]: Briefly, we find the 3×3 matrix $\mathcal{Q}$ such that $\mathcal{A}_i\mathcal{Q}$ is part of a scaled rotation matrix for $i = 1, \ldots, m$. This provides linear constraints on $\mathcal{Q}\mathcal{Q}^T$, and allows the estimation of this symmetric matrix via linear least-squares. The matrix $\mathcal{Q}$ can then be computed via Cholesky decomposition [29,45].

Modeling results. Figure 7 shows a complete model of the teddy bear, along with the directions of the affine cameras. Figure 8 shows the models (but not the cameras) for seven other objects. The current implementation of our modeling approach is quite reliable, but rather slow: The teddy bear shown in Figure 7 is our largest model, with 4014 model patches computed from 20 images (24 image pairs). Image matching takes about 75 minutes per pair using the general matching procedure (Section 2.3), for a total of 29.9 hours. (All computing times in this presentation are given for C++ programs executed on a 3Ghz Pentium 4 running Linux.) The remaining steps to assemble the model run in 1.5 hours. The greatest single expense in our modeling procedure is patch refinement, and this can be sped up by loosening convergence criteria and reducing the number of pixels processed, at the cost of a small loss in the number of matches.

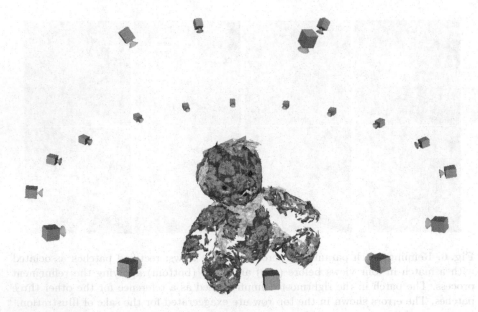

Fig. 7. The bear model, along with the recovered affine viewing directions. These cameras are shown at an arbitrary constant distance from the origin.

4   3D Object Recognition

We now address the problem of identifying instances of 3D models in a test image. This is essentially a matching process, and we apply again the general matching procedure (Section 2.3). The rest of this section describes the specifics of each step of the procedure.

Step 1 – Appearance based selection of potential matches. When patches have high contrast (that is, high variance in the intensity gradient) the SIFT descriptor selects promising matches well. However, in the case of low contrast SIFT becomes less reliable, since the intensity gradient field forms the basis for both the characteristic orientation and the histogram entries. In some situations, SIFT will even place the correct match in the bottom half of the list of candidates (Figure 9). For better reliability, we pre-filter the matches using a color descriptor: a 10×10 histogram of the UV portion of YUV space. We compare the color descriptors using χ^2 distance and eliminate those below a threshold. A contrast measure guides the choice between tight and loose thresholds in the color filtering step. This effectively shifts credence between the color and SIFT descriptors on an individual patch basis.

Step 2 – Robust Estimation. This step finds the largest geometrically consistent set of matches. First, we apply neighborhood constraints to discard obviously inconsistent matches (Figure 10): For each match we construct the projection matrix (since a Euclidean model is available and a match contains three points)

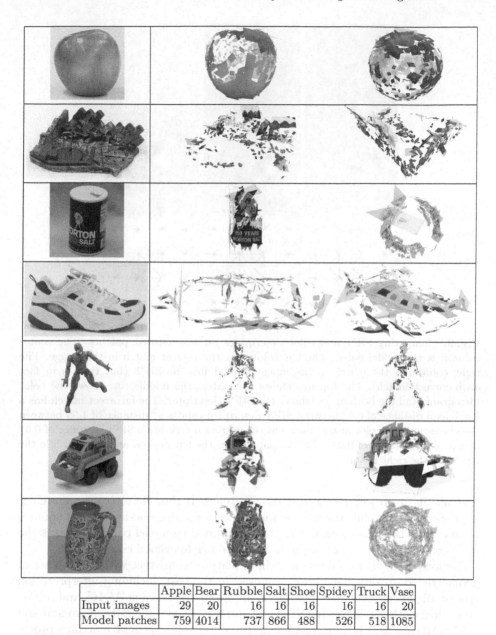

	Apple	Bear	Rubble	Salt	Shoe	Spidey	Truck	Vase
Input images	29	20	16	16	16	16	16	20
Model patches	759	4014	737	866	488	526	518	1085

Fig. 8. Object gallery. Left column: One of several input pictures for each object. Right column: Renderings of each model, not necessarily in the same pose as the input picture. Top to bottom: An apple, rubble (Spiderman base), a salt can, a shoe, Spidey, a toy truck, and a vase.

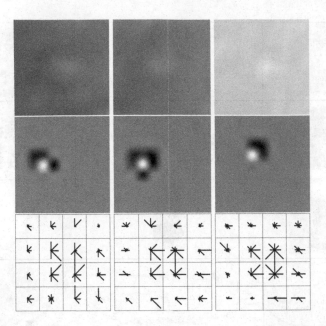

Fig. 9. Comparing SIFT and color descriptors on low-contrast patches. The center column is the model patch. The left column is the correct match in the image. The right column is the match in the image ranked first by SIFT (but that is in fact an incorrect match). The top row shows the patch, the middle row shows the color histogram, and the bottom row shows the SIFT descriptor. The incorrect match has a Euclidean distance of 0.52 between SIFT descriptors and a χ^2 distance of 1.99 between the corresponding color histograms; and the correct match has a SIFT distance of 0.67 and a color distance of 0.03. The two patches on the left are red and green, while the patch on the right is aqua.

and use it to project the surrounding patches. If they lie close, the match is kept. Second, we refine the matched image regions with non-linear least squares to maximize their correlation with the corresponding model patches. This is the most expensive step, so we apply it after the neighborhood constraint.

Various methods for finding matching features consistent with a given set of geometric constraints have been proposed in the past, including interpretation tree or alignment techniques [2,6,11,13,19], geometric hashing [15,16], and robust statistical methods such as RANSAC [8] and its variants [40]. Both alignment and RANSAC can easily be implemented in the context of the general matching procedure (Section 2.3). We used several alternatives in our experiments, and found that the following "greedy" variant performed best: Let M be the number of matches (typically limited to 12,000). For each match, we construct a "seed" model by iteratively adding the next most compatible match, just as in alignment, until the total matches in the seed reach a limit N (typically set to 20). Then we use the model constructed from this seed to collect a consensus set, just as in RANSAC. Thus, the "greedy" variant is a hybrid between alignment and RANSAC.

Fig. 10. An illustration of the neighborhood constraint. The small parallelogram in the upper center is the one used to estimate the projection matrix. The white parallelograms are projections of other forward-facing patches in the 3D model. The "×" surrounded by a circle is the projected center of one of the matches being tested, and the other "×" within the circle is its match in the image.

Step 3 – Geometry-Based Addition of Matches. The matches found by the estimation step provide a projection matrix that places the model into the image. All forward-facing patches in the model could potentially be present in the image. Therefore, we project each such model patch and select the K (typically 5 or 10) closest image patches as new match hypotheses.

Object Detection. Once an object model has been matched to an image, some criterion is needed to decide whether it is present or not. We use the following one:

(number of matches $\geq m$ OR matched area/total area $\geq a$) AND distortion $\leq d$,

where nominal values for the parameters are $m = 10$, $a = 0.1$, and $d = 0.15$. Here, the measure of distortion is

$$\frac{a_1^T a_2}{|a_1||a_2|} + \left(1 - \frac{\min(|a_1|, |a_2|)}{\max(|a_1|, |a_2|)}\right),$$

where a_i^T is the ith row of the leftmost 2×3 portion $\mathcal{A}$ of the projection matrix, and it reflects how close this matrix is to the top part of a scaled rotation matrix. The matched surface area of the model is measured in terms of the patches whose normalized correlation is above the usual thresholds, and it is compared to the total surface area actually visible from the predicted viewpoint.

Recognition results. Our recognition experiments match all eight of our object models against a set of 51 images. Each image contains instances of up to five object models, though the typical image only contains one or two. Using the nominal values for the detection parameters given above, the method gives no false positives and a recognition rate (averaged over the eight object models) of 94%.

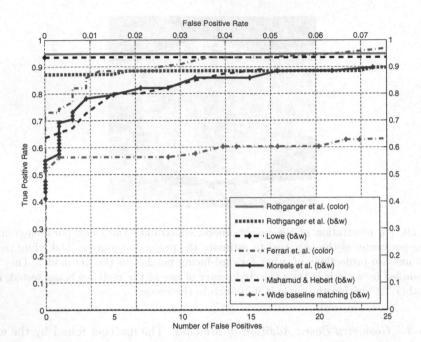

Fig. 11. True positive rate plotted against number of false positives for several different recognition methods

Figure 11 shows a comparison study including our method and several other state-of-the-art object recognition systems. Our dataset is publicly available at http://www-cvr.ai.uiuc.edu/ponce_grp/data, and several other research groups graciously provided test results on it using their systems. The specific algorithms tested were the ones proposed by Ferrari, Tuytelaars & Van Gool [7], Lowe [20], Mahamud & Hebert [21], and Moreels, Maire & Perona [25]. In addition, we performed a test using our wide-baseline matching procedure between a database of training images and the test set, without using 3D models. For details of the comparative study, see [33].

Figure 12 shows sample results of some challenging (yet successful) recognition experiments, with a large degree of occlusion and clutter. Figure 13 shows the images where recognition fails. Note the views where the shoe fails. These are separated by about 60° from the views used during modeling. The surface of the shoe has a very sparse texture, so it is difficult to reconstruct some of the shape details. These details become more significant when the viewpoint moves from nearly parallel to the surface normal to nearly perpendicular.

5 Video

Modeling from video (contiguous image sequences) is similar in many respects to modeling from still images. In particular, we can use the same methods for

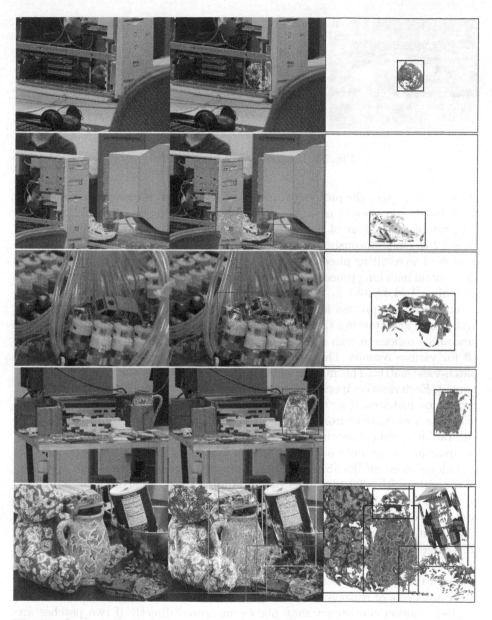

Fig. 12. Some challenging but successful recognition results. The recognized models are rendered in the poses estimated by our program, and bounding boxes for the reprojections are shown as rectangles.

describing the appearance and the geometric structure of affine-covariant patches. Establishing correspondence between multiple views of the same patch is actually easier in video sequences, since successive frames are close to each other in space and time, and it is sufficient to use tracking rather than wide-baseline matching.

Fig. 13. Images where recognition fails

On the other hand, the problem of modeling from video is made *much* more difficult by the presence of multiple independently moving objects. To cope with this, we take advantage of the factorization and error measure presented in Section 2.2 to simultaneously segment the moving components and build their 3D models. The resulting piecewise-rigid 3D models can be directly compared using the general matching procedure (Section 2.3), promising a method for video shot matching [1,34,37,46].

The modeling process for video starts by extracting affine regions from the first frame and tracking them through subsequent frames. It continues to add new affine regions in each subsequent frame as old ones move out of view or die off for various reasons. The collection of all the tracked patches again forms a patch-view matrix. This matrix will in general contain more than one rigid component. Each rigid component has a different motion, producing a different set of projection matrices. If we attempt to construct a 3D patch for a track (column) using a set of cameras from a different rigid component, the reprojection error will be high, while constructing a 3D patch using cameras from the same rigid component will produce a low error. This fact leads to a motion segmentation technique based on RANSAC [9,41]. The basic procedure is to locate a section of the video with a large number of overlapping tracks (that is, a large number of visible patches), select a random pair of them to reconstruct a set of cameras, and then construct a consensus set by measuring the reprojection error associated with each of the remaining tracks and adding those below a threshold. The largest consensus set becomes the basis of a new rigid component. The new model is propagated forward and backward through time, adding all compatible tracks. Finally, we remove the entire set of tracks, and repeat the procedure until all components of reasonable size have been found.

Rigid motion consistency may not be measured directly if two patches are not visible at the same time in the video. It is therefore necessary to extend the range of frames in the video covered by the working model as more consistent patches are found. The stitching method described in Section 3, while very accurate, is too expensive and not suited for building a model incrementally. Instead, we use a method called "bilinear incremental SFM" to add sparse measurements from the patch-view matrix to an existing model. Essentially, the method adds one row or column at a time from the patch-view matrix to a model,

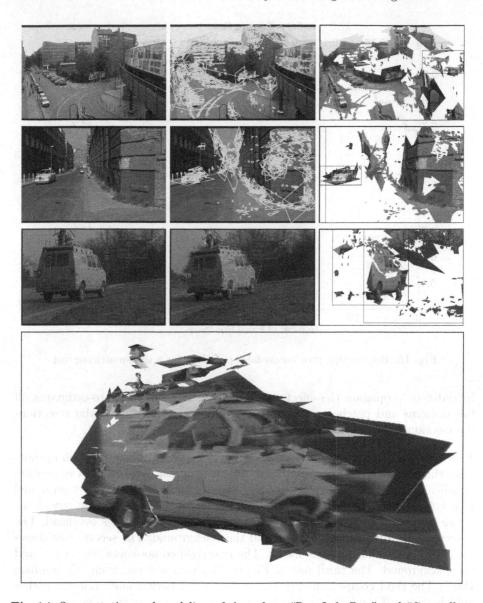

Fig. 14. Segmentation and modeling of shots from "Run Lola Run" and "Groundhog Day"

reconstructing one camera or patch respectively. It reconstructs patches using known cameras associated with the sparse set of image measurements in the new column, and similarly it reconstructs cameras using known patches associated with the image measurements in a row. At each step it always selects the next row or column that has the most image measurements overlapping the current model.

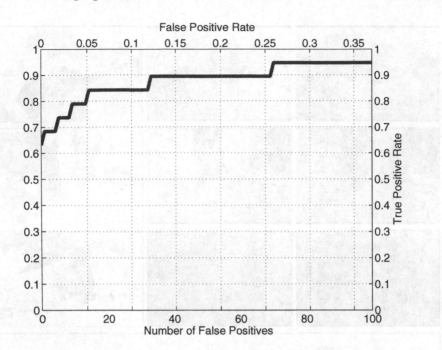

Fig. 15. Recognition rate versus false positives for a shot-matching test

In order to propagate the effects of new data, it periodically re-estimates all the cameras and patches currently in the model, exactly as in the resection-intersection method of bundle adjustment [42].

Experimental results. Figure 14 shows results of segmenting and modeling shots from the movies "Run Lola Run" and "Groundhog Day". These movies contain significant perspective effects, so we have used a more general projection model that is beyond the scope of this chapter, see [32] for details. The first row of the figure shows a scene from "Run Lola Run" where a train passes overhead. The detected components are the train and the background. The second row shows a corner scene from the same movie. The two rigid components are the car and the background. The third row of Figure 14 shows a scene from "Groundhog Day". The rigid components are the van and the background. Later, another vehicle turns off the highway and is also found as a component. The last row of the figure is a reprojection of the 3D model of the van. Note that the viewpoint of the reprojection is significantly different than any in the original scene.

Figure 15 shows the results of a recognition test over a set of 27 video shots collected from various sources: the movies "Run, Lola, Run" and "Groundhog Day", as well as several videos taken in the laboratory. Each scene appeared in 2 or 3 of the shots. We selected 10 different 3D components in turn to act as queries, and used the general matching procedure (Section 2.3) between each query model and the rest of the set, see [32] for details.

Fig. 16. Some correctly matched shots. The left image is the original frame of the test shot. The right image shows the query model reprojected into the test video.

Figure 16 shows some of the correctly matched models. It shows a video frame from the recognized shot and a projection of the 3D model of the query shot. This demonstrates how well the two models are registered in 3D. These results are best viewed in motion, and sample videos appear on our web site: http://www-cvr.ai.uiuc.edu/ponce_grp/research/3d.

6   Discussion

We have proposed in this article to revisit invariants as a local object description that exploits the fact that smooth surfaces are always planar in the small. Combining this idea with the affine regions of Mikolajczyk and Schmid [24] has allowed us to construct a normalized representation of local surface appearance that can be used to select promising matches in 3D object modeling and recognition tasks. We have used multi-view geometric constraints to represent the larger 3D surface structure, retain groups of consistent matches, and reject incorrect ones. Our experiments demonstrate the promise of the proposed approach to 3D object recognition.

We have extended our approach to automatically perform simultaneous motion segmentation and 3D modeling in video sequences containing multiple independently moving objects. Multi-view geometric constraints guide the selection of patches that move together rigidly and again represent their 3D surface structure, resulting in a set of rigid 3D components.

We have reduced 2D images, 3D models, image sequences and video scenes to a simple representation: a collection of affine patches. Any such collection may be matched to any other, aided by a representation of the geometric relationship between the two. We have presented three examples of such matching: between a pair of images (wide-baseline matching), between a 3D model and an image (object recognition), and between two 3D models (shot matching). In all cases, we first select match hypotheses based on appearance similarity and then find a subset that are geometrically consistent; and finally expand this set guided by both geometry and appearance.

Let us close by sketching several directions for improvement of the existing method. One such direction is increasing the computational efficiency of our current implementation. Two key changes would be to use a voting or indexing scheme rather than naive all-to-all matching, and to avoid patch refinement by developing more robustness to noise in the image measurements. Next, we plan to pursue various improvements to the feature extraction method. The current scheme depends in large part on corner-like Harris interest points, which often fall across object boundaries, and therefore cannot be matched or tracked reliably. To help overcome this problem, we could use maximally stable extremal regions [22], which tend to be detected on relatively "flat" regions of an object's surface. More generally, some 3D objects, such as bicycles and lamp-posts, are not amenable to representation by planar patches at all. In such cases, a hybrid system that models point, edge, and planar features would be more suitable. Finally, many interesting objects are non-rigid, the prime example being human actors. Thus, an important future research direction is extending our approach to deal with non-rigid, articulated objects.

Acknowledgments

This research was partially supported by the National Science Foundation under grants IIS-0308087 and IIS-0312438, Toyota Motor Corporation, the UIUC-CNRS Research Collaboration Agreement, the European FET-open project VIBES, the UIUC Campus Research Board, and the Beckman Institute.

References

1. A. Aner and J. R. Kender. Video summaries through mosaic-based shot and scene clustering. In *European Conference on Computer Vision*, pages 388–402, Copenhagen, Denmark, 2002.
2. N. Ayache and O. D. Faugeras. Hyper: a new approach for the recognition and positioning of two-dimensional objects. *IEEE Transactions on Pattern Analysis and Machine Intelligence*, 8(1):44–54, January 1986.
3. A. Baumberg. Reliable feature matching across widely separated views. In *Conference on Computer Vision and Pattern Recognition*, pages 774–781, 2000.
4. J. B. Burns, R. S. Weiss, and E. M. Riseman. View variation of point-set and line-segment features. *IEEE Transactions on Pattern Analysis and Machine Intelligence*, 15(1):51–68, January 1993.
5. O. D. Faugeras, Q. T. Luong, and T. Papadopoulo. *The Geometry of Multiple Images*. MIT Press, 2001.
6. O. D. Faugeras and M. Hebert. The representation, recognition, and locating of 3D objects. *International Journal of Robotics Research*, 5(3):27–52, 1986.
7. V. Ferrari, T. Tuytelaars, and L. Van Gool. Simultaneous object recognition and segmentation by image exploration. In *European Conference on Computer Vision*, 2004.
8. M. A. Fischler and R. C. Bolles. Random sample consensus: a paradigm for model fitting with application to image analysis and automated cartography. *Communications ACM*, 24(6):381–395, June 1981.

9. A. W. Fitzgibbon and A. Zisserman. Multibody structure and motion: 3D reconstruction of independently moving objects. In *European Conference on Computer Vision*, pages 891–906. Springer-Verlag, June 2000.
10. J. Gårding and T. Lindeberg. Direct computation of shape cues using scale-adapted spatial derivative operators. *International Journal of Computer Vision*, 17(2):163–191, 1996.
11. W. E. L. Grimson and T. Lozano-Pérez. Localizing overlapping parts by searching the interpretation tree. *IEEE Transactions on Pattern Analysis and Machine Intelligence*, 9(4):469–482, 1987.
12. C. Harris and M. Stephens. A combined edge and corner detector. In 4th *Alvey Vision Conference*, pages 189–192, Manchester, UK, 1988.
13. D. P. Huttenlocher and S. Ullman. Object recognition using alignment. In *International Conference on Computer Vision*, pages 102–111, 1987.
14. J. J. Koenderink and A. J. van Doorn. Affine structure from motion. *Journal of the Optical Society of America*, 8(2):377–385, February 1991.
15. Y. Lamdan and H. J. Wolfson. Geometric hashing: A general and efficient model-based recognition scheme. In *International Conference on Computer Vision*, pages 238–249, 1988.
16. Y. Lamdan and H. J. Wolfson. On the error analysis of 'geometric hashing'. In *Conference on Computer Vision and Pattern Recognition*, pages 22–27, Maui, Hawaii, 1991.
17. T. Lindeberg. Feature detection with automatic scale selection. *International Journal of Computer Vision*, 30(2):77–116, 1998.
18. T. Lindeberg and J. Gårding. Shape-adapted smoothing in estimation of 3D depth cues from affine distortions of local 2D brightness structure. In *European Conference on Computer Vision*, pages 389–400, Stockholm, Sweden, May 2-5 1994. Springer-Verlag Lecture Notes in Computer Science, vol. 800.
19. D. Lowe. The viewpoint consistency constraint. *International Journal of Computer Vision*, 1(1):57–72, 1987.
20. D. G. Lowe. Distinctive image features from scale-invariant keypoints. *International Journal of Computer Vision*, 60(2):91–110, 2004.
21. S. Mahamud and M. Hebert. The optimal distance measure for object detection. In *Conference on Computer Vision and Pattern Recognition*, 2003.
22. J. Matas, O. Chum, M. Urban, and T. Pajdla. Robust wide baseline stereo from maximally stable extremal regions. In *British Machine Vision Conference*, volume I, pages 384–393, 2002.
23. K. Mikolajczyk and C. Schmid. Indexing based on scale invariant interest points. In *International Conference on Computer Vision*, pages 525–531, Vancouver, Canada, July 2001.
24. K. Mikolajczyk and C. Schmid. An affine invariant interest point detector. In *European Conference on Computer Vision*, volume I, pages 128–142, 2002.
25. P. Moreels, M. Maire, and P. Perona. Recognition by probabilistic hypothesis construction. In *European Conference on Computer Vision*, 2004.
26. J. L. Mundy and A. Zisserman. *Geometric Invariance in Computer Vision*. MIT Press, 1992.
27. J. L. Mundy, A. Zisserman, and D. Forsyth. *Applications of Invariance in Computer Vision*, volume 825 of *Lecture Notes in Computer Science*. Springer-Verlag, 1994.
28. H. Murase and S. K. Nayar. Visual learning and recognition of 3D objects from appearance. *International Journal of Computer Vision*, 14:5–24, 1995.

29. C. J. Poelman and T. Kanade. A paraperspective factorization method for shape and motion recovery. *IEEE Transactions on Pattern Analysis and Machine Intelligence*, 19(3):206–218, 1997.

30. J. Ponce. On computing metric upgrades of projective reconstructions under the rectangular pixel assumption. In *Second SMILE Workshop*, pages 18–27, 2000.

31. P. Pritchett and A. Zisserman. Wide baseline stereo matching. In *International Conference on Computer Vision*, pages 754–760, Bombay, India, 1998.

32. F. Rothganger, S. Lazebnik, C. Schmid, and J. Ponce. Segmenting, modeling, and matching video clips containing multiple moving objects. In *Conference on Computer Vision and Pattern Recognition*, volume 2, pages 914–921, Washington, D.C., June 2004.

33. F. Rothganger, S. Lazebnik, C. Schmid, and J. Ponce. 3D object modeling and recognition using local affine-invariant image descriptors and multi-view spatial constraints. *International Journal of Computer Vision*, 66(3), 2006.

34. F. Schaffalitzky and A. Zisserman. Automated scene matching in movies. In *Proceedings of the Challenge of Image and Video Retrieval*, London, 2002.

35. F. Schaffalitzky and A. Zisserman. Multi-view matching for unordered image sets, or "how do I organize my holiday snaps?". In *European Conference on Computer Vision*, volume I, pages 414–431, 2002.

36. C. Schmid and R. Mohr. Local grayvalue invariants for image retrieval. *IEEE Transactions on Pattern Analysis and Machine Intelligence*, 19(5):530–535, May 1997.

37. J. Sivic and A. Zisserman. Video Google: A text retrieval approach to object matching in videos. In *International Conference on Computer Vision*, 2003.

38. D. Tell and S. Carlsson. Wide baseline point matching using affine invariants computed from intensity profiles. In *Proc 6th ECCV*, pages 814–828, Dublin, Ireland, June 2000. Springer LNCS 1842-1843.

39. C. Tomasi and T. Kanade. Shape and motion from image streams: a factorization method. *International Journal of Computer Vision*, 9(2):137–154, 1992.

40. P. Torr and A. Zisserman. Mlesac: A new robust estimator with application to estimating image geometry. *Computer Vision and Image Understanding*, 78(1):138–156, 2000.

41. P. Torr. *Motion Segmentation and Outlier Detection*. PhD thesis, University of Oxford, 1995.

42. B. Triggs, P. F. McLauchlan, R. I. Hartley, and A. W. Fitzgibbon. Bundle adjustment - a modern synthesis. In B. Triggs, A. Zisserman, and R. Szeliski, editors, *Vision Algorithms*, pages 298–372, Corfu, Greece, September 1999. Spinger-Verlag. LNCS 1883.

43. M. Turk and A. Pentland. Eigenfaces for recognition. *Journal of Cognitive Neuroscience*, 3(1):71–86, Winter 1991.

44. T. Tuytelaars and L. Van Gool. Matching widely separated views based on affine invariant regions. *International Journal of Computer Vision*, 59(1):61–85, 2004.

45. D. Weinshall and C. Tomasi. Linear and incremental acquisition of invariant shape models from image sequences. *IEEE Transactions on Pattern Analysis and Machine Intelligence*, 17(5):512–517, 1995.

46. M. M. Yeung and B. Liu. Efficient matching and clustering of video shots. In *International Conference on Image Processing*, volume 1, pages 338–341, Washington D.C., October 1995.

Video Google: Efficient Visual Search of Videos

Josef Sivic and Andrew Zisserman

Department of Engineering Science
University of Oxford
Oxford, OX1 3PJ1
{josef,az}@robots.ox.ac.uk
http://www.robots.ox.ac.uk/~vgg

Abstract. We describe an approach to object retrieval which searches for and localizes all the occurrences of an object in a video, given a query image of the object. The object is represented by a set of viewpoint invariant region descriptors so that recognition can proceed successfully despite changes in viewpoint, illumination and partial occlusion. The temporal continuity of the video within a shot is used to track the regions in order to reject those that are unstable.

Efficient retrieval is achieved by employing methods from statistical text retrieval, including inverted file systems, and text and document frequency weightings. This requires a visual analogy of a word which is provided here by vector quantizing the region descriptors. The final ranking also depends on the spatial layout of the regions. The result is that retrieval is immediate, returning a ranked list of shots in the manner of Google.

We report results for object retrieval on the full length feature films 'Groundhog Day' and 'Casablanca'.

1 Introduction

The aim of this work is to retrieve those key frames and shots of a video containing a particular object with the ease, speed and accuracy with which Google retrieves text documents (web pages) containing particular words. This chapter investigates whether a text retrieval approach can be successfully employed for this task.

Identifying an (identical) object in a database of images is now reaching some maturity. It is still a challenging problem because an object's visual appearance may be very different due to viewpoint and lighting, and it may be partially occluded, but successful methods now exist [7,8,9,11,13,14,15,16,20,21]. Typically an object is represented by a set of overlapping regions each represented by a vector computed from the region's appearance. The region extraction and descriptors are built with a controlled degree of invariance to viewpoint and illumination conditions. Similar descriptors are computed for all images in the database. Recognition of a particular object proceeds by nearest neighbour matching of the descriptor vectors, followed by disambiguating using local spatial coherence (such as common neighbours, or angular ordering), or global relationships (such as epipolar geometry or a planar homography).

J. Ponce et al. (Eds.): Toward Category-Level Object Recognition, LNCS 4170, pp. 127–144, 2006.
© Springer-Verlag Berlin Heidelberg 2006

We explore whether this type of approach to recognition can be recast as text retrieval. In essence this requires a visual analogy of a word, and here we provide this by vector quantizing the descriptor vectors. However, it will be seen that pursuing the analogy with text retrieval is more than a simple optimization over different vector quantizations. There are many lessons and rules of thumb that have been learnt and developed in the text retrieval literature and it is worth ascertaining if these also can be employed in visual retrieval.

The benefits of this approach is that matches are effectively pre-computed so that at run-time frames and shots containing any particular object can be retrieved with no-delay. This means that any object occurring in the video (and conjunctions of objects) can be retrieved even though there was no explicit interest in these objects when descriptors were built for the video. However, we must also determine whether this vector quantized retrieval misses any matches that would have been obtained if the former method of nearest neighbour matching had been used.

Review of text retrieval: Text retrieval systems generally employ a number of standard steps [2]: the documents are first parsed into words, and the words are represented by their stems, for example 'walk', 'walking' and 'walks' would be represented by the stem 'walk'. A stop list is then used to reject very common words, such as 'the' and 'an', which occur in most documents and are therefore not discriminating for a particular document. The remaining words are then assigned a unique identifier, and each document is represented by a vector with components given by the frequency of occurrence of the words the document contains. In addition the components are weighted in various ways (described in more detail in section 4), and in the case of Google the weighting of a web page depends on the number of web pages linking to that particular page [4]. All of the above steps are carried out in advance of actual retrieval, and the set of vectors representing all the documents in a corpus are organized as an *inverted file* [22] to facilitate efficient retrieval. An inverted file is structured like an ideal book index. It has an entry for each word in the corpus followed by a list of all the documents (and position in that document) in which the word occurs.

A text is retrieved by computing its vector of word frequencies and returning the documents with the closest (measured by angles) vectors. In addition the degree of match on the ordering and separation of the words may be used to rank the returned documents.

Chapter outline: Here we explore visual analogies of each of these steps. Section 2 describes the visual descriptors used. Section 3 then describes their vector quantization into visual 'words', and sections 4 and 5 weighting and indexing for the vector model. These ideas are then evaluated on a ground truth set of six object queries in section 6. Object retrieval results are shown on two feature films: 'Groundhog Day' [Ramis, 1993] and 'Casablanca' [Curtiz, 1942].

Although previous work has borrowed ideas from the text retrieval literature for image retrieval from databases (e.g. [19] used the weighting and inverted file schemes) to the best of our knowledge this is the first systematic application of these ideas to object retrieval in videos.

(a)   (b)

Fig. 1. Object query example I. (a) Top row: (left) a frame from the movie 'Ground-hog Day' with an outlined query region and (right) a close-up of the query region de-lineating the object of interest. Bottom row: (left) all 1039 detected affine covariant regions superimposed and (right) close-up of the query region. (b) (left) two retrieved frames with detected regions of interest and (right) a close-up of the images with affine covariant regions superimposed. These regions match to a subset of the regions shown in (a). Note the significant change in foreshortening and scale between the query image of the object, and the object in the retrieved frames. For this query there are four correctly retrieved shots ranked 1, 2, 3 and 9. Querying all the 5,640 keyframes of the entire movie took 0.36 seconds on a 2GHz Pentium.

2 Viewpoint Invariant Description

Two types of viewpoint covariant regions are computed for each frame. The first is constructed by elliptical shape adaptation about a Harris [5] interest point. The method involves iteratively determining the ellipse centre, scale and shape. The scale is determined by the local extremum (across scale) of a Laplacian, and the shape by maximizing intensity gradient isotropy over the elliptical region [3,6]. The implementation details are given in [11,15]. This region type is referred to as Shape Adapted (SA).

The second type of region is constructed by selecting areas from an intensity watershed image segmentation. The regions are those for which the area is ap-proximately stationary as the intensity threshold is varied. The implementation details are given in [10]. This region type is referred to as Maximally Stable (MS).

Two types of regions are employed because they detect different image areas and thus provide complementary representations of a frame. The SA regions tend to be centred on corner like features, and the MS regions correspond to blobs of high contrast with respect to their surroundings such as a dark window on a grey wall. Both types of regions are represented by ellipses. These are computed at twice the originally detected region size in order for the image appearance to be more discriminating. For a 720×576 pixel video frame the number of regions computed is typically 1,200. An example is shown in Figure 1.

Each elliptical affine invariant region is represented by a 128-dimensional vec-tor using the SIFT descriptor developed by Lowe [7]. In [12] this descriptor was shown to be superior to others used in the literature, such as the response of a set of steerable filters [11] or orthogonal filters [15], and we have also found SIFT to be superior (by comparing scene retrieval results against ground truth [18]). One reason for this superior performance is that SIFT, unlike the other descriptors, is designed to be invariant to a shift of a few pixels in the region position, and this localization error is one that often occurs. Combining the SIFT descriptor with affine covariant regions gives region description vectors which are invariant to affine transformations of the image. Note, both region detection and the description is computed on monochrome versions of the frames, colour information is not currently used in this work.

To reduce noise and reject unstable regions, information is aggregated over a sequence of frames. The regions detected in each frame of the video are tracked using a simple constant velocity dynamical model and correlation. Any region which does not survive for more than three frames is rejected. This 'stability check' significantly reduces the number of regions to about 600 per frame.

3   Building a Visual Vocabulary

The objective here is to vector quantize the descriptors into clusters which will be the visual 'words' for text retrieval. The vocabulary is constructed from a subpart of the movie, and its matching accuracy and expressive power are evaluated on the entire movie, as described in the following sections. The running example is for the movie 'Groundhog Day'.

The vector quantization is carried out here by K-means clustering, though other methods (K-medoids, histogram binning, etc) are certainly possible.

3.1   Implementation

Each descriptor is a 128-vector, and to simultaneously cluster all the descriptors of the movie would be a gargantuan task. Instead a random subset of 437 frames is selected. Even with this reduction there are still 200K descriptors that must be clustered.

The Mahalanobis distance is used as the distance function for the K-means clustering. The distance between two descriptors x_1, x_2, is then given by

$$d(x_1, x_2) = \sqrt{(x_1 - x_2)^\top \Sigma^{-1} (x_1 - x_2)}.$$

The covariance matrix Σ is determined by (i) computing covariances for descriptors throughout tracks within several shots, and (ii) assuming Σ is the same for all tracks (i.e. independent of the region) so that covariances for tracks can be aggregated. In this manner sufficient measurements are available to estimate all elements of Σ. Details are given in [18]. The Mahalanobis distance enables the more noisy components of the 128–vector to be weighted down, and also decorrelates the components. Empirically there is a small degree of correlation. As is standard, the descriptor space is affine transformed by the square root of Σ so that Euclidean distance may be used.

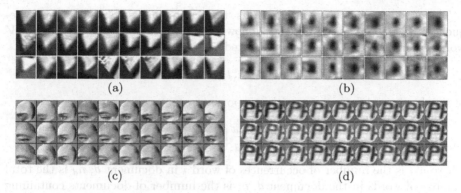

Fig. 2. Samples of normalized affine covariant regions from clusters corresponding to a single visual word: (a,c,d) Shape Adapted regions; (b) Maximally Stable regions. Note that some visual words represent generic image structures, e.g. corners (a) or blobs (b), and some visual words are rather specific, e.g. an eye (c) or a letter (d).

About 6K clusters are used for Shape Adapted regions, and about 10K clusters for Maximally Stable regions. The ratio of the number of clusters for each type is chosen to be approximately the same as the ratio of detected descriptors of each type. The number of clusters was chosen empirically to maximize matching performance on a ground truth set for scene retrieval [18]. The K-means algorithm is run several times with random initial assignments of points as cluster centres, and the lowest cost result used.

Figure 2 shows examples of regions belonging to particular clusters, i.e. which will be treated as the same visual word. The clustered regions reflect the properties of the SIFT descriptors which penalize intensity variations amongst regions less than cross-correlation. This is because SIFT emphasizes orientation of gradients, rather than the position of a particular intensity within the region.

The reason that SA and MS regions are clustered separately is that they cover different and largely independent regions of the scene. Consequently, they may be thought of as different vocabularies for describing the same scene, and thus should have their own word sets, in the same way as one vocabulary might describe architectural features and another the material quality (e.g. defects, weathering) of a building.

4   Visual Indexing Using Text Retrieval Methods

In text retrieval each document is represented by a vector of word frequencies. However, it is usual to apply a weighting to the components of this vector [2], rather than use the frequency vector directly for indexing. Here we describe the standard weighting that is employed, and then the visual analogy of document retrieval to frame retrieval.

The standard weighting is known as 'term frequency–inverse document frequency', *tf-idf*, and is computed as follows. Suppose there is a vocabulary of V words, then each document is represented by a vector

$$\boldsymbol{v}_d = (t_1, ..., t_i, ..., t_V)^\top$$

of weighted word frequencies with components

$$t_i = \frac{n_{id}}{n_d} \log \frac{N}{n_i}$$

where n_{id} is the number of occurrences of word i in document d, n_d is the total number of words in the document d, n_i is the number of documents containing term i and N is the number of documents in the whole database. The weighting is a product of two terms: the *word frequency* n_{id}/n_d, and the *inverse document frequency* $\log N/n_i$. The intuition is that word frequency weights words occurring often in a particular document, and thus describes it well, whilst the inverse document frequency downweights words that appear often in the database.

At the retrieval stage documents are ranked by their normalized scalar product (cosine of angle)

$$f_d = \frac{\boldsymbol{v}_q^\top \boldsymbol{v}_d}{\sqrt{\boldsymbol{v}_q^\top \boldsymbol{v}_q} \sqrt{\boldsymbol{v}_d^\top \boldsymbol{v}_d}} \tag{1}$$

between the query vector $\boldsymbol{v}_q$ and all document vectors $\boldsymbol{v}_d$ in the database.

In our case the query vector is given by the visual words contained in a user specified sub-part of an image, and the frames are ranked according to the similarity of their weighted vectors to this query vector.

4.1   Stop List

Using a stop list analogy the most frequent visual words that occur in almost all images are suppressed. The top 5% and bottom 5% are stopped. In our case the very common words are due to large clusters of over 3K points. These might correspond to small specularities (highlights), for example, which occur throughout many scenes. The stop list boundaries were determined empirically to reduce the number of mismatches and size of the inverted file while keeping sufficient visual vocabulary.

Figure 4 shows the benefit of imposing a stop list – the very common visual words occur at many places in the image and are responsible for mis-matches. Most of these are removed once the stop list is applied. The removal of the remaining mis-matches is described next.

4.2   Spatial Consistency

Google increases the ranking for documents where the searched for words appear close together in the retrieved texts (measured by word order). This analogy is

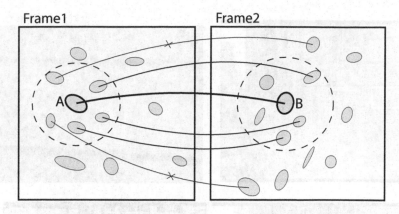

Fig. 3. Illustration of spatial consistency voting. To verify a pair of matching regions (A,B) a circular search area is defined by the k (=5 in this example) spatial nearest neighbours in both frames. Each match which lies within the search areas in both frames casts a vote in support of match (A,B). In this example three supporting matches are found. Matches with no support are rejected.

especially relevant for querying objects by an image, where matched covariant regions in the retrieved frames should have a similar spatial arrangement [14,16] to those of the outlined region in the query image. The idea is implemented here by first retrieving frames using the weighted frequency vector alone, and then re-ranking them based on a measure of spatial consistency.

Spatial consistency can be measured quite loosely simply by requiring that neighbouring matches in the query region lie in a surrounding area in the retrieved frame. It can also be measured very strictly by requiring that neighbouring matches have the same spatial layout in the query region and retrieved frame. In our case the matched regions provide the affine transformation between the query and retrieved image so a point to point map is available for this strict measure.

We have found that the best performance is obtained in the middle of this possible range of measures. A search area is defined by the 15 nearest spatial neighbours of each match, and each region which also matches within this area casts a vote for that frame. Matches with no support are rejected. The final score of the frame is determined by summing the spatial consistency votes, and adding the frequency score f_d given by (1). Including the frequency score (which ranges between 0 and 1) disambiguates ranking amongst frames which receive the same number of spatial consistency votes. The object bounding box in the retrieved frame is determined as the rectangular bounding box of the matched regions after the spatial consistency test. The spatial consistency voting is illustrated in figure 3. This works very well as is demonstrated in the last row of figure 4, which shows the spatial consistency rejection of incorrect matches. The object retrieval examples presented in this chapter employ this ranking measure and amply demonstrate its usefulness.

Fig. 4. Matching stages. Top row: (left) Query region and (right) its close-up. Second row: Original matches based on visual words. Third row: matches after using the stoplist. Last row: Final set of matches after filtering on spatial consistency.

1. **Pre-processing (off-line)**
   - Detect affine covariant regions in each keyframe of the video. Represent each region by a SIFT descriptor (section 2).
   - Track the regions through the video and reject unstable regions (section 2).
   - Build a visual dictionary by clustering stable regions from a subset of the video. Assign each region descriptor in each keyframe to the nearest cluster centre (section 3).
   - Remove stop-listed visual words (section 4.1).
   - Compute tf-idf weighted document frequency vectors (section 4).
   - Build the inverted file indexing structure (section 5).

2. **At run-time (given a user selected query region)**
   - Determine the set of visual words within the query region.
   - Retrieve keyframes based on visual word frequencies (section 4).
   - Re-rank the top $N_s(= 500)$ retrieved keyframes using the spatial consistency check (section 4.2).

Fig. 5. The Video Google object retrieval algorithm

Other measures which take account of the affine mapping between images may be required in some situations, but this involves a greater computational expense.

5 Object Retrieval Using Visual Words

We first describe the off-line processing. A feature length film typically has 100K-150K frames. To reduce complexity one keyframe is used per second of the video. Descriptors are computed for stable regions in each keyframe (stability is determined by tracking as described in section 2). The descriptors are vector quantized using the centres clustered from the training set, i.e. each descriptor is assigned to a visual word. The visual words over all frames are assembled into an inverted file structure where for each word all occurrences and the position of the word in all frames are stored.

At run-time a user selects a query region. This specifies a set of visual words and their spatial layout. Retrieval then proceeds in two steps: first frames are retrieved based on their tf-idf weighted frequency vectors (the bag of words model), then they are re-ranked using spatial consistency voting. The frequency based ranking is implemented using the Matlab sparse matrix engine. The spatial consistency re-ranking is implemented using the inverted file structure. The entire process is summarized in figure 5.

It is worth examining the time complexity of this retrieval architecture and comparing it to that of a method that does not vector quantize the descriptors.

The huge advantage of the quantization is that all descriptors assigned to the same visual word are considered matched. This means that the burden on the run-time matching is substantially reduced as descriptors have effectively been pre-matched off-line.

In detail, suppose there are N frames, a vocabulary of V visual words, and each frame contains R regions and M distinct visual words. $M < R$ if some regions are represented by the same visual word. Each frame is equivalent to a vector in $\mathbb{R}^V$ with M non-zero entries. Typical values are $N = 10,000$, $V = 20,000$ and $M = 500$. At run time the task is to compute the score of (1) between the query frame vector v_q and each frame vector v_d in the database (another situation might be to only return the n closest frame vectors). The current implementation exploits sparse coding for efficient search as follows. The vectors are pre-normalized (so that the denominator of (1) is unity), and the computation reduces to one dot product for each of the N frames. Moreover, only the $m \leq M$ entries which are non-zero in both v_q and v_d need to be examined during each dot product computation (and typically there are far less than R regions in v_q as only a subpart of a frame specifies the object search). In the worst case if $m = M$ for all documents the time complexity is $O(MN)$.

If vector quantization is *not* used, then two architectures are possible. In the first, the query frame is matched to each frame in turn. In the second, descriptors over all frames are combined into a single search space. As SIFT is used the dimension D of the search space will be 128. In the first case the object search requires finding matches for *each* of the R descriptors of the query frame, and there are R regions in each frame, so there are R searches through R points of dimension D for N frames, a worst case cost of $O(NR^2D)$. In the second case, over all frames there are NR descriptors. Again, to search for the object requires finding matches for *each* of the R descriptors in the query image, i.e. R searches through NR points, again resulting in time complexity $O(NR^2D)$.

Consequently, even in the worst case, the vector quantizing architecture is a factor of RD times faster than not quantizing. These worst case complexity results can, of course, be improved by using efficient nearest neighbour or approximate nearest neighbour search [9].

6   Experiments

In this section we evaluate object retrieval performance over the entire movie. The object of interest is specified by the user as a sub-part of any keyframe. In part this retrieval performance assesses the expressiveness of the visual vocabulary, since invariant descriptors from the test objects (and the frames they appear in) may not have been included when clustering to form the vocabulary.

Baseline method: The performance is compared to a baseline method implementing standard frame to frame matching. The goal is to evaluate the potential loss of performance due to the descriptor quantization. The same detected regions

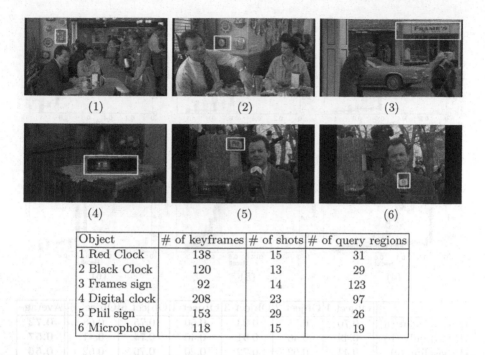

Object	# of keyframes	# of shots	# of query regions
1 Red Clock	138	15	31
2 Black Clock	120	13	29
3 Frames sign	92	14	123
4 Digital clock	208	23	97
5 Phil sign	153	29	26
6 Microphone	118	15	19

Fig. 6. Query frames with outlined query regions for the six test queries with manually obtained ground truth occurrences in the movie Groundhog Day. The table shows the number of ground truth occurrences (keyframes and shots) and the number of affine covariant regions lying within the query rectangle for each query.

and descriptors (after the stability check) in each keyframe are used. The detected affine covariant regions within the query area in the query keyframe are sequentially matched to all 5,640 keyframes in the movie. For each keyframe, matches are obtained based on the descriptor values using nearest neighbour matching with a threshold on the distance. Euclidean distance is used here. Keyframes are ranked by the number of matches and shots are ranked by their best scoring keyframes.

Comparison on ground truth: The performance of the proposed method is evaluated on six object queries in the movie Groundhog Day. Figure 6 shows the query frames and corresponding query regions. Ground truth occurrences were manually labelled in all the 5,640 keyframes (752 shots). Retrieval is performed on keyframes as outlined in section 4 and each shot of the video is scored by its best scoring keyframe. Performance is measured using a precision-recall plot for each query. Precision is the number of retrieved ground truth shots relative to the total number of shots retrieved. Recall is the number of retrieved ground truth shots relative to the total number of ground truth shots in the movie. Precision-recall plots are shown in figure 7. Results are summarized using Average

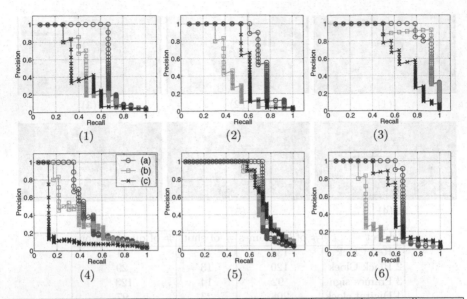

	Object 1	Object 2	Object 3	Object 4	Object 5	Object 6	Average
AP freq+spat (a)	0.70	0.75	0.93	0.50	0.75	0.68	**0.72**
AP freq only (b)	0.49	0.46	0.91	0.40	0.74	0.41	**0.57**
AP baseline (c)	0.44	0.62	0.72	0.20	0.76	0.62	**0.56**

Average precision (AP) for the six object queries.

Fig. 7. Precision-recall graphs (at the shot level) for the six ground truth queries on the movie Groundhog Day. Each graph shows three curves corresponding to (a) frequency ranking followed by spatial consensus (circles), (b) frequency ranking only (squares), and (c) baseline matching (stars). Note the significantly improved precision at lower recalls after spatial consensus re-ranking (a) is applied to the frequency based ranking (b). The table shows average precision (AP) for each ground truth object query for the three different methods. The last column shows mean average precision over all six queries.

Precision (AP) in the table in figure 7. Average Precision is a single valued measure computed as the area under the precision-recall graph and reflects performance over all recall levels.

It is evident that for all queries the average precision of the proposed method exceeds that of using frequency vectors alone – showing the benefits of the spatial consistency in improving the ranking. On average (across all queries) the frequency ranking method performs comparably to the baseline method. This demonstrates that using visual word matching does not result in a significant loss in performance against the standard frame to frame matching.

Figures 1, 8 and 9 show example retrieval results for three object queries for the movie 'Groundhog Day', and figure 10 shows example retrieval results for black and white film 'Casablanca'. For the 'Casablanca' retrievals, the film

Fig. 8. Object query example II: Groundhog Day. (a) Keyframe with user specified query region in yellow (phil sign), (b) close-up of the query region and (c) close-up with affine covariant regions superimposed. (d-g) (first row) keyframes from the 1st, 4th, 10th, and 19th retrieved shots with the identified region of interest shown in yellow, (second row) a close-up of the image, and (third row) a close-up of the image with matched elliptical regions superimposed. The first false positive is ranked 21st. The precision-recall graph for this query is shown in figure 7 (object 5). Querying 5,640 keyframes took 0.64 seconds.

is represented by 5,749 keyframes, and a new visual vocabulary was built as described in section 3.

Processing time: The region detection, description and visual word assignment takes about 20 seconds per frame (720×576 pixels) but can be done off-line. The average query time for the six ground truth queries on the database of 5,640 keyframes is 0.82 seconds with a Matlab implementation on a 2GHz pentium. This includes the frequency ranking and spatial consistency re-ranking. The spatial consistency re-ranking is applied only to the top $N_s = 500$ keyframes ranked by the frequency based score. This restriction results in no loss of performance (measured on the set of ground truth queries).

The query time of the baseline matching method on the same database of 5,640 keyframes is about 500 seconds. This timing includes only the nearest

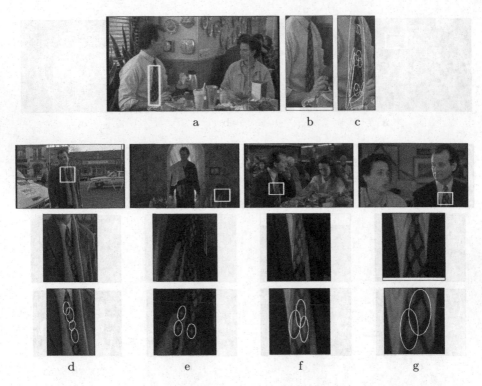

Fig. 9. Object query example III: Groundhog Day. (a) Keyframe with user specified query region in yellow (tie), (b) close-up of the query region and (c) close-up with affine covariant regions superimposed. (d-g) (first row) keyframes from the 1st, 2nd, 4th, and 19th retrieved shots with the identified region of interest shown in yellow, (second row) a close-up of the image, and (third row) a close-up of the image with matched elliptical regions superimposed. The first false positive is ranked 25th. Querying 5,640 keyframes took 0.38 seconds.

neighbour matching performed using linear search. The region detection and description is also done off-line. Note that on this set of queries our proposed method has achieved about 600-fold speed-up.

Limitations of the current method: Examples of frames from low ranked shots are shown in figure 11. Appearance changes due to extreme viewing angles, large scale changes and significant motion blur affect the process of extracting and matching affine covariant regions. The examples shown represent a significant challenge to the current object matching method.

Searching for objects from outside the movie: Figure 12 shows an example of searching for an object outside the 'closed world' of the film. The object (a Sony logo) is specified by a query image downloaded from the internet. The image was

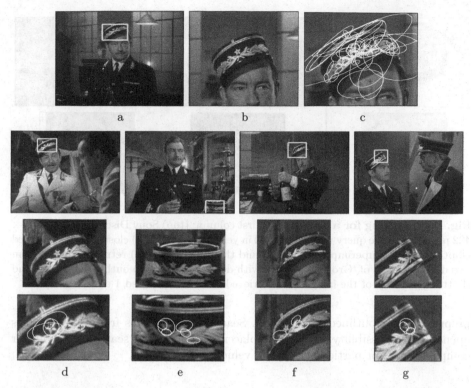

Fig. 10. Object query example IV: Casablanca. (a) Keyframe with user specified query region in yellow (hat), (b) close-up of the query region and (c) close-up with affine covariant regions superimposed. (d-g) (first row) keyframes from the 4th, 5th, 11th, and 19th retrieved shots with the identified region of interest shown in yellow, (second row) a close-up of the image, and (third row) a close-up of the image with matched elliptical regions superimposed. The first false positive is ranked 25th. Querying 5,749 keyframes took 0.83 seconds.

Fig. 11. Examples of missed (low ranked) detections for objects 1,2 and 4. In the left image the two clocks (object 1 and 2) are imaged from an extreme viewing angle and are barely visible – the red clock (object 2) is partially out of view. In the right image the digital clock (object 4) is imaged at a small scale and significantly motion blurred. Examples shown here were also low ranked by the baseline method.

Fig. 12. Searching for a Sony logo. First column: (top) Sony Discman image (640 × 422 pixels) with the query region outlined in yellow and (bottom) close-up with detected elliptical regions superimposed. Second and third column: (top) retrieved frames from two different shots of 'Groundhog Day' with detected Sony logo outlined in yellow and (bottom) close-up of the image. The retrieved shots were ranked 1 and 4.

preprocessed as outlined in section 2. Searching for images from other sources opens up the possibility for product placement queries, or searching movies for company logos, or particular types of vehicles or buildings.

7   Conclusions

We have demonstrated a scalable object retrieval architecture by the use of a visual vocabulary based on vector quantized viewpoint invariant descriptors. The vector quantization does not appear to introduce a significant loss in retrieval performance (precision or recall) compared to nearest neighbour matching.

The method in this chapter allows retrieval for a particular visual aspect of an object. However, temporal information within a shot may be used to group visual aspects, and enable object level retrieval [17].

A live demonstration of the 'Video Google' system on a publicly available movie (Dressed to Kill) is available on-line at [1].

Acknowledgements

Funding for this work was provided by EC Project Vibes and EC Project CogViSys.

References

1. http://www.robots.ox.ac.uk/~vgg/research/vgoogle/.
2. R. Baeza-Yates and B. Ribeiro-Neto. *Modern Information Retrieval.* ACM Press, ISBN: 020139829, 1999.

3. A. Baumberg. Reliable feature matching across widely separated views. In *Proceedings of the IEEE Conference on Computer Vision and Pattern Recognition*, pages 774–781, 2000.
4. S. Brin and L. Page. The anatomy of a large-scale hypertextual web search engine. In *7th Int. WWW Conference*, 1998.
5. C. J. Harris and M. Stephens. A combined corner and edge detector. In *Proceedings of the 4th Alvey Vision Conference, Manchester*, pages 147–151, 1988.
6. T. Lindeberg and J. Gårding. Shape-adapted smoothing in estimation of 3-d depth cues from affine distortions of local 2-d brightness structure. In *Proceedings of the 3rd European Conference on Computer Vision, Stockholm, Sweden*, LNCS 800, pages 389–400, May 1994.
7. D. Lowe. Object recognition from local scale-invariant features. In *Proceedings of the 7th International Conference on Computer Vision, Kerkyra, Greece*, pages 1150–1157, September 1999.
8. D. Lowe. Local feature view clustering for 3D object recognition. In *Proceedings of the IEEE Conference on Computer Vision and Pattern Recognition, Kauai, Hawaii*, pages 682–688. Springer, December 2001.
9. D. Lowe. Distinctive image features from scale-invariant keypoints. *International Journal of Computer Vision*, 60(2):91–110, 2004.
10. J. Matas, O. Chum, M. Urban, and T. Pajdla. Robust wide baseline stereo from maximally stable extremal regions. In *Proceedings of the British Machine Vision Conference*, pages 384–393, 2002.
11. K. Mikolajczyk and C. Schmid. An affine invariant interest point detector. In *Proceedings of the 7th European Conference on Computer Vision, Copenhagen, Denmark*. Springer-Verlag, 2002.
12. K. Mikolajczyk and C. Schmid. A performance evaluation of local descriptors. In *Proceedings of the IEEE Conference on Computer Vision and Pattern Recognition*, 2003.
13. S. Obdrzalek and J. Matas. Object recognition using local affine frames on distinguished regions. In *Proceedings of the British Machine Vision Conference*, pages 113–122, 2002.
14. F. Schaffalitzky and A. Zisserman. Automated scene matching in movies. In *Proceedings of the Challenge of Image and Video Retrieval, London*, LNCS 2383, pages 186–197. Springer-Verlag, 2002.
15. F. Schaffalitzky and A. Zisserman. Multi-view matching for unordered image sets, or "How do I organize my holiday snaps?". In *Proceedings of the 7th European Conference on Computer Vision, Copenhagen, Denmark*, volume 1, pages 414–431. Springer-Verlag, 2002.
16. C. Schmid and R. Mohr. Local greyvalue invariants for image retrieval. *IEEE Transactions on Pattern Analysis and Machine Intelligence*, 19(5):530–534, May 1997.
17. J. Sivic, F. Schaffalitzky, and A. Zisserman. Object level grouping for video shots. In *Proceedings of the 8th European Conference on Computer Vision, Prague, Czech Republic*. Springer-Verlag, May 2004.
18. J. Sivic and A. Zisserman. Video Google: A text retrieval approach to object matching in videos. In *Proceedings of the International Conference on Computer Vision*, October 2003.
19. D.M. Squire, W. Müller, H. Müller, and T. Pun. Content-based query of image databases: inspirations from text retrieval. *Pattern Recognition Letters*, 21:1193–1198, 2000.

20. D. Tell and S. Carlsson. Combining appearance and topology for wide baseline matching. In *Proceedings of the 7th European Conference on Computer Vision, Copenhagen, Denmark*, LNCS 2350, pages 68–81. Springer-Verlag, May 2002.
21. T. Tuytelaars and L. Van Gool. Wide baseline stereo matching based on local, affinely invariant regions. In *Proceedings of the 11th British Machine Vision Conference, Bristol*, pages 412–425, 2000.
22. I. H. Witten, A. Moffat, and T. Bell. *Managing Gigabytes: Compressing and Indexing Documents and Images*. Morgan Kaufmann Publishers, ISBN:1558605703, 1999.

Simultaneous Object Recognition and Segmentation by Image Exploration*

Vittorio Ferrari[1], Tinne Tuytelaars[2], and Luc Van Gool[1,2]

[1] Computer Vision Group (BIWI), ETH Zürich, Switzerland
[2] ESAT-PSI, University of Leuven, Belgium

Abstract. Methods based on local, viewpoint invariant features have proven capable of recognizing objects in spite of viewpoint changes, occlusion and clutter. However, these approaches fail when these factors are too strong, due to the limited repeatability and discriminative power of the features. As additional shortcomings, the objects need to be rigid and only their approximate location is found. We present an object recognition approach which overcomes these limitations. An initial set of feature correspondences is first generated. The method anchors on it and then gradually explores the surrounding area, trying to construct more and more matching features, increasingly farther from the initial ones. The resulting process covers the object with matches, and simultaneously separates the correct matches from the wrong ones. Hence, recognition and segmentation are achieved at the same time. Only very few correct initial matches suffice for reliable recognition. Experimental results on still images and television news broadcasts demonstrate the stronger power of the presented method in dealing with extensive clutter, dominant occlusion, large scale and viewpoint changes. Moreover non-rigid deformations are explicitly taken into account, and the approximative contours of the object are produced. The approach can extend any viewpoint invariant feature extractor.

1   Introduction

The modern trend in object recognition has abandoned model-based approaches (e.g. [2]), which require a 3D model of the object as input, in favor of appearance-based ones, where some example images suffice. Two kinds of appearance-based methods exist: *global* and *local*. Global methods build an object representation by integrating information over an entire image (e.g [4,17,27]), and are therefore very sensitive to background clutter and partial occlusion. Hence, global methods only consider test images without background, or necessitate a prior segmentation, a task which has proven extremely difficult. Additionally, robustness to large viewpoint changes is hard to achieve, because the global object appearance varies in a complex and unpredictable way (the object's geometry is unknown). Local methods counter problems due to clutter and occlusion by representing images as a

---

* This research was supported by EC project VIBES, the Fund for Scientific Research Flanders, and the IST Network of Excellence PASCAL.

J. Ponce et al. (Eds.): Toward Category-Level Object Recognition, LNCS 4170, pp. 145–169, 2006.
© Springer-Verlag Berlin Heidelberg 2006

collection of features extracted based on local information only (e.g. [25]). After the influential work of Schmid [24], who proposed the use of rotation-invariant features, there has been important evolution. Feature extractors have appeared [12,14] which are invariant also under scale changes, and more recently recognition under general viewpoint changes has become possible, thanks to extractors adapting the complete *affine* shape of the feature to the viewing conditions [1,13,15,23,31,30]. These *affine invariant* features are particularly significant: even though the global appearance variation of 3D objects is very complex under viewpoint changes, it can be approximated by simple affine transformations on a local scale, where each feature is approximately planar (a *region*). Local invariant features are used in many recent works, and provide the currently most successful paradigm for object recognition (e.g. [12,15,18,21,30]). In the basic common scheme a number of features are extracted *independently* from both a model and a test image, then characterized by invariant descriptors and finally matched.

In spite of their success, the robustness and generality of these approaches are limited by the repeatability of the feature extraction, and the difficulty of matching correctly, in the presence of large amounts of clutter and challenging viewing conditions. Indeed, large scale or viewpoint changes considerably lower the probability that any given model feature is re-extracted in the test image. Simultaneously, occlusion reduces the number of visible model features. The combined effect is that only a small fraction of model features has a correspondence in the test image. This fraction represents the maximal number of features that can be correctly matched. Unfortunately, at the same time extensive clutter gives rise to a large number of non-object features, which disturb the matching process. As a final outcome of these combined difficulties, only a few, if any, correct matches are produced. Because these often come together with many mismatches, recognition tends to fail.

Even in easier cases, to suit the needs for repeatability in spite of viewpoint changes, only a sparse set of *distinguished* features [18] are extracted. As a result, only a small portion of the object is typically covered with matches. Densely covering the visible part of the object is desirable, as it increases the *evidence* for its presence, which results in higher detection power. Moreover, it would allow to find the contours of the object, rather than just its location.

The image exploration approach. In this chapter we tackle these problems with a new, powerful technique to match a model view to the test image which no longer relies solely on matching viewpoint invariant features. We start by producing an initial large set of unreliable region correspondences, so as to maximize the number of correct matches, at the cost of introducing many mismatches. Additionally, we generate a grid of regions densely covering the model image. The core of the method then iteratively alternates between *expansion* phases and *contraction* phases. Each expansion phase tries to construct regions corresponding to the coverage ones, based on the geometric transformation of nearby existing matches. Contraction phases try to remove incorrect matches, using filters that tolerate non-rigid deformations.

This scheme anchors on the initial matches and then *looks around* them trying to construct more. As new matches arise, they are exploited to construct even more, in a process which gradually *explores* the test image, recursively constructing more and more matches, increasingly farther from the initial ones. At each iteration, the presence of the new matches helps the filter taking better removal decisions. In turn, the cleaner set of matches makes the next expansion more effective. As a result, the number, percentage and extent of correct matches grow with every iteration. The two closely cooperating processes of expansion and contraction gather more evidence about the presence of the object *and* separate correct matches from wrong ones *at the same time*. Hence, they achieve simultaneous recognition and segmentation of the object.

By constructing matches for the coverage regions, the system succeeds in covering also image areas which are not interesting for the feature extractor or not discriminative enough to be correctly matched by traditional techniques. During the expansion phases, the shape of each new region is adapted to the local surface orientation, allowing the exploration process to follow curved surfaces and deformations (e.g. a folded magazine).

The basic advantage of our approach is that each single correct initial match can expand to cover a smooth surface with *many* correct matches, even when starting from a large number of mismatches. This leads to filling the visible portion of the object with matches. Some interesting direct advantages derive from it. First, robustness to scale, viewpoint, occlusion and clutter are greatly enhanced, because most cases where traditional approaches generate only a few correct matches are now solvable. Secondly, discriminative power is increased, because decisions about the object's identity are based on information densely distributed over the entire portion of the object visible in the test image. Thirdly, the approximate boundary of the object in the test image is suggested by the final set of matches. Fourthly, non-rigid deformations are explicitly taken into account.

Chapter organization. Sections 2 to 8 explain the image exploration technique. A discussion of related work can be found in section 10, while experimental results are given in section 9. Finally, section 11 closes the chapter with conclusions and possible directions for future research. A preliminary version of this work appeared in [8,9].

2 Overview of the Method

Figure 2-left shows a challenging example, which is used as case-study throughout the chapter. There is a large scale change (factor 3.3), out-of-plane rotation, extensive clutter and partial occlusion. All these factors make the life of the feature extraction and matching algorithms hard.

A scheme of the approach is illustrated in figure 1. We build upon a multiscale extension of the extractor of [30]. However, the method works in conjunction with any affine invariant region extractor [1,13,15]. In the first phase (*soft matching*), we form a large set of initial region correspondences. The goal is to obtain some correct matches also in difficult cases, even at the price of including a large majority of mismatches. Next, a grid of circular regions covering the model image is generated (coined *coverage regions*). The *early expansion* phase tries to propagate these coverage regions based on the geometric transformation of nearby initial matches. By *propagating* a region, we mean constructing the corresponding one in the test image. The propagated matches and the initial ones are then passed through a local filter, during the *early contraction* phase, which removes some of the mismatches. The processing continues by alternating faster expansion phases (*main expansion*), where coverage regions are propagated over a larger area, with contraction phases based on a global filter (*main contraction*). This filter exploits both topological arrangements and appearance information, and tolerates *non-rigid deformations*. The 'early' phases differ from the 'main' phases in that they are specialized to deal with the extremely low percentage of correct matches given by the initial matcher in particularly difficult cases.

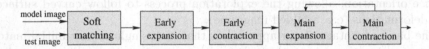

Fig. 1. Phases of the image exploration technique

3   Soft Matching

The first stage is to compute an initial set of region matches between a *model image* I_m and a *test image* I_t. The region extraction algorithm [30] is applied to both images independently, producing two sets of regions Φ_m, Φ_t, and a vector of invariants describing each region [30]. Test regions Φ_t are matched to model regions Φ_m in two steps, explained in the next two subsections. The matching procedure allows for *soft matches*, i.e. more than one model region is matched to the same test region, or vice versa.

3.1   Tentative Matches

For each test region $T \in \Phi_t$ we first compute the Mahalanobis distance of the descriptors to all model regions $M \in \Phi_m$. Next, the following appearance similarity measure is computed between T and each of the 10 closest model regions:

$$\overline{\text{sim}}(M,T) = \text{NCC}(M,T) + (1 - \frac{\overline{\text{dRGB}}(M,T)}{100}) \tag{1}$$

where NCC is the normalized cross-correlation between the regions' greylevel patterns, while $\overline{\text{dRGB}}$ is the average pixel-wise Euclidean distance in *RGB* colorspace after independent normalization of the 3 colorbands (necessary to achieve photometric invariance). Before computation, the two regions are aligned by the affine transformation mapping T to M.

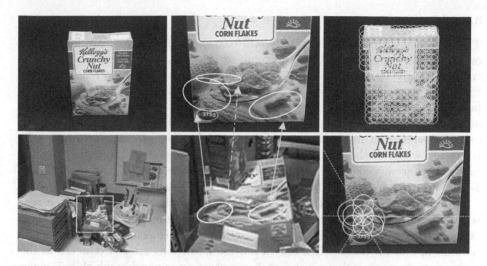

Fig. 2. Left: case-study, with model image (top), and test image (bottom). Middle: a close-up with 3 initial matches. The two model regions on the left are both matched to the same region in the test image. Note the small occluding rubber on the spoon. Right-top: the homogeneous coverage Ω. Right-bottom: a support region (dark), associated sectors (lines) and candidates (bright).

Each of the 3 test regions most similar to T above a low threshold t_1 are considered tentatively matched to T. Repeating this operation for all regions $T \in \Phi_t$, yields a first set of *tentative matches*. At this point, every test region could be matched to either none, 1, 2 or 3 model regions.

3.2 Refinement and Re-thresholding

Since all regions are independently extracted from the two images, the geometric registration of a correct match is often not optimal. Two matching regions often do not cover exactly the same physical surface, which lowers their similarity. The registration of the tentative matches is now *refined* using our algorithm [6], that efficiently looks for the affine transformation that maximizes the similarity. This results in adjusting the region's location and shape in one of the images. Besides raising the similarity of correct matches, this improves the quality of the forthcoming *expansion* stage, where new matches are constructed based on the affine transformation of the initial ones.

After refinement, the similarity is re-evaluated and only matches scoring above a second, higher threshold t_2 are kept[1] . Refinement tends to raise the similarity of correct matches much more than that of mismatches. The increased *separation* between the similarity distributions makes the second thresholding more effective. At this point, about 1/3 to 1/2 of the tentative matches are left.

---

[1] The R, G, B colorbands range in $[0, 255]$, so $\overline{sim}$ is within $[-4.41, 2]$. A value of 1.0 indicates good similarity. In all experiments the matching thresholds are $t_1 = 0.6, t_2 = 1.0$.

3.3   Motivation

The obtained set of matches usually still contains *soft matches*, i.e. more than
one region in Φ_m is matched to the same region in Φ_t, or vice versa. This contrasts with previous works [1,12,15,18,30], but there are two good reasons for it.
First, the scene might contain repeated, or visually similar elements. Secondly,
large viewpoint and scale changes cause loss of resolution which results in a less
accurate geometric correspondence and a lower similarity. When there is also
extensive clutter, it might be impossible, based *purely* on local appearance [22],
to decide which of the best 3 matches is correct, as several competing regions
might appear very similar, and score higher than the correct match. A classic
1-to-1 approach may easily be distracted and fail to produce the correct match.

The proposed process outputs a large set of plausible matches, all with a reasonably high similarity. The goal is to maximize the number of correct matches,
even at the cost of accepting a substantial fraction of mismatches. This is important in difficult cases, when only a few model regions are re-extracted in the
test image, because each correct match can start an expansion which will cover
significant parts of the object.

Figure 2-left shows the case-study, for which 3 correct matches out of 217
are found (a *correct-ratio* of 3/217). The large scale change, combined with the
modest resolution (720x576), causes heavy image degradation which corrupts
edges and texture. In such conditions only a few model regions are re-extracted
in the test image and many mismatches are inevitable. In the rest of the chapter,
we refer to the current set of matches as the *configuration Γ*.

How to proceed ? Global, robust geometry filtering methods, like detecting
outliers to the epipolar geometry through RANSAC [29] fail, as they need a minimal portion of inliers of about 1/3 [3,12]. Initially, this may very well not be the
case. Even if we could separate out the few correct matches, they would probably
not be sufficient to draw reliable conclusions about the presence of the object.
In the following sections, we explain how to gradually increment the number of
correct matches and simultaneously decrease the number of mismatches.

4   Early Expansion

4.1   Coverage of the Model Image

We generate a grid Ω of overlapping circular regions densely covering the model
image I_m (figure 2-top-right). In our implementation the grid is composed of a
first layer of regions of radius 25 pixels, spaced 25 pixels, and a second layer with
radius 13 pixels and spaced 25 pixels [2]. No regions are generated on the black
background. According to various experiments, this choice of the parameters
is not crucial for the overall recognition performance. The choice of the exact
grid pattern, and consequently the number of regions in Ω, trades segmentation
quality for computational cost, and could be selected based on the user's desires.

---

[2] These values are for an image of 720x576 pixels, and are proportionally adapted for
images of other sizes.

At this point, none of the regions in Ω is matched to the test image I_t. The expansion phases will try to construct in I_t as many regions corresponding to them as possible.

4.2 Propagation Attempt

We now define the concept of *propagation attempt* which is the basic building-block of the expansion phases and will be used later. Consider a region C_m in model image I_m without match in the test image I_t and a nearby region S_m, matched to S_t. If C_m and S_m lie on the same physical facet of the object, they will be mapped to I_t by similar affine transformations. The *support* match (S_m, S_t) *attempts to propagate* the *candidate* region C_m to I_t as follows:

1. Compute the affine transformation A mapping S_m to S_t.
2. Project C_m to I_t via $A : C_t = AC_m$.

The benefits of exploiting previously established geometric transformations was also noted by [23].

4.3 Early Expansion

Propagation attempts are used as a basis for the first expansion phase as follows. Consider as supports $\{S^i = (S^i_m, S^i_t)\}$ the soft-matches configuration Γ, and as candidates Λ the coverage regions Ω. For each support region S^i_m we partition I_m into 6 circular sectors centered on the center of S^i_m (figure 2-bottom-right).

Each S^i_m attempts to propagate the closest candidate region in each sector. As a consequence, each candidate C_m has an associated subset $\Gamma_{C_m} \subset \Gamma$ of supports that will *compete* to propagate it. For a candidate C_m and each support S^i in Γ_{C_m} do:

1. Generate C^i_t by attempting to propagate C_m via S^i.
2. Refine C^i_t. If C^i_t correctly matches C_m, this adapts it to the local surface orientation (handles curved and deformable objects) and perspective effects (the affine approximation is only valid on a local scale).
3. Compute the color transformation $T^i_{RGB} = \{s_R, s_G, s_B\}$ between S^i_m and S^i_t. This is specified by the scale factors on the three colorbands.
4. Evaluate the quality of the refined propagation attempt, after applying the color transformation T^i_{RGB}

$$sim_i = sim(C_m, C^i_t, T^i_{RGB}) =$$
$$\mathrm{NCC}(T^i_{RGB}C_m, C^i_t) + (1 - \tfrac{\mathrm{dRGB}(T^i_{RGB}C_m, C^i_t)}{100})$$

Applying T^i_{RGB} allows to use the unnormalized similarity measure sim, because color changes are now compensated for. This provides more discriminative power over using $\overline{sim}$.

We retain C_t^{best}, with $best = \arg\max_i sim_i$, the best refined propagation attempt. C_m is considered successfully propagated to C_t^{best} if $sim_{best} > t_2$ (the matching threshold). This procedure is applied for all candidates $C_m \in \Lambda$.

Most support matches may actually be mismatches, and many of them typically lie around each of the few correct ones (e.g. several matches in a single soft-match, figure 2-middle). In order to cope with this situation, each support concentrates its efforts on the nearest candidate in each direction, as it has the highest chance to undergo a similar geometric transformation. Additionally, every propagation attempt is refined before evaluation. Refinement raises the similarity of correctly propagated matches much more than the similarity of mispropagated ones, thereby helping correct supports to win. This results in a limited, but controlled growth, maximizing the chance that each correct match propagates, and limiting the proliferation of mispropagations. The process also restricts the number of refinements to at most 6 per support (contains computational cost).

For the case-study, 113 new matches are generated and added to the configuration Γ. 17 of them are correct and located around the initial 3 (figure 5, middle of top row). The correct-ratio of Γ improves to 20/330, but it is still very low.

5   Early Contraction

The early expansion guarantees good chances that each initial correct match propagates. As initial filter, we discard all matches that did not succeed in propagating any region. The correct-ratio of the case-study improves to 20/175 (no correct match is lost), but it is still too low for applying a global filter. Hence, we developed the following local filter.

A local group of regions in the model image have uniform shape, are arranged on a grid and intersect each other with a specific pattern. If all these regions are correctly matched, the same regularities also appear in the test image, because the surface is contiguous and smooth (regions at depth discontinuities cannot be correctly matched anyway). This holds for curved or deformed objects as well, because the affine transformation varies slowly and smoothly across neighboring regions (figure 3-left). On the other hand, mismatches tend to be randomly located over the image and to have different shapes.

We propose a local filter based on this observation. Let $\{N_m^i\}$ be the neighbors of a region R_m in the model image. Two regions A, B are considered neighbors if they intersect, i.e. if $\text{Area}(A \cap B) > 0$. Only neighbors which are actually matched to the test image are considered. Any match (R_m, R_t) is removed from Γ if

$$\sum_{\{N_m^i\}} \left| \frac{\text{Area}(R_m \cap N_m^i)}{\text{Area}(R_m)} - \frac{\text{Area}(R_t \cap N_t^i)}{\text{Area}(R_t)} \right| > t_s \tag{2}$$

with t_s some threshold[3]. The filter, illustrated in figure 3-middle, tests the preservation of the pattern of intersections between R and its neighbors (the ratio of areas is affine invariant). Hence, a removal decision is based solely on *local*

---

[3] This is set to 1.3 in all our experiments.

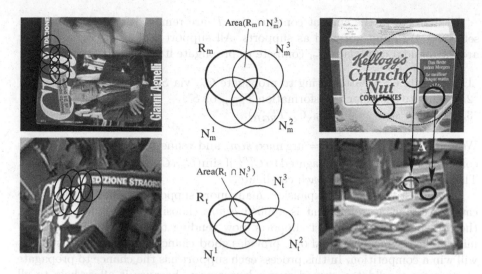

Fig. 3. Left: the pattern of intersection between neighboring correct region matches is preserved by transformations between the model and the test images, because the surface is contiguous and smooth. Middle: the surface contiguity filter evaluates this property by testing the conservation of the area ratios. Right: top: a candidate (thin) and 2 of 20 supports within the large circular area; bottom: the candidate is propagated to the test image using the affine transformation A of the support on the right (thick). Refinement adapts the shape to the perspective effects (brighter). The other support is mismatched to a region not visible in this close-up.

information. As a consequence, this filter is unaffected by the current, low overall ratio of correct matches.

Shape information is integrated in the filter, making it capable of spotting insidious mismatches which are roughly correctly located, yet have a wrong shape. This is an advantage over the (semi-) local filter proposed by [24], and later also used by others [22,26], which verifies if a minimal amount of regions in an area around R_m in the model image also match near R_t in the test image.

The input regions need not be arranged in a regular grid, the filter applies to a general set of (intersecting) regions. Note that isolated mismatches, which have no neighbors in the model image, will not be detected. The algorithm can be implemented to run in $O((|\Gamma| + x)\log(|\Gamma|))$, with $x \ll |\Gamma|^2$ the number of region intersections [5, pp 202-203].

Applying this filter to the case-study brings the correct-ratio of Γ to 13/58, thereby greatly reducing the number of mismatches.

6 Main Expansion

The first early expansion and contraction phases brought several additional correct matches and removed many mismatches, especially those that concentrated around the correct ones. Since Γ is cleaner, we can now try a faster expansion.

All matches in the current configuration Γ are removed from the candidate set $\Lambda \leftarrow \Lambda \backslash \Gamma$, and are used as supports. All support regions S_m^i in a circular area[4] around a candidate C_m compete to propagate it:

1. Generate C_t^i by attempting to propagate C_m via S^i.
2. Compute the color transformation T_{RGB}^i of S^i.
3. Evaluate $sim_i = \mathrm{sim}(C_m, C_t^i, T_{RGB}^i)$.

We retain C_t^{best}, with $best = \arg\max_i sim_i$ and refine it, yielding C_t^{ref}. C_m is considered successfully propagated to C_t^{ref} if $\mathrm{sim}(C_m, C_t^{ref}) > t_2$ (figure 3-right). This scheme is applied for each candidate.

In contrast to the early expansion, many more supports compete for the same candidate, and no refinement is applied *before* choosing the winner. However, the presence of more correct supports, now tending to be grouped, and fewer mismatches, typically spread out, provides good chances that *a* correct support will win a competition. In this process each support has the chance to propagate many more candidates, spread over a larger area, because it offers help to all candidates within a wide circular radius. This allows the system to grow a *mass* of correct matches. Moreover, the process can jump over small occlusions or degraded areas, and costs only one refinement per candidate. For the case-study, 185 new matches, 61 correct, are produced, thus lifting the correct-ratio of Γ up to 74/243 (31%, figure 5, second row).

7   Main Contraction

At this point the chances of having a sufficient number of correct matches for applying a global filter are much better. We propose here a global filter based on a topological constraint for triples of region matches. In contrast to the local filter of section 5, this filter is capable of finding also isolated mismatches. The next subsection introduces the constraint on which the filter is based, while the following two subsections explain the filter itself and discuss its qualities.

7.1   The Sidedness Constraint

Consider a triple (R_m^1, R_m^2, R_m^3) of regions in the model image and their matching regions (R_t^1, R_t^2, R_t^3) in the test image. Let $\mathbf{c}_v^j$ be the center of region R_v^j ($v \in \{m, t\}$). The function

$$\mathrm{side}(R_v^1, R_v^2, R_v^3) = \mathrm{sign}((\mathbf{c}_v^2 \times \mathbf{c}_v^3)\mathbf{c}_v^1) \tag{3}$$

takes value -1 if c_v^1 is on the right side of the directed line $\mathbf{c}_v^2 \times \mathbf{c}_v^3$, going from c_v^2 to c_v^3, or value 1 if it's on the left side. The equation

$$\mathrm{side}(R_m^1, R_m^2, R_m^3) = \mathrm{side}(R_t^1, R_t^2, R_t^3) \tag{4}$$

---

[4] In all experiments the radius is set to 1/6 of the image size.

states that $\mathbf{c}^1$ should be on the same side of the line in both views (figure 4-left). This *sidedness constraint* holds for all correctly matched triples of coplanar regions, because in this case property (3) is viewpoint invariant. The constraint is valid also for most non-coplanar triples. A triple violates the constraint if at least one of the three regions is mismatched, or if they are not coplanar and there is important camera translation in the direction perpendicular to the 3D plane containing their centers (*parallax-violation*). This can create a parallax effect strong enough to move $\mathbf{c}^1$ to the other side of the line. Nevertheless, this phenomenon typically affects only a small minority of triples. Since the camera can only translate in one direction between two views, the resulting parallax can only corrupt few triples, because those on planes oriented differently will not be affected.

The region matches violate or respect equation (4) independently of the order in which they appear in the triple. The three points should be cyclically ordered in the same orientation (clockwise or anti-clockwise) in the two images in order to satisfy (4).

Topological configurations of points and lines were also used by Tell and Carlsson [28] in the wide-baseline stereo context, as a mean for guiding the matching process.

7.2 Topological Filter

A triple including a mismatched region has higher chances to violate the sidedness constraint. When this happens, it indicates that probably at least one of the matches is incorrect, but it does not tell which one(s). While one triple is not enough to decide, this information can be recovered by considering all triples simultaneously. By integrating the weak information each triple provides, it is possible to robustly discover mismatches. The key idea is that we expect incorrectly located regions to be involved in a higher share of violations.

The constraint is checked for all unordered triples $(R^i, R^j, R^k), R^i, R^j, R^k \in \Gamma$. The share of violations for a region match R^i is

$$\text{err}_{\text{topo}}(R^i) = \frac{1}{v} \sum_{R^j, R^k \in \Gamma \setminus R^i, j > k} |\text{side}(R^i_m, R^j_m, R^k_m) - \text{side}(R^i_t, R^j_t, R^k_t)| \qquad (5)$$

with $v = (n-1)(n-2)/2, n = |\Gamma|$. $\text{err}_{\text{topo}}(R^i) \in [0, 1]$ because it is normalized w.r.t. the maximum number of violations v any region can be involved in.

The topological error share (5) is combined with an appearance term, giving the total error

$$\text{err}_{\text{tot}}(R^i) = \text{err}_{\text{topo}}(R^i) + (t_2 - \overline{\text{sim}}(R^i_m, R^i_t))$$

The filtering algorithm starts from the current set of matches Γ, and then iteratively removes one match at a time as follows:

1. (Re-)compute $\text{err}_{\text{tot}}(R^i)$ for all $R^i \in \Gamma$.
2. Find the worst match R^w, with $w = \arg \max_i \text{err}_{\text{tot}}(R^i)$

3. If $\mathrm{err}_{\mathrm{tot}}(R^w) > 0$, remove R^w from Γ. R^w will not be used for the computation of $\mathrm{err}_{\mathrm{topo}}$ in the next iteration. Iterate to 1.
   If $\mathrm{err}_{\mathrm{tot}}(R^w) \leq 0$, or if all matches have been removed, then stop.

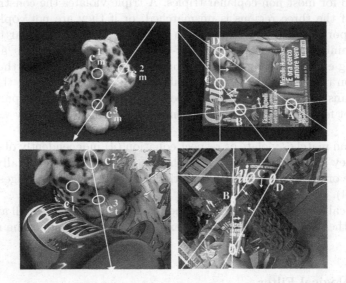

Fig. 4. Sidedness constraints. Left: $\mathbf{c}^1$ should be on the same side of the directed line from $\mathbf{c}^2$ to $\mathbf{c}^3$ in both images. Right: the constraints hold also for deformed objects. The small arrows indicate 'to the right' of the directed lines $A \to B, B \to C, C \to D, D \to A$.

At each iteration the most probable mismatch R^w is removed. During the first iterations many mismatches might still be present. Therefore, even correct matches might have a moderately large error, as they take part in triples including mismatches. However, mismatches are likely to have an even larger error, because they are involved in the very same triples, plus other violating ones. Hence, the worst mismatch R^w, the region located in I_t farthest from where it should be, is expected to have the largest error. After removing R^w all errors decrease, including the errors of correct matches, because they are involved in less triples containing a mismatch. After several iterations, ideally only correct matches are left. Since these have only a low error, due to occasional parallax-violations, the algorithm stops.

The second term of $\mathrm{err}_{\mathrm{tot}}$ decreases with increasing appearance similarity, and it vanishes when $\mathrm{sim}(R_m^i, R_t^i) = t_2$, the matches acceptance threshold. The removal criterion $\mathrm{err}_{\mathrm{tot}} > 0$ expresses the idea that topological violations are accepted up to the degree to which they are compensated by high similarity. This helps finding mismatches which can hardly be judged by only one cue. A typical mismatch with similarity just above t_2, will be removed unless it is perfectly topologically located. Conversely, correct matches with $\mathrm{err}_{\mathrm{topo}} > 0$ due to parallax-violations are in little danger, because they typically have good similarity. Including appearance makes the filter more robust to low correct-ratios, and remedies the potential drawback (parallax-violations) of a purely topological filter [6].

In order to achieve good computational performance, we store the terms of the sum in function (5) during the first iteration. In the following iterations, the sum is quickly recomputed by retrieving and adding up the necessary terms. This makes the computational cost almost independent of the number of iterations. The algorithm can be implemented to run in $O(n^2 \log(n))$, based on the idea of constructing, for each point, a list with a cyclic ordering of all other points (a complete explanation is given in [5, pp. 208-211]).

7.3   Properties and Advantages

The proposed filter has various attractive properties, and offers several advantages over detecting outliers to the epipolar geometry through RANSAC [29], which is traditionally used in the matching literature [13,15,22,23,30]. In the following, we refer to it as RANSAC-EG. The main two advantages are (more discussion in [5, pp. 75-77]):

It allows for non-rigid deformations. The filter allows for non-rigid deformations, like the bending of paper of cloth, because the structure of the spatial arrangements, captured by the sidedness constraints, is stable under these transformations. As figure 4-right shows, sidedness constraints are still respected even in the presence of substantial deformations. Other filters, which measure a geometrical distance error from an estimated model (e.g. homography, fundamental matrix) would fail in this situation. In the best case, several correct matches would be lost. Worse yet, in many cases the deformations would disturb the estimation of the model parameters, resulting in a largely random behavior. The proposed filter does not try to capture the transformations of all matches in a single, overall model, but it relies instead on simpler, weak properties, involving only three matches each. The discriminative power is then obtained by integrating over all measurements, revealing their strong, collective information.

It is insensitive to inaccurate locations. The regions' centers need not be exactly localized, because err_{topo} varies slowly and smoothly for a region departing from its ideal location. Hence, the algorithm is not affected by perturbations of the region's locations. This is precious in the presence of large scale changes, not completely planar regions, or with all kinds of image degradation (motion blur, etc.), where localization errors become more important. In RANSAC-EG instead, the point must lie within a tight band around the epipolar line. Worse yet, inaccurate localization of some regions might compromise the quality of the fundamental matrix, and therefore even cause rejection of many accurate regions [33]. In [5, pp. 84-85] we report experiments supporting this point, where the topological filter could withstand large random shifts on the regions' locations (about 25 pixels, in a 720x576 image).

7.4   Main Contraction on the Case-Study

After main expansion, the correct-ratio of the case-study was of 74/243. Applying the filter presented in this section brings it to 54/74, which is a major improvement (figure 5 second row). 20 correct matches are lost, but many more mismatches are removed (149). The further processing will recover the correct matches lost and generate even more.

8   Exploring the Test Image

The processing continues by iteratively alternating main expansion and main contraction phases.

1. Do a main expansion phase. All current matches Γ are used as supports. This produces a set of propagated region matches Υ, which are added to the configuration: $\Gamma \leftarrow (\Gamma \bigcup \Upsilon)$.
2. Do a main contraction phase on Γ. This removes matches from Γ.
3. If at least one newly propagated region survives the contraction, i.e. if $|\Upsilon \bigcap \Gamma| > 0$, then iterate to point 1, after updating the candidate set to contain $\Lambda \leftarrow (\Omega \backslash \Gamma)$, all original candidate regions Ω which are not yet in the configuration. Stop if no newly propagated regions survived, or if all regions Ω have been propagated.

In the first iteration, the expansion phase generates some correct matches, along with some mismatches. Because a correct match tends to propagate more than a mismatch, the correct ratio increases. The first main contraction phase removes mostly mismatches, but might also lose several correct matches: the amount of noise (percentage of mismatches) could still be high and limit the filter's performance. In the next iteration, this cleaner configuration is fed into the expansion phase again which, less distracted, generates more correct matches and fewer mismatches. The new correct matches in turn help the next contraction stage in taking better removal decisions, and so on. As a result, the number, percentage and spatial extent of correct matches increase at every iteration, reinforcing the confidence about the object's presence and location (figure 6). The two goals of separating correct matches and gathering more information about the object are achieved *at the same time*.

Correct matches erroneously killed by the contraction step in an iteration get another chance during the next expansion phase. With even fewer mismatches present, they are probably regenerated, and this time have higher chances to survive the contraction (higher correct-ratio, more positive evidence present).

Thanks to the refinement, each expansion phase adapts the shape of the newly created regions to the local surface orientation. Thus the whole exploration process follows curved surfaces and deformations.

The exploration procedure tends to 'implode' when the object is not in the test image, typically returning only a few matches. Conversely, when the object is present, the approach fills the visible portion of the object with many high

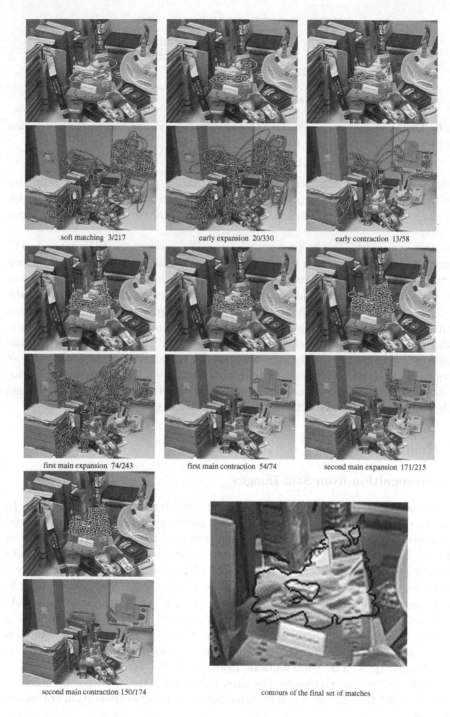

Fig. 5. Evolution of Γ for the case-study. Top rows: correct matches; bottom rows: mismatches.

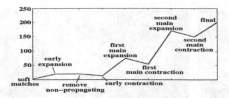

Fig. 6. The number of correct matches for the case-study increases at every iteration (compare the points after each contraction phase)

confidence matches. This yields high discriminative power and the qualitative shift from only *detecting* the object to knowing its extent in the image and which parts are occluded. Recognition and segmentation are two aspects of the *same* process.

In the case-study, the second main expansion propagates 141 matches, 117 correct, which is better than the previous 61/185. The second main contraction starts from 171/215 and returns 150/174, killing a lower percentage of correct matches than in the first iteration. After the 11th iteration 220 matches cover the whole visible part of the object (202 are correct). Figure 5 depicts the evolution of the set of matches Γ. The correct matches gradually cover more and more of the object, while mismatches decrease in number. The system reversed the situation, by going from only very few correct matches in a large majority of mismatches, to hundreds of correct matches with only a few mismatches. Notice the accuracy of the final segmentation, and in particular how the small occluding rubber has been correctly left out (figure 5 bottom-right).

9   Results

9.1   Recognition from Still Images

The dataset in this subsection[5] consists of 9 model objects and 23 test images. In total, the objects appear 43 times, as some test images contain several objects. To facilitate the discussion, the images are referred to by their coordinates as in figure 7, where the arrangement is chosen so that a test image is adjacent to the model object(s) it contains. There are 3 planar objects, each modeled by a single view, including a *Kellogs* box[6] and two magazines, *Michelle* (figure c2) and *Blonde* (analog model view). Two objects with curved shapes, *Xmas* (b1) and *Ovo* (e2), have 6 model views. *Leo* (d3), *Car* (a2), *Suchard* (d1) feature more complex 3D shapes and have 8 model views. Finally, one frontal view models the last 3D object, *Guard* (b3). Multiple model views are taken equally spaced around the object. The contributions from all model views of a single object are combined by superimposing the area covered by the final set of matched regions (to find the contour), and by summing their number (detection criterion).

---

[5] The dataset is available at www.vision.ee.ethz.ch/~ferrari.

[6] The kellogs box is used throughout the chapter as a case-study.

Fig. 7. Recognition results (see text)

All images are shot at a modest resolution (720x576) and all experiments are conducted with the same set of parameters. In general, in the test cases there is considerable clutter and the objects appear smaller than in the models (all model images have the same resolution as the test images and they are shown at the same size).

Tolerance to non-rigid deformations is shown in c1, where *Michelle* is simultaneously strongly folded and occluded. The contours are found with a good accuracy, extending to the left until the edge of the object. Note the extensive clutter. High robustness to viewpoint changes is demonstrated in c3, where *Leo* is only half visible and captured in a considerably different pose than any of the model views, while *Michelle* undergoes a very large out-of-plane rotation of about 80 degrees. *Guard*, occluding *Michelle*, is also detected in the image, despite a scale change of factor 3. In d2, *Leo* and *Ovo* exhibit significant viewpoint changes, while *Suchard* is simultaneously scaled by factor 2.2 and 89% occluded. This very high occlusion level makes this case challenging even for a human observer. A scale change of factor 4 affecting *Suchard* is illustrated in e1. In figure a1, *Xmas* is divided in two by a large occluder. Both visible parts are correctly detected by the presented method. On the right side of the image, *Car* is found even if half occluded and very small. *Car* is also detected in spite of a considerable viewpoint change in a3. The combined effects of strong occlusion, scale change and clutter make b2 an interesting case. Note how the boundaries of *Xmas* are accurately found, and in particular the detection of the part behind the glass. As a final example, 8 objects are detected at the same time in e3 (for clarity, only 3 contours are shown). Note the correct segmentation of the two deformed magazines and the simultaneous presence of all the aforementioned difficulties.

Figure 8-bottom-left presents a close-up on one of 93 matches produced between a model view of *Xmas* (left) and test case b2 (right). This exemplifies the great appearance variation resulting from combined viewpoint, scale and illumination changes, and other sources of image degradation (here a glass). In these cases, it is very unlikely for the region to be detected by the initial region extractor, and hence traditional methods fail.

As a proof of the method's capability to follow deformations, we processed the case in figure 8-bottom-right starting with only one match (dark). 356 regions, covering the whole object, were produced. Each region's shape fits the local surface orientation (for clarity, only 3 regions are shown).

The performance of the system was quantified by processing all pairs of model-object and test images, and counting the resulting number of region matches. The highest ROC curve in figure 8-top-left depicts the detection rate versus false-positive rate, while varying the detection threshold from 0 to 200 matches. An object is detected if the number of produced matches, summed over all its model views, exceeds this threshold. The method performs very well, and can achieve 98% detection with 6% false-positives. For comparison, we processed the dataset also with 4 state-of-the-art affine region extractors [1,15,18,30], and

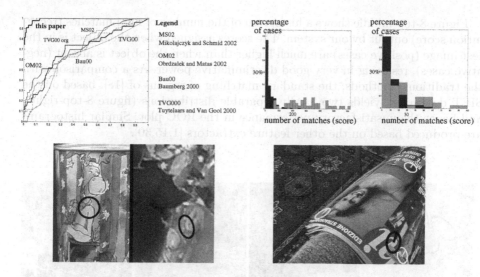

Fig. 8. Top: left: ROC plot. False-positives on the X-axis, detection rate on the Y-axis; middle: distribution of scores for our method (percentage; bright = positive cases; dark = negative cases); right: for the traditional matching of the regions of Matas et al. Bottom: left: close-up on one match of case b2; right: starting from the black region only, the method covers the magazine with 365 regions (3 shown).

described the regions with the SIFT [12] descriptor[7] , which has recently been demonstrated to perform best [4]. The matching is carried out by the 'unambiguous nearest-neighbor' approach[8] advocated in [1,12]: a model region is matched to the region of the test image with the closest descriptor if it is closer than 0.7 times the distance to the second-closest descriptor (the threshold 0.7 has been empirically determined to optimize results). Each of the central curves illustrates the behavior of a different extractor. As can be seen, none is satisfactory, which demonstrates the higher level of challenge posed by the dataset and therefore suggests that our approach can broaden the range of solvable object recognition cases. Closer inspection reveals the source of failure: typically only very few, if any, correct matches are produced when the object is present, which in turn is due to the lack of repeatability and the inadequacy of a simple matcher under such difficult conditions. The important improvement brought by the proposed method is best quantified by the difference between the highest curve and the central thick curve, representing the system we started from [30] ('TVG00 org' in the plot).

---

[7] All region extractors and the SIFT descriptor are implementations of the respective authors. We are grateful to J. Matas, K. Mikolajczyk, A. Zisserman, C. Schmid and D. Lowe.

[8] We have also tried the standard approach, used in [15,4,18,30], which simply matches two nearest-neighbors if their distance is below a threshold, but it produced slightly worse results.

Figure 8-top-middle shows a histogram of the number of final matches (recognition score) output by our system. The scores assigned when the object is in the test image (positive cases) are much higher than when the object is absent (negative cases), resulting in very good discriminative power. As a comparison with the traditional methods, the standard matching of regions of [18], based on the SIFT descriptor, yields two hardly separable distributions (figure 8-top-right), and hence the unsatisfactory performance in the ROC plot. Similar histograms are produced based on the other feature extractors [1,15,30].

Fig. 9. Video retrieval results. The parts of the model-images not delineated by the user are blanked out.

As last comparison, we consider the recent system [21], which constructs a 3D model of each object prior to recognition. We asked the authors to process our dataset. As they reported, because of the low number of model views, their system couldn't produce meaningful models, and therefore couldn't perform recognition. Conversely, we have processed the dataset of [21] with our complete system (including multi-view integration [7]). It performed well, and achieved 95% detection rate for 6% false-positives (see [21] for more details).

9.2   Video Retrieval

In this experiment, the goal is to find a specific object or scene in a test video. The object is only given as delineated by the user in one model image. In [26] another region-based system for video object retrieval is presented. However, it focuses on different aspects of the problem, namely the organization of regions coming from several shots, and weighting their individual relevance in the wider context of the video. At the feature level, their work still relies solely on regions from standard extractors.

Because of the different nature of the data, the system differs in a few points from the object recognition one. At recognition time the test video is segmented into shots, and a few representative keyframes are selected in each shot by the algorithm of [19]. The object is then searched in each keyframe separately, by a simplified version of the image exploration technique. Specifically, it has a simple one-to-one nearest neighbor approach for the initial matching instead of the soft-matching phase, there are no 'early' phases, and there is only one layer of coverage regions. This simpler version runs faster (about twice as fast), though it is not as powerful. It takes about 2 minutes to process a (object,keyframe) pair on a common workstation (2.4 Ghz PC).

We present results on challenging, real-world video material, namely news broadcast provided by the RTBF Belgian television. The data comes from 4 videos, captured on different days, each of about 20 minutes. The keyframes have low resolution (672x528) and many of them are visibly affected by compression artifacts, motion blur and interlacing effects. We selected 13 diverse objects, including locations, advertising products, logos and football shirts, and delineated each in one keyframe. Each object is searched in the keyframes of the video containing its model-image. On average, a video has 325 keyframes, and an object occurs 7.4 times. The number of keyframes not containing an object (negatives), is therefore much greater than the number of positives, allowing to collect relevant statistics. A total of 4236 (object,keyframe) image pairs have been processed.

Figure 9.1 show some example detections. A large piece of quilt decorated with various flags (a2) is found in a3 in spite of non-rigid deformation, occlusion and extensive clutter. An interesting application is depicted in b1-b2-b3. The shirts of two football teams are picked out as query objects (b2), and the system is asked to find the keyframes where each team is playing. In b1 the Fortis shirt is successfully found in spite of important motion blur (close-up in a1). Both teams are identified in b3, where the shirts appear much smaller and the Dexia player is turned 45 degrees (viewpoint change on the shirt). The keyframe in c1 instead, has not been detected. Due to the intense blur, the initial matcher does not return any correct correspondence. Robustness to large scale changes and occlusion is demonstrated in a4, where the UN council, modeled in b4, is recognized while enlarged by a scale factor 2.7, and heavily occluded (only 10% visible). Equally intriguing is the image of figure c4, where the UN council is seen from an opposite viewpoint. The large painting on the left of b4 is about the only thing still visible in the test keyframe, where it appears on the right side. The system matched the whole area of the painting, which suffers from out-of-plane rotation. As a last example, a room with Saddam Hussein is found in figure c3 (model in c2). The keyframe is taken under a different viewpoint and substantially corrupted by motion blur.

The retrieval performance is quantified by the *detection rate* and *false-positive rate*, averaged over all objects. An object is detected if the number of final matches, divided by the number of model coverage regions, exceeds 10% (detections of model-keyframes are not counted). The system performs well, by achieving an average detection rate of 82.4%, for a false-positive rate of 3.6%. As a comparison, we repeated the experiment with [30], the method we started from. It only managed a 33.3% detection rate, for a false-positive rate of 4.6%, showing that our approach can substantially boost the performance of standard affine invariant matching procedures.

10   Related Work

The presented technique belongs to the category of appearance-based object recognition. Since it can extend any approach which matches affine invariant regions between images, it is tightly related to this class of methods. The novelties and improvements brought by our approach are enumerated in the introduction section and demonstrated in the result section 9.

Beyond the realm of local invariant features, there are a few works which are related to ours, in that they also combine recognition with segmentation. Leibe and Schiele [10] present a method to detect an unknown object instance of a given category and segment it from a test image. The category (e.g. cows) is learnt from example instances (images of particular cows). However, the method does not support changes in camera viewpoint or orientation. In [32], low-level grouping cues based on edge responses, high-level cues from a part detector and spatial consistency of detected parts, are combined in a graph partitioning framework. The scheme is shown to recognize and segment a human body in a cluttered image. However, the part detectors need a considerable number of training examples, and the very parts to be learned are manually indicated (head, left arm, etc.). Moreover, there is no viewpoint, orientation or scale invariance. Both methods are suited for categorization, and not specialized in the recognition of a particular objects.

While we believe our approach to be essentially original, some components are clearly related to earlier research. The filter in section 7 is constructed around the sidedness constraint. A similar constraint, testing the cyclic ordering of points, was used for wide-baseline matching in [28]. Moreover, the 'propagation attempt' at the heart of the expansion phases is an evolution of the idea of 'growing matches' proposed by [20,23,22]. While they use existing affine transformations only to *guide the search* for further matches, our approach actively *generates* new regions, which have not been originally extracted. This is crucial to counter the repeatability problems stated in the introduction. Finally, a different, pixel-by-pixel propagation strategy was previously proposed in [11], but it is applicable only in case of small differences between the images.

11   Conclusion and Outlook

We have presented an approach to object recognition capable of solving particularly challenging cases. Its power roots in the 'image exploration' technique. Every single correct match can lead to the generation of many correct matches covering the smooth surface on which it lies, even when starting from an overwhelming majority of mismatches. Hence, the method can boost the performance of any algorithm which provides affine regions correspondences, because very few correct initial matches suffice for reliable recognition. Moreover, the approximate boundaries of the object are found during the recognition process, and non-rigid deformations are explicitly taken into account, two features lacking in competing approaches (e.g. [1,12,15,18,21,22,30]).

Some individual components of the scheme, like the topological filter and GAMs, are useful in their own right, and can be used profitably beyond the scope of this chapter.

In spite of the positive points expressed above, our approach is not without limitations. One of them is the computational expense: in the current implementation, a 2.4 Ghz computer takes about 4-5 minutes, on average, to process a pair of model and test images. Although we plan a number of speedups, the method is unlikely to reach the speed of the fastest other systems (the system of Lowe [12] is reported to perform recognition within seconds). As another limitation, our method is best suited for objects which have some texture, much like the other recognition schemes based on invariant regions. Uniform objects (e.g. a balloon) cannot be dealt with and seem out of the reach of this kind of approaches. They should be addressed by techniques based on contours [4,25]. Hence, a useful extension would be to combine some sort of 'local edge regions' with the current textured regions. An important evolution is the systematic exploitation of the relationships between multiple overlapping model views. We have tackled this issue in a separate publication [7]. Finally, using several types of affine invariant regions simultaneously, rather than only those of [30], would push the performance further upwards.

References

1. A. Baumberg. Reliable feature matching across widely separated views. In *Proceedings of the International Conference on Computer Vision*, pages 774–781, 2000.
2. G. Bebis, M. Georgiopoulos, and N. V. Lobo. Learning geometric hashing functions for model-based object recognition. In *Proceedings of the International Conference on Computer Vision*, pages 543–548, 1995.
3. O. Chum, J. Matas, and S. Obdrzalek. Epipolar geometry from three correspondences. In *Proceedings of Computer Vision Winter Workshop*, 2003.
4. C. Cyr and B. Kimia. 3d object recognition using similarity-based aspect graph. In *Proceedings of the International Conference on Computer Vision*, 2001.
5. V. Ferrari. *Affine Invariant Regions* ++. PhD Thesis, Selected Readings in Vision and Graphics, Springer Verlag, Zuerich, CH, 2004.

6. V. Ferrari, T. Tuytelaars, and L. Van-Gool. Wide-baseline multiple-view correspondences. In *Proceedings of the IEEE Conference on Computer Vision and Pattern Recognition*, 2003.
7. V. Ferrari, T. Tuytelaars, and L. Van-Gool. Integrating multiple model views for object recognition. In *Proceedings of the IEEE Conference on Computer Vision and Pattern Recognition*, 2004.
8. V. Ferrari, T. Tuytelaars, and L. Van-Gool. Simultaneous object recognition and segmentation by image exploration. In *Proceedings of the European Conference on Computer Vision*, 2004.
9. V. Ferrari, T. Tuytelaars, and L. Van-Gool. Simultaneous object recognition and segmentation from single or multiple model views. *to appear in International Journal of Computer Vision*, 2006.
10. B. Leibe and B. Schiele. Scale-invariant object categorization using a scale-adaptive mean-shift search. In *Proceedings of DAGM*, pages 145–153, 2004.
11. M. Lhuillier and L. Quan. Match propagation for image-based modeling and rendering. *IEEE Transactions on Pattern Analysis and Machine Intelligence*, 24(12), 2002.
12. D. Lowe. Distinctive image features from scale-invariant keypoints. *to appear in International Journal of Computer Vision*, 2004.
13. J. Matas, O. Chum, M. Urban, and T. Pajdla. Robust wide baseline stereo from maximally stable extremal regions. In *Proceedings of the British Machine Vision Conference*, 2002.
14. K. Mikolajczyk and C. Schmid. Indexing based on scale-invariant interest points. In *Proceedings of the International Conference on Computer Vision*, 2001.
15. K. Mikolajczyk and C. Schmid. An affine invariant interest point detector. In *Proceedings of the European Conference on Computer Vision*, 2002.
16. K. Mikolajczyk and C. Schmid. A performance evaluation of local descriptors. In *Proceedings of the IEEE Conference on Computer Vision and Pattern Recognition*, volume II, pages 257–263, 2003.
17. H. Murase and S. Nayar. Visual learning and recognition of 3d objects from appearance. *International Journal of Computer Vision*, 14(1), 1995.
18. S. Obrdzalek and J. Matas. Object recognition using local affine frames on distinguished regions. In *Proceedings of the British Machine Vision Conference*, pages 414–431, 2002.
19. M. Osian and L. Van-Gool. Video shot characterization. In *Proceedings of the TRECVID Workshop*, 2003.
20. P. Pritchett and A. Zisserman. Wide baseline stereo matching. In *Proceedings of the IEEE Conference on Computer Vision and Pattern Recognition*, 1998.
21. F. Rothganger, S. Lazebnik, C. Schmid, and J. Ponce. 3d object modeling and recognition using affine-invariant image descriptors and multi-view spatial constraints. *to appear in International Journal of Computer Vision*, 2005.
22. F. Schaffalitzky and A. Zisserman. Automated scene matching in movies. In *Proceedings of the Workshop on Content-based Image and Video Retrieval*, 2002.
23. F. Schaffalitzky and A. Zisserman. Multi-view matching for unordered image sets. In *Proceedings of the European Conference on Computer Vision*, 2002.
24. C. Schmid. Combining greyvalue invariants with local constraints for object recognition. In *Proceedings of the IEEE Conference on Computer Vision and Pattern Recognition*, pages 872–877, 1996.
25. A. Selinger and R. C. Nelson. A perceptual grouping hierarchy for appearance-based 3d object recognition. *Computer Vision and Image Understanding*, 76(1):83–92, 1999.

26. J. Sivic and A. Zisserman. Video google: A text retrieval approach to object matching in videos. In *Proceedings of the International Conference on Computer Vision*, 2003.
27. M. J. Swain and B. H. Ballard. Color indexing. *International Journal of Computer Vision*, 7(1):11–32, 1991.
28. D. Tell and S. Carlsson. Combining appearance and topology for wide baseline matching. In *Proceedings of the European Conference on Computer Vision*, pages 68–81, 2002.
29. P.H.S. Torr and D. W. Murray. The development and comparison of robust methods for estimating the fundamental matrix. *International Journal of Computer Vision*, 24(3):271–300, 1997.
30. T. Tuytelaars and L. Van-Gool. Wide baseline stereo based on local, affinely invariant regions. In *Proceedings of the British Machine Vision Conference*, 2000.
31. T. Tuytelaars, L. Van-Gool, L. Dhaene, and R. Koch. Matching affinely invariant regions for visual servoing. In *Proceedings of the IEEE Conference on Robotics and Automation*, pages 1601–1606, 1999.
32. S. X. Yu, R. Gross, and J. Shi. Concurrent object recognition and segmentation by graph partitioning. In *Neural Information Processing Systems*, 2002.
33. Z. Zhang, R. Deriche, O. Faugeras, and Q. Luong. A robust technique for matching two uncalibrated images through the recovery of the unknown epipolar geometry. *Artificial Intelligence*, 78:87–119, 1995.

Part III

Recognition of Object Categories

Part III

Recognition of Object Categories

Comparison of Generative and Discriminative Techniques for Object Detection and Classification

Ilkay Ulusoy[1] and Christopher M. Bishop[2]

[1] METU, Computer Vision and Intelligent Systems Research Lab.
06531 Ankara, Turkey
http://www.eee.metu.edu.tr/~ilkay
[2] Microsoft Research,
7 J J Thompson Avenue,
Cambridge, U.K.
http://research.microsoft.com/~cmbishop

Abstract. Many approaches to object recognition are founded on probability theory, and can be broadly characterized as either generative or discriminative according to whether or not the distribution of the image features is modelled. Generative and discriminative methods have very different characteristics, as well as complementary strengths and weaknesses. In this chapter we introduce new generative and discriminative models for object detection and classification based on weakly labelled training data. We use these models to illustrate the relative merits of the two approaches in the context of a data set of widely varying images of non-rigid objects (animals). Our results support the assertion that neither approach alone will be sufficient for large scale object recognition, and we discuss techniques for combining the strengths of generative and discriminative approaches.

1 Introduction

In recent years many studies, both in machine learning and computer vision areas, have focussed on the problem of object recognition. The key challenge is to be able to recognize any member of a category of objects in spite of wide variations in visual appearance due to changes in the form and colour of the object, occlusions, geometrical transformations (such as scaling and rotation), changes in illumination, and potentially non-rigid deformations of the object itself. Since detailed hand-segmentation and labelling of images is very labour intensive, learning object categories from 'weakly labelled' data has been studied in recent years. Weakly labelled data means that training images are labelled only according to the presence or absence of each category of object. A major challenge presented by this problem is that the foreground object is accompanied by widely varying background clutter, and the system must learn to distinguish the foreground from the background without the aid of labelled data.

J. Ponce et al. (Eds.): Toward Category-Level Object Recognition, LNCS 4170, pp. 173–195, 2006.
© Springer-Verlag Berlin Heidelberg 2006

Many of the current approaches to this problem rely on the use of local features obtained from small patches of the image. One motivation for this is that local patches can give information about an object even it is occluded. An other motivation is that the variability of small patches is much less than that of whole images and so there are much better prospects for generalization, in other words for recognizing that a patch from a test image is similar to patches in the training images. However, the patches must be sufficiently variable, and therefore sufficiently large, to be able to discriminate between the different object categories and also between objects and background clutter. A good way to balance these two conflicting requirements is to determine the object categories present in an image by fusing together partial ambiguous information from multiple patches. Probability theory provides a powerful framework for combining such uncertain information in a principled manner, and will form the basis for our research. We will also focus on the detection of objects within images by combining information from a large number of patches of the image.

Local features are obtained from small patches which are extracted from the local neighbourhood of interest points obtained in the image. Some of the interest point operators such as saliency [8], Difference of Gaussian (DoG) [11] and Harris-Laplace (HL) [12] are invariant to location, scale and orientation, and some are also affine invariant [12] to some extent. For the purposes of this chapter we shall consider the use of such generic operators. We will use some very common operators (Section 2) and feature description methods and will compare their effect in learning performance (Section 5).

Also, the locations of the patches which provide strong evidence for an object can give an indication of the location and spatial extent of that object. The probabilistic model of Fergus et al. [5] performed the localization of the object in an image by learning jointly the appearances and relative locations of a small set of parts whose potential locations are determined by the saliency detector [8]. Since their algorithm is computationally complex, the number of parts has to be kept small. In [10] a discriminative framework for the classification of image regions by incorporating neighborhood interactions is presented. But for two class classification only. In [4], the spatial relationship between patches was not considered but informative features (i.e. object features) were selected based on information criteria such as likelihood ratio and mutual information. However, in this supervised approach, hundreds of images were hand segmented. Finally, [19] extended the Gaussian Mixture Model (GMM) based approach of [4] to a semi-supervised case where a multi-modal GMM was trained to model foreground and background feature together. In their study, some uncluttered images of foreground were also used for the purpose of training their model. In this chapter, we do not attempt to model the spatial relationship between patches but instead focus on the comparison of generative with discriminative methods in the context of local patch labelling.

The object recognition problem is basically a classification problem and there are many different modelling approaches for the solution. These approaches can be classified into two main categories such as generative and discriminative. To understand the distinction between discriminative and generative approaches, consider a scenario in which an image described by a vector $\mathbf{X}$ (which might comprise raw pixel intensities, or some set of features extracted from the image) is to be assigned to one of K classes $k = 1, \ldots, K$. From basic decision theory [2] we know that the most complete characterization of the solution is expressed in terms of the set of posterior probabilities $p(k|\mathbf{X})$. Once we know these probabilities it is straightforward to assign the image $\mathbf{X}$ to a particular class to minimize the expected loss (for instance, if we wish to minimize the number of misclassifications we assign $\mathbf{X}$ to the class having the largest posterior probability).

In a discriminative approach we introduce a parametric model for the posterior probabilities, $p(k|\mathbf{X})$, and infer the values of the parameters from a set of labelled training data. This may be done by making point estimates of the parameters using maximum likelihood, or by computing distributions over the parameters in a Bayesian setting (for example by using variational inference).

By contrast, in a generative approach we model the joint distribution $p(k, \mathbf{X})$ of images and labels. This can be done, for instance, by learning the class prior probabilities $p(k)$ and the class-conditional densities $p(\mathbf{X}|k)$ separately. The required posterior probabilities are then obtained using Bayes' theorem

$$p(k|\mathbf{X}) = \frac{p(\mathbf{X}|k)p(k)}{\sum_j p(\mathbf{X}|j)p(j)} \tag{1}$$

where the sum in the denominator is taken over all classes.

Each modelling approach has some advantages as well as disadvantages. There are many recent studies dealing with the comparison of these two approaches with the final goal of combining the two in the best way. In [14] it was concluded that although the discriminative learning has lower asymptotic error, a generative classifier approaches its higher asymptotic error much faster. Very similar results were also obtained by [3] but they showed on a simulated data that this is only true when the models are appropriate for the data, i.e. the generative model models the data distribution correctly. Otherwise, if a mis-matched model was selected then generative and discriminative models behaved similarly, even with a small number of data points. In both [3] and [14] it was observed that as the number of data points is increased the discriminative model performs better. In [3] and [7] discriminative and generative learning were combined in an ad-hoc manner using a weighting parameter and the value of this parameter defines the extend to which discriminative learning is effective over generative learning. In [18] discriminative learning was performed on a generative model where background posterior probability was modelled with a constant.

In this chapter we will provide two different models, one from each approach, which are able to provide labels for the individual patches, as well as for the image as a whole, so that each patch is identified as belonging to one of the object categories or to the background class. This provides a rough indication of the location of the object or objects within the image. Again these individual patch labels must be learned on the basis only of overall image class labels. Our training set is weakly labelled where each image is labelled only according to the presence or absence of each category of object. Our goal in this chapter is not to find optimal object recognition system, but to compare alternative learning methodologies. For this purpose, we shall use a fixed data set. In particular, we consider the task of detecting and distinguishing cows and sheep in natural images. This set is chosen for the wide variability of the objects in order to present a non-trivial classification problem. We do not have any data set for background only. Various features used in this study are explained in Section 2. Our discriminative and generative models are introduced in Sections 3 and 4 respectively.

We use $\mathbf{t}_n$ to denote the image label vector for image n with independent components $t_{nk} \in \{0, 1\}$ in which $k = 1, \ldots K$ labels the class. In our case $K = 3$ where the classes are cow, sheep and background. Each class can be present or absent independently in an image, and we make no distinction between foreground and background classes within the model itself. $\mathbf{X}_n$ denotes the observation for image n and this comprises as set of J_n patch vectors $\{\mathbf{x}_{nj}\}$ where $j = 1, \ldots, J_n$. Note that the number J_n of detected interest points will in general vary from image to image.

We shall compare the two models in various aspects. First we will investigate how the models behave with weakly labelled data and then we will test how strongly labelled (i.e. images are segmented as foreground and background) and weakly labelled data can be used together in training the models. Experiments and results for this is given in Section 5.1. Secondly, we will test the models with various types of feature as inputs to see how feature type effects the models. Experiments and results for this is given in Section 5.2. Finally, as many previous studies did, we will see how training data quantity affects learning in the two different model types. Experiments and results for this is given in Section 5.3.

2   Feature Extraction

Due to the reasons that we have mentioned in the previous section,we will follow several recent approaches and use interest point detectors to focus attention on a small number of local patches in each image. This is followed by invariant feature extraction from a neighbourhood around each interest point.

We choose to work with Harris-Laplace (HL) [12] and Difference of Gaussian (DoG) [11] interest point operators because they are invariant to orientation and scale changes. In our earlier study [16] we have used DoG interest point detector with SIFT (Scale Invariant Feature Transform) descriptor. SIFT is invariant to illumination and affine (to some degree) changes and very suitable for DoG interest point detectors. However SIFT, being a 128 dimentional vector, brings a high computational load for model learning. Thus, in this chapter we will use 15 dimensional Local Jet (LJ) descriptor instead [9,6].

For the purpose of comparison, we will train our models using different feature types and see how they are effected by these choices. The two feature point operators, HL and DoG, will be used with the same feature descriptor (LJ). In Figure 1 a cow image is shown together with with HL and DoG feature point detectors in order to give more insight into these two types of operators. Here only feature points which have scale grater than 5 pixels are shown. As can be observed from the images, the DoG operator extracts uniform regions (leftmost image in Figure 1) and HL extracts corners (middle image in the figure) where the number of features extracted by HL is usually less than DoG.

The feature descriptor may be concatenated with colour information. The colour information is extracted from each patch based on [1]. Averages and standard deviations of (R, G, B), (L, a, b) and $(r = R/(R+G+B), g = G/(R+G+B))$ constitute the colour part of the feature vector. Lab is a device-independent colour space that attempts to uniformly represent colour as we perceive it. L is the lightness value, a is the red/green opponency and blue/yellow is represented on the b axis. As a result, if colour is also used as a feature descriptor then we will have a 31 dimensional feature vector.

Just for comparison purposes, we will also use square random patches as interest regions which are selected at random sizes and random positions all over the image. Since the size of a patch can vary between 1 pixel to the full size of the image, the patches will be scaled to 16 by 16 size. If each pixel's colour information is used directly to form a feature vector, this makes a feature vector of size 768 ($16 \times 16 \times 3$) and it is impossible to use this directly in our models (especially in the generative model). Thus, we compute first 15 Principle Component Analysis (PCA) coefficients for the gray scale patch and we obtain the colour feature as described in the previous paragraph. Again this makes a 31 dimensional feature vector. The number of random patches is selected to be approximately the same as the number of patches found by other interest point operators, which is around 100 for each image. In the rightmost image in Figure 1 the cow image with some of the random patches is also shown. We only show 10 random patches here. In Section 5.2, comparison of the two models when used with different features will be given in terms of patch labelling and image labelling. We will compare HL and DoG operators with LJ and colour feature, and random patches with PCA coefficients and colour feature.

Fig. 1. Different interest point operators. Feature point locations are the centers of the squares and the size of a square shows the scale of that feature point. The three images show (left to right) DoG interest points, HL interest points and random patches.

3   The Discriminative Model with Patch Labelling

In a discriminative setting, the purpose is to learn the posterior probabilities. Since our goal is to determine the class membership of individual patches also, we associate with each patch j in an image n a binary label $\tau_{njk} \in \{0,1\}$ denoting the class k of the patch. For the models developed in this chapter we shall consider these labels to be mutually exclusive, so that $\sum_{k=1}^{K} \tau_{njk} = 1$, in other words each patch is assumed to be either cow, sheep or background. Note that this assumption is not essential, and other formulations could also be considered. These components can be grouped together into vectors $\boldsymbol{\tau}_{nj}$. If the values of these labels were available during training (corresponding to strongly labelled images) then the development of recognition models would be greatly simplified. For weakly labelled data, however, the $\{\boldsymbol{\tau}_{nj}\}$ labels are hidden (latent) variables, which of course makes the training problem much harder.

We now introduce a discriminative model, which corresponds to the directed graph shown in Figure 2.

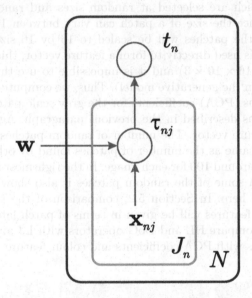

Fig. 2. Graphical representation of the discriminative model for object recognition

Consider for a moment a particular image n (and omit the index n to keep the notation uncluttered). We build a parametric model $y_k(\mathbf{x}_j, \mathbf{w})$ for the probability that patch $\mathbf{x}_j$ belongs to class k. For example we might use a simple linear-softmax model with outputs

$$y_k(\mathbf{x}_j, \mathbf{w}) = \frac{\exp(\mathbf{w}_k^{\mathrm{T}} \mathbf{x}_j)}{\sum_l \exp(\mathbf{w}_l^{\mathrm{T}} \mathbf{x}_j)} \tag{2}$$

which satisfy $0 \leqslant y_k \leqslant 1$ and $\sum_k y_k = 1$. More generally we can use a multi-layer neural network, a relevance vector machine, or any other parametric model that gives probabilistic outputs and which can be optimized using gradient-based methods. The probability of a patch label τ_j is then given by

$$p(\tau_j|\mathbf{x}_j) = \prod_{k=1}^{K} y_k(\mathbf{x}_j, \mathbf{w})^{\tau_{jk}} \tag{3}$$

where the binary exponent τ_{jk} simply pulls out the required term (since $y_k^0 = 1$ and $y_k^1 = y_k$).

Next we assume that if one, or more, of the patches carries the label for a particular class, then the whole image will. For instance, if there is at least one local patch in the image which is labelled 'cow' then the whole image will carry a 'cow' label (recall that an image can carry more than one class label at a time). Thus the conditional distribution of the image label, given the patch labels, is given by

$$p(\mathbf{t}|\boldsymbol{\tau}) = \prod_{k=1}^{K} \left[1 - \prod_{j=1}^{J}[1 - \tau_{jk}]\right]^{t_k} \left[\prod_{j=1}^{J}[1 - \tau_{jk}]\right]^{1-t_k}. \tag{4}$$

In order to obtain the conditional distribution $p(\mathbf{t}|\mathbf{X})$ we have to marginalize over the latent patch labels. Although there are exponentially many terms in this sum, it can be performed analytically for our model due to the factorization implied by the graph in Figure 2 to give

$$p(\mathbf{t}|\mathbf{X}) = \sum_{\boldsymbol{\tau}} \left\{ p(\mathbf{t}|\boldsymbol{\tau}) \prod_{j=1}^{J} p(\tau_j|\mathbf{x}_j) \right\}$$

$$= \prod_{k=1}^{K} \left[1 - \prod_{j=1}^{J}[1 - y_k(\mathbf{x}_j, \mathbf{w})]\right]^{t_k} \left[\prod_{j=1}^{J}[1 - y_k(\mathbf{x}_j, \mathbf{w})]\right]^{1-t_k}. \tag{5}$$

This can be viewed as a probabilistic version of the 'noisy OR' function [15].

Given a training set of N images, which are assumed to be independent, we can construct the likelihood function from the product of such distributions, one for each data point. Taking the negative logarithm then gives the following error function

$$E(\mathbf{w}) = -\sum_{n=1}^{N} \sum_{k=1}^{C} \{t_{nk} \ln[1 - Z_{nk}] + (1 - t_{nk}) \ln Z_{nk}\} \tag{6}$$

where we have defined

$$Z_{nk} = \prod_{j=1}^{J_n} [1 - y_k(\mathbf{x}_{nj}, \mathbf{w})]. \tag{7}$$

The parameter vector $\mathbf{w}$ can be determined by minimizing this error (which corresponds to maximizing the likelihood function) using a standard optimization algorithm such as scaled conjugate gradients [2]. More generally the likelihood function could be used as the basis of a Bayesian treatment, although we do not consider this here.

Once the optimal value $\mathbf{w}_{ML}$ is found, the corresponding functions $y_k(\mathbf{x}, \mathbf{w}_{ML})$ for $k = 1, \ldots, K$ will give the posterior class probabilities for a new patch feature vector $\mathbf{x}$. Thus the model has learned to label the patches even though the training data contained only image labels. Note, however, that as a consequence of the 'noisy OR' assumption, the model only needs to label one foreground patch correctly in order to predict the image label. It will therefore learn to pick out a small number of highly discriminative foreground patches, and will classify the remaining foreground patches, as well as those falling on the background, as 'background' meaning non-discriminative for the foreground class. This will be illustrated in Section 5.1.

3.1 Soft Discriminative Model

In our discriminative model with probabilistic noisy OR assumption, if only one patch is labelled as belonging to a class, then the whole image is labelled as belonging to that class. We can soften this assumption by modelling the posterior probability of the image label using the logistic sigmoid function

$$p\left(t_k = 1|\mathbf{X}\right) = \frac{1}{1 + e^{-Z_k}} \tag{8}$$

where Z_k is the sum over all patches

$$Z_k = \sum_{j=1}^{J} y_k\left(\mathbf{x}_j, \mathbf{w}\right) \tag{9}$$

where

$$y_k(\mathbf{x}_j, \mathbf{w}) = \mathbf{w}_k^{\mathrm{T}} \mathbf{x}_j \tag{10}$$

so that we are adding the log odds. It follows that the conditional distribution of target labels is given by

$$p\left(t_k|\mathbf{X}\right) = \left(\frac{1}{1 + e^{-Z_k}}\right)^{t_{n_k}} \left(1 - \frac{1}{1 + e^{-Z_k}}\right)^{1 - t_k}. \tag{11}$$

The distribution for the vector of target variables is then given by

$$p\left(\mathbf{t}|\mathbf{X}\right) = \prod_{k=1}^{K} p\left(t_k|\mathbf{X}\right). \tag{12}$$

However outputs of this model can not be directly used as patch label probabilities because they are not normalized and they don't satisfy $\sum_k y_k = 1$. This does not cause a problem in finding the most probable patch label. We can directly use the model outputs and choose the biggest one as patch label. However, when we need patch label probabilities then we need to normalize the model outputs over all possible patches and labels.

The error function for this soft discriminative model is given by the negative log likelihood, and takes the form

$$E\left(\mathbf{w}\right) = -\sum_{n=1}^{N}\sum_{k=1}^{K}\left\{Z_{nk}\left(t_{nk} - 1\right) - \ln\left(1 + e^{-Z_{nk}}\right)\right\}. \tag{13}$$

With this soft version, an improvement in both patch labelling and image labelling is obtained. Comparative results for the two discriminative models (probabilistic noisy OR and soft) are given in Section 5.1.

4   The Generative Model with Patch Labelling

Next we turn to a description of our generative model, whose graphical representation is shown in Figure 3. The structure of this model mirrors closely that

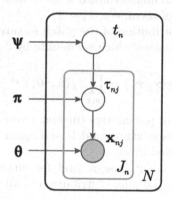

Fig. 3. Graphical representation of the generative model for object recognition

of the discriminative model. In particular, the same class-label variables τ_{nj} are associated with the patches in each image, and again these are unobserved and must be marginalized out in order to obtain maximum likelihood solutions.

In the discriminative model we represented the conditional distribution $p(\mathbf{t}|\mathbf{X})$ directly as a parametric model. By contrast in the generative approach we model $p(\mathbf{t}, \mathbf{X})$, which we decompose into $p(\mathbf{t}, \mathbf{X}) = p(\mathbf{X}|\mathbf{t})p(\mathbf{t})$ and then model the two factors separately. This decomposition would allow us, for instance, to employ large numbers of 'background' images (those containing no instances of the object classes) during training to determine $p(\mathbf{X}|\mathbf{t})$ without concluding that the prior probabilities $p(\mathbf{t})$ of objects is small.

Again, we begin by considering a single image n. The prior $p(\mathbf{t})$ is specified in terms of K parameters ψ_k where $0 \leqslant \psi_k \leqslant 1$ and $k = 1, \ldots, K$, so that

$$p(\mathbf{t}) = \prod_{k=1}^{K} \psi_k^{t_k} (1 - \psi_k)^{1-t_k}. \tag{14}$$

In general we do not need to learn these from the training data since the prior occurrences of different classes is more a property of the way the data was collected than of the real world frequencies. (Similarly in the discriminative model we will typically wish to correct for different priors between the training set and test data using Bayes' theorem.)

The remainder of the model is specified in terms of the conditional probabilities $p(\boldsymbol{\tau}|\mathbf{t})$ and $p(\mathbf{X}|\boldsymbol{\tau})$. The probability of generating a patch from a particular class is governed by a set of parameters π_k, one for each class, such that $\pi_k \geqslant 0$, constrained by the subset of classes actually present in the image. Thus

$$p(\boldsymbol{\tau}_j|\mathbf{t}) = \left(\sum_{l=1}^{K} t_l \pi_l \right)^{-1} \prod_{k=1}^{K} (t_k \pi_k)^{\tau_{jk}}. \tag{15}$$

Note that there is an overall undetermined scale to these parameters, which may be removed by fixing one of them, e.g. $\pi_1 = 1$.

For each class k, the distribution of the patch feature vector $\mathbf{x}$ is governed by a separate mixture of Gaussians which we denote by $\phi_k(\mathbf{x}; \boldsymbol{\theta}_k)$, so that

$$p(\mathbf{x}_j|\boldsymbol{\tau}_j) = \prod_{k=1}^{K} \phi_k(\mathbf{x}_j; \boldsymbol{\theta}_k)^{\tau_{jk}} \tag{16}$$

where $\boldsymbol{\theta}_k$ denotes the set of parameters (means, covariances and mixing coefficients) associated with this mixture model, and again the binary exponent τ_{jk} simply picks out the required class.

If we assume N independent images, and for image n we have J_n patches drawn independently, then the joint distribution of all random variables is

$$\prod_{n=1}^{N} p(\mathbf{t}_n) \prod_{j=1}^{J_n} [p(\mathbf{x}_{nj}|\boldsymbol{\tau}_{nj}) p(\boldsymbol{\tau}_{nj}|\mathbf{t}_n)]. \tag{17}$$

Since we wish to maximize likelihood in the presence of latent variables, namely the $\{\boldsymbol{\tau}_{nj}\}$, we use the EM algorithm. The expected complete-data log likelihood is given by

$$\sum_{n=1}^{N} \sum_{j=1}^{J_n} \left\{ \sum_{k=1}^{K} \langle \tau_{njk} \rangle \ln[t_{nk} \pi_k \phi_k(\mathbf{x}_{nj})] - \ln\left(\sum_{l=1}^{K} t_{nl} \pi_l \right) \right\}. \tag{18}$$

In the E-step the expected values of τ_{nkj} are computed using

$$\langle \tau_{njk} \rangle = \sum_{\{\boldsymbol{\tau}_{nj}\}} \tau_{njk} p(\boldsymbol{\tau}_{nj}|\mathbf{x}_{nj}, \mathbf{t}_n) = \frac{t_{nk} \pi_k \phi_k(\mathbf{x}_{nj})}{\displaystyle\sum_{l=1}^{K} t_{nl} \pi_l \phi_l(\mathbf{x}_{nj})}. \tag{19}$$

Notice that the first factor on the right hand side of (15) has cancelled in the evaluation of $\langle \tau_{njk} \rangle$.

For the M-step we first set the derivative with respect to one of the parameters π_k equal to zero (no Lagrange multiplier is required since there is no summation constraint on the $\{\pi_k\}$) and then re-arrange to give the following re-estimation equations

$$\pi_k = \left[\sum_{n=1}^{N} J_n t_{nk} \left(\sum_{l=1}^{K} t_{nl} \pi_l \right)^{-1} \right]^{-1} \sum_{n=1}^{N} \sum_{j=1}^{J_n} \langle \tau_{njk} \rangle. \tag{20}$$

Since these represent coupled equations we perform several (fast) iterations of these equations before proceeding with the next EM cycle (note that for this purpose the sums over j can be pre-computed since they do not depend on the $\{\pi_k\}$).

Now consider the optimization with respect to the parameters $\boldsymbol{\theta}_k$ governing the distribution $\phi_k(\mathbf{x}; \boldsymbol{\theta}_k)$. The dependence of the expected complete-data log likelihood on $\boldsymbol{\theta}_k$ takes the form

$$\sum_{n=1}^{N} \sum_{j=1}^{J_n} \langle \tau_{njk} \rangle \ln \phi_k(\mathbf{x}_{nj}; \boldsymbol{\theta}_k) + \text{const}. \tag{21}$$

This is easily maximized for each class k separately using the EM algorithm (in an inner loop), since (21) simply represents a log likelihood function for a weighted data set in which patch (n, j) is weighted with $\langle \tau_{njk} \rangle$. Specifically, we use a model in which $\phi_k(\mathbf{x}; \boldsymbol{\theta}_k)$ is given by a Gaussian mixture distribution of the form

$$\phi_k(\mathbf{x}; \boldsymbol{\theta}_k) = \sum_{m=1}^{M} \rho_{km} \mathcal{N}(\mathbf{x}|\boldsymbol{\mu}_{km}, \boldsymbol{\Sigma}_{km}). \tag{22}$$

The E-step is given by

$$\gamma_{njkm} = \frac{\rho_{km} \mathcal{N}(\mathbf{x}_{nj}|\boldsymbol{\mu}_{km}, \boldsymbol{\Sigma}_{km})}{\sum_{m'} \rho_{km'} \mathcal{N}(\mathbf{x}_{nj}|\boldsymbol{\mu}_{km'}, \boldsymbol{\Sigma}_{km'})} \tag{23}$$

while the M-step equations are weighted by the coefficients $\langle \tau_{njk} \rangle$ to give

$$\boldsymbol{\mu}_{km}^{\text{new}} = \frac{\sum_n \sum_j \langle \tau_{njk} \rangle \gamma_{njkm} \mathbf{x}_{nj}}{\sum_n \sum_j \langle \tau_{njk} \rangle \gamma_{njkm}}$$

$$\boldsymbol{\Sigma}_{km}^{\text{new}} = \frac{\sum_n \sum_j \langle \tau_{njk} \rangle \gamma_{njkm} (\mathbf{x}_{nj} - \boldsymbol{\mu}_{km}^{\text{new}})(\mathbf{x}_{nj} - \boldsymbol{\mu}_{km}^{\text{new}})^{\text{T}}}{\sum_n \sum_j \langle \tau_{njk} \rangle \gamma_{njkm}}$$

$$\rho_{km}^{\text{new}} = \frac{\sum_n \sum_j \langle \tau_{njk} \rangle \gamma_{njkm}}{\sum_n \sum_j \langle \tau_{njk} \rangle}.$$

If one EM cycle is performed for each mixture model $\phi_k(\mathbf{x}; \boldsymbol{\theta}_k)$ this is equivalent to a global EM algorithm for the whole model. However, it is also possible to perform several EM cycle for each mixture model $\phi_k(\mathbf{x}; \boldsymbol{\theta}_k)$ within the outer

EM algorithm. Such variants yield valid EM algorithms in which the likelihood never decreases.

The incomplete-data log likelihood can be evaluated after each iteration to ensure that it is correctly increasing. It is given by

$$\sum_{n=1}^{N}\sum_{j=1}^{J_n}\left\{\ln\left(\sum_{k=1}^{K}t_{nk}\pi_k\phi_k(\mathbf{x}_{nj})\right)-\ln\left(\sum_{l=1}^{K}t_{nl}\pi_l\right)\right\}.$$

Note that, for a data set in which all $t_{nk}=1$, the model simply reduces to fitting a flat mixture to all observations, and the standard EM is recovered as a special case of the above equations.

This model can be viewed as a generalization of that presented in [19] in which a parameter is learned for each mixture component representing the probability of that component being foreground. This parameter is then used to select the most informative N components in a similar approach to [4] and [17] where the number N is chosen heuristically. In our case, however, the probability of each feature belonging to one of the K classes is learned directly.

Inference in the generative model is more complicated than in the discriminative model. Given all patches $\mathbf{X} = \{\mathbf{x}_j\}$ from an image, the posterior probability of the label τ_j for patch j can be found by marginalizing out all other hidden variables

$$p(\tau_j|\mathbf{X}) = \sum_{\mathbf{t}}\sum_{\tau/\tau_j} p(\tau, \mathbf{X}, \mathbf{t})$$

$$= \sum_{\mathbf{t}} p(\mathbf{t}) \frac{1}{\left(\sum_{l=1}^{K}\pi_l t_l\right)^J}\prod_{k=1}^{K}(\pi_k t_k \phi_k(\mathbf{x}_j))^{\tau_{jk}}\prod_{i\neq j}\left[\sum_{k=1}^{K}\pi_k t_k \phi_k(\mathbf{x}_i)\right] \quad (24)$$

where $\tau = \{\tau_j\}$ denotes the set of all patch labels, and τ/τ_j denotes this set with τ_j omitted. Note that the summation over all possible $\mathbf{t}$ values, which must be done explicitly, is computationally expensive.

For the inference of image label we require the posterior probability of image label $\mathbf{t}$, which can be computed using

$$p(\mathbf{t}|\mathbf{X}) \propto p(\mathbf{X}|\mathbf{t})\,p(\mathbf{t}) \quad (25)$$

in $p(\mathbf{t})$ is computed from the coefficients $\{\psi_k\}$ for each setting of $\mathbf{t}$ in turn, and $p(\mathbf{X}|\mathbf{t})$ is found by summing out patch labels

$$p(\mathbf{X}|\mathbf{t}) = \sum_{\tau}\prod_{j=1}^{J} p(\mathbf{X}, \tau_j|\mathbf{t}) = \prod_{j=1}^{J_n}\frac{\sum_{k=1}^{K}t_k\pi_k\phi_k(\mathbf{x}_j)}{\sum_{l=1}^{K}t_l\pi_l}. \quad (26)$$

5   Experiments and Results

In this chapter, we have used a test bed of weakly labelled images each containing either cows or sheep, in which the animals vary widely in terms of number, pose, size, colour and texture. There are 167 images in each class, and 10-fold cross-validation is used to measure performance. For the discriminative model we used a two-layer nonlinear network having 10 hidden units with 'tanh' activation functions. The network had 31 inputs, corresponding to the LJ or PCA coefficient with colour feature as discussed in Section 2 and 3 outputs (cow, sheep, background). For the generative model we used a separate Gaussian mixture for cow, sheep and background, each of which has 10 components with diagonal covariance matrices. In our earlier study [16] we used input vector of size 144 which consists of SIFT and colour features. Using a smaller feature vector this time brings computational benefit such as speed and computable covariance matrixes.

In the test phase of both discriminative and generative models, we input the patch features to the models and obtain the posterior probabilities of the patch labels as the outputs using (2) for probabilistic noisy OR discriminative model or (10) with normalization for soft discriminative model and (24) for the generative model. The posterior probability of the image label is computed as in (5) for probabilistic noisy OR model or (12) for the soft discriminative model and (25) for the generative case. We can therefore investigate the ability of the models both to predict the class labels of whole images and of their constituent patches. The latter is important for object localization.

5.1   Combining Strongly Labelled and Weakly Labelled Data for Training

Initial results with the generative model showed that with random initialization of the mixture model parameters it is incapable of learning a satisfactory solution [16]. We conjectured that this is due to the problem of multiple local maxima in the likelihood function (a similar effect was found by [19]). To test this, we used some segmented images for initialization purposes (but not for optimization) in our earlier study [16]. 30 cow and 30 sheep images were hand-segmented, and a patch which has any foreground pixel was labelled as foreground and a patch which has no foreground pixel was labelled as background. Features obtained from the patches belonging to each class were clustered using the K-means algorithm and the component centers of a class mixture model were assigned to the cluster centers of the respective class. The mixing coefficients were set to the number of points in the corresponding cluster divided by the total number of points in that class. Similarly, covariance matrices were computed using the data points assigned to the respective center.

In this chapter, we use these segmented images also for training optimization in order to give both models the same chance. In the generative case, including the segmented data into learning requires only a slight change in the expected complete-data log likelihood which becomes partially expected in this case:

$$\sum_{n\in US}\sum_{j=1}^{J_n}\left\{\sum_{k=1}^{K}\langle\tau_{njk}\rangle\ln\left[t_{nk}\pi_k\phi_k(\mathbf{x}_{nj})\right]-\ln\left(\sum_{l=1}^{K}t_{nl}\pi_l\right)\right\}$$

$$+\sum_{n\in S}\sum_{j=1}^{J_n}\left\{\sum_{k=1}^{K}\tau_{njk}\ln\left[t_{nk}\pi_k\phi_k(\mathbf{x}_{nj})\right]-\ln\left(\sum_{l=1}^{K}t_{nl}\pi_l\right)\right\} \qquad (27)$$

where S and US denote segmented and unsegmented image sets respectively. For segmented images $n \in S$, τ_{nkj} values are already known. Including the segmented data to the generative model is very easy where we only need to assign known patch labels instead of their expected labels in the outer E step (19) mentioned in Section 4.

For the probabilistic noisy OR discriminative model, the error function becomes

$$E(\mathbf{w}) = - \sum_{n \in US} \sum_{k=1}^{K} \{t_{nk} \ln[1 - Z_{nk}] + (1 - t_{nk}) \ln Z_{nk}\}$$

$$- \sum_{n \in S} \sum_{j=1}^{J_n} \sum_{k=1}^{K} \tau_{njk} \ln(y_k(\mathbf{x}_{nj}, \mathbf{w})) \qquad (28)$$

where the first term on the right hand side of the error function includes unsegmented images and is the image labelling error, while the second term includes segmented images and is the patch labelling error.

Similarly, for the soft discriminative model, the error function (29) consists of two parts: one with unlabelled data and the other with labelled data. These two parts need to be treated differently during all optimization steps.

$$E(\mathbf{w}) = - \sum_{n \in US} \sum_{k=1}^{K} \{Z_{nk}(t_{nk} - 1) - \ln(1 + e^{-Z_{nk}})\}$$

$$- \sum_{n \in S} \sum_{j=1}^{J_n} \sum_{k=1}^{K} (y_k(\mathbf{x}_{nj}, \mathbf{w}) - \tau_{njk}) \qquad (29)$$

To test the effect of labelled data on the generative model, we train the same generative model with and without labelled data and compared the results. When only unlabelled data is used (i.e. no initialization is performed) overall correct rate (ocr) for image labelling is obtained to be 46.50% which is worse than random labelling. When segmented data is used for initialization only then there is a significant increase in the performance where ocr becomes 59.37%. When the segmented data is used for training as well the performance is not effected much where ocr stays at 59.37%. In Figure 4 examples for generative model patch labelling are given for different situations where most probable label is assigned for each patch. Patch centers are shown by coloured dots where colour denotes the class (red, white, green for cow, sheep and background respectively). As can be observed from the image, without initialization patch labelling is as random (top image of the figure). Image labelling result for this particular sheep image is $\mathbf{t} = [1\ 0\ 1]$ for this sample run which means that this is a cow image. With initialization, most of the patches are labelled correctly (middle image in the figure). Image label for the same sheep is $\mathbf{t} = [1\ 1\ 1]$ this time which means there are both cow and sheep (as well as background) present in the image. When segmented data is also used for training (bottom image) patch labelling performance becomes better and sheep image is labelled correctly as $\mathbf{t} = [0\ 1\ 1]$.

Using segmented data for the probabilistic noisy OR discriminative model brings some problems. When labelled data is also used for training, although the patch labelling performance increases significantly image labelling performance degrades. For example, in Figure 4 patch labelling results during a sample run are given where the most probable label is assigned to each patch. Top image is an example which is obtained when segmented data is not used in training and ocr for this case is 62.50%. Image labelling result is correct for this particular cow with $t = [0.99\,0.50\,1]$ which becomes $t = [1\,0\,1]$ when 0.5 is used as a threshold for image label probability. Middle image is obtained when segmented data is used for training the model and ocr for this case is very low, 30%. In this case patch labelling is better but image label for this particular cow image is $t = [1\ 0.83\ 1]$ which means that there is a high probability of sheep also. This is caused by a white (sheep) patch in the cow image. The bottom image is when the soft discriminative model is trained with segmented data where ocr becomes 78.1%. Patch labelling is as good as the previous case but this time image labelling is also correct $t = [1\ 0\ 1]$ for this particular cow image although there are two white (sheep) patches. This shows that when we use segmented data and force the probabilistic noisy OR discriminative model to learn those patches as they are labelled then the discriminative power decreases because those patches may not be that discriminative. However this is not the case for soft discriminative model.

As we mentioned in Section 3.1 outputs are linear for our soft discriminative model and this means that outputs can take any real value. Thus, normalization is required for this model when we need patch label probabilities.

5.2   Comparison with Different Feature Types

In this section we will provide comparative results between our generative (G) and soft discriminative (D) model when they are used with different types of features such as HL operator with LJ and colour feature (HL-LJ+C), DoG operator with LJ and colour (DoG-LJ+C) and random patches with PCA coefficients and colour feature (R-PCA+C). Usually DoG feature point operator finds more points than HL operator does when applied on the same image. In the random selection case we define the number of feature points and their local extension. In order to eliminate the effect of data quantity in the comparison, we arranged the feature point extraction algorithms so that they produce roughly the same amount of feature points (around 100) for each image. Means and standard deviations of overall correct rate results over 10 fold runs are given in Table 1. Columns are for different feature types and rows are for different models.

As can be observed from the table, ocr for discriminative model is not effected much when different feature types are used. The best overall correct rate for the discriminative model is obtained by DoG-LJ+C feature and R-PCA+C feature causes the worst performance. The generative model produces highly different overall correct rates with different feature types. The best performance for the generative model is obtained by the random patches. With DoG-LJ+C and HL-LJ+C the performance is worse than the random patches.

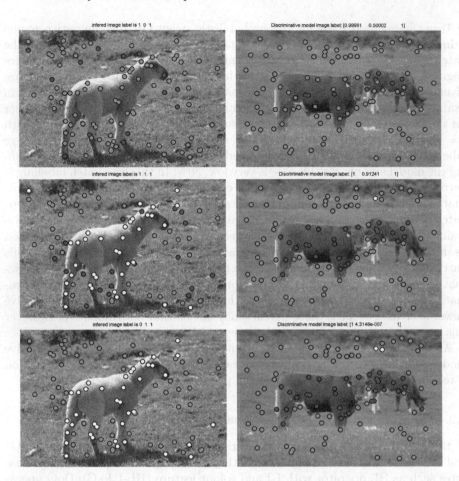

Fig. 4. Patch labelling results (red, white, green for cow, sheep and background respectively). Left column: Labelling results for the generative model where the most probable label is assigned to each patch. Patch labelling result in the top image is obtained when the generative model is trained without initialization. The middle image is when labelled data is used only for initializing the model. The bottom image is when the segmented images are used for both initializing and training the model. Right column: Labelling results for discriminative models where the most probable label is assigned to each patch. Top image is obtained when segmented data is not used in training of probabilistic noisy OR discriminative model. Middle row is when segmented data is used for training the same model. The bottom row is when the soft discriminative model is trained with segmented data.

It is also interesting to investigate the extent to which the discriminative and generative models correctly label the individual patches. In order to make a comparison in terms of patch labelling we use 12 hand segmented test images for each class. These segmented images are different from those we have used for initializing and training the models. Patch labels are obtained by (24) for the

Table 1. Means (M) and standard deviations (SD) of overall correct image label rate for different feature types: HL with LJ and colour (HL-LJ+C), DoG with LJ and colour (DoG-LJ+C) and random patches with PCA coefficients and colour (R-PCA+C)

	HL–LJ+C	DoG–LJ+C	R-PCA+C
D (M)(%)	80.63	89.38	78.13
D (SD)(%)	7.13	4.74	3.83
G (M)(%)	56.25	56.25	75.62
G (SD)(%)	6.25	9.88	2.61

generative model and by (10) for the soft discriminative model. Normalization is required for the discriminative model in order to obtain patch label probabilities. Various thresholds are used on patch label probabilities in order to produce ROC curves for the generative model and the soft discriminative model, as shown in Figure 5.

As can be observed from the plots the generative model patch labelling is better than the discriminative model patch labelling for all types of features and patch labelling with DoG operator with LJ and colour feature is better than other feature types.

Some examples of patch labelling for test images are given in Figure 6 for random patches and for DoG patches, and in Figure 7 for HL patches. In these figures each patch is assigned to the most probable class and patch centers are given with coloured dots where colour denotes the patch label.

5.3   Comparison for Training Data Quantity

We trained our models with various number of training data. We used 50 to 150 images with 25 intervals from each class for training and plot overall correct rate versus number of images used in training for both models in Figure 8. The left figure corresponds to the use of random patches, while the right figure corresponds to the use of DoG patches.

Similar results as [14] and [3] are obtained in this chapter also. Since the generative model performs the best with random patches (Section 5.2) we were expecting that with less data the generative model performance should be better than discriminative model. As can be observed from the left plots in Figure 8 the generative model performance is much better than the discriminative one for less data and as the quantity of data is increased discriminative model performance increases much faster than the generative model's performance. When DoG-LJ+C features are used, since the generative model does not perform well with this feature type, we were not expecting same type of behaviour. As can be seen in the right hand plots in Figure 8, the generative and the discriminative models behave nearly the same as we increase the data quantity but the discriminative model performs better than the generative model all the time.

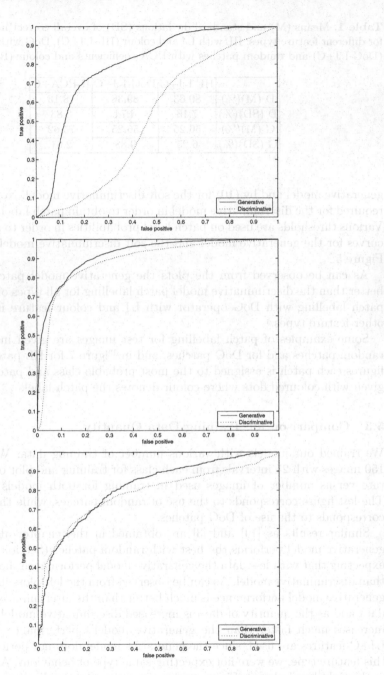

Fig. 5. ROC curves of patch labelling. Each figure contains two curves. One for the generative model and the other one for the discriminative model. Upper figure is for R-PCA+C patches. Center one is for DoG-LJ+C. Bottom one is for HL-LJ+C.

Fig. 6. Patch labelling examples for random patches (a) and for DoG patches (b). Results are shown for discriminative model (top row) and generative model (bottom row) for cow (left column) and sheep (right column) image. Red, white, green dots denote cow, sheep and background patches respectively and patch labels are obtained by assigning each patch to the most probable class.

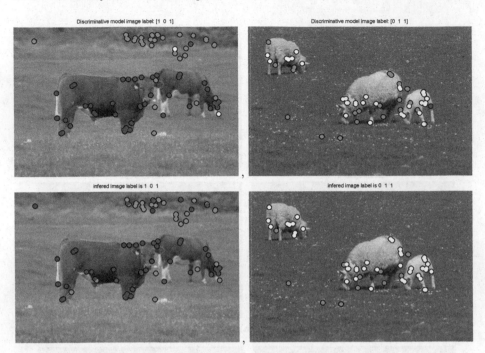

Fig. 7. Patch labelling examples for HL patches. Results for discriminative model (top row) nd generative model (bottom row) for cow (left column) and sheep (right column) image. Red, white, green dots denote cow, sheep and background patches respectively and patch labels are obtained by assigning each patch to the most probable class.

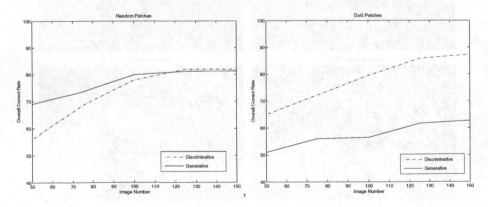

Fig. 8. Overall correct rate versus data number plots to show how the models behave as the data quantity is increased. Left figure is when random patches are used and the right figure is when DoG features are used.

6 Discussion

In our earlier study [16], we introduced novel discriminative (probabilistic noisy OR) and generative models. We used SIFT features only and showed that the probabilistic noisy OR discriminative model and the generative model have complementary strengths and limitations. The discriminative model is able to focus on highly informative features, while the generative model gives high classification accuracy, and also has some ability to localize the objects within the image. However, the generative model required careful initialization in order to achieve good results. Also, inference in such a generative model can be very complex. A discriminative model, on the other hand, is typically very fast once trained.

In this chapter, we have introduced a soft version of our previous probabilistic noisy OR discriminative model [16]. The soft discriminative model introduced here has a better patch labelling capability than probabilistic noisy OR one.

We have compared our soft discriminative and generative models in terms of using strongly labelled and weakly labelled data together in training. Combining these two data types is very easy in the generative model training but needs lots of variations in the discriminative case. The generative model, unlike the discriminative ones, could also benefit from the use of completely unlabelled images, although we have not conducted any experiments on this so far.

We have used several different feature point operators and feature extractors, and experimented with the effect of different feature types on the learning capacity of the models. First, we have compared the models in terms of image labelling performance. We have observed that the discriminative model is not effected very much when different feature types are used and the model performs the best with DoG-LJ+C (DoG operator with local jet and colour features). Random patches with PCA coefficients and colour features caused the worst performance for the discriminative model, while the opposite results are observed for the generative model. The performance of the generative model depends significantly on the choice of feature types, and the best performance is obtained with random features. We also compared the models in terms of patch labelling. In all cases the generative model outperforms the discriminative model in patch labelling. But the best patch labelling performance is obtained with DoG-LJ+C feature for both models. This is a very reasonable result because DoG operator extracts uniform regions as patches and in most cases a patch is either fully background or fully foreground. However in other cases most of the time, a patch may contain some foreground pixels as well as background pixels. In randomly selected patches this is more serious.

We have also compared the two models when different number of images are used for training. When this comparative experiment is performed using random patches as features, we have observed that with small number of data the generative model performs better than the discriminative model and as the data quantity increases the performances for both models increase but this increase is more marked for the discriminative model, so that the performance of the two approaches is similar for large data sets. When this comparative experiment is performed using DoG-LJ+C features, both models behaved nearly the same for all data quantities but the discriminative model performs better all the time as we increase the data quantity.

Our investigations suggest that the most fruitful approaches will involve some combination of generative and discriminative models. Indeed, this is already found to be the case in speech recognition where generative hidden Markov models are used to express invariance to non-linear time warping, and are then trained discriminatively by maximizing mutual information in order to achieve high predictive performance.

One promising avenue for investigation is to use a fast discriminative model to locate regions of high probability in the parameter space of a generative model, which can subsequently refine the inferences. Indeed, such coupled generative and discriminative models can mutually train each other, as has already been demonstrated in a simple context in [13].

One of the limitations of the techniques discussed here is the use of interest point detectors that are not tuned to the problem being solved (since they are hand-crafted rather than learned) and which are therefore unlikely in general to focus on the most discriminative regions of the image. Similarly, the invariant features used in our study were hand-selected. We expect that robust recognition of a large class of object categories will require that local features be learned from data.

Classifying individual patches is very hard because patches from different classes may seem similar due to the effects of illumination, pose, noise or similarity. This ambiguity can be solved by modeling the interactions between patches. The contextual information can be used in the form of spatial dependencies in the images. Markov Random Field models are traditional interaction models used in vision because they can incorporate spatial relationship constraints in a principled manner. For the purposes of this study we have ignored spatial information regarding the relative locations of feature patches in the image. However, most of our conclusions remain valid if a spatial model is combined with the local information provided by the patch features.

Acknowledgements

We would like to thank Antonio Criminisi, Geoffrey Hinton, Fei Fei Li, Tom Minka, Markus Svensen and John Winn for numerous discussions. The idea of replacing noise OR with with sum of log-odds arose in a discussion with Geoffrey Hinton.

References

1. K. Barnard, P. Duygulu, D. Forsyth, N. Freitas, D. Blei, and M. I. Jordan. Matching words and pictures. *Journal of Machine Learning Research*, 3:1107–1135, 2003.
2. C. M. Bishop. *Neural Networks for Pattern Recognition*. Oxford University Press, 1995.
3. G. Bouchard and B. Triggs. The trade-off between generative and discriminative classifiers. In *COMPSTAT*, 2004.

4. G. Dorko and C. Schmid. Selection of scale invariant parts for object class recognition. In *ICCV*, 2003.
5. R. Fergus, P. Perona, and A. Zisserman. Object class recognition by unsupervised scale invariant learning. In *CVPR*, 2003.
6. B. M. ter Haar Romay, L. M. J. Florach, A. H. Salden, and M. A. Viergever. Representation of local geometry in the visual system. *Biological cybernetics*, 55:367–375, 1987.
7. A. Holub and P. Perona. A discriminative framework for modelling object classes. In *CVPR*, 2005.
8. T. Kadir and M. Brady. Scale, saliency and image description. *International Journal of Computer Vision*, 45(2):83–105, 2001.
9. J. J. Koenderink and A. J. van Doorn. Representation of local geometry in the visual system. *Biological Cybernetics*, 55:367–375, 1987.
10. S. Kumar and M. Hebert. Discriminative random fields: A discriminative framework for contextual interaction in classification. In *ICCV*, 2003.
11. D. Lowe. Distinctive image features from scale invariant keypoints. *International Journal of Computer Vision*, 60(2):91–110, 2004.
12. K. Mikolajczyk and C. Schmid. Scale and affine invariant interest point detectors. *International Journal of Computer Vision*, 60:63–86, 2004.
13. R. Neal P. Dayan, G. E. Hinton and R. S. Zemel. The helmholtz machine. *Neural Computation*, pages 1022–1037, 1995.
14. A. Y. Ng and M. I. Jordan. On discriminative vs. generative classifiers: A comparison of logistic regression and naive bayes. In *Advances in Neural Information Processing Systems 14*, 2002.
15. J. Pearl. *Probabilistic Reasoning in Intelligent Systems: Net- works of Plausible Inference*. Morgan Kaufmann Publishers, 1998.
16. I. Ulusoy and C. M. Bishop. Generative versus discriminative methods for object recognition. In *CVPR*, 2005.
17. M. Vidal-Naquet and S. Ullman. Object recognition with informative features and linear classification. In *ICCV*, 2003.
18. A. Bar-Hillel, T. Hertz, and D. Weinshall. Object class recognition by boosting a part-based model. In *CVPR*, 2005.
19. L. Xie and P. Perez. Slightly supervised learning of part-based appearance models. In *IEEE Workshop on Learning in CVPR*, 2004.

Synergistic Face Detection and Pose Estimation with Energy-Based Models

Margarita Osadchy[1], Yann Le Cun[2], and Matthew L. Miller[3]

[1] Computer Science Department,
University of Haifa,
Mount Carmel, Haifa 31905, Israel
rita@cs.haifa.ac.il
[2] The Courant Institute of Mathematical Sciences,
New York University,
715 Broadway, New York, NY 10003, USA
yann@cs.nyu.edu
[3] NEC Labs America,
4 Independence Way Princeton,
NJ 08540, USA
mlm@nec-labs.com

Abstract. We describe a novel method for real-time, simultaneous multi-view face detection and facial pose estimation. The method employs a convolutional network to map face images to points on a manifold, parametrized by pose, and non-face images to points far from that manifold. This network is trained by optimizing a loss function of three variables: image, pose, and face/non-face label. We test the resulting system, in a single configuration, on three standard data sets – one for frontal pose, one for rotated faces, and one for profiles – and find that its performance on each set is comparable to previous multi-view face detectors that can only handle one form of pose variation. We also show experimentally that the system's accuracy on *both* face detection and pose estimation is improved by training for the two tasks together.

1   Introduction

The detection of human faces in natural images and videos is a key component in a wide variety of applications of human-computer interaction, search and indexing, security, and surveillance. Many real-world applications would profit from *multi-view* detectors that can detect faces under a wide range of poses: looking left or right (yaw axis), up or down (pitch axis), or tilting left or right (roll axis).

In this paper we describe a novel method that not only detects faces independently of their poses, but simultaneously estimates those poses. The system is highly-reliable, runs at near real time (5 frames per second on standard hardware), and is robust against variations in yaw ($\pm 90°$), roll ($\pm 45°$), and pitch ($\pm 60°$).

The method is motivated by the idea that multi-view face detection and pose estimation are so closely related that they should not be performed separately.

J. Ponce et al. (Eds.): Toward Category-Level Object Recognition, LNCS 4170, pp. 196–206, 2006.

The tasks are related in the sense that they must be robust against the same sorts of variation: skin color, glasses, facial hair, lighting, scale, expressions, etc. We suspect that, when trained together, each task can serve as an inductive bias for the other, yielding better generalization or requiring fewer training examples [2].

To exploit the synergy between these two tasks, we train a convolutional network to map face images to points on a *face manifold*, and non-face images to points far away from that manifold. The manifold is parameterized by facial pose. Conceptually, we can view the pose parameter as a latent variable that can be inferred through an *energy-minimization process* [4]. To train the machine we derive a new type of *discriminative loss function* that is tailored to such detection tasks.

Previous Work: Learning-based approaches to face detection abound, including real-time methods [16], and approaches based on convolutional networks [15,3]. Most multi-view systems take a *view-based* approach, which involves building separate detectors for different views and either applying them in parallel [10,14,13,7] or using a pose estimator to select a detector [5]. Another approach is to estimate and correct in-plane rotations before applying a single pose-specific detector [12]. Closer to our approach is that of [8], in which a number of Support Vector Regressors are trained to approximate smooth functions, each of which has a maximum for a face at a particular pose. Another machine is trained to convert the resulting values to estimates of poses, and a third is trained to convert the values into a face/non-face score. The resulting system is very slow.

2   Integrating Face Detection and Pose Estimation

To exploit the posited synergy between face detection and pose estimation, we must design a system that integrates the solutions to the two problems. We hope to obtain better results on *both* tasks, so this should not be a mere cascaded system in which the answer to one problem is used to assist in solving the other. Both answers must be derived from one underlying analysis of the input, and both tasks must be trained together.

Our approach is to build a trainable system that can map raw images X to points in a low-dimensional space. In that space, we pre-define a *face manifold* $F(Z)$ that we parameterize by the pose Z. We train the system to map face images with known poses to the corresponding points on the manifold. We also train it to map non-face images to points far away from the manifold. Proximity to the manifold then tells us whether or not an image is a face, and projection to the manifold yields an estimate of the pose.

Parameterizing the Face Manifold: We will now describe the details of the parameterizations of the face manifold. Let's start with the simplest case of one pose parameter $Z = \theta$, representing, say, yaw. If we want to preserve the natural topology and geometry of the problem, the face manifold under yaw variations in the interval $[-90°, 90°]$ should be a half circle (with constant curvature). We embed this half-circle in a three-dimensional space using three equally-spaced shifted cosines.

$$F_i(\theta) = \cos(\theta - \alpha_i); \quad i = 1, 2, 3; \quad \theta = [-\frac{\pi}{2}, \frac{\pi}{2}]; \quad \alpha = \{-\frac{\pi}{3}, 0, \frac{\pi}{3}\} \quad (1)$$

A point on the face manifold parameterized by the yaw angle θ is $F(\theta) = [F_1(\theta), F_2(\theta), F_3(\theta)]$. When we run the network on an image X, it outputs a vector $G(X)$. The yaw angle $\overline{\theta}$ corresponding to the point on the manifold that is closest to $G(X)$ can be expressed analytically as:

$$\overline{\theta} = \arctan \frac{\sum_{i=1}^{3} G_i(X) \cos(\alpha_i)}{\sum_{i=1}^{3} G_i(X) \sin(\alpha_i)} \quad (2)$$

The point on the manifold closest to $G(X)$ is just $F(\overline{\theta})$.

$$F_{ij}(\theta, \phi) = \cos(\theta - \alpha_i) \cos(\phi - \beta_j); \quad i, j = 1, 2, 3; \quad (3)$$

For convenience, we rescale the roll angles to the range $[-90, 90]$ which allows us to set $\beta_i = \alpha_i$. With this parameterization, the manifold has constant curvature, which ensures that the effect of errors will be the same regardless of pose. Given a 9-dimensional output vector from the convolutional network $G_{ij}(X)$, we compute the corresponding yaw and roll angles $\overline{\theta}, \overline{\phi}$ as follows:

$$cc = \sum_{ij} G_{ij}(X) \cos(\alpha_i) \cos(\beta_j); \quad cs = \sum_{ij} G_{ij}(X) \cos(\alpha_i) \sin(\beta_j)$$
$$sc = \sum_{ij} G_{ij}(X) \sin(\alpha_i) \cos(\beta_j); \quad ss = \sum_{ij} G_{ij}(X) \sin(\alpha_i) \sin(\beta_j)$$
$$\overline{\theta} = 0.5(atan2(cs + sc, cc - ss) + atan2(sc - cs, cc + ss)) \quad (4)$$
$$\overline{\phi} = 0.5(atan2(cs + sc, cc - ss) - atan2(sc - cs, cc + ss))$$

The process can easily be extended to include pitch in addition to yaw and roll, as well as other parameters if necessary.

Note that the dimension of the face manifold is much lower than that of the embedding space. This gives ample space to represent non-faces away from the manifold. Having lots of free space to represent non-face images may be necessary, due to the considerable amount of variability in non-face images.

3   Learning Machine

To build a learning machine for the proposed approach we refer to the *Minimum Energy Machine* framework described in [4].

Energy Minimization Framework: We can view our system as a scalar-value function $E_W(Y, Z, X)$, where X and Z are as defined above, Y is a binary label ($Y = 1$ for face, $Y = 0$ for a non-face), and W is a parameter vector subject to learning. $E_W(Y, Z, X)$ can be interpreted as an *energy function* that measures the degree of compatibility between X, Z, Y. If X is a face with pose Z, then we want: $E_W(1, Z, X) \ll E_W(0, Z', X)$ for any pose Z', and $E_W(1, Z', X) \gg E_W(1, Z, X)$ for any pose $Z' \neq Z$.

Operating the machine consists in clamping X to the observed value (the image), and finding the values of Z and Y that minimize $E_W(Y, Z, X)$:

$$(\overline{Y}, \overline{Z}) = \mathrm{argmin}_{Y \in \{Y\}, \, Z \in \{Z\}} E_W(Y, Z, X) \quad (5)$$

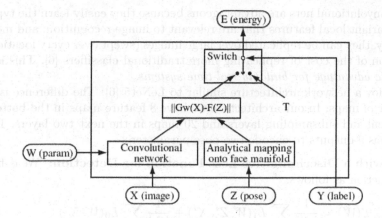

Fig. 1. Architecture of the Minimum Energy Machine

where $\{Y\} = \{0, 1\}$ and $\{Z\} = [-90, 90] \times [-45, 45]$ for yaw and roll variables. Although this inference process can be viewed probabilistically as finding the most likely configuration of Y and Z according to a model that attributes high probabilities to low-energy configurations (e.g. a Gibbs distribution), we view it as a non probabilistic decision making process. In other words, we make no assumption as to the finiteness of integrals over $\{Y\}$ and $\{Z\}$ that would be necessary for a properly normalized probabilistic model. This gives us considerable flexibility in the choice of the internal architecture of $E_W(Y, Z, X)$.

Our energy function for a face $E_W(1, Z, X)$ is defined as the distance between the point produced by the network $G_W(X)$ and the point with pose Z on the manifold $F(Z)$:

$$E_W(1, Z, X) = \|G_W(X) - F(Z)\| \qquad (6)$$

The energy function for a non-face $E_W(0, Z, X)$ is equal to a constant T that we can interpret as a threshold (it is independent of Z and X). The complete energy function is:

$$E_W(Y, Z, X) = Y\|G_W(X) - F(Z)\| + (1 - Y)T \qquad (7)$$

The architecture of the machine is depicted in Figure 1. Operating this machine (finding the output label and pose with the smallest energy) comes down to first finding: $\overline{Z} = \mathrm{argmin}_{Z \in \{Z\}} \|G_W(X) - F(Z)\|$, and then comparing this minimum distance, $\|G_W(X) - F(\overline{Z})\|$, to the threshold T. If it smaller than T, then X is classified as a face, otherwise X is classified as a non-face. This decision is implemented in the architecture as a *switch*, that depends upon the binary variable Y.

Convolutional Network: We employ a Convolutional Network as the basic architecture for the $G_W(X)$ image-to-face-space mapping function. Convolutional networks [6] are "end-to-end" trainable system that can operate on raw pixel images and learn low-level features and high-level representation in an integrated fashion. Convolutional nets are advantageous because they easily learn the types of shift-invariant local features that are relevant to image recognition; and more importantly, they can be replicated over large images (swept over every location) at a fraction of the cost of replicating more traditional classifiers [6]. This is a *considerable advantage for building real-time systems.*

We employ a network architecture similar to LeNet5 [6]. The difference is in the number of maps. In our architecture we have 8 feature maps in the bottom convolutional and subsampling layers and 20 maps in the next two layers. The last layer has 9 outputs to encode two pose parameters.

Training with a Discriminative Loss Function for Detection: We define the loss function as follows:

$$\mathcal{L}(W) = \frac{1}{|S_1|} \sum_{i \in S_1} L_1(W, Z^i, X^i) + \frac{1}{|S_0|} \sum_{i \in S_0} L_0(W, X^i) \qquad (8)$$

where S_1 is the set of training faces, S_0 the set of non-faces, $L_1(W, Z^i, X^i)$ and $L_0(W, X^i)$ are loss functions for a face sample (with a known pose) and non-face, respectively[1].

The loss $\mathcal{L}(W)$ should be designed so that its minimization for a particular positive training sample $(X^i, Z^i, 1)$, will make $E_W(1, Z^i, X^i) < E_W(Y, Z, X^i)$ for $Y \neq Y^i$ or $Z \neq Z^i$. To satisfy this, it is sufficient to make $E_W(1, Z^i, X^i) < E_W(0, \overline{Z}, X^i)$. For a particular negative training sample $(X^i, 0)$, minimizing the loss should make $E_W(1, Z, X^i) > E_W(0, Z, X^i) = T$ for any Z. To satisfy this, it is sufficient to make $E_W(1, \overline{Z}, X^i) > T$.

Let W be the current parameter value, and W' be the parameter value after an update caused by a single sample. To cause the machine to achieve the desired behavior, we need the parameter update to decrease the difference between the energy of the desired label and the energy of the undesired label. In our case, since $E_W(0, Z, X) = T$ is constant, the following condition on the update is sufficient to ensure the desired behavior:

Condition 1. *For a face example $(X, Z, 1)$, we must have:*

$$E_{W'}(1, Z, X) < E_W(1, Z, X)$$

For a non-face example $(X, 1)$, we must have:

$$E_{W'}(1, \overline{Z}, X) > E_W(1, \overline{Z}, X)$$

We choose the following forms for L_1 and L_0:

$$L_1(W, 1, Z, X) = E_W(1, Z, X)^2; \quad L_0(W, 0, X) = K \exp[-E(1, \overline{Z}, X)] \qquad (9)$$

where K is a positive constant.

---

[1] Although face samples whose pose is unknown can easily be accommodated, we will not discuss this possibility here.

Next we show that minimizing (9) with an incremental gradient-based algorithm will satisfy condition 1. With gradient-based optimization algorithms, the parameter update formula is of the form: $\delta W = W' - W = -\eta A \frac{\partial L}{\partial W}$. where A is a judiciously chosen symmetric positive semi-definite matrix, and η is a small positive constant.

For $Y = 1$ (face): An update step will change the parameter by

$$\delta W = -\eta A \frac{\partial E_W(1, Z, X)^2}{\partial W} = -2\eta E_W(1, Z, X) A \frac{\partial E_W(1, Z, X)}{\partial W}$$

To first order (for small values of η), the resulting change in $E_W(1, Z, X)$ is given by:

$$\left(\frac{\partial E_W(1, Z, X)}{\partial W} \right)^T \delta W =$$

$$-2\eta E_W(1, Z, X) \left(\frac{\partial E_W(1, Z, X)}{\partial W} \right)^T A \frac{\partial E_W(1, Z, X)}{\partial W} < 0$$

because $E_W(1, Z, X) > 0$ (it's a distance), and the quadratic form is positive. Therefore $E_{W'}(1, Z, X) < E_W(1, Z, X)$.

For $Y = 0$ (non-face): An update step will change the parameter by

$$\delta W = -\eta A \frac{\partial K \exp[-E(1, \overline{Z}, X)]}{\partial W} = \eta K \exp[-E_W(1, \overline{Z}, X)] \frac{\partial E_W(1, \overline{Z}, X)}{\partial W}$$

To first order (for small values of η), the resulting change in $E_W(1, \overline{Z}, X)$ is given by:

$$\left(\frac{\partial E_W(1, Z, X)}{\partial W} \right)^T \delta W =$$

$$\eta K \exp[-E_W(1, \overline{Z}, X)] \left(\frac{\partial E_W(1, \overline{Z}, X)}{\partial W} \right)^T A \frac{\partial E_W(1, \overline{Z}, X)}{\partial W} > 0$$

Therefore $E_{W'}(1, \overline{Z}, X) > E_W(1, \overline{Z}, X)$.

Running the Machine: Our detection system works on grayscale images and it applies the network to each image at a range of scales, stepping by a factor of $\sqrt{2}$. The network is replicated over the image at each scale, stepping by 4 pixels in x and y (this step size is a consequence of having two, 2x2 subsampling layers). At each scale and location, the network outputs are compared to the closest point on the manifold, and the system collects a list of all instances closer than our detection threshold. Finally, after examining all scales, the system identifies groups of overlapping detections in the list and discards all but the strongest (closest to the manifold) from each group. No attempt is made to combine detections or apply any voting scheme. We have implemented the system

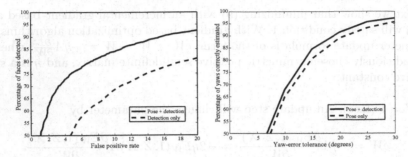

Fig. 2. Synergy test. Left: ROC curves for the pose-plus-detection and detection-only networks. Right: frequency with which the pose-plus-detection and pose-only networks correctly estimated the yaws within various error tolerances.

in C. The system can detect, locate, and estimate the pose of faces that are between 40 and 250 pixels high in a 640 × 480 image at roughly 5 frames per second on a 2.4GHz Pentium 4.

4   Experiments and Results

Using the above architecture, we built a detector to locate faces and estimate two pose parameters: yaw from left to right profile, and in-plane rotation from −45 to 45 degrees. The machine was trained to be robust against pitch variation.

In this section, we first describe the training regimen for this network, and then give the results of two sets of experiments. The first set of experiments tests whether training for the two tasks together improves performance on both. The second set allows comparisons between our system and other published multi-view detectors.

Training: Our training set consisted of 52, 850, 32x32-pixel faces from natural images collected at NEC Labs and hand annotated with appropriate facial poses (see [9] for a description of how the annotation was done). These faces were selected from a much larger annotated set to yield a roughly uniform distribution of poses from left profile to right profile, with as much variation in pitch as we could obtain. Our initial negative training data consisted of 52, 850 image patches chosen randomly from non-face areas of a variety of images. For our second set of tests, we replaced half of these with image patches obtained by running the initial version of the detector on our training images and collecting false detections. Each training image was used 5 times during training, with random variations in scale (from $x\sqrt{2}$ to $x(1 + \sqrt{2})$), in-plane rotation (±45°), brightness (±20), contrast (from 0.8 to 1.3).

To train the network, we made 9 passes through this data, though it mostly converged after about the first 6 passes. Training was performed using LUSH [1], and the total training time was about 26 hours on a 2Ghz Pentium 4. At the end of training, the network had converged to an equal error rate of 5% on the training data and 6% on a separate test set of 90,000 images.

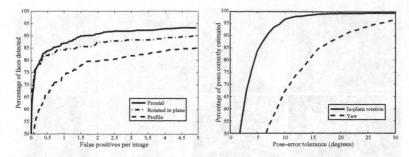

Fig. 3. Results on standard data sets. Left: ROC curves for our detector on the three data sets. The x axis is the average number of false positives per image over all three sets, so each point corresponds to a single detection threshold. Right: frequency with which yaw and roll are estimated within various error tolerances.

Synergy tests: The goal of the synergy test was to verify that both face detection and pose estimation benefit from learning and running in parallel. To test this claim we built three networks with almost identical architectures, but trained to perform different tasks. The first one was trained for simultaneous face detection and pose estimation (combined), the second was trained for detection only and the third for pose estimation only. The "detection only" network had only one output for indicating whether or not its input was a face. The "pose only" network was identical to the combined network, but trained on faces only (no negative examples). Figure 2 shows the results of running these networks on our 10,000 test images. In both these graphs, we see that the pose-plus-detection network had better performance, confirming that training for each task benefits the other.

Standard data sets: There is no standard data set that tests all the poses our system is designed to detect. There are, however, data sets that have been used to test more restricted face detectors, each set focusing on a particular variation in pose. By testing a single detector with all of these sets, we can compare our performance against published systems. As far as we know, we are the first to publish results for a single detector on all these data sets. The details of these sets are described below:

• MIT+CMU [14,11] – 130 images for testing frontal face detectors. We count 517 faces in this set, but the standard tests only use a subset of 507 faces, because 10 faces are in the wrong pose or otherwise not suitable for the test. (Note: about 2% of the faces in the standard subset are badly-drawn cartoons, which we do not intend our system to detect. Nevertheless, we include them in the results we report.)

• TILTED [12] – 50 images of frontal faces with in-plane rotations. 223 faces out of 225 are in the standard subset. (Note: about 20% of the faces in the standard subset are outside of the ±45° rotation range for which our system is designed. Again, we still include these in our results.)

Fig. 4. Some example face detections. Each white box shows the location of a detected face. The angle of each box indicates the estimated in-plane rotation. The black crosshairs within each box indicate the estimated yaw.

- PROFILE [13] – 208 images of faces in profile. There seems to be some disagreement about the number of faces in the standard set of annotations: [13] reports using 347 faces of the 462 that we found, [5] reports using 355, and we found 353 annotations. However, these discrepencies should not significantly effect the reported results.

We counted a face as being detected if 1) at least one detection lay within a circle centered on the midpoint between the eyes, with a radius equal to 1.25 times the distance from that point to the midpoint of the mouth, and 2) that detection came at a scale within a factor of two of the correct scale for the face's size. We counted a detection as a false positive if it did not lie within this range for any of the faces in the image, including those faces not in the standard subset.

The left graph in Figure 3 shows ROC curves for our detector on the three data sets. Figure 4 shows a few results on various poses. Table 1 shows our detection rates compared against other systems for which results were given on these data sets. The table shows that our results on the TILTED and PROFILE sets are similar to those of the two Jones & Viola detectors, and even approach those of the Rowley *et al* and Schneiderman & Kanade non-real-time detectors. Those detectors, however, are not designed to handle all variations in pose, and do not yield pose estimates.

The right side of Figure 3 shows our performance at pose estimation. To make this graph, we fixed the detection threshold at a value that resulted in about 0.5 false positives per image over all three data sets. We then compared the pose estimates for all detected faces (including those not in the standard subsets) against our manual pose annotations. Note that this test is more difficult than typical tests of pose estimation systems, where faces are first localized by hand. When we hand-localize these faces, 89% of yaws and 100% of in-plane rotations are correctly estimated to within 15°.

Table 1. Comparisons of our results with other multi-view detectors. Each column shows the detection rates for a given average number of false positives per image (these rates correspond to those for which other authors have reported results). Results for real-time detectors are shown in bold. Note that ours is the only single detector that can be tested on all data sets simultaneously.

Data set →	TILTED		PROFILE		MIT+CMU	
False positives per image →	4.42	26.90	.47	3.36	.50	1.28
Our detector	**90%**	**97%**	**67%**	**83%**	**83%**	**88%**
Jones & Viola [5] (tilted)	**90%**	**95%**	x		x	
Jones & Viola [5] (profile)	x		**70%**	**83%**	x	
Rowley et al [11]	89%	96%	x		x	
Schneiderman & Kanade [13]	x		86%	93%	x	

5   Conclusion

The system we have presented here integrates detection and pose estimation by training a convolutional network to map faces to points on a manifold, parameterized by pose, and non-faces to points far from the manifold. The network is trained by optimizing a loss function of three variables – image, pose, and face/non-face label. When the three variables match, the energy function is trained to have a small value, when they do not match, it is trained to have a large value.

This system has several desirable properties:

- The use of a convolutional network makes it fast. At typical webcam resolutions, it can process 5 frames per second on a 2.4Ghz Pentium 4.
- It is robust to a wide range of poses, including variations in yaw up to $\pm 90°$, in-plane rotation up to $\pm 45°$, and pitch up to $\pm 60°$. This has been verified with tests on three standard data sets, each designed to test robustness against a single dimension of pose variation.
- At the same time that it detects faces, it produces estimates of their pose. On the standard data sets, the estimates of yaw and in-plane rotation are within $15°$ of manual estimates over 80% and 95% of the time, respectively.

We have shown experimentally that our system's accuracy at *both* pose estimation and face detection is increased by training for the two tasks together.

References

1. L. Bottou and Y. LeCun. *The Lush Manual.* http://lush.sf.net, 2002.
2. R. Caruana. Multitask learning. *Machine Learning*, 28:41–75, 1997.
3. C. Garcia and M. Delakis. A neural architecture for fast and robust face detection. *IEEE-IAPR Int. Conference on Pattern Recognition*, pages 40–43, 2002.
4. F. J. Huang and Y. LeCun. Loss functions for discriminative training of energy-based graphical models. Technical report, Courant Institute of Mathematical Science, NYU, June 2004.

5. M. Jones and P. Viola. Fast multi-view face detection. Technical Report TR2003-96, Mitsubishi Electric Research Laboratories, 2003.
6. Y. LeCun, L. Bottou, Y. Bengio, and P. Haffner. Gradient-based learning applied to document recognition. *Proceedings of the IEEE*, 86(11):2278–2324, November 1998.
7. S. Z. Li, L. Zhu, Z. Zhang, A. Blake, H. Zhang, and H. Shum. Statistical learning of multi-view face detection. In *Proceedings of the 7th European Conference on Computer Vision-Part IV*, 2002.
8. Y. Li, S. Gong, and H. Liddell. Support vector regression and classification based multi-view face detection and recognition. In *Face and Gesture*, 2000.
9. H. Moon and M. L. Miller. Estimating facial pose from sparse representation. In *International Conference on Image Processing*, Singapore, 2004.
10. A. Pentland, B. Moghaddam, and T. Starner. View-based and modular eigenspaces for face recognition. In *CVPR*, 1994.
11. H. A. Rowley, S. Baluja, and T. Kanade. Neural network-based face detection. *PAMI*, 20:22–38, 1998.
12. H. A. Rowley, S. Baluja, and T. Kanade. Rotation invariant neural network-based face detection. In *Computer Vision and Pattern Recognition*, 1998.
13. H. Schneidermn and T. Kanade. A statistical method for 3d object detection applied to faces and cars. In *Computer Vision and Pattern Recognition*, 2000.
14. K. Sung and T. Poggio. Example-based learning of view-based human face detection. *PAMI*, 20:39–51, 1998.
15. R. Vaillant, C. Monrocq, and Y. LeCun. Original approach for the localisation of objects in images. *IEE Proc on Vision, Image, and Signal Processing*, 141(4):245–250, August 1994.
16. P. Viola and M. Jones. Rapid object detection using a boosted cascade of simple features. In *Proceedings IEEE Conf. on Computer Vision and Pattern Recognition*, pages 511–518, 2001.

Generic Visual Categorization Using Weak Geometry

Gabriela Csurka, Christopher R. Dance, Florent Perronnin,
and Jutta Willamowski

Xerox Research Centre Europe
6 Rue de Maupertuis, 38240 Meylan, France
{gsurka,cdance,fperronn,willamow}@xrce.xerox.com

Abstract. In the first part of this chapter we make a general presentation of the bag-of-keypatches approach to generic visual categorization (GVC). Our approach is inspired by the bag-of-words approach to text categorization. This method is able to identify the object content of natural images while generalizing across variations inherent to the object class. To obtain a visual vocabulary insensitive to viewpoint and illumination, rotation or affine invariant orientation histogram descriptors of image patches are vector quantized. Each image is then represented by one visual word occurrence histogram. To classify the images we use one-against-all SVM classifiers and choose the best ranked category. The main advantages of the method are that it is simple, computationally efficient and intrinsically invariant. We obtained excellent results as well for multi-class categorization as for object detection.

In the second part we improve the categorizer by incorporating geometric information. Based on scale, orientation or closeness of the keypatches we can consider a large number of simple geometrical relationships, each of which can be considered as a simplistic classifier. We select from this multitude of classifiers (several millions in our case) and combine them effectively with the original classifier. Results are shown on a new challenging 10 class dataset.

1 Introduction

The proliferation of digital imaging sensors in mobile phones and consumer-level cameras is producing a growing number of large digital image collections and increasing the pervasiveness of images on the web and in other documents. To search and manage such collections it is useful to have access to high-level information about objects contained in the images. We are therefore interested in recognizing several objects or image categories within a multi-class categorization system, but not in the localization of the objects which is unnecessary for most applications involving tagging and search. In this chapter we describe a generic visual categorization (GVC) system which is sufficiently generic to cope with many object types simultaneously and which can readily be extended to new categories. It can handle variations in view, background clutter, lighting and occlusion as well as intra-class variations.

J. Ponce et al. (Eds.): Toward Category-Level Object Recognition, LNCS 4170, pp. 207–224, 2006.
© Springer-Verlag Berlin Heidelberg 2006

Before describing the approach we underline the distinction of visual categorization from three related problems:

- *Recognition*: This concerns the identification of particular object instances. For instance, recognition would distinguish between images of two structurally distinct cups, while categorization would place them in the same class.
- *Content Based Image Retrieval*: This refers to the process of retrieving images on the basis of low-level image features, given a query image or manually constructed description of these low-level features. Such descriptions frequently have little relation to the semantic content of the image.
- *Detection*: This refers to deciding whether or not a member of one visual category is present in a given image. While it would be possible to perform generic categorization by applying a detector for each class of interest to a given image, this approach becomes inefficient given a large number of classes. In contrast to the technique proposed in this paper, most existing detection techniques require precise manual alignment of the training images and the segregation of these images into different views, neither of which is necessary in our case.

Our generic visual categorization system is a bag-of-keypatches approach which was motivated by an analogy to learning methods using the bag-of-words representation for text categorization [9,24,13]. In the bag-of-words representation, a text document is encoded as a histogram of the number of occurrences of each word. Similarly, one can characterize an image by a histogram of visual word counts. The visual vocabulary provides a "mid-level" representation which helps to bridge the semantic gap between the low-level features extracted from an image and the high-level concepts to be categorized [1]. However, the main difference from text categorization is that there is no given vocabulary for images. Instead we generate a visual vocabulary automatically from a training set.

The idea of adapting text categorization approaches to visual categorization is not new. Zhu *et al* [27] investigated the vector quantization of small square image windows, which they called keyblocks. They showed that these features produced more "semantics-oriented" results than color and texture based approaches, when combined with analogues of the well-known vector-, histogram-, and n-gram-models of text retrieval. In contrast to our approach, their keyblocks do not possess any invariance properties. Our visual vocabulary [4] is obtained by clustering rotation or affine invariant orientation histogram descriptors using the K-means algorithm. In a similar way Sivic and Zisserman [23] used vector quantized SIFT descriptors of shape adapted regions and maximally stable regions to localize all the occurrences of a given object in a video sequence.

In these cases each centroid corresponds to a visual word and, to build a histogram, each feature vector is assigned to its closest centroid. In [8], Hsu and Chang argue that the clusters obtained with K-means have a high correlation with the low-level features but a weak correlation with the concepts. They devised a visual cue cluster construction based on the information bottleneck principle. More recently soft clustering using Gaussian Mixture Model (GMM) was proposed as an alternative to K-means [5,19]. In this case, a low-level feature is not assigned to one visual word but to all words probabilistically, resulting in a continuous histogram representation.

Others have explored the post-processing of K-means clustering. For instance Sivic *et al* [22] use Probabilistic Latent Semantic Analysis (PLSA) to discover topics in a corpus of unlabelled images. Test images were then categorized based on the most relevant topic.

In order to improve the accuracy of our system we further exploit a boosting approach based on keypatches and simple geometrical relationships (similar scales, similar orientation, closeness) between them. We chose to adopt the boosting approach because there are many possible geometric relationships and boosting offers an effective way to select from this multitude of possible features. Boosting was used with success in [16] to detect the presence of bikes, persons, cars or airplanes against background. However their approach differs from ours as they do not include any geometry and consider every appearance descriptor without considering a vocabulary.

The main advantage of our approach is that geometric constraints are introduced as weak conditions in contrast to others such as [6,11], where due to the use of relatively strong geometric models, such previous methods requires the alignment and segregation of different views of objects in the dataset.

Several other categorization approaches have recently been developed that are based on image segmentation [2,12,17,3], rather than the interest point descriptors. In [2] geometry has been included through generative MRF models of neighboring relations between segmented regions. In contrast we prefer to take a discriminative classifier approach in order to optimize overall accuracy.

The remainder of this paper is organized as follows: section 2 describes the original bag of keypatches approach; in section 3 we introduce an alternative based on the boosting framework; in section 4 we then describe how to incorporate weak geometry in the boosting approach; we present experimental results in section 5 and conclude in section 6.

2   The Bag-of-Keypatch Approach

The main steps of the bag-of-keypatches approach introduced in [4] are as follows (see also Figure 1):

- Detect image patches and assign each of them to one of a set of predetermined clusters (a visual vocabulary) on the basis of their appearance descriptors.
- Construct a bag-of-keypatches by counting the number of patches assigned to each cluster.
- Apply a multi-class classifier, treating the bag-of-keypatches as the feature vector, and thus determine which categories to assign to the image. The multi-class classifier is built from a combination of one-against-all classifiers.

The extracted descriptors of image patches should be invariant to the variations that are irrelevant to the categorization task (viewpoint change, lighting

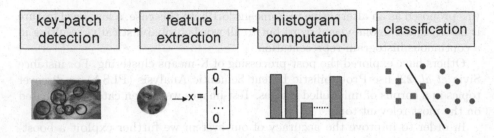

Fig. 1. The main steps of the bag-of-keypatches approach

variations and occlusions) but rich enough to carry all necessary information to be discriminative at the category level. We used Lowe's SIFT approach [14] to detect and describe image patches. This produces scale-invariant circular patches that are associated with 128-dimensional feature vectors of Gaussian derivatives. While in [4] we used affine invariant elliptical patches [15], similar performance was obtained with circular patches. Moreover, the use of circular patches makes it simpler to deal with geometric issues.

The visual vocabulary was constructed using the K-means algorithm applied to a set of over 10000 patches obtained from a set of images that was completely independent from the images used to train or test the classifier. We are not interested in a *correct clustering* in the sense of feature distributions, but rather in an accurate categorization. Therefore, to overcome the initialization dependence of K-means, we run it several times with different initial cluster centers and select the final clustering giving the highest categorization accuracy using an SVM classifier (without any geometric properties) on a subset of the dataset.

For categorization we use the SVM which finds the hyperplane that separates two-class data with maximal margin [26]. The margin is defined as the distance of the closest training point to the separating hyperplane. The SVM decision function can be expressed as:

$$f(\mathbf{x}) = \text{sign}(\sum_i y_i \alpha_i K(\mathbf{x}, \mathbf{x}_i) + b)$$

where $\mathbf{x}_i$ are the training features from data space and $y_i \in \{-1, 1\}$ is the label of $\mathbf{x}_i$. The parameters α_i are zero for most i, so the sum is taken only over a selected set of $\mathbf{x}_i$ known as support vectors. It can be shown that the support vectors are those feature vectors lying nearest to the separating hyperplane.

In this chapter, the input features $\mathbf{x}_i$ are the binned histograms formed by the number of occurrences of keypatches in the input image. K is a kernel function corresponding to an inner product between two transformed feature vectors, usually in a high and possibly infinite dimensional space. In the experiments described here we used a linear kernel, which is the dot product of $\mathbf{x}$ and $\mathbf{x}_i$.

In order to apply the SVM to multi-class problems we took the one-against-all approach. Given an m-class problem, we trained m SVM's, each of which distinguishes images from some category i from images from all the other $m-1$

categories j not equal to i. Given a query image, we assigned it to the class with
the largest SVM output.

3   The Boosting Approach

An alternative to the SVM classifier is the boosting approach. Here we exploit
the generalized version of the AdaBoost algorithm described in [21]. Boosting is a
method of finding an accurate classifier H by combining M simpler classifiers h_m:

$$H(\mathbf{x}) = \Big(\sum_{m=1}^{M} \alpha_m h_m(\mathbf{x}) \Big) / \Big(\sum_{m=1}^{M} \alpha_m \Big). \tag{1}$$

Each simpler classifier $h_m(\mathbf{x}) \in [-1,1]$ needs only to be moderately accurate and
is therefore known as a *weak classifier*. They are chosen from a classifier space
to maximize correlation[1] of the predictions and labels:

$$r_m = \sum_i D^m(i) h_m(\mathbf{x}_i) y_i,$$

where $D^m(i)$ is a set of weights (distribution) over the training set. At each step
the weights are updated by increasing the weights of the incorrectly predicted
training examples:

$$D^{m+1}(i) = D^m(i) \exp\{-\alpha_m y_i h_m(\mathbf{x}_i)\}/Z_m \tag{2}$$

where

$$\alpha_m = \frac{1}{2} \log \frac{1 + r_m}{1 - r_m} \tag{3}$$

and Z_m is a normalization constant, such that $\sum_i D^{m+1}(i) = 1$.

To define the weak classifiers we consider the same inputs as for the SVM,
i.e. the binned histograms $\mathbf{x}_i$. The simplest keypatch-based weak classifier $h^{k,T}$
counts the number of patches whose SIFT features belong to cluster k, which is
equivalent to comparing $\mathbf{x}_i^k$ to some threshold T. If this number is at least T,
then the classifier output is 1, otherwise -1:

$$h^{k,T}(\mathbf{x}_i) = \begin{cases} 1 \text{ if } \mathbf{x}_i^k \geq T \\ -1 \text{ otherwise} \end{cases}.$$

We may build similar weak classifiers $h^{kl,T}$ from a pair of keypatch types k, l. If
at least T keypatches of both types are observed, then the classifier output is 1:

$$h^{kl,T}(\mathbf{x}_i) = \begin{cases} 1 \text{ if } \mathbf{x}_i^k \geq T \text{ and } \mathbf{x}_i^l \geq T \\ -1 \text{ otherwise} \end{cases}.$$

---

[1] This is equivalent to minimizing the weighted training error which is equal to
$(1 - r_m)/2$.

In practice we select weak classifiers by searching over a predefined set of thresholds such as $\{1, 5, 10\}$. The opposite weak classifier $h^{k,\bar{T}}$ can also be defined by inverting the inequality $(\mathbf{x}^k < T)$. Four such definitions are possible for pairs of keypatches $h^{kl,T}$, $h^{kl,\bar{T}}$, $h^{kl,T\bar{T}}$ and $h^{kl,\bar{T}T}$, e.g:

$$h^{kl,T\bar{T}}(\mathbf{x}_i) = \begin{cases} 1 \text{ if } \mathbf{x}_i^k \geq T \text{ and } \mathbf{x}_i^l < T \\ -1 \text{ otherwise} \end{cases}.$$

In practice, we search over the full set of different possibilities when working with weak classifiers and refer to them collectively as h^k and h^{kl}. Obviously, it would be possible to further extend the definition for pairs to applying a different threshold to each keypatch type (T_k and T_l). In practice, we avoid this as it results in a prohibitively large number of possible weak classifiers.

4   Incorporating Geometric Information

In this section we describe some ways to construct geometric weak classifiers. As input, we assume each patch i in a query image has been labeled according to its appearance via the index of the cluster centre k_i to which it is assigned. Each patch is associated with its orientation θ_i and a ball (circular patch) B_i which has center position p_i and scale σ_i.

A simple way to incorporate geometrical information in weak classifiers depending on one keypatch is to threshold the number of interest points belonging to a cluster k and having a particular *orientation*:

$$h_\theta^{k,T}(I) = \begin{cases} 1 \text{ if } \exists \theta \text{ such that } |\{i \in \mathcal{P}_I : k_i = k, \theta_i = \theta\}| \geq T \\ -1 \text{ otherwise} \end{cases}$$

where $|A|$ denotes the cardinality of the set A and $\mathcal{P}_I$ denotes the set of patches in image I.

Note that a large number of different orientations are produced by the interest point detectors. Therefore we exploit a coarse quantization of the orientations into eight bins. Two keypatches are considered to have the same orientation if they fall into the same bin[2]. This does not constitute exact orientation invariance, as a small rotation could cause two keypatches in one bin to move to different bins. However, this approach is more efficient than directly measuring and thresholding the difference in orientations $\|\theta_i - \theta_j\|$ between pairs of keypatches.

Likewise, we define sets of weak classifiers that count the number of keypatches with the same *scale* or a set that count patches with both the same *scale and orientation*. The scale bins are selected with logarithmic spacing, in order to approximate scale invariance. Collectively[3] these classifiers are denoted by $h_\theta^k, h_\sigma^k, h_{\sigma,\theta}^k$.

---

[2] The equality in the notation $\theta_i = \theta$ should be interpreted in this way.

[3] Considering similar threshold reversals as for h^k and h^{kl}, e.g. $h_\theta^{k,\bar{T}}$ and $h_{\sigma,\theta}^{kl,\bar{T}T}$.

$$h_\sigma^{y,5},\ h_{\sigma\theta}^{y,4},\ h_\sigma^{ry,2},\ h_\theta^{ry,5},\ h_{\sigma\theta}^{ry,2},\ h_{y\cap r}^1\ \text{and}\ h_{y\in r}^1 = 1$$
$$h^{r,6},\ h_\theta^{y,6},\ h^{ry,6},\ h_{\sigma=}^{ry,1},\ h_{\theta=}^{ry,1},\ h_{\sigma\theta=}^1\ \text{and}\ h_{r\subset r}^1 = -1$$

Fig. 2. Examples of weak classifiers on a typical image for keypatches of type r, y (red or yellow). For clarity, only the patches of type r and y are shown. In these examples, the threshold T on which the weak classifiers depend has been chosen as large as possible for output 1 (first row) and as small as possible for output -1 (second row).

Another way to incorporate geometry is to count the *number of interest points in the ball* around a keypatch of a given type. This count is made irrespective of the type of keypatches in the ball. As with the other weak classifiers, this property is invariant to shift, scaling and rotation. In a given image, there may be multiple keypatches of a given type containing different numbers of points. We define h_B^k in terms of the keypatch of type k with the maximum number of points in its ball:

$$h_B^{k,T}(I) = \begin{cases} 1 \text{ if } \exists i \text{ such that } k_i = k \text{ and } \left|\{j \in \mathcal{P}_I : p_j \in B_i\}\right| \geq T \\ -1 \text{ otherwise} \end{cases}$$

where $p_j \in B_i$ means that the center of the patch j is inside of the ball B_i defined by the patch i.

Taking two types of keypatches k and l into consideration, there are more ways to introduce geometry. Classifiers based on common scale or orientation can be extended in two obvious ways. Firstly we can require that the patches of type k and those of type l have *identical* scale and/or orientation, giving $h_{\sigma=}^{kl}, h_{\theta=}^{kl}, h_{\sigma\theta=}^{kl}$. Alternatively we can allow each type to have their own independent scales or

Table 1. Complete list of weak classifiers investigated. $p \propto q$ indicates that p is the closest point to q and $\aleph_{p_j}^N$ is the set of the N closest neighbors of p_j.

h	$h = \begin{cases} 1 \text{ if this quantity} \geq T \\ -1 \text{ otherwise} \end{cases}$	h	$h = \begin{cases} 1 \text{ if this quantity} \geq T \\ -1 \text{ otherwise} \end{cases}$
$h_\sigma^{k,T}$	$\max_\sigma \left| \{ i : k_i = k, \sigma_i = \sigma \} \right|$	$h_{\sigma\theta}^{k,T}$	$\max_{\sigma,\theta} \left| \{ i : k_i = k, \sigma_i = \sigma, \theta_i = \theta \} \right|$
$h_\sigma^{kl,T}$	$\min_{u \in \{k,l\}} \max_\sigma \left| \{ i : k_i = u, \sigma_i = \sigma \} \right|$	$h_{\sigma\theta}^{kl,T}$	$\min_{u \in \{k,l\}} \max_{\sigma,\theta} \left| \{ i : k_i = u, \sigma_i = \sigma, \theta_i = \theta \} \right|$
$h_\theta^{k,T}$	$\max_\theta \left| \{ i : k_i = k, \theta_i = \theta \} \right|$	$h_{\sigma\theta=}^{kl,T}$	$\max_{\sigma,\theta} \min_{u \in \{k,l\}} \left| \{ i : k_i = u, \sigma_i = \sigma, \theta_i = \theta \} \right|$
$h_\theta^{kl,T}$	$\min_{u \in \{k,l\}} \max_\theta \left| \{ i : k_i = u, \theta_i = \theta \} \right|$	$h_{k \in l}^T$	$\left| \{ j : k_j = l, \exists k_i = k, p_i \in B_j \} \right|$
$h_{\sigma=}^{kl,T}$	$\max_\sigma \min_{u \in \{k,l\}} \left| \{ i : k_i = u, \sigma_i = \sigma \} \right|$	$h_{k \subset l}^T$	$\left| \{ j : k_j = l, \exists k_i = k, B_i \subset B_j \} \right|$
$h_{\theta=}^{kl,T}$	$\max_\theta \min_{u \in \{k,l\}} \left| \{ i : k_i = u, \theta_i = \theta \} \right|$	$h_{k \cap l}^T$	$\left| \{ j : k_i = l, \exists k_i = k, B_i \cap B_j \neq \emptyset \} \right|$
$h_B^{k,T}$	$\max_i \left| \{ j : k_i = k, p_j \in B_i \} \right|$	$h_{k \propto l}^T$	$\left| \{ j : k_j = l, \exists k_i = k, p_i \propto p_j \} \right|$
$h_B^{kl,T}$	$\max_i \min_{u \in \{k,l\}} \left| \{ j : k_i = u, p_j \in B_i \} \right|$	$h_{k \in \aleph_i^N}^T$	$\left| \{ j : k_j = l, \exists k_i = k, p_i \in \aleph_{p_j}^N \} \right|$

orientations, giving $h_\sigma^{kl}, h_\theta^{kl}, h_{\sigma\theta}^{kl}$. The latter corresponds to a Boolean combination of single point classifiers, e.g. h_σ^k and h_σ^l.

A weak classifier h_B^{kl} can be constructed similarly to h_B^k that checks for the existence of a pair of interest points labeled k, l such that both of them have at least T interest points inside their balls.

We additionally consider five other ways of exploiting the position information associated with patches:

- $h_{k \in l}$ tests if there are at least T keypatches labeled l which contain an interest point labeled k within their ball.
- $h_{k \subset l}$ tests if there are at least T keypatches labeled l whose balls contain the whole ball of an interest point labeled k.
- $h_{k \cap l}$ tests if there are at least T keypatches labeled l whose balls intersect with the ball of at least one interest point labeled k.
- $h_{k \propto l}$ tests if there are at least T keypatches labeled l such that their closest neighboring interest points in the image are labeled k.
- $h_{k \in \aleph_i^N}$ tests if there are at least T keypatch labeled l such that there exist a keypatch labeled k among its N closest neighbors.

Fig. 3. Examples from our 10 class dataset

The set of weak classifiers we considered is summarized in Table 1 and Figure 2 illustrates some of them. Of course there are a lot of other possibilities that could be experimented with.

5 Results

This section presents some results from our experiments. First we compare our bag-of-keypatch approach with the method described in [6]. Therefore we used the object classes from their FPZ dataset that are freely available, i.e. five object classes - 1074 airplane side images, 651 car rear images, 720 car side images, 450 frontal face images, and 826 motorbike side images - and a set of 451 background images.

The second set of experiments were done on a more challenging in-house dataset. This test was made to test larger number of classes, more variable poses and intra-class variations and significant amounts of background clutter. The images have resolutions between 0.3 and 2 mega-pixels and were acquired with a diverse set of cameras. The images are color but only the luminance component is used in our method. They were gathered by XRCE and Graz University. This dataset[4] contains 3084 images from 10 categories. The number of images per class are: bikes (237), boats (434), books (270), cars (307), chairs (346), flowers (242), phones (250), road signs (211), shoes (525) and soft toys (262). Figure 3 shows some images from this database.

We used the confusion matrix (4) to evaluate the multi-class classifiers and the overall correct rate (5) for the object detection:

$$M_{ij} = \frac{\left|\{I \in \mathbf{C}_j : H_i(I) \geq H_m(I), \forall m\}\right|}{|\mathbf{C}_j|}, \tag{4}$$

and

$$R = 1 - \frac{\sum_{j=1}^{N_c} |\mathbf{C}_j| M_{jj}}{\sum_{j=1}^{N_c} |\mathbf{C}_j|} \tag{5}$$

where N_c is the number of considered classes, $i, j \in \{1, \cdots, N_c\}$, $\mathbf{C}_j$ is the set of test images from category j and $H_m(I)$ is the real output of the classifier H_m which was trained to distinguish class m from the rest of the classes.

Vocabulary size. There exist methods allowing to automatically select the number of clusters for K-means. For example, Pelleg *et al* [18] use cluster splitting, where the splitting decision depend on the Bayesian Information Criterion. However, in the present case we do not really know anything about the density or the compactness of our clusters. Moreover, we are not even interested in a "correct clustering" in the sense of feature distributions, but rather in accurate categorization. We therefore simply compare error rates for different values of K.

Figure 4 presents the overall error rates using the bag-of-keypatches approach on our in-house dataset as a function of the number of clusters K. Each point in Figure 4 is the "best"[5] of 10 random trials of K-means. We can notice that the error rate only improves slightly as we move from k = 1000 to k = 2500. We therefore assert that k = 1000 presents a good trade-off between accuracy and speed and in all of our experiments we worked with the "best" vocabulary of size 1000.

Object Detection. Table 2 compares our results with the ones obtained by Fergus *et al* as far as they are available from their paper [6] on the FPZ dataset. They were obtained using 2-fold cross-validation and the correct rates reported correspond to the equal error operating point. As they did, we train our classifiers to recognize foreground images, i.e. images belonging to the considered class, and reject background images. The difference between SVM_1 and SVM_2 is that to build the visual vocabulary (K-means) in the former case we used a subset of images from the FPZ database and in the latter case a completely independent image set. We can observe only a slight difference between the performances of SVM_1 and SVM_2, showing a low influence of the initial sample feature set on the classification results.

---

[4] The dataset is publicly available on ftp://ftp.xrce.xerox.com/pub/ftp-ipc
[5] Best in the sense of lowest empirical risk in categorization [26].

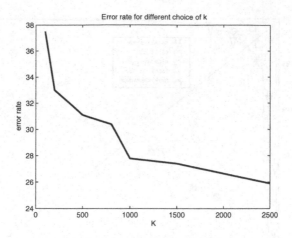

Fig. 4. The lowest overall error rate (percentage) found for different choices of k

Table 2. Correct rates for all classes obtained in 2-fold cross-validation at the equal error rate point by Fergus *et al* (FPZ) with our bag-of-keypatches method (SVM_i) and a PLSA based approach ($PLSA$) described in [22]. The best results for each class are shown in bold face.

method	Airplanes	Cars(rear)	Cars(side)	Faces	Motorbikes
FPZ	90.2	N/A	**88.5**	96.4	92.5
SVM_1	**97.1**	**98.6**	87.3	**99.3**	**98**
SVM_2	96.4	97.9	86.1	98.9	97.3
$PLSA$	96.6	88.1	N/A	94.7	84.6

Except for cars (side) all the classifiers trained with our method perform much better, no matter which set of keypatches we use. The small difference on the cars (side) dataset is probably not significant. One possible reason why we do not perform so well on this category is that the cars (side) images are small and contain few keypatches (only about 50 keypatches compared with 500-1000 for the other classes).

Figure 5 shows the ROC curves for the classifiers obtained for SVM_1 with the different classes using 2-fold cross-validation. It shows that even for classifiers with a very small false positive rate the recall is very high.

Multi-class Classifier. Tables 3 and 4 report the results we obtain using our method for training a multi-class classifier on the above mentioned five-class dataset. Table 3 shows the results with 2-fold cross-validation. This allows to compare the results with those from the object detection case (Table 2). It shows that in all cases except cars (side) the correct rates observed in the multi-class case are inferior to those obtained in the object detection case. Again this might be linked to the small number of keypatches present in the images belonging to this category.

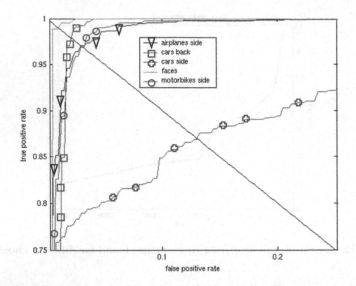

Fig. 5. Zoomed-in view of the ROC curves obtained with keypatch set 2. The x-axis corresponds to false positive rate (1-precision), while the y-axis corresponds to the true positive rate (recall). The diagonal indicates the equal error rate (false negative rate = false positive rate).

Table 3. Overall correct rates for all classes obtained with 2-fold cross-validation with the different keypatch sets

method	Airplanes	Cars(rear)	Cars(side)	Faces	Motorbikes
SVM_1	96.4	97.1	97.1	92.4	92.4
SVM_2	94.4	94.6	97.3	89.8	90.5
$SREZF1$	95.2	98.1	N/A	94	83.6
$SREZF2$	97.5	99.3	N/A	99.5	96.5

In two last rows of Table 3 ($SREZF1$ and $SREZF2$) we show the recent results obtained by Sivic et al [22] on this dataset using PLSA. They do not used cars (side) images. The inclusion of cars (side) is belived to confuse the classifier and significantly increase error rates.

They first used the training images (one fold) plus about 200 background images without their label and searched for 7 topics. In this way the PLSA discovered 3 topics related to background content and 4 topics corresponding to the 4 categories. In $SREZF1$ the test images were assigned to the most probable of the 7 topics. In $SREZF2$ test images were assigned only to the most probable of the 4 topics corresponding to categories (excluding the background topic from the ranking).

The results shows that using PLSA for automatic topic detection is promising and has the advantage that it do not need individual labeling of images. However it is difficult to judge how it scales with the number of categories and as shown in Table 2 it works less well for binary classification against background.

Table 4. Confusion matrix for SVM_1 with 10-fold cross validation using a linear kernel

True classes →	Airplanes	Cars(rear)	Cars(side)	Faces	Motorbikes
Airplanes	**96.7**	0.2	0.6	2	3.4
Cars(rear)	0.4	**98.2**	1	1.1	2.4
Cars(side)	0.2	0	**97.6**	0.2	0.3
Faces	1	0.6	0.1	**94.2**	0.6
Motorbikes	1.8	1.1	0.8	2.4	**93.4**
Mean ranks	1.04	1.03	1.06	1.06	1.09

Table 4 shows the confusion matrix and the mean ranks[6] for SVM_1 with 10-fold cross-validation for comparison. The results obtained with 10-fold cross-validation outperform those obtained with 2-fold cross-validation. This is natural, as the number of training images increases.

10 Class Dataset. For the experiments with our 10 class database we only used the independently built visual vocabulary. Therefore in the following we ignore the subscript 2 from SVM_2. Table 5 shows the confusion matrix and the mean ranks obtained for this dataset using a 5-fold cross-validation.

Table 5. Confusion matrix and mean ranks for SVM

classes	bikes	boats	books	cars	chairs	flowers	phones	r. signs	shoes	s. toys
bikes	**69.2**	1.7	1.9	1	5.3	1.2	0.4	3.2	1.2	1.3
boats	3.7	**79.3**	5.2	4.6	7.7	1.7	1.2	1.3	1.8	1.7
books	1.3	2.2	**70.3**	2.4	2.7	0.6	4.6	4.5	0.6	1.7
cars	4.2	3.7	2.4	**72.1**	8.3	0.3	3.1	3.1	1.5	0.8
chairs	10.8	3.9	5.3	5.4	**58.8**	2.2	2.7	5.8	1.3	1.1
flowers	1.2	1.2	1.3	1.6	1.2	**86.7**	1.6	1.6	0.7	0.8
phones	1.9	0.7	4.1	3.7	2.8	1.4	**70.4**	1.7	1.3	1.4
road signs	1.7	1.9	2.4	1.9	4.9	1.1	2.7	**69**	1.4	1.2
shoes	3.6	5.2	4.5	6.4	6.7	1.6	11.6	8.3	**86.3**	10.8
soft toys	2.4	0.2	2.6	0.9	1.6	3.2	1.7	1.5	3.9	**79.2**
mean ranks	1.5	1.3	1.5	1.3	1.9	1.3	1.9	1.7	1.3	1.2

Incorporating Geometry Information. Table 6 shows the correct classification rates (M_{ii}) for each class obtained with the boosting approach without adding geometric information. The first row corresponds to the approach h_k where only single keypatch based weak classifiers were selected, and the second row shows results of the $h_{k,l}$ approach corresponding to weak classifiers based on pair of keypatches. In the third row we show the results of the SVM (the diagonal of the confusion matrix shown in Table 5) for comparison. All results were obtained by 5-fold cross-validation.

---

[6] These are the mean position of the correct labels when labels output by the multiclass classifier are sorted by the classifiers' scores.

Table 6. Correct classification rates for: boosting without geometry $(h_k, h_{k,l})$; SVM with a linear kernel; boosting all types of weak classifiers h_{all} and boosting SVM with all types of weak classifiers (SVM_{all}). The standard error on the correct rate for each category is about 0.4%.

classes	bikes	boats	books	cars	chairs	flowers	phones	r. signs	shoes	s. toys	mean
h_k	61.7	74.5	67.0	55.6	50.7	82.5	67.6	61.4	73.9	68.9	**66.4**
$h_{k,l}$	64.6	76.1	68.5	61.0	50.7	84.6	69.6	64.8	76.6	69.2	**68.6**
SVM	69.2	79.3	70.3	72.1	58.8	86.7	70.4	69.0	86.3	79.2	**74.1**
h_{all}	70.0	73.8	68.2	64.1	57.4	82.9	68.0	61.9	75.2	76.2	**69.8**
SVM_{all}	74.6	81.8	78.2	77.5	65.2	89.6	76.0	76.2	83.8	83.8	**78.7**

We can see that $h_{k,l}$ outperforms h_k, but both boosting approaches have much lower performance than the linear SVM. We also tested the quadratic kernel for SVM as it implicitly considers keypatch pairs but the results were very similar to those of the linear kernel.

Furthermore, we investigated how well each weak classifier type performed when it was used exclusively for boosting. Results are given in Table 7 and selected weak classifier examples are shown in Figure 6.

Table 7. Mean correct rates when boosting individual weak classifier types (first row) and their percentage of being chosen when combined with SVM

h_σ^k	h_σ^{kl}	$h_{\sigma=}^{kl}$	h_θ^k	h_θ^{kl}	$h_{\theta=}^{kl}$	$h_{\sigma\theta}^k$	$h_{\sigma\theta}^{kl}$	$h_{\sigma\theta=}^{kl}$	h_B^k	h_B^{kl}	$h_{k\cap l}$	$h_{k\in l}$	$h_{k\subset l}$	$h_{k\propto l}$	$h_{k\in\aleph_l^5}$	$h_{k\in\aleph_l^{10}}$
63.6	66.5	46.2	62.1	62.6	48.8	61.6	64.5	48.8	62.8	63.8	63.3	64.1	53.8	58.5	62.4	64.5
2	21.2	2.8	0.4	13.5	3.2	0.4	9	1.6	3.8	35.7	2.7	0.8	0.1	0.3	0.9	1.6

Table 8. Confusion matrix and mean ranks for SVM_{all}

classes	bikes	boats	books	cars	chairs	flowers	phones	r. signs	shoes	s. toys
bikes	**74.6**	1.6	1.5	0.6	5.5	1.2	0	1	0.6	0.8
boats	3.3	**81.8**	4.1	4.7	4.6	1.2	0.4	1	2.1	0.8
books	0	2.1	**78.2**	1.3	2.3	0	4.8	3.3	0.7	1.1
cars	3.8	3.7	2.2	**77.5**	7	0.4	2	3.3	1.3	0.4
chairs	10.4	2.8	4.4	4.8	**65.2**	2.1	2.8	4.3	2.5	0
flowers	1.2	0.9	0	0.6	1.8	**89.6**	0	1.4	0.6	0.8
phones	0.8	0.7	3	2.9	2.3	0.4	**76**	1	2.1	0.4
road signs	1.3	0.9	2.2	1.6	4.6	1.3	2.4	**76.2**	1.3	0
shoes	2.9	5.3	3.7	6	5.5	1.3	10.4	7.6	**83.8**	11.9
soft toys	0.4	0.2	0.7	0	1.2	2.5	1.2	0.9	5	**83.8**
mean ranks	1.4	1.3	1.4	1.3	1.8	1.2	1.9	1.5	1.5	1.1

Fig. 6. The three most relevant single keypatches h^k for the "chair" classifier are shown in (a). The following images show the single most relevant weak classifier based on pairs of patches for types (b) h_σ^{kl}, (c) $h_{k\subset l}$ and (d) $h_{k\cap l}$ respectively in the case of "road sign", "flowers" and "boat" classifiers. In each case we show *all* patches of type k (in blue) and *all* patches of type l (in green). Not all of these patches verify the respective geometric condition. For (d) $h_{k\cap l}$ it happends that the most relevant weak classifier $h_{k\subset l}$ for the "boat" classifier was obtained for $k = l$ hence only blue circles are shown.

We then combined the 17 types of geometric weak classifiers with hypotheses h_k and $h_{k,l}$. This (see fourth row of Table 6) slightly improved on the boosting results without geometry (first two rows) but gave still lower performance than the SVM.

Finally, we combined the SVM outputs with the weak classifiers using generalized AdaBoost. First the SVM outputs were normalized to $[-1, 1]$ using a sigmoid fit[7] [20]. This classifier was considered as first "weak" classifier h_1 of the boosting approach (see Eqn (1)) and the corresponding α_1 and $D^2(i)$ were accordingly computed (see Eqn's (3) and (2)). Other weak classifiers were selected from the full set of 19's h's. The second row of Table 7 shows how often each classifier type was used. Clearly h_B^{kl} and h_σ^{kl} are importnat complements to the SVM.

The SVM performance was significantly improved (see Table 6 fifth row). Table 8 shows the confusion matrix and the mean ranks for this combined classifier.

6   Conclusions

In this chapter we have presented a simple approach to generic visual categorization using feature vectors constructed from clustered descriptors of image patches. This approach can easily handle variations in view and lighting. Furthermore it is robust to background clutter, occlusion as well as intra-class variations. It was tested on different datasets which showed the strength and the weaknesses of the method. Using an easy dataset (FPZ) we obtained excellent results both for object detection and for multi-class categorization. However our in-house dataset which is much more challenging showed that further improvements are necessary.

We explored the possibility of improving the accuracy using geometric information. In contrast to approaches such as [6,11], where due to relatively strong geometrical (shape) constraints the method requires the alignment and segregation of different views of objects in the dataset, we proposed to incorporate geometric constraints as weak conditions. We defined and selected from a multitude of geometry based weak classifiers (several millions) and combine them effectively with the original SVM classifier using generalized AdaBoost. Results have been given on a challenging 10-class dataset which is publicly available. The benefits of the proposed method are its invariance and good accuracy. Overall improvement in error rate has been demonstrated through the use of geometric information, relative to results obtained in the absence of geometric information.

While we have explored 19 types (17 with geometry) of weak classifier, many more can be envisaged for future work. Geometric properties are of course widely used in matching. It will be interesting to explore how recent progress in this domain such as techniques in [7,10] can be exploited for categorization. It will also be interesting to evaluate other approaches to boosting in the multi-class case such as the joint-boosting proposed in [25], which promises improved generalization performance and the need for fewer weak classifiers.

However, one of the main inconveniences of the proposed approach is the cost of the training which does not scale well with the number of images and number of classes (all weak classifiers must be tested on the whole training set at each step of the boosting). One way to reduce the search is to build a vocabulary of doublets (pair of keypatches) using only the most relevant visual words as in [22].

---

[7] This transformation of SVM outputs to confidence was also applied when we ranked the outputs from different classes.

More recently, in [19] we have shown that approaches based on soft clustering using GMM rather than K-means can enable substantial improvements in accuracy. It was also shown that when combined with adaptation techniques drawn from speech recognition, such approaches can scale well with the number of classes. It will be an interesting challenge to incorporate geometric information with such soft clustering approaches.

Acknowledgments

This work was supported by the European Project IST-2001-34405 LAVA (Learning for Adaptable Visual Assistants, http://www.l-a-v-a.org). We are grateful to DARTY for their permission to acquire images in their shops, to INRIA for the use of their multi-scale interest point detector and to TU Graz for the bikes image database.

References

1. A. Amir, J. Argillander, M. Berg, S.-F. Chang, M. Franz, W. Hsu, G. Iyengar, J. Kender, L. Kennedy, C.-Y. Lin, M. Naphade, A. Natsev, J. Smith, J. Tesic, G. Wu, R. Yang, and D. Zhang. IBM research TRECVID-2004 video retrieval system. In *Proc. of TREC Video Retrieval Evaluation*, 2004.
2. P. Carbonetto, N. de Freitas, and K. Barnard. A statistical model for general contextual object recognition. In *Proc. ECCV*, volume 1, pages 350–362, 2004.
3. Y. Chen and J. Z. Wang. Image categorization by learning and reasoning with regions. *JMLR*, 5:913–939, 2004.
4. G. Csurka, C. Dance, L. Fan, J. Willamowski, and C. Bray. Visual categorization with bags of keypoints. In *Proc. ECCV International Workshop on Statistical Learning in Computer Vision*, 2004.
5. J. Farquhar, S. Szedmak, H. Meng, and J. Shawe-Taylor. Improving "bag-of-keypoints" image categorisation. Technical report, University of Southampton, 2005.
6. R. Fergus, P. Perona, and A. Zisserman. Object class recognition by unsupervised scale-invariant learning. In *Proc. CVPR*, volume 2, pages 264–271, 2003.
7. V. Ferrari, T. Tuytelaars, and L. Van Gool. Simultaneous object recognition and segmentation by image exploration. In *Proc. ECCV*, volume 1, pages 40–54, 2004.
8. W. H. Hsu and S.-F. Chang. Visual cue cluster construction via information bottleneck principle and kernel density estimation. In *Proc. CIVR*, 2005.
9. T. Joachims. Text categorization with support vector machines: learning with many relevant features. In *Proc. ECML*, volume 1398, pages 137–142, 1998.
10. S. Lazebnik, C. Schmid, and J. Ponce. Semi-local affine parts for object recognition. In *Proc. BMVC*, volume 2, pages 959–968, 2004.
11. B. Leibe, A. Leonardis, and B. Schiele. Combined object categorization and segmentation with an implicit shape model. In *Proc. ECCV Workshop on Statistical Learning in Computer Vision*, pages 17–32, 2004.
12. Y. Li, J. A. Bilmes, and L. G. Shapiro. Object class recognition using images of abstract regions. In *Proc. ICPR*, volume 1, pages 40–44, 2004.

13. H. Lodhi, J. Shawe-Taylor, N. Christianini, and C. Watkins. Text classification using string kernels. In *Advances in Neural Information Processing Systems*, volume 13, 2001.
14. D.G. Lowe. Object recognition from local scale-invariant features. In *Proc. ICCV*, pages 1150–1157, 1999.
15. K. Mikolajczyk and C. Schmid. An affine invariant interest point detector. In *Proc. ECCV*, volume 1, pages 128–142, 2002.
16. A. Opelt, M. Fussenegger, A. Pinz, and P. Auer. Weak hypotheses and boosting for generic object detection and recognition. In *Proc. ECCV*, volume 2, pages 71–84, 2004.
17. J.-Y. Pan, H.-J. Yang, C. Faloutsos, and P. Duygulu. GCap: Graph-based automatic image captioning. In *Proc. CVPR Workshop on Multimedia Data and Document Engineering*, 2004.
18. D. Pelleg and A. Moore. X-means: Extending k-means with efficient estimation of the number of clusters. In *Proc. ICML*, 2000.
19. F. Perronnin, C. Dance, G. Csurka, and M. Bressan. Adapted vocabularies for generic visual categorization. Submitted to ECCV 2006.
20. J. C. Platt. Probabilistic outputs for support vector machines and comparison to regularized likelihood methods. In *Advances in Large Margin Classifiers*. MIT Press, 1999.
21. R.E. Schapire and Y. Singer. Improved boosting algorithms using confidence-rated predictions. *Machine Learning*, 37(3):297–336, 1999.
22. J. S. Sivic, B. C. Russell, A. A. Efros, A. Zisserman, and W. F. Feeman. Discovering objects and their localization in images. In *Proc. ICCV*, pages 370–377, 2005.
23. J. S. Sivic and A. Zisserman. Video google: A text retrieval approach to object matching in videos. In *Proc. ICCV*, volume 2, pages 1470–1477, 2003.
24. S. Tong and D. Koller. Support vector machine active learning with applications to text classification. In *Proc. ICML*, 2000.
25. A. Torralba, K. P. Murphy, and W. T. Freeman. Sharing features: Efficient boosting procedures for multiclass object detection. In *Proc. CVPR*, volume 2, pages 762–769, 2004.
26. V. Vapnik. *Statistical Learning Theory*. Wiley, 1998.
27. L. Zhu, A. Rao, and A. Zhang. Theory of keyblock-based image retrieval. *ACM Transactions on Information Systems*, 20(2):224–257, 2002.

Components for Object Detection and Identification

Bernd Heisele[1,2], Ivaylo Riskov[1], and Christian Morgenstern[1]

[1] Center for Biological and Computational Learning, M.I.T.,
Cambridge, MA 02142, USA
riskov@mit.edu, christian.morgenstern@upc.edu
[2] Honda Research Institute US
Boston, MA 02111, USA
bheisele@honda-ri.com

Abstract. We present a component-based system for object detection and identification. From a set of training images of a given object we extract a large number of components which are clustered based on the similarity of their image features and their locations within the object image. The cluster centers build an initial set of component templates from which we select a subset for the final recognizer. The localization of the components is performed by normalized cross-correlation. Two types of components are used, gray value components and components consisting of the magnitudes of the gray value gradient.

In experiments we investigate how the component size, the number of the components, and the feature type affects the recognition performance. The system is compared to several state-of-the-art classifiers on three different data sets for object identification and detection.

1 Introduction

Object detection and identification systems in which classification is based on local object features have become increasingly common in the computer vision community over the last couple of years, see e.g. [24,8,11,26,4]. These systems have the following two processing steps in common: In a first step, the image is scanned for a set of characteristic features of the object. For example, in a car detection system a canonical gray-value template of a wheel might be cross-correlated with the input image to localize the wheels of a car. We will refer to these local object features as the components of an object, other authors use different denotations such as parts, patches or fragments. Accordingly, the feature detectors will be called component detectors or component classifiers. In a second step, the results of the component detector stage are combined to determine whether the input image contains an object of the given class. We will refer to this classifier as the combination classifier.

An alternative approach to object classification is to search for the object as a whole, for example by computing the cross-correlation between a template of the object and the input image. In contrast to the component-based approach, a single classifier takes as input a feature vector containing information about the

J. Ponce et al. (Eds.): Toward Category-Level Object Recognition, LNCS 4170, pp. 225–237, 2006.
© Springer-Verlag Berlin Heidelberg 2006

whole object. We will refer to this category of techniques as the global approach; examples of global face detection systems are described in [23,13,18,14,7]. There are systems which fall in between the component-based and the global approach. The face detection system in [25], for example, performs classification with an ensemble of simple classifiers, each one operating on locally computed image features, similar to component detectors. However, each of these simple classifiers is only applied to a fixed x-y-position within the object window. In the component-based approach described above, the locations of the components relative to each other are not fixed: each component detector performs a search over some part of the image to find the best matching component.

In the following we briefly motivate the component-based approach:

(a) A major problem in detection is the variation in the appearance of objects belonging to the same class. For example, a car detector should be able to detect SUVs as well as sports cars, even though they significantly differ in their shapes. Building a detector based on components which are visually similar across all objects of the class might solve this problem. In the case of cars, these indicator components could be the wheels, the headlights or the taillights.

(b) Components usually vary less under pose changes than the image pattern of the whole object. Assuming that sufficiently small components correspond to planar patches on the 3D surface of the object, changes in the viewpoint of an object can be modeled as affine transformations on the component level. Under this assumption, view invariance can be achieved by using affine invariant image features in the component detector stage as proposed in [4]. A possibility to achieve view invariance in the global approach is to train a set of view-tuned, global classifiers as suggested in [15].

(c) Another source of variations in an objects appearance is partial occlusion. In general it is difficult to collect a training set of images which covers the spectrum of possible variations caused by occlusion. In the component-based approach, partial occlusion will only affect the outputs of a few component detectors at a time. Therefore, a solution to the occlusion problem might be a combination classifier which is robust against changes in a small number of its input features, e.g. a voting-based classifier. Another possibility is to add artificial examples of partially occluded objects to the training data of the combination classifier, e.g. by decreasing the component detector outputs computed on occlusion-free examples. Experiments on detecting partially occluded pedestrians with a component-based system similar to the one describe in our chapter have been reported in [11].

One of the main problems that has to be addressed in the component-based approach is how to choose a suitable set of components. A manually selected set of five components containing the head, the upper body, both arms, and the lower body has been used in [11] for person detection. Although there are intuitively obvious choices of components for many types of objects, such as the eyes, the nose and the mouth for faces, a more systematic approach is to automatically select the components based on their discriminative power. In [24] components of various sizes were cropped at random locations in the training images of an object. The mutual information between the occurrence of a component in a training image and the class label of the image was used as a measure to rank and select components. Another strategy to automatically determine an initial set of components is to apply a generic interest operator to the training images and to select components located in the vicinity of the detected points of interest [5,4,10]. In [4], this initial set was subsequently reduced by selecting components based on mutual information and likelihood ratio. Using interest operators has the advantage of providing a quick and reliable way to locate component candidates in a given input image. However, forcing the locations of the components to coincide with the points detected by the interest operator considerably restricts the choice of possible components—important components might be lost. Furthermore, interest operators have a tendency to fail for objects with little texture and objects at a low pixel resolution.

How to include information about the spatial relationship between components is another important question. In the following we assume that scale and translation invariance are achieved by sliding an object window of fixed size over the input image at different resolutions—the detection task is then reduced to classifying the pattern within the current object window. Intuitively, information about the location of the components is important in cases where the number of components is small and each component carries only little class-specific information.

We adopt the component-based classification architecture similar to the one suggested in [8,12]. It consists of two levels of classifiers; component classifiers at the first level and a single combination classifier at the second level. The component classifiers are trained to locate the components and the combination classifier performs the final detection based on the outputs of the component classifiers. In contrast to [8], where support vector machines (SVM) were used at both levels, we use component templates and normalized cross-correlation for detecting the components and a linear classifier to combine the correlation values.

2   System Description

2.1   Overview

An overview of our two-level component-based classifier is shown in Fig. 1. At the first level, component classifiers independently detect components of the object. Each component classifier consists of a single component template which is matched against the image within a given search region using normalized cross-correlation. We pass the maximum correlation value of each component to the combination classifier at the second level. The combination classifier produces a binary recognition result which classifies the input image as either belonging to the background class or to the object class.

2.2   Features

The applicability of a certain feature type depends on the recognition task at hand–some objects are best described by texture features, others by shape

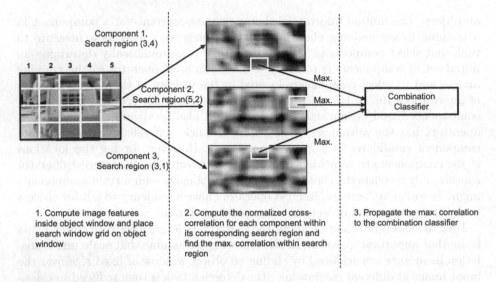

1. Compute image features inside object window and place search window grid on object window

2. Compute the normalized cross-correlation for each component within its corresponding search region and find the max. correlation within search region

3. Propagate the max. correlation to the combination classifier

Fig. 1. The component-based architecture: At the first level, the component templates are matched against the input image within predefined search regions using normalized cross-correlation. Each component's maximum correlation value is propagated to the combination classifier at the second level.

features. The range of variations in the pose of an object might also influence the choice of features. For example, the recognition of cars and pedestrians from a car-mounted camera does not require the system to be invariant to in-plane rotation; the recognition of office objects on a desk, on the other hand, requires invariance to in-plane rotation. Invariance to in-plane rotation and to arbitrary rotation of planar objects can be dealt with on a feature level by computing rotation-invariant or affine invariant features, e.g. see [10,4]. In the general case, however, pose invariance requires an altogether different classification architecture such as a set of view-tuned classifiers [15]. Looking at biological visual systems for clues about useful types of features is certainly a legitimate strategy. Recently, a biologically motivated system which uses Gabor wavelet features at the lowest level has shown good results on a wide variety of computer vision databases [21]. With broad applicability and computational efficiency in mind, we chose gray values and the magnitudes of the gradient as feature types.[1]

2.3 Geometrical Model

Omitting any spatial information leads to a detection system similar to the biologically plausible object recognition models proposed in [16,24,21]. In [16],

---

[1] We computed the gradient by convolving the image with the derivatives of a 2D-Gaussian with $\sigma = 1$.

the components were located by searching for the maximum outputs of the detectors across the full image. The only data propagated to the higher level classifiers were the outputs of the component detectors.

A framework in which the geometry is modeled as a prior on the locations of the components by a graphical model has been proposed in [3]. The complexity of the graphical model could be varied between the simple naïve Bayesian model and the full joint Gaussian model. The experimental results were inconclusive since the number of components was small and the advantages of the two implemented models over the naïve Bayesian model were in the range a few percent. In cases where the number of components and the number of detections per component are large, complex models might become computationally too expensive. A standard technique to keep the number of detections small is to apply interest operators to the image. The initial detections are then solely appearance-based which has the disadvantage that configurations with a high geometrical prior might be discarded early in the recognition process. A technique in which both appearance and geometry are used at an early stage has been proposed in [2].

We introduce geometrical constraints by restricting the location of each component to be within a pre-defined search region inside the object window. The search regions can be interpreted as a simple geometrical model in which the prior for finding a component within its search region is uniform and the prior of finding it outside is zero.

2.4   Selecting Components

As shown in Fig. 1 we divided the image into non-overlapping search regions. For each of the object images in the training set and for each search region we extracted 100 squared patches of fixed size whose centers were randomly placed within the corresponding search region. We then performed a data reduction step by applying k-means clustering to all components belonging to the same search region. The k-means clustering algorithm has been applied before the context of computing features for object recognition [17,20]. The resulting cluster centers built our initial set of component templates. For each component template we built a corresponding component classifier which returned a single output value for every training image. This value was computed as the maximum of the correlation between the component template and the input image within the search region. The next step was to select a subset of components from the pool of available component templates. We added a negative training set containing non-object images which had the same size as the object images and either used Adaboost [19] or Gentle-boost [6] to select the component templates. In a previous study [12] we evaluated two other feature selection techniques on an object identification database: a method based on the individual performance (ROC area) of the component templates and forward stepwise regression [27]. The technique based on the ROC area performed about the same as Adaboost, forward stepwise regression did worse.

3 Experiments

3.1 The MIT Office Object Database

In this identification task, the positive training and test data consisted of images of four objects, a telephone, a coffee machine, a fax machine, and a small bird figurine.[2] The object images were manually cropped from high resolution color images recorded with a digital camera. The aspect ratio of the cropping window was kept constant for each object but varied between the four objects. After cropping we scaled the object images to a fixed size. For all objects we used randomly selected 4,000 non-object training images and 9,000 non-object test images. Some examples of training and test images of the four objects are shown in Fig. 2. We kept the illumination and the distance to the object fixed when we took the training images and only changed the azimuthal orientation of the camera. When we took the test pictures, we changed the illumination, the distance to the object, and the background for the small objects. We freely moved the hand-held camera around the objects allowing all three degrees of freedom in the orientation of the camera.

Fig. 2. Examples of training and test images for the four objects. The first four images in each row show training examples, the last four were taken from the test set.

Before we trained the final recognition systems we performed a couple of quick tests on one of the four objects (telephone) to get an idea of how to choose the size the components and the number of components for further experiments. We also verified the usefulness of search regions:[3]

- We compared a system using search regions to a system in which the maximum output of the component classifiers was computed across the whole object window. Using search regions improved the recognition rate by more

---

[2] Fax machine: 44 training images and 157 test images of size 89×40. Phone: 34 training images and 114 test images of size 69×40 pixels. Coffee machine: 54 training and 87 test images of size 51×40. Bird: 32 training images and 131 test images of size 49×40.

[3] The ROC curves for the experiments can be found in [12].

than 20% up to a false positive (FP) rate of 0.1. Search regions were used in all following experiments.

- We trained four classifiers on gray value components of size 3×3, 5×5, 10×10 and 15×15. All four classifiers used 30 components selected by Adaboost. The classifiers for sizes 5×5, 10×10 and 15×15 performed about the same while the 3×3 classifier was significantly worse. We eliminated components of size 3×3 from all further experiments.
- We trained a classifiers on gray value components of size 5×5 with the number of components ranging between 10 and 400. For more than 100 components the performance of the classifier did not improve significantly.
- We evaluated the two feature types by selecting 100 components from a set of gray value components, a set of gradient components, and the combination of both sets. The gray values outperformed the combination slightly, the gradient components performed worst. The differences, however, were subtle (in the 2% range) and did not justify the exclusion of gradient features from further experiments.

In the final experiment we trained a separate classifier for each of the four objects. We randomly cropped gray value and gradient components from the positive training images at sizes 5×5, 10×10, and 15×15. Components of the same size and the same feature type, belonging to the same search region were grouped into 30 clusters of which only the components at the cluster centers entered the following selection process. Of the 3,600 components we selected a subsets of 100 and 400 components. As as baseline system we trained four SVMs with on the raw gray values of the objects.[4] Fig. 3 shows the ROC curves for the four different objects for the component-based system and the global SVM classifier. Except for the fax machine, where both systems were on par, the component based system performed better. Both systems had problems recognizing the bird. This can be explained by the strong changes in the silhouette of the figure under rotation. Since we extracted the object images with a fixed aspect ratio, some of the training images of the bird contained a significant amount of background. Considering the fact that the background was the same on all training images but was different on the test images, the relatively poor performance is not surprising.

3.2   The MIT Face Database

In this set of experiments we applied the system with a 4×4 search region grid to a face detection database. The positive training set consisted of about 9,000 synthetic face images of size 58×58, the negative training set contained about 13,700 background patches of the same size. The test set included 5,000 non-face patterns which were selected by a 19×19 low-resolution LDA classifier as the most similar to faces out of 112 background images. The positive test set

---

[4] We did experiments with Gaussian and linear kernels and also applied histogram-equalization in the preprocessing stage. Fig. 3 shows the best results achieved with global systems.

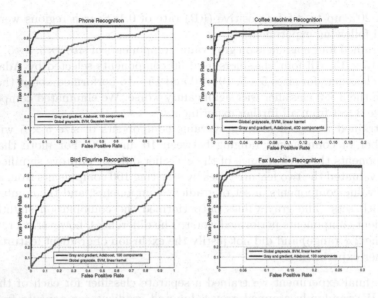

Fig. 3. Final identification results for the four different objects using a combination of gray value and gradient components in comparison to the performance of a global classifier

consisted of a subset of the CMU PIE database [22] that we randomly sampled across the individuals, illumination and expressions. The faces were extracted based on the coordinates of facial feature points given in the CMU PIE database. We resized these images to 70×70 such that the faces in test and training set were at about the same scale. Some examples from the training and test sets are shown in Fig. 4. When testing on the 70×70 images we applied the shifting object window technique.

Fig. 4. Examples from the face database. The images on the left half show training examples, the images on the right test examples taken from the CMU PIE database. Note that the test images show a slightly larger part of the face than the training images.

In the following we summarize the experiments on the face database:

– We compared Adaboost, previously used on the office database, with Gentle-boost. Gentle-boost produced consistently better results. The improvements were subtle, the largest increase in ROC area achieved in any of the comparisons was 0.01. In all of the following experiments we used Gentle-boost to select the components.

- We compared systems using gray value components of size 5×5, 10×10, and 15×15. The systems performed about the same.
- When increasing the number of gray value components of size 5×5 from 10 up to 80 the ROC area increased by 0.016. Adding more components did not improve the results.
- Gradient components performed poorly on this database. In a direct comparison using 100 5×5 components the ROC area of the gradient system was about 0.2 smaller than that of the gray value system.

In conclusion, systems with 80 gray value components of size 5×5 or 10×10 selected by Gentle-boost gave best results for face detection. Gradient components were not useful for this database, adding them to the pool of gray value components lead to a decrease in the system's performance. A comparison to the 14 component system using SVMs [8][5] and the biologically inspired model in [21] is given in Table I.

Table 1. Comparison between our system with 80 gray value components and two baseline systems. Given are the ROC area and the recognition rate at the point of equal error rates (EER).

	Our system	14 components SVM [8]	Biological model [21]
ROC area	0.995	0.960	0.993
1− EER	0.962	0.904	0.956

3.3   The MIT Car Database

This database was collected at MIT as part of a larger project on the analysis of street scenes [1]. It includes around 800 positive images of cars of size 128×128 and around 9,000 negative background patterns of the same size. Since no explicit separation of training and testing images was given, we followed the procedure in [1] and randomly selected two thirds of the images for training and the rest for testing. As for faces, we used a 4×4 search region grid. As the samples in Fig. 5 show, the set included different types of cars, strong variations the viewpoint (side, front and rear views), partial occlusions, and large background parts.

Fig. 5. Examples from the car database. Note the large variations in pose and illumination.

It turned out thats small components performed the best on this database. The ROC area for gray value components of a fixed size decreased by 0.12 when

---

[5] A different training set of faces was used in this paper.

increasing the size of the components from 5×5 to 15×15. The appearance of the cars in this database varied strongly making it unlikely to find large components which are shared amongst the car images. Since the shadow below the car was a salient feature across most of the car images, it did not surprise that the gradient components outperformed the gray components on this task.

In Fig. 6 we compare the ROC curves published in [1] with our system using 100 gradient components of size 5×5 selected by Gentle-boost. We did not train the systems on the same data since the database did not specify exactly how to split into training and test sets. However, we implemented a global classifier similar to the one used in [1] and applied it to our training and test sets. The right diagram shows two wavelet-based systems labeled "C1" and "C2", the latter is similar to [21], a global gray value classifier using an SVM, labeled "global grayscale", a part-based system according to [9], and a patch-based approach in which 150 out of a pool of 1024 12×12 patches were selected for classification. In a direct comparison, our system performs similar to the "C2" system and slightly worse than the "C1" system. This comparison should be taken with a grain of salt since the global gray value classifier performed very differently on the two tests (compare the two curves labeled "global grayscale").

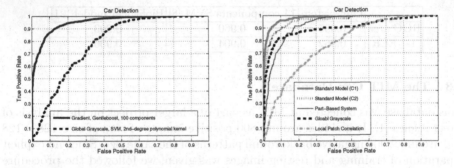

Fig. 6. The ROC curves on the left compare the component system to a global system, the curves on the right are taken from [1]. The curves in both diagrams have been computed on the MIT car detection database, however, the splits into training and test sets were different.

4   Conclusion

We presented a component-based system for detecting and identifying objects.

From a set of training images of a given object we extracted a large number of gray value and gradient components which were split into clusters using the k-means algorithm. The cluster centers built an initial set of component templates. We localized the components in the image by finding the maxima of the normalized cross-correlation inside search regions. The final classifier was built by selecting components with Adaboost or Gentle-boost.

In most of our experiments, selecting around 100 components from a pool of several thousands seemed to be sufficient. The proper choice of the size of the components proved to be task-dependent. Intermediate component sizes between 5×5 and 15×15 pixels led to good results on the objects in our databases, which varied in resolution between 50×50 and 130×130 pixels. We also noticed that the optimal choice of the feature type depends on the task. While the gray value components outperformed the gradient components in the office object and face experiments, the gradient components proved to be better for detecting cars.

We showed that our system can compete with state-of-the-art detection and identification systems. Only on one of the databases our system was outperformed by a detection system using wavelet-type features. We see the main advantages of our approach in its conceptual simplicity and its broad applicability. Since both the computation of the features and the matching algorithm are computationally simple, the system has the potential of being implemented in real-time.

Acknowledgements

The authors would like to thank S. Bileschi for providing the car database and experimental results on this database.

This chapter describes research done at the Center for Biological and Computational Learning, which is in the McGovern Institute for Brain Research at MIT, as well as in the Department of Brain and Cognitive Sciences, and which is affiliated with the Computer Sciences and Artificial Intelligence Laboratory (CSAIL). This research was sponsored by grants from: Office of Naval Research (DARPA) Contract No. MDA972-04-1-0037, Office of Naval Research (DARPA) Contract No. N00014-02-1-0915, National Science Foundation-NIH (CRCNS) Contract No. EIA-0218506, and National Institutes of Health (Conte) Contract No. 1 P20 MH66239-01A1. Additional support was provided by: Central Research Institute of Electric Power Industry (CRIEPI), Daimler-Chrysler AG, Eastman Kodak Company, Honda Research Institute USA, Komatsu Ltd., Merrill-Lynch, NEC Fund, Oxygen, Siemens Corporate Research, Inc., Sony, Sumitomo Metal Industries, and the Eugene McDermott Foundation.

References

1. S. Bileschi and L. Wolf. A unified system for object detection, texture recognition, and context analysis based on the standard model feature set. In *British Machine Vision Conference (BMVC)*, 2005.
2. S. M. Bileschi and B. Heisele. Advances in component-based face detection. In *Proceedings of Pattern Recognition with Support Vector Machines, First International Workshop, SVM 2002*, pages 135–143, Niagara Falls, 2002.
3. D. Crandall, P. Felzenszwalb, and D. Huttenlocher. Spatial priors for part-based recognition using statistical model. In *Proc. IEEE Conference on Computer Vision and Pattern Recognition (CVPR)*, pages 10–17, 2005.

4. G. Dorko and C. Schmid. Selection of scale invariant neighborhoods for object class recognition. In *International Conference on Computer Vision (ICCV)*, pages 634–640, 2003.
5. R. Fergus, P. Perona, and A. Zisserman. Object class recognition by unsupervised scale-invariant learning. In *Proceedings of the IEEE Conference on Computer Vision and Pattern Recognition*, pages 264–271, 2003.
6. J. Friedman, T. Hastie, and R. Tibshirani. Additive logistic regression: a statistical view of boosting. Tecnical report, Dept. of Statistics, Stanford University, 1998.
7. B. Heisele, T. Serre, S. Mukherjee, and T. Poggio. Hierarchical classification and feature reduction for fast face detection with support vector machines. *Pattern Recognition*, 36(9):2007–2017, 2003.
8. B. Heisele, T. Serre, M. Pontil, T. Vetter, and T. Poggio. Categorization by learning and combining object parts. In *Neural Information Processing Systems (NIPS)*, Vancouver, 2001.
9. B. Leibe, A. Leonardis, and B. Schiele. Combined object categorization and segmentation with an implicit model. In *ECCV'04 Workshop on Statistical Learning in Computer Vision*, 2004.
10. D. G. Lowe. Distinctive image features from scale-invariant keypoints. *International Journal of Computer Vision*, 60(2):91–110, 2004.
11. A. Mohan, C. Papageorgiou, and T. Poggio. Example-based object detection in images by components. In *IEEE Transactions on Pattern Analysis and Machine Intelligence*, volume 23, pages 349–361, April 2001.
12. C. Morgenstern and B. Heisele. Component-based recognition of objects in an office environment. A.I. Memo 232, Center for Biological and Computational Learning, M.I.T., Cambridge, MA, 2003.
13. M. Oren, C. Papageorgiou, P. Sinha, E. Osuna, and T. Poggio. Pedestrian detection using wavelet templates. In *IEEE Conference on Computer Vision and Pattern Recognition*, pages 193–199, San Juan, 1997.
14. E. Osuna. *Support Vector Machines: Training and Applications*. PhD thesis, MIT, Department of Electrical Engineering and Computer Science, Cambridge, MA, 1998.
15. T. Poggio and S. Edelman. A network that learns to recognize 3-D objects. *Nature*, 343:163–266, 1990.
16. M. Riesenhuber and T. Poggio. Hierarchical models of object recognition in cortex. *Nature Neuroscience*, 2(11):1019–1025, 1999.
17. M. Riesenhuber and T. Poggio. The individual is nothing, the class everything: Psychophysics and modeling of recognition in object classes. A.I. Memo 1682, Center for Biological and Computational Learning, M.I.T., Cambridge, MA, 2000.
18. H. A. Rowley, S. Baluja, and T. Kanade. Neural network-based face detection. *IEEE Transactions on Pattern Analysis and Machine Intelligence*, 20(1):23–38, 1998.
19. R. Schapire, Y. Freund, P. Bartlett, and W. S. Lee. Boosting the margin: A new explanation of effectiveness of voting methods. *The Annals of Statistics*, 26(5):1651–1686, 1998.
20. T. Serre, J. Louie, M. Riesenhuber, and T. Poggio. On the role of object-specific features for real world recognition in biological vision. In *Biologically Motivated Computer Vision, Second International Workshop (BMCV 2002)*, pages 387–397, Tuebingen, Germany., 2002.
21. T. Serre, L. Wolf, and T. Poggio. A new biologically motivated framework for robust object recognition. A.I. Memo 2004-26, Center for Biological and Computational Learning, M.I.T., Cambridge, USA, 2004.

22. T. Sim, S. Baker, and M. Bsat. The CMU pose, illumination, and expression database. *IEEE Trans. Pattern Analysis and Machine Intelligence (PAMI)*, 25(12):1615–1618, 2003.
23. K.-K. Sung. *Learning and Example Selection for Object and Pattern Recognition*. PhD thesis, MIT, Artificial Intelligence Laboratory and Center for Biological and Computational Learning, Cambridge, MA, 1996.
24. S. Ullman, M. Vidal-Naquet, and E. Sali. Visual features of intermdediate complexity and their use in classification. *Nature Neuroscience*, 5(7):682–687, 2002.
25. P. Viola and M. Jones. Rapid object detection using a boosted cascade of simple features. In *Proc. IEEE Conference on Computer Vision and Pattern Recognition (CVPR)*, pages 511–518, 2001.
26. M. Weber, W. Welling, and P. Perona. Towards automatic dscovery of object categories. In *Proc. IEEE Conference on Computer Vision and Pattern Recognition*, June 2000.
27. S. Weisberg. *Applied Linear Regression*. Wiley, New York, 1980.

Cross Modal Disambiguation

Kobus Barnard[1], Keiji Yanai[2], Matthew Johnson[3], and Prasad Gabbur[4]

[1] Department of Computer Science, University of Arizona
kobus@cs.arizona.edu
[2] Department of Computer Science, The University of Electro-Communications,
1-5-1 Chofugaoka, Chofu-shi, Tokyo, 182-8585 Japan
yanai@cs.uec.ac.jp
[3] Department of Engineering, University of Cambridge
mj293@cam.ac.uk
[4] Electrical and Computer Engineering,
University of Arizona
pgsangam@ece.arizona.edu

Abstract. We consider strategies for reducing ambiguity in multi-modal data, particularly in the domain of images and text. Large data sets containing images with associated text (and vice versa) are readily available, and recent work has exploited such data to learn models for linking visual elements to semantics. This requires addressing a correspondence ambiguity because it is generally not known which parts of the images connect with which language elements. In this paper we first discuss using language processing to reduce correspondence ambiguity in loosely labeled image data. We then consider a similar problem of using visual correlates to reduce ambiguity in text with associated images. Only rudimentary image understanding is needed for this task because the image only needs to help differentiate between a limited set of choices, namely the senses of a particular word.

1 Introduction

Recent work suggests that the semantics of images and associated text can be better learned from data if they are considered together. For example, to build a system for searching and browsing large data sets, one should take advantage of available textual information. However, text alone cannot capture all that is of interest in an image. Furthermore, images with detailed text descriptions are rare. Thus there has been recent interest in integrating available text with visual information. This includes providing methods for searching and browsing which use both image features and text [21,22], and learning links between visual representations and words from loosely labeled training data [13,25,10,20]. In this paradigm, the models learned can be used to add labels to new images (auto-annotate), or even image regions (region-labeling). Alternatively, the links can be implicit, and simply help queries based on visual descriptors to return more semantically meaningful results [13,46].

J. Ponce et al. (Eds.): Toward Category-Level Object Recognition, LNCS 4170, pp. 238–257, 2006.

The underlying key idea in these methods is the observation that images with associated text have substantive supervisory information that can be exploited. The main confound is ambiguity. For example, in an image labeled with the words "tiger", "water", and "grass", it is not known which parts of the image correspond to which of these words. The work cited above addresses this correspondence ambiguity by building models for the various visual concepts that are consistent over a number of images. In our example, the single image does not have sufficient information to determine which words go with which features. However, additional images with, for example, tigers without water, and water without tigers, the ambiguity can be reduced. The process of reducing the ambiguity by using large training sets is analogous to statistical machine translation.

Now consider a program for automatically labeling our example image based on a learned model. Labeling images is clearly a difficult task. However, it becomes easier if we assume that the labels must come from the associated words. In our example, this means that instead of choosing among potentially hundreds, or thousands of words, we only need to choose between three of them.

This constrained labeling of the training data is implicit in some of the learning approaches mentioned above. However, we find it useful to consider it more explicitly. Doing so emphasizes that there are two parts of the problem. First, we wish to migrate semi-supervised data towards supervised data. This is important if we are to use large, loosely labeled data sets in a more supervisory fashion. Second, we need to develop algorithms and models that are targeted for inference on new data. As mentioned above, current approaches deal with the dependence between these two problems by iteratively solving one and then the other. However, as the required models and inference become more complex, it may be beneficial to consider the tasks separately. For example, a simple model may be able to give a reasonable approximate labeling of training data. This labeling can then be used to develop inference approaches which might be difficult to integrate into the initial labeling method. Further, augmenting strategies, such as integrating supervisory data and language modeling, can be simplified if we explicitly reduce correspondence ambiguity in the training data first, and then build models for inference.

In this paper, we will suggest how language models can be used to reduce correspondence ambiguity. In the work reported so far, language models have been limited to a "bag of words" model. Further, the words are generally assumed to be nouns. However, different parts of speech such as nouns, adjectives, and prepositions relate to visual attributes differently. Further, since modern parts of speech tagging [16,17] is relatively effective, there is opportunity to better exploit associated text through language tools. For example, certain (visual) adjectives embody specific image region features, and this is assumed to be consistent over multiple objects. If this relationship is known, it can help resolve the correspondence between words and image regions. Thus one can simultaneously learn the meaning of words such as "red", and use natural language analysis to exploit the occurrence of the modifier "red" to help learn the meaning of "ball" from an image annotated with "red ball". Similarly, if we assume that certain simple prepositions reflect spatial relations, we should be able to simultaneously learn the meaning of those prepositions, and exploit that meaning to help learn the visual representation of nouns being spatially related.

Reciprocally, images can also help disambiguate language meaning. In particular, words in natural language are ambiguous because they have multiple meanings (senses). For example, the word "bank" has a number of meanings including "financial institution" and that suggested by "river bank". Intuitively, an image could help determine the senses in a sentence like: "He ate his lunch by the bank". All that is required is that we have an image that is more correlated with the correct sense. The image need not even contain a bank, nor do we need to identify banks; the image features only need to correlate better with the correct sense as compared with the incorrect sense.

It is important that a complete understanding of the image is not required, as this would make the approach impractical given the current state of automated and image understanding. Notice that the disambiguation task is made much easier because we only need to select among a limited number of choices; namely the senses of the word being considered. Again, the disambiguation task is simpler than a complete understanding, but reducing the ambiguity can help move towards an understanding.

In what follows we first review recently developed approaches for dealing with multi-modal data with correspondence ambiguity. We then consider two instances of cross modality disambiguation in further detail. Here we discuss how adjectives can reduce correspondence ambiguity in images with associated text. We also propose a method to prune adjectives that are not visual, relative to our features. Finally, we outline a method for using images to disambiguate words in natural language.

2   Matching Words and Pictures

A number of methods have been recently developed for predicting words from image data, based on a large training data of images with associated text. Critically, the correspondence between particular words and particular visual elements is not required, as large quantities of such data is not readily available and expensive to obtain. Current approaches include:

- Simultaneously learning a model and reducing ambiguity, with latent entities (concepts) competing with each other for image elements and words [13,25,10,20]. This competition means that an image element that is more likely to be associated with one word (e.g. "tiger") is less likely to be associated with another one (e.g. "water"). Included here are translation approaches which constructs a model for words conditioned on image elements.
- Cross-media relevance models which predict words for entire images (auto-annotation) based on a statistical match of the image with components in the training data [35,28].

- Multiple instance learning which builds a separate classifier for the presence or absence of each word in the vocabulary in the face of multiple possibilities of which image element is relevant [38,39,4,52,53,5,6]. While not explicitly developed to do so, these methods support region labeling, and have recently been evaluated on this task [12].
- Object category recognition efforts [15,29,27,48], which are focused on identifying the existence of an object category, are related to the task of predicting words for images, and could be evaluated in the same way. Here the data is typically of an instance of an object category, with non-trivial clutter.

Here we review one method from the first approach which we build on below. Specifically we will consider the *dependent* model ([8]) with linear topology (no document clustering). This model owes much to previous work in the text domain [34] and statistical machine translation [18,19,40].

The general idea, common with many models in this genre, is that image are generated from latent factors (concepts) which contribute both visual entities and words. The fact that visual entities and words come from the same source is what enables the model to link them. Because we train the models without knowing the correspondence, we need an assumption of how multiple draws from the pool of factors lead to the observed data with ambiguity. The dependent model is distinguished by assuming that multiple draws are first made to produce the observed image entities. The same group of factors is then sampled to produced the image words. Because words are generated conditioned on the observed image, we consider this to be a translation approach.

This approach will work with any characterization of image entities (e.g. regions with features). However, a key assumption is that image semantics is compositional, and thus each image typically needs to be described by multiple visual entities. Without compositionally, we would need to model all possible combinations of entities. For example, we would have to model tigers on grass, tigers in water, tigers on sand, and so on. Clearly, one tiger model should be reused when possible.

In what follows, we use feature vectors associated with image regions obtained using normalized cuts [45]. For each image region we compute a feature vector representing color, texture, size, position, shape [8], and color context [11]. As in earlier work, we will refer to region, together with its feature vector, as a *blob*. Our segmentations are limited to grouping pixels together with coherent color and texture, and thus should be considered very low level.

2.1   An Exemplar Multi-modal Translation Model

We model the joint probability of a particular blob, b, and a word w, as

$$P(w, b) = \sum_{l} P(w|l)P(b|l)P(l) \tag{1}$$

where l indexes over concepts, $P(l)$ is the concept prior, $P(w|l)$ is a frequency table, and $P(b|l)$ is a Gaussian distribution over features. We further assume a diagonal covariance matrix (independent features) because fitting a full covariance is generally too difficult for a large number of features. This independence assumption is less troublesome because we only require conditional independence, given the concept. Intuitively, each concept generates some image regions according to the particular Gaussian distribution for that concept. Similarly, it generates one ore more words for the image according to a learned table of probabilities.

To go from the blob oriented expression (1) to one for an entire image, we assume that the observed blobs, B, yield a posterior probability, $P(l|B)$, which is proportional to the sum of $P(l|b)$. Words are then generated conditioned on the blobs from:

$$P(w|B) \propto \sum_l P(w|l)P(l|B) \tag{2}$$

where by assumption

$$P(l|B) \propto \sum_b P(l|b) \tag{3}$$

and Bayes rule is used to compute $P(l|b) \propto P(b|l)P(l)$.

Some manipulation [9] shows that this is equivalent to assuming that the word posterior for the image is proportional to the sum of the word posteriors for the regions:

$$P(w|B) \propto \sum_b^N P(w|b) \tag{4}$$

We limit the sum over blobs to the largest N blobs (in this work N is sixteen). While training, we also normalize the contributions of blobs and words to mitigate the effects of differing numbers of blobs and words in the various training images. The probability of the observed data, $W \cup B$, given the model, is thus:

$$P(W \cup B) = \prod_{b \in B} \left(\sum_l P(b|l)P(l) \right)^{\frac{max(N_b)}{N_b}} \prod_{w \in W} \left(\sum_l P(w|l)P(l|B) \right)^{\frac{max(N_w)}{N_w}} \tag{5}$$

where $max(N_b)$ (similarly $max(N_w)$) is the maximum number of blobs (words) for any training set image, N_b (similarly N_w)is the number of blobs (words) for the particular image, and $P(l|B)$ is computed from (3).

Since we do not know which concept is responsible for which observed blobs and words in the training data, determining the maximum likelihood values for the model parameters ($P(w|l)$, $P(b|l)$, and $P(l)$) is not tractable. We thus estimate values for the parameters using expectation maximization (EM) [23], treating the hidden factors (concepts) responsible for the blobs and words as missing data.

The model generalizes well because it learns about image components. These components can occur in different configurations and still be recognized. For example, it is possible to learn about "sky" regions in images of tigers, and then predict "sky" in giraffe images. Of course, predicting the word giraffe requires having giraffes in the training set.

3   Reducing Correspondence Ambiguity with Adjectives

We assume that descriptive text of an image can be parsed into parts of speech with reasonable accuracy [16,17]. We further assume that the nouns that adjectives bind to can be identified. Finally, in order to be useful, adjectives need to be *visual* relative to a set of features. Examples of visual adjectives include color words (e.g. "red"), and texture words (e.g. "furry"). We address pruning non-visual adjectives from our vocabulary in the next section (§4).

Under these assumptions, it should be clear that adjectives have the potential to help with correspondence disambiguation. If we are not (yet) able to link a red ball to a circular red region, but we have the binding "red ball", and we have a model for red, then we have evidence that "ball" should link to red image regions, and not other ones. We assume that if an adjective, a, binds to a noun, n, then:

$$P(n|b) \propto P(b|n) \propto P(b|a) \propto P_{adj}(a|b) \tag{6}$$

where P_{adj} indicates that we use an adjective model. It is conceivable to construct a process to jointly learns an adjective model and a noun model. However, it is simpler to compute an adjective model first, using (for example) (5) restricted to adjectives, and then use (6) as a prior probability for the nouns (6). That prior is than used with a noun model, such as(5) applied to nouns.

To test the hypothesis that visual adjectives can help reduce correspondence ambiguity in training data, we constructed a small data by labeling many of the nouns associated with 1900 Corel ^{TM} images with one of fifteen adjectives which were expected to have good visual properties (11 were color words). We then built a prediction model for the adjectives alone using the model reviewed above (§2.1). Thus we learned a model that could predict, to a certain extent, "red" for a red region. We then applied the adjective based posterior to get a noun prior via the linking of nouns with adjectives. We assumed that most of the probability mass for this prior should be distributed among the associated words for that image, but since the annotations often do not cover all blobs, we allowed 10% of the probability mass for words not in the annotation. We also build an instance of the same model (§2.1) for nouns. We then combined the evidence from the noun model and adjective model used to predict the nouns that they modify.

The results are much as one would expect. Some difficult to characterize nouns are relatively easy to label given this kind of additional, semi-supervisory, information. Almost invariably the labeling of the training data was improved by including the adjective information. Often it was a more reliable source of information than the noun model. This is likely partly due to the nature of our "toy" data set, which has more nouns associated with visual adjectives than would commonly be the case.

A main use of adjective information is to help label data that is not strongly correlated with simple visual features. A good example is the car image (Figure 1). Since cars come in all colors, learning to recognize cars as an object class by color is not possible. However, color can be used to identify a particular instance of a car. Several examples can further ensure that that cars are dissociated from a narrow range of colors. Given the identified examples, we are then in a better position to construct a car model.

The fact that we chose to learn the meaning of the adjectives from a small, weakly labeled data set, means that there were some labeling errors due to the imperfect adjective model. This could be improved by more data, or by adding some truly supervisory information. A second problem with our current system is that good labellings based on adjectives are often better than the combined result. We are currently pursuing better integration of the two sources of information.

4   Identifying Visual Words

The above proof of concept relied on having nouns associated with adjectives that had a good chance of being linked with our features. When we apply the methods discussed above to larger data sets with free form text, our vocabularies will gain many entries that have no chance to be linked with visual properties measured by a given feature set. It is thus reasonable to attempt to prune vocabularies in advance, removing words that do not have significant correlations with our features. While is is conceivable that our models can simply absorb these words without any ill effect, it is more likely that the noise created by words with no visual properties will be detrimental. At a minimum, the computation cost can be reduced by excluding such words.

We consider determining the visualness of a word based on a large external data set that is not necessarily the target data set. While the visualness of a word is somewhat relative to the data set, many words may not occur frequently enough in a particular data set that a clear distinction can be made. We want to keep words that might be subtly visual in our data set, and prune as many as we can that have little chance of being visual at all.

Thus our approach is to actively seek many images that might be relevant to each word under consideration, and determine how visual that word is in general. Fortunately, with web image search engines such as Google Image Search, finding a large number of images that have a fair chance of being relevant to a given word is relatively straightforward.

Having selected the images, we face a familiar problem. Even if a word is relevant to an image in general, it likely correlates with the features of only a small part of the image. We expect the bulk of any image to be irrelevant to the word. Hence to estimate whether a word correlates with image features, we need to estimate which parts of the image are relevant. Not surprisingly, this requires an iterative algorithm which alternates between determining an appropriate characterization for the word, and determining which regions are relevant.

To implement this we prepare a large Gaussian mixture model for the regions of a large number of images. A concept is characterized as probability distribution over the mixture components. We iteratively estimate that distribution and

Fig. 1. Example of using adjectives to reduce correspondence ambiguity in training data. The upper left image is the original image containing a red car with a green vegetation backdrop. It is annotated with "red:automobile red:vehicle red:car exotic drago ferrari". The upper right image shows the nouns with maximal posterior probability for each region, based on the adjective model. Specifically, the red regions in the image are labeled by one of the nouns linked to "red". Regions that have low posterior given "red" are labeled by one of the words not linked to red (e.g. "exotic"). In this example, all words also refer to the car but this is not known at this point, and by exclusion, the non red regions get labeled with these other words. The bottom left image shows the labeling using the noun model alone, but with a strong prior (90%) on choosing among the associated words. This ensures that most of the words are good words for the image, but correspondence can be a problem, as is quite noticeable with "automobile" in a tree region. The bottom right image image shows the combined result. The correspondence has been enhanced by the adjective, promoting "car" to be the label for the body of the car. Several other words are reasonable, such as two instances of "trees". These words are not in the annotation, but they have sufficiently high posterior to overcome the prior that tends to restrict words to the ones from the annotation. Finally, it is clear that the word "exotic" is still ambiguous, due to being in the annotation of many car images with many backdrops, but having no clear visual properties.

the whether or not each image region is relevant to the concept. After sufficient iterations we compute the entropy of the distribution. If that distribution has low entropy, then we designate the word as visual. Otherwise, the process suggests that it is hard to distinguish the regions linked to the word with from a random selection of regions. In that case we consider that word not sufficiently visual, and prune it from the words that we try to link to image features. Some details follow.

4.1   Data Gathering and Pre-processing

For each concept (e.g. adjective) we use Google^{TM} image search to find several hundred images. As in the previous section, we simplify the data using low level segmentation. However, due to the volume of data, we segment images with JSEG [24] instead of normalized cuts, which is more expensive. For all processing that follows we used the same feature set described above.

4.2   Detecting Regions Associated with a Concept

We process each concept in sequence. For each concept "X" we process the regions from the associated images, as well as an equal number of randomly selected other images, providing "non-X" regions. To obtain $P(X|r_i)$, which represents the probability that a region is associated with the concept "X" we use the following iterative process.

At first, we select "X" regions from the "X" images, and some "non-X" regions from the "non-X" images at random. We then fit a Gaussian mixture model for the image region features for both "X" and "non-X", and assign components of the mixture model according to the following formula:

$$p_j^X = \sum_{i=1}^{n_X} P(c_j|r_i^X, X) \tag{7}$$

$$= \sum_{i=1}^{n_X} P(X|c_j, r_i^X)P(c_j) \tag{8}$$

where c_j is the j-th component of the mixture model, n_X is the number of "X" regions, and r_i^X is the i-th "X" region.

The top m components in terms of p_j^X are regarded as the model of "X" and the rest are the model of "non-X". With these models of "X" and "non-X", we can compute $P(X|r_i)$ for all the regions which come from "X" images. Assuming that $p1(X|r_i)$ is the output of the model of "X" and $p2(nonX|r_i)$ is the output of the model of "non-X", given r_i, we can obtain $P(X|r_i)$ as follows:

$$P(X|r_i) = \frac{p1(X|r_i)}{p1(X|r_i) + p2(nonX|r_i)} \tag{9}$$

For the next iteration, we select the top n regions regarding $P(X|r_i)$ as "X" regions and the top $n/2$ regions regarding $P(nonX|r_i)$ as "non-X" regions. Add $n/2$ regions randomly selected from "non-X" images to "non-X" regions. In this way, we mix newly estimated "non-X" regions and randomly selected regions from "non-X" images after the second iteration. We adopt mixing rather than using only newly estimated "non-X" regions based on the results of the preliminary experiments. After computing the entropy, we repeat estimation of the model of "X" and "non-X", and computation of $P(X|r_i)$.

4.3 Computing the Entropy of Concepts

We estimate the entropy of the image features of all the regions weighted by $P(X|x_i)$ with respect to a generic model for image regions. For this model we use a Gaussian mixture model (GMM) for fifty thousand randomly selected regions from all the images. To reduce the impact of initialization in the EM process, we average the results over k GMM's fit with different starting points.

The average probability of image features of "X" weighted by $P(X|x_i)$ with respect to the j-th component of the l-th generic base represented by the GMM is given by

$$P(X|c_j, l) = \frac{w_{j,l} \sum_{i=1}^{N_X} P(f_{X,i}; \theta_{j,l}) P(X|r_i)}{\sum_{i=1}^{N_X} P(X|r_i)} \tag{10}$$

where $f_{X,i}$ is the image feature of the i-th region of "X", $P(f_{X,i}; \theta_{j,l})$ is the generative probability of $f_{X,i}$ from the j-th component, $w_{j,l}$ is the weight of the j-th component of the l-th base, and N_X is the number of all the regions which come from "X" images,

The entropy for "X" is given by

$$E(X) = \frac{1}{k} \sum_{l=1}^{k} \sum_{j=1}^{N_{\text{base}}} -P(X|c_j, l) \log_2 P(X|c_j, l) \tag{11}$$

where N_{base} is the number of the components of the base (250 in our experiments), and k is number of GMM's with different starting points (5 in our experiments). We use this entropy as a measure of the visualness of a concept.

4.4 Experiments

We experimented with 150 adjectives which are the 150 most common adjectives used for indexing images in the Hemera Photo-Object collection. We used each of these adjectives as the search term for Google Image search. We used the first 250 web images returned. Thus the entire experiment considered nearly forty thousand images associated with adjectives.

We used 15 mixture components in (7). Because we expect adjectives to be associated with visual properties more directly than nouns, we simply use a single mixture component to model "X" (i.e., $m=1$).

Figure 2 shows "yellow" images after one iteration. In the figure, the regions with high probability $P(\text{yellow}|r_i)$ are labeled as "yellow", while the regions with high probability $P(\text{non\_yellow}|r_i)$ are labeled as "non-yellow". Figure 3 shows "yellow" images after five iterations. This indicates the iterative region selection worked well in case of "yellow".

Table 1 shows the 15 top adjectives and their image entropy. In this case, the entropy of "dark" is the lowest, so in this sense "dark" is the most "visual" adjective among the 150 adjectives under the condition we set in this experiment. Figure 4 shows some of the "dark" images. Most of the region labeled with "dark" are uniform black ones. Other highly-ranked adjectives, "senior" and "beautiful" include many human faces, and "visual", which, interestingly, are not photos but graphical images such as screen shots of Windows or Visual C. This suggests that addressing biases due to what images are common on the web may be helpful.

We provide the ranking of color adjectives in Table 1. They are relatively high, even though images from the Web included many irrelevant images. This suggests that our pruning approach is promising.

Notice that the method identifies many words which, at first glance, do not appear to be truly visual. A good example in our results is "professional" which is ranked relatively high. The connection is through the sampling bias for "professional sports" which yields low entropy because of a limited number of textures and backgrounds (e.g. fields and courts) that go with those images. It would seem to depend on the application as to whether these words are a liability. If the goal is to help image search, then such associations can be helpful. However, we have clearly not captured the essence of "professional", and thus for recognition we would hope that the ambiguity can be resolved in subsequent steps.

This is conceivable in many cases. In the "professional sports" case, if we assume relatively rich descriptions and sufficient data, then in the generative model above, words like "field" and "court" would *compete* with "professional" for probability. This can promote "professional" as a more general term that is less directly associated with local features.

Table 2 lists the 15 adjectives with lowest entropy among the 150 tested. In case of "religious" (Figure 5), which is ranked as 145-th, the region-adjective linking did not work well, and the entropy is thus relatively large. This reflects the fact that the image features of the regions included in "religious" images have no prominent tendency. Thus we can say that "religious" has no or only a few visual properties.

5   Using Pictures to Understand Language

Links between visual features and words can also be exploited for understanding text and other documents. The idea is very simple and very familiar — illustrations can help clarify and enhance the meaning of documents. As an initial step in making this operational in an automatic setting, we have studied the problem of using images to help disambiguate word senses [14].

Words used in natural language are often ambiguous because language has evolved so that many words have several distinct meanings (senses). For example, the word "bank" can mean a financial institution or a step or edge as in "snow bank" or "river bank". Words which are spelled the same but have different meanings (polysemes) confound attempts to automatically understand natural language.

Because such words are very prevalent, determining the correct sense (word sense disambiguation) has been identified as an important problem in natural language processing research. As such, it has been studied by many researchers leading to a large body of work [7,37,51,50,32,3,2,42,43,49].

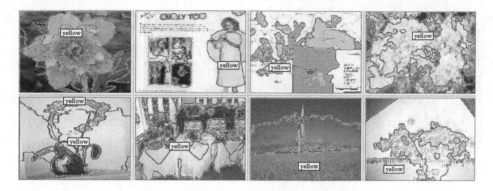

Fig. 2. "Yellow" regions after one iteration. At this stage many of the images do not have much yellow in them, and there are many labeling errors. For example, the flower in the top right image is green-blue, as is the region in the third image in the top row. The region marked yellow in the second image of the second row is white, whereas the two smaller, un-labeled, regions to either side are in fact yellow.

Fig. 3. "Yellow" regions after five iterations. These images all have significant yellow regions, and they are generally correctly labeled.

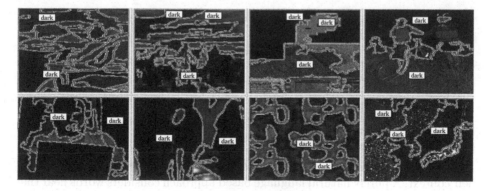

Fig. 4. "Dark" regions after five iterations

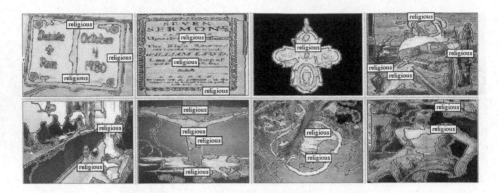

Fig. 5. "Religious" regions after five iterations

Table 1. Words with the top 15 entropy rankings

rank	adjective	entropy
1	dark	0.0118
2	senior	0.0166
3	beautiful	0.0178
4	visual	0.0222
5	rusted	0.0254
6	musical	0.0321
7	purple	0.0412
8	black	0.0443
9	ancient	0.0593
10	cute	0.0607
11	shiny	0.0643
12	scary	0.0653
13	professional	0.0785
14	stationary	0.1201
15	electric	0.1411

Table 2. Words with the bottom 15 entropy rankings

rank	adjective	entropy
136	medical	2.5246
137	assorted	2.5279
138	large	2.5488
139	playful	2.5541
140	acoustic	2.5627
141	elderly	2.5677
142	angry	2.5942
143	sexy	2.6015
144	open	2.6122
145	religious	2.7242
146	dry	2.8531
147	male	2.8835
148	patriotic	3.0840
149	vintage	3.1296
150	mature	3.2265

Table 3. Rankings of color adjectives

(color adjectives)		
7	purple	0.0412
8	black	0.0443
36	red	0.9762
39	blue	1.1289
46	yellow	1.2827

Since the words are spelled the same, resolving their sense requires considering their context. A purely natural language based approach considers words near the one in question. Thus in the bank example, words like "financial" or "money" are strong hints that the financial institution sense is meant. Interestingly, despite much work, and a number of innovative ideas, doing significantly better than choosing the most common sense remains difficult [49].

To use our word prediction model for word sense disambiguation, we constrain the predicted words to be from the set of senses for the word being analyzed. In general, when word prediction is constrained to a narrow set of choices (such as possible senses), reasonable performance is possible. This is the key point. A very limited understanding of what is in the image can be helpful for sense disambiguation. All that is required is that the image is more likely to be associated with the correct sense, compared to a handful of others.

Associated images can help improve document retrieval. Invariably the senses of the words available in unstructured data are not sense disambiguated. Being able to automatically reduce the ambiguity should improve the quality of results.

Notice that in this scenario, we assume that the user is willing to indicate the query term sense. However, the general thrust of the method can take an implicit role. Specifically, even without sense information, retrieved documents can be organized on semantic lines for searching, browsing and relevance feedback based on a combination of words and visual features of associated images. To the extent that the later are linked to semantics based on training data, the associated images can help specify text semantics.

5.1 Predicting Senses Based on Visual Information

In the context of word sense disambiguation, our vocabulary is assumed to be sense disambiguated. Formally, we use an extended vocabulary S, which contains the senses of the words in a vocabulary W. Notationally, if the word *bank* $\in W$ then $\{bank\_1, bank\_2, \ldots\} \in S$. Thus, every sense $s \in S$ is the sense of only one word $w \in W$. Once a model has been trained on S, we can use the annotation process to compute $P(s|B)$. Different than annotation, word sense disambiguation has the additional characteristic that we are trying to *only* distinguish between the senses, s, for a particular word, w, rather than produce a number of good choices from all of S, which is clearly more difficult.

Thus given a word, w, we assume that senses for all other words should not be predicted. Operationally we simply take the posterior probability over all the senses in our vocabulary, and set those not corresponding to w to zero. We then rescale the posterior so that it sums to one. This computation yields the probability of a word sense, s, given w, and the visual context, B, which we denote as $P(s|w, B)$.

5.2 Combining Word Prediction with Text Based Word Sense Disambiguation

The quantity $P(s|w, B)$ can be used as is for word sense disambiguation, and we provide results for this strategy. It is also natural to combine it with text based methods, as it seems to provide an orthogonal source of information. Here we assume that a text based method can provide a second estimate of the probability

$P(s|w, W)$ for the sense, s, for w, based on the observed words, W (the senses are not known a priori). We discuss our choice of $P(s|w, W)$ below (§5.3).

We assume that these two estimates are relatively independent, which gives the following simple expression for combining them:

$$P(s|w, B, W) \propto P(s|w, B)P(s|w, W). \qquad (12)$$

5.3   Text Based Word Sense Disambiguation

The probability $P(s|w, W)$ in (12) is assumed to come from a traditional text based word sense disambiguation algorithm. We report results using the state of the art SMUaw algorithm [43]. This algorithm, and a recent derivative, Sense-Learner [41]), have performed very well in word sense disambiguation challenges [26,1]. We modified the SMUaw algorithm to give softer output so that it would work better with our approach ([14]).

5.4   ImCor

To develop and test methods for using images to disambiguate text, one requires a data set that has images linked to sense disambiguated text. As no such data was readily available, we developed a new corpus, ImCor with these properties. This data is available for research purposes [36].

To construct ImCor we linked images from the Corel^{TM} data set to passages from the already sense-attributed corpus, SemCor [43,47,33,44]. SemCor, short for the WordNet Semantic Concordance [31], consists of 25% of the Brown corpus [30] files which have been fully tagged with part-of-speech and is sense disambiguated. Since the SemCor files contain sizable text passages, we selected the relevant subset of a file to link with each image. Two participants carefully linked 1633 images with an overlap of 1/6 to verify consistency. We then automatically expanded the set to 20,153 image/text pairings by exploiting the semantic redundancy in the Corel^{TM} data, by linking images that shared two or more keywords with the manually linked images.

5.5   Experiments

To test our approach we created twenty different splits of ImCor into training and testing sets (90% training, 10% testing). Since there are a number of images which are used multiple times, we took care to ensure that all duplicate images were considered to be in either the training or testing sets for a given run. For each split, we then determined the vocabulary from the training data. First we removed stop words from the corpus. Then we eliminated word senses which occurred less than 20 times. If this produced images without words, they were removed, and the vocabulary was recomputed, iteratively, if needed. Typical vocabulary sizes were 3800 senses from about 3100 sense blind words.

We trained the word prediction model (§2) on the combined image sense data. We used the features described above for the 16 largest regions. If there were fewer than 16 regions, the we used all of them. We then applied the model to the test data to predict senses according to (4), by restricting word prediction to the sense for each word being processed as described above. We them combined visual and textual cues as described in §5.2.

We computed performance using *only* documents which have at least one ambiguous word. We used the performance of the empirical distribution of the training set for a baseline. Baseline performance on sense prediction was roughly 60%. This baseline provides a harsher standard than the simple "most common sense" method, as the empirical distribution gives the common sense for the em particular corpus.

In Table 4 provides the average absolute sense prediction scores over the 20 samples. More detailed results have been reported elsewhere [14]. The results of

Table 4. Word sense prediction results. The first row is for the extended ImCor data set (20,153 text passages paired with images). The second row shows the result using the manually produced seed data set (1,633 pairs), even though the data is a bit sparse for our learning method. The numbers tabulated are the fraction of times the sense was correctly chosen. Every document processed has at least one ambiguous word. Some unambiguous can accompany those, and all algorithms score correctly on them by construction. All results are the average of 20 different splits of training and testing. The error, as estimated from the variance over the 20 test/training splits, is about 0.003 for the first row, and about 0.01 for the second row. tests.

Data set	Minimum sense count	Baseline	Text only using [43]	Image only	Combined (using (12))
Full	20	0.615	0.683	0.791	0.817
Seed	20	0.571	0.693	0.687	0.741

combining the two sources of information are very promising. The performance exceeds that of either method alone, which was what we were trying to achieve. On the large data set we were able to increase performance over the baseline by nearly 20% yielding nearly 80% absolute performance. In the small data set, the performance increase was more modest, yielding 5% improvement. We emphasize that our domain was constructed somewhat artificially to test our ideas, and that some of the improvement going from the small (seed) data set to the larger one is likely due to the system taking advantage of the structure of the Corel^{TM} data. However, even in the seed data case, where there was only limited training data (but the corpus was more pure), including image data produced a statistically significant improvement in word sense disambiguation performance.

6   Conclusion

Data with multiple modalities present great opportunities to learn semantics beyond what is possible considering the modes separately. In general, we will be more successful if we combine information from all available sources. We have presented several examples for doing this in the case of images with associated text and vice versa.

We have demonstrated how language structure can help reduce correspondence ambiguities in loosely labeled data. In particular, adjectives extracted from text can be help push loosely labeled data towards labeled data. Such an approach is important because many current methods for learning recognition rely on non-negligible quantities of data. Since labeled data is rare, but loosely labeled data is relatively easy to acquire, strategies for reducing the ambiguity of the labeling are clearly useful. Because these efforts are on a large scale, we have also studied the problem of how to prune words that are not visual given a feature set. Such pre-processing will be helpful for developing systems that learn for large scale data with free form text. In particular, the method addresses the problem that noise from non-visual words can overwhelm attempts to automatically learn the meaning of others that have more substantive links to features.

We have also summarized recent work on using images to help the understanding of natural language. In particular, correlations with visual attributes can help disambiguate word senses. Because the word prediction machinery is applied to merely choosing among the various senses of one word, visual information can be quite helpful, despite current limitations in image understanding.

We remark that it is also the limited number of choices that makes obtaining reasonable labeled data from loosely labeled image data reasonable. Here we only need to differentiate among the visual words associated with the images, which is generally a relatively small set compared to the entire vocabulary. Once the correspondence ambiguity has been reduced, we are then in a better position to learn more sophisticated processes and models which are necessary for inference on novel data.

References

1. *Proceedings of Senseval-3: The Third International Workshop on the Evaluation of Systems for the Semantic Analysis of Text*, 2004.
2. E. Agirre and G. Rigau. Word sense disambiguation using conceptual density. In *Proceedings of COLING'96*, pages 16–22, Copenhagen, Denmark, 1996.
3. E. Agirre and G. Rigau. A proposal for word sense disambiguation using conceptual distance. In *Proceedings of the 1st International Conference on Recent Advances in Natural Language Processing*, 1995.
4. R.A. Amar, D.R. Dooly, S.A. Goldman, and Q. Zhang. Multiple instance learning of real-valued data. In *18th Int. Conf. Machine Learning*, 2001.
5. S. Andrews, T. Hofmann, and I. Tsochantaridis. Multiple instance learning with generalized support vector machines. In *AAAI*, 2002.
6. S. Andrews, I. Tsochantaridis, and T. Hofmann. Support vector machines for multiple-instance learning. In *Advances in Neural Information Processing Systems*, 15, 2002.
7. Y. Bar-Hillel. The present status of automatic translation of languages. In Donald Booth and R.E. Meagher, editors, *Advances in Computers*, pages 91–163, New York, 1960. Academic Press.

8. K. Barnard, P. Duygulu, N. de Freitas, D. Forsyth, D. Blei, and M. I. Jordan. Matching words and pictures. *Journal of Machine Learning Research*, 3:1107–1135, 2003.

9. K. Barnard, P. Duygulu, and D. Forsyth. Exploiting text and image feature co-occurrence statistics in large datasets. In Remco Veltkamp, editor, *Trends and Advances in Content-Based Image and Video Retrieval*. Springer, to appear.

10. K. Barnard, P. Duygulu, N. de Freitas, D. Forsyth, D. Blei, and M. I. Jordan. Matching words and pictures. *Journal of Machine Learning Research*, 3:1107–1135, 2003.

11. K. Barnard, P. Duygulu, K. G. Raghavendra, P. Gabbur, and D. Forsyth. The effects of segmentation and feature choice in a translation model of object recognition. In *IEEE Conference on Computer Vision and Pattern Recognition*, pages II:675–682, 2003.

12. K. Barnard, Q. Fan, R. Swaminathan, A. Hoogs, R. Collins, P. Rondot, and J. Kaufhold. Evaluation of localized semantics: data, methodology, and experiments. Technical report, University of Arizona, 2005.

13. K. Barnard and D. Forsyth. Learning the semantics of words and pictures. In *International Conference on Computer Vision*, pages II:408–415, 2001.

14. K. Barnard and M. Johnson. Word sense disambiguation with pictures. *Artificial Intelligence*, 167:13–30, 2005.

15. A. C. Berg, T. L. Berg, and J. Malik. Shape matching and object recognition using low distortion correspondence. In *CVPR*, 2005.

16. E. Brill. A simple rule-based part of speech tagger. In *Third Conference on Applied Natural Language Processing*. ACL, 1992.

17. E. Brill. Transformation-based error-driven learning and natural language processing: A case study in part-of-speech tagging. *Computational Linguistics*, 21(4):543–565, 1995.

18. P. F. Brown, J. Cocke, S.A. Della Pietra, V.J. Della Pietra, Fedrick Jelinek, John D. Lafferty, Robert L. Mercer, and Paul S. Roossin. A statistical approach to machine translation. *Computational Linguistics*, 16:79–85, 1990.

19. P. F. Brown, S. A. Della Pietra, V. J. Della Pietra, and R. L. Mercer. The mathematics of machine translation: parameter estimation. *Computational Linguistics*, 19(10):263–311, 1993.

20. P. Carbonetto, N. de Freitas, and K. Barnard. A statistical model for general contextual object recognition. In *European Conference on Computer Vision*, pages I:350–362, 2004.

21. C. Carson, M. Thomas, S. Belongie, J. M. Hellerstein, and J. Malik. Blobworld: A system for region-based image indexing and retrieval. In *Third International Conference on Visual Information Systems*. Springer, 1999.

22. M. La Cascia, S. Sethi, and S. Sclaroff. Combining textual and visual cues for content based image retrieval on the web. In *IEEE Workshop on Content Based Access of Image and Video Libraries*, pages 24–28, 1998.

23. A.P. Dempster, N.M. Laird, and D.B. Rubin. Maximum likelihood from incomplete data via the em algorithm. *Journal of the Royal Statistical Society. Series B (Methodological)*, 39(1):1–38, 1977.

24. Y. Deng and B. S. Manjunath. Unsupervised segmentation of color-texture regions in images and video. *IEEE Transactions on Pattern Analysis and Machine Intelligence*, 23(8):800–810, 2001.

25. P. Duygulu, K. Barnard, J.F.G de Freitas, and D.A. Forsyth. Object recognition as machine translation: Learning a lexicon for a fixed image vocabulary. In *The Seventh European Conference on Computer Vision*, pages IV:97–112, 2002.

26. P. Edmonds and A. Kilgarriff, editors. *Journal of Natural Language Engineering*, volume 9, January 2003.
27. L. Fei-Fei, R. Fergus, and P. Perona. Learning generative visual models from few training examples: an incremental bayesian approach tested on 101 object categories. In *Workshop on Generative-Model Based Vision*, 2004.
28. S.L. Feng, R. Manmatha, and V. Lavrenko. Multiple bernoulli relevance models for image and video annotation. In *Proceedings of CVPR'04*, volume 2, pages 1002–1009, 2004.
29. R. Fergus, P. Perona, and A. Zisserman. Object class recognition by unsupervised scale-invariant learning. In *IEEE Conference on Computer Vision and Pattern Recognition*, 2003.
30. W. N. Francis and H. Kucera. *Frequency Analysis of English Usage. Lexicon and Grammar*. Houghton Mifflin, 1981.
31. G. Miller, C. Leacock, T. Randee, and R. Bunker. A semantic concordance. In *Procedings of the 3rd DARPA Workshop on Human Language Technology*, pages 303–308, 1993.
32. W. Gale, K. Church, and D. Yarowsky. One sense per discourse. In *DARPA Workshop on Speech and Natural Language*, pages 233–237, 1992.
33. J. Gonzalo, F. Verdejo, I. Chugur, and J. Cigarran. Indexing with wordnet synsets can improve text retrieval. In *Proceedings of the COLING/ACL '98 Workshop on Usage of WordNet for NLP*, pages 38–44, Montreal, Canada, 1998.
34. T. Hofmann and J. Puzicha. Statistical models for co-occurrence data. Technical report, Massachusetts Institute of Technology, 1998.
35. J. Jeon, V. Lavrenko, and R. Manmatha. Automatic image annotation and retrieval using cross-media relevance models. In *SIGIR*, pages 119–126, 2003.
36. M. Johnson and K. Barnard. *ImCor: A linking of SemCor sense disambiguated text to corel image data*. http://kobus.ca/research/data/index.html, 2004.
37. A. Kaplan. An experimental study of ambiguity in context, 1950.
38. O. Maron and T. Lozano-Perez. A framework for multiple-instance learning. In *Neural Information Processing Systems*. MIT Press, 1998.
39. O. Maron and A.L. Ratan. Multiple-instance learning for natural scene classification. In *The Fifteenth International Conference on Machine Learning*, 1998.
40. D. Melamed. *Empirical methods for exploiting parallel texts*. MIT Press, Cambridge, Massachusetts, 2001.
41. R. Mihalcea and E. Faruque. Senselearner: Minimally supervised word sense disambiguation for all words in open text. In *Proceedings of ACL/SIGLEX Senseval-3*, Barcelona, Spain, July 2004.
42. R. Mihalcea and D. Moldovan. Word sense disambiguation based on semantic density. In *Proceedings of the COLING/ACL Workshop on Usage of WordNet in Natural Language Processing Systems*, Montreal, Canada, August 1998.
43. R. Mihalcea and Dan Moldovan. An iterative approach to word sense disambiguation. In *Proceedings of Florida Artificial Intelligence Research Society Conference (FLAIRS 2000)*, pages 219–223, Orlando, FL, May 2000.
44. P. M. Montoyo. Wordnet enrichment with classification systems. In *Proceedings of NAACL Workshop 'WordNet and Other Lexical Resources: Applications, Extensions and Customizations'*, pages 101–106, Carnegie Mellon University, Pittsburgh, USA, 2001.
45. J. Shi and J. Malik. Normalized cuts and image segmentation. *IEEE Transactions on Pattern Analysis and Machine Intelligence*, 22(9):888–905, 2000.
46. N. V. Shirahatti and K. Barnard. Evaluating image retrieval. In *Proceedings of CVPR'05*, volume 1, pages 955–961, 2005.

47. J. Stetina, S. Kurohashi, and M. Nagao.   General word sense disambiguation method based on A full sentential context. In Sanda Harabagiu, editor, *Use of WordNet in Natural Language Processing Systems: Proceedings of the Conference*, pages 1–8. Association for Computational Linguistics, Somerset, New Jersey, 1998.
48. A. Torralba, K. P. Murphy, and W. T. Freeman. Sharing features: efficient boosting procedures for multiclass object detection. In *IEEE Conference on Computer Vision and Pattern Recognition*, pages II:762–769, 2004.
49. J. Traupman and R. Wilensky. Experiments in improving unsupervised word sense disambiguation. Technical report, University of California at Berkeley, 2003.
50. D. Yarowsky. Unsupervised word sense disambiguation rivaling supervised methods. In *33rd Conference on Applied Natural Language Processing*. ACL, 1995.
51. V. Yngve. Syntax and the problem of multiple meaning. In W. Locke and D. Booth, editors, *Machine Translation of Languages*, pages 208–226, New York, 1955. Wiley.
52. Q. Zhang and S.A. Goldman. Em-dd:an improved multiple-instance learning technique. In *Neural Information Processing Systems*, 2001.
53. Q. Zhang, S.A. Goldman, W. Yu, and J.E. Fritts. Content-based image retrieval using multiple-instance learning. In *19th Int. Conf. Machine Learning*, 2001.

Translating Images to Words for Recognizing Objects in Large Image and Video Collections

Pınar Duygulu[1], Muhammet Baştan[1], and David Forsyth[2]

[1] Department of Computer Engineering, Bilkent University, Ankara, Turkey
{duygulu,bastan}@cs.bilkent.edu.tr
[2] University of Illinois
405 N. Mathews Avenue, Urbana, IL 61801, USA
dforsyth@uiuc.edu

Abstract. We present a new approach to the object recognition problem, motivated by the recent availability of large annotated image and video collections. This approach considers object recognition as the translation of visual elements to words, similar to the translation of text from one language to another. The visual elements represented in feature space are categorized into a finite set of blobs. The correspondences between the blobs and the words are learned, using a method adapted from Statistical Machine Translation. Once learned, these correspondences can be used to predict words corresponding to particular image regions (region naming), to predict words associated with the entire images (auto-annotation), or to associate the speech transcript text with the correct video frames (video alignment). We present our results on the Corel data set which consists of annotated images and on the TRECVID 2004 data set which consists of video frames associated with speech transcript text and manual annotations.

1 Introduction

Object recognition is one of the major problems in computer vision and there have been many efforts to solve this problem (see [13] for a detailed review of recent approaches). However, recognition on the large scale is still a challenge. We consider the object recognition problem as translating the visual elements to semantic labels. This view of object recognition allows us to recognize large number of objects in the large image and video collections.

Classical object recognition systems require supervised data where regions corresponding to objects are manually labeled. However, creation of such data is labor intensive and error-prone. Recently, many annotated image and video collections have become available. Examples include stock photographs annotated with keywords, museum image collections with metadata, captioned news photographs on the web, and news videos associated with captions or speech recognition transcripts (Figure 1). These annotated data sets, provide labels not on the region level but on the image level. Although, that is only loosely labeled data, it is available in large quantities. By making use of this data, the

J. Ponce et al. (Eds.): Toward Category-Level Object Recognition, LNCS 4170, pp. 258–276, 2006.

plane jet su-27   sky tiger cat grass water   diver fish ocean   memorial flags grass

Forest Snow
FemaleSpeech
TextOverlay

Sky WaterBody
Beach Building
MaleSpeech People

Music Car
SpaceVehicleLaunch

StudioSetting
MaleNewsPerson
Monologue

Fig. 1. Examples of annotated images. **Top:** Corel data set. **Bottom:** TRECVID news videos data set.

object recognition problem can be transformed into finding the correspondences between image structures and annotation words.

Recent studies show that, with careful use of these large annotated data sets, it is possible to predict words for the images by integrating visual and textual data [22,30,19,24,27]. More recently, probabilistic models are proposed to capture the joint statistics between images and words, including the hierarchical aspect model [5,4], relevance based models [16,18,12], mixture of multi-modal latent Dirichlet allocation model [3], and a method based on Hidden Markov Model [15].

Predicting words for the images, which is referred as **auto-annotation**, is helpful since considerable amount of work for manually annotating the images can be eliminated. However, that is not a solution to the recognition problem, since the correspondences between image structures and words are unknown. For example, an image with the keyword `tiger` is likely to contain a tiger object, but we don't know which part of the image corresponds to tiger (Figure 2).

The correspondence problem is very similar to the correspondence problem faced in statistical machine translation literature (Figure 3). There is one form of data (image structures or English words) and we want to transform it into another form of data (keywords or French words). Learning a lexicon (a device that can predict one representation given the other representation) from large data sets (referred as aligned bitext) is a standard problem in the statistical machine translation literature [8,23,17,21]. Aligned bitexts consist of many small blocks of text in both languages, corresponding to each other at paragraph or sentence level, but not at the word level. Using the aligned bitexts the problem of lexicon learning is transformed into the problem of finding the correspondences between words of different languages, which can then be tackled by machine learning methods.

Due to the similarity of the problems, correspondence problem between image structures and keywords can be attacked as a problem of translating visual features into words, as first proposed in [10]. Given a set of training images, the

tiger grass cat

Fig. 2. The correspondence problem between image regions and words. The keywords **tiger**, **cat** and **grass** are associated with the image, but the word-to-region correspondences are unknown. If there are other images, the correct correspondences can be learned and used to automatically label each region in the image with correct words or to auto-annotate a given image.

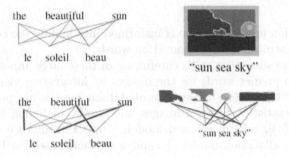

Fig. 3. The analogy with the statistical machine translation. We want to transform one form of data (image structures or English words) to another form of data (keywords or French words).

problem is to create a probability table that associates words and visual elements. This translation table can then be used to find the corresponding words for the given test images (**auto-annotation**) or to label the image components with words as a novel approach to recognition (**region labeling**).

A similar correspondence problem occurs in video data. There are sets of video frames and transcripts extracted from the audio speech narrative, but the semantic correspondences between them are not fixed because they may not be co-occurring in time. If there is no direct association between text and video frames, a query based on text may produce incorrect visual results. For example, in most news videos (see Figure 4) the anchorperson talks about an event, place or person, but the images related to the event, place, or person appear later in the video. Therefore, a query based only on text related to a person, place, or event, and showing the frames at the matching narrative, may yield incorrect frames of the anchorperson as the result.

The goal is to determine the correspondences between the video frames and speech transcript text in order to associate the video frames with more reliable

... (1) so today it was an energized president **CLINTON** who formally presented his one point seven three trillion dollar budget to the congress and told them there'd be money left over first of the white house a.b.c's sam donaldson (2) ready this (3) morning here at the whitehouse and why not (4) next year's projected budget deficit zero where they've presidential shelf and tell *this* (5) *budget marks the hand of an era and ended decades of deficits that have shackled our economy paralyzed our politics and held our people back* ..... (6) [empty] (7) [empty] (8) administration officials say this balanced budget are the results of the president's sound policies he's critics say it's merely a matter of benefiting from a strong economy that other forces are driving for the matter why it couldn't come at a better time just another upward push for mr **CLINTON**'s new sudden sky high job approval rating peter thanks very ...

Fig. 4. Keyframes and corresponding speech transcripts for a sample sequence of shots for a story related to Clinton. Italic text shows Clinton's speech, and capitalized letters show when Clinton's name appears in the transcript. Note that, Clinton's name is mentioned when an anchorperson or reporter is speaking, but not when he is in the picture.

labels and descriptions, which we refer as **video alignment**. This enables a textual query to return more accurate semantically corresponding images. We will show that, a modified version of the translation model can be used to solve the correspondence problem faced in video data.

Other models proposed to attack the correspondence problem include the simple co-occurrence model [25], Correlation Latent Dirichlet Allocation (LDA) model [6] and an extension of translation approach using MRFs [9].

2   Translation Approach

Brown *et al.* [8] propose a set of models for statistical machine translation. These models aim to maximize the conditional probability density $p(\mathbf{f} \mid \mathbf{e})$, which is called as the likelihood of translation $(\mathbf{f}, \mathbf{e})$, where $\mathbf{f}$ is a set of French words, and $\mathbf{e}$ is a set of English words.

In machine translation, a lexicon links a set of discrete objects (words in one language) onto another set of discrete objects (words in the other language). In our case, the data consist of visual elements associated with words. The **words** are in discrete form. In order to exploit the analogy with machine translation, the visual data, represented as a set of feature vectors also need to be broken up into discrete items. For this purpose, the features are grouped by vector quantization techniques such as k-means and the labels of the classes, which we call as **blobs**, are used as the discrete items for the visual data. Then, an aligned bitext, consisting of the blobs and the words for each image is obtained and used to construct a probability table linking blobs with words.

In our case, the goal is to maximize $p(\mathbf{w} \mid \mathbf{b})$, where $\mathbf{b}$ is a set of blobs and $\mathbf{w}$ is a set of words. Each word is aligned with the blobs in the image. The alignments (referred as **a**) provide a correspondence between each word and all the blobs. The model requires the sum over all possible assignments for each pair of aligned sentences, so that $p(\mathbf{w} \mid \mathbf{b})$ can be written in terms of the conditional probability density $p(\mathbf{w}, \mathbf{a} \mid \mathbf{b})$ as

$$p(\mathbf{w} \mid \mathbf{b}) = \sum_{\mathbf{a}} p(\mathbf{w}, \mathbf{a} \mid \mathbf{b}) \tag{1}$$

The simplest model (Model-1), assumes that all connections for each French position are equally likely. This model is adapted to translate blobs into words, since there is no order relation among the blobs or the words in the data [29]. In Model-1 it is assumed that each word is aligned exactly with a single blob. If the image has l blobs and m words, the alignment is determined by specifying the values of a_j such that if the jth word is connected to the ith blob, then $a_j = i$, and if it is not connected to any blob $a_j = 0$. Assuming a uniform alignment probability (each alignment is equally probable), given a blob the joint likelihood of a word and an alignment is then can be written as:

$$p(\mathbf{w}, \mathbf{a} \mid \mathbf{b}) = \frac{\epsilon}{(l+1)^m} \prod_{j=1}^{m} t(w_j \mid b_{a_j}) \tag{2}$$

where $t(w_j \mid b_{a_j})$ is the translation probability of the word w_j given the blob b_{a_j}, and ϵ is a fixed small number.

The alignment is determined by specifying the values of a_j for j from 1 to m each of which can take a value from 0 to l. Then, $p(\mathbf{w} \mid \mathbf{b})$ can be written as:

$$p(\mathbf{w} \mid \mathbf{b}) = \frac{\epsilon}{(l+1)^m} \sum_{a_1=0}^{l} \cdots \sum_{a_m=0}^{l} \prod_{j=1}^{m} t(w_j \mid b_{a_j}) \tag{3}$$

Our goal is to maximize $p(\mathbf{w} \mid \mathbf{b})$ subject to the constraint that for each b

$$\sum_{w} t(w \mid b) = 1 \tag{4}$$

This maximization problem can be solved with the EM (Expectation Maximization) formulation [8,10]. In this study, we use the Giza++ tool [1,26] -which is a part of the Statistical Machine Translation toolkit developed during summer 1999 at CLSP at Johns Hopkins University- to learn the probabilities. Note that, we use the direct translation model throughout the study.

The learned association probabilities are kept in a translation probability table, and then used to predict words for the test data.

3   Associating Visual Elements with Words

In this study, we attack two types of correspondence problems between visual elements and words. The first problem is between the image regions and words in annotated image collections. The second problem is between the frames of a video sequence and the corresponding speech transcript text.

In the annotated image and video collections, the images are usually annotated with a few keywords which describe the images. However, correspondences between image regions and words are unknown. In order to solve this correspondence problem, first we segment the images into regions and represent each region with a set of visual features. A vector quantization technique, such as k-means, is used to transform the visual features into labels which are called as blobs. The words are in the form of keywords, therefore no further processing is required. The blobs and words are associated with certain probabilities using the translation approach. The translation table can then be used for two purposes: region naming and auto-annotation.

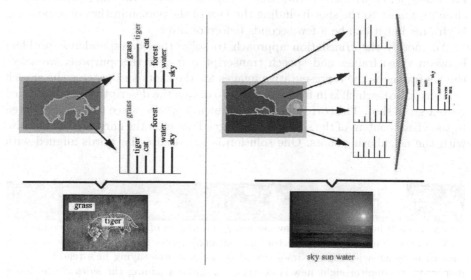

Fig. 5. Left: Region naming. **Right:** Auto-annotation. For region naming, the word with the highest probability is used to label the region. For auto-annotation the word posterior probabilities of the image regions are marginalized to obtain the probabilities for the entire image and then the top N words with the highest probabilities are used to annotate the image.

Region naming refers to predicting the labels for the regions, which is clearly recognition. For region naming, given a blob b corresponding to the region, the word w with the highest probability ($p(w \mid b)$) is chosen and used to label the region (Figure 5).

In order to automatically annotate the images, the word posterior probabilities for the entire image are obtained by marginalizing the word posterior probabilities of all the blobs in the image as:

$$p(w|I_b) = 1/|I_b| \sum_{b \in I_b} p(w|b) \tag{5}$$

where b is a blob, I_b is the set of all blobs of the image and w is a word. Then, the word posterior probabilities are normalized. The first N words with the highest posterior probabilities are used as the annotation words (Figure 5).

The other correspondence problem that we attack is the video alignment problem. Specifically, we will concentrate on the video alignment problem in the news videos. In these videos, the speech transcript text is temporally aligned with the video frames and each shot is associated with a portion of the transcript that falls within its boundary. Most of the retrieval systems use the speech recognition text aligned with the shots to search for persons, places or events. However, the frames of the resulting shots may not visually correspond to the query (Figure 4). For example, in [31], it is shown that for person queries the name appears in a close proximity to the shot including the face of the person in the corresponding keyframe, but it can be a few seconds before or after.

We modify the translation approach to solve the correspondence problem between video frames and speech transcript text. For this purpose, we select the keyframes as the representative images for the shots and process the speech transcript text -which is in free text form- to obtain the descriptive words aligned with a given shot. The correspondence problem appears, since the words related to the visual content of the shot may be aligned not with the current shot but also with the neighboring shots. One solution is to use also the words aligned with

Story 1: (1-3) he says the u.s. may use force in a matter of weeks to try to compelling rock to allow u.n. weapons inspectors unrestricted access to suspected weapons sites russian news agencies reports iraqi president saddam was saying he's ready to allow inspectors to monitor eight new sites must the ground joining the sides of the latest u.s. defense secretary william cohen says that he's not an appropriate solution
Story 2: (4-5) darkness has led air transportation officials in the philippines to temporarily call of the helicopter searched for a missing passenger plane bound teams are continuing to look for the cebu pacific and d.c. nine it was carrying one hundred four people when it disappeared on its way from manila tuned and other parts of the southern philippines the pilot last contacted the airport tower minutes before that plane was supposed to land he made no mention of any trouble with the plane
Story 3: (6-7) the sarbes extending to unbeaten streak to five games we'll fight to win over the panthers final singer with the bow ahead goal detroit rallied with three goals in the final period
Story 4: (8) this is orelon sidney with your headline news weather update a low pressure storm moving out of the james bay region will mean a chance of snow flurries for the upper peninsula if michigan cold temperatures are due in the forecast for the north as the cold front moves into the mississippi and ohio river valleys

Fig. 6. Keyframes and speech transcripts for some stories from TRECVID2004 news videos. Numbers in parenthesis correspond to the keyframes of the stories.

the preceding and the following shots during the learning phase [11]. However, this strategy may use incorrect annotation words, since the speech transcript text a few shots before or after may correspond to other stories that are not related with the current shot.

News videos consist of story segments each corresponding to different topics (Figure 6). Using this characteristics of news videos, we use a story based approach. Each story is taken as the basic unit, and the correspondence problem is turned into finding the associations between the keyframes and the speech transcript words of the story segments. To make the analogy with the correspondence problem between image regions and annotation keywords, the story corresponds to the image, the keyframes correspond to the regions and the speech transcript text corresponds to the annotation keywords. The features extracted from the entire images of the keyframes are vector quantized to represent each image with a single label which is again referred as blob. Then, the translation tables are constructed similar to the one constructed for annotated images. The associations can then be used either to align the keyframes with the correct words or for predicting words for the entire story.

4   Data Sets and Input Representation

In this study, we use the annotated images from Corel stock photograph data set and the news videos from TRECVID2004 corpus.

The Corel data set consists of images annotated with 3-5 keywords. We segment the images using the Normalized Cuts algorithm [28] and represent the 8 largest regions in each image with 30 features including the region size, position, color, texture and shape features. Regions are then clustered into blobs using k-means.

The TRECVID 2004 corpus [2] provided by NIST consists of over 150 hours of CNN and ABC broadcast news videos. The shot boundaries, and the keyframes extracted from each shot are provided by NIST. The keyframes are represented by a set of features including global color histogram, and mean and standard deviation of color, edge and texture features extracted from 5x7 grids. Videos are manually annotated with a collaborative effort of the TRECVID participants with a few keywords [20]. The automatic speech recognition (ASR) transcripts provided by LIMSI are aligned with the shots on the time basis [14]. The speech transcripts are in the free text form and requires preprocessing. First, we use Brill's part of speech tagger [7] to extract nouns which are expected to correspond to object names. Then, we apply a stemmer and remove the stop words and also the least frequent words appearing less than 300 times to obtain the descriptive words.

5   Measuring the Performance

The trivial way to measure the performance of region naming is to check the labels of each region visually. However, considering the huge size of the data sets, this is not a practical solution. One alternative is to label the regions of a small set of images manually and then compare the predictions with the manual labels. Then, the performance can be measured in terms of recall and precision where recall is defined as the number of correct predictions of the word over the number of times that the word is a label word, and precision is defined as the number of correct predictions of the word over the number of times that the word is predicted.

Another solution, applicable to large number of images, is to predict the words for the entire images and use the annotation performance as a proxy. If the image has N annotation keywords, the system will also predict N words. A word prediction measure (WP) [3] can then be defined as:

$$WP = c/N \tag{6}$$

where c is the number of words predicted correctly. Thus, if there are three keywords, sky, water, and sun, then N=3, and we allow the model to predict 3 words for that image. The range of this score is clearly from 0 to 1.

Recall and precision can also be used to measure the annotation performance. In this case, the word is defined to be predicted correctly, if it is predicted as one of the best N words (where N is the number of words in the manual annotation) and it matches with one of the annotation keywords. Then, recall is defined as the number of times that the word is predicted correctly over the number of times that the word is used as an annotation keyword throughout the entire data set, and precision is defined as the number of times that the word is predicted correctly over the total number of times that the word is predicted.

The performance of video alignment can be measured similarly. We predict N words with the highest probability for a given story and compare them with the actual speech transcript words.

6   Results on Corel Data Set

For the experiments, we used 160 CD's, each consisting of 100 images on a relatively specific topic. The words occurring less than 20 times are excluded, resulting in vocabularies in the order of 155 words. As the visual features, color is represented by the average and standard deviation of (R,G,B) and (L,a,b) over the region; texture is represented using the average of 12 oriented energy filters aligned in 30 degree increments; and shape is represented by the ratio of the area to the perimeter squared, the moment of inertia and the region of the area to that of its convex hull. The features are quantized into 500 blobs using k-means.

Figure 7 shows some examples of region labeling. The label words are the words predicted with the highest probability for the corresponding blobs. We are generally successful in predicting words like sky and buildings. Rare words such as plane and fish are also predicted correctly in these examples.

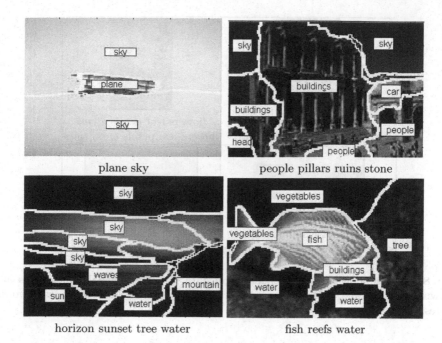

plane sky   people pillars ruins stone

horizon sunset tree water   fish reefs water

Fig. 7. Sample images and the word prediction results for the Corel data set. Manual annotations are shown for comparison.

In order to test the performance of region labeling, 450 images are manually labeled with a set of 117 words. Table 1 shows the region labeling performances in the form of recall and precision for a set of words.

Table 1. Region labeling performance for some words on the Corel data set

word	recall	precision	word	recall	precision	word	recall	precision
sea	0.67	0.50	sky	0.31	0.34	windows	0.33	0.25
snake	0.20	0.33	water	0.40	0.20	buildings	0.16	0.17
tree	0.28	0.15	pillars	0.17	0.11	clouds	0.19	0.06
people	0.32	0.04	grass	0.09	0.19	flowers	0.08	0.16
car	0.10	0.12	coral	0.05	0.20	lion	0.05	0.17

Figure 8 shows some auto-annotation examples. Most of the words are predicted correctly and most of the incorrect matches are due to the missing manual annotations. For instance, although tree appears at the top left image, the word **tree** it is not in the manual annotations.

In order to measure the performance of auto-annotation, we create ten experimental data set each consisting of 80 CDs which are randomly chosen. Each experimental data set is further split up into training and standard test sets, containing

field foals horses mare *tree* horses foals mare field	flowers leaf petals *stems* flowers leaf petals *grass* *tulip*
people pool swimmers water swimmers pool people water *sky*	jet plane sky sky plane jet *tree* *clouds*

Fig. 8. Auto-annotation examples for Corel data set. The manual annotations are shown at the top, and the top 5 predicted words are shown at the bottom. Italic words correspond to incorrect matches.

75% and 25% of the images respectively. The images from the remaining CD's are used to form a more difficult novel test set.

Table 2 shows the word prediction results for each of the ten data sets on training, standard test and novel test sets. The average number of annotation words per image is three. The prediction performances show that on the average we are predicting one of the three words correctly.

Table 2. Word prediction measures for each of the ten experimental data sets

set	training	standard test	novel test
001	0.2708	0.2171	0.2236
002	0.2799	0.2262	0.2173
003	0.2763	0.2288	0.2095
004	0.2592	0.1925	0.2172
005	0.2853	0.2370	0.2059
006	0.2776	0.2198	0.2163
007	0.2632	0.2036	0.2217
008	0.2799	0.2363	0.2102
009	0.2659	0.2223	0.2114
010	0.2815	0.2297	0.1991

7   Results on TRECVID Data Set

In the TRECVID 2004 corpus, there are 229 videos in the training set and 128 videos in the test set. On the average, there are around 300 keyframes for each shot. 114 videos from the training set are manually annotated by the TRECVID participants. We only use the annotations for the keyframes, and therefore eliminate the videos where the annotations are provided for the frames which are not keyframes, resulting in 92 videos. The original annotations consisting of 614 words have many spelling and format errors. After correcting the errors and removing the least frequent words we pruned the vocabulary down to 76 words.

StudioSetting Graphics FemaleNewsPerson MaleNewsSubject Person	People Basketball	WaterBody Boat
FemaleNewsPerson StudioSetting People MaleFace Graphics Person SceneText	People Graphics Basketball FemaleNewsPerson SceneText MaleNewsSubject StudioSetting	Sky Graphics WaterBody Building Boat Person MaleNewsPerson
Sky Building Road Car Graphics	Tree Snow People	Forest MaleNewsSubject FemaleFace Person Graphics
Road ManMadeObject People Sky Building Car ManMadeScene	Graphics People Person MaleFace MaleNewsSubject Tree Snow	People Person Graphics MaleFace Greenery SceneText FemaleFace

Fig. 9. Auto-annotation examples for the TRECVID data set. The manual annotations are shown at the top, and the predicted words (top 7 words with the highest probability) are shown at the bottom.

We use the manually annotated data set for learning the correspondences between image regions (which are in the form of fixed sized grids) and the keywords for region labeling and for auto-annotation similar to the Corel data set. The grids are represented by the mean and standard deviation of HSV values. The features are clustered into 500 blobs. On the test data, we obtain word prediction

performance as 0.27, and average recall and precision values for the words that
are predicted at least once as 0.15 and 0.21 respectively.

Figure 9 shows the auto-annotation results for some sample shots. The results
show that when the annotations are not available the predicted words can be
used for a better retrieval. Figure 10 shows some region labeling results. Note
that words like `female-news-person`, `female-face`, `studio-setting`, sky and
`building` are correctly predicted.

For video alignment, 114 videos are used for training and 39 videos are used for
testing. The story boundaries provided by NIST are used. Speech transcript text

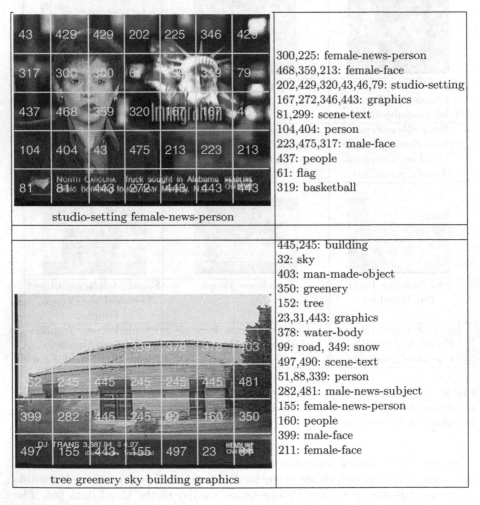

300,225: female-news-person
468,359,213: female-face
202,429,320,43,46,79: studio-setting
167,272,346,443: graphics
81,299: scene-text
104,404: person
223,475,317: male-face
437: people
61: flag
319: basketball

studio-setting female-news-person

445,245: building
32: sky
403: man-made-object
350: greenery
152: tree
23,31,443: graphics
378: water-body
99: road, 349: snow
497,490: scene-text
51,88,339: person
282,481: male-news-subject
155: female-news-person
160: people
399: male-face
211: female-face

tree greenery sky building graphics

Fig. 10. Region labeling results for the TRECVID dataset. Manual annotations are
shown for comparison.

(ASR) is processed by applying tagging, stemming and stop word elimination steps and only the nouns having frequencies more than 300 are used in the final vocabulary. We remove the stories associated with less than 4 words, and use the remaining 2165 stories consisting of 30801 keyframes for training and 1050 stories consisting of 10326 keyframes for testing. The number of words corresponding to the stories vary between 4 and 105, and the average number of words per story is 15. Each keyframe is represented with a blob obtained by vector quantization of the global HSV color histogram values and also with another blob corresponding to the number of faces in the keyframe. Color feature is represented with 1000 blobs and face count is represented with 4 blobs.

The translation probabilities are used to predict words for the individual shots (Figure 11) and for the stories (Figure 12). The results show that especially for the stories related to weather, sports or economy, which frequently appear in the broadcast news, the system can predict the correct words. Note that, the system can predict words which are better than the original speech transcript words. This characteristic is important for a better retrieval. The prediction performance obtained by comparing the predicted words for a given story with the original ASR words is 0.15 and the average recall and precision values are 0.13 and 0.16 respectively.

An important aspect of predicting words for the video segments is to retrieve the related shots when speech transcript is not available or include unrelated words. In such cases it would not be possible to retrieve such shots with a text based retrieval system if the predicted words were not available. Figure 13 shows that the proposed system is able to detect the associations between the sport word and different types of sport scenes, and therefore can be used in retrieving sport shots even when the ASR is not available. Similarly, the system is successful in capturing the relationships between the visual features and words for scenes such as snow, night or office as in Figure 14 or objects such as plane, house, water or car as in Figure 15. Note that, these examples include objects and scenes which can be described by color information.

One of the main goals of solving the video alignment problem is to associate the words with the correct shots. Figure 16 shows an example to the solution of video alignment problem. Originally the word clinton was aligned with the anchorperson shot. After correcting the association problem, the shot which predicts clinton inside the story corresponds to the shot where Clinton appears. We should mention here that, this is not a solution to face recognition. In this example, the goal is to find the shot which has the highest probability to be associated with the clinton word inside the story segment. The third shot has the highest probability to be associated with clinton since it includes faces and also the black suits which can be described by color information. The second shot is probably eliminated since there were no faces detected, and the first shot is eliminated since the anchorperson shots having the studio setting at the background are associated with many words.

| temperature weather forecast | point nasdaq stock | sport time game | jenning people evening |

Fig. 11. Top three words predicted for some shots using the ASR outputs

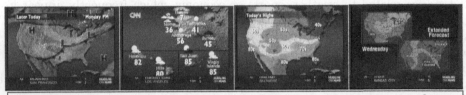

ASR : center headline thunderstorm morning line move state area pressure chance shower lake head monday west end weekend percent temperature gulf coast tuesday
PREDICTED : weather thunderstorm rain temperature system shower west coast snow pressure

ASR : check peace york morning charge dollar share nasdaq market issue percent consumer month
PREDICTED : market stock york nasdaq street check point yesterday record share

ASR : night game sery story
PREDICTED : game headline sport goal team product business record time shot

Fig. 12. For sample stories corresponding ASR outputs and top 10 words predicted

Fig. 13. Shots having no attached ASR output but including **sport** keyword in their top 2 predicted words

Fig. 14. Shots having no related ASR output but including **snow**, **night** and **office** keywords in their top 7 predicted words respectively

Fig. 15. Example shots predicting **plane**, **house**, **water** and **car** as their top 7th, 1st, 3rd and 7th words respectively

ASR outputs : (1) home washington president clinton (2) office president state
department (3) deal

Fig. 16. For a story about Clinton with three shots, the keyframes and the ASR outputs associated with each of the shots on the time basis are shown. Note that, `clinton` is associated with the first shot where the anchorperson appears. When we search over the predicted words, the shot corresponding to `clinton` word with the highest probability is the third shot where Clinton actually appears.

8 Conclusion and Future Work

We associate visual features with words using the translation approach. The proposed method allows novel applications on image and video databases including region naming as a way of recognizing objects, auto-annotation for better access to image databases and video alignment which is a crucial process for effective retrieval of video data.

In video data, motion information also plays an important role. Usually, moving objects have more importance than still objects. The regions corresponding to these objects can be extracted using the motion information rather than using any segmentation algorithm. Also, besides associating the visual features such as color, texture and shape with nouns for naming the objects, the motion information can be associated with verbs for naming the actions.

Translation approach can also be used as a novel method for face recognition. The correspondence problem that appears between the face of a person and his/her name can be attacked similarly for naming the people. The example about Clinton story promises that such an approach is possible for naming large number of faces.

Acknowledgements

This research is partially supported by TÜBİTAK Career grant number 104E065 and grant number 104E077.

References

1. Giza++. http://www.fjoch.com/GIZA++.html.
2. TREC Video Retrieval Evaluation.   http://www-nlpir.nist.gov/projects/
   trecvid.

3. K. Barnard, P. Duygulu, N. de Freitas, D. A. Forsyth, D. Blei, and M. Jordan. Matching words and pictures. *Journal of Machine Learning Research*, 3:1107–1135, 2003.
4. K. Barnard, P. Duygulu, and D. A. Forsyth. Clustering art. In *IEEE Conference on Computer Vision and Pattern Recognition*, volume 2, pages 434–439, 2001.
5. K. Barnard and D. A. Forsyth. Learning the semantics of words and pictures. In *International Conference on Computer Vision (ICCV)*, volume 2, pages 408–415, 2001.
6. D. Blei and M. I. Jordan. Modeling annotated data. In *26th Annual International ACM SIGIR Conference*, pages 127–134, Toronto, Canada, July 28-August 1 2003.
7. E. Brill. A simple rule-based part of speech tagger. In *Proceedings of the Third Conference on Applied Natural Language Processing*, pages 152–155, Trento, Italy, 1992.
8. P. Brown, S. A. D. Pietra, V. J. D. Pietra, and R. L. Mercer. The mathematics of statistical machine translation: Parameter estimation. *Computational Linguistics*, 19(2):263–311, 1993.
9. P. Carbonetto, N. de Freitas, and K. Barnard. A statistical model for general contextual object recognition. In *Eight European Conference on Computer Vision (ECCV)*, Prague, Czech Republic, May 11-14 2004.
10. P. Duygulu, K. Barnard, N. Freitas, and D. A. Forsyth. Object recognition as machine translation: learning a lexicon for a fixed image vocabulary. In *Seventh European Conference on Computer Vision (ECCV)*, volume 4, pages 97–112, Copenhagen Denmark, May 27 - June 2 2002.
11. P. Duygulu and H. Wactlar. Associating video frames with text. In *Multimedia Information Retrieval Workshop in conjuction with the 26th annual ACM SIGIR conference on Information Retrieval*, Toronto, Canada, August 1 2003.
12. S. Feng, R. Manmatha, and V. Lavrenko. Multiple bernoulli relevance models for image and video annotation. In *the Proceedings of the International Conference on Pattern Recognition (CVPR 2004)*, volume 2, pages 1002–1009, 2004.
13. D. A. Forsyth and J. Ponce. *Computer Vision: A Modern Approach*. Prentice-Hall, 2002.
14. J. Gauvain, L. Lamel, and G. Adda. The limsi broadcast news transcription system. *Speech Communication*, 37(1-2):89–108, 2002.
15. A. Ghoshal, P. Ircing, and S. Khudanpur. Hidden markov models for automatic annotation and content based retrieval of images and video. In *The 28th International ACM SIGIR Conference*, Salvador, Brazil, August 15-19 2005.
16. J. Jeon, V. Lavrenko, and R. Manmatha. Automatic image annotation and retrieval using cross-media relevance models. In *26th Annual International ACM SIGIR Conference*, pages 119–126, Toronto, Canada, July 28-August 1 2003.
17. D. Jurafsky and J. H. Martin. *Speech and Language Processing: An Introduction to Natural Language Processing Computational Linguistics and Speech Recognition*. Prentice-Hall, 2000.
18. V. Lavrenko, R. Manmatha, and J. Jeon. A model for learning the semantics of pictures. In *the Proceedings of the Seventeenth Annual Conference on Neural Information Processing Systems*, volume 16, pages 553–560, 2003.
19. J. Li and J. Wang. Automatic linguistic indexing of pictures by a statistical modeling approach. *IEEE Trans. on Pattern Analysis and Machine Intelligence*, 25(9):1075–1088, September 2003.

20. C.-Y. Lin, B. L. Tseng, and J. R. Smith. Video collaborative annotation forum:establishing ground-truth labels on large multimedia datasets. In *NIST TREC-2003 Video Retrieval Evaluation Conference*, Gaithersburg, MD, November 2003.
21. C. D. Manning and H. S. utze. *Foundations of Statistical Natural Language Processing*. MIT Press, Cambridge Massachusetts, 1999.
22. O. Maron and A. L. Ratan. Multiple-instance learning for natural scene classification. In *The Fifteenth International Conference on Machine Learning*, pages 341–349, 1998.
23. I. D. Melamed. *Empirical Methods for Exploiting Parallel Texts*. MIT Press, Cambridge Massachusetts, 2001.
24. F. Monay and D. Gatica-Perez. On image auto-annotation with latent space models. In *Proc. ACM Int. Conf. on Multimedia (ACM MM)*, Berkeley, CA, USA, November 2003.
25. Y. Mori, H. Takahashi, and R. Oka. Image-to-word transformation based on dividing and vector quantizing images with words. In *First International Workshop on Multimedia Intelligent Storage and Retrieval Management*, 1999.
26. F. J. Och and H. Ney. A systematic comparison of various statistical alignment models. *Computational Linguistics*, 1(29):19–51, 2003.
27. J.-Y. Pan, H.-J. Yang, C. Faloutsos, and P. Duygulu. Automatic multimedia crossmodal correlation discovery. In *Proceedings of the 10th ACM SIGKDD Conference*, Seatle, WA, August 22-25 2004.
28. J. Shi and J. Malik. Normalized cuts and image segmentation. *IEEE Transactions on Pattern Analysis and Machine Intelligence*, 22(8):888–905, August 2000.
29. P. Virga and P. Duygulu. Systematic evaluation of machine translation methods for image and video annotation. In *The Fourth International Conference on Image and Video Retrieval (CIVR 2005)*, Singapore, July 20-22 2005.
30. L. Wenyin, S. Dumais, Y. Sun, H. Zhang, M. Czerwinski, and B. Field. Semiautomatic image annotation. In *Proc. INTERACT : Conference on Human-Computer Interaction*, pages 326–333, Tokyo Japan, July 9-13 2001.
31. J. Yang, M.-Y. Chen, and A. Hauptmann. Finding person x: Correlating names with visual appearances. In *International Conference on Image and Video Retrieval (CIVR'04)*, Dublin City University Ireland, July 21-23 2004.

A Semi-supervised Learning Approach to Object Recognition with Spatial Integration of Local Features and Segmentation Cues

Peter Carbonetto[1], Gyuri Dorkó[2], Cordelia Schmid[2],
Hendrik Kück[1], and Nando de Freitas[1]

[1] University of British Columbia, Vancouver, Canada
{pcarbo,kueck,nando}@cs.ubc.ca
[2] INRIA Rhône-Alpes, Grenoble, France
{Gyuri.Dorko,Cordelia.Schmid}@inrialpes.fr

Abstract. This chapter presents a principled way of formulating models for automatic local feature selection in object class recognition when there is little supervised data. Moreover, it discusses how one could formulate sensible spatial image context models using a conditional random field for integrating local features and segmentation cues (superpixels). By adopting sparse kernel methods and Bayesian model selection and data association, the proposed model identifies the most relevant sets of local features for recognizing object classes, achieves performance comparable to the fully supervised setting, and consistently outperforms existing methods for image classification.

1 Introduction

Over the past few years, researchers in high-level vision have shifted their focus from matching specific objects to the significantly more challenging problem of recognizing visual categories of objects. Since solutions exists to some image classification problems, there is a push to address more difficult problems such as object localization (segmenting an object from the background). There has also been success in learning robust representations of specific classes in constrained situations, notably frontal faces [33] and pedestrians in street scenes [17,22], but models that can be trained to recognize generic object categories remain elusive.

A wealth of complementary developments in vision and machine learning have lead to improvements in general representations of object classes [1,9,26,11]. This paper furthers the state-of-the-art by adopting a principled probabilistic model for data association and model selection in object recognition. Our approach consists of the following three steps:

1. Extract a sparse set of *a priori* informative regions of the scene [9,21], also called *keypoints* [7,19]. Local interest regions bring tolerance to clutter, occlusion and deformable objects, and their sparsity reduces the complexity of subsequent learning and inference. Good detectors extract a sparse set

J. Ponce et al. (Eds.): Toward Category-Level Object Recognition, LNCS 4170, pp. 277–300, 2006.
© Springer-Verlag Berlin Heidelberg 2006

of interest regions without sacrificing information content, and select the same regions when observed at different viewpoints and scales. There exist many definitions as to what constitutes a good interest region, predicated on maximizing disparate criteria. Therefore, we expect that using multiple detectors will provide complementary information, and hence improve recognition. Sec. 6.1 describes how interest regions are extracted and represented as feature vectors.

2. Train the Bayesian classification model developed in [15] with an efficient Markov Chain Monte Carlo (MCMC) algorithm for Bayesian learning. The algorithm learns a sparse object class representation from the interest region descriptors, and does so with little supervision by explicitly modeling data association. See Sections 2-4 for more details.

3. For localization of objects, integrate two types of visual cues: interest regions and low-level segmentation using *superpixels* [27]. On their own, independent, local interest regions do not contain enough information to segment the object from the background, so we propose a simple conditional random field [16] that propagates information across neighbouring superpixels and weights the superpixel labels by the scores of overlapping interest regions. It is described in detail in Sec. 5.

The resulting representations accurately detect and locate objects in a wide variety of scenes at different poses and scales, even when training under very little supervision from the user.

We start with an example that illustrates the need for a model of data association in object recognition. After that, we motivate our proposed Bayesian hierarchical model for data association and object recognition.

1.1   A Case for Data Association in Object Recognition

Consider the toy training set in Fig. 1. It consists of three images, each with a caption indicating the presence or absence of cars in the scene. The circles depict some of the extracted features at their characteristic scale. The first image does not contain a car, so we can justifiably say that none of the circles are car features. In the second and third training images, however, we cannot conclude with certainty which features belong to a car. The conventional approach to this problem is to treat unlabeled features in the background as noise [1,9,11], an approach which degrades significantly when the object in question occupies only a small part of the unlabeled image, as in the second image. A more sensible strategy is to explicitly model the feature labels, allowing the learning algorithm to exploit the unlabeled background features instead of being hindered by them. This is precisely the solution we propose in this paper.

Each feature label is a binary variable indicating whether it belongs to a car (positive) or to the background (negative). In this setting, data association is closely related to the multiple instance learning problem [2,8]. In the classical multiple instance formulation, a positive group label (the images are the groups) indicates that *at least one* of the individuals in the group has a positive label (this

Fig. 1. Three annotated images from the INRIA car training set. The circles represent some of the extracted features. The feature labels y_1 to y_3 in the first image are known. In the second and third images, we don't know the correspondence between the features and the labels, hence the question marks on the y_i's. Notice there is no image that contains only car features, and the size of the cars varies considerably. The correct correspondence is likely $y_4 = -1, y_5 = 1, y_6 = -1, y_7 = 1, y_8 = 1, y_9 = -1$ (1 means "car" and -1 signifies "not car").

corresponds to a "contains cars" caption), while a negative group label implies that *all* individuals in the group have a negative label. For our purposes, this formulation is not sufficiently informative for learning the correct association, since an image may contain *hundreds* of unlabeled points and in the multiple instance setting only one of them is enforced to have a positive label.[1] We propose two alternatives. In the first, we introduce image-level constraints enforcing a certain number of the features to belong to the positive class.

The problem is that it may be hard to identify appropriate constraints. Referring back to Fig. 1, the cars in the third image occupy much more space than in the second, so the third image is likely to contain more features associated with the car class. The best we can do with hard constraints to set a conservative lower bound on the number of positives per image. We suggest a better route: specify a ratio that indicates the expected fraction of individuals with a positive label, along with a level of confidence in such an expectation. When objects vary widely in size, a low confidence on the expected fraction allows the model to adapt the number of positive labels to each image. We call this approach data association with group statistics. It was first proposed in [13].

One might be skeptical that it is possible to achieve recognition in this setting, given the wide variability exhibited in the training images, the high dimension of the features, and the fact that there are hundreds of unlabeled points per image. However, the alternative, complete supervision, is not only unappealing but also unrealistic for general object recognition problems. Complete supervision requires the user to annotate and segment objects from the background. This is not only a time-consuming task, but also poorly defined since people tend to segment scenes differently. It also inhibits exploitation of the vast quantities of

---

[1] Data association is also commonly studied as a case of *semi-supervised learning* [34]. This formulation is less compatible since it has no notion of groups.

Fig. 2. Two sample images from the MIT-CSAIL database [32]. Yellow lines indicate car annotations. The annotations are incomplete in both images, so learning from data association is still appropriate in the presence of annotated data.

captioned images available on the Internet (in the form of news photos, for example [25]). The experiments in Sec. 6.3 show that our data association scheme largely compensates for the lack of annotation data.

Even when annotations are provided, a recognition system might still benefit from multiple instance learning. Consider images from the MIT-CSAIL database [32], pain-stakingly annotated with more than 30 object classes, including cars, fire hydrants and coffee machines. Despite the effort in producing the scene labelings, the annotations shown in Fig. 2 are still far from complete. By learning the labels in the unannotated areas, the model can better exploit such training data.

There have been several previous attempts in tackling the problem of data association in object recognition, but they failed to extend to realistic domains. Duygulu *et al.* [10] studied the problem from the perspective of statistical machine translation. They formulated data association as a mixture model, using expectation maximization (EM) to learn the parameters and the unknown labels. Later, the translation model was extended to handle continuous image features [4] and spatial relations [5]. The problem with their approach is that the posterior over the parameters of the mixture model is highly multimodal, so EM tends to get stuck in local minima. The situation is no better when applying MCMC simulation techniques to mixture models, due to a factorial explosion in the number of modes [6]. More complex representations only exacerbate the issue, so mixture models are limited to simple, unimodal object classes. While [5,4,10] tackle multi-category classification, we can do likewise by combining responses from multiple binary classifiers [31]. Others have extended the multiple instance learning paradigm. We refer the reader to [13] for further references.

1.2   A Case for Bayesian Learning in Object Recognition

We employ the augmented Bayesian classification model developed in [15] with an efficient Markov Chain Monte Carlo (MCMC) algorithm for Bayesian learning. The algorithm accomplishes two things simultaneously: 1.) it learns the unobserved labels, and 2.) it selects a sparse object class representation from the high-dimensional feature vectors of the interest regions. We introduce a generalized Gibbs sampler to explore the space of labels that satisfy the constraints or group statistics.

Bayesian learning comprehends approximation of the posterior distribution through integration of multiple hypotheses. This is a crucial ingredient for robust performance in noisy environments, and helps resolve sensitivity to initialization. In the presence of uncertainty about the labels, Bayesian learning allows us to be open about multiple possible interpretations, and is honest regarding its confidence in a hypothesis. The latter is of particular importance for integrating multiple visual cues for recognition (see Sec. 5), since it helps weigh the decisions of multiple models. The same cannot be said for learning through optimization of the model posterior, using EM for example.

Another advantage over other methods is that we do not need to reduce the dimension of the features through unsupervised techniques which may purge valuable information. Monte Carlo methods have received little attention in high-level vision, but our results show that they can be both effective and efficient in solving difficult problems.

In effect, what we describe is a *bag of keypoints* model [7] that chooses the features that best identify an object (e.g. the car model should select features that describe wheels or rear-view mirrors). It is widely appreciated that bag of keypoints methods — which treat individual features as being independent — are inadequate for identifying and locating objects in scenes (a person is not just an elbow!), and there has been much success in learning relations between parts [11] and global context [5,32]. Despite these objections, independent parts models are not only efficient and simple to implement, but also remain the state-of-the-art in detection systems [7,28] and, as we show, can function as a basis for more complex localization systems.

2 Bayesian Kernel Machine for Classification

We start by assuming complete supervision. In other words, each data point x_i has a known label $y_i^k \in \{-1, 1\}$. The next section considers the case when some of the labels are unknown.

The training data consists of a set of D labeled images, and each image j, for $j = 1, 2, \ldots, D$, contains a set of exemplars or feature vectors $\{x_i \mid i \in d_j\}$. The set of exemplars for all the images used during training is $\boldsymbol{x} = \{x_1, x_2, \ldots, x_N\}$, where N is the total number of training exemplars. Sec. 6.1 describes how to obtain the feature vectors beginning with the raw pixel data.

We use a sparse kernel machine to classify the interest region descriptors. The classification output depends on the feature being classified, x_i, and its relation to a subset of relevant exemplars. The outputs of the classifier are then mapped to the probability of the discrete labels using the probit link function. Following Tham, Doucet and Kotagiri [30], we have

$$p(y_i = 1 \mid x_i, \boldsymbol{\beta}, \boldsymbol{\gamma}) = \Phi\left(f(x_i, \boldsymbol{\beta}, \boldsymbol{\gamma})\right), \tag{1}$$

where the unknown regression function f is given by

$$f(x_i, \beta, \gamma) = \sum_{k=1}^{N} \gamma_k \beta_k \psi(x_i, x_k).$$

The probit link $\Phi(\cdot)$ is the cumulative density function of the standard Normal distribution. By convention, researchers tend to adopt a logistic (sigmoidal) link function, but from a Bayesian computational point of view, the probit link has many advantages and is equally valid.

The kernel function is denoted by ψ. We use the Gaussian kernel $\psi(x_i, x_k) = \exp(-(x_i - x_k)^2/\sigma)$ since it worked well in our experiments, but other choices are possible. We denote the vector of regression coefficients by $\boldsymbol{\beta} \triangleq [\beta_1 \ \beta_2 \ \cdots \ \beta_N]^T$. Our model is *discriminative* because it is specified as a conditional probability distribution of labels given observations, and not the other way around as in a *generative* mixture model.

We introduce sparsity through a set of feature selection parameters $\boldsymbol{\gamma} \triangleq [\gamma_1 \ \gamma_2 \ \cdots \ \gamma_N]$, where $\gamma_k \in \{0, 1\}$. Most of these binary variables will be zero and so the classification probability for feature vector x_i will only depend on a small subset of exemplars. By learning $\boldsymbol{\gamma}$, we learn the relevant set of feature vectors, or prototypes, for each class.

It is convenient to express (1) in matrix notation,

$$p(y_i = 1 \mid x_i, \beta, \gamma) = \Phi(\boldsymbol{\Psi}_{i,\gamma}\boldsymbol{\beta}_\gamma), \qquad (2)$$

where $\boldsymbol{\Psi} \in \mathbb{R}^{N \times N}$ is the kernel matrix with entries $\boldsymbol{\Psi}_{i,k} = \psi(x_i, x_k)$, $\boldsymbol{\Psi}_{i,\gamma}$ is the ith row of the kernel matrix with zeroed columns corresponding to inactive entries of $\boldsymbol{\gamma}$, and $\boldsymbol{\beta}_\gamma$ is the reduced version of $\boldsymbol{\beta}$ containing only the coefficients of the active kernels. Thus, the vector product in (2) is shorthand for

$$\boldsymbol{\Psi}_{i,\gamma}\boldsymbol{\beta}_\gamma = \left[\psi(x_i, x_1)\beta_1 \ \psi(x_i, x_2)\beta_2 \cdots \psi(x_i, x_N)\beta_N \right].$$

We follow a hierarchical Bayesian strategy [3], where the unknown parameters $\{\gamma, \beta\}$ are drawn from appropriate prior distributions. The intuition behind this hierarchical approach is that by increasing the levels of inference, we can make the higher level priors increasingly more diffuse. That is, we avoid having to specify sensitive parameters and therefore are more likely to obtain results that are independent of parameter tuning.

We place a regularized maximum entropy g-prior on the regression coefficients $p(\beta \mid \delta, \gamma) = \mathcal{N}(0, \delta^2 \mathbf{S}_\gamma)$, where $\mathbf{S}_\gamma = (\boldsymbol{\Psi}_\gamma^T \boldsymbol{\Psi}_\gamma + \epsilon I_N)^{-1})$ and ϵ is a small value that helps maintain a prior covariance with full rank. The regularization term δ^2 is in turn assigned an inverse Gamma prior with two hyperparameters $\frac{\mu}{2}, \frac{\nu}{2}$ specified by the user. One could argue that this is worse than the single parameter δ^2. However, the parameters of this hyperprior have much less direct influence than δ^2 itself, and therefore are less critical in determining the performance of the model [3]. Typically, we set μ and ν to near-uninformative values.

Following [15], each γ_k follows a Bernoulli distribution with success rate $\tau \in [0, 1]$, which in turn follows a Beta distribution with parameters $a, b \geq 1$. This allows the data to automatically determine the complexity of the model

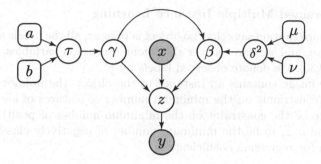

Fig. 3. The directed graphical representation of the fully-supervised classification model. Shaded nodes are observed during training, and square nodes are fixed hyperparameters.

according to the principle of Occam's razor, while allowing the user some control over the prior. Setting $b \gg a$ on large data sets initializes the learning algorithm to a reasonable number of active kernels.

The model is highly intractable. In particular, it is non-linear and the posterior of the coefficients $\beta \in \mathbb{R}^N$ is a correlated, hard to sample, high-dimensional distribution. However, we can simplify the problem enormously by introducing easy to sample low-dimensional variables z. Then, by conditioning on the samples of these latent variables, we can solve for the posterior of β analytically. This is accomplished by ensuring that the variables $z \triangleq \{z_1, z_2, \ldots, z_N\}$ have distribution

$$p(z_i \mid \gamma, \beta, x_i) = \mathcal{N}(\Psi_{i,\gamma}\beta_\gamma, 1). \tag{3}$$

It then follows that, conditioned on z, the posterior of the high-dimensional coefficients β is a Gaussian distribution that can be obtained analytically. This simple trick, first introduced by Nobel Laureate Daniel McFadden, is important to Bayesian data analysis since it reduces a difficult high-dimensional inference problem to a much simpler problem of sampling independent low-dimensional variables [20]. To recover the binary labels, we have

$$y_i = \begin{cases} 1 & \text{if } f(x_i, \beta, \gamma) > 0, \\ -1 & \text{otherwise.} \end{cases}$$

The directed graphical model in Fig. 3 summarizes the Bayesian kernel machine for classification.

3   Two Augmented Models for Data Association

The model presented up to this point is nearly identical to the one proposed in [30]. It assumes all the labels in the training data are known. In this section, we augment the model with either constraints (Sec. 3.1) or group statistics (Sec. 3.2) in order to handle weak supervision.

3.1   Constrained Multiple Instance Learning

When the image caption says that no object is present, all the labels are observed to be negative, and we can recover the latent regression variables z_i following (3), as in [20,30]. We denote observed labels by y_i^k.

When the image contains an instance of the object, the unknown labels y_i^u must satisfy constraints on the minimum number of features of each class. We define $n_{(+)}$ to be the constraint on the minimum number of positive points in an image, and $n_{(-)}$ to be the minimum number of negatively classified points. The prior on the regression coefficients is

$$p(\{z_i^u\}|\gamma,\beta,\{x_i\}) \propto \prod_i \mathcal{N}(z_i^u|\mathbf{\Psi}_{\gamma,i}\beta,1)\,\mathbb{I}_{C_{(-)}}(\{z_i^u\})\mathbb{I}_{C_{(+)}}(\{z_i^u\}),$$

where i ranges over the set of exemplars in the image, $C_{(-)}$ is the set of assignments to y_i^u (and accordingly z_i^u) that obey the negative labels constraint $n_{(-)}$, $C_{(+)}$ is the set of assignments to y_i^u that satisfy the constraint $n_{(+)}$, and $\mathbb{I}_\Omega(\omega)$ is the set indicator: 1 if $\omega \in \Omega$, and 0 otherwise. Discrete constraints in non-convex continuous optimization problems can be highly problematic. However, they can be realistically handled by MCMC algorithms [15].

3.2   Learning with Group Statistics

An alternative to constrained data association is to augment the training data with two user-defined statistics: an estimate of the fraction of positive instances for each image j, $m_j \in [0,1]$, and a global parameter χ quantifying the confidence in these guesses. Higher values indicate higher confidence, while $\chi = 0$ is a complete lack of confidence, resulting in unsupervised learning.

The observed value m_j is an estimate of the true fraction of positives, λ_j, which in turn is deterministically computed from the labels in the image according to

$$\lambda_j = \frac{1}{N_j} \sum_{i \in d_j} \mathbb{I}_{(0,+\infty)}(z_i^u), \tag{4}$$

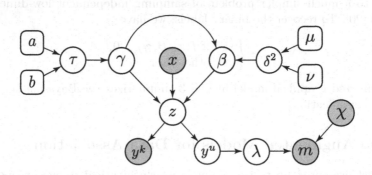

Fig. 4. The directed graphical representation of the classification model with group statistics. Shaded nodes are observed during training, and square nodes are fixed hyperparameters.

where N_j is the total number of extracted feature vectors in image j. Note that we implicitly integrate out y_i^u in (4). We use the Beta distribution to model this noisy measurement process, so the prior on m_j is

$$p(m_j \mid \lambda_j, \chi) = \text{Beta}\left(\chi\lambda_j + 1, \chi(1 - \lambda_j) + 1\right) \propto m_j^{\chi\lambda_j}(1 - m_j)^{\chi(1-\lambda_j)}.$$

The augmented classification model with group statistics is summarized in Fig. 4.

4   Model Computation

The classification objective is to estimate the density

$$p(y_{N+1}=1 \mid x_{N+1}, \boldsymbol{x}, \boldsymbol{y}^k) = \int p(y_{N+1}=1 \mid x_{N+1}, \theta)p(\theta \mid \boldsymbol{x}, \boldsymbol{y}^k)d\theta$$

for an unseen point x_{N+1}, given the training data $\{\boldsymbol{x}, \boldsymbol{y}^k\}$, where $\theta = \{\boldsymbol{\gamma}, \boldsymbol{\beta}\}$ is the set of parameters that directly influence prediction. Obtaining this probability requires a solution to an intractable integral, so we approximate it with the Monte Carlo point-mass estimate

$$p(y_{N+1}=1 \mid x_{N+1}, \boldsymbol{x}, \boldsymbol{y}^k) \approx \frac{1}{n_s}\sum_{s=1}^{n_s} p(y_{N+1}=1 \mid x_{N+1}, \theta^{(s)})$$

$$\approx 1 - \frac{1}{n_s}\sum_{s=1}^{n_s} \Phi\left(- \boldsymbol{\Psi}_{N+1,\boldsymbol{\gamma}^{(s)}}\boldsymbol{\beta}_{\boldsymbol{\gamma}}^{(s)}\right),$$

where n_s is the number of samples, and each sample $\theta^{(s)} = \{\boldsymbol{\gamma}^{(s)}, \boldsymbol{\beta}^{(s)}\}$ is distributed according to the posterior $p(\boldsymbol{\gamma}, \boldsymbol{\beta} \mid \boldsymbol{x}, \boldsymbol{y}^k)$. Kück et al. [15] develop an MCMC algorithm for sampling from the posterior by augmenting the original blocked Gibbs sampler [30] to the data association scenario. We follow their strategy for sampling these variables efficiently using Rao-Blackwellisation for variance reduction and the Morrison-Sherman lemma for fast matrix updates. One key difference is that [15] uses rejection sampling to sample the unknown labels subject to the constraints or group statistics, while we adopt a more efficient MCMC scheme and sample from the full conditionals in each document.

5   Conditional Random Field for Integration of Multiple Cues

Even though positively classified local features often lie on the object (see the experimental results of Sec. 6.3), they are inadequate for separating the object from the background. Interest regions have been used successfully as a basis for image classification, but there are few positive results extending to the localization of objects. Here, we add an additional layer to localize the objects in an image.

The basic intuition behind our approach is that labels on nearby interest regions and neighbouring segments should be useful in predicting a segment label. We propose a simple conditional random field that incorporates segmentation cues and the interest region labels predicted by our Bayesian kernel machine. Spatial integration is achieved in a generic fashion, so we expect our localization scheme applies to a variety of object classes.

The first step is to learn a classifier using the Bayesian learning algorithm described in Sections 2-4. Next, the image is decomposed into *superpixels* — small segments which induce a low compression [27]. We use the Normalized Cuts algorithm [29] to segment images, but other (less expensive) methods could possibly be used with similar returns. The extracted features of small segments are hardly sufficient for locating object classes in cluttered scenes, so the novel step is the construction of a conditional random field [16] (CRF) that propagates information across an image's neighbouring superpixels and interest regions.

Interest region labels influence the segment labels through CRF potentials. The strength of a potential is determined according to the overlap between the interest region and the segment. Defining a_i to be the area occupied by interest region i, and a_{ik} to be the overlap between segment k and interest region i, the potential on the kth segment label y_k^s is defined to be

$$\phi_k(y_k^s) = \sum_i \frac{a_{ik}}{a_i} \delta(y_k^s = y_i),\tag{5}$$

where y_i is the interest region label predicted by the sparse kernel machine classifier (1), i ranges over the set of interest regions in the image, and $\delta(x=y)$ is the delta-Dirac indicator which returns 1 when x is equal to y, and 0 otherwise.

Next, we define the potential between two adjacent segments k and l to be

$$\mu_{kl}(y_k^s, y_l^s) = \theta_\mu + \left(\frac{b_{kl}}{2b_k} + \frac{b_{kl}}{2b_l} \right) \delta(y_k^s = y_l^s),\tag{6}$$

where b_k is the contour length of segment k and b_{kl} is the length of the border shared by segments k and l. The pairwise potential (6) is the prior compatibility of the labels of neighbouring segments.

Putting the potentials (5,6) together, the joint probability of the segment labels $\boldsymbol{y}^s$ is given by

$$p(\boldsymbol{y}^s \mid \boldsymbol{y}) = \frac{1}{Z(\boldsymbol{y})} \prod_k \phi_k(y_k^s) \prod_l \mu_{kl}(y_k^s, y_l^s),\tag{7}$$

where the partition function $Z(\boldsymbol{y}) = \sum_{\boldsymbol{y}^s} \prod_k \phi_k(y_k^s) \prod_l \mu_{kl}(y_k^s, y_l^s)$ ensures that the probabilities sum to unity. There is only a single free parameter, θ_μ, which controls the strength of the potential. At this point, there is no learning; we tune the parameter by hand. In our experiments, we set θ_μ to a relatively strong prior, 0.1, which encourages neighbouring segments to have the same labels.

Even though equation (7) contains a product over all pairs (k, l) of segments in the image, the adjacency graph is sparse since only a few superpixels will share a border, so it is reasonable to run an inference algorithm suitable for sparse graphs. We use the tree sampling algorithm of [12] to infer the hidden labels y^s.

6   Experiments

We conduct three sets of experiments. First, we measure the model's ability to detect the presence or absence of objects in scenes, comparing performance with previously proposed models. Second, we assess the model's capacity for learning the correct associations between local features and class labels by training the model with varying levels of supervision. Third, by integrating local feature and segmentation cues in a principled manner, we demonstrate reliable localization of objects. We start by describing the setup used in our experiments.

6.1   Experiment Setup

We use interest region detectors which select informative or stable regions of the image. We use three different scale-invariant detectors: the Harris-Laplace detector [24] which finds corner-like features, the Kadir-Brady detector [14] which proposes circular regions with maximum grey-level entropy, and the Laplacian method [18] which detects blob-like structures. Based on earlier studies [23], we chose the Scale Invariant Feature Transform (SIFT) [19] to describe the normalized regions extracted by the detectors. We compute each SIFT description using 8 orientations and a 4×4 grid, resulting in a 128-dimension feature vector.

For fair comparison, we adjust the thresholds of all the detectors in order to obtain an average of 100 interest regions per training image. The combination scenario has an average of 300 detections per image. Note Fergus *et al.* [11] extract only 20 features per image on average, owing in part to the expense of training, while Opelt *et al.* [26] learn from several hundred regions per image.

For all our experiments using the constrained data association model (Sec. 3.1), we fix the label constraint n_0 to 0 and set n_1 between 15 and 30, depending on the object in question. Our constraints tend to be conservative, the advantage being that they do not force too many points to belong to objects that occupy only a small portion of the scene. When employing the group statistics model (Sec. 3.2), we set the parameters to be approximately $m = 0.3$ and $\chi = 400$. We set $a = 1$ and b according to a feature selection prior of approximately 200 active kernel centres, and we bestow near uninformative priors on the rest of the model parameters. In all our experiments, we set σ to $1/100$ because our MCMC algorithm reliably converged to a good solution. (Scale selection is an unsolved problem.) We found that 2000 MCMC samples with a burn-in period of 100 was sufficient for a stable approximation of the model posterior. Prediction by integrating the samples is fast: it takes about 1 second per image on a 2 GHz Pentium machine. The code and data for our experiments are available at http://lear.inrialpes.fr/objrecls.

6.2   Image Classification

The experiments in this section quantify our model's capacity for identifying the presence or absence of objects in images. We refer to this task as image classification. One should take caution, however, in generalizing the results to recognition: unless the image data is well-constructed, one cannot legitimately make the case that image classification is equivalent to object recognition. It is important to ensure the model learns to recognize cars, not objects associated with cars, such as stop signs. We address these concerns by proposing new experiment data consisting of images arising from the same environment: parking lots with and without cars. The outdoor scenes exhibit a significant amount of variation in scale, pose and lighting conditions. In addition, the new data set poses a challenge to learning with weak supervision, since the cars often occupy a small portion of the scene. See Fig. 1 for some example images. For purposes of comparison with other methods, we also present results on some existing databases of airplanes, motorbikes, wildcats, bicycles and people. The experiment data is summarized in Table 1.

Table 1. Summary of experiment data. The sources are the Caltech motorbikes (side) and airplanes (side) categories (http://www.vision.caltech.edu/html-files/archive.html), the Corel Image database for the Wildcats, the Graz bicycles and people data sets (http://www.emt.tugraz.at/~pinz/data/GRAZ_01), and the INRIA car database (http://lear.inrialpes.fr/data).

class	Training images with object	without	Test images with object	without
airplanes	400	450	400	450
motorbikes	400	450	400	450
wildcats	100	450	100	450
bicycles	100	100	50	50
people	100	100	50	50
cars	50	50	29	21

We adopt a simple voting scheme for image classification by summing over the feature label probabilities assigned by the model. Results of the image classification experiments are shown in Table 2. We report performance using the Receiver Operating Characteristic (ROC) equal error rate, a standard evaluation criterion [26,11]. It is defined to be the point on the ROC curve — obtained by varying the classification threshold — when the proportion of true positives is equal to the proportion of true negatives. We used the constrained data association model for these experiments, since constraints were easier to specify for most of the existing data sets.

Table 2. Image classification performance on test sets measured using the ROC equal error rate. The two three columns refer to the performance reported by Fergus *et al.* [11] and Opelt *et al.* [26]. The third column from the right is a reimplementation of the bag-of-keypoints model of Csurka *et al.* [7] using affine-invariant Harris-Laplace interest regions. All the other columns state the performance obtained using the proposed Bayesian model with regions extracted by various detectors (from left to right): Harris-Laplace [24], Kadir-Brady entropy detector [14], Laplacian of Gaussians [18], and combination of the three detectors.

data set	H-L	K-B	LoG	Combo	Csurka	Fergus	Opelt
airplanes	0.985	0.993	0.938	0.998	0.962	0.902	0.889
motorbikes	0.988	0.998	0.983	1.000	0.980	0.925	0.922
wildcats	0.960	0.980	0.930	0.990	0.920	0.900	—
bicycles	0.920	0.880	0.840	0.900	0.880	—	0.865
people	0.800	0.740	0.840	0.820	0.780	—	0.808
cars	0.966	0.897	0.897	0.931	—	—	—

Observe that our model in combination with the three detectors always produces the best image classification (at least when comparisons with other methods are available). Moreover, our model does very well in classifying car images in spite of the aforementioned challenges posed by the training examples. We omitted error bars because independent MCMC trials with fixed priors exhibited little variance.

One of the more interesting results of Table 2 is that no single detector dominates over the rest. This highlights the importance of having a wide variety of feature types for object class recognition.

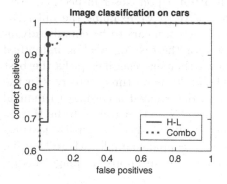
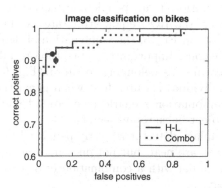

Fig. 5. The graph on the left plots the ROC curve for classification performance of car test images using the Harris-Laplace detector (blue solid line) and the combination of three detectors (red dotted line). The graph on the right shows analogous results for the bicycles test set. In both cases, the equal error rate (indicated by a large dot) is inferior in the combination, but according to the full ROC curve it may perform slightly better.

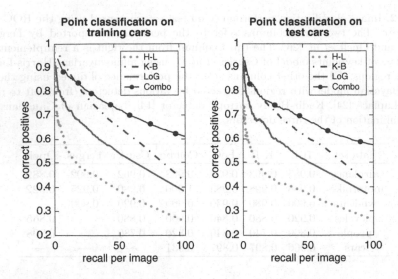

Fig. 6. Plots of precision (percentage of correct positives) versus average recall per image for the task of labeling individual features as belonging to cars. Our definition of recall here is not standard since we do not divide by the number of regions in the image. The combination scenario extends to 300 along the x-axis, but we cut it off at 100. Our algorithm learns which features are best in the combination, but this performance does not necessarily translate to better image classification (shown in Table 2).

Training with the combination of the Harris-Laplace, Kadir-Brady and LoG detectors often — albeit inconsistently — improves the equal error rate. For instance, we see that the ROC equal error rate decreases in the combination scenario for car, people and bicycle classification. Upon closer inspection, however, the ROC equal error rate can be deceptive. If we examine the full ROC plots in Fig. 5, the combination of detectors now appears to be equally advantageous. Importantly, a precision-recall plot for the task of labeling individual features as belonging to cars in Fig. 6 shows that our classifier picks the best individual features first when given the choice between three detectors in the combination scenario (the ground truth was determined according to manual object-background segmentations of the scenes). Note that in Fig. 6 the Harris-Laplace detector is overly penalized because it often selects corner-like features that are near, but not on, cars. Fig. 7 shows a couple examples where learning a model with a combination of detectors results in an improved image classification.

We show examples of correctly and incorrectly classified images, along with the interest regions extracted by the detectors, in Fig. 8. Incorrectly classified images tended to be unlike any of the images observed during training, such as the van and the child's bicycle. Problematic images also tended to exhibit unusual illumination conditions.

Fig. 7. Two examples in which the combination of detectors (top row) results in improved image classification over the Harris-Laplace detector (middle row). The circles represent the 9 interest regions that are most likely to belong to cars or bicycles. The bottom row shows the top features along with feature type and probability of positive classification. The combination is an improvement precisely because the Harris-Laplace detector fails to select good features in these two images.

6.3 Investigation of Data Association

In this section, we ask to what extent our proposed scheme for data association correctly labels the individual features, given that it is provided very little information. In some sense, this task is unfair since many individual interest regions cannot discriminate the object class. Fig. 9 shows two Kadir-Brady interest regions that do not help discriminate bicycles. Even under the best of conditions, we should not expect the classifier to predict the feature labels perfectly.

Fig. 8. Test images correctly (top four images) and incorrectly (bottom four) classified using interest regions extracted by the Harris-Laplace (for cars and bicycles) or
LoG detector (for people). Dark blue circles represent local interest regions that are
more likely to belong to the object, while yellow circles more probably belong to the
background.

We frame the data association question as follows: if manual segmentations
were provided, how much would we gain over image caption data? The answer of
course depends on the nature and quality of the data. At the very least, we should
expect that our model predicts the correct labels of the discriminative features

Fig. 9. The yellow circles are two interest regions extracted by the entropy detector. By looking only at the pixels inside the yellow circle, it is difficult to tell which one belongs to the bicycle and which one belongs to the background.

in the INRIA car database, since it appears to exhibit sufficient information to delineate positive and negative instances.

We conduct the experiment on the car database using the interest regions extracted from the Harris-Laplace detector. We use both hard constraints and group statistics. We increase supervision by setting some unknown labels y_i^u known to fall on cars to $y_i^k = 1$. Note that there is some noise in this process, since an interest region near a car may or may nor be associated with it. The results are presented in Fig. 10. The ROC curves show how the accuracy in labeling individual features changes with different levels of supervision. As expected, the addition of a few hand-labeled points improves recognition in training images. However, further upgrades in supervision result in almost no gains to recognition in test images. This shows that our data association schemes largely compensate for the lack of annotations in the data. Fig. 11 demonstrates this effect on a single image.

6.4   Object Localization

In this section, we evaluate the proposed object localization model. In order to quantify its effectiveness, we compare the object-background segmentation predicted by the model with those drawn by hand. Some examples of manual

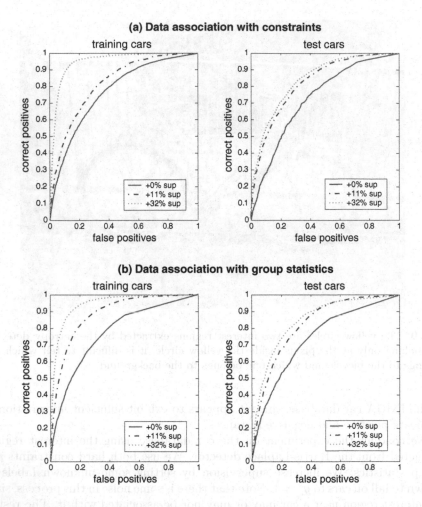

Fig. 10. The ROC plots demonstrate how learning with different proportions of hand-labeled points affects performance on labeling individual car features. *(a)* Labeling accuracy using the constrained data association model (Sec. 3.1). *(b)* Labeling accuracy using the data association with group statistics model (Sec. 3.2). The Harris-Laplace detector is used for both these experiments. With a lot of supervision, the models predict near-perfect feature labels in the training images, but there is little improvement in the test images.

segmentations are shown in Fig. 12. Perfect localization requires: 1.) that the boundaries of the segments follow the object boundaries, and 2.) that the conditional random field predicts the segment labels correctly. Even then, the evaluation may not be precise since the ground truth annotations contain some error, as evidenced by the examples in Fig. 12.

Fig. 11. Labeling of individual interest regions using the model augmented with data association constraints. The model was trained with various levels of supervision (see Fig. 10). *Left:* Car test image, no observed car labels during training. *Right:* The same image, except that the model was trained with an additional 11% observed feature labels. Dark blue circles are more likely than not to belong to the object, and light yellow circles are more likely to belong to the background.

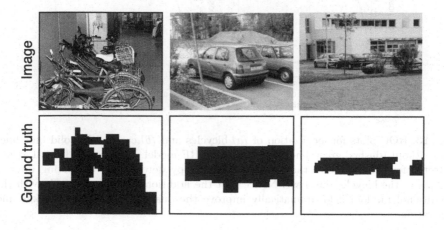

Fig. 12. Examples of ground truth segmentations from the bicycle and car databases

The ROC curves in Fig. 13 report the quality of the estimated segmentations in the car and bicycle databases. The ROC plots are obtained by thresholding the label probabilities on the segments and then finding the intersection with the ground truth segmentations. We use the Harris-Laplace detector for the car images and the Kadir-Brady entropy detector for the bicycles. The "without CRF" results in Fig. 13 do not use the superpixels; the spatial information is acquired from the location and scale of the interest regions. Our results show that we gain a lot in localization by using the segments to propagate interest

(a) Localization of cars

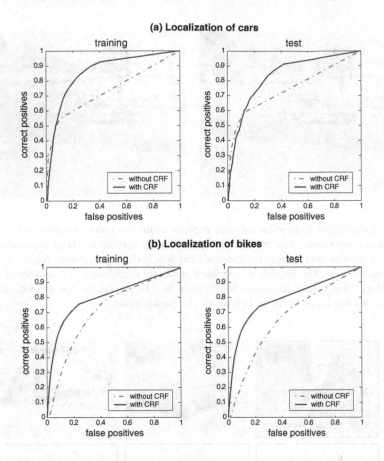

Fig. 13. ROC plots for localization of *(a)* bicycles and *(b)* cars, with (solid blue line) and without (dashed green line) the proposed CRF model. We use the Harris-Laplace detector for the cars, and the Kadir-Brady entropy detector for extracting interest regions in the bicycles database. Notice that the addition of the superpixels with the conditional random field dramatically improve the quality of the object-background separation.

region labels. The results in Fig. 13 show that our method is more reliable for locating cars in images. Without the CRF, Fig. 13a shows that the first selected labels selected are almost always within the boundary of cars, but the model cannot make any predictions in areas where no interest regions are extracted by the detector.

Some successful predictions in car test images are shown in Fig. 14, and some less successful car recognition results are displayed in Fig. 15. Localization failed when the interest regions and superpixels failed to complement each other. Notice we did not tailor the CRF to an object class, so recognition performance might very well generalize to other visual object classes.

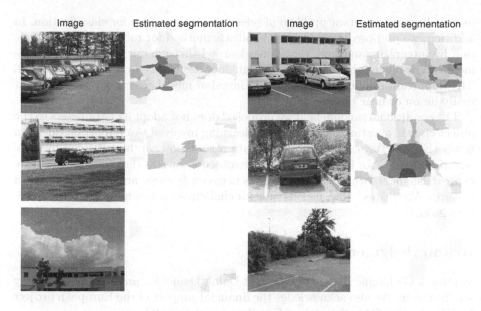

Fig. 14. Good localization results on car test images. Darker patches are more likely to correspond to cars.

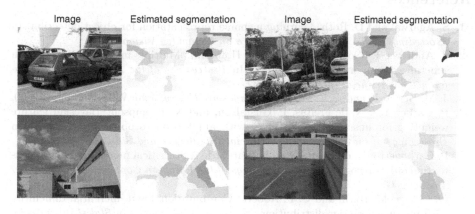

Fig. 15. Poor localization results on car test images. Darker patches are more likely to belong to the car class.

7   Conclusions and Discussion

In this paper, we extended the discriminative power of local scale-invariant features using Bayesian learning. We showed that both models for generalized multiple instance learning — constrained data association and learning with group statistics — are remarkably well-behaved in the face of noisy high-dimensional features and wide variability in the unlabeled training data. Our method allows us to solve the important problem of selecting local features for classification. In addition, we proposed a generic, probabilistic method for robust object localization by integrating multiple visual cues learned through our model. The experiments show our method successfully segments the object from the background. The important implication is that our Bayesian model selects the features that really lie on or near the object.

The conditional random field we proposed does not adapt its parameters to the object class in question since there is no learning involved. An important question is whether our Bayesian methods for data association can be extended to more advanced models for learning to recognize objects, such as those that incorporate context, shape information, correlations between features and different types of features. We suspect that it is as much a challenge for machine learning as it is for vision.

Acknowledgments

We thank Guillaume Bouchard, Navneet Dalal, Daniel Eaton and Kevin Murphy for their help. We also acknowledge the financial support of the European project LAVA, the PASCAL Network of Excellence and NSERC.

References

1. S. Agarwal and D. Roth. Learning a sparse representation for object detection. In *Proceedings of the European Conference on Computer Vision*, 2002.
2. S. Andrews, I. Tsochantaridis, and T. Hofmann. Multiple instance learning with generalized support vector machines. In *Proceedings of the AAAI National Conference on Artificial Intelligence*, 2002.
3. J. M. Bernardo and A. F. M. Smith. *Bayesian Theory*. John Wiley and Sons, 2000.
4. P. Carbonetto, N. de Freitas, P. Gustafson, and N. Thompson. Bayesian feature weighting for unsupervised learning, with application to object recognition. In *Proceedings of the Workshop on Artificial Intelligence and Statistics*, 2003.
5. P. Carbonetto, N. de Freitas, and K. Barnard. A Statistical model for general contextual object recognition. In *Proceedings of the European Conference on Computer Vision*, 2004.
6. G. Celeux, M. Hurn, and C. P. Robert. Computational and inferential difficulties with mixture posterior distributions. *Journal of the American Statistical Association*, 95:957–970, 2000.
7. G. Csurka, C. R. Dance, L. Fan, J. Willamowski, and C. Bray. Visual categorization with bags of keypoints. In *Proceedings of the ECCV International Workshop on Statistical Learning in Computer Vision*, 2004.
8. T. G. Dietterich, R. H. Lathrop, and T. Lozano-Perez. Solving the multiple instance learning with axis-parallel rectangles. *Artificial Intelligence*, 89(1):31–71, 1997.
9. G. Dorkó and C. Schmid. Selection of scale invariant neighborhoods for object class recognition. In *Proceedings of the International Conference on Computer Vision*, 2003.
10. P. Duygulu, K. Barnard, N. de Freitas, and D. A. Forsyth. Object recognition as machine translation: learning a lexicon for a fixed image vocabulary. In *Proceedings of the European Conference on Computer Vision*, 2002.

11. R. Fergus, P.Perona, and A.Zisserman. Object class recognition by unsupervised scale-invariant learning. *Proceedings of the IEEE Conference on Computer Vision and Pattern Recognition*, 2003.
12. F. Hamze and N. de Freitas. From fields to trees. In *Proceedings of the Conference on Uncertainty in Artificial Intelligence*, 2004.
13. K. Hendrik and N. de Freitas. Learning about individuals from group statistics. In *Proceedings of the Conference on Uncertainty in Artificial Intelligence*, 2005.
14. T. Kadir and M. Brady. Scale, saliency and image description. *International Journal of Computer Vision*, 45(2):83–105, 2001.
15. H. Kück, P. Carbonetto, and N. de Freitas. A Constrained semi-supervised learning approach to data association. In *Proceedings of the European Conference on Computer Vision*, 2004.
16. J. Lafferty, A. McCallum, and F. Pereira. Conditional random fields. In *Proceedings of the International Conference on Machine Learning*, 2001.
17. B. Leibe, E. Seemann, and B. Schiele. Pedestrian detection in crowded scenes. In *Proceedings of the IEEE Conference on Computer Vision and Pattern Recognition*, 2005.
18. T. Lindeberg. Feature detection with automatic scale selection. *International Journal of Computer Vision*, 30(2), 1998.
19. D. G. Lowe. Distinctive image features from scale-invariant keypoints. *International Journal of Computer Vision*, 60(2):91–110, 2004.
20. D. McFadden. A Method of simulated moments for estimation of discrete response models without numerical integration. *Econometrica*, 57:995–1026, 1989.
21. K. Mikolajczyk and C. Schmid. Indexing based on scale invariant interest points. In *Proceedings of the International Conference on Computer Vision*, 2001.
22. K. Mikolajczyk, C. Schmid, and A. Zisserman. Human detection based on a probabilistic assembly of robust part detectors. In *Proceedings of the European Conference on Computer Vision*, 2004.
23. K. Mikolajczyk and C. Schmid. A Performance evaluation of local descriptors. In *Proceedings of the IEEE Conference on Computer Vision and Pattern Recognition*, 2003.
24. K. Mikolajczyk and C. Schmid. Selection of scale-invariant parts for object class recognition. In *Proceedings of the International Conference on Computer Vision*, 2001.
25. T. Miller, A. C. Berg, J. Edwards, M. Maire, R. White, Y. W. Teh, E. Learned-Miller, and D. A. Forsyth. Faces and names in the news. In *Proceedings of the IEEE Conference on Computer Vision and Pattern Recognition*, 2004.
26. A. Opelt, M. Fussenegger, A. Pinz, and P. Auer. Weak hypotheses and boosting for generic object detection and recognition. In *Proceedings of the European Conference on Computer Vision*, 2004.
27. X. Ren and J. Malik. Learning a classification model for segmentation. In *Proceedings of the International Conference on Computer Vision*, 2003.
28. T. Serre, L. Wolf, and T. Poggio. Object recognition with features inspired by visual cortex. In *Proceedings of the IEEE Conference on Computer Vision and Pattern Recognition*, 2005.
29. J. Shi and J. Malik. Normalized cuts and image segmentation. In *Proceedings of the IEEE Conference on Computer Vision and Pattern Recognition*, 1997.
30. S. S. Tham, A. Doucet, and R. Kotagiri. Sparse Bayesian learning for regression and classification using Markov Chain Monte Carlo. In *Proceedings of the International Conference on Machine Learning*, 2002.

31. M. E. Tipping. Sparse Bayesian learning and the relevance vector machine. *Journal of Machine Learning Research*, 1:211–244, 2001.
32. A. Torralba, K. P. Murphy, W. T. Freeman, and M. A. Rubin. Context-based vision system for place and object recognition. In *Proceedings of the International Conference on Computer Vision*, 2003.
33. P. Viola and Michael J. Jones. Robust real-time face detection. *International Journal of Computer Vision*, 57(2):137–154, May 2004.
34. X. Zhu, Zoubin Ghahramani, and John Lafferty. Semi-supervised learning using gaussian fields and harmonic functions. In *Proceedings of the International Conference on Machine Learning*, 2003.

Towards the Optimal Training of Cascades of Boosted Ensembles

S. Charles Brubaker, Jianxin Wu, Jie Sun, Matthew D. Mullin,
and James M. Rehg

College of Computing and GVU Center, Georgia Institute of Technology
Atlanta, GA 30332
{brubaker,wujx,sun,mdmullin,rehg}@cc.gatech.edu

Abstract. Cascades of boosted ensembles have become a popular technique for face detection following their introduction by Viola and Jones. Researchers have sought to improve upon the original approach by incorporating new techniques such as alternative boosting methods, feature sets, etc. We explore several avenues that have not yet received adequate attention: global cascade learning, optimal ensemble construction, stronger weak hypotheses, and feature filtering. We describe a probabilistic model for cascade performance and its use in a fully-automated training algorithm.

1 Introduction

In order for object recognition to be useful in real-world applications such as robotics, surveillance, or video indexing, recognizers must have the ability to localize objects of interest in images under viewpoint changes (e.g. changes in object size or position) and must be robust to complex background clutter. This aspect of object recognition can be studied from the standpoint of object detection, where the goal is to develop efficient and accurate classifiers capable of discriminating a target object from the background. In this chapter, we explore the efficient and optimal training of cascade classifiers for face detection.

Given an input image, our goal is to return a list of (location, scale)-tuples that describe the position and size of detected faces. A natural search strategy in this context is to quantize the location $\times$ scale space and search it in a brute-force fashion. In this setting, object instances will frequently occupy only a small part of the image's scale space. In this sense, we may say that objects are "rare events" in the image, hidden among a large background class [32]. This results in a strongly asymmetric classification problem, since the error rate for the background class must be on the order of 10^{-7} to avoid littering the image with misclassified non-objects, while error rates of a few percent may be acceptable for the target class.

As popularized by Viola and Jones [29], the rarity of positive examples in object detection tasks can be exploited for computational efficiency via the cascade architecture. Each stage of the cascade either rejects an input region immediately as a non-object, or passes it on to the next stage for further analysis.

J. Ponce et al. (Eds.): Toward Category-Level Object Recognition, LNCS 4170, pp. 301–320, 2006.
© Springer-Verlag Berlin Heidelberg 2006

Inputs which survive all classifier stages are accepted as object instances. The cascade is efficient because most instances are non-objects and can be rejected by the first few stages with a minimal amount of computation. In this approach, the running time of the detector is no longer simply a function of the size of the image but also reflects the image's complexity. Blanchard and Geman have recently presented a general theoretical analysis of such classifier systems [1].

Each stage in the cascade architecture is an ensemble classifier node. These nodes are typically trained in a sequential manner, starting with the top node in the cascade and proceeding to the last. This training process raises several questions about the optimality and efficiency of cascade induction:

1. How should we handle the trade-off between the detection rate and false positive rate goals for each node in the cascade, so that the overall cascade performance is optimized? This decision is complicated by the fact that each node in the cascade experiences a different distribution of data, as a result of the filtering performed by earlier nodes.
2. How should we decide when to stop training one stage and move on to the next one? How should we decide when to stop adding nodes to a given cascade? In the absence of a fully-automated solution to these questions, human intervention is required. The resulting lack of repeatability makes it very difficult to perform experimental comparisons between different cascade learning methods.
3. Given a desired operating point for a node classifier, how can we ensure that it will be met? In the standard approach, an ensemble classifier is trained to minimize misclassification error and then its threshold is adjusted to achieve the desired tradeoff between error types. How can we address the requirements of the node classifier more directly, so that the performance goal informs the training process in a meaningful way?
4. What is the most efficient feature selection method for a node classifier? Given a large number of potentially-redundant features, are there any filtering schemes which can quickly reduce the number of feature sets that need to be considered?

We address this first point by developing a probabilistic model for the overall performance of a cascade classifier during training. We show that distribution over possible cascade operating points can be modeled as a product of beta variables (see Sec. 4.2). The stage-wise goal can then be chosen to optimize the expected overall performance. We address the second issue by defining a global cascade loss function which is optimized at each stage. The loss function results in an automatic stopping criteria. The third point is met by a new ensemble rule which we call the Linear Asymmetric Classifier (LAC) [30] (see Sec. 5.1). This method re-assigns weights to a set of weak hypotheses and combines them into an ensemble that is designed for the asymmetric nature of the stage classification task. Finally, we present experimental results for feature filtering. We also show that combining Adaboost with CART-based weak learning can improve the detector's final output.

2   Cascade of Boosted Ensembles

We begin by defining the Cascade of Boosted Ensembles (CoBE) architecture which provides a mathematical model for the cascade classifier. We express the CoBE architecture as follows. Let X be the instance space and let $c: X \rightarrow \{0,1\}$ be the target concept. The stages of the cascade $\{s_i\}_{i=1}^N$ consist of a set of weak classifiers $\{h_{ij}\}_{j=1}^{M_i}$ and a threshold θ_i such that for all $x \in X$

$$s_i(x) = \mathbf{I} \left[\sum_{j=1}^{M_i} h_{ij}(x) > \theta_i \right], \tag{1}$$

where $\mathbf{I}[\cdot]$ is the indicator function. Here we follow the convention of using confidence rated classifiers that return an unbounded real value, instead of $\{0,1\}$ or $\{-1,1\}$, removing the need for a weighting coefficient.[1] The hypotheses for the entire cascade can then be expressed as $\bigwedge_{i=1}^N s_i(x)$. It is important to note, however, that while a stage concept s_i is defined over all X, it will only ever be applied to the set $X_i = \{x \in X : \bigwedge_{k=1}^{i-1} s_k(x)\}$. Thus, a stage that performs well on such a subset might perform poorly on all of X and still fulfill its role in the detector.

2.1   Training a CoBE

A generic version of the original Viola-Jones training algorithm is presented in the LEARN-CoBE procedure. The subroutines serve as placeholders for a variety of solutions from the literature that apply to a given subproblem. Before training a stage, we first apply the standard bootstrapping practice [23] to acquire appropriate training and validation data. Positive examples that would be rejected by the current cascade are removed from the training and validation sets, and false positives of the current cascade are extracted from an image corpus, in which the object is either absent or blacked out, to form the negative examples (BOOTSTRAP). Thus, these data sets consist only of instances not rejected by any stage of the cascade that has already been trained. Since the set of features available is often too large (134,736 for the original Viola-Jones set), we then filter the set down to a manageable size (FILTER-FEATURES).

   To build the ensemble of classifiers, we first learn a classifier (WEAK-LEARN) based on the current set of weights. We then re-weight the examples (REWEIGHT-EXAMPLES), giving the misclassified examples more weight. Finally, we search for a suitable θ_i to balance the detection versus false positive tradeoff (FIND-BEST-THRESHOLD).[2] To assess the performance, we apply the stage to the validation set to calculate the false positive and detection rate pair $\langle \hat{f}_i, \hat{d}_i \rangle$ (VALIDATE). This

---

[1] Schapire and Singer use the same convention in Sec. 4 of [20], saying that the weight coefficients are "folded into" the hypothesis.

[2] We use the same "validation" data in the FIND-BEST-THRESHOLD step as we do in the VALIDATE step. We find that this works well in practice.

Let F be the set of features and E the set of examples. We denote the weights for E as W. No more than L iterations of Adaboost are permitted. G refers to the goal cost for the cascade, and $\langle \hat{f}_i, \hat{d}_i \rangle$ denotes the false positive and detection rate pair for the ith stage.

procedure LEARN-CoBE()

    $C \leftarrow \emptyset$ { C initialize an empty cascade}

    for each stage i **do**

        $E \leftarrow$ BOOTSTRAP()

        $F' \leftarrow$ FILTER-FEATURES()

        $s_i \leftarrow \emptyset$

        $W \leftarrow$ INITIALIZE-WEIGHTS()

        repeat

            $h \leftarrow$ WEAK-LEARN()

            $W \leftarrow$ REWEIGHT-EXAMPLES()

            $s_i \leftarrow s_i \cup h$

            $\theta_i \leftarrow$ FIND-BEST-THRESHOLD()

            $\langle \hat{f}_i, \hat{d}_i \rangle \leftarrow$ VALIDATE()

        until $|s_i| > L$ or PREDICT-COST() $\leq G$

        $\langle s_i, \theta_i \rangle \leftarrow$ REWEIGHT-HYPOTHESES

        $C \leftarrow C \cup \langle s_i, \theta_i \rangle$

Let P be the set of partitions of the examples induced by the classifier's form; e.g. thresholding on a single feature.

procedure WEAK-LEARN()

    $\epsilon \leftarrow \infty$

    for all $p \in P$ **do**

        $h_p \leftarrow$ CONFIDENCE(p)

        if $\epsilon >$ ERROR(h_p) **then**

            $h_{\text{best}} \leftarrow h_p$

            $\epsilon \leftarrow$ ERROR(h_p)

    return h_{best}

---

measurement and the analogous measurements for all previous stages are used to predict an overall cost for the cascade that is to be minimized (PREDICT-COST). If this cost is too high, then we repeat the cycle of learning a new hypothesis, re-weighting the examples, and evaluating the ensemble. Once the cost has been sufficiently reduced or the maximum number of hypotheses is reached, we may re-weight the hypotheses and select a new ensemble threshold (REWEIGHT-HYPOTHESES). Note that it is also possible to re-weight the ensemble of hypotheses each time a new one is added, as is done in [17]. Having completed the training process for a stage, we begin training the next one.

It should be noted that in choosing the stage thresholds θ_i, the goal should not be to maximize the performance of the stage in isolation, but rather to maximize the performance of the cascade as a whole. We will shown how to address this problem in Sec. 4.

Next, we turn to the WEAK-LEARN routine, which outlines the standard procedure for training weak classifiers. The form of the classifier defines partitions P of the instance space considered by the algorithm. For instance, if the classifier thresholds a single feature to make its decision, then the set P could contain all dichotomies produced by all possible thresholds of all features in F'. For a given partition p we denote the corresponding disjoint sets of the instance space as $\{X_j^p\}$, where j indexes over the sections of the partition. We denote the weight of the positive and negatives examples in these sets as $\{W_j^+\}$ and $\{W_j^-\}$. The WEAK-LEARN routine builds a hypothesis for each partition p by deciding on a confidence value for each subset of the instance space X_j^p based on the weights W_j^+ and W_j^-. It then evaluates each hypothesis and returns the best hypothesis for use in the ensemble.

Although not all changes made to the original Viola and Jones implementation strictly fit into the above architecture, we believe it provides a useful abstraction of the CoBE approach.

3   Previous Work

Despite the critical importance of the FIND-BEST-THRESHOLD and PREDICT-COST functions to the performance of the final detector, these aspects of the training process have received comparatively little attention in the literature. A preliminary version of our approach was published in [22]. Likewise, there have been few controlled, comparative studies that address questions about which factors have the greatest impact on cascade performance. One exception is [16], which also examines CART features. See [2] for a detailed comparison to the present work.

Huitao Luo has recently published a method for adjusting the stage thresholds after the full cascade has been trained [18]. While the success of this method illustrates the importance of the stage thresholds for classification performance, it does not address how the thresholds should be chosen in the cascade training phase (FIND-BEST-THRESHOLD), which critically influences the bootstrapped data, or when it is appropriate to begin training a new stage (PREDICT-COST).

Much of the early research on the CoBE architecture focused on the boosting algorithm. In [27], Viola and Jones propose Asymmetric Adaboost, which changes the REWEIGHT-EXAMPLES routine to keep most of the weight on the positive examples (instead of treating positive and negative examples equally), ensuring that a high percentage is detected by each weak classifier. Similar strategies from the machine learning literature include AdaUBoost [12], AdaCost [4], and [24]. Also similar to our work are the BMPM [11], and MRC [3] methods. A more detailed discussion of the relationships between these methods and LAC can be found in [30].

Li and Zhang have applied another alternative boosting algorithm to face detection in their paper on FloatBoost [15], which instead of greedily adding hypotheses to the ensemble, allows backtracking to eliminate the less useful or even harmful hypotheses. In other respects, the algorithm proceeds as RealBoost.

Liu and Shum [17] found that using KL-boost combined with weak classifiers based on histograms of 1D projections in feature space improved detection performance over the original approach. However, it is not clear whether it is the changes to the weighting scheme or the means of forming the weak hypotheses that is critical to the improvement.

A more radical departure from the LEARN-COBE routine is due to Xiao et al. [33]. Inspired by the observation that the operating point of a stage may not minimize error, they allow the hypothesis formed by the minimum error threshold of the previous stage to play the role of a weak hypothesis in the next stage of the cascade. Having thus produced a cascaded detector, they convert it to a single weighted voting scheme and train an SVM to relearn the confidence (vote) weights.

Others have changed the feature set while keeping the other key aspects of the CoBE architecture. Lienhart et al. [16] proposed another Haar-like feature set including diagonal features that can also be quickly computed via an integral image. Froba and Ernst [6] use a modified census transform and achieve state of the art performance using only three cascade stages. Levi and Weiss [14] also achieve state of the art performance using a small number of training examples with features based on edge oriented histograms.

CoVEs. A class of detectors closely related to the CoBE family are the cascades of voting ensembles. By a voting ensemble, we mean a classifier of the form[3]

$$\sum_i h_i(x) > \theta, \tag{2}$$

where x is an instance and h_i returns an unbounded real. Included in this class are the cascade of semi-Naive Bayes classifiers used by Schneiderman [21], the cascades of SVMs used by Heisele et al. [10], and the linear classifiers of Keren et al. [13], Elad et al. [3], and Romdhani et al. [19]. The critical difference between these detectors and the CoBEs is that they do not use boosting. Nevertheless, the cascade learning algorithm and some of the empirical results may have implications for these architectures as well.

The material in this chapter is taken primarily from [2] and [30], and the LAC method is also described in [31]. For a detailed survey of face detection see [34].

4   Cascade Learning

Two of the most important decisions in building a cascade of boosted ensembles are:

---

[3] A more strict definition of a voting ensemble might require that the classifier be of the form $\sum_i a_i h_i(x) > \theta$, where h_i is a concept returning either 0 or 1. This restriction causes a vote's weight to be fixed; whereas the h in the confidence-rated hypotheses used in Eqn. 2 might adjust their weight according to x. If the confidence-rated hypotheses return only two distinct values, then the two definitions are equivalent, but if they can take on more values, then the classifier described in Eqn. 2 does not meet the more strict definition.

1. When to stop training a stage to move on to the next one.
2. How to balance the detection versus false positive trade-off within a stage.

In terms of our LEARN-COBE algorithm these decisions are determined by the function FIND-BEST-THRESHOLD, which chooses θ_i, fixing the stage's operating point, and by the function PREDICT-COST which determines when to move on to the next stage of the cascade.

4.1 Fixed Stage Goal

If the true false positive and detection rates for the stages are $\{f_i\}$ and $\{d_i\}$, then the false positive and detection rates for the whole cascade are $F = \prod_{i=1}^{N} f_i$ and $D = \prod_{i=1}^{N} d_i$. This is not a statement of independence, but a factorization of the probability that all stages accept an instance as,

$$\Pr[s_1(x), \ldots, s_N(x) | c(x) = y] = \prod_{i=1}^{N} \Pr[s_i(x) | s_{i-1}(x), \ldots, s_1(x), c(x) = y], \quad (3)$$

where y is either 0 or 1 (non-face or face). Knowing the relationship between $\{f_i\}$ and $\{d_i\}$ will enable us to reason about F and D and thus about the overall performance of the cascade.

The standard approach to addressing the cascade training goals, as outlined in [28,27], is to choose a goal operating point $\langle F_g, D_g \rangle$ and then take its Lth root to obtain $\langle f_g, d_g \rangle$, where L is the intended number of stages in the cascade. Each stage is constrained to achieve one of f_g or d_g (typically f_g works better) and then terminates when either the other goal criterion is achieved or the maximum number of boosting iterations is exceeded.

This goal-based strategy leaves something to be desired, however. First, it rigidly fixes the number of stages in the cascade before any training is done. Second, it does not permit any trade-off between the detection and false positive rates within the stages. For instance, when selecting the threshold of a stage, one might be able to significantly improve the false positive rate at a small expense to the detection rate, improving the chances of meeting the goal criteria. The extra leeway on the false positive criterion might also be used at a later stage to improve a stage's detection at the expense of the false positive rate. By fixing one element of the operating point, this strategy precludes taking advantage of such trade-offs.

4.2 Cascade Learning with Beta Variables

We now describe an adaptive method for setting the stage classifier goals. It is based on our earlier work in [22] and is described in detail in [2]. The inputs to this alternative method are:

1. A goal operating point for the entire cascade $\langle F_g, D_g \rangle$.
2. A ratio η that reflects the relative importance of the false positive and detection criteria.
3. A maximum number of stages L.

The cascade learner then builds the fastest detector it can while achieving the goal performance with high probability.

A key element of our approach is that the algorithm views the performance of the cascade $\langle F, D \rangle$ as a random variable and treats the empirical results on validation data for the individual stages, $\{\hat{f}_i\}$ and $\{\hat{d}_i\}$, as evidence. A statistical model estimates the distribution of full cascade operating points, and each stage is trained to use the minimum number of features that ensure that the probability of meeting the performance goals is sufficiently high.

The key assumption underlying the statistical model is that the results on the validation data for the current stage can be repeated at all subsequent stages. We call this the "repeatability assumption" [22]. It is important to note that a similar assumption is implied in the fixed stage goal framework, where it is assumed that a particular operating point will be achieved in each stage. Although, the repeatability assumption is not strictly true in practice, it provides a guiding principle for applying our statistical model during training. The advantage of this model is that it affords a principled and practical way to make detection and false positive rate trade-offs in the individual stages.

Cost Function. Because a reasonable goal might not be known a priori, the algorithm must be robust to unattainable goals and produce results that are as close as possible. Depending on the attainability of the goal, therefore, we adjust our cost function. For simplicity, assume that $\eta > 1.0$, meaning that the false positive criterion is more important. We consider the following cases

1. If $\Pr[D < D_g] < \gamma$ and $\Pr[F > F_g] < \gamma$, then

$$\text{cost} = \Pr[D < D_g] + \eta \Pr[F > F_g].$$

2. If $\Pr[F > F_g] < \gamma$, then $\text{cost} = 2 + \eta - D$.
3. Otherwise, $\text{cost} = 2 + \eta + F$.

The first cost function is suitable when both goals are attainable with some substantial probability, say γ. However, when this is not possible, then the function provides no incentive to trade a small decrease in the false positive rate for a large improvement in the detection rate (an analogous statement holds if $\eta < 1.0$, giving detection greater importance). Therefore, if both criteria cannot be met with probability γ, then we constrain the false positive rate to be met with probability γ and maximize the detection rate. Finally, if the criterion for false positive rate cannot be met with probability γ, we simply minimize the false positive rate. Typically, this means that the false positive rate is reduced to zero, effectively terminating the training process.

Cost Prediction. Minimizing this cost function requires the ability to compute $\Pr[D < D_g]$ and $\Pr[F > F_g]$. We will only treat the detection criterion, because the false positive one is analogous. Consider the likelihood $\Pr[\hat{d}_i | d_i]$, where $\hat{d}_i$ is the measured detection rate over M positive examples. Given the true detection

Assume that the cascade has already been trained through stage i and that we are predicting the cost if the measured operating point of the next stage is $\langle \hat{f}_{i+1}, \hat{d}_{i+1} \rangle$.

PREDICT-COST-SAMPLE *maintains a set of sampled operating points for the currently trained cascade* $\{\langle F_i^k, D_i^k \rangle\}_{k=1}^{K}$. *All measurements are made with validation sets of M negative examples and the same number of positive examples.*

procedure PREDICT-COST-SAMPLE()
   for $j = i+1$ **to** N **do**
      for $k = 1$ **to** K **do**
         $F_j^k \leftarrow F_{j-1}^k \cdot \beta_{\hat{f}_i}$, where $\beta_{\hat{f}_i}$ is a random beta deviate with parameters $\hat{f}_i M + 1$
         and $(1 - \hat{f}_i)M + 1$.
         $D_j^k \leftarrow D_{j-1}^k \cdot \beta_{\hat{d}_i}$, where $\beta_{\hat{d}_i}$ is a random beta deviate with parameters $\hat{d}_i M + 1$
         and $(1 - \hat{d}_i)M + 1$.
         $G_f \leftarrow |\{k : F_j^k > F_g\}|/M$
         $G_d \leftarrow |\{k : D_j^k < D_g\}|/M$
         $\text{cost}_j \leftarrow \text{COST}(G_f, G_d)$.
   return $\min_j \text{cost}_j$.

The above procedure is used for PREDICT-COST.
procedure FIND-BEST-THRESHOLD()
   choose θ_i for which PREDICT-COST() is lowest.

---

rate d_i, the probability of m out of M examples being detected is just the binomial distribution

$$\binom{M}{m} (1 - d_i)^{M-m} d_i^m.$$

Taking a uniform prior $\Pr[d_i]$ over $[0, 1]$ and applying Bayes rule gives

$$\Pr[d_i|m, M] = \frac{\Pr[m|d_i, M]\,\Pr[d_i]}{\int_0^1 \Pr[m|p, M]\,\Pr[p]\,dp} = \frac{(1 - d_i)^{M-m} d_i^m}{\int_0^1 (1 - p)^{M-m} p^m\,dp},$$

which is precisely the beta distribution with parameters $m + 1$ and $M - m + 1$.

Therefore, conditioned on the validation measurements, D is the product of beta variables. The exact distribution only admits a clean analytic form in a few specialized cases [8], but it can easily be approximated. One strategy is to sample from the distribution for D by taking a sample from the distribution d_i for each stage and taking their product. The quantity $\Pr[D > D_g]$ can be estimated by counting the fraction of samples greater than D_g. This method is used in the PREDICT-COST-SAMPLE procedure. A final set of samples for a fully trained cascade is shown in Fig. 1.

This procedure allows us to estimate the cost once the cascade is fully trained. It remains to specify the final cascade training procedure. It is here that we apply the repeatability assumption, meaning that if we can achieve $\langle \hat{f}_i, \hat{d}_i \rangle$ on a validation set for the current stage, then we assume that we can achieve the same result for all subsequent stages. Therefore, as we are training the ith stage, we use the results on the validation set to estimate $\langle \hat{f}_j, \hat{d}_j \rangle$ for all previous stages

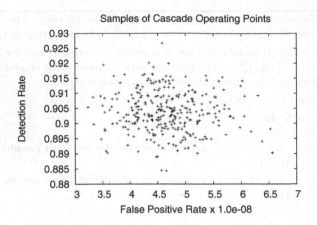

Fig. 1. Samples generated by PREDICT-COST-SAMPLE of the operating point for a fully trained cascade. Note the diversity of the sample set.

$(j < i)$, but we use the results for the ith stage on validation data for any subsequent stages $(j > i)$. The operating point having the lowest cost according to this estimate is chosen for each stage, as shown in the FIND-BEST-THRESHOLD procedure.

4.3   Discussion

The advantage of this approach is that it offers the control of the goal-based strategy over the cascade's overall performance, while allowing some subtle tradeoffs between detection and false positive rates in the stages. Moreover, it can "remember" past trade-offs to help decide whether a new trade-off will improve the chances of achieving the cascade's goal operating point. Note that though we specify a maximum number of stages, we do not specify a minimum. If the learner predicts better performance with fewer stages, then it will plan for fewer stages.

To demonstrate the effectiveness and robustness of our improved cascade learning algorithm, we point out that all thirty-five detectors used in the experiments of [2] were trained automatically using a single set of parameters. This set of experiments ranges from a cascade using four level deep CART trees that achieves state of the art performance, to a cascade where the feature pool was reduced to 200 randomly selected features (see Sec. 6.2).

It sometimes happens that the early stages of the cascades produced by our method contain more hypotheses than those prodcued by other approaches. In most other systems, the number of hypotheses in a stage is manually specified, and in an effort to create a fast detector the early stages are forced to contain only a few hypotheses. We could incorporate such a heuristic into the cascade learning strategy presented here, so long as the cascade learner is provided with measurement of the earlier stages' detection and false positive rates.

5   Adjusting Weights in the Ensemble

When no re-weighting is applied, the stage decision can be rewritten as

$$s(x) = \mathbf{I}\left[\mathbf{1}^T \mathbf{h}(x) > \theta)\right],\tag{4}$$

which is just a restatement of Eqn. 1 where $\mathbf{h}$ denotes the vector of hypotheses and the subscripts on s and θ have been dropped. In this section, we seek to replace the weight vector $\mathbf{1}$ and scalar θ of Eqn. 4 with a new weight vector $\mathbf{a}$ and with a new threshold b that are better suited to stage classification task, which is to reject a significant portion of negative examples while detecting almost all of the positive examples. This task corresponds to the REWEIGHT-HYPOTHESES procedure in the LEARN-COBE algorithm.

5.1   The Linear Asymmetric Classifier

For convenience, we will denote the hypothesis vector of a positive example as $\mathbf{x}$, of a negative example as $\mathbf{y}$, and of an unknown class label as $\mathbf{z}$ for the remainder of this section. We can now state our stage learning goal as the program

$$\begin{aligned} \max_{\mathbf{a}\neq 0,\theta} \quad & \Pr_{\mathbf{x}\sim(\bar{\mathbf{x}},\Sigma_{\mathbf{x}})} \{\mathbf{a}^T\mathbf{x} \geq b\} \\ \text{s.t.} \quad & \Pr_{\mathbf{y}\sim(\bar{\mathbf{y}},\Sigma_{\mathbf{y}})} \{\mathbf{a}^T\mathbf{y} \leq b\} = \beta, \end{aligned}\tag{5}$$

where β is some constant. In general this problem has no closed-form solution; however, we will develop an approximation for it. Empirically, it has been found that setting a false positive goal of 0.5 is effective in the fixed stage goal cascade learning strategy. Thus, we will give a closed-form (approximate) solution when $\beta = 0.5$.

Let $\mathbf{x} \sim (\bar{\mathbf{x}}, \Sigma_{\mathbf{x}})$ denote that $\mathbf{x}$ is drawn from a distribution with mean $\bar{\mathbf{x}}$ and covariance matrix $\Sigma_{\mathbf{x}}$. Note that we do not assume any specific form of the distribution. The only assumption is that its mean and covariance can be estimated from samples. We are dealing with binary classification problems with two classes $\mathbf{x} \sim (\bar{\mathbf{x}}, \Sigma_{\mathbf{x}}), \mathbf{y} \sim (\bar{\mathbf{y}}, \Sigma_{\mathbf{y}})$, which are fixed but unknown.

The key idea to solve this learning problem is to use the cumulative distribution functions of $\mathbf{a}^T\mathbf{x}$ and $\mathbf{a}^T\mathbf{y}$ to replace the $\Pr\{\}$ function. Let $\mathbf{x_a}$ denote the standardized version of $\mathbf{a}^T\mathbf{x}$ ($\mathbf{x}$ projected onto the direction of $\mathbf{a}$), i.e.

$$\mathbf{x_a} = \frac{\mathbf{a}^T(\mathbf{x} - \bar{\mathbf{x}})}{\sqrt{\mathbf{a}^T \Sigma_{\mathbf{x}}\mathbf{a}}},\tag{6}$$

obviously we have $\mathbf{x_a} \sim (0,1)$. Let $\Phi_{\mathbf{x,a}}$ denotes the cumulative distribution function (c.d.f.) of $\mathbf{x_a}$, i.e.

$$\Phi_{\mathbf{x,a}}(b) = \Pr\{\mathbf{x_a} \leq b\}.\tag{7}$$

$\mathbf{y_a}$ and $\Phi_{\mathbf{y,a}}$ are defined similarly as

$$y_{\mathbf{a}} = \frac{\mathbf{a}^T(\mathbf{y} - \bar{\mathbf{y}})}{\sqrt{\mathbf{a}^T \Sigma_{\mathbf{y}} \mathbf{a}}}, \tag{8}$$

$$\Phi_{\mathbf{y},\mathbf{a}}(b) = \Pr\{y_{\mathbf{a}} \leq b\}. \tag{9}$$

The constrained optimization problem (5) is equivalent to

$$\min_{\mathbf{a} \neq 0} \Phi_{\mathbf{x},\mathbf{a}} \left(\frac{\mathbf{a}^T(\bar{\mathbf{y}} - \bar{\mathbf{x}}) + \Phi_{\mathbf{y},\mathbf{a}}^{-1}(\beta)\sqrt{\mathbf{a}^T \Sigma_{\mathbf{y}} \mathbf{a}}}{\sqrt{\mathbf{a}^T \Sigma_{\mathbf{x}} \mathbf{a}}} \right). \tag{10}$$

where $\Phi_{\mathbf{y},\mathbf{a}}^{-1}$ is the inversion function of $\Phi_{\mathbf{y},\mathbf{a}}$ (The equivalence of these two equations are proved in detail in [30]). In Eqn. (10), $\Phi_{\mathbf{x},\mathbf{a}}$ and $\Phi_{\mathbf{y},\mathbf{a}}^{-1}$ depend upon the distributions of $\mathbf{x}$ and $\mathbf{y}$, in addition to the projection direction $\mathbf{a}$. Because we have no knowledge of these distributions, we cannot solve Eqn. (10) analytically. We need to make some approximations to simplify it.

First, let us give a bound for Φ and Φ^{-1}. It is easy to prove the following bound (see [30] for details):

$$\Phi^{-1}(\beta) \leq \kappa(\beta), \text{ where } \kappa(\beta) = \sqrt{\frac{\beta}{1-\beta}} \tag{11}$$

and Φ is the cdf of any random variable that has zero mean and unit variance. From the definition, it is clear that $\mathbf{x}_{\mathbf{a}} \sim (0,1)$. Thus, instead of minimizing $\Phi_{\mathbf{x},\mathbf{a}}(\xi)$ in Eqn. (10), we can instead minimize its upper bound $\kappa(\xi)$. Furthermore, since $\kappa(\xi)$ is an increasing function, it is equivalent to minimizing ξ. Thus, we can *approximately* solve Eqn. (10) by solving

$$\min_{\mathbf{a} \neq 0} \frac{\mathbf{a}^T(\bar{\mathbf{y}} - \bar{\mathbf{x}}) + \Phi_{\mathbf{y},\mathbf{a}}^{-1}(\beta)\sqrt{\mathbf{a}^T \Sigma_{\mathbf{y}} \mathbf{a}}}{\sqrt{\mathbf{a}^T \Sigma_{\mathbf{x}} \mathbf{a}}}, \tag{12}$$

or, equivalently,

$$\max_{\mathbf{a} \neq 0} \frac{\mathbf{a}^T(\bar{\mathbf{x}} - \bar{\mathbf{y}}) - \Phi_{\mathbf{y},\mathbf{a}}^{-1}(\beta)\sqrt{\mathbf{a}^T \Sigma_{\mathbf{y}} \mathbf{a}}}{\sqrt{\mathbf{a}^T \Sigma_{\mathbf{x}} \mathbf{a}}}. \tag{13}$$

This transformation is approximate because in Eqn. (10), the function $\Phi_{\mathbf{x},\mathbf{a}}$ depends on $\mathbf{a}$, while $\mathbf{a}$ also appears in the argument of $\Phi_{\mathbf{x},\mathbf{a}}$. However, if we assume that $\mathbf{a}^T \mathbf{x}$ is Gaussian for any $\mathbf{a}$, then $\mathbf{x}_{\mathbf{a}}$ is the standard normal distribution. Under this assumption, $\Phi_{\mathbf{x},\mathbf{a}}$ does not depend on $\mathbf{a}$ any more, and Eqn. (13) is exactly equivalent to Eqn. (5).

Second, we assume that the median value of the distribution $\mathbf{y}_{\mathbf{a}}$ is close to its mean. This assumption is true for all symmetric distributions and is reasonable for many others. Under this assumption, we have $\Phi_{\mathbf{y},\mathbf{a}}^{-1}(0.5) \approx 0$. Thus for $\beta = 0.5$ (which is used in the cascade framework), Eqn. (13) can be further approximated by

$$\max_{\mathbf{a} \neq 0} \frac{\mathbf{a}^T(\bar{\mathbf{x}} - \bar{\mathbf{y}})}{\sqrt{\mathbf{a}^T \Sigma_{\mathbf{x}} \mathbf{a}}}. \tag{14}$$

If in addition we can assume that $\mathbf{y_a}$ is a symmetric distribution and $\beta = 0.5$, we have $\Phi_{\mathbf{y,a}}^{-1}(0.5) = 0$ in addition to Eqn. (13). The implication is that under these assumptions, Eqn. (14) is exactly equivalent to the node learning goal in Eqn. (5). We call the linear discriminant function determined by Eqn. (14) the Linear Asymmetric Classifier (LAC) and use it in the cascade learning framework.

The form of Eqn. (14) is similar to the Fisher Discriminant Analysis (FDA) [7], which can be written as:

$$\max_{\mathbf{a} \neq 0} \frac{\mathbf{a}^T(\bar{\mathbf{x}} - \bar{\mathbf{y}})}{\sqrt{\mathbf{a}^T(\Sigma_{\mathbf{x}} + \Sigma_{\mathbf{y}})\mathbf{a}}}. \tag{15}$$

The only difference between FDA and LAC is that the pooled covariance matrix $\Sigma_{\mathbf{x}} + \Sigma_{\mathbf{y}}$ is replaced by $\Sigma_{\mathbf{x}}$. This analogy immediately gives us the solution to Eqn. (14) as:

$$\mathbf{a}^* = \Sigma_{\mathbf{x}}^{-1}(\bar{\mathbf{x}} - \bar{\mathbf{y}}), b^* = \mathbf{a}^{*T}\bar{\mathbf{y}}, \tag{16}$$

under the assumption that $\Sigma_{\mathbf{x}}$ is positive definite. In applications where $\Sigma_{\mathbf{x}}$ happens to be positive semi-definite, $\Sigma_{\mathbf{x}} + \lambda I$ can be used to replace $\Sigma_{\mathbf{x}}$, where λ is a small positive number.

Note that if that $\mathbf{x}$ and $\mathbf{y}$ have equal covariance matrices, LAC is equivalent to FDA. If the covariance are not equal, however, the $\mathbf{a}$ vectors can differ dramatically. In [30], we present empirical evidence that supports the assumptions underlying the LAC approach.

5.2   Analysis

To assess the effectiveness of the LAC approach, we measure the performance of individual stages rather than the cascade as a whole. We compare stages trained using Adaboost with no re-weighting, with FDA re-weighting, and with LAC re-weighting. Training and validation sets for each stage of the cascade were obtained via bootstrapping during the training process. This produced training and validation sets for all stages the cascade for each re-weighting scheme. Each re-weighting scheme was then trained on each of these training sets. Fig. 2 shows the false negative rate (the number of mistakes on faces) on the validation data when the false positive rate is set to 0.5.

From the results in Fig. 2, it is clear that both FDA and LAC can greatly reduce the false negative rates (i.e. increase the detection rates). In Fig. 2(a), averaged over the 11 nodes shown, AdaBoost+FDA reduces the false negative rates by 31.5% compared to AdaBoost, while in 2(c) AdaBoost+LAC reduces it by 22.5%.

6   Speed-Ups for Ensemble Learning

A significant practical obstacle to the wider use of cascades of boosted ensembles is their long training times. In [32], we showed how Adaboost with threshold-based weak learners can be replaced with Forward Feature Selection (FFS). Without significant loss in detection performance, we were able to dramatically

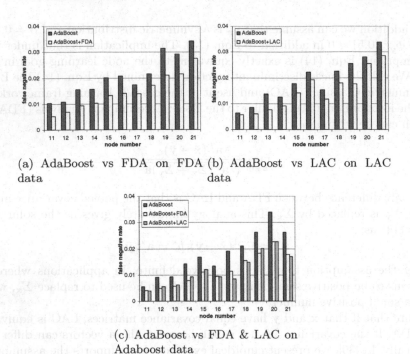

(a) AdaBoost vs FDA on FDA data   (b) AdaBoost vs LAC on LAC data

(c) AdaBoost vs FDA & LAC on Adaboost data

Fig. 2. Experiments comparing different linear discriminant functions. The y axis shows the false negative rate when $\beta = 0.5$. In 2(a), training sets are collected from the AdaBoost+FDA cascades for nodes 11 to 21 (x axis shows the node number). AdaBoost and AdaBoost+FDA are compared using these training sets. Similarly, 2(b) and 2(c) use training sets from AdaBoost+LAC and Adaboost, respectively.

improve the training time of an ensemble over a naive implementation of Adaboost. The key to the improved training time is that in FFS the best feature thresholds can be precomputed and re-used during training. In [30], we show how a similar strategy can be applied to Adaboost by sorting feature values in a precomputation step. This removes the most expensive part of the threshold-based weak learning routine. In both cases, the precomputation strategy offers a dramatic speed-up, though FFS remains slightly faster than the faster implementation of Adaboost.

The training time of the three algorithms are summarized as follows. Detailed analysis can be found in [30].

1. **Naive AdaBoost.** The naive algorithm requires $O(|F'||E|)$ time for precomputation and $O(|F'||E|\log|E|)$ time per iteration, where F' is the set of selected features and E is the set of examples.
2. **Forward Feature Selection.** The FFS algorithm requires $O(|F'||E|\log|E|)$ for precomputation and $O(|F'||E|)$ time per iteration.
3. **Faster Adaboost.** The faster implementation of Adaboost has the same asymptotic training time as that of FFS, but with a larger constant.

6.1   Fast Feature Selection

A primary issue in the training cost of the cascade classifier is the fact that in every round of boosting the WEAK-LEARN routine examines every example for every feature. Since reducing the example corpus weakens the generalization, reducing the feature pool via the FILTER-FEATURES routine is an attractive option.

To actually improve the training time, however, the filtering algorithm itself must be faster than Adaboost. Unfortunately, few filtering algorithms offer an asymptotic improvement in training time. Nevertheless, asymptotically equivalent methods often admit implementation speed-ups, which make the actual run-time faster than the worst-case analysis time would indicate. Moreover, because Adaboost's greedy selection of features is not optimal, limiting the feature pool available to Adaboost may actually improve the results. The idea is that Adaboost may produce a better classifier when it is presented with a small set of features, all of which are good, rather than a large set containing these same good features in addition to many spurious ones.

For purposes of this discussion, therefore, we divide filtering techniques into two broad categories:

Fast Filters: This category consists primarily of ranking schemes which examine each feature once and sort according to some measure of the feature's discriminative power. These filters are typically much faster than Adaboost and run in $O(|F| \log |F|)$ time. From this category, we test random selection and ranking by mutual information. For the latter, we choose a feature threshold that maximizes the mutual information between the resulting binarized feature and the class label, and then select the features that have the largest mutual information (see [25] for a related method).

Slow Filters: This category includes methods that examine each feature in F before choosing the next feature to add to the selected pool F'. These filters run in $O(|F'||F||E|)$ time and are about as fast as Adaboost with a thresholding weak learner. From this category, we use the Conditional Mutual Information Maximization (CMIM) method of [5] and Forward Feature Selection [32]. Note that the algorithm in [5] represents a significant speed-up over the original CMIM method in [26].

Notice that the running times given above assume that the precomputation of best feature thresholds has been performed. With this strategy, the evaluation of a feature, either for selection or for use in a weak classifier, can be performed in $O(|E|)$ time, where E is the set of examples. It is also important to realize that although these filtering methods sometimes choose a threshold value for the feature during selection, the original feature values are retained for the boosting or ensemble learning phase of the training process.

In this context, we hypothesize that filters from the first category might improve the training time significantly without diminishing the quality of the results. On the other hand, we hypothesize that filters from the second category could improve the quality of the results and perhaps offer a modest improvement in training time.

6.2   Results

Fast Filters. Each of the fast methods was used to reduce the feature pool by 90% (RND13473 and RANK13473) and 99% (RND1347 and RANK1347) during the training of several detectors. Results on the CMU-MIT data set for a detector using Adaboost and no re-weighting are shown in Fig. 3.

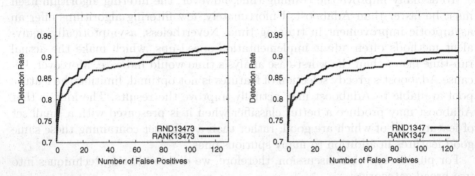

Fig. 3. Comparison of ROC curves for detectors trained with random feature selection (RND) and ranking by mutual information (RANK) for 90% feature reduction (left) and 99% feature reduction (right). Results for discrete Adaboost shown.

In both cases, random selection gives comparable performance to the ranking method. At first, this may seem counter-intuitive. The ranking method does, after all, include the most discriminative features. How can a random selection of features produce detectors that perform just as well or better? The answer is

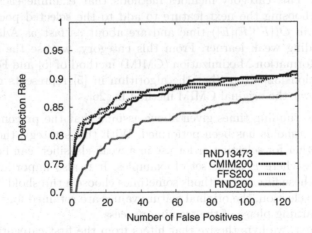

Fig. 4. ROC curves for detectors using CMIM and FFS filtering methods. Results for random feature pools also shown for comparison. Both "slow" filtering methods perform than random selection (RND200), but do no better than not filtering at all (RND13473). Results shown with Gentleboost.

the well known redundancy problem [9]. The "best" features tend to misclassify the same examples, making it difficult for Adaboost to learn an ensemble of hypotheses that classifies these examples correctly.

Slow Filters. To assess the asymptotically slower methods, conditional mutual information maximization (CMIM) and forward feature selection (FFS), we first randomly selected 10% of the features and then used these methods to filter down to 200 features. For a baseline comparison we also trained a detector with 200 randomly selected features (RND200). The ROC curves for the resulting detectors trained with Gentleboost are shown in Fig. 4. Both FFS and CMIM produce ROC curves comparable to the one produced by RND13473. That is, the detectors perform as well as they would if no filtering had been applied at all. Thus, although these methods offer a modest improvement in training time, they do not outperform the greedy selection naturally employed by Adaboost.

7 Weak Learning

Although thresholding on a single feature has been the dominant practice in CoBEs for object detection, Adaboost does not restrict how the weak learning takes place. The thresholding strategy may be efficient in terms of training or execution time, but it seems doubtful that such a simple weak learner would give the best results. We therefore explore the use of CART-based weak hypotheses, which we found to significantly improve the cascade performance.

Our experiments show that CART-based detectors offer improved detection rates with only small drops in speed. As shown in [2], this result holds across Discrete Adaboost, RealBoost, and Gentleboost. The ROC curve of Fig. 5 shows the improvement that results from using CART trees of depth 2, 4, and 6, as opposed to stumps (i.e. threshold-based hypotheses).

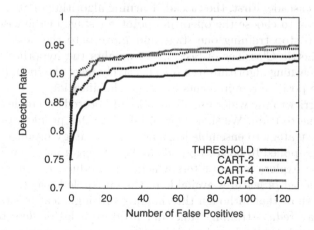

Fig. 5. CART depths up to 4 significantly and consistently improve performance. Results shown for discrete Adaboost.

Table 1. A comparison of detection rates at fixed numbers of false positives on the CMU-MIT data set for several standard detectors

Detector	False Positives							
	6	10	31	46	50	65	78	95
Viola-Jones [29]	–	0.761	0.884	–	0.914	0.920	0.921	0.929
Viola-Jones [29] (voting)	–	0.811	0.897	–	0.921	0.931	0.931	0.932
Luo [18]	0.866	0.874	0.903	–	0.911	–	–	–
Li and Zhang [15]	–	0.836	0.902	–	–	–	–	–
Schneiderman [21]	0.897	–	–	0.957	–	–	–	–
CART-4 w/ Realboost	0.891	0.905	0.931	0.935	0.935	0.943	0.948	0.951

Table 1 gives a comparison between our best detector and other published cascade training methods. While a comprehensive comparison would include testing speed as well as classification performance, these numbers suggest that the current method produces results which are comparable to published work that is based on substantial modifications to the basic Adaboost learning method. Our results show that the basic method can yield excellent performance if stronger weak hypotheses are employed. Moreover these results can be obtained without hand-tweaking cascade parameters during training, as a consequence of our automatic global training method. Promising directions for future studies include an evaluation of these methods from the standpoint of testing speed and the use of our global training method of Sec. 4.2 in conjunction with previously-published stage learning algorithms.

8   Conclusion

We argue that the cascade architecture is well-suited for the rare event nature of object detection problem, and present two algorithms that address challenges specific to the cascade. First, the cascade learning algorithm of Sec. 4.2 provides a principled way to choose the operating point for stage of the cascade and to decide when to stop training one stage and move onto the next. Second, the Linear Asymmetric Classifier of Sec. 5.1 re-weights the hypotheses chosen by the ensemble learning algorithm to more effectively meet the high detection and moderate false positive requirements for stage classification.

A major barrier to the wider use of cascades of boosted ensembles is that they take a long time to train. We show how to alleviate this problem by applying a precomputation strategy to ensemble learning. This strategy produces a dramatic speed-up when applied to both FFS and Adaboost over a more naive implementation. We also explore feature filters which can produce a moderate speed-up by reducing the set of features available to the ensemble learner.

Finally, we show that although thresholding on single features to form weak hypotheses may reduce training time and produce a faster detector, combining Adaboost with CART-based weak learning can improve the detector's final output.

Acknowledgments

This material is based upon work which was supported in part by the National Science Foundation under NSF Award IIS-0133779 and IIS-0205507.

References

1. G. Blanchard and D. Geman. Sequential testing designs for pattern recognition. *Annals of Statistics*, 33(3):1155–1202, 2005.
2. S. C. Brubaker, J. Wu, J. Sun, M. D. Mullin, and J. M. Rehg. On the design of cascades of boosted ensembles for face detection. Technical Report GIT-GVU-05-28, Georgia Institute of Technology, 2005.
3. M. Elad, Y. Hel-Or, and R. Keshet. Pattern detection using a maximal rejection classifier. *Pattern Recognition Letters*, 23(12):1459–1471, 2002.
4. W. Fan, S. J. Stolfo, J. Zhang, and P. K. Chan. Adacost: Misclassification cost-sensitive boosting. In *Proc. 16th Int'l Conf Machine Learning*, pages 97–105, 1999.
5. F. Fleuret. Fast binary feature selection with conditional mutual information. *J. Mach. Learn. Res.*, 5:1531–1555, November 2004.
6. B. Froba and A. Ernst. Face detection with the modified census transform. In *6th IEEE Int'l Conf Automatic Face and Gesture Recognition*, pages 91–96, May 2004.
7. K. Fukunaga. *Introduction to Statistical Pattern Recognition*. Academic Press, San Diego, 1990.
8. A. K. Gupta and S. Nadarajah, editors. *Handbook of Beta Distribution and its applications*. Marcel Dekker, Inc., 2004.
9. I. Guyon and A. Elisseeff. An introduction to variable and feature selection. *J. Mach. Learn. Res.*, 3:1157–1182, 2003.
10. B. Heisele, T. Serre, S. Mukherjee, and T. Poggio. Feature reduction and hierarchy of classifiers for fast object detection in video images. In *CVPR*, volume II, pages 18–24, 2001.
11. K. Huang, H. Yang, I. King, and M. R. Lyu. Learning classifiers from imbalanced data based on biased minimax probability machine. In *CVPR*, volume II, pages 558–563, 2004.
12. G. J. Karakoulas and J. Shawe-Taylor. Optimizing classifiers for imbalanced training sets. In *NIPS 11*, pages 253–259, 1999.
13. D. Keren, M. Osadchy, and C. Gotsman. Antifaces: A novel, fast method for image detection. *IEEE Trans. on PAMI*, 23(7):747–761, 2001.
14. K. Levi and Y. Weiss. Learning object detection from a small number of examples: The importance of good features. In *CVPR*, volume II, pages 53–60, 2004.
15. S. Z. Li and Z. Q. Zhang. Floatboost learning and statistical face detection. *IEEE Trans. on PAMI*, 26(9):1112–1123, 2004.
16. R. Lienhart, A. Kuranov, and V. Pisarevsky. Empirical analysis of detection cascades of boosted classifiers for rapid object detection. In *Pattern Recognition LNCS 2781*, pages 297–304, 2003.
17. C. Liu and H.-Y. Shum. Kullback-leibler boosting. In *CVPR*, volume II, pages 587–594, 2003.
18. H. Luo. Optimization design of cascaded classifiers. In *CVPR*, volume I, pages 480–485, 2005.
19. S. Romdhani, P. Torr, B. Schoelkopf, and A. Blake. Computationally efficient face detection. In *Proc. ICCV*, pages 695–700, 2001.

320   S.C. Brubaker et al.

20. R. E. Schapire and Y. Singer. Improved boosting using confidence-rated predictions. *Machine Learning*, 37(3):297–336, 1999.
21. H. Schneiderman. Feature-centric evaluation for efficient cascaded object detection. In *CVPR*, volume II, pages 29–36, 2004.
22. J. Sun, J. M. Rehg, and A. F. Bobick. Automatic cascade training with perturbation bias. In *CVPR*, volume II, pages 276–283, 2004.
23. K. Sung and T. Poggio. Example-based learning for view-based human face detection. *IEEE Trans. on PAMI*, 20(1):39–51, 1998.
24. K. M. Ting. A comparative study of cost-sensitive boosting algorithms. In *Proc. 17th Int'l Conf Machine Learning*, pages 983–990, 2000.
25. N. Vasconcelos. Feature selection by maximum marginal diversity: Optimality and implications for visual recognition. In *CVPR*, volume 1, pages 762–772, 2003.
26. M. Vidal-Naquet and S. Ullman. Object recognition with informative features and linear classification. In *Proc. ICCV*, pages 281–288, 2003.
27. P. Viola and M. Jones. Fast and robust classification using asymmetric AdaBoost and a detector cascade. In *NIPS 14*, pages 1311–1318, 2002.
28. P. Viola and M. J. Jones. Robust real-time object detection. Technical Report CRL 2001/01, Compaq Cambridge Research Laboratory, Feb 2001.
29. P. Viola and M. J. Jones. Robust real-time face detection. *Int. J. Comput. Vision*, 57(2):137–154, 2004.
30. J. Wu, S. C. Brubaker, M. D. Mullin, and J. M. Rehg. Fast asymmetric learning for cascade face detection. Technical Report GIT-GVU-05-27, Georgia Institute of Technology, 2005.
31. J. Wu, M. Mullin, and J. Rehg. Linear asymmetric classifier for cascade detectors. In *Proc. 22nd Int'l Conf Machine Learning*, pages 993–1000, 2005.
32. J. Wu, J. M. Rehg, and M. D. Mullin. Learning a rare event detection cascade by direct feature selection. In *NIPS 16*, pages 1523–1530, 2004.
33. R. Xiao, L. Zhu, and H.-J. Zhang. Boosting chain learning for object detection. In *Proc. ICCV*, volume 1, pages 709–715, 2003.
34. M.-H. Yang, D. J. Kriegman, and N. Ahuja. Detecting faces in images: A survey. *IEEE Trans. on PAMI*, 24(1):34–58, 2002.

Visual Classification by a Hierarchy of Extended Fragments

Shimon Ullman and Boris Epshtein

Weizmann Institute of Science,
67100, Rehovot, Israel
{shimon.ullman,boris.epshtein}@weizmann.ac.il

Abstract. The chapter describes visual classification by a hierarchy of semantic fragments. In fragment-based classification, objects within a class are represented by common sub-structures selected during training. The chapter describes two extensions to the basic fragment-based scheme. The first extension is the extraction and use of feature hierarchies. We describe a method that automatically constructs complete feature hierarchies from image examples, and show that features constructed hierarchically are significantly more informative and better for classification compared with similar non-hierarchical features. The second extension is the use of so-called semantic fragments to represent object parts. The goal of a semantic fragment is to represent the different possible appearances of a given object part. The visual appearance of such object parts can differ substantially, and therefore traditional image similarity-based methods are inappropriate for the task. We show how the method can automatically learn the part structure of a new domain, identify the main parts, and how their appearance changes across objects in the class. We discuss the implications of these extensions to object classification and recognition.

Introduction

Object classification involves two main stages: feature extraction, and then using these features to classify a novel image. Many different features have been proposed in the past, ranging from simple local ones such as Wavelets or Gabor filters [23], to complex features such as geons [3],[13] which are view-invariant 3-D primitive shapes. Most of the features used in the past, from the simple to the more complex, were usually generic in the sense that the same limited set of features was used for all objects and object classes.

In several recent classification schemes, objects are represented as a combination of informative image parts [1],[6],[9],[21]. This approach was shown to be effective for various classification problems. Unlike previous schemes, these features are class-specific: different features are extracted automatically for different classification tasks from the training data. The present work extends this approach in two directions: the use of hierarchical features, and the representation of object parts by equivalence classes of features, called 'semantic features'.

J. Ponce et al. (Eds.): Toward Category-Level Object Recognition, LNCS 4170, pp. 321–344, 2006.

The idea of representing objects in a class by their informative parts can be extended recursively: the informative object parts can themselves be represented as an arrangement of informative sub-parts, the sub-parts can then be split into smaller parts and so on. This general scheme raises a number of questions, related to the creation of such a hierarchy: a method for selecting the best parts and sub-parts, a stopping rule for decomposing the features, and the optimal selection of parameters such as the size of search region for each part. There are also questions related to the use of the hierarchy: how to perform classification using this structure, and how to best detect sub-parts of the object using their context. We discuss these questions in Part 2 of the chapter.

Each object part and sub-part (say, an eye) can be represented not just by a single representative image fragment, but by a collection of semantically equivalent fragments, representing different appearances of the part, such as an open eye, closed eye, or eyes of different shapes. Questions related to this issue include: how to extract such sets of semantically equivalent fragments, and how to use them for classification. These issues are discussed in Part 3.

The two components discussed above, hierarchical representation and semantic features, can be used independently, but can also be used naturally in a combined manner. Taken together, they give rise to the following feature organization: an object or a class are represented by a hierarchy of parts and sub-parts. This hierarchy can be represented as a tree, with semantic fragments at each node, as as illustrated schematically in Figure 1. In the remaining of this chapter we will discuss how this hierarchy of semantic fragments is constructed and used. The chapter is divided into three parts. The first briefly summarizes the extraction of informative features, the second describes the construction of

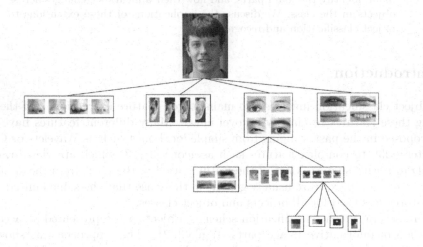

Fig. 1. Representing a class by a hierarchy of semantic fragments. A face is represented as an arrangement of parts such as nose, eyes, ear and mouth. Each of these parts is represented as a semantic equivalence set. The parts are represented in turn in terms of their sub-parts. For simplicity, only the sub-parts of the eye part are shown.

feature hierarchies, and the third describes the extraction and use of semantically equivalent parts. We conclude with a discussion of using the feature hierarchies and semantic equivalence sets together.

1   Informative Classification Fragments

In this section we describe the algorithm for extracting informative images fragments and learning their associated parameters, such as the detection threshold for each fragment. This family of features proved to be highly effective for classification. An empirical comparisons with other classification features can be found in [22].

Fragments are selected from the training data using the the procedure in [21]. The process proceeds by identifying fragments that deliver the maximal amount of information about the class. A large number (tens of thousands) of candidate fragments are extracted from the training images at multiple locations and sizes. For each fragment, the optimal detection threshold is computed as explained below. This detection threshold indicates the minimal visual similarity that a fragment must have within an image, to be detected. Normalized cross-correlation was used in the past as a similarity measure, but other similarity measures, such as SIFT [12], can also be used. A binary variable can then be associated with each fragment depending on its presence in the image I:

$$f_i(I, \theta_i) = \begin{cases} 1, & \text{if } S(I, f_i) > \theta_i \\ 0, & otherwise \end{cases} \tag{1}$$

$S(I, f_i)$ is the maximal visual similarity between fragment f_i and image I, θ_i is the threshold associated with f_i. The class variable variable $C(I)$ is defined as 1 if the image belongs to the class being detected, and 0 otherwise. We can then derive the mutual information between the two binary variables:

$$MI(f_i(\theta_i); C) = \sum_{f_i, C} p(f_i, C) \log \frac{p(f_i, C)}{p(f_i)p(C)} \tag{2}$$

The mutual information in this expression depends on the detection threshold θ_i. If the threshold is too low, the information delivered by the fragment about the class will be low, because the fragment will be detected with high frequency in both the class and non-class images. A high threshold will also yield low mutual information, since the fragment will be seldom detected in both the class and non-class images. At some intermediate value of threshold, the mutual information reaches a maximum. The value θ_i of threshold yielding maximal information for the fragment f_i is therefore associated with the fragment. The most informative fragments are selected successively, using the following max-min procedure. After finding the first fragment with the highest mutual information score, the search identified the next fragment that delivered the maximal amount of additional information. At iteration i the fragment f_i is selected to increase the mutual information of the fragment set by maximizing the minimal addition in mutual information with respect to each of the first i-1 fragments.

$$f_i = \arg \max_{f_k \in K_i} \min_{f_j \in S_i} (MI(f_k, f_j; C) - MI(f_j; C)) \tag{3}$$

K_i is the set of candidate fragments, S_i is the set of already selected fragments at iteration i, f_i is the new fragment to be selected at iteration i. The update rule for the fragment sets is:

$$\begin{aligned} K_{i+1} &= K_i \backslash \{f_i\} \\ S_{i+1} &= S_i \cup \{f_i\} \end{aligned} \tag{4}$$

The initial K_0 is the set of all candidate fragments; S_0 is the set containing a single fragment with the highest mutual information with the class. The iterations end when adding new fragment to the set S makes only a small increment to the mutual information, less than some small threshold ε. Once the set of informative fragments is determined, the optimal size of the region of interest (ROI) for each selected fragment is computed. The ROI defines the area in novel images where the fragment is searched for. For each fragment f, the amount of information it delivers about the class depends on the size of its ROI. When the ROI is too small, the information is low, because in many class images the fragment will fall outside the search region, and therefore will not be detected. If the size of the ROI is too large, the number of false detections will increase. At some intermediate size of the ROI, the mutual information reaches a maximum (Figure 6). The algorithm therefore evaluates different ROI sizes from zero to half the size of the full search window, and identifies the size that brings the MI to its maximum. The full search window is a fixed region within the input image, where the algorithm looks for the entire object. This window was set in the experiments described in this chapter to size 200x200 pixels. To detect an object within a larger image, the search window can either scan the image, or move only to selected salient locations [10]. The locations of the ROIs of the informative fragments are defined relative to the center of the search window.

2   Feature Hierarchies for Object Classification

In this part we describe a method for extracting complete feature hierarchies from training examples. The method includes the construction of the feature hierarchies, and learning the required parameters, such as the combination weight for each part. We briefly discuss a method of using the feature hierarchy for classification. Experimental comparisons with other classification features illustrate the advantages offered by the use of feature hierarchies compared with non-hierarchical features.

2.1   Construction of Hierarchical Features

The search for useful sub-fragments is similar to the search of useful top-level classification features. The top-level features are selected based on their usefulness for detected class examples. In an analogous manner, useful sub-fragments should appear with high frequency in regions containing the 'parent' feature, but infrequently elsewhere. As for the top-level fragments, a useful selection criterion is the mutual information between the sub-fragment and its parent fragment. To evaluate this information, we need for each 'parent' fragment f a set of positive examples, namely, image regions containing the fragment f, and a set of negative examples, where the detection of f should be avoided. The positive examples for the fragment f are provided by identifying all the locations in the class images where the fragment f was detected. This set is then increased, since the goal of the fragment decomposition is to successfully detect additional examples, which were not captured by the fragment f alone. The positive set is increased by lowering the detection threshold of the fragment f, yielding examples where f is either detected or almost detected. The reduced threshold was determined to increase the positive set by 20%. This amount of increase was chosen to add a significant number of almost-detected examples, and avoid examples that are dissimilar to f. A set of negative examples was similarly derived from the non-class images. Negative examples are selected from non-class images that give "false alarms", and therefore supply negative instances which lie close to the boundary between class and non-class instances. The reduced detection threshold used for the positive examples is applied here as well, to obtain non-class examples where the feature was incorrectly detected, or almost detected.

In terms of the positions of the fragment examples within the training images, examples come from regions in class images where the parent feature was detected or almost detected within its ROI, and negative examples come from regions in the non-class images where the feature was detected. In this case, the feature position in the training images was determined by the computation of optimal positions of all the hierarchy nodes together (Part 2.2) so that at most one example was taken from each training image.

Once the positive and negative examples of the feature f are established, sub-fragments are selected by exactly the same information maximization procedure used at the first level. The candidate sub-fragments in this case are the sub-images with their center point within the parent fragment, and having an area up to $1/4$ of the parent's area. Sub-features are added to the tree, until the additional information falls below a threshold (0.08). Experimentally, fragments with smaller contributions did not improve significantly the detection of the parent feature. If the decomposition of f into simpler features increased the information delivered by the entire hierarchy, the same decomposition was also applied to f's sub-features. Each of the sub-fragments is considered in turn a parent fragment, positive and negative examples are found and the set of its informative sub-fragments is selected. Otherwise, the decomposition is terminated, with f considered an atomic fragment. Atomic fragments were usually simple, typically containing edges, corners or lines. Hierarchy examples are shown in Figure 4. Examples of atomic fragments are shown in Figure 5.

During the classification stage, only the atomic features are directly correlated with the input image, and their responses are combined using weights learned at the training stage (Part 2.2).

2.2   Optimizing the Parameters of the Hierarchy

For each hierarchy node (fragment or sub-fragment), a region of positional tolerance is extracted, which is the feature's region of interest (ROI) (as in Part 1). The locations of the ROIs of sub-fragments in every image are determined relative to the detected position of their parent fragment. The dimensions of the ROI for all the sub-fragments are adjusted during learning to maximize the information delivered by the feature hierarchy. During the hierarchy construction, the initial ROI size of a sub-fragment is set to the size of its parent. After the hierarchy is completed, additional optimization of the ROI sizes is performed in a top-down manner: first, the ROI of the uppermost node is optimized to maximize the mutual information between the class variable and hierarchy's detection variable, while all other ROIs are fixed. A similar process is then applied to its sub-fragments, and the optimization proceeds down the hierarchy, where at each stage the ROIs of the higher levels are kept fixed.

An additional set of hierarchy parameters used for classification is the combination weights of the sub-features responses. The optimization of the combination weights is described below together with the use of these weights in the classification process.

The classification performance of the hierarchy was evaluated using a network model similar to HMAX [16], with layers performing maximization and weighted sum operations. For a given feature, the maximal response of each sub-feature is taken over the sub-feature's ROI, and then the responses of all sub-features are combined linearly:

$$r = w_0 + \sum_{i=1}^{n} w_i s_i \tag{5}$$

where r is the combined response, s_i the maximal response of sub-feature i within its ROI, w_i are the weights of the combination, and n the number of sub-features. For the atomic sub-features, the response was equal to the maximal normalized cross-correlation between the sub-feature and the image within the ROI. The final response s_p of the parent feature was obtained by a sigmoid function,

$$s_p = \frac{2}{1 + e^{-r}} - 1 \tag{6}$$

which normalizes s_p to the range [-1,1].

The response of the topmost node of the hierarchy, which determines the presence or absence of the entire object, is then compared to a detection threshold. The amount of information about the class carried by the hierarchy is defined as the mutual information between the class variable C and the hierarchy detection variable H, which is equal to 1 when the response of the topmost node is higher than threshold and 0 otherwise.

The combination weights are adjusted during training using iterative optimization that alternates between optimizing positions and weights, as described below. First, the weights are initialized randomly in the range (0,1). The scheme then alternates between the following two steps.

Positions Step: fix the weights, optimize feature positions. For every position of the parent fragment within its ROI the positions of sub-fragments (within their relative ROIs) that maximize the responses of the sub-fragments are found. Then, the position of the parent fragment that maximizes its response s_p is chosen. This routine can be implemented efficiently using Dynamic Programming.

Weights Step: fix feature positions, optimize weights. The combination weights of the features are optimized using the standard Back-Propagation algorithm with batch training protocol. The algorithm ends when no feature changes its position during the Positions Step.

This weight selection procedure can be shown to converge to a local minimum of classification error. Experimentally, we found that the algorithm converged in less than 10 iterations, average just 3 iterations. The obtained optimum was found to be stable, since starting from multiple random initial weights the algorithm terminated with similar performance.

2.3 Experiments

Empirical testing was used to test two main aspects of the hierarchical scheme. First, we compared the classification performance of the hierarchical features with similar features used in a holistic, non-hierarchical manner. Second, we compared the use of adaptive against a uniform hierarchy. The adaptive hierarchy adjusted the center positions and individual ROI for all the features as described above. The uniform hierarchy used instead a hierarchy where both ROI sizes and the sub-fragments were chosen in a fixed manner on a uniform grid.

In comparing the adaptive with a fixed grid hierarchy, the fixed ROI size was set at each hierarchy level to the average size of the units in the adaptive scheme, which simulations showed to be a good average size. Comparisons were averaged for all units with more than a single hierarchical level. To compare a fixed-grid hierarchy with the adaptable scheme above, each parent feature was divided into k sub-features, where k was set to the average number of sub-features in the adaptive hierarchy (6 for faces, airplanes, 9 for cows). The horizontal and vertical dimensions of the sub-features were similarly set at each level to the average dimensions in the adaptive hierarchy, shown by simulations to be a good average size.

Training images for features extraction contained 200 faces, 95 cows, 320 airplanes. The images were grey-level, 120-210 pixels in each dimension. Non-class images included a random collection of landscape, fruits, toys, etc., with a similar grey-level range. Feature detection experiments were performed on a new set of 1770 images (800 faces, 220 cows, 750 airplanes), repeated by randomly partitioning the full set into training and test images.

In computing the ROC curves [8] of a feature, the hits and false alarms were defined by using the feature as a single feature classifier. That is, test images were classified based on the feature in question; hits corresponded to class image identified correctly, false alarms to non-class images identified incorrectly. By varying the classification threshold, the complete ROC curves were obtained.

2.4 Summary of the Results

We first compared the non-hierarchical top level fragments with the same fragments detected in a hierarchical manner, in terms of information supplied and classification performance. The information supplied by the first-level hierarchical features increased in the test set for all fragments (n=150, 3 classes), and was significantly higher compared with the corresponding holistic features (average increase 46.6%, s.d. 30.5%, $p < 10^{-9}$ one-tailed paired t-test). The holistic and hierarchical features were also compared using their complete ROC curves, showing a significant advantage of the hierarchical detection over the entire range, (0-90% false alarm, n=150, $p < 0.000001$, Figure 3b). These comparisons clearly show that hierarchical features are more informative and produce better classification.

Further decomposition into a multi-level hierarchy provided additional significant gain in information (n=97 features, average increase 10.0%, s.d. 10.7% $p < 10^{-9}$ one-tailed paired t-test). The ROC detection curves also improved significantly (example in Figure 3a).

The full hierarchy also proved considerably more robust than holistic features. This is of interest particularly when the feature hierarchies are considered as a possible biological model for object processing. A biological system cannot be expected to converge to the exact optimal parameters, but we found that introducing size and position errors (13%, 25% of feature size) reduced the MI on average by 10.8% for the full hierarchy, compared with 35.3% for holistic features (n =41, $p < 10^{-10}$, paired t-test).

Using the optimal ROI sizes adds significantly to the MI compared with a fixed ROI size, that was optimized for each level separately (average 8.1% s.d. 13.7% $p < 0.0055$), and different subunits had different optimal ROI size. Adapting the relative positions of the subunits is also significant: if the subunits' centers were arranged on a uniform grid, rather than selecting their optimal locations during training, the MI decreases (N=153, average 43% s.d. = 35% $p < 10^{-10}$ paired t-test), and the detection performance of the units decreases (Figure 3a).

These results can be used to compare the use of hierarchical and holistic features in both computer vision and biological modelling. Most computational models of recognition and classification in the past did not use hierarchical features. This is in contrast to the primate visual system where objects are analyzed by a hierarchy of features. Our analysis and testing shows that hierarchical features are significantly more informative and better for classification than holistic features. It also shows that this improvement requires the learning of positions and sizes; without this the hierarchical scheme is not significantly better than a single layer of top-level features.

Some previous biological models ([11],[16]) used a hierarchy of features, to simulate the cortical structure. However, these models used fixed uniform architecture in contrast with the adaptive scheme used here, and which proved valuable to the construction of a successful hierarchy. The method of selecting the features, based on the information they contribute, also proved to produce better results than either fixed features [16], or features extracted by back-propagation

Fig. 2. Informative fragments (examples on the left) and their optimal sub-fragments (right), selected automatically from three object classes by maximizing mutual information

neural network model [11]. See [5] for more details on experimental comparisons with other types of features.

3   Semantically Equivalent Features

In this part we consider the problem of detecting semantically equivalent parts of objects belonging to the same class. By 'semantic' equivalence we mean parts of the same type in similar objects, often having the same part name, such as a nose in a face, an animal's tail, a car's headlight and the like. The aim is to identify such parts, although their visual appearance can be highly dissimilar. The input to the algorithm is a set of images belonging to the same object class, together with an image patch (called below a "root fragment"), depicting a part of an object. The output is a set of image patches from the input images, containing object parts which are semantically equivalent to the one depicted in the root fragment. Examples of semantically equivalent fragments are shown in Figure 7. In each row, the leftmost image contains the root fragment, the other images are semantically equivalent fragments discovered by the algorithm. The identification of equivalent object parts has two main goals. First, the correct detection and identification of object parts is important on its own right, and can be useful for various applications that depend on identifying parts, such as recognizing facial expressions, visual aid for speech recognition, visual inspection, surveillance and so on. Second, the correct identification of semantically equivalent object parts improves the performance of object recognition algorithms. In several recent object recognition schemes [1],[6],[9],[21] image fragments depicting object components are used as classification features. Our results show that the performance of such schemes can be improved when an object component is represented not by a single fragment, but by a set of semantically equivalent fragments.

The general idea behind our approach is to use common context to identify equivalent parts. Given an image fragment F depicting a part of an object, we

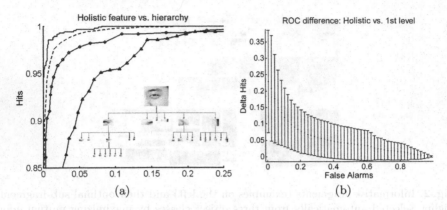

(a)   (b)

Fig. 3. Comparing recognition by hierarchical and holistic features. (a) ROC of a single fragment comparing detection by a holistic feature (third from top), optimal decomposition into sub-features (second from top), full hierarchical decomposition (top curve), and decomposition on a fixed grid (lowest curve). y-axis: percent correct identification of class images by the fragment (hits), x-axis: percent incorrect identification of non-class images (false alarms). (b) Average gain in ROC, vertical axis: increase in hit rate, horizontal: false alarm rate (n = 150 fragments). See text for further details.

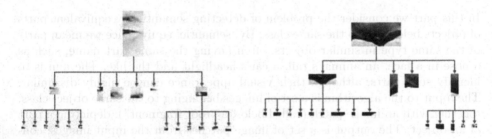

Fig. 4. Examples of full feature hierarchies, (bottom nodes are atomic features)

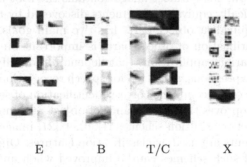

E   B   T/C   X

Fig. 5. Atomic features, derived from three classes. Most are tuned to oriented edges (E), bars (B), terminations/corners (T/C); some are more complex (X).

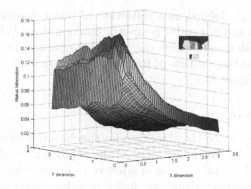

Fig. 6. Increase in mutual information as a function of search region size, for one sub-feature (inset). Color code: increase in mutual information, horizontal axes: ROI size, (size of parent feature is taken as '1'). Optimal x-size: 0.27, y-size: 0.43.

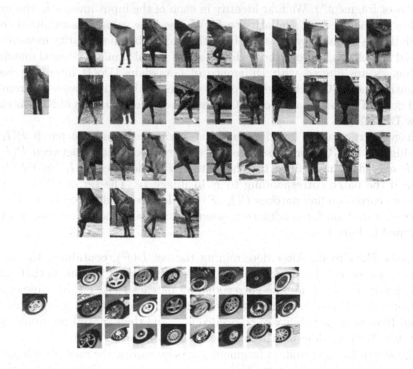

Fig. 7. Examples of semantically equivalent fragments, extracted by the algorithm. The leftmost image in each set is the input root fragment, the others are equivalent parts identified by the algorithm (horse torso with forelegs, car wheels). The algorithm identifies semantically similar parts that can have markedly different appearance in the image.

look for a context C, defined as a collection of image fragments that co-occur with F consistently and in a stable geometric configuration. When such context is found, we look for all images where the context fragments are detected, and infer from their positions the location of fragments that are likely to be semantically equivalent to F (Figure 8).

3.1 Description of the Algorithm

In this section, we describe the algorithm for the detection of semantically equivalent image fragments. The main stages of the algorithm are the identification of common context (3.1) and the use of context to extract equivalent parts (3.1). We begin with describing visual similarity matching used as a pre-processing step.

Visual Similarity Matching. The input to the algorithm consists of a set of images of different objects within a class, I_k, and a single fixed fragment F (the "root fragment"). We first identify in each of the input images I_k the image patch with the maximal similarity to F. We used the value of normalized cross-correlation as a similarity measure, but other image-based similarity measure can be used as well. To improve the performance of visual similarity-based matching, the images are filtered with Difference of Gaussians (DoG) filter [12] before computing the NCC. This filter emphasizes the gradients in images and removes small noise. The combination of DoG filtering with computation of NCC is called below DNCC.

Image patches at all locations in I_k are examined, and the patch $P(I_k, F)$ with highest DNCC score is selected. If the cross-correlation between $P(I_k, F)$ and F exceeds a pre-defined threshold, then F is detected in I_k, and $P(I_k, F)$ is called the patch corresponding to F in image I_k. The set of all the images I_k where corresponding patches $P(I_k, F)$ are detected is denoted by $D(F)$. The detection threshold for candidate context patches was chosen automatically as explained in Part 1.

Context Retrieval. After determining the set $D(F)$, containing the images where F was detected , the next goal is to identify context fragments that consistently co-occur with F and its corresponding patches $P(I_k, F)$. Reliable context fragments should meet two criteria: the context fragment f and root fragment F should have high probability of co-occurrence, and their spatial relations should be stable. We next describe the selection based on these criteria.

The search for good context fragment starts by pairing the root F with patches f_i in each image in $D(F)$ at multiple sizes and positions. These patches are the candidate context patches for F. In practice, we limited the search to patch sizes ranging from 50% of F size up to 150% in each dimension, with scaling step of 1.5. For each patch size, we examine patches in positions placed on a regular grid with step equal to 1/4 of the size of a patch. The exact position and size of a context patch is eventually optimized as described later in this section. For every candidate patch f, we find the set $D(f)$ of images containing patches visually similar to f, as described in Part 3.1.

The first context condition above was high co-occurrence, that is, a good context fragments should satisfy $p(F|f) > p(F)$. We also want to focus on context fragments that appear together with F at least some minimal number of times, and therefore require:

$$P(f|F) > \theta_p \qquad p(F|f) > p(F) \tag{7}$$

The value of θ_p was computed automatically by sampling a set of candidate patches from $D(f)$, computing their probabilities of co-occurrence with F, and setting the threshold to average co-occurrence probability plus one standard deviation.

Second, F and f should appear in a stable spatial configuration. If the variations in scale and orientation between the images are assumed to be small, then the relative location of F and f when they are detected together should be similar. We therefore test the variance of coordinate differences:

$$Var(F_x - f_x) < \theta_{VarX} \qquad Var(F_y - f_y) < \theta_{VarY} \tag{8}$$

Here F_x and f_x are vectors of x-coordinates of the centers of image patches corresponding to F and f, respectively, in images from $D(F) \cap D(f)$, similarly for F_y and f_y. The thresholds θ_{VarX} and θ_{VarY} determine the flexibility of the geometric model of the object. These thresholds are also set automatically by computing the values of $Var(F_x - f_x)$ and $Var(F_y - f_y)$ for the sampled fragments, for which $P(f|F) > \theta_p$ and setting the thresholds to the average of these values plus one standard deviation.

To identify the best context fragments, we first remove from the set of candidates all fragments that do not meet requirements (7) and (8). We next select from the remaining set the fragments with the highest probability of co-occurrence with F, and smallest variances of coordinate differences (indicating a stable geometric relation with the root F). To combine these criteria, we compute a 'consistency weight', w_f:

$$w_f = P(f|F) \cdot \frac{1}{1 + \sqrt{\max(Var(F_x - f_x), Var(F_y - f_y))}} \tag{9}$$

The fragment with the highest w_f is then selected as a context fragment. Since the initial search for context fragments was limited to a fixed grid, we refine the optimal position and size of the context fragment by searching locally for the best fragment position and size that maximize w_f. We add the optimized fragment to the set of context fragments.

To avoid redundancy, and prefer conditionally independent context fragments (see Part 3.1 for details), we remove from the set of remaining candidates all the fragments that intersect the selected one by more than 25% of their area, and repeat the process until no candidates are left. The final context set contains fragments f_i that have high co-occurrence with F, and with stable relative positions. Typically this set contains between 6 and 12 fragments.

Fig. 8. Left: a root fragment (mouth) together with context fragments (ear and eye). Right: the same context detected in another image; a semantically equivalent part is identified by the context.

Identifying Semantically Equivalent Parts. After the set of context fragments has been selected, they are used to infer the positions of fragments that are semantically equivalent to the root fragment F. Using a probabilistic model, we identify for each image I_k, in which at least one context fragment has been detected, the most likely position of F_k, a semantically equivalent fragment to F.

Assume for simplicity first that our context set consists of a single fragment C. Our modelling assumption is that if C is detected in some image I_k at coordinates (x_c, y_c); then the probability density of F being found at coordinates (x, y) is 2D Gaussian centered at $(\hat{x}_c, \hat{y}_c)$, where $\hat{x}_c$ and $\hat{y}_c$ are the expected coordinates of the root fragment's center, predicted by context fragment C. The values of $\hat{x}_c$ and $\hat{y}_c$ are computed as:

$$\hat{x}_c = x_c + \overline{\Delta x_c} \qquad \hat{y}_c = y_c + \overline{\Delta y_c} \tag{10}$$

where $\overline{\Delta x_c}$ and $\overline{\Delta y_c}$ are the mean coordinate differences between the centers of F and C, estimated during training.

$$P(F(x, y)|C) = P(F|C) \cdot N(x - \hat{x}_c, y - \hat{y}_c; \Sigma_c) \tag{11}$$

where Σ_c is the covariance matrix of coordinate differences between the centers of fragments F and C, estimated during training.

If the context fragment C is not detected in the image I_k, we assume 2D uniform probability density of F being found at coordinates (x, y):

$$P(F(x, y)|\bar{C}) = P(F|\bar{C}) \cdot U(W, H) \tag{12}$$

here the distribution bounds W and H are set to the width and height of the image.

When the context consists of several fragments, we assume conditional independence between them given the detection of F at position (x, y):

$$P(C_1, ..., C_N|F(x, y)) = \prod_{i=1}^{N} P(C_i|F(x, y)) \tag{13}$$

The modelling assumption of the conditional independence is motivated by the observation that if geometric relation between fragments is stable, the positions of the context fragments are determined by the position of the root fragment. The fluctuations of the positions are due to noise, which is assumed to be independent for the context fragments. Modelling of higher-order geometric relations between fragments is also possible, but we found in testing that it did not make a significant contribution. Applying Bayes rule to (13):

$$P(F(x,y)|C_1, ..., C_N) = \frac{P(F(x,y))}{P(C_1, ..., C_N)} \prod_{i=1}^{N} P(C_i|F(x,y)) \tag{14}$$

We assume the prior probability $P(F(x,y))$ of finding F at the coordinates (x, y) to be uniform, consequently not depending on x and y. It is also straightforward to use non-uniform prior. The probability $P(C_1, ..., C_N)$ similarly does not depend on (x, y). Therefore, we can write:

$$P(F(x,y)|C_1, ..., C_N) \propto \prod_{i=1}^{N} P(C_i|F(x,y)) \tag{15}$$

For the individual factors $P(C_i|F(x,y))$ we use equations (11) or (12), depending on whether or not the context fragment C_i was detected in the image. Applying the Bayes rule again, if C_i was detected in the image:

$$P(C_i|F(x,y)) = \frac{P(C_i) \cdot P(F(x,y)|C_i)}{P(F(x,y))} = \frac{P(C_i) \cdot P(F|C_i) \cdot N(x - \hat{x}_{ci}, y - \hat{y}_{ci}; \Sigma_{Ci})}{P(F(x,y))} \tag{16}$$

If C_i was not detected in the image:

$$P(\overline{C_i}|F(x,y)) = \frac{(1 - P(C_i)) \cdot P(F(x,y)|\bar{C_i})}{P(F(x,y))} = \frac{(1 - P(C_i)) \cdot P(F|\overline{C_i}) \cdot U(W, H)}{P(F(x,y))} \tag{17}$$

Now we can find the values of coordinates x and y that maximize (15), i.e. find a Maximum Likelihood solution for the coordinates of the center of the fragment F:

$$(x, y) = \arg\max_i \prod N(x - \hat{x}_{ci}, y - \hat{y}_{ci}; \Sigma_{ci}) \tag{18}$$

where each 2D Gaussian can be explicitly written in terms of its parameters: mean position and covariance matrix. Note that the product is taken over only the detected context fragments. Taking the log of the product, differentiating with respect to x and y, and setting the derivatives to zero, yields a system of equation of the form:

$$xA - yB + C = 0 \qquad yD - xB + E = 0 \tag{19}$$

where

$$A = \sum_i \frac{1}{(1-\rho_{xyi}^2)\sigma_{xi}^2}$$

$$B = \sum_i \frac{\rho_{xyi}}{\sigma_{xi}\sigma_{yi}}$$

$$C = \sum_i \left(\frac{\rho_{xyi}(y_{ci}+\overline{\Delta y_{ci}})}{\sigma_{xi}\sigma_{yi}} - \frac{x_{ci}+\overline{\Delta x_{ci}}}{(1-\rho_{xyi}^2)\sigma_{xi}^2} \right) \qquad (20)$$

$$D = \sum_i \frac{1}{(1-\rho_{xyi}^2)\sigma_{yi}^2}$$

$$E = \sum_i \left(\frac{\rho_{xyi}(x_{ci}+\overline{\Delta x_{ci}})}{\sigma_{xi}\sigma_{yi}} - \frac{y_{ci}+\overline{\Delta y_{ci}}}{(1-\rho_{xyi}^2)\sigma_{yi}^2} \right)$$

$$\sigma_{xi} = \sqrt{Var(x - x_{ci})}, \quad \sigma_{yi} = \sqrt{Var(y - y_{ci})}, \quad \rho_{xyi} = \frac{CoVar((x - x_{ci}),(y - y_{ci}))}{\sigma_{xi}\sigma_{yi}}$$

Solving (19), we obtain:

$$y = \frac{AE + BC}{B^2 - AD} \qquad x = \frac{By - C}{A} \qquad (21)$$

After obtaining the maximal likelihood solution for the coordinates (x, y), we extract a fragment centered at (x, y) with size equal to the size of F, and add it to the set of fragments semantically equivalent to F.

The set of semantically equivalent fragments constructed in this manner is called the "equivalence set" of the part. We next sort it by measuring the strength of the evidence used to select the fragments. This is obtained by setting the optimal values found for (x, y) into (15) and taking the log. The resulting quantity is equal to the log-likelihood of the optimal solution plus a constant factor. This value is then used to sort the equivalence set: the log-likelihood will be smaller when only a few context fragments are detected in a particular image, or when their evidence was inconsistent, i.e. they predict different locations of a semantic fragment. The decision regarding the number of fragments from the equivalence set to be used is application-dependent. For the object recognition experiments we used the upper 30% of the sorted equivalence set. For the part detection experiments we used the entire set and counted the number of errors.

The section above describes the main computation; its accuracy can be improved by incorporating a number of additional steps. We used in particular simple criteria to reject outliers, based on the fact that they will be detected at highly variable image locations. We therefore computed the average value of coordinate differences between the detected positions of F and f, and removed the farthest outliers, until the variance of coordinate differences is below threshold. The same procedure for outlier rejection is used when performing the Maximum Likelihood estimation, since some of the context fragments can correspond to false detections.

3.2   Experimental Results

Object Parts Detection. We selected first for testing 7 root fragments depicting different parts of the human face (shown in Table 1), and applied the algorithm described in Section 3.1 to detect semantically equivalent parts in new face images independently for each root fragment. For comparison, we applied the algorithm for detecting face parts based on their visual similarity to the root fragment, as described in Section 3.1, using the same input image set and root fragments. The visual similarity for testing was computed using two different measures - DNCC and SIFT [12]. We applied both algorithms to a database of 1000 face images (about 150x200 pixels in size, roughly the same scale and orientation) and counted the number of images where all the parts were simultaneously detected correctly. The numbers of face images where all 7 fragments were simultaneously detected correctly were 379 using semantic equivalence, 5 using DNCC visual similarity and 7 using SIFT visual similarity. As can be seen, the method is successful in recovering a large number of correct part configurations, that cannot be identified by their visual similarity. The percentage of correctly identified matches, verified by humans, for semantic equivalence and DNCC visual similarity was also computed for each individual part, yielding the results in Table 1. Using the SIFT similarity measure produced similar results to DNCC. See [4] for the details of the experiments on other object classes.

Object Recognition. The classifier we used for the experiments is an extension of a classifier described in [21]. Briefly, an object from a general class is represented by a collection of object parts. A set of fragments (either visually similar or semantically equivalent) selected automatically, is used to represent each part. An object part is detected in the image if one of the fragments representing it is detected within a detection window. Each fragment is assigned a weight w_i determined by the log-likelihood ratio:

$$w_i = \log \frac{P(F_i|C=1)}{P(F_i|C=0)} \tag{22}$$

where C is a class variable (1 in images containing an object, 0 otherwise) and F_i is a fragment variable (1 when the fragment was detected, 0 otherwise). Final detection is based on a Bayesian decision,

$$\sum_i w_i F_i > \theta \tag{23}$$

where θ is decision threshold; by varying θ complete ROC curves are obtained (Figure 9).

Face detection performance was compared using 7 face parts, shown in Table 1. Each part was then represented by 20 representative image fragments selected to optimize performance. The two schemes we compared used an identical classifier, but differed in the selection of the image fragments representing each part. In the 'semantic' scheme, each part was represented by a set of 20 semantically equivalent fragments, selected by the algorithm described in Part 3.1. In the 'visual similarity' scheme, each part was represented by 20 representative image fragments, selected from the set of visually similar fragments so as to optimize performance.

The selection of representative fragments for each face part was done in a greedy fashion, using a mutual information criterion: the fragment delivering the highest information between the classifier response and the true class was selected first. Next, all the remaining fragments were examined, to determine the fragment contributing the largest amount of additional information when added to the first one. The process was repeated until 20 fragments have been selected. An identical selection procedure was used to select the best representatives from the set of visually similar fragments.

The image set was divided randomly into a training set (300 images) and test set (700 images), and the computation was repeated 50 times. The results are presented in Figure 9. Figure 9a shows the comparison of ROC curves of a single root fragment (the mouth in Table 1): the ROC curve of the classifier based on this fragment alone (line with circles), the ROC curve of the classifier based on visually similar fragments (dashed line) and the ROC curve of the classifier based

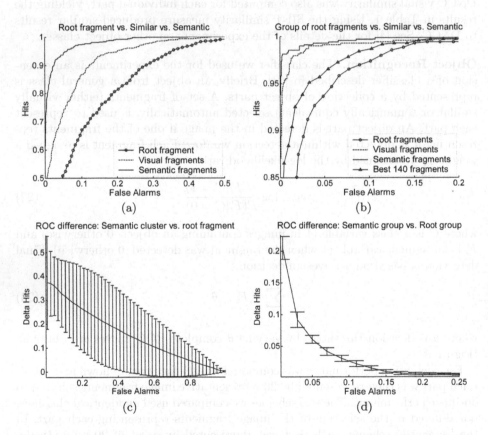

Fig. 9. Comparing recognition by semantic equivalence and visual similarity. (a) ROC curves for a single part (mouth); (b) classification by 7 parts; (c) average gain in ROC between semantic and visual similarity for single parts; (d) average gain in ROC for classification by 7 parts, using semantic vs. visual similarity. See text for further details.

Table 1. Percentage of correctly identified fragments representing object parts in three classes: faces, car rear views and toy cars. See text for further details.

Root fragment	Semantic equivalence	Visual similarity (DNCC)
	94%	33%
	92%	39%
	92%	71%
	89%	20%
	90%	29%
	88%	51%
	84%	26%
	65%	41%
	55%	18%
	64%	25%
	71%	59%
	42%	32%

on semantic equivalence class (solid line). Figure 9b shows the performance of 7 root fragments, compared to the performance of visually similar and semantic fragments, where each of 7 parts was represented by a set of 20 fragments. The graph also shows the performance based on the selection of 140 individual fragments. Figure 9c shows the mean difference between the ROC curves of the classifier based on visually similar fragments, and the classifier that uses semantic equivalence classes for single parts. Figure 9d shows the mean difference between the ROC curves of the classifier based on the group of 7 parts, represented by semantically equivalent fragments, compared with the performance of 7 root fragments used together.

Image similarity was based in the scheme above on normalized cross-correlation. Other, more robust image comparison measures can be used to compensate for scale changes, affine transformations, and small local distortions (see [15] for a review). Comparisons in [14] have shown that in the absence of scale changes and affine transformations, the performance of normalized cross-correlation is comparable to the performance of the SIFT descriptor [12] and better than the results obtained with other measures. Since we tested the algorithm under these conditions, the use of DNCC was appropriate. We also compared the performance of DNCC and SIFT, in the following way. For each face image, the fragment semantically equivalent to the root and the fragment most visually similar to the root were determined by the algorithm (only the images where both fragments were found by the algorithms were considered). The images where the computed semantic fragment was correct (as determined by an observer), but the fragment selected by visual similarity was incorrect, were chosen for comparison. For each image, we then normalized the three fragments (the root, the semantically equivalent and the most visually similar) by an affine transform to a normal form [15], and compared the SIFT distance between the root and semantic fragment, to the SIFT distance between the root and the visually similar fragment. In 74.6% of the cases, the SIFT made the incorrect selection: the visually similar fragment was closer to the root fragment than the semantic fragment. We conclude that the SIFT distance did not overcome the incorrect choice of the visually similar fragment made by the DNCC.

3.3   Other Methods of Obtaining Equivalent Fragments

The scheme described above identifies sets of semantically equivalent fragments in the training images. These semantically equivalent fragments depict corresponding parts in different objects of the same class, such as different hairlines, aircraft wings, car wheels and the like. They can also identify different views of the same object part under different conditions, such as a smiling vs. neutral mouth, or open vs. closed eye. Other methods have been developed in the past for identifying the same object part under changes in viewing conditions, in particular, changes in viewing direction and illumination conditions. These equivalence relations then play a crucial part in identifying specific objects under different conditions. We briefly review in this section past methods for identifying such equivalent fragments, and comment in the final discussion on their use in object identification.

Motion-Based Fragment Equivalence. Motion can serve as a powerful cue for identifying the same object part under different viewing conditions. If an image region transforms in a smooth continuous manner over time, then its image at different times are likely to represent the same part under different conditions. In particular, when the object moves rigidly in space, such motion-based equivalence can be used to identify different appearances of an object part from different viewing directions. Motion-based equivalence has been used to deal with the problem of position invariance [7] as well as more complex transformations [17],[19],[20].

In [19], the problem of obtaining fragment sets representing the same object part under different viewing angles was considered, and a method for identifying informative equivalent parts was developed based on motion correspondence. The method first extracts a large pool of so-called extended fragments, which are sets of fragments representing the same object part under different viewing conditions, in this case different viewing directions. The correspondence between fragments in different views is established using motion tracking [18]. From this initial pool of motion-related fragments, informative extended fragments are extracted based on the mutual information supplied by the extended fragments for view-invariant recognition. The selection of informative fragments is similar to the algorithm described in Part 1, but applied to extended fragments rather than to individual fragments. The selection process is initialized by selecting the extended fragment with the highest mutual information. Extended fragments are then added one by one by the max-min procedure described above, until the gain in mutual information is small, or a pre-selected size of fragment bank is reached. Fragment detection is done by computing the maximal similarity between the fragment and underlying image patch over the entire image, and comparing it to a pre-determined threshold. The optimal thresholds were computed automatically, by a procedure similar to the one described in Part 1.

In the recognition stage, the system was given a single image of a novel object from the learned class, for example, a face in frontal view. The task was then to identify the same object from a side view, from a large set of both frontal and side-view faces. The identification was based on the activation of the identified extended fragments. The main underlying assumption is that after learning, a frontal face F and a corresponding side view F' share the same extended fragment. If a particular fragment f is found in the frontal view, then its corresponding counterpart f' should be present in the side view. In order to identify the corresponding side view, the activation pattern for the query frontal view was computed. The activation pattern is a binary vector containing 1 in n-th position if the n-th fragment in the object representation was active in the image, and 0 otherwise. Similarly, the activation patterns were computed for all the images in the test set. The test image, whose activation pattern was the closest to the one of the query image, was then selected as the corresponding side view.

Equivalence Under Arbitrary Changes in Viewing Conditions. The motion-based correspondence of object parts proved useful for dealing with view-invariance under changes in viewing direction. However, motion-based correspondence is not always applicable for identifying the same object part under different conditions. For example, views of the same object under different illumination conditions are usually not related by continuous motion. In [2], a different criterion for obtaining fragment equivalence sets was therefore employed, without relying on motion correspondence. Fragment equivalence was established instead based on the consistency in parts appearance in different objects in which these parts are present. If two fragments, F_1 and F_2 represent the same object part under different viewing conditions (such as different illuminations, or also different viewing directions), C_1 and C_2, then their detections should be consistent – namely, if F_1 is detected is an image of some object O under viewing condition C_1, then F_2 should also be detected in an image of O under condition C_2. In contrast, two unrelated fragments will be in general significantly less consistent. Therefore, this consistency criterion can be used for identifying equivalent object fragments.

Given a set of images $I_{11}...I_{1N}$ of N objects taken under condition C_1 and a set of images $I_{21}...I_{2N}$ taken under condition C_2, the activation patterns A_1 and A_2 of fragments F_1 and F_2 respectively can be computed. Their consistency can be derived, for example by the simple score:

$$S(F_1, F_2) = \frac{NCC(A_1, A_2) + 1}{2}$$

This is just the correlation of the activation patterns, but re-normalized to lie between 0 and 1. To make the scheme robust to noise and to within-object redundancy, this consistency measure was augmented with a measure based on geometric consistency, which used a simple proximity assumption: if two object parts are located nearby, their matching parts also should lie close to each other. This constraint was implemented using a hierarchical representation of proximity relations. The scheme was shown to deal effectively with changes in illumination and pose without relying on motion correspondence.

4   Summary and Discussion

In this chapter we have presented two extensions of the fragment-based object recognition scheme. The basic scheme uses informative image fragments as classification features. Here we proposed a hierarchical decomposition of the features into parts and sub-parts at multiple levels. The second extension was to use semantic equivalence sets of features, depicting different appearances of the same object part. We have shown that hierarchical features are more informative and better for classification compared with the same features used non-hierarchically. For semantic features, we have shown how the method can automatically learn the part structure of a new domain and extract sets of semantically equivalent fragments. Semantic features are an example of the more general concept of extended features, which are sets of fragments representing the same or similar object parts under different viewing conditions. Different methods were described above for extracting extended fragments based on common context, motion, and consistency across transformations. Extended features are used in the proposed scheme as the basis for making broad generalizations in object recognition, at the level of general classification as well as specific object identification. For example, a particular object can be recognized across changes in pose, illumination, and complex local shape changes, based on the representation of its components in terms of extended features. The capacity of the recognition system to deal with large variability in appearance at the objects level is inherited in this scheme from learning the variability at the level of common informative components.

The two aspects described above, hierarchical representation and the use of extended fragments, can be combined into a representation using a hierarchy of sub-parts, were each sub-part is represented by extended fragments. This representation can be extended in several directions. For example, in terms of the classification algorithm using this representation, instead of the bottom-up computation described above, we have also used a full Bayesian network which produced a significantly better interpretation of the constituent parts. A second general direction is the extension of the hierarchy from a single class to a multi-class representation. The issues here include, for example, the optimal construction of a feature hierarchy for multiple classes simultaneously, extracting semantically equivalent fragments across different classes, sharing features across classes at multiple levels in the hierarchy, and using the hierarchy to make fine distinctions between similar classes. Finally, given the hierarchical nature of objects representation in the primate visual cortex, it will be of interest to use the computational studies of feature hierarchies and extended features to model aspects of the human visual system.

Acknowledgements

This work was supported by grant no. 3-992 from the Israeli Ministry of Science and Technology, and conducted at the Moross Laboratory for Vision and Motor Control.

References

1. S. Agarwal, A. Awan, D. Roth. Learning to detect objects in images via a sparse, part-based representation. IEEE TPAMI, Vol. 26(11). (2004) 1475–1490
2. E. Bart, S. Ullman. Class-based matching of object parts, Proc. CVPR Workshop on Image and Video Registration, (2004)
3. I. Biederman. Recognition-by-Components: A Theory of Human Image Understanding. Psychological Review, Vol. 94(2) (1987) 115–147.
4. B. Epshtein, S. Ullman. Identifying Semantically Equivalent Object Fragments. CVPR, (2005) 2–9
5. B. Epshtein, S. Ullman. Feature Hierarchies for Object Classification. ICCV, (2005), to appear.
6. R. Fergus, P. Perona, A. Zisserman. Object Class Recognition by Unsupervised Scale-Invariant Learning. CVPR, (2003) 264–271
7. P. Foldiak. Learning invariance from transformation sequences. Neural Computation, Vol. 3(2). (1991) 194–200
8. D. Green, J. Swets. Signal Detection Theory and Psychophysics. Wiley, NY, (1966)
9. B. Heisele, T. Serre, M. Pontil, T. Vetter, T. Poggio. Categorization by learning and combining object parts. NIPS, (2001)
10. L. Itti, C. Kosh, E. Niebur. A model of saliency-based visual attention for rapid scene analysis. IEEE TPAMI, Vol. 20(11) (1998) 1254–1259
11. Y. LeCun, B. Boser, J. Denker, D. Henderson, R. Howard, W. Hubbard, L. Jackel. Backpropagation applied to handwritten zip code recognition. Neural Computation, Vol. 1(4) (1989) 541–551
12. D. Lowe. Distinctive image features from scale-invariant keypoints. Int. J. Comp. Vis, Vol. 60(2) (2004) 91–100
13. D. Marr, H. Nishihara. Representation and recognition of the spatial organization of three dimensional structure. Proceedings of the Royal Society of London B, Vol. 200 (1978) 269–294.

14. Mikolajczyk, K., Schmidt, C.: A performance evaluation of local descriptors. CVPR, (2003) 257–264.
15. K. Mikolajczyk, C. Schmidt. Scale and affine invariant point detectors. Int. J. Comp. Vis, Vol. 60(1) (2004) 63–86
16. M. Riesenhuber, T. Poggio. Hierarchical models of object recognition in cortex. Nature Neuroscience, Vol. 2(11) (1999) 1019–1025
17. S. Stringer, E. Rolls. Invariant object recognition in the visual system with novel view of 3D objects. Neural Computation, Vol. 14. (2002) 2585–2596
18. C. Tomasi, T. Kanade. Detecting and tracking of point features. Technical Report CMU-CS-91-132, Carnegie Mellon University (1991)
19. S. Ullman, E. Bart. Recognition invariance obtained by extended and invariant features. Neural Networks, Vol. 17. (2004) 833–848
20. S. Ullman, S. Soloviev. Computation of pattern invariance in brain-like structures. Neural Networks, Vol. 12. (1999) 1021–1036
21. S. Ullman, M. Vidal-Naquet, E. Sali. Visual features of intermediate complexity and their use in classification. Nature Neuroscience, Vol. 5(7) (2002) 1–6
22. M. Vidal-Naquet, S. Ullman. Object Recognition with Informative Features and Linear Classification. ICCV, (2003) 281–288
23. L. Wiskott, J. Fellous, N. Kruger, C. von der Malsburg. Face Recognition by Elastic Bunch Graph Matching, IEEE TPAMI, Vol. 19(7), (1997) 775–779

Shared Features for Multiclass Object Detection

Antonio Torralba[1], Kevin P. Murphy[2], and William T. Freeman[1]

[1] Computer Science and Artificial Intelligence Laboratory,
Massachusetts Institute of Technology, USA
[2] Departments of computer science and statistics
University of British Columbia, Canada

Abstract. We consider the problem of detecting a large number of different classes of objects in cluttered scenes. We present a learning procedure, based on boosted decision stumps, that reduces the computational and sample complexity, by finding common features that can be shared across the classes (and/or views). Shared features, emerge in a model of object recognition trained to detect many object classes efficiently and robustly, and are preferred over class-specific features. Although that class-specific features achieve a more compact representation for a single category, the whole set of shared features is able to provide more efficient and robust representations when the system is trained to detect many object classes than the set of class-specific features. Classifiers based on shared features need less training data, since many classes share similar features (e.g., computer screens and posters can both be distinguished from the background by looking for the feature "edges in a rectangular arrangement").

1 Introduction

A long-standing goal of machine vision has been to build a system which is able to recognize many different kinds of objects in a cluttered world. Although the general problem remains unsolved, progress has been made on restricted versions of this goal. One succesful special case considers the problem of detecting individual *instances* of highly textured objects, such as magazine covers or toys, despite clutter, occlusion and affine transformations. The method exploits features which are invariant to various transformations, yet which are very specific to a particular object [9,15]. This can be used to solve tasks such as "find an object that looks just like this one", where the user presents a specific instance; but it cannot be used to solve tasks such as "find an object that looks like a car", which requires learning an appearance model of a generic car.

The problem of detecting a generic category of object in clutter is often posed as a binary classification task, namely distinguishing between object class and background class. Such a classifier can be turned into a detector by sliding it across the image (or image pyramid), and classifying each such local window [1,6,20]. Alternatively, one can extract local windows at locations and scales returned by an interest point detector and classify these, either as an object or as part of an object (see e.g., [4]). In either case, the classifier will be applied to

J. Ponce et al. (Eds.): Toward Category-Level Object Recognition, LNCS 4170, pp. 345–361, 2006.

a large number of image locations, and hence needs to be fast and to have a low false positive rate.

Various classifiers have been used, such as SVMs [17], naive Bayes [22], mixtures of Gaussians [4], boosted decision stumps [26], etc. In addition, various types of image features have been considered, ranging from generic wavelets [21,26] to class-specific fragments [6,25]. Since it is expensive to compute these features at run-time, many classifiers will try to select a small subset of useful features.

The category-level object detection work mentioned above is typically only concerned with finding a single class of objects (most work has concentrated on frontal and profile faces and cars). To handle multiple classes, or multiple views of a class, separate classifiers are trained and applied independently. There has been work on training a single multi-class classifier, to distinguish between different classes of object, but this typically assumes that the object has been separated from the background (see e.g., [12,16]).

We consider the combined problem of distinguishing classes from the background and from each other. This is harder than standard multi-class isolated object classification problems, because the background class is very heterogeneous in appearance (it represents "all other classes"), and is much more likely to appear than the various object classes (since most of the image is background).

The first key insight of our work [24] is that training multiple binary classifiers at the same time needs less training data, since many classes share similar features (e.g., computer screens and posters can both be distinguished from the background by looking for the feature "edges in a rectangular arrangement"). This observation has previously been made in the multi-task learning literature (see e.g., [3,23]). However, nearly all of this work focuses on feedforward neural networks, whereas we use a quite different kind of classifier, based on boosted decision stumps[19]. Transfering knowledge between objects to improve generalization has also been studied in several recent papers [2,13,22].

The second key insight of our work is that training multiple binary classifiers at the same time results in a much faster classifier at run time, since the computation of many of the features can be shared for the different classes. This observation has previously been made in the neural network literature [10,11]. However, in these systems, the architecture of the network (and hence its computational complexity) is fixed in advance, whereas we effectively learn the structure.

2   Sharing Features

As objects tend to share many properties, an efficient visual dictionary of objects should capture those commonalities. Since objects are typically embedded in cluttered backgrounds, the representations have to be robust enough to allow for reliable discrimination between members of an object class and background distractors (non-objects). Here we show that shared features emerge in a model of object recognition trained to detect many object classes efficiently and robustly, and are preferred over class-specific features. Note that edge features emerge here from a visual recognition task, rather than from a statistical criterion such as sparse coding or maximizing statistical independence. We show that, although that class-specific features achieve a more compact representation for a single category, the whole set of shared features is able to provide more efficient and robust representations when the system is trained to detect many object classes than the set of class-specific features.

Fig. 1 illustrates the difference between two representations for objects. The first representation (Fig. 1a-left), obtained when training a set of classifiers to detect each object independently, is based on class-specific features of intermediate complexity, which have been shown to maximize the information delivered about the presence of an object class [25]. One drawback of class-specific features is that they might be too finely tuned, preventing them from being useful for other objects classes. The second representation is obtained when training the system to detect 29 object classes by allowing the classifiers to share features. The resulting representation is based on a vocabulary of shared visual features where each feature is used by a subset of the 29 object classes. Each object is represented as configurations of simple features that resemble edge and line detectors instead of relying on configurations of class-specific features.

Our learning algorithm, based on multiclass Boosting [19], is an iterative procedure that adds one feature at each step in order to build a dictionary of visual features. Each feature is found by selecting, from all possible class groupings and features, the combination that provides the largest reduction of the multiclass error rate. The feature added in the first iteration will have to be as informative as possible for as many objects as possible, since only the object classes for which the feature is used will have their error rate reduced. In the second iteration the same selection process is repeated but with a larger weight given to the training examples that were incorrectly classified by the previous feature. Once the second feature is selected, new weights are given to each training example to penalize more the examples incorrectly classified using both features. This process is iterated until a desired level of performance is reached. The algorithm has the flexibility to select class-specific features if it finds that the different object classes do not share any visual property.

2.1 Boosting for Binary Classification

Boosting [5,19,20] provides a simple way to sequentially fit additive models of the form

$$H(v) = \sum_{m=1}^{M} h_m(v),$$

where v is the input feature vector, M is the number of boosting rounds, and $H(v) = \log P(c = 1|v)/P(c = 0|v)$ is the log-odds of being in class c. (Hence $P(c = 1|v) = \sigma(H(v))$, where $\sigma(x) = 1/(1 + e^{-x})$ is the sigmoid or logistic function.) In the boosting literature, the $h_m(v)$ are often called weak learners, and $H(v)$ is called a strong learner.

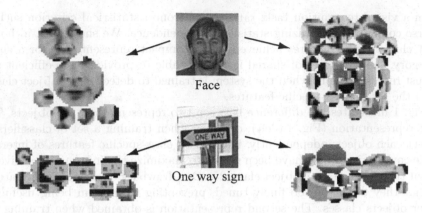

Fig. 1. Example of specific (left) and generic (right) features, and their class-conditional response distributions. Two possible representations of objects (e.g., face and one-way sign). The number of features used for each representation is selected so that both representations achieve the same detection performance (area under ROC is 0.95). The first representation (left) uses class-specific features (optimized for detecting each object class in cluttered scenes). Each feature is shown in object-centered coordinates. In contrast, the second representation is built upon the best features that can be shared across 29 object categories.

Boosting optimizes the following cost function one term of the additive model at a time:

$$J = E\left[e^{-zH(v)}\right] \tag{1}$$

where z is the class membership label (± 1). The term $zH(v)$ is called the "margin", and is related to the generalization error (out-of-sample error rate). The cost function can be thought of as a differentiable upper bound on the misclassification rate [20] or as an approximation to the likelihood of the training data under a logistic noise model [5].

There are many ways to optimize this function. We chose to base our algorithm on the version of boosting called "gentleboost" [5], because it is simple to implement, numerically robust, and has been shown experimentally [14] to outperform other boosting variants for the face detection task. In gentleboost, the optimization of J is done using adaptive Newton steps, which corresponds to minimizing a weighted squared error at each step. Specifically, at each step m, the function H is updated as $H(v) := H(v) + h_m(v)$, where h_m is chosen so as to minimize a second order Taylor approximation of the cost function:

$$\arg\min_{h_m} J(H + h_m) \simeq \arg\min_{h_m} E\left[e^{-zH(v)}(z - h_m)^2\right] \tag{2}$$

Replacing the expectation with an empirical average over the training data, and defining weights $w_i = e^{-z_i H(v_i)}$ for training example i, this reduces to minimizing the weighted squared error:

$$J_{wse} = \sum_{i=1}^{N} w_i (z_i - h_m(v_i))^2, \tag{3}$$

where N is the number of training examples. How we minimize this cost depends on the specific form of the weak learners h_m.

It is common to define the weak learners to be simple functions of the form $h_m(v) = a\delta(v^f > \theta) + b$, where v^f denotes the f'th component (dimension) of the feature vector v, θ is a threshold, δ is the indicator function, and a and b are regression parameters. (Note that we can replace $\sum_m b_m$ by a single global offset in the final strong classifier.) In this way, the weak learners perform feature selection, since each one picks a single component f.

These weak learners are called decision or regression "stumps", since they can be viewed as degenerate decision trees with a single node. We can find the best stump just as we would learn a node in a decision tree: we search over all possible features f to split on, and for each one, we search over all possible thresholds θ induced by sorting the observed values of f; given f and θ, we can estimate the optimal a and b by weighted least squares. Specifically, we have

$$b = \frac{\sum_i w_i z_i \delta(v_i^f \le \theta)}{\sum_i w_i \delta(v_i^f \le \theta)}, \tag{4}$$

$$a + b = \frac{\sum_i w_i z_i \delta(v_i^f > \theta)}{\sum_i w_i \delta(v_i^f > \theta)}, \tag{5}$$

We pick the f and θ, and corresponding a and b, with the lowest cost (using Eq. 3), and add this weak learner to the previous ones for each training example: $H(v_i) := H(v_i) + h_m(v_i)$. Finally, boosting makes the following multiplicative update to the weights on each training sample:

$$w_i := w_i e^{-z_i h_m(v_i)}$$

This update increases the weight of examples which are missclassified (i.e., for which $z_i H(v_i) < 0$), and decreases the weight of examples which are correctly classified. The overall algorithm is summarized in Fig. 2.

2.2   Multiclass Boosting and Shared Stumps

In the multiclass case, we modify the cost function as in Adaboost.MH [19]:

$$J = \sum_{c=1}^{C} E\left[e^{-z^c H(v,c)}\right] \tag{6}$$

where z^c is the membership label (± 1) for class c and

$$H(v,c) = \sum_{\dot{m}=1}^{M} h_m(v,c).$$

1. Initialize the weights $w_i = 1$ and set $H(v_i) = 0$, $i = 1..N$.
2. Repeat for $m = 1, 2, \ldots, M$
   (a) Fit stump:
   $$h_m(v_i) = a\delta(v_i^f > \theta) + b$$
   (b) Update class estimates for examples $i = 1, \ldots, N$:
   $$H(v_i) := H(v_i) + h_m(v_i)$$
   (c) Update weights for examples $i = 1, \ldots, N$:
   $$w_i := w_i e^{-z_i h_m(v_i)}$$

Fig. 2. Boosting for binary classification with regression stumps. v_i^f is the f'th feature of the i'th training example, $z_i \in \{-1, +1\}$ are the labels, and w_i are the *unnormalized* example weights. N is the number of training examples, and M is the number of rounds of boosting.

where $H(v, c) = \log P(c = 1|v)/P(c = 0|v)$, so $P(c|v) = e^{H(v,c)}/\sum_{c'} e^{H(c',v)}$ (the softmax function).

Proceeding as in the regular gentleBoost algorithm, we must solve the following weighted least squares problem at each iteration:

$$J_{wse} = \sum_{c=1}^{C} \sum_{i=1}^{N} w_i^c (z_i^c - h_m(v_i, c))^2 \tag{7}$$

where $w_i^c = e^{-z_i^c H(v_i, c)}$ are the weights[1] for example i and for the classifier for class c. Here, we use the same procedure as in Adaboost.MH, but we change the structure of the multiclass weak classifiers. The key idea is that at each round m, the algorithm will choose a subset of classes $S(m)$ to be considered "positive"; examples from the remaining classes can be considered "negative" (i.e., part of the background) or ignored. This gives us a binary classification problem, which can be solved by fitting a binary decision stump as outlined above. (Some small modifications are required when we share classes, which are explained below.) The goal is to pick a subset and a weak learner that reduces the cost for all the classes. At the next round, a different subset of classes may be chosen. For classes in the chosen subset, $c \in S(n)$, we can fit a regression stump as before. For classes not in the chosen subset, $c \notin S(n)$, we define the weak learner to be a class-specific constant k^c. The form of a shared stump is:

$$h_m(v, c) = \begin{cases} a\delta(v_i^f > \theta) + b & \text{if } c \in S(n) \\ k^c & \text{if } c \notin S(n) \end{cases} \tag{8}$$

---

[1] Note that each training example has C weights, one for each binary problem. It is important to note that the weights cannot be normalized for each binary problem independently, but a global normalization does not affect the results.

The purpose of the class-specific constant k^c is to prevent a class being chosen for sharing just due to the imbalance between negative and positive training examples. (The constant gives a way to encode a prior bias for each class, without having to use features from other classes that happen to approximate that bias.) Note that this constant does not contribute to the final strong classifier, but it changes the way features are shared, especially in the first iterations of boosting.

---

1. Initialize the weights $w_i^c = 1$ and set $H(v_i, c) = 0$, $i = 1..N$, $c = 1..C$.
2. Repeat for $m = 1, 2, \ldots, M$
   (a) Repeat for $n = 1, 2, \ldots, 2^C - 1$
      i. Fit shared stump:

$$h_m^n(v_i, c) = \begin{cases} a\delta(v_i^f > \theta) + b & \text{if } c \in S(n) \\ k^c & \text{if } c \notin S(n) \end{cases}$$

   ii. Evaluate error

$$J_{wse}(n) = \sum_{c=1}^{C} \sum_{i=1}^{N} w_i^c (z_i^c - h_m(v_i, c))^2$$

   (b) Find best subset: $n^* = \arg\min_n J_{wse}(n)$.
   (c) Update the class estimates

$$H(v_i, c) := H(v_i, c) + h_m^{n^*}(v_i, c)$$

   (d) Update the weights

$$w_i^c := w_i^c e^{-z_i^c h_m^{n^*}(v_i, c)}$$

Fig. 3. Boosting with shared regression stumps. v_i^f is the f'th feature of the i'th training example, $z_i^c \in \{-1, +1\}$ are the labels for class c, and w_i^c are the *unnormalized* example weights. N is the number of training examples, and M is the number of rounds of boosting.

Minimizing Eq. 7 gives

$$b = \frac{\sum_{c \in S(n)} \sum_i w_i^c z_i^c \delta(v_i^f \leq \theta)}{\sum_{c \in S(n)} \sum_i w_i^c \delta(v_i^f \leq \theta)}, \tag{9}$$

$$a + b = \frac{\sum_{c \in S(n)} \sum_i w_i^c z_i^c \delta(v_i^f > \theta)}{\sum_{c \in S(n)} \sum_i w_i^c \delta(v_i^f > \theta)}, \tag{10}$$

$$k^c = \frac{\sum_i w_i^c z_i^c}{\sum_i w_i^c} \quad c \notin S(n) \tag{11}$$

Thus each weak learner contains 4 parameters (a, b, f, θ) for the positive class, $C - |S(n)|$ parameters for the negative class, and 1 parameter to specify which subset $S(n)$ was chosen.

Fig. 3 presents the simplest version of the algorithm, which involves a search over all $2^C - 1$ possible sharing patterns at each iteration. Obviously this is very slow. Instead of searching among all possible $2^C - 1$ combinations, we use best-first search and a forward selection procedure. This is similar to techniques used for feature selection but here we group classes instead of features (see [7] for a review of feature selection techniques). We start by computing the best feature for each leaf (single class), and pick the class that maximally reduces the overall error. Then we select the second class that has the best error reduction jointly with the previously selected class. We iterate until we have added all the classes. Finally we select from all the sets we have examined the one that provides the largest error reduction.

The complexity is quadratic in the number of classes, requiring us to explore $C(C + 1)/2$ possible sharing patterns instead of $2^C - 1$. We can improve the approximation by using beam search considering at each step the best $N_c < C$ classes. However, we have found empirically that the maximally greedy strategy (using $N_c = 1$) gives results which are as good as exhaustive search.

Fig. 4 compares two features, one optimized for one class only (faces) and another selected for optimal sharing.

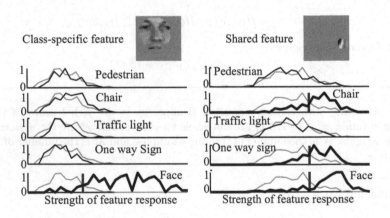

Fig. 4. These graphs compare the behavior of the two types of features for five object classes. Each graph shows the response distribution of a feature for non-objects (gray) and objects (black) of several classes. On the left side, the feature is class-specific and is optimized for detecting faces. The distributions show that the feature responds strongly when a face is present in its receptive field and weakly for non-objects or other object classes. When other object classes are present, the feature has no selectivity and is unable to discriminate between other object classes and non-objects, as expected. The plots on the right show the behavior of a feature selected for optimal sharing. This feature has elevated activation for a variety of objects (chairs, one-way signs, and faces).

3   Multiclass Object Detection

We are interested in the problem of object detection in cluttered scenes. In the rest of sections, we provide some experimental results and discuss some of the benefits of sharing features between a large number of object detectors.

3.1   LabelMe Database for Multiclass Object Detection

One important problem when developing algorithms for multiclass object detection is the lack of databases with labeled data. Most of existing databases for object recognition are inadequate for the task of learning to detect many object categories in cluttered real-world images. For this reason we have build a large database of hand-labeled images. Fig. 5 shows some examples of annotated images from the LabelMe database [18]. The LabelMe database and the online annotation tool for labeling new objects, can be found at:

http://www.csail.mit.edu/~brussell/research/LabelMe/intro.html

Fig. 5. Some examples of images from the LabelMe database

For the experiments presented here we used 21 object categories: 13 indoor objects (screen, keyboard, mouse, mouse pad, speaker, computer, trash, poster, bottle, chair, can, mug, light); 7 outdoor objects (frontal view car, side view car, traffic light, stop sign, one way sign, do not enter sign, pedestrians); and heads (which can occur indoors and outdoors).

3.2   Local Features

For each 32x32 window in the image, we compute a feature vector. The features we use are inspired by the fragments proposed by [25]. Specifically, we extract a random set of 2000 patches or fragments from a subset of the 32x32 training images from all the classes (Fig. 6). The fragments have sizes ranging from 4x4 to 14x14 pixels. When we extract a fragment g_f, we also record the location from which it was taken (within the 32x32 window); this is represented by a binary spatial mask w_f. To compute the feature vector for a 32x32 window, we perform the following steps for each of the 2000 fragments f:

1. Apply normalized cross correlation between the window and the fragment to find where the fragment occurs;
2. Perform elementwise exponentiation of the result, using exponent p. With a large exponent, this has the effect of performing template matching. With $p = 1$, the feature vector encodes the average of the filter responses, which are good for describing textures.
3. Weight the response with the spatial mask (to test if the fragment occurs in the expected location).
4. Sum the result across all 32x32 pixels.
5. Perform element wise exponentiation using exponent $1/p$.

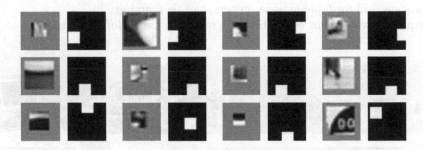

Fig. 6. Each feature is composed of a template (image patch on the left) and a binary spatial mask (on the right) indicating the region in which the response will be averaged. The patches vary in size from 4x4 pixels to 14x14.

This procedure converts each 32x32 window into a single positive scalar for each fragment f. This operation, for all image locations and scales, can be summarized as:

$$v^f(x, y, \sigma) = (w_f * |I_\sigma \otimes g_f|^p)^{1/p} \tag{12}$$

where I_σ is the image at scale σ, g_f is the fragment, w_f is the spatial mask, $\otimes$ represents the normalized correlation, and $*$ represents the convolution operator.

In this chapter, we use $p = 10$; this is good for template matching as it approximates a local maximum operator (although we feel that other values of p will be useful for objects defined as textures like buildings, grass, etc.). Using 2000 fragments give us a 2000 dimensional feature vector for each window. However, by only using M rounds of boosting, we will select at most M of these features, so the run time complexity of the classifier is bounded by M.

3.3 Dictionary of Visual Shared Features

One important consequence of training object detectors jointly is in the nature of the features selected for multiclass object detection. When training objects jointly, the system will look for features that generalize across multiple classes. These features tend to be edges and generic features typical of many natural structures.

Fig. 7 shows the final set of features selected (the parameters of the regression stump are not shown) and the sharing matrix that specifies how the different features are shared across the 21 object classes. Each column corresponds to one feature and each row shows the features used for each object. A white entry in cell (i, j) means that object i uses feature j. The features are sorted according to the number of objects that use each feature. From left to right the features are sorted from generic features (shared across many classes) to class-specific features (shared among very few objects).

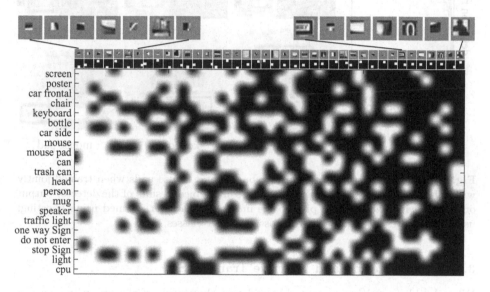

Fig. 7. Matrix that relates features to classifiers, which shows which features are shared among the different object classes. The features are sorted from left to right from more generic (shared across many objects) to more specific. Each feature is defined by one filter, one spatial mask and the parameters of the regression stump (not shown). These features were chosen from a pool of 2000 features in the first 40 rounds of boosting.

Fig. 1 illustrates the difference between class-specific and generic features. In this figure we show the features selected for detecting a traffic sign. This is a well-defined object with a very regular shape. Therefore, a detector based on template matching will be able to perform perfectly. Indeed, when training a single detector using boosting, most of the features are class-specific and behave like a template matching detector. But when we need to detect thousands of other objects, we cannot afford to develop such specific features for each object. This is what we observe when training the same detector jointly with 20 other objects. The new features are more generic (configuration of edges) which can be reused by other objects.

Fig. 8 shows some typical results for the detection of office objects. Note that not all the objects achieve the same performance after training. The figure shows some results for the detection of computer monitors, keyboards and mouse pads. The three classifiers have been trained jointly with 18 other objects.

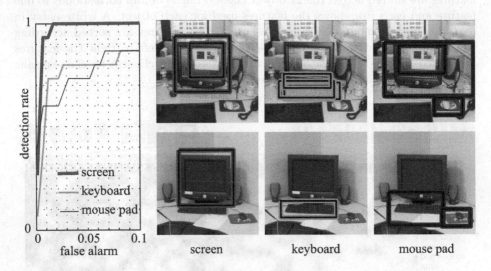

Fig. 8. ROC for detection of screens, keyboards and mouse pads when trained jointly with other 18 objects. On the right, we show some typical results of the detector output on images with size 256x256 pixels. The multiclass classifier, trained using boosting, uses 500 features (stumps) shared across 21 object classes.

3.4   Generalization and Effective Training Set

When building a vision system able to detect thousands of objects, using a set of independent classifiers will require a large amount of computations that will grow linearly with respect to the number of object classes. Most of those computations are likely to be redundant.

One important consequence of feature sharing is that the number of features needed grows sub-linearly with respect to the number of classes. Fig. 9.a shows the number of features necessary to obtain a fixed performance as a function of the number of object classes to be detected. When using C independent classifiers, the complexity grows linearly as expected. However, when sharing features among classifiers, the complexity grows sublinearly. (A similar result has been reported by Krempp, et. al ([8]) using character detection as a test bed.) In fact, as more and more objects are added, we can achieve good performance in all the object classes even using fewer features than objects.

Another important consequence of joint training is that the amount of training data required is reduced. If different classes share common features, the learning of such features should benefit from the multiple classes reducing the amount of data required for each class. In the case where we are training C object class

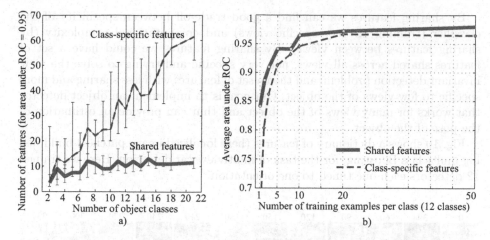

Fig. 9. Efficiency and generalization improve when objects are trained jointly allowing them to share features. a) Number of features needed in order to reach a fix level of performance (area under the ROC equal to 0.95). The results are averaged across 20 training sets. The error bars show the variability between the different runs (80% interval). b) Detection performance as a function of number of training examples per class when training 12 detectors of different object categories.

detectors and we have N positive training examples for each class, by jointly training the detectors we expect that the performance will be equivalent to training each detector independently with N^e positive examples for each class, with $N \leq N^e \leq NC$. The number of equivalent training samples N^e will depend on the degree of sharing between objects.

Fig. 9.b shows the detection performance as a function of number of training examples per class when training 12 detectors of different object categories (we used 600 features in the dictionary, and 1000 negative examples). Sharing features improves the generalization when few training samples are available, especially when the classes have many features in common. The boosting procedure (both with class-specific and shared features) is run for as many rounds as necessary to achieve maximal performance on the test set. From Fig. 9.b, we get that $N^e \approx 2.1N$ (i.e., we need to double the size of the training set to get the same performance out of class-specific features).

3.5   Multiview Object Detection

In the case of multiple views, some objects have poses that look very similar. For instance, in the case of a car, both frontal and back views have many common features, and both detectors should share a lot of computations. However, in the case of a computer monitor, the front and back views are very different, and we will not be able to share many features. Our algorithm will share features as much as possible, but only if it does not hurt performance.

By sharing features we can find a good trade-off between specificity of the classifier (training on very specific views) and computational complexity (by sharing features between views). By sharing features we could have a set of features shared across all views, not very specific and trying to solve the view invariant detection problem, and then a set of features with less sharing and more specific to few views of the object. Our goal is to implement an object detector that works for many views of the object and that can provide an estimation of the pose of the object.

Fig. 10 shows a dictionary of features (here localized image patches) build, using multiclass Boosting, for the task of multiview car detection. Here we trained 12 detectors each one tuned to one orientation.

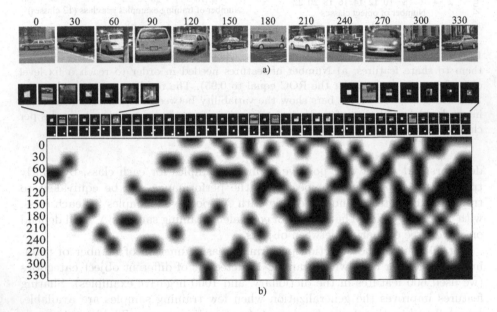

Fig. 10. Matrix that relates features to classifiers, which shows which features are shared among the different car views (orientation is discretized in 12 groups). The features are sorted from left to right from more generic (shared across many objects) to more specific.

Fig. 11 shows the results of multiview car detectors and compares the classifiers obtained with specific and shared features. In both cases, we limit the number of stumps to 70 and training is performed with 20 samples per view (12 views). Both classifiers have the same computational cost. The top row shows typical detection results obtained by combining 12 independent binary classifiers, each one trained to detect one specific view. When the detection threshold is set to get 80% detection rate, independent classifiers produce over 8 false alarms per image on average, whereas the joint classifier results in about 1 false alarm per image (averages obtained on 200 images not used for training). Test images were

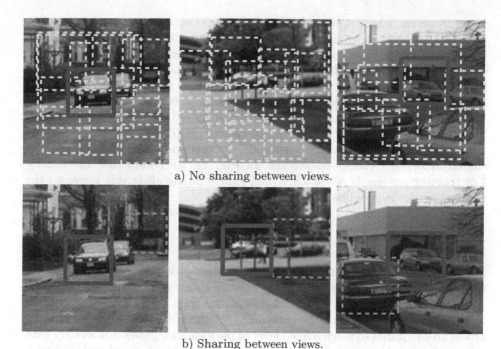

a) No sharing between views.

b) Sharing between views.

Fig. 11. View invariant car detection (dashed boxes are false alarms, and solid boxes are correct detections). a) No feature sharing, b) feature sharing. The joint training provides more robust classifiers with the same complexity.

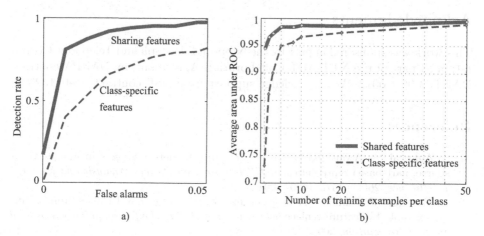

a)   b)

Fig. 12. a) ROC for view invariant car detection. b) Detection performance as a function of number of training examples per class (each class correspond to one out of the 12 car orientations) when using view-specific and shared features. Detection performance is measured as the average area under the ROC for all the classes.

128x128 pixels, which produced more than 17000 patches to be classified. The detector is trained on square regions of size 24x24 pixels. Fig. 12 summarizes the result showing the ROC for detectors using specific and shared features.

Intuitively, we expect that more features will be shared in the multi*view* case than in the multi*class* case. The experiment confirms this intuition. In order to be comparable with the results of fig. 9.b, we used 600 features in the dictionary (created from patches extracted from cars), and 1000 negative examples. Specifically, we find that in the multiclass case (fig. 9.b), each feature was shared amongst 5.4 classes on average, whereas in the multiview case, each feature was shared amongst 7 classes on average. In Fig. 12, we obtain that the equivalent training set size is $N^e \approx 4.8N$ (i.e., joint training effectively increases the training set for every class by almost a factor of 5).

4   Conclusion

We have introduced an algorithm for multi-class object detection that shares features across objects. The result is a classifier that runs faster (since it computes fewer features) and requires less data to train (since it can share data across classes) than independently trained classifiers. In particular, the number of features required to reach a fixed level of performance grows sub-linearly with the number of classes, as opposed to the linear growth observed with independently trained classifiers. We believe the computation of shared features will be an essential component of object recognition algorithms as we scale up to large numbers of object classes.

Acknowledgments

This work was sponsored in part by the Nippon Telegraph and Telephone Corporation as part of the NTT/MIT Collaboration Agreement, by DARPA contract DABT63-99-1-0012. We acknowledge support from NSF contract IIS-0413232.

References

1. S. Agarwal, A. Awan and D. Roth. Learning to detect objects in images via a sparse, part-based representation. *IEEE Trans. on Pattern Analysis and Machine Intelligence*, 26(11):1475–1490, 2004.
2. E. Bart and S. Ullman. Cross-generalization: learning novel classes from a single example by feature replacement. In *Proc. IEEE Conf. Computer Vision and Pattern Recognition*, 2005.
3. R. Caruana. Multitask learning. *Machine Learning*, 28(1):41–75, 1997.
4. R. Fergus, P. Perona, and A. Zisserman. Object class recognition by unsupervised scale-invariant learning. In *Proc. IEEE Conf. Computer Vision and Pattern Recognition*, 2003.
5. J. Friedman, T. Hastie, and R. Tibshirani. Additive logistic regression: a statistical view of boosting. *Annals of statistics*, 28(2):337–374, 2000.

6. B. Heisele, T. Serre, S. Mukherjee, and T. Poggio. Feature reduction and hierarchy of classifiers for fast object detection in video images. In *Proc. IEEE Conf. Computer Vision and Pattern Recognition*, 2001.
7. R. Kohavi and G. H. John. Wrappers for feature subset selection. *Artificial Intelligence*, 1.
8. S. Krempp, D. Geman, and Y. Amit. Sequential learning of reusable parts for object detection. Technical report, CS Johns Hopkins, 2002. http://cis.jhu.edu/cis-cgi/cv/cisdb/pubs/query?id=geman.
9. S. Lazebnik, C. Schmid, and J. Ponce. Affine-invariant local descriptors and neighborhood statistics for texture recognition. In *Intl. Conf. on Computer Vision*, 2003.
10. Y. LeCun, L. Bottou, Y. Bengio, and P. Haffner. Gradient-based learning applied to document recognition. *Proceedings of the IEEE*, 86(11):2278–2324, November 1998.
11. Y. LeCun, Fu-Jie Huang, and L. Bottou. Learning methods for generic object recognition with invariance to pose and lighting. In *Proceedings of CVPR'04*. IEEE Press, 2004.
12. B. Leibe and B. Schiele. Analyzing appearance and contour based methods for object categorization. In *IEEE Conference on Computer Vision and Pattern Recognition (CVPR'03)*, Madison, WI, June 2003.
13. K. Levi, M. Fink, and Y. Weiss. Learning from a small number of training examples by exploiting object categories. In *Workshop of Learning in Computer Vision*, 2004.
14. R. Lienhart, A. Kuranov, and V. Pisarevsky. Empirical analysis of detection cascades of boosted classifiers for rapid object detection. In *DAGM 25th Pattern Recognition Symposium*, 2003.
15. D. G. Lowe. Object recognition from local scale-invariant features. In *Proc. of the International Conference on Computer Vision ICCV, Corfu*, pages 1150–1157, 1999.
16. H. Murase and S. Nayar. Visual learning and recognition of 3-d objects from appearance. *Intl. J. Computer Vision*, 14:5–24, 1995.
17. C. Papageorgiou and T. Poggio. A trainable system for object detection. *Intl. J. Computer Vision*, 38(1):15–33, 2000.
18. B. C. Russell, A. Torralba, K. P. Murphy, W. T. Freeman. LabelMe: a database and web-based tool for image annotation. MIT AI Lab Memo AIM-2005-025, September, 2005.
19. R. Schapire and Y. Singer. BoosTexter: A boosting-based system for text categorization. *Machine Learning*, 39(2/3):135–168, 2000.
20. R. Schapire. The boosting approach to machine learning: An overview. In *MSRI Workshop on Nonlinear Estimation and Classification*, 2001.
21. H. Schneiderman and T. Kanade. A statistical model for 3D object detection applied to faces and cars. In *Proc. IEEE Conf. Computer Vision and Pattern Recognition*, 2000.
22. E. Sudderth, A. Torralba, W.T. Freeman, and A. Willsky. Learning hierarchical models of scenes, objects, and parts. In *IEEE Conf. on Computer Vision and Pattern Recognition*, 2005.
23. S. Thrun and L. Pratt, editors. *Machine Learning. Special issue on Inductive Transfer*. 1997.
24. A. Torralba, K. Murphy, and W. Freeman. Sharing features: efficient boosting procedures for multiclass object detection. In *Proc. IEEE Conf. Computer Vision and Pattern Recognition*, 2004.
25. M. Vidal-Naquet and S. Ullman. Object recognition with informative features and linear classification. In *IEEE Conf. on Computer Vision and Pattern Recognition*, 2003.
26. P. Viola and M. Jones. Robust real-time object detection. *Intl. J. Computer Vision*, 57(2):137–154, 2004.

Generative Models for Labeling Multi-object Configurations in Images

Yali Amit[1] and Alain Trouvé[2]

[1] Department of Statistics, University of Chicago, Chicago, IL 60637
amit@marx.uchicago.edu
[2] CMLA, ENS-Cachan,
61 Ave du President Wilson, 94235 Cachan cedex, France
trouve@cmla.ens-cachan.fr

Abstract. We propose a generative approach to the problem of labeling images containing configurations of objects from multiple classes.
The main building blocks are dense statistical models for individual objects. The models assume conditional independence of binary oriented
edge variables conditional on a hidden instantiation parameter, which
also determines an *object support*. These models are then be composed
to form models for object configurations with various interactions including occlusion. Choosing the optimal configuration is entirely likelihood
based and no decision boundaries need to be pre-learned. Training involves estimation of model parameters for each class separately. Both
training and classification involve estimation of hidden pose variables
which can be computationally intensive. We describe two levels of approximation which facilitate these computations: the Patchwork of Parts
(POP) model and the coarse part based models (CPM). A concrete implementation of the approach is illustrated on the problem of reading
zip-codes.

1 Introduction

Work in object recognition has focused on two main areas. The first area involves classifying images of segmented objects or images known to contain only
one object. The problems are formulated in different ways, sometimes a decision among several classes [3,7], and at times a decision class vs. background
[15]. The second area involves the detection of instances of an object class in
large images, which may contain any number of these objects or none at all,
[24,4,16,27,26]. In [25] several objects are detected simultaneously. These two
areas are of course closely related, and raise important issues such as how is
photometric and geometric variability handled? How is the background defined?
What type of training is used?

There is a rather clear dividing line in the literature between those that emphasize non-parametric discriminative learning of decision boundaries and those
that employ parametric modeling of the different object classes. For example in
handwritten digit recognition the work in [11,3] involves discriminative learning

J. Ponce et al. (Eds.): Toward Category-Level Object Recognition, LNCS 4170, pp. 362–381, 2006.
© Springer-Verlag Berlin Heidelberg 2006

using different algorithms, whereas a generative modeling approach is proposed in [23]. For object detection the work in [27] uses large numbers of examples of faces and massive numbers of non-face examples to train a classifier between face and non-face. These ideas are extended in [25]. On the other hand in [17] training is performed on several hundred object examples alone. Although the method there is described as a cascade of classifiers, it is shown in [5] that these can be viewed as approximations to an underlying stochastic model for face images. The approach in [12,15] is also generative.

Yet both detection and classification are in fact reductions of the real goal of labeling images with multiple instances of different object classes, with various types of interactions between the objects. If we put aside the approach of bottom up segmentation and subsequent classification, we need to be able to combine detection and classification for multi-object configurations. This issue arises even when detecting a single object class, say faces. When several faces are present close to each other, or even occluding each other, or when trying to determine how to prune clusters of very close detections, one encounters the issue of object configurations which are not accounted for with simple object/background discriminative boundaries. All the more so when multiple object classes are present.

One interesting example of a coherent *discriminative* framework for dealing with object configurations, in the context of reading handwritten digits, is found in [20]. A well defined cost function is proposed involving an interaction between segmentations and outputs of classification. However for the system to work the authors needed to train the network with massive numbers of digits presented with *flanking* digits so that the pretrained classifiers would be robust to clutter in the subwindow being processed. It does not appear that such an approach can scale to multiple objects and novel types of configurations. Moreover the requirements on the training set size are prohibitive.

In terms of generative approaches [18,9] provide an overall *theoretical* proposal for compositional scene models involving hierarchies of parts/objects that are successively composed, ultimately to provide an explanation of the entire scene. In [5] a concrete attempt is made to compose object models into scene models. The notion of an *object support* is defined in terms of the model and the object instantiation. This concept is crucial in composing object models, defining object configurations, occlusion and other forms of interactions. In [5] it is assumed the object supports do not overlap, and the range of poses is rather limited. The main challenge comes from the presence of clutter and noise. Object supports can be defined naturally when one employs dense data models, such as the Bernoulli edge based model proposed in [2] and used in [5]. Sparse models such as the constellation models of [15,13], or [14] do not provide an object support, and could in fact be viewed as approximations to dense models. In [21] object supports are derived from constellation models.A related non-generative approach to computing object supports is proposed in [10].

In this chapter the ideas of [5] are extended to highly deformable objects, e.g. handwritten digits. We start with the formulation of single object deformable Bernoulli models and their composition into scene models (section 2). In section 3 we outline the patchwork of parts (POP) approximation to the Bernoulli model, which allows for tractable and efficient training and testing. In section 4 we describe a further coarse part based approximation which can be used to efficiently discover clusters within object classes, as well as quickly scan a large image for candidate detections. Results on combining the two approximations for isolated digit classification are given in section 5. In section 6 we explain how an image containing multiple objects is processed using the above models and how the optimal scene labelling is computed. Finally in 7 we provide some experimental results on hand written zip-codes from the US postal CEDAR database.

2   The Deformable Bernoulli Model

2.1   Oriented Edge Features

The data models defined below are all based on a set of eight binary oriented edge features defined originally in [4], and employed in multiple applications see e.g. [2,5,6]. The edge features are binary and computed at each point in the image which is defined on a grid L. Several edges can be present at one location - they are not mutually exclusive. These features arc highly robust to intensity variations. Each detected edge is spread to its immediate 3×3 neighborhood. This spreading operation providing robustness to small local deformations which are very difficult to model, and greatly improves performance of any classifier implemented on the data. We write the binary data (after spreading) as $X = \{X_e(x) \mid x \in L, e = 1, \cdots, E\}$, where $E = 8$, corresponding to 8 orientations at increments of 45 degrees. In figure 1 we show the edges extracted on a typical zip-code for two different orientations. The darker points are the original edges and the gray areas the spreading regions.

Fig. 1. Left: A sample zip-code. Middle: Horizontal edges. Right: Vertical edges. Dark points original edges, gray points after spreading.

2.2   One Object

We start with a data model for the edge features in an image containing only one object.

There are several components in the description of the model.

Instantiation set. A set $\Theta = L \times \Theta_0$ describing the possible instantiations of the object, where L is the image lattice and indicates all possible locations of the object, and Θ_0 describes the linear and non-linear deformations of the object. We write $\theta = (\xi, \vartheta)$ where $\xi \in L, \vartheta \in \Theta_0$. There will be a product prior distribution $P(\theta) = P(\xi)P(\vartheta)$, indicating that the deformation of the object is independent of its location. Typically with one object $P(\xi)$ is uniform on L.

Probability maps. A probability map on a reference grid G.
$$p_e \equiv p_e(z), z \in G, e = 1, \ldots, 8.$$

Probability instantiation. For any $\theta \in \Theta$ and any point $x \in L$ define an operator $\theta p_e(x)$ which assigns a probability of finding edge e at x as a function of the instantiation θ, and the probability map p_e. For example if θ is a map of $G \to L$ one reasonable form would be

$$\theta p_e(x) = \begin{cases} p_e(\theta^{-1}x) & \text{if } x \in \theta G \\ p_{e,bgd} & x \notin \theta G \end{cases}, \tag{1}$$

where $p_{e,bgd}$ is a generic background probability for edge e, and $\theta^{-1}x = \vartheta^{-1}(x - \xi)$. We will propose a different form in the context of the POP models below.

Given only one object of this class is present in the image at instantiation (ξ, ϑ) we assume the edges in the image are independent and have marginal probabilities at each point x given by $\theta p_e(x)$. Specifically we write

$$P(X|\theta) = \prod_e \prod_{x \in L} \theta p_e(x)^{X_e(x)} (1 - \theta p_e(x))^{1 - X_e(x)}. \tag{2}$$

Let the *object support* for edge type e be defined as

$$S_{\theta,e} = \{x \in L : \theta p_e(x) \neq p_{e,bgd}\}, \tag{3}$$

namely the set of pixels with probabilities different from the generic background probability, which bear some information regarding the presence of the object. The probability model is rewritten as

$$P(X|\theta) = \prod_e \left[\prod_{x \in S_{\theta,e}} \theta p_e(x)^{X_e(x)} (1 - \theta p_e(x))^{1 - X_e(x)} \cdot \prod_{x \notin S_{\theta,e}} p_{e,bgd}^{X_e(x)} (1 - p_{e,bgd})^{1 - X_e(x)} \right]$$

$$= P_{bgd}^{-1} \prod_e \prod_{x \in S_{\theta,e}} \left(\frac{\theta p_e(x)}{p_{e,bgd}} \right)^{X_e(x)} \left(\frac{1 - \theta p_e(x)}{1 - p_{e,bgd}} \right)^{1 - X_e(x)}, \tag{4}$$

where P_{bgd} can be viewed as the probability of the data given *no object* is present in the image.

If Θ_0 consists of smooth mappings of G into L we have described a deformable template model. However since typically a semantic object class can contain more than several distinct smoothly deformable structures we model classes as *mixtures* of Bernoulli models. In other words introduce a discrete variable $m \in \{1, \ldots, K\}$ denoting the component and a distribution $P(m)$. For each

m we have a specific distribution on instantiations Θ, denoted $P(\theta|m)$, and a specific probability map $p_{e,m}$. Write the joint distribution of observables, deformation and component as

$$P(X, \theta, m) = P(X|\theta, m)P(\theta|m)P(m), \tag{5}$$

where $P(X|\theta, m)$ has the same form as equation (4) with the probability maps $p_{e,m}$.

For each component of each object class we denote the probability maps as $p_{e,m,c}, m = 1, \ldots, K$. Given an image with a single object of unknown class we may ask for the maximum posterior on class

$$\tilde{c} = \mathrm{argmax}_c P(c|X) = \mathrm{argmax}_c P(c)P(X|c)$$
$$= \mathrm{argmax}_c P(c) \sum_m \int_\Theta P(X|\theta, m, c)P(\theta|m, c)d\theta P(m|c), \tag{6}$$

where the key data term $P(X|\theta, m, c)$ is given in equation (4). The integration above is very difficult to compute so we substitute a maximization for integration and summation and define the classifier as

$$\hat{c} = \mathrm{argmax}_c P(c) \max_{\theta, m} P(X|\theta, m, c)P(\theta|m, c)P(m|c). \tag{7}$$

There may be an advantage to computing $\hat{c}$ since is comes together with an estimate of the instantiation. Note that in the standard classification problems with segmented data it is assumed that $\xi = 0$.

2.3   Scene Models

Define a scene as a set of objects $c_1, \ldots, c_k$ with their instantiations and components $\theta_1, m_1, \ldots, \theta_k, m_k$, and a partial ordering determining an occlusion relation between the objects. For simplicity we can assume that if $i < j$ than c_j can not occlude c_i. Denote a scene as

$$\mathbf{D} = \{k, c_1, m_1, \theta_1, \ldots, c_k, m_k, \theta_k\}. \tag{8}$$

Let S_i denote the support of object i (equation (3)). Let the occluding region of object c_i for edge type e be the union of the supports of all previous objects,

$$O_{i,e} = \cup_{j=1}^{i-1} S_{j,e}. \tag{9}$$

The likelihood of the data given a scene $\mathbf{D}$ is then

$$P(X|\mathbf{D}) = P_{bgd}^{-1} \prod_e \prod_{i=1}^k \prod_{x \in S_{i,e} \setminus O_{i,e}} \left(\frac{\theta_i p_{e,c_i,m_i}(x)}{p_{e,bgd}} \right)^{X_e(x)} \left(\frac{1 - \theta p_{e,c_i,m_i}(x)}{1 - p_{e,bgd}} \right)^{1 - X_e(x)}.$$
$$\tag{10}$$

We introduce a prior on scenes with a probability distribution $P(k)$ on the number of elements in the scene and an interaction term between the objects involving their instantiation parameters. Assuming no interaction between the class and component labels we have

$$P(\mathbf{D}) = P(k) \left(\exp[U_k(\theta_1, \ldots, \theta_k)] \prod_{i=1}^{k} P(\theta_i, m_i, c_i) \right) / Z_k, \qquad (11)$$

where $P(\theta_i|m, c)$ are the original distributions on Θ for the component m of class c. Again given the edge data of an image the scene label is obtained by maximizing the posterior on the entire *scenes* parameter

$$\hat{\mathbf{D}} = \text{argmax}_{\mathbf{D} \in \mathcal{D}} P(\mathbf{D}) P(X|\mathbf{D}), \qquad (12)$$

yielding a set of pose parameters in addition to the labels of the objects.

The introduction of interactions between the instantiations introduces significant complications in the form of the distribution $P(\mathbf{D})$. For example in our application these interactions involve constraints on the intersections of the supports of objects. Thus Z_k involves the normalization of the product on the right on a subset of admissible k-tuples. In general computing Z_k is a challenge but it is essential for comparing the posterior on scenes with different numbers of elements. This is the fundamental challenge of compositional models (see [9].)

In our particular setting of reading zip-codes we have $k = 5$ so that Z_k is irrelevant in comparing different admissible instantiations. Another simpler setting is where the interaction term involves only the locations ξ_i of the objects:

$$U_k(\theta_1, \ldots, \theta_k) = U_k(\xi_1, \ldots, \xi_k).$$

Since $P(\theta_i|c, m)$ is independent of ξ_i the normalization constant Z_k is computed independently in terms of the ξ. In other circumstances if there is a very good data model, the likelihood component of the posterior should overwhelmingly point towards a particular value of k in which case there is no problem. But in general this issue remains a challenge.

3   Approximations I: Patchwork of Parts (POP) Models

So far we have considered Θ_0 as a set of smooth maps of the reference grid G into the lattice L, with the operator $\theta p_e(x)$ defined in terms of equation (1). The main problem in this formulation is the complex form of the posterior distribution on θ conditional on the data. This presents computational challenges which effect both training and labeling. In [6] a convenient approximation is introduced which we describe in brief.

3.1   POP Model Formulation

Instead of describing a full map of the reference grid the instantiation is summarized as the mapping of a moderate number of reference points $y_1, \ldots, y_n$ in the

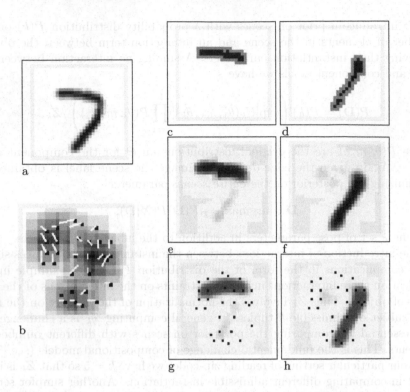

Fig. 2. a: Sample seven. b. The function $\mathcal{I}(x)$ for instantiation θ. Black dots are the reference points y_i. White arrows show the shifts $z_i - y_i$. Darker areas are correspond to higher values. (c,d) Extracted horizontal and vertical edges. (e,f) The global POP model for the two edge types given θ. (g,h) The model probability map for the two edge types (mean global POP), black dots are the reference points.

reference grid into the image lattice. Let $z_i = \theta y_i, i = 1, \ldots, n$ and with some abuse of notation write $\theta = (z_1, \ldots, z_n)$. Define *parts* Q_i of the full probability map

$$Q_{i,e}(s) \doteq p_e(y_i + s), e = 1, \ldots, 8, s \in W, \qquad (13)$$

where W is some fixed size subwindow around the origin. Now imagine that the part Q_i is 'moved' to the point z_i. Edges at points in the image lattice that are not covered by any of the windows $z_i + W$ get assigned background probabilities. At points covered by one or more of the translated parts edges are assigned the average of the contributed probabilities. Specifically for each $x \in L$ let $\mathcal{I}(x) = \{i : x \in z_i + W\}$ be the set of shifted reference points whose W neighborhood covers x. The marginal probability at each point x is then given by the following average of the contributions of the parts:

$$\theta p_e(x) = P(X_e(x) = 1|\theta) = \begin{cases} \frac{1}{|\mathcal{I}(x)|} \sum_{i \in I(x)} Q_{i,e,x-z_i} & \text{if } |\mathcal{I}(x)| > 0 \\ p_{e,bgd} & \text{if } |\mathcal{I}(x)| = 0, \end{cases} \qquad (14)$$

where $p_{e,bgd}$ is a generic background probability for edge type e.

This *patchwork* of the local models using the pointwise average of all local submodels covering the point x motivates the term *patchwork of parts (POP)* model. With this new definition of $\theta p_e(x)$, and staying with the conditional independence assumption, we write the global POP model conditional on the points θ as

$$P(X|\theta) = P(X|z_1, \ldots, z_n) = \prod_x \prod_e [\theta p_e(x)]^{X_e(x)} [1 - \theta p_e(x)]^{(1 - X_e(x))}, \quad (15)$$

with $\theta p_e(x)$ defined in (14). Let $\bar{\theta} = (y_i)_{i=1,\ldots,n}$, i.e. the original reference points. The original probability map $p_e(y), y \in G$ is given by $\bar{\theta} p_e(y)$. Since the windows have not been moved the probabilities in the average in (14) are all the same and equal to $p_{e,y}$.

In 2(a) we show a sample '7', with the function $\mathcal{I}(x)$ in 2(b), together with white arrows connecting the reference points y_i to the instantiation points z_i. In panels (c,d) we show two edge types extracted from the image, in (e,f) we show the global POP model conditional on $z_1, \ldots, z_n$, and in (g,h) the original probability map. The gray areas in panels (g,h) show areas in the reference grid where $p_e = p_{bgd}$, the remaining areas are the *object support* at reference pose. The same holds for (e,f) - the object support includes all pixels outside the gray areas.

3.2 Training

This simplified model lends itself to a very simple and effective approximate estimation procedure. Given a fixed collection of start points x_i on a coarse subgrid of the reference grid, separately estimate a Bernoulli model $\tilde{Q}_i$ supported on a window of size W, for the data around x_i. For each local model, the unobserved variable - the instantiation - is simply a shift τ of the start point x_i, constrained within a fixed window V. For estimation assume that conditional on the shift τ the data is generated independently according to $\tilde{Q}_i$ inside $x_i + \tau + W$ and according to the homogeneous background model *everywhere else* in the image. Since we can enumerate all the shifts in V a full EM algorithm can be implemented. Some of the local Bernoulli models $\tilde{Q}_i$ end up being very close to a homogeneous background model and are eliminated.

The reference points y_i are obtained from this procedure as $x_i + \bar{\tau}_i$ where $\bar{\tau}_i$ is the average shift, estimated through the EM procedure, over all training points. Finally the full probability map is created by patching together the local models using equations (14),(15) with $\theta = (y_1, \ldots, y_n)$. The probability maps shown in figure 2 (g,h) were estimated in this manner. Despite the separate training of each part Q_i the data imposes consistency between models estimated at neighboring windows and the final probability map is smooth and has the form of a seven. For more details see [6].

3.3 Computing an Instantiation

Once the probability map and the reference points of the POP model have been estimated it is possible to run the model on a test image. Around each reference point y_i, find the optimal shift τ_i^* for the submodel Q_i defined in equation (13), in terms of the likelihood ratio to the background model, within the range V of shifts. This is done independently of all other shifts. Setting $z_i = y_i + \tau_i^*$, compute the likelihood under the global POP model $P(X|z_1, \ldots, z_n)$. The instantiation shown in 2 (b) was obtained in this manner. Joint optimization of the shifts τ_i to optimize the full likelihood is computationally very intensive.

3.4   Training Additional Parameters

Once the probability map is estimated other parameters of the model can be estimated by computing an instantiation for each training data using the method outlined in 3.3. One can obtain the distribution of the computed likelihoods, which are assumed to be Gaussian and summarized with a mean and standard deviation μ, σ. Furthermore we estimate a joint distribution $p(\theta)$ for the computed instantiations. Assuming a joint Gaussian we take the means to be $y_i, i = 1, \ldots, n$ and a $2n \times 2n$ covariance matrix Γ, whose dimension is twice the number of reference points. A POP model for a class c can be summarized as the collection

$$\mathcal{M}_c^{pop} = \{Q_{i,c}, y_{i,c}, i = 1, \ldots, n, \Gamma_c, \mu_c, \sigma_c\}, \tag{16}$$

where each $Q_{i,c}$ is the local model in the window W around point y_i.

4   Approximations II: Coarse Part Based Mixture Models

Whereas the estimation of the probability maps with a POP model proves to be rather simple, estimating a mixture of POP models is quite a challenge. One can formulate a more complex EM procedure that involves both the unobserved instantiation parameters and the discrete component parameter, see for example [1]. However this is quite computationally demanding. We propose the following simplification which involves introducing a further approximation of the POP model in terms of part models on a coarse grid.

4.1   Generic Part Library with Rotational Symmetry

It is intuitively clear that the local Bernoulli models, i.e. the restriction of the full model to small windows, can be well approximated by a moderate number of fixed models - a fixed library of parts. We thus consider local edge maps in a window W arbitrarily placed in the image as coming from a mixture distribution of local Bernoulli models. Since it is sensible to assume that any local structure occurs at all rotations we assume the mixture includes a discrete set of A equally spaced rotations of a small number of base components. This both simplifies the problem of chosing the number of components and provides a means for rotating models.

We do not want to model 'background' windows in this mixture, i.e. windows with no real structure. These are assumed to be distributed according to a

Bernoulli model with homogeneous probabilities $p_{e,bgd}$ for each edge. We reject the null background hypothesis on a subwindow if its probability under the background model is less than .01. For example if $p_{e,bgd} \equiv p_{bgd}$ this reduces to setting a minimal number of edges τ_e in the window. The training sample then consists of windows $W + x$ around random points in a set of images, where the background hypothesis has been rejected. Write the mixture as

$$P(X_W) = \sum_{f=1}^{K_F} \sum_{\alpha=0}^{A-1} \tau_{f,\alpha} P_{f,\alpha}(X_W) \tag{17}$$

$$P_{f,\alpha}(X_W) = \prod_{s \in W} \prod_e p_{e,f,\alpha}(s)^{X_e(s)} (1 - p_{e,f,\alpha}(s))^{(1-X_e(s))}.$$

Theoretically one would want to write $p_{e,f,\alpha}(s) = p_{\alpha^{-1}e,f}(\alpha^{-1}s)$ for some base probabilities $p_{e,f}$. This however is problematic since it is unclear how to rotate the edge by angles that are not multiples of $\pi/4$ and the square domain W is not invariant under rotations. Instead we assume that if the edge map - X_{W+x} - in a subwindow is from component (f, α), then after rotation of the *original image* around x by angle a the resulting edge map in the same window is a sample from component $(f, \alpha + a)$, i.e. it is distributed according to $P_{f,\alpha+a}$. We take the addition of the angle indices to be *modulo A*.

Thus for each point x which is the center of a valid 'non-background' subwindow we rotate the original gray level image *around* x at the A angles and compute the edge maps $X_{x+W}^{(a)}, a = 0, \ldots, A - 1$ from the rotated images. We denote the resulting training set as $X_W^{t,a}, t = 1, \ldots, T, a = 0, \ldots, A - 1$. Suppose $X_W^{t,0}$ is a sample from P_{f_t,α_t} then $X_W^{t,a}$ is a sample from P_{f,α_t+a}. But f_t, α_t are unobserved and are dealt with in the framework of the EM algorithm. The estimate of $p_{e,f,\alpha}$ with fully observed data (i.e. knowing α_t, f_t for each training sample $X_W^{(t)}$) would reduce to

$$\hat{p}_{e,f,\alpha}(s) = \frac{1}{T_f} \sum_{t:f_t=f} X^{(t,\alpha-\alpha_t)}(s), \alpha = 0, \ldots, A - 1 \tag{18}$$

where T_f is the number of training subwindows from component f. Instead, denoting by $\pi_{f,\alpha,t}$ the estimated conditional expectation on (f, α) for training sample t, the EM algorithm produces the following estimate

$$\hat{p}_{e,f,\alpha}(s) = \frac{1}{w_f} \sum_{t=1}^{T} \sum_{a=0}^{A-1} \pi_{f,a,t} X_e^{(t,\alpha-a)}(s), \ \alpha = 0, \ldots, A - 1$$

$$w_f = \frac{1}{T} \sum_{t=1}^{T} \sum_{a=0}^{A-1} \pi_{f,a,t}. \tag{19}$$

The resulting features are very easy to interpret. In the first column of figure 3 we show the mean gray level images with $K_F = 6$ parts at angle $\alpha = 0$ found on the MNIST data base. In other words we show the mean of all subwindows

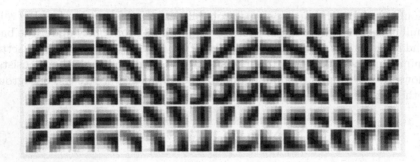

Fig. 3. Left column $K_F = 6$ parts at angle $\alpha = 0$. Subsequent columns rotations of parts at multiples of $\pi/8$. All together 96 parts.

assigned to each cluster. In the subsequent columns are the parts corresponding to the rotations $\alpha = 1, \ldots, 16(A = 16)$. The mean images are easier to visualize than the actual probability maps, but the clustering based on edge maps is essential for photometric invariance. The same process can be performed on generic gray level images with widely varying lighting and gray scale maps. The unsupervised clustering process has discovered several basic local structures - curves with different curvatures, 'junctions' and 'endings'. We have not yet developed a rigorous framework for choosing the number of components K_F, but experiments show that the results are not very sensitive to this choice if a sufficient number of angles is used. The only price for using more angles is computational. In this chapter, since the rotation information of the features is not used, we relabel the $A \cdot K_F$ features with the index $f = 1, \ldots, F$.

4.2   Feature Labeling, Spreading and Subsampling

Having estimated a set of local features, a local feature map $Y_f(x)$, $f = 1, \ldots, F$ is computed. At each point x for which the local edge data X_{x+W} is found to be *non-background*, the most likely feature under the mixture model is recorded, i.e.

$$Y_f(x) = \begin{cases} 1 & \text{if } f = \text{argmax}_{f'} \; \log P_{f'}(X_{x+W}) \\ 0 & \text{otherwise} \end{cases}$$

Note that the computation of the log-likelihood at all locations is simply a linear convolution on the *binary edge data*, not the original image data.

The result is a new set of feature maps on the image lattice L. Since each feature encodes an entire local structure, its exact position is no longer as important as the exact edge positions. We take advantage of this fact by *spreading* the detected features to a neighborhood B of the original location and subsampling to a sublattice L_b at spacing b of the original lattice L.

$$Y_f^s(x) = \max_{\xi \in B+b \cdot x} Y_f(\xi) \tag{20}$$

for $x \in L_b$. Note that after subsampling several features can occur at the same point $x \in L_b$.

4.3 Part Based Object Models -CPM's

The local features - parts - on the coarse subgrid were motivated as approximations of the original POP model. After spreading and subsampling one assumes
that the local deformations are accounted for and there is no need for a deformation variable ϑ and the instantiation is determined by the location ξ. Thus each
class is modeled as a mixture of K_c Bernoulli models based on the new features
in a coarse reference grid G_b. That is, conditional on the model component m,
each feature Y_f^s is assumed to occur independently at each location z in L with
some probability $p_{f,m,c}(z)$:

$$P(Y^s|M = m, C = c, \xi = x)$$
$$= \prod_{y \in x+G_b} \prod_f p_{f,m,c}(y-x)^{Y_f^s(y)} (1 - p_{f,m,c}(y-x))^{(1-Y_f^s(y))} \qquad (21)$$

In this context the independence assumption is blatantly wrong unless one uses
a very large number of components; after all if one conditions on 'enough' all
variables become independent. Nonetheless these mixture models give rise to a
well defined estimation procedure based on the EM algorithm. Our experience
is that due to the simplicity of the model - the parameters involve simple proportions - the EM algorithm is very stable and does not depend heavily on the
initialization. For each component we also estimate the mean and standard de-
viation of the log-likelihood - $\mu_{c,m}^{coarse}, \sigma_{c,m}^{coarse}$. We denote the final coarse part
based model (CPM) for a class c as

$$\mathcal{M}_c^{coarse} = \{p_{f,m,c}(z), z \in G_b, \mu_{c,m}^{coarse}, \sigma_{c,m}^{coarse}, f = 1, \ldots, F, m = 1, \ldots, K_c\}.$$
$$(22)$$

The value K_c is chosen so that on average there would be approximately 20
samples per component which is sufficient to provide good estimates of each of
the marginal probabilities.

In [8] we show that such coarse models yield very powerful likelihood based
classifiers on the MNIST dataset, as well as good single object detectors, see also
section 5.2. In training they are used to obtain class clusters which become the
components of the POP models. Finally for the purpose of scene analysis these
models will be used as an indexing mechanism to prune the number of locations
and classes on which to compute the more detailed POP models.

5   Combining CPM's and POP Models

5.1   Mixtures of POP Models

Given K_c mixture components of the coarse object models each training image
will have one component with highest likelihood. It is almost always the case
that the likelihood of one component is much higher than all the rest and there

is no ambiguity. In the top row of figure 4 we show the mean image for each of the components of the coarse model. It is already clear that the estimation procedure using the coarse features discovers interesting subclasses of each digit class. The same phenomenon is observed with a dataset of face images.

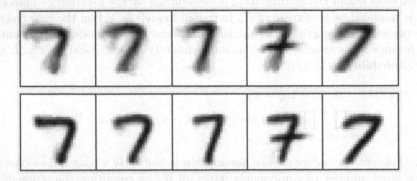

Fig. 4. Top: Mean images of training data in each cluster estimated from coarse feature based models. Bottom: *Mean global image* for the POP model estimated from the data points in each cluster.

Now use the images assigned to each component m to train a full POP model on the original reference grid G. To visualize the effect of the estimation of the POP models it is possible to create a *global mean image* as opposed to visualizing the probability maps of each model. Given the original images of the training data: $I^{(t)}, t = 1, \ldots, T$, and for each start point x_i, take the average of the shifted subimages:

$$J_{W,i} = 1/T \sum_{t=1}^{T} I^{(t)}_{x_i + \tau_i^{(t)} + W},$$

where $\tau_i^{(t)}$ is the most likely shift, as computed in the EM procedure. Now create a *global mean image* using the patchwork operation with the subimages $J_{W,i}$ using the estimated reference points y_i,

$$J(x) = \begin{cases} \frac{1}{|\mathcal{I}(x)|} \sum_{i \in \mathcal{I}(x)} J_{W,i}(x - y_i) & \text{if } |\mathcal{I}(x)| > 0 \\ 0 & \text{else} \end{cases}. \tag{23}$$

In figure 4 we show the global mean image for the POP models for the five clusters of sevens below the regular mean images of the sevens in each cluster. The subsequent estimation of the POP models creates a much crisper model since the local variations are accounted for.

5.2   Hierarchical Classification

The hierarchy of coarse feature based models and refined POP models leads to a natural organization of computation. For example in simple standardized classification problems one can first run a classifier based on the CPM's and only when the log-likelihood ratio between the top two classes is below some threshold run the more computationally intensive and refined POP models. The results of this procedure on the MNIST data set is summarized in table 1. We see that generative models with no discriminative training are able to obtain state of the art classification rates (under 1% error) with small training samples. However this classification problem, so intensively studied in the machine learn-

Table 1. Error rates on MNIST

No. of Training data per class	Components per model	CPM error rate	CPM+POP error rate	SVM Error rate
30	2	4.26	3.43	6.57
100	5	2.68	1.73	3.02
500	20	1.71	1.12	1.47
1000	30	1.51	.9	1.15

ing community is very artificial. The objects are not only cleanly segmented, they are also scaled and centered. This is hardly the case when trying to analyze unsegmented scenes even as 'simple' as a zip-code. In section 6 we approach the issue from a top down model based approach.

5.3   Scale and Slant Clusters

The characters in the MNIST dataset are well centered and scaled. In real zip-codes there is much larger variability in terms of scale, and other linear parameters such as slant or shear. In one zip-code one can find a 2:1 ratio in size of characters, some upright characters and some heavily slanted ones. In principle one could add a linear parameter to the instantiation parameter θ. However within a small neighborhood of the identity map the linear variations are easily accommodated by the configurations of the reference points. For the larger variations we produce additional components to the mixture models indexed by a linear parameter. Specifically define a discrete set of scales and slants Σ. For each $\sigma \in \Sigma$ apply σ to the training data of component m and retrain a POP model. The end result is $K_m \times |\Sigma|$ POP models covering a large range of linear variations and the non-linear variations governed by the ϑ parameter.

In addition, to expedite certain computations we also store a simple estimate $\mathcal{M}_{c,\sigma}^{simple}$ of marginal probabilities of the edges for the training data in each component m, *with no accounting for local shifts*. We now write

$$\mathcal{M}_c^{fine} = \{\mathcal{M}_{c,m,\sigma}^{pop}, \mathcal{M}_{c,m,\sigma}^{simple}, m = 1, \ldots, K_c, \ \sigma \in \Sigma\} \tag{24}$$

where each $\mathcal{M}_{c,m,\sigma}^{pop}$ is a POP model as in equation (16).

6 Analyzing a Scene

The scene labeling is defined as the optimizer in equation (12) over the set $\mathcal{D}$. This is of course an intractable computation and some short cuts need to be defined. First extract a moderate number of candidate detections, i.e. class-component-instantiation triples (c, m, θ), *ignoring their interactions*. Many of these detections may have substantial overlaps in their supports. The goal is to make sure the correct objects are among these detections at the price of having say several hundred false positives. This is done in several stages.

6.1 Stage I: Candidate Detections Using CPM's

The coarse grid L_b is labeled with the collection of part variables $Y_f, f = 1, \ldots, F$ as detailed in section 4.2. At each point $x \in L_b$ run all the CPM's on Y_{x+G_b} and keep those models for which the likelihood is higher than $\mu_{c,m}^{coarse} - \alpha \cdot \sigma^{coarse} \_c, m$ where α is a parameter usually set to 2 or 3. This yields a list Δ^{coarse} of candidate detections (c, ξ), where $\xi = x \cdot b$ denotes a location on the original lattice L. In the present setting we omit the m variable denoting the component index from the detection. Note that this step is the only one involving a full scan of the image on the coarse grid.

Even though the coarse models yield good classifiers on segmented and normalized data, they do not provide precise information regarding object support and hence are not as useful when constructing probability models for object configurations. Therefore each candidate CPM detection is subsequently analyzed with the POP models.

6.2 Stage II: Refining Candidate Detections

For each detection in $(c, \xi) \in \Delta^{coarse}$ choose the most likely POP component. It is inefficient to compute the full instantiation (see section 3.3) for each pair (m, σ), which involves optimization on each reference point y_i. Instead we use $\mathcal{M}_{c,m,\sigma}^{simple}$ and compute the likelihood ratio to the background for each (m, σ) and for a range of locations around ξ. The optimal likelihood ratio then determines the preferred component (m^*, σ^*), and a location x. An optimal instantiation ϑ is only computed for the POP model $\mathcal{M}_{c,m^*,\sigma^*}^{pop}$ at location x. The result is a list Δ^{fine} of quintuples $\delta = (c, m, \sigma, \vartheta, x)$ derived from the original list of class location pairs Δ^{coarse}.

6.3 Finding the Optimal Scene Labeling

From the list of detections Δ^{fine} we now want to extract the optimal scene $\mathbf{D}$ of the image. Even if the distribution on scenes is fully specified (see discussion in section 2.3) this would be a complex computation and one can not guarantee that a global optimum will be found. Rather one would need to develop a sequence of reasonable approximations.

Table 2. Parameters used in zip-code experiment

Reference grid sizes	$G - 40 \times 40, G_b - 5 \times 5, b = 6$
Number of local features	$K = 96, K_F = 6$, 6 components, 16 angles.
Window sizes	$W - 6 \times 6, V - 5 \times 5$
Background prob.	$p_{e,bgd} \equiv .1$
Min. no. of edges for non-bgd. window	$\tau_e = 40$
Scales and slants	5 - scales .7 - 1.8, 3 slants.
Coarse models	Training - 100 per class, 5 components per class.
Fine models	Training - 500 per class, 20 components per class.

On the other hand in the particular problem of reading zip-codes this is not an issue since we know there are 5 objects, and these are more or less linearly organized. Thus in equation (11) $k = 5$ and the interaction term only involves hard constraints on the arrangements of the objects. First there is an upper limit on the area of the intersection of the supports of any two objects relative to the areas of each of the objects. Then assuming the objects are ordered left to right, which also determines the order of occlusion, given two consecutive objects $\delta = (c, m, \sigma, \vartheta, x), \delta' = (c', m', \sigma', \vartheta', x')$ we assume $x_1 < x'_1$ and impose an upper limit on $|x - x'|$. We also impose an upper limit on the angle between x and x'. One could add some soft constraints such as penalizing large differences in the linear pose index σ between two consecutive objects, we have not done so.

Since object $i-1$ can not occlude object $i+1$ rewrite the likelihood of equation (10) for an admissible sequence of 5 objects $\delta_1, \ldots, \delta_5$ as

$$P(X|\mathbf{D}) = P_{bgd}^{-1} \prod_e \prod_{i=1}^{k} \prod_{x \in S_{i,e} \setminus S_{i-1,e}} \left(\frac{\theta_i p_{e,i}(x)}{p_{e,bgd}} \right)^{X_e(x)} \left(\frac{1 - \theta_i p_{e,i}(x)}{1 - p_{e,bgd}} \right)^{1 - X_e(x)},$$

(25)

where $p_{e,i} = p_{e,c_i,m_i,\sigma_i}$, $S_{i,e}$ is the support of object δ_i and $S_{0,e} = \emptyset$.

Now the likelihood is a product of terms only involving consecutive pairs of detections, and the constraints on configurations are also given in terms of pairs. Consequently optimizing the likelihood over all admissible sequences of five objects from the list of candidate detections can be efficiently done with dynamic programming. The state space for each of the five 'slots' is the set of detections in Δ^{fine}. Since the same pair (δ, δ') of detections can be entertained several times we precompute the value

$$\Phi(\delta, \delta') = \sum_e \sum_{x \in S_{\delta',e} \setminus S_{\delta,e}} X_e(x) \log \left(\frac{\theta' p_{e,\delta}(x)}{p_{e,bgd}} \right) + (1 - X_e(x)) \log \left(\frac{1 - \theta' p_{e,\delta}(x)}{1 - p_{e,bgd}} \right),$$

but only for those pairs which satisfy the pairwise hard constraints. Once Φ is precomputed dynamic programming reduces to lookups and summations. It is also an easy matter to compute L top sequences which could be further processed if needed.

7   Experimental Results

Table 2 summarizes the parameter settings in the experiments. In figure 5.a we show all locations of detections of class 2 in the coarse pass on a zip-code. In 5 (b,c,d) we show the support of a number of these detections after computation of the optimal (m, σ) and the instantiation θ of the corresponding POP model. Note that due to the range of sizes of the models, the algorithm finds 2's in strange places. There is no apriori way to know the correct size, since in some zip-codes the size of the digits ranges quite drastically.

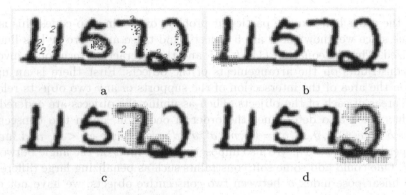

Fig. 5. a. Coarse detections of class 2. b-d Support of some fine model detections of 2's after optimizing over model component, linear parameter and instantiation. The supports shown are the union of the supports $S_{e,\theta}$ for the different edge types.

In figure 6 we show the top two scene labelings obtained with dynamic programming for three different zip-codes. These examples illustrate several interesting aspects. First we see that due to the clutter in the form of the horizontal bar in the first zip-code there is a well formed 2 shown in figure 5(c). This instance appears in the second best labeling shown in figure 6(b). It appears with some overlap with the subsequent detection. As indicated above some percent overlap between supports is allowed and is then modeled as if one object partially occludes the other. This is necessary since indeed sometimes digits share some parts of the stroke. The dynamic programming happens to select the correct labeling in the first zip-code despite the presence of the bar. However since there is no explicit modeling of structures other than digits, other types of clutter could lead to false positives and incorrect labeling. In both the second and third zip-code one sees the large differences in object size as well as the difficulty in computing a bottom up segmentation; The flanking 4 and 6 in the second zip-code and the connected 0's in the third. Indeed any labeling obtained by the algorithm, together with the object supports provides a top down object based segmentation.

Finally table 3 shows some of the results on a set of 1000 zip-codes from the US postal CEDAR data base. For comparison we show two reported results from

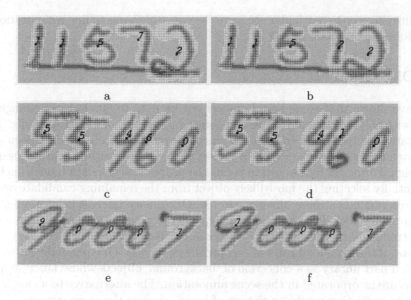

Fig. 6. Zip-code labeling. For three different zip-codes we show the top 2 labelings, together with the support (white dots) of each detection.

the literature in the mid-90's. All the reported methods used quite a number of dedicated preprocessing steps tailored to the problem. In our implementation no preprocessing or normalization is performed on the zip-code image, nor is there any presegmentation. The overall full zip-code recognition rate is 85.8, with 20% rejection the rate rises to 93.1%, reaching 97.6% at 50% rejection. The models employed in this implementation correspond to the third row of table 1 reporting an error rate just under 1% on the normalized MNIST images. One would then expect a lower error rate on the zipcodes. However as mentioned above, error rates on presegmented and centered images is misleading. If the scene labeling algorithm is run on individual MNIST images just as it is run on the zip-codes, assuming 1 object per image ($k = 1$) but assuming the location and pose are *not* known, the error rate increases significantly, to around 4%.

The computation time on a 2Ghz P-IV is approximately 10-15 seconds per zip-code where the largest computation is the massive loop over components and linear poses using the simple Bernoulli step. There are many ways one could

Table 3. Left: Comparison of zip-code classification results. Right: Scene Model classification rate against rejection rate.

Author	n	% corr.	% corr. at % rej	% rej.	% corr.
[19]	436	85%	97% - 34%	10%	89.1%
[22]	1566	*	96.5% - 32%	19%	93.1%
[28]	1000	72%	95.4% - 43%	30%	95.5%
Scene Models	1000	**85.8 %**	**96.3% - 33%**	50%	97.6%

expedite this step in particular are more clever use of coarse to fine computational techniques as proposed in [16].

8   Discussion

We have shown that scene based models can be used to label object configurations with no preprocessing or presegmentation, yielding competitive results. The application o zipcodes is constrained since the number of objects is known and their arrangement is linear. Still, a variety of greedy algorithms can be used to find high scoring configurations in terms the proposed scene data model, such as sequentially selecting the most likely object from the remaining candidate detections *conditional* on those already selected. Of primary interest is improving the background model. The conditional independence assumption for background is very strong and the result is that clutter in the background can score very high in terms of the likelihood ratio of certain object models. One possibility is to use the fixed part library as a collection of 'background' objects whose labels and locations are incorporated in the scene annotation. The alternative to a candidate object instantiation would be the set of parts covering the same support.

Acknowledgement. Yali Amit was supported in part by NSF Grant 0427223, and by L2TI, Université Paris XIII, Villetaneuse.

References

1. S. Allassonnière, Y. Amit, and A. Trouvé. Toward a coherent statistical framework for dense deformable template estimation. Technical report, Department of Statistics, University of Chicago, 2005.
2. Y. Amit. *2d Object Detection and Recognition: Models, Algorithms and Networks.* MIT Press, Cambridge, Mass., 2002.
3. Y. Amit and D. Geman. Shape quantization and recognition with randomized trees. *Neural Computation,* 9:1545–1588, 1997.
4. Y. Amit and D. Geman. A computational model for visual selection. *Neural Computation,* 11:1691–1715, 1999.
5. Y. Amit, D. Geman, and X. Fan. A coarse-to-fine strategy for multi-class shape detection. *IEEE PAMI,* 26:1606–1621, 2004.
6. Y. Amit and A. Trouvé. Pop: Patchwork of parts models for object recognition. Technical report, Department of Statistics, University of Chicago, 2004.
7. S. Belongie, J. Malik, and S. Puzicha. Shape matching and object recongition using shape context. *IEEE PAMI,* 24:509–523, 2002.
8. E. J. Bernstein and Yali Amit. Part-based statistical models for object classification and detection. In *CVPR (2),* pages 734–740, 2005.
9. E. Bienenstock, Geman S., and D. Potter. Compositionality, mdl priors, and object recognition. In M. C. Mozer, M. I. Jordan, and T. Petsche, editors, *Advances in Neural Information and Processing Systems,* volume 9, pages 834–844, Cambridge, Mass., 1997. MIT Press.
10. E. Borenstein, E. Sharon, and Ullman S. Combining bottom up and top down segmentation. In *Proceedings CVPRW04,* volume 4. IEEE, 2004.

11. L. Bottou, C. Cortes, J. S. Denker, H. Drucker, I. Guyon, L. D. Jackel, Y. LeCun, U. A. Muller, E. Sackinger, P. Simard, and V. Vapnik. Comparison of classifier methods: a case study in handwritten digit recognition. In *Proc. IEEE Inter. Conf. on Pattern Recognition*, pages 77–82, 1994.

12. M.C. Burl, M. Weber, and P. Perona. A probabilistic approach to object recognition using local photometry and global geometry. In *Proc. of the 5th European Conf. on Computer Vision, ECCV 98*, pages 628–641, 1998.

13. Michael Burl, Markus Weber, and Perona Pietro. A probabilistic approach to object recognition using local photometrie and global geometry. In *Proc ECCV*, pages 628–641, 1998.

14. D. Crandall, P. Felzenszwalb, and D. Huttenlocher. Spatial priors for part-based recognition using statistical models. In *to appear, Proceedings CVPR 2005*, 2005.

15. L. Fei-Fei, R. Fergus, and P. Perona. A bayesian approach to unsupervised one-shot learning of object categories. In *Proceedings of the International Conference on Computer Vision*, volume 1, 2003.

16. F. Fleuret and D. Geman. Coarse-to-fine face detection. *International Journal of Computer Vision*, 41:85–107, 2001.

17. F. Fleuret and D. Geman. Fast face detections with precise pose estimation. In *Proceedings of ICPR2002, I*, pages 235–238, 2002.

18. S. Geman, D. Potter, and Z. Chi. Composition systems. *Quarterly J. Appl. Math.*, LX:707–737, 2002.

19. T. M. Ha, M. Zimmermann, and H. Bunke. Off-line handwritten numeral string recognition by combining segmentation-based and segmentation-free methods. *Pattern Recognition*, 31:257–272, 1998.

20. Y. LeCun, L. Bottou, Y. Bengio, and P. Haffner. Gradient-based learning applied to document recognition. *Proceedings of the IEEE*, 86(11):2278–2324, November 1998.

21. B Leibe and B Schiele. Interleaved object categorization and segmentation. In *BMVC'03*, 2003.

22. P Palumbo and S. Srihari. Postal address reading in real time. *Intr. Jour. of Imaging Science and Technology*, 1996.

23. M. Revow, C. K. I. Williams, and G. E. Hinton. Using generative models for handwritten digit recognition. *IEEE PAMI*, 18:592–606, 1996.

24. H. A. Rowley, S. Baluja, and T. Kanade. Neural network-based face detection. *IEEE Trans. PAMI*, 20:23–38, 1998.

25. A. Torralba, K. P. Murphy, and W. T. Freeman. Sharing visual features for multi-class and multiview object detection. Technical Report AI-Memo 2004-008, MIT, 2004.

26. S. Ullman, M. Vida-Naquet, and E. Sali. Visual features of intermediate complexity and their use in classification. *Nature Neuroscience*, 5:682–687, 2002.

27. P Viola and M. J. Jones. Robust real time object detection. *Intl. Jour. Comp. Vis.*, 2002.

28. S. C. Wang. *A statistical model for computer recognition of sequences of handwritten digits, with applications to zip codes*. PhD thesis, University of Chicago, 1998.

Object Detection and Localization
Using Local and Global Features

Kevin Murphy[1], Antonio Torralba[2], Daniel Eaton[1], and William Freeman[2]

[1] Department of Computer Science, University of British Columbia
[2] Computer Science and AI Lab, MIT

Abstract. Traditional approaches to object detection only look at local pieces of the image, whether it be within a sliding window or the regions around an interest point detector. However, such local pieces can be ambiguous, especially when the object of interest is small, or imaging conditions are otherwise unfavorable. This ambiguity can be reduced by using global features of the image — which we call the "gist" of the scene — as an additional source of evidence. We show that by combining local and global features, we get significantly improved detection rates. In addition, since the gist is much cheaper to compute than most local detectors, we can potentially gain a large increase in speed as well.

1 Introduction

The most common approach to generic[1] object detection/ localization is to slide a window across the image (possibly at multiple scales), and to classify each such local window as containing the target or background. This approach has been succesfully used to detect rigid objects such as faces and cars (see e.g., [26,24,27,35]), and has even been applied to articulated objects such as pedestrians (see e.g., [20,36]). A natural extension of this approach is to use such sliding window classifiers to detect object parts, and then to assemble the parts into a whole object (see e.g., [19,20]). Another popular approach is to extract local interest points from the image, and then to classify each of the regions around these points, rather than looking at all possible subwindows (see e.g., [5,11]).

A weakness shared by all of the above approaches is that they can fail when local image information is insufficient e.g. because the target is very small or highly occluded. In such cases, looking at parts of the image outside of the patch to be classified — that is, by using the context of the image as a whole — can help. This is illustrated in Figure 1.

---

[1] By generic detection, we mean detecting classes (categories) of objects, such as any car, any face, etc. rather than finding a specific object (class instance), such as a particular car, or a particular face. For one of the most succesful approaches to the instance-level detection problem, see [18]. The category-level detection problem is generally considered harder, because of the need to generalize over intra-class variation. That is, approaches which memorize idiosyncratic details of an object (such as particular surface pattern or texture) will not work; rather, succesful techniques need to focus on generic object properties such as shape.

J. Ponce et al. (Eds.): Toward Category-Level Object Recognition, LNCS 4170, pp. 382–400, 2006.

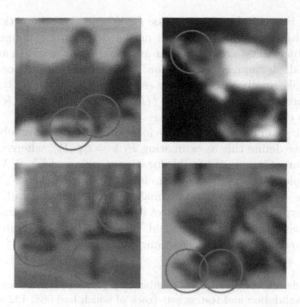

Fig. 1. An image blob can be interpreted in many different ways when placed in different contexts. The blobs in the circled regions have identical pixel values (except for rotation), yet take on different visual appearances depending on their context within the overall image. (This image is best viewed online.)

An obvious source of context is other objects in the image (see e.g., [10,30], [31,7,15] for some recent examples of this old idea), but this introduces a chicken-and-egg situation, where objects are mutually dependent. In this chapter, we consider using global features of the image — which we call the "gist" of the image — as a source of context. There is some psychological evidence [22,3,28] that people use such global scene factors before analysing the image in detail.

In [23,34], Oliva and Torralba showed how one can use the image gist to predict the likely location and scale of an object. without running an object detector. In [21], we showed that combining gist-based priming with standard object detection techniques based on local image features lead to better accuracy, at negligible extra computational cost. This chapter is an extension of [21]: we provide a more thorough experimental comparison, and demonstrate much improved performance.[2]

---

[2] These improvements are due to various changes: first, we use better local features; second, we prepare the dataset more carefully, fixing labeling errors, ensuring the objects in the test set are large enough to be detected, etc; finally, we have subsantially simplified the model, by focusing on single-instance object localization, rather than pixel labeling i.e., we try to estimate the location of one object, $P(X = i)$, rather than trying to classify every pixel, $P(C_i = 1)$; thus we replace N binary variables with one N-ary variable. Note that in this chapter, in order to focus on the key issue of local vs global features, we do not address the scene categorization problem; we therefore do not need the graphical model machinery used in [21].

We consider two closely related tasks: Object-presence detection and object localization. Object-presence detection means determining if one or more instances of an object class are present (at any location or scale) in an image. This is sometimes called "image classification", and can be useful for object-based image retrieval. Formally we define it as estimating $P(O = 1|f(I))$, where $O = 1$ indicates the presence of class O and $f(I)$ is a set of features (either local or global or both) extracted from the image.

Object localization means finding the location and scale of an object in an image. Formally we define this as estimating $P(X = i|f(I))$, where $i \in \{1, \ldots, N\}$ is a discretization of the set of possible locations/ scales, so $\sum_i P(X = i|\cdot) = 1$. If there are multiple instances of an object class in an image, then $P(X|\cdot)$ may have multiple modes. We can use non-maximal suppression (with radius r, which is related to the expected amount of object overlap) to find these, and report back all detections which are above threshold. However, in this chapter, we restrict our attention to single instance detection.

Table 1. Some details on the dataset: number of positive (+) and negative (-) images in the training, validation and testing sets (each of which had 668, 132 and 537 images respectively). We also show the size of the bounding box which was used for training the local classifier.

	Train +	Train -	Valid +	Valid -	Test +	Test -	Size (hxw)
Screen	247	421	49	84	199	337	30x30
Keyboard	189	479	37	95	153	384	20x66
CarSide	147	521	29	104	119	417	30x80
Person	102	566	20	113	82	454	60x20

For training/testing, we used a subset of the MIT-CSAIL database of objects and scenes[3], which contains about 2000 images of indoor and outdoor scenes, in which about 30 different kinds of objects have been manually annotated. We selected images which contain one of the following 4 object classes: computer screens (front view), keyboards, pedestrians, and cars (side view). (These classes were chosen because they had enough training data.) We then cropped and scaled these so that each object's bounding box had the size indicated in Table 1. The result is about 668 training images and 537 testing images, most of which are about 320x240 pixels in size.

The rest of the chapter is structured as follows. In Section 2, we will discuss our implementation of the standard technique of object detection using sliding window classifiers applied to local features. In Section 3, we will discuss our implementation of the ideas in [34] concerning the use of global image features for object priming. In Section 4, we discuss how we tackle the object presence detection problem, using local and global features. In Section 5, we discuss how we tackle the object localization problem, using local and global features. Finally, in Section 6, we conclude.

---

[3] http://web.mit.edu/torralba/www/database.html

2   Object Detection Using Local Image Features

The standard approach to object detection is to classify each image patch/ window as foreground (containing the object) or background. There are two main decisions to be made: what kind of local features to extract from each patch, and what kind of classifier to apply to this feature vector. We discuss both of these issues below.

2.1   Feature Dictionary

Following standard practice, we first convolve each image with a bank of filters (shown in Figure 2). These filters were chosen by hand, but are similar to what many other groups have used. After filtering the images, we then extract image fragments from one of the filtered outputs (chosen at random). The size and location of these fragments is chosen randomly, but is constrained to lie inside the annotated bounding box. (This approach is similar to the random intensity patches used in [37], and the random filtered patches used in [29].) We record the location from which the fragment was extracted by creating a spatial mask centered on the object, and placing a blurred delta function at the relative offset of the fragment. This process is illustrated in Figure 3. We repeat this process for multiple filters and fragments, thus creating a large ($N \sim 150$) dictionary of features. Thus the i'th dictionary entry consists of a filter, f_i, a patch fragment P_i, and a Gaussian mask g_i. We can create a feature vector for every pixel in the image in parallel as follows:

$$v_i = [(I * f_i) \otimes P_i] * g_i$$

where $*$ represents convolution, $\otimes$ represents normalized cross-correlation and $v_i(x)$ is the i'th component of the feature vector at pixel x. The intuition behind this is as follows: the normalized cross-correlation detects places where patch P_i occurs, and these "vote" for the center of the object using the g_i masks (c.f., the Hough transform). Note that the $D \sim 10$ positive images used to create the dictionary of features are not used for anything else.

Fig. 2. The bank of 13 filters. From left to right, they are: a delta function, 6 oriented Gaussian derivatives, a Laplace of Gaussian, a corner detector, and 4 bar detectors.

2.2   Patch Classifier

Popular classifiers for object detection include SVMs [20], neural networks [26], naive Bayes classifiers [22], boosted decision stumps [26], etc. We use boosted

Fig. 3. Creating a random dictionary entry consisting of a filter f, patch P and Gaussian mask g. Dotted blue is the annotated bounding box, dashed green is the chosen patch. The location of this patch relative to the bounding box is recorded in the g mask.

decision stumps[4], since they have been shown to work well for object detection [26,17] they are easy to implement, they are fast to train and to apply, and they perform feature selection, thus resulting in a fairly small and interpretable classifier.

We used the gentleBoost algorithm [9], because we found that it is more numerically stable than other confidence-rated variants of boosting; a similar conclusion was reached in [14].

Our training data for the classifier is created as follows. We compute a bank of features for each labeled image, and then sample the resulting filter "jets" at various locations: once near the center of the object (to generate a positive training example), and at about 20 random locations outside the object's bounding box (to generate negative training examples): see Figure 4. We repeat this for each training image. These feature vectors and labels are then passed to the classifier.

We perform 50 rounds of boosting (this number was chosen by monitoring performance on the validation set). It takes 3–4 hours to train each classifier (using about 700 images); the vast majority of this time is spent computing the feature vectors (in particular, performing the normalized cross correlation).[5] The resulting features which are chosen for one of the classes are shown in Figure 5. (Each classifier is trained independently.)

Once the classifier is trained, we can apply it to a novel image at multiple scales, and find the location of the strongest response. This takes about 3 seconds for an image of size 240x320.

The output of the boosted classifier is a score b_i for each patch, that approximates $b_i \approx \log P(C_i = 1|I_i)/P(C_i = 0|I_i)$, where I_i are the features extracted from image patch I_i, and C_i is the label (foreground vs background) of patch i. In order to combine different information sources, we need to convert the output of the discriminative classifier into a probability. A standard way to do this [25] is by taking a sigmoid transform: $s_i = \sigma(w^T[1 \ b_i]) = \sigma(w_1 + w_2 b_i)$,

---

[4] A decision stump is a weak learner of the form $h(v) = a\delta(v_i > \theta) + b$, where v_i is the i'th dimension (feature) of v, θ is a threshold, a is a regression slope and b an offset.

[5] All the code is written in matlab, except for normalized cross-correlation, for which we use OpenCV, which is written in C++.

$$[(I * f) \otimes P] * g$$

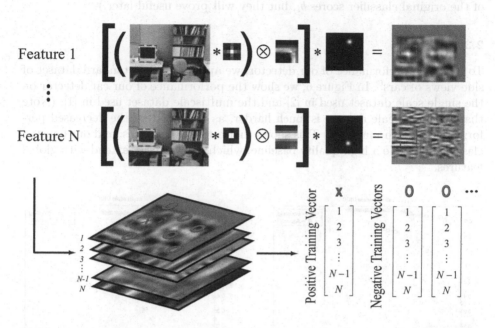

Fig. 4. We create positive (X) and negative (O) feature vectors from a training image by applying the whole dictionary of $N = 150$ features to the image, and then sampling the resulting "jet" of responses at various points inside and outside the labeled bounding box

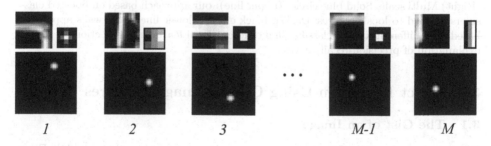

Fig. 5. Some of the $M = 50$ features which were chosen from the dictionary for the screen classifier. Within each group, there are 3 figures, representing (clockwise from upper left): the filtered image data; the filter; the location of that feature within the analysis region.

where the weights w are fit by maximum likelihood on the validation set, so that $s_i \approx P(C_i = 1 | I_i)$. This gives us a per-patch probability; we will denote this vector of local scores computed from image I as $L = L(I)$. Finally we convert this into a probability distribution over possible object locations by normalizing:

$P(X = i|L) = s_i/(\sum_{j=1}^{N} s_j)$, so that $\sum_i P(X = i|L) = 1$. (None of these operations affect the performance curves, since they are monotonic transformations of the original classifier scores b_i, but they will prove useful later.)

2.3   Results

To illustrate performance of our detector, we applied it to a standard dataset of side views of cars[6]. In Figure 6, we show the performance of our car detector on the single scale dataset used in [2] and the multiscale dataset used in [1]. (Note that the multiscale dataset is much harder, as indicated by the decreased performance of both methods.) This shows that our local features, and our boosted classifier, provide a high quality baseline, which we will later extend with global features.

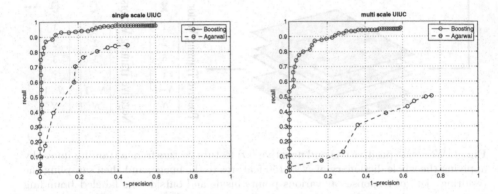

Fig. 6. Localization performance features on UIUC carSide data. (Left) Single scale. (Right) Multi scale. Solid blue circles (upper line): our approach based on boosted classifiers applied to local features; Dashed black circles (lower line): Agarwal's approach, based on a different kind of classifier and different local features. See Section 5.1 for an explanation of precision-recall curves.

3   Object Detection Using Global Image Features

3.1   The Gist of an Image

We compute the gist of an image using the procedure described in [32]. First we compute a steerable pyramid transformation, using 4 orientations and 2 scales; second we divide the image into a 4x4 grid, and compute the average energy of each channel in each grid cell, giving us $4 \times 2 \times 4 \times 4 = 128$ features; finally, we reduce dimensionality by performing PCA, and taking the first 80 dimensions. We will denote the resulting global feature vector derived from image I by $G = G(I)$. Note that this procedure is similar to the one used in [34], except in that chapter, Torralba used Gabor filters instead of steerable pyramids.

---

[6] http://l2r.cs.uiuc.edu/~cogcomp/Data/Car/

We have found both methods to work equally well, and mainly chose steerable pyramids because there is a good implementation available in Matlab/C.[7] We have also performed some preliminary experiments where we replace the steerable pyramids with the 13 filters in Figure 2; this has the advantage that some of the work involved in computing L and G can be shared. Performance seems to be comparable; however, the results in this chapter are based on the steerable pyramid version of gist.

The gist captures coarse texture and spatial layout of an image. This is illustrated in Figure 7, where we show a real image I and a noise image J, both of which have roughly the same gist, i.e., $G(I) \approx G(J)$. (J was created by initializing it to a random image, and then locally perturbing it until $||G(I) - G(J)||$ was minimized.)

Fig. 7. An illustration of the gist of an image. Top row: original image I; bottom row: noise image J for which gist(I) = gist(J). We see that the gist captures the dominant textural features of the overall image, and their coarse spatial layout. (This figure is best viewed online.)

3.2   Location Priming Using the Gist

As shown in [34], it is possible to predict the rough location and scale of objects based on the gist, before applying a local detector. We will denote this as $P(X|G)$. (Note that this is typically much more informative than the unconditional prior marginal, $P(X)$: see Figure 9.) This information can be used in

---

[7] http://www.cns.nyu.edu/~eero/STEERPYR/

two ways: We can either threshold $P(X|G)$ and apply the local detector only to the locations deemed probable by the gist (to increase speed), or we can can apply the detector to the whole image and then combine $P(X|L)$ and $P(X|G)$ (to increase accuracy). In this chapter, we adopt the latter approach. We will discuss how we perform the combination in Section 5.2, but first we discuss how to compute $P(X|G)$.

Location priming learns a conditional density model of the form $p(X = x, y, s|G)$. Following [34], we assume scale and location are conditionally independent, and learn separate models for $p(x, y|G)$ and $p(s|G)$. As shown in [34], we can predict the y value of an object class from the gist reasonably well, but it is hard to predict the x value; this is because the height of an object in the image is correlated with properties which can be inferred from the gist, such as the depth of field [33], location of the ground plane, etc., whereas the horizontal location of an object is essentially unconstrained by such factors. Hence we take $p(x|G)$ to be uniform and just learn $p(y|G)$ and $p(s|G)$.

In [34], Torralba used cluster weighted regression to represent $p(X, G)$:

$$p(X,G) = \sum_q P(q)P(G|q)P(X|G,q) = \sum_q \pi(q)\mathcal{N}(G; \mu_q^{(1)}, \Sigma_q^{(1)})\mathcal{N}(X; W_qG + \mu_q^{(2)}, \Sigma_q^{(2)})$$

where $\pi(q)$ are the mixing weights, W_q is the regression matrix, $\mu_q^{(i)}$ are mean (offset) vectors, and $\Sigma_q^{(i)}$ are (diagonal) covariance matrices for cluster q. These parameters can be estimated using EM. A disadvantage of this model is that it is a generative model of X and G. An alternative is a mixture of experts model [16], which is a conditional model of the form

$$p(X|G) = \sum_q P(q|G)P(X|G,q) = \sum_q \text{softmax}(q; w_q^T G)\mathcal{N}(X; W_qG, \Psi_q)$$

This can also be fit using EM, although now the M step is slightly more complicated, because fitting the softmax (multinomial logistic) function requires an iterative algorithm (IRLS). In this chapter, we use a slight variant of the mixture of experts model called mixture density networks (MDNs) [4]. MDNs use a multilayer perceptron to represent $P(q|G)$, $E[X|G,q]$ and $\text{Cov}[X|G,q]$, and can be trained using gradient descent. The main reason we chose MDNs is because they are implemented in the netlab software package.[8] Training (using multiple restarts) only takes a few minutes, and application to a test image is essentially instantaneous. When applied to the dataset used in [34], we get essentially the same results using MDN as those achieved with cluster weighted regression. (We have also performed some preliminary experiments using boosted stumps for regression [12]; results seem comparable to MDNs.)

To evaluate performance, the prior $P(X|G)$ can be evaluated on a grid of points for each scale: $G_i = P(x, y|G)P(s|G)$, where $i = (x, y, s)$. We then normalize to get $P(X = i|G) = G_i/(\sum_j G_j)$ so that $\sum_i P(X = i|G) = 1$. We can visualize this density by multiplying it elementwise by the image: see Figure 8

---

[8] http://www.ncrg.aston.ac.uk/netlab

for an example. We can evaluate the performance of the density estimate more quantitatively by comparing the predicted mean, $EX = \int Xp(X|G)dX$, with the empirical mean $\hat{X}$: see Figure 9. We see that we can predict the y value reasonably well, but the scale is harder to predict, especially for pedestrians.

Fig. 8. Example of location priming for screens, keyboards, cars and people using global features. In each group, the image on the left is the input image, and the image on the right is the input image multiplied by the probability, given the gist, of the object being present at a given location, i.e., $I * P(x|G(I))$.

4   Object Presence Detection

Object presence detection means determining if one or more instances of an object class are present (at any location or scale) in an image. A very successful approach to this problem, pioneered by [6], is as follows: first, extract patches around the interest points in an image; second, convert them to codewords using vector quantization; third, count the number of occurrences of each possible codeword; finally, classify the resulting histogram. Unfortunately, if this method determines the object is present, it is not able to say what its location is, since all spatial information has been lost. We therefore use the more straightforward approach of first running a local object detector, and then using its output as input to the object presence classifier. More specifically, we define $L_m = \max_i L_i$ as the largest local detection score, and take $P(O = 1|L) = \sigma(w^T [1\ L_m])$, so that $0 \leq P(O = 1|L) \leq 1$.

As shown in [34], it is possible to use the gist to predict the presence of objects, without needing to use a detector, since gists are correlated with object presence. Torralba used a mixture of (diagonal) Gaussians as a classifier:

$$P(O = 1|G) = \frac{P(G|O = 1)}{P(G|O = 1) + P(G|O = 0)} = \frac{\sum_q \pi_q^+ N(G; \mu_q^+, \Sigma_q^+)}{\sum_q \pi_q^+ N(G; \mu_q^+, \Sigma_q^+) + \sum_q \pi_q^- N(G; \mu_q^-, \Sigma_q^-)}$$

where each class-conditional density $P(G|O = \pm, q)$ is modeled as a Gaussian with diagonal covariance. We have found that using a single mixture component

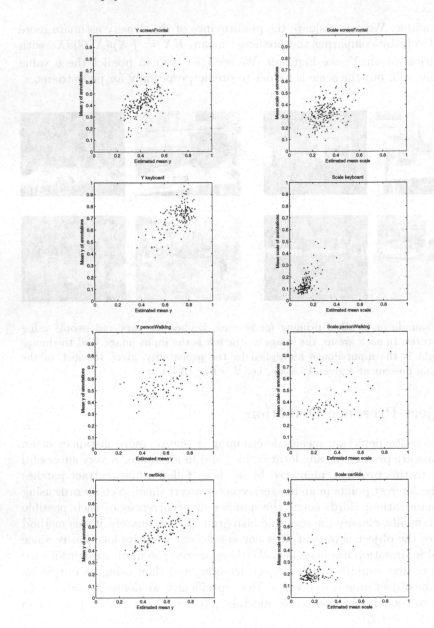

Fig. 9. Localization performance of screens, keyboards, people and cars using global features. Left column: vertical location of object; right column: scale of object. Vertical axis = truth, horizontal axis = prediction. We see that the gist provides a coarse localization of the object in vertical position and scale c.f., [34].

(i.e., a naive Bayes classifier) is sufficient, and has the advantage that EM is not necessary for learning. (We have also performed preliminary experiments using boosted decisions stumps; results were slightly better, but in this chapter, we stick to the naive Bayes classifier for simplicity.)

To combine the local and global features, we treat $P(O = 1|G)$ and $P(O = 1|L)$ as scalar features and combine them with logistic regression:

$$P(O = 1|L, G) = \sigma(w^T [1 \ P(O = 1|L) \ P(O = 1|G)])$$

We estimate the weights w using maximum likelihood on the validation set, just in case either $P(O = 1|L)$ or $P(O = 1|G)$ is overconfident. Applying one classifier inside of another is a standard technique called "stacking". Other approaches to combining the individual $P(O = 1|L)$ and $P(O = 1|G)$ "experts" will be discussed in Section 5.2.

We compare the performance of the 3 methods (i.e., $P(O|L)$, $P(O|G)$ and $P(O|L, G)$) using ROC curves, as shown in Figure 10. We summarize these results using the area under the curve (AUC), as shown in Table 2. We see that the combined features always work better than either kind of feature alone. What is perhaps surprising is that the global features often perform as well as, and sometimes even better than, the local features. The reason for this is that in many of the images, the object of interest is quite small; hence it is hard to detect using a local detector, but the overall image context is enough to suggest the object presence (see Figure 11).

Table 2. AUC for object presence detection

	Screen	Kbd	Car	Ped
L	0.93	0.81	0.85	0.78
G	0.93	0.90	0.79	0.79
L,G	0.96	0.91	0.88	0.85

5   Object Localization

Object localization means finding the location and scale of an object in an image. Formally, we can define the problem as estimating $P(X = i|\cdot)$. We will compare 3 methods: $P(X|L)$, $P(X|G)$ and $P(X|L, G)$.

5.1   Performance Evaluation

We evaluate performance by comparing the bounding box B_p corresponding to the most probable location, $i^* = \arg\max P(X = i|\cdot)$, to the "true" bounding box B_t in manually annotated data. We follow the procedure adopted in the Pascal VOC (visual object class) competition[9], and compute the area of overlap

$$a = \frac{\text{area}(B_p \cap B_t)}{\text{area}(B_p \cup B_t)} \tag{1}$$

---

[9] http://www.pascal-network.org/challenges/VOC/

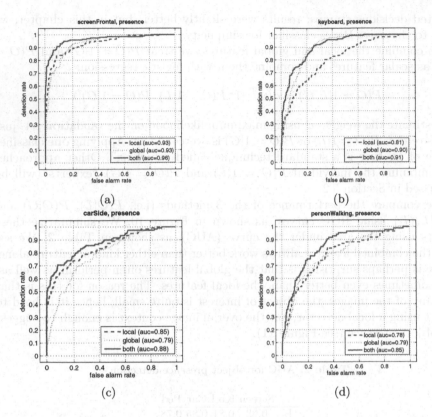

Fig. 10. Performance of object presence detection. (a) Screens, (b) keyboards, (c) cars, (d) pedestrains. Each curve is an ROC plot: $P(O|G)$: dotted blue, $P(O|L)$: dashed green, $P(O|L,G)$: solid red. We see that combining the global and local features improves detection performance.

If $a > 0.5$, then B_p is considered a true positive, otherwise it is considered a false positive.[10] (This is very similar to the criterion proposed in [1].)

We assign the best detection a score, $s(i^*) = P(O = 1|\cdot)$, which indicates the the probability that the class is present. By varying the threshold on this confidence, we can compute a precision-recall curve, where we define recall = TP/nP and precision = TP/ (TP+FP), where TP is the number of true positives (above threshold), FP is the number of false positives (above threshold), and nP is the number of positives (i.e., objects) in the data set.

We summarize performance of the precision-recall curves in a single number called the F1 score:

$$F = \frac{2 \cdot \text{Recall} \cdot \text{Precision}}{\text{Recall} + \text{Precision}}$$

---

[10] We used a slightly stricter criterion of $a > 0.6$ for the case of pedestrians, because the variation in their height was much less than for other classes, so it was too easy to meet the 0.5 criterion.

We use precision-recall rather than the more common ROC metric, since the latter is designed for binary classification tasks, not detection tasks. In particular, although recall is the same as the true positive rate, the false positive rate, defined as FP/nN where nN is the number of negatives, depends on the size of the state space of X (i.e., the number of patches examined), and hence is not a solution-independent performance metric. (See [1] for more discussion of this point.)

5.2   Combining Local and Global Features

We combine the estimates based on local and global features using a "product of experts" model [14]

$$P(X = i|L, G) = \frac{1}{Z} P(X = i|L)^\gamma P(X = i|G)$$

The exponent γ can be set by cross-validation, and is used to "balance" the relative confidence of the two detectors, given that they were trained independently (a similar technique was used in [15]). We use $\gamma = 0.5$.

Another way to interpret this equation is to realise that it is just a log-linear model:

$$P(X = i|L, G) \propto e^{\gamma \psi_L(X=i) + \psi_G(X=i)}$$

where the fixed potentials/features are $\psi_L(X) = \log P(X|L)$ and $\psi_G(X) = \log P(X|G)$. Since $Z = \sum_{i=1}^{N} P(X = i|L, G)$ is tractable to compute, we could find the optimal γ using gradient descent (rather than cross validation) on the validation set. A more ambitious approach would be to jointly learn the parameters inside the models $P(X = i|L)$ and $P(X = i|G)$, rather than fitting them independently and then simply learning the combination weight γ. We could optimize the contrastive divergence [14] instead of the likelihood, for speed. However, we leave this for future work.

Note that the product of experts model is a discriminative model, i.e. it defines $P(X|I)$ rather than $P(X, I)$. This gives us the freedom to compute arbitrary functions of the image, such as $G(I)$ and $L(I)$. Also, it does not make any claims of conditional independence: $P(X|L)$ and $P(X|G)$ may have features in common. This is in contrast to the generative model proposed in [34], where the image was partitioned into disjoint features, $I = I_G \cup I_L$, and the global features were used to define a "prior" $P(X|I_G)$ and the local features were used to define a "likelihood" $P(I_L|X)$:

$$
\begin{aligned}
P(X|I) &= \frac{P(I_L, I_G, X)}{P(I_L, I_G)} \\
&= \frac{P(I_L|X, I_G)P(X|I_G)P(I_G)}{P(I_L|I_G)P(I_G)} \\
&\propto P(I_L|X, I_G)P(X|I_G) \\
&\approx P(L(I)|X)P(X|G(I))
\end{aligned}
$$

Fig. 11. Examples of localization of screens, keyboards, cars and pedestrians. Within each image pair, the top image shows the most likely location/scale of the object given local features ($\arg\max P(X|L)$), and the bottom image shows the most likely location/scale of the obhect given local and global features ($\arg\max P(X|L, G)$).

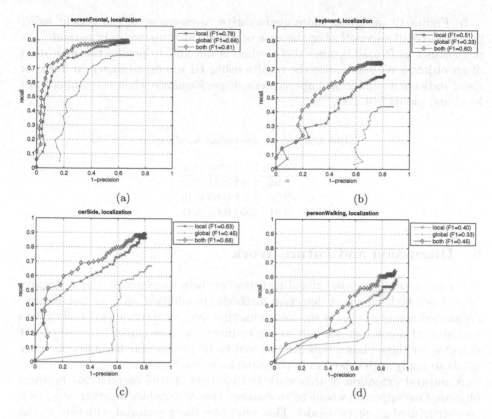

Fig. 12. Localization performance for (a) screens, (b) keyboards, (c) cars, (d) pedestrians. Each curve shows precision-recall curves for $P(X|G)$ (bottom blue line with dots), $P(X|L)$ (middle green line with crosses), and $P(X|L,G)$ (top red line with diamonds). We see significant performance improvement by using both global and local features.

The disadvantage of a product-of-experts model, compared to using Bayes' rule as above, is that the combination weights are fixed (since they are learned offline). However, we believe the advantages of a discriminative framework more than compensate.

The advantages of combining local and global features are illustrated qualitatively in Figure 11. In general, we see that using global features eliminates a lot of false positives caused by using local features alone. Even when the local detector has correctly detected the location of the object, sometimes the scale estimate is incorrect, which the global features can correct. We see a dramatic example of this in the right-most keyboard picture, and some less dramatic examples (too small to affect the precision-recall results) in the cases of screens and cars. The right-most pedestrian image is an interesting example of scale ambiguity. In this image, there are two pedestrians; hence both detections are considered correct. (Since we are only considering single instance detection in this chapter, neither method would be penalized for missing the second object.)

In Figure 12 we give a more quantitative assessement of the benefit using precision-recall curves.[11] (For the case of global features, we only measure the peformance of $P(y, s|G)$, since this method is not able to predict the x location of an object.) We summarize the results using F1 scores, as shown in Table 3; these indicate a significant improvement in performance when combining both local and global features.

Table 3. F1 scores for object localization

	Screen	Kbd	Car	Ped
G	6.66	0.33	0.45	0.33
L	0.78	0.51	0.63	0.40
L,G	0.81	0.60	0.68	0.45

6   Discussion and Future Work

We have shown how using global features can help to overcome the ambiguity often faced by local object detection methods. In addition, since global features are shared across all classes and locations, they provide a computationally cheap first step of a cascade: one only needs to invoke a more expensive local object detector for those classes that are believed to be present; furthermore, one only needs to apply such detectors in plausible locations/ scales.

A natural extension of this work is to model spatial correlations between objects. One approach would be to connect the X variables together, e.g., as a tree-structured graphical model. This would be like a pictorial structure model [8] for scenes. However, this raises several issues. First, the spatial correlations between objects in a scene are likely to be much weaker than between the parts of an object. Second, some object classes might be absent, so X^c will be undefined; we can set X^c to a special "absent" state in such cases (thus making the O^c nodes unnecessary), but the tree may still become effectively disconnected (since location information cannot propagate through the "absent" states). Third, some objects might occur more than once in an image, so multiple X^c nodes will be required for each class; this raises the problem of data association, i.e., which instance of class c should be spatially correlated with which instance of class c'.

An alternative approach to directly modeling correlations between objects is to recognize that many such correlations have a hidden common cause. This suggests the use of a latent variable model, where the objects are considered conditionally independent given the latent variable. In [21], we showed how we could introduce a latent scene category node to model correlations amongst the O variables (i.e., patterns of object co-occurrence). Extending this to model correlations amongst the X variables is an interesting open problem. One promising approach is to estimate the (approximate) underlying 3D geometry of the scene

---

[11] Note that the results for the car detector in Figure 12 are much worse than in Figure 6; this is because the MIT-CSAIL dataset is much harder than the UIUC dataset.

[13]. This may prove helpful, since e.g., the keyboard and screen appear close together in the image because they are both supported by a (potentially hidden) table surface. We leave this issue for future work.

References

1. S. Agarwal, A. Awan, and D. Roth. Learning to detect objects in images via a sparse, part-based representation. *IEEE Trans. on Pattern Analysis and Machine Intelligence*, 26(11):1475–1490, 2004.
2. S. Agarwal and D. Roth. Learning a sparse representation for object detection. In *ECCV*, 2002.
3. I. Biederman. On the semantics of a glance at a scene. In M. Kubovy and J. Pomerantz, editors, *Perceptual organization*, pages 213–253. Erlbaum, 1981.
4. C. M. Bishop. Mixture density networks. Technical Report NCRG 4288, Neural Computing Research Group, Department of Computer Science, Aston University, 1994.
5. G. Bouchard and B. Triggs. A hierarchical part-based model for visual object categorization. In *CVPR*, 2005.
6. G. Csurka, C. Dance, C. Bray, L. Fan, and J. Willamowski. Visual categorization with bags of keypoints. In *ECCV workshop on statistical learning in computer vision*, 2004.
7. P. Carbonetto, N. de Freitas, and K. Barnard. A statistical model for general contextual object recognition. In *ECCV*, 2004.
8. P. Felzenszwalb and D. Huttenlocher. Pictorial structures for object recognition. *Intl. J. Computer Vision*, 61(1), 2005.
9. J. Friedman, T. Hastie, and R. Tibshirani. Additive logistic regression: a statistical view of boosting. *Annals of statistics*, 28(2):337–374, 2000.
10. M. Fink and P. Perona. Mutual boosting for contextual influence. In *Advances in Neural Info. Proc. Systems*, 2003.
11. R. Fergus, P. Perona, and A. Zisserman. A sparse object category model for efficient learning and exhaustive recognition. In *CVPR*, 2005.
12. J. Friedman. Greedy function approximation: a gradient boosting machine. *Annals of Statistics*, 29:1189–1232, 2001.
13. D. Hoiem, A.A. Efros, and M. Hebert. Geometric context from a single image. In *IEEE Conf. on Computer Vision and Pattern Recognition*, 2005.
14. G. Hinton. Training products of experts by minimizing contrastive divergence. *Neural Computation*, 14:1771–1800, 2002.
15. X. He, R. Zemel, and M. Carreira-Perpinan. Multiscale conditional random fields for image labelling. In *CVPR*, 2004.
16. M. I. Jordan and R. A. Jacobs. Hierarchical mixtures of experts and the EM algorithm. *Neural Computation*, 6:181–214, 1994.
17. R. Lienhart, A. Kuranov, and V. Pisarevsky. Empirical analysis of detection cascades of boosted classifiers for rapid object detection. In *DAGM 25th Pattern Recognition Symposium*, 2003.
18. D. G. Lowe. Distinctive image features from scale-invariant keypoints. *Intl. J. Computer Vision*, 60(2):91–110, 2004.
19. A. Mohan, C. Papageorgiou, and T. Poggio. Example-based object detection in images by components. *IEEE Transactions on Pattern Analysis and Machine Intelligence*, 23(4):349–361, 2001.

20. K. Mikolajczyk, C. Schmid, and A. Zisserman. Human detection based on a probabilistic assembly of robust part detectors. In *Proceedings of the 8th European Conference on Computer Vision, Prague, Czech Republic*, May 2004.
21. K. Murphy, A. Torralba, and W. Freeman. Using the forest to see the trees: a graphical model relating features, objects and scenes. In *Advances in Neural Info. Proc. Systems*, 2003.
22. D. Navon. Forest before the trees: the precedence of global features in visual perception. *Cognitive Psychology*, 9:353–383, 1977.
23. A. Oliva and A. Torralba. Modeling the shape of the scene: a holistic representation of the spatial envelope. *Intl. J. Computer Vision*, 42(3):145–175, 2001.
24. C. Papageorgiou and T. Poggio. A trainable system for object detection. *Intl. J. Computer Vision*, 38(1):15–33, 2000.
25. J. Platt. Probabilistic outputs for support vector machines and comparisons to regularized likelihood methods. In A. Smola, P. Bartlett, B. Schoelkopf, and D. Schuurmans, editors, *Advances in Large Margin Classifiers*. MIT Press, 1999.
26. H. A. Rowley, S. Baluja, and T. Kanade. Human face detection in visual scenes. In *Advances in Neural Info. Proc. Systems*, volume 8, 1995.
27. H. Schneiderman and T. Kanade. A statistical model for 3D object detection applied to faces and cars. In *CVPR*, 2000.
28. P. Schyns and A. Oliva. From blobs to boundary edges: Evidence for time and spatial scale dependent scene recognition. *Psychological Science*, 5:195–200, 1994.
29. T. Serre, L. Wolf, and T. Poggio. A new biologically motivated framework for robust object recognition. In *CVPR*, 2005.
30. A. Singhal, J. Luo, and W. Zhu. Probabilistic spatial context models for scene content understanding. In *CVPR*, 2003.
31. A. Torralba, K. Murphy, and W. Freeman. Contextual models for object detection using boosted random fields. In *Advances in Neural Info. Proc. Systems*, 2004.
32. A. Torralba, K. Murphy, W. Freeman, and M. Rubin. Context-based vision system for place and object recognition. In *Intl. Conf. Computer Vision*, 2003.
33. A. Torralba and A. Oliva. Depth estimation from image structure. *IEEE Trans. on Pattern Analysis and Machine Intelligence*, 24(9):1225, 2002.
34. A. Torralba. Contextual priming for object detection. *Intl. J. Computer Vision*, 53(2):153–167, 2003.
35. P. Viola and M. Jones. Robust real-time object detection. *Intl. J. Computer Vision*, 57(2):137–154, 2004.
36. P. Viola, M. Jones, and D. Snow. Detecting pedestrians using patterns of motion and appearance. In *IEEE Conf. on Computer Vision and Pattern Recognition*, 2003.
37. M. Vidal-Naquet and S. Ullman. Object recognition with informative features and linear classification. In *IEEE Conf. on Computer Vision and Pattern Recognition*, 2003.

The Trace Model for Object Detection and Tracking

Sachin Gangaputra[1] and Donald Geman[2]

[1] Dept. of Electrical and Computer Engineering
The Johns Hopkins University
Baltimore, MD 21218
sachin@jhu.edu
[2] Dept. of Applied Mathematics and Statistics
The Johns Hopkins University
Baltimore, MD 21218
geman@jhu.edu

Abstract. We introduce a stochastic model to characterize the online computational process of an object recognition system based on a hierarchy of classifiers. The model is a graphical network for the conditional distribution, under both object and background hypotheses, of the classifiers which are executed during a coarse-to-fine search. A likelihood is then assigned to each history or "trace" of processing. In this way, likelihood ratios provide a measure of confidence for each candidate detection, which markedly improves the selectivity of hierarchical search, as illustrated by pruning many false positives in a face detection experiment. This also leads to a united framework for object detection and tracking. Experiments in tracking faces in image sequences demonstrate invariance to large face movements, partial occlusions, changes in illumination and varying numbers of faces.

1 Introduction

The two main categories of traditional pattern classification methods are generative and discriminative [8]. Generative methods involve the design and estimation of a probability distribution over features, both observed and unobserved, which capture the appearance of patterns in each class. Recent variations include work on spatial arrangements of parts [4], Boolean models [1], reusable parts [13] and compositional vision [11]. Such methods usually require intense computation (e.g., computing MAP estimators) and extensive modeling. Nonetheless, in principle, they can account for context and semantic labels at many levels, thereby providing a comprehensive analysis of natural scenes. In contrast, discriminative methods usually aim at inducing decision surfaces directly from training data. Popular methods include support vector machines [21,15], neural networks [17] and Adaboost [22]. Some are well-grounded in the theory of inductive learning and achieve high performance in classification. However, they often require very large training sets and their extension to global, full-scale scene interpretation is

J. Ponce et al. (Eds.): Toward Category-Level Object Recognition, LNCS 4170, pp. 401–420, 2006.
© Springer-Verlag Berlin Heidelberg 2006

by no means obvious. Of course, these categories are hardly disjoint and many methods, including those proposed here, involve components of both.

Recently, a different approach has been applied to pattern recognition [3,10,2]. In *computational modeling*, the primary object of analysis is the online computational process rather than probability distributions or decision surfaces. Hierarchies of binary classifiers which cover varying subsets of hypotheses are built from standard discriminative methods by exploiting shared properties of the appearance of shapes. Online, the hierarchy is traversed using a coarse-to-fine (CTF) search strategy: a classifier is evaluated if and only if all its ancestors have been evaluated and were positive. One important consequence is that computation is concentrated on ambiguous regions of the image; in particular, the "object hypothesis" is rejected as quickly as possible in background regions. A limitation of this approach is that statistical interactions among the classifiers in the hierarchy is not taken into account; in particular, no global likelihoods are assigned.

Here, we extend computational modeling, and take a step towards contextual analysis, by introducing a global stochastic network to model classifier interactions. The central concept is the *trace* of processing, which encodes the *computational history* – the family of classifiers performed, together with their outcomes, during CTF search. Notice that the trace is a far richer structure than the output of a decision tree; it is in fact a data-driven subtree of the original hierarchy since many branches may be partially traversed before a negative result is encountered or a leaf is reached. The trace space is represented by a tree-structured graphical network and a likelihood is assigned to each trace under both object and background hypotheses. This provides a generative framework for the hierarchy of classifiers. Detections (full chains of positive responses) can then be analyzed using likelihood ratio tests, adding a statistical component to sequential search strategies.

We test the effectiveness of our trace model in experiments in face detection and face tracking. Single-frame detection is based on the CTF framework proposed in [10], where a hierarchy of linear classifiers is used to efficiently reject non-face patterns and focus computation on face-like regions. Likelihood ratios of observed traces represent a measure of confidence for each detection, allowing for higher discrimination than with purely CTF search. This is illustrated by successfully pruning false positives to produce a strictly superior ROC curve. Tracking of faces in a video sequence is accomplished by integrating frame-based probability measures within a spatial-temporal Markov model for the joint evolution of poses and traces. Due to continuously updating detections, there are no restrictions on face movements. Unlike existing approaches, the motion model is not used to restrict the search domain but rather only to link detections between consecutive frames. This framework then unites detection and tracking within a single stochastic model.

In Section 2, we provides an overview of hierarchical object detection. The trace model is introduced in Section 3, along with the construction of a probability distribution on the space of traces relative to a general hierarchy of classifiers.

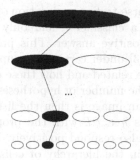

Fig. 1. Hierarchical class/pose decomposition. Each cell represents a subset of classes and poses. An alarm is identified with a fine (leaf) cell Λ if the classifiers for every coarser cell (i.e containing Λ) responds positively.

In Section 4, we specialize to the case of learning a trace model for a hierarchy based on the pose of a frontal view of a face and in Section 5 we demonstrate how this model can eliminate false positives in hierarchical face detection. In Section 6, the spatial trace model is integrated into a spatial-temporal Markov model in order to produce a real-time face tracking system. Concluding remarks are provided in Section 7.

2 Hierarchical Object Detection

Object detection refers to discovering and localizing instances from a list of object classes based on a grey level image of an underlying scene. The basic hierarchical framework can be found in [3,10,2,18]. In hierarchical detection, both learning and parsing algorithms are based on a tree-structured representation of hypotheses – a sequence of nested partitions – which captures shared structure, e.g., common shape features. Hypotheses correspond to individual class/pose pairings, although the framework is more general. Whereas scene interpretations may involve multiple, inter-connected pairings, we shall focus on pure detection. Each cell of the hierarchy corresponds to a subset of hypotheses and is included in exactly one of the cells in the preceding, coarser partition (see Fig.1). Fine cells may not correspond to individual hypotheses.

A binary classifier X_η is associated with the cell at each $\eta \in T$, where T denotes the tree graph underlying the hierarchy. Classifier X_η is designed to respond positively ($X_\eta = 1$) to all images labeled by the cell at η and negatively ($X_\eta = -1$) to as many images as possible which fall into a suitable alternative category. These classifiers range from those near the root of T, which accommodate many hypotheses simultaneously, to those near the leaves of T, which are more dedicated (and hence selective). In principle, the classifiers could be constructed by any learning algorithm, but under the constraint that each classifier maintain a very small false negative error rate, which facilitates early termination of the search.

Scenes are parsed by a coarse-to-fine exploration of the hierarchy, i.e., starting at the root and evaluating a classifier if and only if all ancestors have been evaluated and returned a positive answer. This processing strategy is known to be theoretically optimal [3] under certain assumptions about how the power and cost of the classifiers are related and how these quantities interact with the "scope" of the classifiers – the number of hypotheses covered.

The result of processing an image is then the list of hypotheses determined by the union of all leaf cells $\eta \in \partial T$ with the property that $X_\eta = 1$ and all classifiers at ancestors of η also respond positively. This can be visualized as a *chain of positive responses* in the hierarchy of cells (see Fig. 1). Areas of the image rejected by coarse tests are then rapidly processed, whereas ambiguous areas are not labeled until at least some fine classifiers have been evaluated. The resulting distribution of processing is highly skewed and detection is rapid at the expense of some false positives.

On an empirical level, the success of this technique has been demonstrated in several contexts, including experiments in face detection [10,18] and multi-class character recognition [2]. In the former case, for example, parsing an image results in a binary decision labeling each non-overlapping $k \times k$ window (e.g., $k = 16$) as either "background" or "face". Although this method is quite fast and accurate (see Section 5 for comparisons with other methods), it does not assign any numeric confidence measure to each detection, which can aid in resolving competing interpretations. More generally, there is no global stochastic model for the hierarchy of classifiers.

The key to introducing a model, and accounting for context, is to exploit the rich information provided by hierarchical search. Information is lost by only collecting the list of complete chains. Clues about the semantic identity of image regions, specifically the existence and presentations of objects of interest, can be accumulated by considering the global history of the search process. More specifically, processing a subimage leaves a fairly distinctive "signature" because *every test tells us something about every possible interpretation.* That is, if $y \in Y$ is an interpretation (e.g., face at some pose), then each classifier X_η in the hierarchy offers some evidence for the presence or absence of y, *even if X_η is based on a subset $\Lambda_\eta \subset Y$ which does not contain y.* The trace model is intended to capture this type of global information.

3   The Trace of Coarse-to-Fine Search

Our approach is to model the computational history using a graphical stochastic network indexed by certain subtrees of T. This then provides a joint probability distribution over all possible processing records. The nature of the coarse-to-fine processing makes this feasible as the search imposes major restrictions on the possible records – subtrees – that can be observed. This in turn leads to a simple distribution on the search histories or "traces" and provides a natural likelihood-ratio test for weeding out false detections.

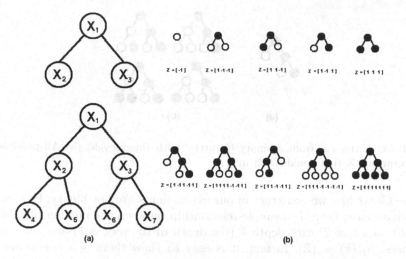

Fig. 2. The result of CTF search is a labeled subtree where dark circles indicate a positive classifier result and light circles a negative result. The traces are depicted together with the outcomes of the classifiers performed. Top panel: (a) A hierarchy of three classifiers; (b) The 5 different traces that can result from CTF search. Bottom panel: (a) A hierarchy of seven classifiers; (b) Five of the 26 possible traces for this hierarchy.

3.1 Trace Configurations

Depending on the image I, certain nodes $\eta \in T$ are visited during CTF search and their corresponding classifiers $X_\eta \in \{-1, 1\}$ are evaluated. The result of CTF search is then a *labeled subtree* of T, which we call the *trace* of image I. The nodes of the trace correspond to the classifiers evaluated and the labels correspond to the outcomes. Specifically, let $S(I) \subset T$ denote the set of visited nodes, a *random subtree*, and write $Z(I) = \{X_\eta, \eta \in S(I)\} \in \mathcal{Z}$ for the trace, where $\mathcal{Z}$ denotes the set of all possible traces for a given hierarchy. In addition, let $\mathcal{A}_\eta$ denote the set of parent nodes of η. For any trace $Z(I)$, certain constraints result from the fact that a classifier X_η is performed if and only if all ancestor classifiers $\{X_\xi, \xi \in \mathcal{A}_\eta\}$ are performed *and* each one is positive. In particular, i) the classifier at any non-terminal node of $S(I)$ must be positive; ii) the classifier at any node which is terminal in $S(I)$ but not terminal in T must be negative; and iii) the classifier at a terminal node of both $S(I)$ and T can be either positive or negative.

The situation is illustrated in Fig. 2 for two simple binary hierarchies. For three nodes and three corresponding binary classifiers X_1, X_2, X_3, there are 2^3 total possible full realizations but only five possible traces, listed in the upper right of Fig. 2. With seven nodes and classifiers, there are $2^7 = 128$ full realizations and twenty-six possible traces, five of which are shown in the lower right of Fig. 2. In general, the total number of traces depends on T.

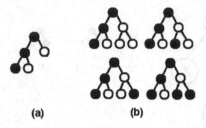

(a)   (b)

Fig. 3. (a) A trace Z from a binary hierarchy with three levels; (b) All possible full configurations $\mathbf{X}$ that could result in Z

The hierarchies we construct in our experiments are not binary. However, in the binary case, there is a simple relationship between the number of subtrees, $n_{sub}(k)$, of a tree T with depth k (the depth of the root is 1) and the number of traces, $n_{tr}(k) = |\mathcal{Z}|$. In fact, it is easy to show there is a one-to-one correspondence between $\mathcal{Z}$ and the subtrees of a tree of depth $k + 1$, and hence $n_{tr}(k) = n_{sub}(k+1)$. Given the trace of a tree of depth k, expanding every "on" node (which is necessarily terminal) into two children gives a subtree of a tree of depth $k + 1$; conversely, every subtree can be identified with a trace by cutting off its terminal leaves. It follows that

$$n_{tr}(k) = n_{sub}(k+1) = n_{sub}^2(k) + 1 = n_{tr}^2(k-1) + 1, \ k \geq 2.$$

In particular, $n_{tr}(1) = 2$, $n_{tr}(2) = 5$ and $n_{tr}(3) = 26$ (see Fig. 2(b)).

3.2   Trace Distributions

CTF search induces a mapping $\tau : \{-1, 1\}^T \to \mathcal{Z}$ from full configurations $\mathbf{X}$ to traces Z. In general, many realizations $\mathbf{X}$ are mapped to the same trace Z. In Fig. 3, the four configurations in (b) are mapped to the trace in (a). This mapping induces a partition of the entire configuration space. Consequently, given any probability distribution $p_{\mathbf{X}}$ for $\mathbf{X}$, we have

$$\sum_{z \in \mathcal{Z}} p_{\mathbf{X}}(\tau^{-1}(z)) = 1. \tag{1}$$

However, in order to construct a distribution on $\mathcal{Z}$ we need not start with a distribution on the full configuration space.

One natural distribution on $\mathcal{Z}$ can be constructed directly along the lines of graphical models. This direct construction has the added advantage that the model requires only one parameter for each node in T. In contrast, learning a graphical model for $\mathbf{X}$ on the full realization space $\{-1, 1\}^T$ can be difficult for large T even with conditional independence assumptions since the number of nodes, as well as the number of parameters determining each conditional probability, increases exponentially with $|T|$. Moreover, in terms of online computation, the original motivation for constructing a hierarchy of classifiers under the zero false negative constraint was the amount of computation involved in evaluating classifiers at many image locations and resolutions.

Theorem 1. *Let* $\{p_\eta, \ \eta \in T\}$ *be any set of numbers with* $0 \le p_\eta \le 1$. *Then*

$$P(z) = \prod_{\eta \in S_z} p_\eta(x_\eta) \tag{2}$$

defines a probability distribution on traces where S_z *is the subtree identified with* z *and* $p_\eta(1) = p_\eta$ *and* $p_\eta(-1) = 1 - p_\eta$.

Proof. There are several ways to prove that (2) implies $\sum_z P(z) = 1$ using the type of "peeling" argument common in graphical models. The "direct" proof proceeds by performing the summation one node at a time starting from the leaves of T. Start with any terminal node η of T and divide all traces into three disjoint groups: those for which S does not contain η; those for which $\eta \in S$ and $x_\eta = 1$; and those for which $\eta \in S$ and $x_\eta = -1$. The second and third groups are of equal size and there is a one-to-one pairing between them in which each pair is the same trace except for the sign of x_η. Adding the probabilities in each pair, and using $p_\eta(1) + p_\eta(-1) = 1$, results in a reformulation of the problem with probabilities identical to those in (2) except that node η does not appear, i.e., the trace space is relative to $T \setminus \{\eta\}$. Recursively looping over all the leaves of T then reduces the problem to a hierarchy of depth $k - 1$; continuing this way, proving $\sum_z P(z) = 1$ eventually reduces to $p_\eta(1) + p_\eta(-1) = 1$ for the root η of T. $\square$

There is obviously a natural connection between the trace distribution given by (2) and a graphical model $p_{\mathbf{X}}$ on the full configuration space, linked by defining

$$p_\eta(x_\eta) = p_{\mathbf{X}}(x_\eta | x_\xi = 1, \xi \in \mathcal{A}_\eta). \tag{3}$$

Here, the distribution $p_{\mathbf{X}}$ on $\{-1, 1\}^T$ is determined by imposing the splitting property of DAGs [16]:

$$p_{\mathbf{X}}(\mathbf{x}) = P(X_\eta = x_\eta, \eta \in T) = \prod_{\eta \in T} P(X_\eta = x_\eta | X_\xi = x_\xi, \xi \in \mathcal{A}_\eta). \tag{4}$$

We can choose any graphical model $p_{\mathbf{X}}$ consistent with (3). Then we only need to show that (2) holds; normalization is guaranteed by the mapping from full realizations to traces. Proving this is again a standard argument in graphical models. In fact, (3) holds relative to *any* sub-configuration on a subtree of T (i.e., whether or not the node histories consist of all positive responses). In particular, if $\Omega(z)$ is the subset of the full configuration space that maps to trace z, we clearly have:

$$P(Z = z) = \sum_{\mathbf{x} \in \Omega(z)} p_{\mathbf{X}}(\mathbf{x})$$

$$= \sum_{\mathbf{x} \in \Omega(z)} \prod_{\eta \in T} p(x_\eta | x_\xi, \xi \in \mathcal{A}_\eta).$$

This reduces to (2) by factoring the product of conditional probabilities into two groups and by extracting common terms in a recursive fashion.

The important point is that the conditional probabilities in the full model are reduced to binomial terms $p_\eta(x_\eta)$ since all the conditional events are "positive histories." *Consequently, specifying a single parameter $p_\eta(1)$ for every node $\eta \in T$ yields a consistent probability model on traces.* In contrast, in the full model with binary trees, 2^k parameters would be required to specify each conditional probability for a history of length k, and hence order 4^k parameters would be required altogether, at least without imposing further Markov assumptions on path histories.

4   Learning Trace Models for a Pose Hierarchy

In this section, we specialize the trace formulation to the case of a pose hierarchy for faces. A reference set of poses is recursively partitioned into finer and finer cells Λ_η and the classifier X_η for cell η is designed to detect all faces with poses in Λ_η. The manner in which the classifiers are constructed from training data, and full scenes are processed, will be reviewed only briefly in the following section since these issues have been discussed in previous work; for example further details may be found in [10] and [2]. Here we review what the hierarchy represents in order to understand what the corresponding trace distributions mean and how they are estimated from data.

4.1   Pose Hierarchy

The space of hypotheses is the set of poses of a face. Each classifier is trained on a specific subset of face subimages which satisfy certain pose restrictions. In detecting frontal views of faces, tilts are restricted to the range $-15° \leq \alpha \leq 15°$. The base detector is designed to detect faces with scales (the number of pixels between the eyes) in the range $8 \leq s \leq 16$. The position of the face (taken to be the midpoint between the eyes) is unrestricted. To detect larger faces, the original image is downsampled before applying the base detector. With four levels of downsampling, one is able to detect faces with sizes from 8 to 128 pixels.

Processing an entire image with a single hierarchy of classifiers would entail building a root classifier which applies to *all* face positions simultaneously, and to tilts and scales in the ranges given above. Instead, the face location in the coarsest cell in the hierarchy is restricted to an 8×8 block and the entire image is processed by visiting each (non-overlapping) 8×8 block and applying the base detector to the surrounding image data. Specifically, then, the classifier at the root of the hierarchy is designed to detect faces with tilts in the range $-15° \leq \alpha \leq 15°$, scales in the range $8 \leq s \leq 16$, and location restricted to an 8×8 window. The leaf cells localize faces to a 2×2 region with $\Delta\alpha = 10°$ and $\Delta s = 2$ pixels. In particular, faces are not detected at the resolution of one specific position, scale and tilt, but rather at the resolution of the leaf cells. For ease of notation, however, each leaf cell $s \in \partial T$ in the hierarchy T is represented by a single pose in that cell, call it θ_s.

The discussion in Section 3 about constructing trace distributions can now be applied conditionally on each leaf cell s, i.e., under the hypothesis that there is a face with pose in Λ_s. Using the representative pose θ_s to signify this hypothesis, the conditional probability of observing a trace z in the pose hierarchy is then

$$P(z|\theta_s) = \prod_{\eta \in S_z} p_\eta(x_\eta|\theta_s).$$
(5)

4.2   Learning

The task of learning is then to estimate the probabilities $p_\eta(1|\theta_s), \eta \in T$, for each leaf cell $s \in \partial T$. Recall that this probability represents the likelihood that the classifier at node η responds positively *given that all its ancestors have re-sponded positively*. In addition, detection will involve a likelihood ratio test for the hypothesis "θ_s" against a universal "background hypothesis," denoted by B. Under B, the trace data follow another distribution estimated from non-face subimages. Consequently, we must also learn the probabilities $p_\eta(1|B), \eta \in T$.

Due to the natural assumption of space-invariance (i.e., the trace distributions are block-independent), we need to only learn the responses of classifiers for all poses contained within a single, reference block. Moreover, two pose cells at the same level in the (reference) hierarchy which differ only in the location of the subset of positions (i.e., cover the same subset of scales and tilts and the same subset of positions up to translation) can evidently be aggregated in collecting statistics. Notice also that, in estimating $p_\eta(1|\theta_s)$ for a fixed η, all the face training data with poses in the leaf cell represented by θ_s are also aggregated in compiling empirical statistics.

The model parameters are learned for the object model by accumulating the results of classification tests over a standard face database and for the back-ground model from subimages randomly sampled from the WWW. Fig. 4 illus-trates the distribution of the model parameters $p_\eta(1|\theta_s)$ for one specific pose θ_s and under the background hypothesis. Only the section of the hierarchy that contains the complete chain corresponding to the pose θ_s is illustrated. A darker circle indicates a higher value of the probability $p_\eta(1|\theta_s)$. As expected, we observe darker circles along the chain that corresponds to the true pose. A consistent decrease in the darkness at deeper levels is observed for the background model.

5   Experiments in Face Detection

We now demonstrate the advantage of the trace model with respect to the base-line detector utilized in previous work [2,3,10] on coarse-to-fine object detection. Briefly, the baseline detector operates as follows: The image is partitioned into disjoint 8×8 blocks and the image data surrounding each block is processed by the hierarchy of classifiers which corresponds to the (reference) pose hierarchy. The search is breadth-first CTF. A detection is declared at a terminal pose cell ξ when there is a chain in the hierarchy, from the root to ξ, for which $X_\xi = 1$ and

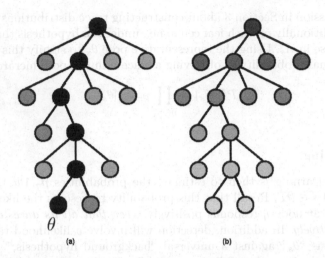

θ

(a)   (b)

Fig. 4. (a) The learned parameters $p_\eta(1|\theta_s)$ under the hypothesis of a face with pose in the cell represented by θ_s; (b) The same parameters for the background model. Only the section of the full hierarchy that contains the complete chain to the cell represented by θ_s is shown. A circle shaded darker indicates a higher value of the parameter.

$X_\eta = 1, \eta \in \mathcal{A}_\xi$. In the baseline system, when multiple detections are recorded for a given block, some criterion must be used to identify a unique detection for that block. The details are not important for our purposes. The important point is that there is no global probabilistic model for assigning likelihoods to detections or measuring one detection against another, or against a background hypothesis. The trace model provides for this.

The general design of the hierarchy and the classifiers follows previous work [10]. In this work, we use a slightly modified pose hierarchy (see §4.1) and make use of both positive (face) and negative (non-face) training instances in constructing the classifiers. We use the Adaboost [22] learning algorithm to build each $X_\eta, \eta \in T$. The features are the same oriented binary edge fragments from [10]. The same learning algorithm is applied to each cell; only the training set changes. More specifically, a standard training dataset is used to build both the hierarchical classifiers and the trace models. 1600 faces are synthesized from the dataset for each different pose and 10000 randomly selected image patches were downloaded from the WWW and used as "non-faces". The non-face instances used at cell η are those which have responded positively to the preceding classifiers $X_\xi, \xi \in \mathcal{A}_\eta$. In this way, in training X_η, the system is competing with those particular non-faces encountered during CTF search, which increasingly resemble faces.

5.1   Trace-Based Likelihood Ratios

Assume the hierarchy of classifiers has been constructed and processed using the baseline detection system, resulting in a susbset (usually empty) of complete chains for a given 8×8 block W. (Recall that the baseline detector is applied to each in a series of downsampled images in order to detect faces at a wide range of scales.) Let $Z(W)$ denote the trace of block W. For each complete chain in W, say arriving at leaf node $s \in \partial T$, we perform a likelihood ratio test, comparing $P(Z(W)|\theta_s)$ to $P(Z(W)|B)$. A detection is declared "at θ_s" if

$$\frac{P(Z(W)|\theta_s)}{P(Z(W)|B)} \geq \tau.$$

An ROC curve may then be constructed by varying τ and collecting statistics on a test set; see below. The smallest value of τ, i.e., the most conservative in terms of retaining faces at the expense of false positives, is determined by studying the distribution of the likelihood ratio over a training set of faces and non-faces and choosing a value that maintains every face.

NOTES:

- The speed of the algorithm is mainly governed by the baseline detection scheme as the evaluation of each trace likelihood is only performed at complete chains.
- However, restricting the search to complete chains is merely a computational shortcut. Very little would change if screening for complete chains was omitted and hence the likelihood ratio was maximized over *every* pose hypothesis in each block. This is due to the underlying false negative constraint on each classifier. Given a face with pose θ, any trace z which does not contain a path to the leaf containing θ, including a positive value at the leaf, has very small probability compared with $P(z|B)$. As a result, the likelihood ratio is smaller than even the smallest value of τ described above and consequently there is no detection at (the leaf cell containing) θ. *Hence, the detector for block W is effectively a true likelihood ratio test.*

5.2   Towards a Global Model

One might ask whether this block-by-block likelihood ratio test can be related to a full-image search based on a global, generative model. Consider a single hierarchy for the entire image; suppose there is a branch from the root to the subset of poses corresponding to each region W_i, $1 \leq i \leq n$, for a partition of the image pixels into non-overlapping 8×8 blocks. Suppose also that the root test is virtual – always positive. How might the global trace Z be used to make inferences about the poses of all faces in the image? Let Θ denote a collection of poses representing a global (image-wide) hypothesis. Suppose the prior distribution $P(\Theta)$ forbides any two components of Θ with positions in the same 8×8 block W; otherwise it is uniform. (This only rules out severe occulsion.) We make no assumptions about the number of faces in the image (up to the number of blocks). Let $\Theta = \{\gamma_1, ..., \gamma_n\}$ where $\gamma_i = B$ signals "no face in block W_i" and $\gamma_i = \theta_i$ is a pose with location in W_i.

Fig. 5. Detection results on the CMU+MIT test set

Let $Z(i)$ correspond to the trace generated with image block W_i. Make the convenient assumptions that that the components of Z are conditionally independent given both Θ and background, that $P(Z(i)|\Theta) = P(Z(i)|\gamma_i)$ and that $P(Z(i)|\gamma_i = B)$ follows a universal "background law" denoted $P(Z|B)$. (The conditional independence assumption is violated in practice because $Z(i)$ depends on the image data surrounding W_i; for example, in the scale range $8 \leq s \leq 16$, faces might occupy a region of order 32×32 and hence adjacent traces have overlapping supports. The other assumptions are reasonable.) Then

$$\frac{P(Z|\Theta)}{P(Z|\mathbf{B})} = \prod_{i=1}^{n} \frac{P(Z(i)|\gamma_i)}{P(Z(i)|B)} = \prod_{i \in F(\Theta)} \frac{P(Z(i)|\theta_i)}{P(Z(i)|B)} \qquad (6)$$

where $F(\Theta) \subset \{1, ..., n\}$ is the set of blocks for which $\gamma_i \neq B$. Maximizing this over all Θ is evidently intractable. However, visiting the blocks one-by-one and performing an individual likelihood ratio test is a reasonable approximation.

5.3   Results

Our algorithm is implemented in C++ on a standard Pentium 4 1.8GHz PC, and we use a subset of the CMU+MIT [17,20] frontal face test set to estimate performance. Images with strong pose variations in 2D and out-of-plane face orientations are removed from the original test set. Figure 5 shows the result of the trace-based system at a high detection rate (i.e., small τ) on a few images of this test set. Processing a 320×240 image takes only a fraction of a second.

Fig. 6 illustrates the difference in detection performance between the trace-based system and the baseline detector on some images from the test set. Typically, true detections and false positives produce different types of traces.

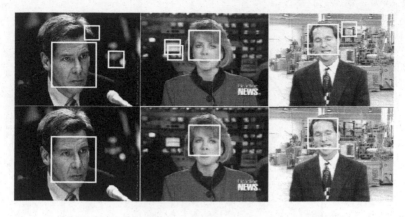

Fig. 6. Top row: The results of pure detection using the baseline CTF system. Bottom row: False positives are eliminated by setting an appropriate threshold on the trace likelihood.

For instance, the trace signatures of false positives tend to have multiple complete chains and generate larger subtrees S. The traces generated by actual faces are usually more locally concentrated with fewer long chains. These phenomena are manifested in the learned trace models, which is why the likelihood ratio test is efficient in reducing false positives while maintaining faces.

Some comparisons with the baseline CTF system as well as other face detection methods are reported in Table 1. A detection rate of 88.8% with 126 false positives is achieved on 164 images from the test set. For the same detection rate, the false positive rate for the trace-based system is lower than that of the baseline CTF system. The trace-based results are also comparable to other well-known systems. It should be noted that the results from each system are reported on slightly different subsets of the CMU+MIT test set. Also, the performance of both the baseline CTF system and the trace-based system could very likely be improved by considering a richer feature set and/or a richer training set.

Table 1. Detection rates for various face detection systems

	Detection	False positives / image
Trace-Based CTF	89.1%	0.77
Baseline CTF	89.1%	1.11
Viola-Jones	90.8%	0.73
Rowley-Baluja-Kanade	89.2%	0.73

5.4   Comparison of ROC Curves

Another way to compare the baseline and trace-based systems is using ROC curves. The ROC principle is based on varying a free parameter (e.g., a threshold) in order to quantify the tradeoff between false positive and false negative

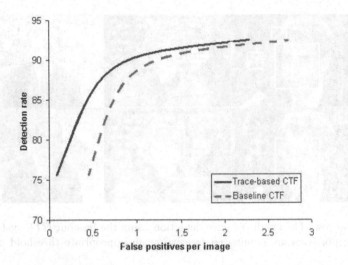

Fig. 7. ROC curve - detection rate vs. false positives on the MIT+CMU test set for the baseline CTF and the trace-based system

error rates. In the case of the baseline CTF system, the parameter τ is the minimum number of complete chains required for an 8×8 window to be classified as containing the location of a face. For example, when $\tau = 1$ the detector produces a high number of false positives but few missed detections. For the trace-based system, the parameter is the threshold on the likelihood ratio, as discussed earlier. If multiple chains yield likelihood ratios above the threshold, the trace-based system chooses the chain (for that 8×8 block) that maximizes the likelihood ratio. For selected values of these thresholds, the false alarm rate and the true detection rate on the CMU+MIT test set are plotted in Fig. 7. The trace ROC curve is strictly superior, indicating that information does indeed reside in the "history of processing."

6   Application to Face Tracking

Face tracking usually involves characterizing the temporal evolution of shapes, features or statistics. Tracking might be keyed by low level features such as color [19] and contours [7]. In some model-based methods [9], foreground regions are segmented by constantly updating a background model. Monte Carlo methods [12] applied to the posterior probability distribution of the object state employ dynamic sampling and Bayesian inference to estimate parameters of interest. Nonparametric methods, such as the mean-shift algorithm [6], have also been proposed for visual tracking. Most of these approaches exploit the temporal correlation between successive frames in order to refine the localization of a target. In most cases, real-time performance is achieved by restricting the search space by way of a highly constrained motion model. In general, work in face tracking has progressed

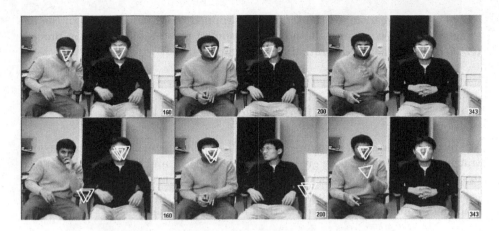

Fig. 8. Top row: The result of our tracker in three different frames. Bottom row: The raw results of pure detection in the same three frames.

largely independently from work in face detection and only a few approaches have attempted to merge them into a single framework [14].

In order to make inferences about a dynamical system, it is customary to specify two models – one that describes the evolution of the state with time (the system model) and one that relates the noisy measurement to the state (the measurement model). In our work, the state at time t is the set of poses of the faces in frame t and the trace is the measurement. A simple joint Markov model provides a natural probabilistic formulation and allows for the updating of information based on new measurements.

6.1 A Model for Face Tracking

In order to illustrate the role of the trace model, we shall only discuss tracking a single face, assumed visible throughout the sequence. We use $\mathbf{I}_{0:t-1}$ and $\theta_{0:t-1}$ to denote the set of observed image frames and the set of observed poses, respectively, from time 0 to $t-1$. The (global) trace for image frame $\mathbf{I}_t$ is denoted by Z_t; recall from Section 4.2 that $Z_t = \{Z_t(i)\}$, where $Z_t(i)$ is the trace for the hierarchy corresponding to the i'th block. The tracking problem is formulated by estimating the pose of a face for every time t, given (i) a new trace, Z_t; (ii) the previously recorded set of traces, $Z_{0:t-1}$; and (iii) the set of previously observed poses, $\theta_{0:t-1}$. The MAP estimate $\hat{\theta}_t$ of the pose at time t is

$$\hat{\theta}_t = \arg\max_{\theta_t} P(\theta_t | Z_{0:t}, \theta_{0:t-1})$$

$$= \arg\max_{\theta_t} \frac{P(Z_{0:t}, \theta_{0:t})}{P(Z_{0:t}, \theta_{0:t-1})}$$

$$= \arg\max_{\theta_t} P(Z_{0:t}, \theta_{0:t})$$

$$= \arg\max_{\theta_t} P(Z_t, \theta_t | Z_{0:t-1}, \theta_{0:t-1})$$

where we have rearranged the terms and dropped those independent of the argument θ_t. The trace and the pose are assumed to be a joint Markov process $(Z_t, \theta_t), t \geq 0$. The maximization is then simplified to

$$\hat{\theta}_t = \arg\max_{\theta_t} P(Z_t, \theta_t | Z_{t-1}, \theta_{t-1})$$
$$= \arg\max_{\theta_t} P(Z_t | Z_{t-1}, \theta_t, \theta_{t-1}) P(\theta_t | Z_{t-1}, \theta_{t-1}).$$

We further assume that the trace Z_t is conditionally independent of the previous trace and the previous pose given the current pose θ_t, and that the current pose θ_t is independent of the previous trace Z_{t-1} given the previous pose θ_{t-1}. These assumptions are reasonable and are consistent with other probabilistic-based tracking approaches. This leads to the following baseline tracker

$$\hat{\theta}_t = \arg\max_{\theta_t} P(Z_t | \theta_t) P(\theta_t | \theta_{t-1}). \tag{7}$$

The likelihood function $P(Z_t | \theta_t)$ of the global trace $Z_t = \{Z_t(i), i = 1, ..., n\}$ is defined in the same way as in Section 5.2, but under the simplifying constraint that all but one of the components of Θ represent "background". Writing $W(i(t))$ for the (unique) block containing the location component of θ_t, this likelihood can be written:

$$P(Z_t | \theta_t) = C(Z_t) \times \frac{P(Z_t(i(t)) | \theta_t)}{P(Z_t(i(t)) | B)} \tag{8}$$

where

$$C(Z_t) = \prod_{i=1}^{n} P(Z_t(i) | B)$$

is independent of θ_t.

A new track is initialized by examining the likelihood ratio as before, i.e., the maximization can be restricted to those θ_t which fall inside terminal pose cells at the end of complete chains. An old track is continued by restricting the pose space to regions in a neighborhood of the previous pose θ_{t-1}. The size of the neighborhood is determined by the variability captured by the pose transition model. The restriction of the pose-space does not limit the ability of the tracker to handle faces with large motions; these faces are detected as new faces by the CTF detection scheme.

The transition probability $P(\theta_t | \theta_{t-1})$ is assumed stationary and captures our prior knowledge about how the pose moves from one frame to another. Our transition model is learned from a set of training video sequences, recorded in a video conference setting with a subject normally seated not far from a fixed camera; there is then limited motion of the subject's face. The training sequences are manually landmarked and provide ground truth data for estimating pose transitions. A histogram of the pose differences $\theta_t - \theta_{t-1}$ is generated for the entire training set and serves as a good estimate for the pose transition model $P(\theta_t | \theta_{t-1})$.

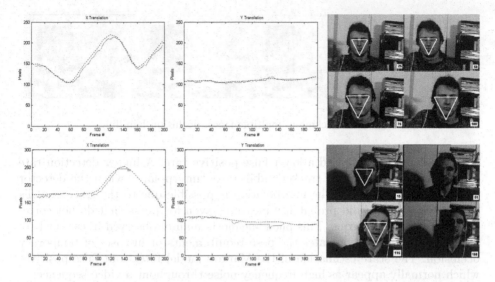

Fig. 9. Trajectories for the x and y coordinates of the estimated position during a tracking sequence. The dashed line represents ground truth and the solid line is the outcome of the trace-based Markov tracker. The right panel illustrates the results in some static frames extracted from the sequence.

Multiple faces and varying numbers of faces can also be accommodated since the evaluation of the trace is global. Multiple faces are tracked by implementing the baseline tracker independently for each new face. We omit the details concerning the initialization of new tracks and the removal of existing ones. Extending the algorithm to accommodate more variations in the pose of a face is straightforward. Pose hierarchies corresponding to left and right profiles are learned separately and are added directly to the original hierarchy (frontal faces) via a virtual node at the root and pose representation is augmented by a parameter indicating whether the view is frontal, left profile or right profile.

6.2   Results

Video sequences from commercial films and the Web are used to test the performance of the tracker. The sequences contain multiple faces per frame under various conditions of illumination and occlusion. With a standard desktop PC and with no MMX optimizations, faces are tracked at around 15 frames per second. Since the evaluation of trace likelihoods is restricted to regions of interest, the speed of the tracker is mainly determined by the efficiency of detection. Real-time performance can be obtained by only executing the full-image detector every few frames or by incorporating global temporal information.

Fig. 6 illustrates the difference in the quality of single-frame detection between the trace-based Markov tracking model and the static algorithm (without the trace model) in [10]. Naturally, exploiting temporal continuity and the trace model removes false detections. In fact, tracking generally results in both

Fig. 10. Tracking of multiple faces: occlusion handling

a higher detection rate and a lower false positive rate. A higher detection rate is achieved because of the tracker's ability to "interpolate" when the detector fails to signal an alarm. The interpolation is possible due to the trace model's ability to produce valid probability measures even for poses that do not correspond to detected alarms. This phenomenon is mainly observed in cases where a subject temporarily violates the pose requirements or in cases of temporary occlusion. The state estimation of the Markov model filters out false positives which normally appear as high-frequency noise throughout a video sequence.

An empirical analysis of the tracker's performance is illustrated in Fig. 9. A single face is tracked in each sequence and its image coordinates are plotted through a segment of 200 frames. The video sequences are provided by [5] and are available at *http://www.cs.bu.edu/groups/ivc/HeadTracking/*. The frames in the right panel of Fig. 9 illustrate the result of the tracker at different points throughout the sequence. The dashed line represents ground truth which is obtained by manually landmarking the video sequence. The solid line is the outcome of the trace-based Markov tracker. As can be observed, the face position is correctly determined through most of the sequences. Some discontinuities are observed and are attributed to a failure of the CTF detection algorithm. The second sequence in Fig. 9 exhibits varying illumination; as a result, the detector provides inconsistent initialization and this propagates to the tracker, generating the observed discontinuity. A slight amount of jitter in position is attributed to inability of the first-order Markov model to integrate information over multiple frames.

Fig. 11. Tracking results on a difficult sequence with high camera instability

Fig. 10 shows the result of tracking multiple faces through occlusions. Fig. 11 depicts the result of tracking a subject in a very challenging video sequence [23]. The face of the subject is successfully tracked despite heavy camera panning and unsteady focus. Unlike most tracking algorithms, the search is global and the influence of the CTF detection model reduces the dependence on accurate motion estimation.

7   Conclusions

We have characterized the online computational process of an object detection system in the context of a graphical model for the history or "trace" of processing. This introduces a generative component into sequential detection strategies based on coarse-to-fine processing of a hierarchy of classifiers. The trace model captures and exploits the interactions among various classifiers within the hierarchy.

The utility of the trace model is demonstrated with experiments in face detection and tracking. There is a substantial gain in selectivity. Roughly speaking, at the same detection rate, the trace model eliminates around 40% of the false positives in deterministic hierarchical search. It also provides a unified framework for static face detection and dynamic face tracking, in which frame-based trace measures are merged with time-varying pose parameters within a simple Markov model. Unlike traditional tracking algorithms, there are no restrictions on the motion of a face. This is possible due to the computational efficiency of CTF detection, allowing for a nearly real-time search for multiple faces over an entire video frame at each instant. Further experiments will appear in forthcoming work.

References

1. Y. Amit. *2D Object Detection and Recognition. MIT Press*, 2002.
2. Y. Amit, D. Geman and X. Fan. A coarse-to-fine strategy for pattern recognition. *IEEE Trans PAMI*, Vol. 26, no. 12, pp. 1606-1621, 2004.
3. G. Blanchard and D. Geman. Sequential testing designs for pattern recognition. *Annals of Statistics*, Vol. 33, pp. 155-1202, June 2005.
4. M. Burl and P. Perona. Recognition of planar object classes. *IEEE Proc. CVPR*, pp 223-230, 1996.
5. M. L. Cascia, S. Sclaroff and V. Athitos. Fast reliable head tracking under varying illumination: An approach based on registration of texture-mapped 3D models. *IEEE. Trans. PAMI*, Vol. 21, No. 6, 1999.
6. D. Comaniciu, V. Ramesh and P. Meer. Kernel based object tracking. *IEEE Trans. PAMI*, Vol. 25. pp:564-577, 2003.
7. D. Decarlo and D. Metaxas. Deformable model based face shape and motion estimation. *Proc. Int'l Conf. Auto. Face and Gesture Recognition*, 1996.
8. R. Duda, P. Hart and D. Stork. Pattern Classification. *John Wiley and Sons*, 2001.
9. C.J. Edwards, C.J. Taylor and T.F Cootes. Learning to identify and track faces in an image sequence. *Proc. Int'l Conf. Auto. Face and Gesture Recognition*, pp 260-265, 1998.

10. F. Fleuret and D. Geman. Coarse-to-fine face detection. *IJCV*, Vol. 41, pp. 85-107, 2001.
11. S. Geman, D. Potter and Z. Chi. Composition systems. *Quaterly of Applied Mathematics*, LX:707-736, 2002.
12. M. Isard and A. Blake. Condensation-conditional density propagation for visual tracking. *IJCV*, vol. 29, pp 5-28, 1998.
13. S. Krempp, D. Geman and Y. Amit, Sequential learning with reusable parts for object detection, Technical Report, Johns Hopkins University, 2002.
14. B. Li and R. Chellappa. A generic approach to simultaneous tracking and verification in video. *IEEE Trans. Image Processing*, 11:530-544, 2002.
15. E. Osuna, R. Freund and F. Girosi. Training support vector machines: an application to face detection. *Proc. IEEE CVPR*, pp. 130-136, 1997.
16. J. Pearl. Probabilistic Reasoning in Intelligent Systems: Networks of Plausible Inference. *Morgan Kaufmann*, 1988.
17. H. Rowley, S. Baluja and T. Kanade. Neural network-based face detection. *IEEE Trans. PAMI*, Vol. 20, pp. 23-38, 1998.
18. H. Sahbi. Coarse-to-fine support vector machines for hierarchical face detection. *PhD thesis*, Versailles University, 2003.
19. K. Schwerdt and J. Crowley. Robust face tracking using colour. *Proc. Int'l Conf. Auto. Face and Gesture Recognition*, pp. 90-95. 2000.
20. K. Sung and T. Poggio. Example-based learning for view-based face detection. *IEEE Trans. PAMI*, Vol. 20,pp. 39-51, 1998.
21. V. Vapnik. The Nature of Statistical Learning Theory. *Springer-Verlag*, 1995.
22. P. Viola and M. Jones. Rapid object detection using a boosted cascade of simple features. *IEEE Proc. CVPR*, 2001.
23. http://www.madonnalicious.com/downloads.html

Part IV

Recognition of Object Categories with Geometric Relations

A Discriminative Framework for Texture and Object Recognition Using Local Image Features

Svetlana Lazebnik[1], Cordelia Schmid[2], and Jean Ponce[1]

[1] Beckman Institute, University of Illinois
405 N. Mathews Avenue, Urbana, IL 61801, USA
{slazebni,jponce}@uiuc.edu
[2] INRIA Rhône-Alpes
665 Avenue de l'Europe, 38330 Montbonnot, France
cordelia.schmid@inrialpes.fr

Abstract. This chapter presents an approach for texture and object recognition that uses scale- or affine-invariant local image features in combination with a discriminative classifier. Textures are represented using a visual dictionary found by quantizing appearance-based descriptors of local features. Object classes are represented using a dictionary of composite *semi-local parts*, or groups of nearby features with stable and distinctive appearance and geometric layout. A discriminative maximum entropy framework is used to learn the posterior distribution of the class label given the occurrences of parts from the dictionary in the training set. Experiments on two texture and two object databases demonstrate the effectiveness of this framework for visual classification.

1 Introduction

By analogy with a text document, an image can be viewed as a collection of parts or "visual words" drawn from a "part dictionary." This parallel has been exploited in recent *bag-of-keypoints* approaches to visual categorization [6,27], unsupervised discovery of visual "topics" [24], and video retrieval [18]. More generally, representations based on *local image features*, or salient regions extracted by specialized interest operators, have shown promise for recognizing textures [13], different views of the same object [9,22], and different instances of the same object class [1,7,8,26]. For textures, appearance-based descriptors of salient local regions are clustered to form characteristic texture elements, or *textons*. For objects, such clusters can also play the role of generic object parts. In our own previous work [15], we have introduced a more expressive representation based on composite *semi-local parts*, defined as geometrically stable configurations of multiple local regions that are robust against approximately rigid deformations and intra-class variations.

In this chapter, we present an approach to visual categorization that first constructs a texture or object representation based on a dictionary of textons or parts, and then learns a discriminative classifier that can effectively distinguish assemblies of parts or occurrence patterns of textons characteristic of different classes.

J. Ponce et al. (Eds.): Toward Category-Level Object Recognition, LNCS 4170, pp. 423–442, 2006.

For the classification step, we adopt a discriminative *maximum entropy* framework, which has been used successfully for text document classification [3,21] and image annotation [10]. This framework has several characteristics that make it attractive for visual categorization as well: It directly models the posterior distribution of the class label given the image, leading to convex (and tractable) parameter estimation; moreover, classification is performed in a true multi-class fashion, requiring no distinguished background class. Because the maximum entropy framework makes no independence assumptions, it offers a principled way of combining multiple kinds of features (e.g., keypoints produced by different detectors), as well as inter-part relations, into the object representation. While maximum entropy has been widely used in the computer vision for *generative* tasks, e.g., modeling of images as Markov random fields [28], where it runs into issues of intractability for learning and inference, it can be far more efficient for *discriminative* tasks. For example, Mahamud et al. [18] have used maximum entropy to combine multiple nearest-neighbor discriminators, and Keysers et al. [12] have applied it to digit recognition. In this chapter, we explore this framework in a part-based object categorization setting.

The rest of our presentation is organized as follows. We review in Section 2 the basics of *exponential models*, which arise from maximum entropy considerations. Sections 3 and 4 describe our approach to texture and object recognition, and Section 5 concludes with a summary and discussion of future directions. The research reported in this chapter has been previously published in [14].

2   The Maximum Entropy Framework

A discriminative maximum entropy approach seeks to estimate the posterior distribution of class labels given image features that matches the statistics of the features observed in the training set, and yet remains as uniform as possible. Intuitively, such a distribution properly reflects our uncertainty about making a decision given ambiguous or inconclusive image data. (By contrast, some generative methods, e.g., mixtures of Gaussians, tend to yield peaky or "overconfident" posterior distributions.) Suppose that we have defined a set of *feature functions* $f_k(I, c)$ that depend both on the image I and the class label c (the definitions of the specific feature functions used in our work will appear in Sections 3 and 4). To estimate the posterior of the class label given the features, we constrain the expected values of the features under the estimated distribution $P(c|I)$ to match those observed in the training set $\mathcal{T}$. The observed "average" value of feature f_k in the training set $\mathcal{T}$ is

$$\hat{f}_k = \frac{1}{|\mathcal{T}|} \sum_{I \in \mathcal{T}} f_k(I, c(I)).$$

Given a particular posterior distribution $P(c|I)$, the expected value of f_k, taken with respect to the observed empirical distribution $P(I)$ over the training set, is

$$E[f_k] = \frac{1}{|\mathcal{T}|} \sum_{I \in \mathcal{T}} \sum_{c} P(c|I) f_k(I, c).$$

We seek the posterior distribution that has the maximum *conditional entropy*

$$H = -\frac{1}{|T|} \sum_{I \in T} \sum_c P(c|I) \log P(c|I)$$

subject to the constraints $E[f_k] = \hat{f}_k$. It can be shown that the desired distribution has the *exponential form*

$$P(c|I) = \frac{1}{Z} \exp\left(\sum_k \lambda_k f_k(I, c)\right), \tag{1}$$

where

$$Z = \sum_c \exp\left(\sum_k \lambda_k f_k(I, c)\right)$$

is the normalizing factor,[1] and the λ_k are parameters whose optimal values are found by maximizing the likelihood of the training data under the exponential model (1). This optimization problem is convex and the global maximum can be found using the improved iterative scaling (IIS) algorithm [3,21]. At each iteration of IIS, we compute an update δ_k to each λ_k, such that the likelihood of the training data is increased. To do this, we bound $L(\lambda + \delta) - L(\lambda)$ from below by a positive function $F(\delta)$, and find the value of δ that maximizes this function. The derivation of updates is omitted here, but it can be shown [3,21] that when the features are *normalized*, i.e., when $\sum_k f_k(I, c)$ is a constant S for all I and c, updates can be found efficiently in closed form:

$$\delta_k = \frac{1}{S}\left(\log \hat{f}_k - \log E_\lambda[f_k]\right). \tag{2}$$

Because of the computational efficiency gained in this case, we use only normalized features in the present work.

Because of the form of (2), zero values of $\hat{f}_k$ cause the optimization to fail, and low values cause excessive growth of the weights. This is a symptom of one of the biggest potential pitfalls of the maximum entropy framework: overfitting. When the training set is small, the observed averages may deviate significantly from the "true" expectations, leading to a poor estimate of the posterior distribution. This problem can be alleviated by adding a zero-mean Gaussian prior on the weights [21]. However, in our experiments, we have achieved better results with a basic IIS setup where simple transformations of the feature functions are used to force expectations away from zero. Specifically, for all the feature functions defined in Sections 3 and 4, we use the standard Laplace smoothing, i.e.,

---

[1] Note that Z involves only a sum over the classes, and thus can be computed efficiently. If we were modeling the distribution of features given a class instead, Z would be a sum over the exponentially many possible combinations of feature values — a major source of difficulty for a generative approach. By contrast, the discriminative approach described here is more related to logistic regression. It is easy to show that (1) yields binary logistic discrimination in the two-class case.

adding one to each feature value and renormalizing. To simplify the subsequent presentation, we will omit this operation from all feature function definitions.

We close this section with a note concerning the technique we use to design feature functions. Instead of directly defining class-dependent features $f_k(I, c)$, it is much more convenient to obtain them from a common pool of *class-independent* features $g_k(I)$, as follows:

$$f_{d,k}(I, c) = \begin{cases} g_k(I) & \text{if } c = d, \\ 0 & \text{otherwise.} \end{cases}$$

Then we have

$$P(c|I) = \frac{1}{Z} \exp\left(\sum_{d,k} \lambda_{d,k} f_{d,k}(I, c)\right) = \frac{1}{Z} \exp\left(\sum_k \lambda_{c,k} g_k(I)\right).$$

Thus, "universal" features g_k become associated with class-specific weights $\lambda_{c,k}$. All our feature functions will be defined in this way. Note, however, that the exponential framework also allows completely different features for representing each class.

3   Texture Recognition

In this section, we describe the application of the maximum entropy framework to texture recognition. Section 3.1 describes our texton-based representation, and Section 3.2 discusses experiments on two large collections of texture images, the Brodatz database [4] and the UIUC database [13].

3.1   Feature Functions

For texture recognition, we use the sparse representation introduced in our earlier work [13], where the locations and shapes of salient image regions are found by a specialized keypoint detector. We use either a scale- or an affine-invariant detector (returning circular and elliptical regions, respectively), depending on the degree of invariance required by a particular database. Next, the extracted regions serve as domains of support for computing appearance-based descriptors (the specific choices of detectors and descriptors used in our experiments are discussed in Section 3.2). After descriptors have been extracted from the training set, a texton dictionary is formed by clustering them, and associating each cluster center with a discrete texton label. Finally, each descriptor from a new image is assigned the label of the closest cluster center.

The next step is to define the feature functions for the exponential model. For text classification, Nigam et al. [21] use scaled counts of word occurrences in a document. By analogy, we define feature functions based on texton frequencies:

$$g_k(I) = \frac{N_k(I)}{\sum_{k'} N_{k'}(I)},$$

where $N_k(I)$ is the number of times texton label k occurs in the image I. To enrich the feature set, we also define functions $g_{k,\ell}$ that encode the probability of co-occurrence of pairs of labels at nearby locations. Let $k \diamond \ell$ denote the event that a region labeled ℓ is adjacent to a region labeled k. Specifically, we say that $k \diamond \ell$ if the center of ℓ is contained in the neighborhood obtained by "growing" the shape (circle or ellipse) of the kth region by a constant factor (4 in the implementation). Let $N_{k \diamond \ell}(I)$ denote the number of times the relation occurs in the image I, and define

$$g_{k,\ell}(I) = \frac{N_{k \diamond \ell}(I)}{\sum_{k',\ell'} N_{k' \diamond \ell'}(I)}.$$

An image model incorporating co-occurrence counts of pairs of adjacent labels is a counterpart of a *bigram language model* that estimates the probabilities of two-word strings in natural text. Just as in language modeling, we must deal with sparse probability estimates due to many relations receiving extremely low counts in the training set. Thus, we are led to consider smoothing techniques for probability estimates [5]. One of the most basic techniques, interpolation with marginal probabilities, leads to the following modified definition of the co-occurrence features:

$$\tilde{g}_{k,\ell}(I) = (1 - \alpha)g_{k,\ell}(I) + \alpha\Big(\sum_{\ell'} g_{k,\ell'}(I)\Big)\Big(\sum_{k'} g_{k',\ell}(I)\Big),$$

where α is a constant (0.1 in our implementation). Informally, a co-occurrence relation $k \diamond \ell$ should have higher probability if both k and ℓ occur frequently in samples of the class, and if they each have many neighbors.

While smoothing addresses the problem of unreliable probability estimates, we are still left with millions of possible co-occurrence relations, and it is necessary to use feature selection to reduce the model to a manageable size. Possible feature selection techniques include greedy selection based on increase of likelihood under the exponential model [3], mutual information [7,21] and likelihood ratio [7]. However, since more frequently occurring relations yield more reliable estimates, we have chosen a simpler likelihood-based scheme: For each class, we find a fixed number of relations that have the highest probability in the training set, and then combine them into a global "relation dictionary."

3.2   Experimental Results

In this section, we show classification results on the Brodatz database (999 images: 111 classes, 9 samples per class) [4] and the UIUC database (1000 images: 25 classes, 40 samples per class) [13]. Figure 1 shows examples of images from the two databases. For the Brodatz database, we use a scale-invariant Laplacian detector [16], which finds salient blob-like circular regions in an image. This level of invariance is sufficient for the Brodatz database, which does not feature any significant geometric deformations between different samples from the same class. By contrast, the UIUC database contains arbitrary rotations, perspective

Brodatz texture database

UIUC texture database

Fig. 1. Examples of five classes each from the Brodatz database (top) and the UIUC database (bottom). The UIUC database is publicly available at http://www-cvr.ai.uiuc.edu/ponce_grp/data.

distortions and non-rigid deformations. This greater degree of geometric variability requires a greater degree of invariance in the low-level features. Therefore, we process the UIUC database with an affinely adapted version of the Laplacian detector, which returns elliptical regions. In both cases, the appearance of the detected regions is represented using SIFT descriptors [17]. The SIFT descriptor consists of gradient orientation histograms within the support region. For each of 8 orientation planes, the gradient image is sampled over a 4 × 4 grid of locations, thus resulting in a 128-dimensional feature vector. We have chosen to use SIFT descriptors because of their impressive performance in a recent comparative evaluation [20].

To form the texton dictionary, we run K-means clustering on a randomly selected subset of all training descriptors. To limit the memory requirements of the K-means algorithm, we cluster each class separately and concatenate the resulting textons. We find $K = 10$ and $K = 40$ textons per class for the Brodatz and the UIUC database, respectively, resulting in dictionaries of size 1110 and 1000. For co-occurrence relations, we select $10K$ features per class; because the relations selected for different classes sometimes coincide, the total number of $g_{k,\ell}$ features is slightly less than ten times the total number of textons.

Table 1 shows a comparison of classification rates obtained using various methods on the two databases. All the rates are averaged over 10 runs with different randomly selected training subsets; standard deviations of the rates are also reported. The training set consists of 3 (resp. 10) images per class for the Brodatz (resp. UIUC) database. The first row shows results for a popular baseline method using nearest-neighbor classification of texton histograms with the χ^2 distance (for an example of such an approach, see, e.g., [25]). The second row shows results for a Naive Bayes baseline using the *multinomial event model* [19]:

Table 1. Texture classification results (see text)

	Brodatz database		UIUC database	
	Mean (%)	Std. dev.	Mean (%)	Std. dev.
χ^2	83.09	1.18	94.25	0.59
Naive Bayes	85.84	0.90	94.08	0.67
Exp. g_k	87.37	1.04	97.41	0.64
Exp. $g_{k,\ell}$	75.20	1.34	92.40	0.93
Exp. $g_k + g_{k,\ell}$	83.44	1.17	97.19	0.57
Exp. $\tilde{g}_{k,\ell}$	80.51	1.09	95.85	0.62
Exp. $g_k + \tilde{g}_{k,\ell}$	83.36	1.14	97.09	0.47

$$P(I|c) = \prod_k P(k|c)^{N_k(I)},$$

where $P(k|c)$ is given by the frequency of texton k in the training images for class c. The results for the two baseline methods on the Brodatz database are comparable, though Naive Bayes has a potential advantage over the χ^2 method, since it does not treat the training samples as independent prototypes, but combines them in order to compute the probabilities $P(k|c)$. This may help to account for the slightly better performance of Naive Bayes on the Brodatz database. The third and fourth rows show results for exponential models based on individual g_k (textons only) features and $g_{k,\ell}$ (relations only) features, respectively, and the fifth row shows results for the exponential model with both kinds of features combined. For both databases, the texton-only exponential model performs much better than the two baseline methods; the relations-only models are inferior to the baseline. Interestingly, combining textons and relations does not improve performance. To test whether this is due to overfitting, we compare performance of the $g_{k,\ell}$ features with the smoothed $\tilde{g}_{k,\ell}$ features (last two rows). While the smoothed features do perform better, combining them with textons-only features once again does not bring any improvement. Thus, texton-only features clearly supercede the co-occurrence relations.

To get a more detailed look at the performance of the exponential model, refer to Figure 2, which shows the histograms of classification rates achieved by the parts-only exponential model for individual classes. With this model, 100% recognition rate is achieved by 61 classes from the Brodatz database and by 8 classes from the UIUC database. The distribution of classification rates, in particular for the Brodatz database, suggests another reason (besides overfitting) for the lack of improvement afforded by co-occurrence features. Namely, most classes in the database can be represented quite well without taking texton co-occurrences into account, while a few are either extremely nonhomogeneous or extremely perceptually similar to another class. Consequently, adding relations to the exponential model cannot improve the recognition of either the "easy" or the "difficult" classes.

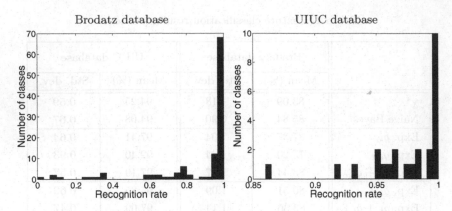

Fig. 2. Histograms of classification rates for the exponential parts-only model for the Brodatz database (left) and the UIUC database (right)

Overall, the g_k exponential model performs the best for both texture databases. For the Brodatz database, our result of 87.37% is comparable to the rate of 87.44% reported in [13]. Note, however, that the result of [13] was obtained using a combination of appearance- and shape-based features. In our case, we use only appearance-based features, so we get as much discriminative power with a weaker representation. For the UIUC database, our result of 97.41% exceeds the highest rate reported in [13], that of 92.61%.

4   Object Recognition

In this section, we describe our approach to object recognition using *semi-local parts* and present results of experiments on two challenging datasets: the CalTech dataset [8] consisting of airplanes, cars, faces, and motorbikes; and a bird dataset that we have collected, consisting of images of six different species.

4.1   Semi-local Parts

For our texture recognition experiments, Laplacian region detectors have proven to be successful. However, we have found them to be much less satisfactory for detecting object parts with complex internal structures, e.g., eyes, wheels, heads, etc. Instead, for object recognition, we have implemented the scale-invariant detector of Jurie and Schmid [11], which finds salient circular configurations of edge points, and is robust to clutter and texture variations inside the regions. Just as in Section 3, the appearance of the extracted regions is represented using SIFT descriptors.

For each object class, we construct a dictionary of composite *semi-local parts* [15], or groups of several nearby regions whose appearance and spatial configuration occurs repeatably in the training set. The key idea is that consistent occurrence of (approximately) rigid groups of simple features in multiple images is very unlikely to be accidental, and must thus be a strong cue for the presence of the object. Semi-local parts are found in a *weakly supervised* manner, i.e., from cluttered, unsegmented training images, via a direct search for visual correspondence.[2] The intractable problem of simultaneous alignment of multiple images is reduced to pairwise matching: *Candidate parts* are initialized by matching several training pairs and then *validated* against additional images.

The key operation of two-image matching is accomplished efficiently with the help of strong appearance (descriptor similarity) and geometric consistency constraints. Specifically, initial constraints on descriptor similarity are used to create a short list of *potential matches* for each region in the other image; semi-local neighborhood constraints [9,23] reduce the set of all potential matches even further. Then, starting from the smallest possible *seed group* of nearby matches that allows us to estimate an aligning transformation, we conduct a greedy search for additional geometrically and photometrically consistent matches lying in the neighborhood of the current group. The aligning transformation can be scaling, similarity, or affine. Originally, we have introduced semi-local parts in the context of an affine alignment model [15]; however, for the two databases used in this chapter, scale and translation invariance are sufficient. Note that in the implementation, we treat all transformation groups within the same computational framework. Namely, we use linear least squares to estimate an affine alignment between the two groups of regions, and then enforce additional geometric constraints by rejecting any alignment that deviates too much from the desired model. In particular, for a scale-and-translation model, we reject transformations that include too much skew, rotation, and anisotropic scaling. The correspondence search terminates when the residual of the transformation grows too large, or when no further consistent matches can be found. Note that the number of regions in the correspondence (the size of the part) is determined automatically as a result.

In existing literature, similar procedures for growing groups of matches based on geometric and appearance consistency have been successfully applied to the recognition of the same object instance in multiple views [9]; one of the key insights of our earlier work [15] is that such procedures are also quite effective for building models of object classes with substantial intra-class variation. Because of the strong geometric and photometric consistency constraints that must be satisfied by semi-local parts, they are much more discriminative than atomic parts, and much less likely to give rise to false detections.

A detected instance of a candidate part in a validation image may have multiple regions missing because of occlusion, failure of the keypoint detector, etc. We define the *repeatability* $\rho_k(I)$ of a detected instance of part k in image I as the number of regions in that instance normalized by the total number of regions in that part. If no instances of part k are detected at all, we have $\rho_k(I) = 0$, and if several instances are detected, we simply select the one with the highest

---

[2] See [2] for another recent approach to object recognition that shares our emphasis on geometric correspondence.

repeatability. This implicitly assumes that an object can contain at most one instance of each part. In the future, we plan to improve our feature representation to allow for multiple detected instances of the same part. This would allow us to perform more accurate localization for classes such as cars (which have two wheels) or faces (which have two eyes).

After recording the repeatability values for a given part in all positive and negative validation images, we compute a *validation score* for the part by taking the χ^2 distance between h_p, the histogram of repeatabilities of the part over the positive class, and h_n, the histogram of its repeatabilities in all the negative images (for examples of these histograms, see Figures 5(b) and 7(b)). The χ^2 distance is defined as follows:

$$d(h_p, h_n) = \frac{1}{2} \sum_{b=1}^{B} \frac{\left(h_p(b) - h_n(b)\right)^2}{h_p(b) + h_n(b)},$$

where B is the number of bins (discrete repeatability levels) in the histograms, and $h_p(b)$ (resp. $h_n(b)$) is the proportion of all part detections in positive (resp. negative) images falling into the bin with index b. The validation score can range from 1, when the two histograms have no overlap at all, to 0, when they are identical. A fixed number of highest-scoring parts is retained for each class, and their union forms our dictionary.

Finally, for each part k and each training image I, we compute a normalized feature function based on its repeatability:

$$g_k(I) = \frac{\rho_k(I)}{\sum_{k'} \rho_{k'}(I)}.$$

Just as in our texture recognition experiments, we also investigate whether, and to what extent, incorporating relations into the object representation improves classification performance. To this end, we define *overlap* relations between pairs of parts that belong to the same class. Let $\omega_{k,\ell}(I)$ be the overlap between detected instances of parts k and ℓ in the image I, i.e., the ratio of the intersection of the two parts to their union. This ratio ranges from 0 (disjoint parts) to 1 (coincident parts). Then we define

$$g_{k,\ell}(I) = \frac{\omega_{k,\ell}(I)}{\sum_{k',\ell'} \omega_{k',\ell'}(I)}.$$

The overlap relations are very flexible — in effect, they enforce only spatial coherence. This flexibility potentially allows us to deal with non-rigid and/or articulated objects. In the future, we plan to experiment with more elaborate relations that take into account the distance, relative scale, or relative orientations of the two parts [1]. Finally, it is important to note that we currently do not use feature selection techniques to reduce the number of overlap relations within the exponential model. Because of the small size of the part dictionaries used in the experiments presented in the next section (namely, 20 parts per class), the resulting number of overlap relations (190 per class) is quite manageable, unlike in our texture recognition experiments, where we had to contend with millions of potential co-occurrence relations.

Fig. 3. One example image per class for the CalTech database (top) and the birds database (bottom). The birds database is publicly available at http://www-cvr.ai.uiuc.edu/ponce_grp/data.

4.2 Experimental Results

This section presents recognition results obtained on two multi-class object databases. The first is a subset of the publicly available CalTech database [8]. We have taken 300 images each from four classes: airplanes, rear views of cars, faces, and motorbikes (Figure 3, top). The second database, which we collected from the Web, consists of 100 images each of six different classes of birds: egrets, mandarin ducks, snowy owls, puffins, toucans, and wood ducks (Figure 3, bottom). For the CalTech database, 50 randomly chosen images per class are used for creating candidate parts. Each image is paired up to two others, for a total of 100 initialization pairs. Of the several hundred candidate parts yielded by this matching process, the 50 largest ones are retained for training and selection. Candidate parts are then matched against every image from another training set, which also contains 50 randomly chosen images per class, and 20 highest-scoring parts per class are retained to form the part dictionary. The repeatability results of the selected parts on this training set are also used as training data to estimate the parameters of the exponential model. Finally, the remaining 200 images per class make up the test set. We follow the same protocol for the bird dataset, except that 20 images per class are used for finding candidate parts, another 30 for part selection, and the remaining 50 for testing. Unlike the texture recognition results of Section 3.2, the results of this section are not averaged over multiple splits of the databases because of the considerably larger computational expense involved in computing semi-local parts. With our current unoptimized MATLAB implementation, a single run through an entire object database (both training and testing) takes about a week.

Figures 5 and 7 illustrate training and part selection. As can be seen from the plots of validation scores for all selected parts, the quality of part dictionaries found for different classes varies widely. Extremely stable, salient parts are formed for faces, motorbikes, and ducks. The classes with the weakest parts are airplanes for the CalTech database and egrets for the bird database. Both airplanes and egrets lack characteristic texture, and often appear against busy backgrounds that generate a lot of detector responses (buildings, people, and airport machinery in case of planes, or grass and branches in case of egrets). In addition, both egrets and airplanes are "thin" objects, so the local regions that overlap the object also capture a lot of background. Thus, the SIFT descriptors computed over these regions end up describing mostly clutter. To alleviate this problem, we plan to experiment with alternative descriptors that capture the shape of the edges close to the boundary of the scale-invariant regions [11], as opposed to the internal texture, as the SIFT descriptor does. Note that our part selection framework is suitable for choosing between semi-local parts based on different descriptors, since it abstracts from the low-level details of matching (i.e., how appearance similarity is computed, what aligning transformation is used, or how the correspondence search is performed), and looks only at the end result of the matching on the training set (i.e., how repeatable the resulting parts are, and whether they can be used to distinguish between positive and negative examples for a given class).

The parts obtained for classes other than airplanes and egrets have higher scores and capture much more salient object features. Interestingly, though, for cars, even the highest-scoring part includes spurious background detections along the horizontal line at the eye level of the image. This comes from the relative visual monotony of the car class: all the rear views of cars were apparently captured through the windshield by a person in the front seat. Thus, the "horizon" formed by the converging sides of the road is approximately in the same location in all the images, and the scenery at the roadside (trees, buildings) gives rise to a lot of features in stable positions that are consistently picked up by the matching procedure.

Tables 2 and 3 show classification performance of several methods with 20 parts per class. The first column of the tables shows the performance of a baseline Naive Bayes approach with likelihood given by

$$P(I|c) = \prod_k P\left(\rho_k(I)|c\right) .$$

The distributions $P(\rho_k|c)$ are found by histogramming the repeatabilities of part k on all training images from class c. Note that we take into account the repeatability of parts on images from *all* classes, not only the class which they describe. Roughly speaking, we expect $P(\rho_k(I)|c)$ to be high if part k describes class c and $\rho_k(I)$ is high, or if part k *does not* describe class c and $\rho_k(I)$ is low or zero. Thus, to conclude that an object from class c is present in the image, we not only have to observe high-repeatability detections of parts from class c, but also low-repeatability detections of parts from other classes. The exponential model, which encodes the same information in its feature functions, also uses this reasoning.

Table 2. Classification rates for the CalTech database using 20 parts per class

CalTech database	Naive Bayes	Exp. parts	Exp. relations	Exp. parts & relations
Airplanes	98.0	88.0	78.0	87.5
Cars (rear)	95.5	99.5	90.5	99.5
Faces	96.5	98.5	96.5	98.0
Motorbikes	97.5	99.5	83.0	99.5
All classes	96.88	96.38	87.0	96.13

Table 3. Classification rates for the birds database using 20 parts per class

Birds database	Naive Bayes	Exp. parts	Exp. relations	Exp. parts & relations
Egret	68	90	72	88
Mandarin	66	90	66	90
Snowy owl	66	98	52	96
Puffin	88	94	94	94
Toucan	88	82	82	82
Wood duck	96	100	86	100
All classes	78.67	92.33	75.33	91.67

The second (resp. third, fourth) columns of Tables 2 and 3 show the classification performance obtained with exponential models using the g_k features only (resp. the $g_{k,\ell}$ only, g_k and $g_{k,\ell}$ combined). For the CalTech database, the

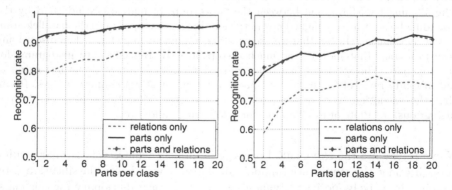

Fig. 4. Classification rate (exp. parts) as a function of dictionary size: CalTech database (left), birds database (right). For the CalTech database, because three of the four classes have extremely strong and redundant parts, performance increases very little as more parts are added. For the bird database, diminishing returns set in as progressively weaker parts are added.

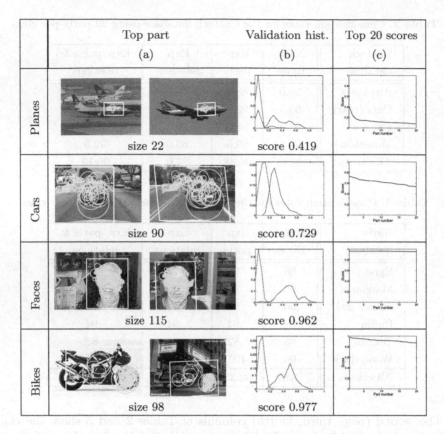

	Top part (a)	Validation hist. (b)	Top 20 scores (c)
Planes	size 22	score 0.419	
Cars	size 90	score 0.729	
Faces	size 115	score 0.962	
Bikes	size 98	score 0.977	

Fig. 5. Learning part vocabularies for the CalTech database. (a) The highest-scoring part for each class. The two training images that were originally matched to obtain the part are shown side by side, with the matched regions (yellow circles) superimposed. The aligning transformation between the two groups of matches is indicated by the bounding boxes: the axis-aligned box in the left image is mapped onto the parallelogram in the right image. (Recall that we use an affine alignment model and then discard any transformation that induces too much distortion.) (b) Repeatability histograms for the top part. The solid red line (resp. dashed blue line) indicates the histogram of repeatability rates of the part in all positive (resp. negative) training images. Recall that the validation score of the part is given by the χ^2 distance between the two histograms. (c) Plots of top 20 part scores following validation.

Naive Bayes and the exponential parts-only models achieve very similar results, though under the exponential model, airplanes have a lower classification rate, which is intuitively more satisfying given the poor part dictionary for this class. Note that our classification accuracy of over 96% on the four CalTech classes is comparable to other recently published results [6,7]. For the bird database, the exponential model outperforms Naive Bayes; for both databases, relations-only features alone perform considerably worse than the parts-only features, and

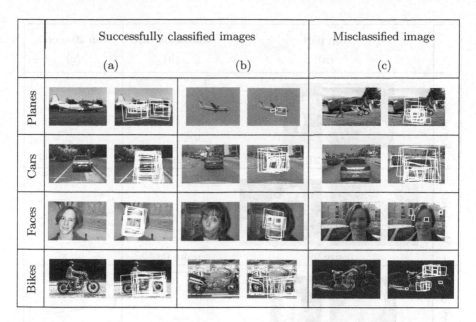

Fig. 6. CalTech results. (a), (b) Two examples of correctly classified images per class. Left of each column: original image. Right of each column: transformed bounding boxes of all detected part instances for the given class superimposed on the image. (c) Examples of misclassified images. Note that localization is poor for airplanes and very good for faces (notice the example a changed facial expression). For motorbikes, the front wheel is particularly salient. Out of the entire test set, only one bike image was misclassified, and it is one in which the front wheel is not properly visible.

combining parts-based with relation-based features brings no improvement. Figure 4 shows a plot of the classification rate for the exponential model as a function of part dictionary size. Note that the curves are not monotonic — adding a part to the dictionary can decrease performance. This behavior may be an artifact of our scoring function for part selection, which is not directly related to classification performance. In the future, we plan to experiment with part selection based on increase of likelihood under the exponential model [3].

Though we did not conduct a quantitative evaluation of localization accuracy, the reader may get a qualitative idea by examining Figures 6 and 8, which show examples of part detection on several test images. A poorer part vocabulary for a class tends to lead to poorer localization quality, though this is not necessarily reflected in lower classification rates. Specifically, an object class represented by a relatively poor part vocabulary may still achieve a high classification rate, provided that parts for other classes do not generate too many false positives on images from this class. The second airplane example in Figure 6 is a good illustration of this phenomenon: only three airplane parts are detected in this image, yet the airplane is recognized correctly since the image does not contain enough clutter to generate false detections of parts from other classes.

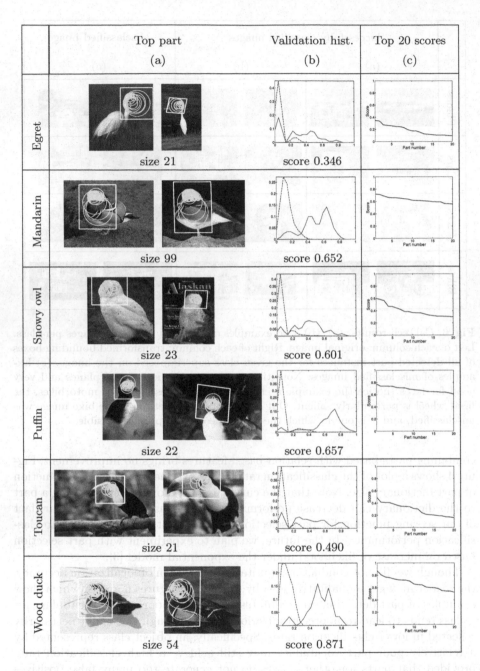

Fig. 7. Learning part vocabularies for the birds database. (a) The highest-scoring part for each class superimposed on the two original training images. (b) Validation repeatability histograms for the top parts. (c) Plots of validation scores for the top 20 parts from each class.

Successfully classified images		Misclassified image
(a)	(b)	(c)

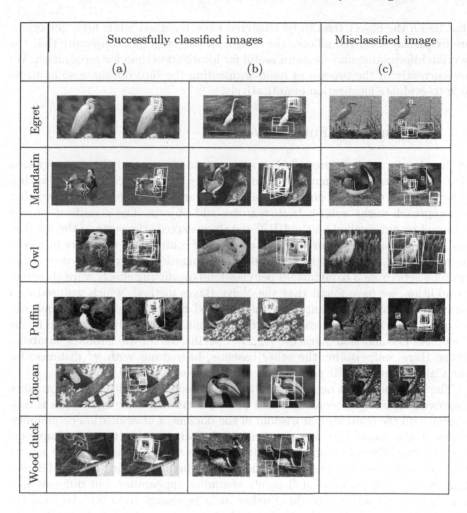

Fig. 8. Birds database results. (a), (b) Two examples of successfully classified images per class. The original test image is on the left, and on the right is the image with superimposed bounding boxes of all detected part instances for the given class. Notice that localization is fairly good for mandarin and wood ducks (the head is the most distinctive feature). Though owl parts are more prone to false positives, they do capture salient characteristics of the class: the head, the eye, and the pattern of the feathers on the breast and wings. (c) Misclassified examples. The wood duck class has no example because it achieved 100% classification rate.

Perhaps the most suprising finding of our experiments is that inter-part relations do not improve classification performance. From examining the part detection examples in Figures 6 and 8, it seems intuitively clear that the pattern of overlap of different part instances encodes useful information: the part detections that lie on the object tend to be clustered close together, while false detections are frequently scattered all over the image. At this stage, we conjecture that the overlap information may be more useful for localization than for recognition. We are currently in the process of hand-segmenting the bird database so as to be able to evaluate localization quantitatively.

5   Summary and Future Work

In this chapter, we have presented an approach to texture and object recognition that uses a visual dictionary of textons or object parts in combination with a discriminative maximum entropy framework. Our experiments have shown that the approach works well for both textures and objects. The classification rate achieved by our method on the UIUC database exceeds the state of the art [13], and our results on the four CalTech classes are comparable to others in recent literature [6,7]. Interestingly, while all our recognition experiments used small training sets (from 3 to 50 images per class), no overfitting effects were observed. In addition, we have found that the Naive Bayes method, which we used as a baseline to evaluate the improvement provided by the exponential model, can be quite powerful in some cases — a finding that is frequently expresssed in the document classification literature [19,21]. Specifically, for the Brodatz database, Naive Bayes outperforms the other baseline, histograms with χ^2 distance; for the CalTech database, it performs as well as the exponential model.

The most important negative result of this chapter is the lack of performance improvement from co-occurrence and overlap relations. Once again, this is consistent with the conventional wisdom in the document classification community, where it was found that for document-level discrimination tasks, a simple orderless "bag-of-words" representtentation is effective. For textures, we expect that co-occurrence features may be helpful for distinguishing between different textures that consist of local elements of similar appearance, but different spatial layouts. To investigate this further, it is necessary to collect larger-scale, more difficult texture databases that include a wider variety of classes. For object recognition, the lack of improvement can be ascribed, at least partly, to the weakness of our overlap relations, especially compared to the strong geometric consistency constraints encoded within semi-local parts. In the future, we plan to investigate geometric relations that capture more discriminative information, and to test their behavior for classification on additional object databases.

Acknowledgments

This research was supported by Toyota, NSF grants IIS-0308087 and IIS-0312438, the European project LAVA (IST-2001-34405), and the CNRS-UIUC Collaboration Agreement.

References

1. S. Agarwal and D. Roth, "Learning a Sparse Representation for Object Detection," In *Proc. ECCV* 2002, vol. 4, pp. 113-130.
2. A. Berg, T. Berg, and J. Malik, "Shape Matching and Object Recognition Using Low-Distortion Correspondence," In *Proc. CVPR* 2005.
3. A. Berger, S. Della Pietra, and V. Della Pietra, "A Maximum Entropy Approach to Natural Language Processing," *Computational Linguistics* 22(1):39–71, 1996.
4. P. Brodatz, *Textures: A Photographic Album for Artists and Designers*, Dover, New York, 1966.
5. S. Chen and J. Goodman, "An Empirical Study of Smoothing Techniques for Language Modeling," In *Proc. Conf. of the Association for Computational Linguistics* 1996, pp. 310-318.
6. G. Csurka, C. Bray, C. Dance, and L. Fan, "Visual Categorization with Bags of Keypoints," In *ECCV Workshop on Statistical Learning in Computer Vision* 2004.
7. G. Dorko and C. Schmid, "Selection of Scale-Invariant Parts for Object Class Recognition," In *Proc. ICCV* 2003, vol. I, pp. 634-640.
8. R. Fergus, P. Perona, and A. Zisserman, "Object Class Recognition by Unsupervised Scale-Invariant Learning," In *Proc. CVPR* 2003, vol. II, pp. 264-271.
9. V. Ferrari, T. Tuytelaars, and L. Van Gool, "Simultaneous object recognition and segmentation by image exploration," In *Proc. ECCV* 2004.
10. J. Jeon and R. Manmatha, "Using Maximum Entropy for Automatic Image Annotation," In *Proc. Conf. on Image and Video Retrieval* 2004, pp. 24-32.
11. F. Jurie and C. Schmid, "Scale-invariant Shape Features for Recognition of Object Categories," In *Proc. CVPR* 2004.
12. D. Keysers, F. Och, and H. Ney, "Maximum Entropy and Gaussian Models for Image Object Recognition," *DAGM Symposium for Pattern Recognition* 2002.
13. S. Lazebnik, C. Schmid, and J. Ponce, "A Sparse Texture Representation Using Local Affine Regions," *IEEE Trans. PAMI* 27(8): 1265-1278, 2005.
14. S. Lazebnik, C. Schmid, and J. Ponce, "A Maximum Entropy Framework for Part-Based Texture and Object Recognition," In *Proc. ICCV* 2005, to appear.
15. S. Lazebnik, C. Schmid, and J. Ponce, "Semi-local Affine Parts for Object Recognition," In *Proc. BMVC* 2004.
16. T. Lindeberg, "Feature Detection with Automatic Scale Selection," *IJCV* 30(2):77-116, 1998.
17. D. Lowe, "Distinctive image features from scale-invariant keypoints," *IJCV* 60(2):91-110, 2004.
18. S. Mahamud, M. Hebert, and J. Lafferty, "Combining Simple Discriminators for Object Discrimination," *ECCV 2002*.
19. A. McCallum and K. Nigam, "A Comparison of Event Models for Naive Bayes Text Classification," *AAAI-98 Workshop on Learning for Text Categorization* 1998, pp. 41-48.
20. K. Mikolajczyk and C. Schmid, "A performance evaluation of local descriptors," In *Proc. CVPR* 2003, vol. 2, pp. 257-263.
21. K. Nigam, J. Lafferty, and A. McCallum, "Using Maximum Entropy for Text Classification," *IJCAI Workshop on Machine Learning for Information Filtering* 1999, pp. 61-67.
22. F. Rothganger, S. Lazebnik, C. Schmid, and J. Ponce, "3D object modeling and recognition using local affine-invariant image descriptors and multi-view spatial constraints," *IJCV*, 2005, to appear.

23. J. Sivic and A. Zisserman, "Video Google: A Text Retrieval Approach to Object Matching in Videos," In *Proc. ICCV* 2003, pp. 1470-1477.
24. J. Sivic, B. Russell, A. Efros, A. Zisserman, and W. Freeman, "Discovering objects and their location in images," In *Proc. ICCV* 2005, to appear.
25. M. Varma and A. Zisserman, "Texture Classification: Are Filter Banks Necessary?" In *Proc. CVPR* 2003, vol. 2, pp. 691-698.
26. M. Weber, M. Welling, and P. Perona, "Unsupervised learning of models for recognition," In *Proc. ECCV* 2000, vol. 1, pp. 18–32.
27. J. Willamowski, D. Arregui, G. Csurka, C. R. Dance, and L. Fan, "Categorizing nine visual classes using local appearance descriptors," In *International Workshop on Learning for Adaptable Visual Systems*, 2004.
28. S.C. Zhu, Y.N. Wu, and D. Mumford, "Filters, Random Fields, and Maximum Entropy (FRAME): Towards a Unified Theory for Texture Modeling," *IJCV* 27(2):1-20, 1998.

A Sparse Object Category Model for Efficient Learning and Complete Recognition

Rob Fergus[1], Pietro Perona[2], and Andrew Zisserman[1]

[1] Dept. of Engineering Science
University of Oxford
Parks Road, Oxford
OX1 3PJ, U.K.
{fergus,az}@robots.ox.ac.uk
[2] Dept. of Electrical Engineering
California Institute of Technology
MC 136–93, Pasadena
CA 91125, U.S.A.
perona@vision.caltech.edu

Abstract. We present a "parts and structure" model for object category recognition that can be learnt efficiently and in a weakly-supervised manner: the model is learnt from example images containing category instances, without requiring segmentation from background clutter.

The model is a sparse representation of the object, and consists of a star topology configuration of parts modeling the output of a variety of feature detectors. The optimal choice of feature types (whose repertoire includes interest points, curves and regions) is made automatically.

In recognition, the model may be applied efficiently in a complete manner, bypassing the need for feature detectors, to give the globally optimal match within a query image. The approach is demonstrated on a wide variety of categories, and delivers both successful classification and localization of the object within the image.

1 Introduction

A variety of models and methods exist for representing, learning and recognizing object categories in images. Many of these are variations on the "Parts and Structure" model introduced by Fischler and Elschlager [10], though the modern instantiations use scale-invariant image fragments [1,2,3,12,15,20,21]. The constellation model [3,8,21] was the first to convincingly demonstrate that models could be learnt from weakly-supervised unsegmented training images (i.e. the only supervision information was that the image contained an instance of the object category, but not the location of the instance in the image). Various types of categories could be modeled, including those specified by tight spatial configurations (such as cars) and those specified by tight appearance exemplars (such as spotted cats). The model was translation and scale invariant both in learning and in recognition.

J. Ponce et al. (Eds.): Toward Category-Level Object Recognition, LNCS 4170, pp. 443–461, 2006.
© Springer-Verlag Berlin Heidelberg 2006

However, the Constellation model of [8] has some serious short-comings, namely: (i) The joint nature of the shape model results in an exponential explosion in computational cost, limiting the number of parts and regions per image that can be handled. For N feature detections, and P model parts the complexity for both learning and recognition is $O(N^P)$; (ii) Since only 20-30 regions per image and 6 parts are permitted by this complexity, the model can only learn from an incredibly sparse representation of the image. Good performance is therefore highly dependent on the consistent firing of the feature detector; (iii) Only one type of feature detector (a region operator) was used, making the model very sensitive to the nature of the class. If the distinctive features of the category happen, say, to be edge-based then relying on a region-based detector is likely to give poor results (though this limitation was overcome in later work [9]); (iv) The model has many parameters resulting in over-fitting unless a large number of training images (typically 200+) are used.

Other models and methods have since been developed which have achieved superior performance to the constellation model on at least a subset of the object categories modeled in [8]. These models range from bag-of-word models (where the words are vector quantized invariant descriptors) with no spatial organization [5,18], through to fragment based models [2,15] with particular spatial configurations. The methods utilize a range of machine learning approaches EM, SVMs and Adaboost.

In this paper we propose a heterogeneous star model (HSM) which maintains the simple training requirements of the constellation model, and also, like the constellation model, gives a localization for the recognized object. The model is translation and scale invariant both in learning and in recognition. There are three main areas of innovation: (i) both in learning and recognition it has a lower complexity than the constellation model. This enables both the number of parts and the number of detected features to be increased substantially; (ii) it is heterogeneous and is able to make the optimum selection of feature types (here from a pool of three, including curves). This enables it to better model objects with significant intra-class variation in appearance, but less variation in outline (for example a guitar), or vice-versa; (iii) The recognition stage can use feature detectors or can be complete in the manner of Felzenswalb and Huttenlocher [6]. In the latter case there is no actual detection stage. Rather the model itself defines the areas of most relevance using a matched filter. This complete search overcomes many false negatives due to feature drop out, and also poor localizations due to small feature displacement and scale errors.

2   Approach

We describe here the structure of the heterogeneous star model, how it is learnt from training data, and how it is applied to test data for recognition.

2.1 Star Model

As in the constellation model of [8], our model has P parts and parameters θ. From each image i, we extract N features with locations $\mathbf{X}^i$; scales $\mathbf{S}^i$ and descriptors $\mathbf{D}^i$. In learning, the aim is to find the value of θ that maximizes the log-likelihood over all images:

$$\sum_i \log\, p(\mathbf{X}^i, \mathbf{D}^i, \mathbf{S}^i | \theta) \tag{1}$$

Since $N \gg P$, we introduce an assignment variable, $\mathbf{h}$, to assign features to parts in the model. The log-likelihood is obtained by marginalizing over $\mathbf{h}$.

$$\sum_i \log \sum_{\mathbf{h}} p(\mathbf{X}^i, \mathbf{D}^i, \mathbf{S}^i, \mathbf{h} | \theta) \tag{2}$$

In the constellation model, the joint density is factored as:

$$p(\mathbf{X}^i, \mathbf{D}^i, \mathbf{S}^i, \mathbf{h} | \theta) = \underbrace{p(\mathbf{D}^i | \mathbf{h}, \theta)}_{Appearance}\, \underbrace{p(\mathbf{X}^i | \mathbf{S}^i, \mathbf{h}, \theta)}_{Rel.\ Locations}\, \underbrace{p(\mathbf{S}^i | \mathbf{h}, \theta)}_{Rel.\ Scale}\, \underbrace{p(\mathbf{h} | \theta)}_{Occlusion} \tag{3}$$

In [8], the appearance model for each part is assumed independent but the relative location of the model parts is represented by a joint Gaussian density. While this provides the most thorough description, it makes the location of all parts dependent on one another. Consequently, the EM-based learning scheme, which entails marginalizing over $p(\mathbf{h} | \mathbf{X}^i, \mathbf{D}^i, \mathbf{S}^i, \theta)$, becomes an $O(N^P)$ operation. We propose here a simplified configuration model in which the location of

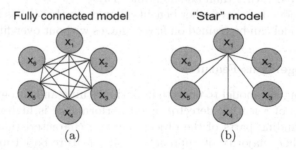

Fig. 1. (a) Fully-connected six part shape model. Each node is a model part while the edges represent the dependencies between parts. **(b)** A six part Star model. The former has complexity $O(N^P)$ while the latter has complexity $O(N^2 P)$ which may be further improved in recognition by the use of distance-transforms [6] to $O(NP)$.

the model part is conditioned on the location of a *landmark* part. Under this model the non-landmark parts are independent of one another given the landmark. In graphical model terms, this is a tree of depth one, with the landmark part being the root node. We call this the "star" model. A similar model, where the reference frame acts as a landmark is used by Lowe [16] and was studied in a probabilistic framework by Moreels *et al.* [17]. Figure 1 illustrates the differences between the full and star models. In the star model the joint probability of the configuration aspect of the model may be factored as:

$$p(\mathbf{X}|\mathbf{S}, \mathbf{h}, \theta) = p(\mathbf{x}_L|h_L) \prod_{j \neq L} p(\mathbf{x}_j|\mathbf{x}_L, s_L, h_j, \theta_j) \qquad (4)$$

where $\mathbf{x}_j$ is the position of part j and L is the landmark part. We adopt a Gaussian model for $p(\mathbf{x}_j|\mathbf{x}_L, s_L, h_j, \theta_j)$ which depends only on the relative position and scale between each part and the landmark. The reduced dependencies of this model mean that the marginalization in Eqn. 2 is $O(N^2P)$, in theory allowing us to cope with a larger N and P in learning and recognition.

In practical terms, we can achieve translation invariance by subtracting the location of the landmark part from the non-landmark ones. Scale invariance is achieved by dividing the location of the non-landmark parts by the locally measured scale of the landmark part.

It is useful to examine what has been lost in the star compared to the constellation model of [8]. In the star model any of the leaf (i.e. non-landmark) parts can be occluded, but (as discussed below) we impose the condition that the landmark part must always be present. With small N this can lead to a model with artificially high variance, but as N increases this ceases to be a problem (since the landmark is increasingly likely to actually be detected). In the constellation model any or several parts can be occluded. This is a powerful feature: not only does it make the model robust to the inadequacies of the feature detector but it also assists the convergence properties of the model by enabling a subset of the parts to be fitted rather than all simultaneously.

The star model does have other benefits though, in that it has less parameters so that the model can be trained on fewer images without over-fitting occurring.

2.2   Heterogeneous Features

By constraining the model to operate in both learning and recognition from the sparse outputs of a feature detector, good performance is highly dependent on the detector finding parts of the object that are characteristic and distinctive of the class. The majority of approaches using feature-based methods rely on region detectors such as Kadir and Brady or multi-scale Harris [11,13] which favour interest points or circular regions. However, for certain classes such as bottles or mugs, the outline of the object is more informative than the textured regions on the interior. Curves have been used to a limited extent in previous models for object categories, for example both Fergus *et al.* [9] and Jurie & Schmid [12] introduce curves as a feature type. However, in both cases the model was constrained to being homogeneous, i.e. consisting only of curves. Here the models can utilize a combination of different features detectors, the optimal selection being made automatically. This makes the scheme far more tolerant to the type of category to be learnt.

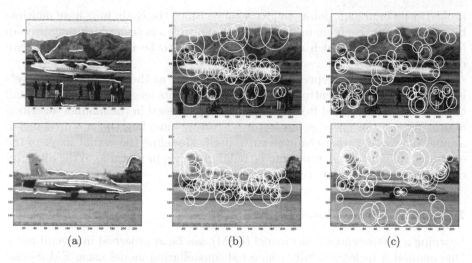

Fig. 2. Output of three different feature detectors on two airplane images. **(a)** Curves.
(b) Kadir & Brady. **(c)** Multi-scale Harris.

In our scheme, we have a choice of three feature types: Kadir & Brady; multi-scale Harris and Curves. Figure 2 shows examples of these 3 operators on two sample airplane images. The detectors were chosen since they are somewhat complementary in their properties: Kadir & Brady favours circular regions; multi-scale Harris prefers interest points, and curves locate the outline of the object.

To be able to learn different combinations of features we use the same representation for all types. Inspired by the performance of PCA-SIFT in region matching [14], we utilize a gradient-based PCA approach in contrast to the intensity-based PCA approach of [8]. Both the region operators give a location and scale for each feature. Each feature is cropped from the image (using a square mask); rescaled to a $k \times k$ patch; has its gradient computed and then normalized to remove intensity differences. Note that we do not perform any orientation normalization as in [14]. The outcome is a vector of length $2k^2$, with the first k elements representing the x derivative, and the second k the y derivatives. The derivatives are computed by symmetric finite difference (cropping to avoid edge effects).

The normalized gradient-patch is then projected into a fixed PCA basis[1] of d dimensions. Two additional measurements are made for each gradient-patch: its unnormalized energy and the reconstruction error between the point in the PCA basis and the original gradient-patch. Each region is thus represented by a vector of length $d + 2$.

Curve features are extracted in the same manner as [9]: a Canny edge detector is run over the image; the edgels are grouped into chains; each chain is then

---

[1] The fixed basis was computed from patches extracted using all Kadir and Brady regions found on all the training images of Motorbikes; Faces; Airplanes; Cars (Rear); Leopards and Caltech background.

broken at its bitangent points to give a curve. Since the chain may have multiple bitangent points, each chain may result in multiple curves (which may overlap in portions). Curves which are very straight tend to be uninformative and are discarded.

The curves are then represented in the same way as the regions. Each curve's location is taken as its centroid with the scale being its length. The region around the curve is then cropped from the image and processed in the manner described above. We use the curve as an feature detector, modeling the textured region around the curve, rather than the curve itself. Modeling the actual shape of the curve, as was done in [9], proved to be uninformative, in part due to the difficulty of extracting the contours consistently enough.

2.3   Learning the Model

Learning a heterogeneous star model (HSM) can be approached in several ways. One method is to learn a fully connected constellation model using EM [8] and then reduce the learnt spatial model to a star by completely trying out each of the parts as a landmark, and picking the one which gives the highest likelihood on the training data. The limitation of this approach is that the fully connected model can only handle a small number of parts and detections in learning. The second method, which we adopt, is to learn the HSM directly using EM as in [8,21], starting from randomly-chosen initial conditions, enabling the learning of many more parts and with more detections/image.

Due to the more flexible nature of the HSM, successful learning depends on a number of factors: To avoid combinatorics inherent in parameter space and to ensure the good convergence properties of the model, an ordering constraint is imposed on the locations of the model parts (e.g. the x-coordinates must be increasing). However, to enable the landmark part to select the most stable feature on the object (recall that we force it to always be present), the landmark is not subject to this constraint. Additionally, each part is only allowed to pick features of a pre-defined type and the ordering constraint only applies within parts of the same type. This avoids over-constraining the shape model. Imposing these constraints prevents exact marginalization in $O(N^2P)$, however by using efficient search methods, an approximation can be computed using all hypotheses within a threshold δ of the best hypothesis that obeys the constraint ($\delta = e^{-10}$ in our experiments). In Figure 3, the mean time per iteration per frame in learning is shown as N and P are varied. In Figure 3(a) P is fixed at 6 and N varied from 20 up to 200 while recording the mean time per image over all EM iterations in learning. The curve has a quadratic shape with the time per image still respectable even for $N = 200$. It should be noted that a full model cannot be learnt with $N > 25$ due to memory requirements. In Figure 3(b) N is fixed at 20 and P varied from 2 to 13 with the mean time per image plotted on a log-scale y-axis. The curve for the full model is a straight line as expected from the $O(N^P)$ complexity, stopping at $P = 7$ owing to the memory overhead. The

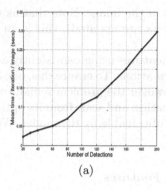
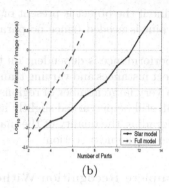

(a)   (b)

Fig. 3. Plots showing the learning time for a star model with different numbers of parts (P) and detections per image (N). (a) P fixed to 6 and N varied from 20 to 200. The curve has a quadratic shape, with a reasonable time even for $N = 200$. (b) N fixed to 20 and P varied from 2 to 13, with a logarithmic time axis. The full model is shown with a dashed line and the star model with a solid line. While both show roughly exponential behavior (i.e. linear in the log-domain), the star model's curve is much flatter than the full model.

star model's curve, while also roughly linear, has a much flatter gradient: a 12 part star model taking the same time to learn as a 6 part full model.

The optimal choice of feature types is made using a validation set. For each dataset, given a pre-defined number of parts, seven models each with different combinations of types are learnt: Kadir & Brady (KB); multi-Scale Harris (MSH); Curves (C); KB + MSH; KB + C; MSH + C; KB + MSH + C. In each case, the parts are split evenly between types. In cases where the dataset is small and the validation set would be too small to give an accurate estimate of the error, the performance on the training set was used to select the best combination.

Learning is fairly robust, except when a completely inappropriate choice of feature type was made in which case the model occasionally failed to converge, despite multiple re-runs. A major advantage of the HSM is the speed of learning. For a 6 part model with 20 detections/feature-type/image the HSM typically takes 10 minutes to converge, as opposed to the 24 hours of the fully connected model – roughly the same time as a 12 part, 100 detections/feature-type/image would with the HSM. Timings are for a 2Ghz Pentium 4.

2.4   Recognition Using Features

For the HSM, as with the fully connected Constellation Model of [8], recognition proceeds in a similar manner to the learning process. For a query image, regions/curves are first found using a feature detector. The learnt model is then applied to the regions/curves and the likelihood of the best hypothesis computed using the learnt model. This likelihood is then compared to a threshold to determine if the object is present or not in the image. Note that as no ordering constraint is needed (since no parameters are updated), this is an $O(N^2P)$ operation.

Good performance is dependent on the features firing consistently across different object instances and varying transformations. To ensure this, one approach is to use a very large number of regions, however the problem remains that each feature will still be perturbed slightly in location and scale from its optimal position so degrading the quality of the match obtainable by the model. We address these issues in the next section.

2.5   Complete Recognition Without Features

Relying on unbiased, crude feature detectors in learning is a necessary evil if we wish to learn without supervision: we have no prior knowledge of what may or may not be informative in the image but we need a sparse representation to reduce the complexity of the image sufficiently for the model learning to pick out consistent structure. However in recognition, the situation is different. Having learnt a model, the appearance densities model the regions of the image we wish to find. Our complete approach relies on these densities having distinctive mean and a sufficiently tight variance so that they can be used for soft template matching.

The scheme, based on Feltzenswalb and Huttenlocher [6], proceeds in two phases: first, the appearance densities are run completely over the entire image (and at different scales). At each location and scale, we compute the likelihood ratio for each part. Second, we take advantage of the Star model for location and employ the efficient matching scheme proposed by [6], which enables the global maximum of both appearance and location to be found within the image. The global match found is clearly superior to the maximum over a sparse set of regions. Additionally, it allows us to precisely localize the object (and its parts) within the image. See figure 4 for an example.

In more detail, each PCA basis vector is convolved with the image (employing appropriate normalizations), so projecting every patch in the image into the PCA basis. While this is expensive ($O(k^2N)$, where N is now the number of pixels in the image and k is the patch size) this only needs to be performed once regardless of the number of category models that will evaluate the image. For a given model, the likelihood ratio of each part's appearance density to the background density is then computed at every location, giving a likelihood-ratio map over the entire image for that part. The cost is $O(dN)$, where the dimension of the PCA space, d is much less than k^2.

We then introduce the shape model, which by the use of distance transforms [6], reduces the cost of finding the optimal match from $O(N^2P)$ to $O(NP)$. Note that we cannot use this trick in learning since we need to marginalize out over all possible matches, not just the optimal. Additionally, the efficient matching scheme requires that the location model be a tree. No ordering constraint is applied to the part locations hence the approximations necessary in learning are not needed.

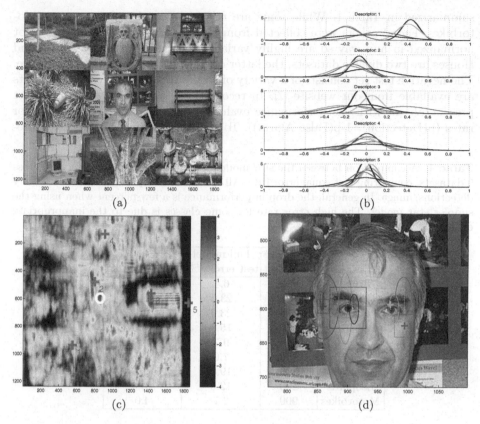

Fig. 4. An example of the complete recognition operation on a query image. **(a)** A mosaic query image. **(b)** First five descriptor densities of a 5 part face model (black is background density). **(c)** Overall matching probability (red is higher). The global optimum indicated by the white circle, while the magenta +'s show the maximum of each part's response. Note they are not in the same location, illustrating the effect of the shape term. **(d)** Close-up of optimal fit with shape model superimposed. Crosses indicates matched location of each part, with the squares showing their scale. The ellipses show the variance of the shape model at 1 standard deviation.

3 Experiments

We investigate the performance of the HSM in a number of ways: (i) we compare to the fully connected model; (ii) the effect of increasing the number of parts and detections/image; (iii) the difference between feature-based and complete recognition.

3.1 Datasets

Our experiments use a variety of datasets. Evaluation of the HSM using feature-based detection is done using nine widely varying, unnormalized, datasets summarized in Table 1. While some are relatively consistent in nature (Motorbikes, Faces) others were collected from Google's image search and are not normalized in any way so are highly variable (Camels, Bottles). Guitars and Houses are two diverse datasets, the latter of which is highly variable in nature. The negative test set consists of a variety of scenes around Caltech. All datasets are available from our website [7]. In recognition, the test is a simple object present/absent with the performance evaluated by comparing the equal error rates (p(Detection)=1-p(False Alarm)). To test the difference between feature-

Table 1. A comparison between the star model and the fully connected model across 9 datasets, comparing test equal error rate. All models used 6 parts, 20 Kadir & Brady detections/image. In general, the drop in performance is a few percent when using the simpler star model. The high error rate for some classes is due to the inappropriate choice of feature type.

Dataset	Total size of dataset	Full model test error (%)	Star model test error (%)
Airplanes	800	6.4	6.8
Bottles	247	23.6	27.5
Camels	350	23.0	25.7
Cars (Rear)	900	15.8	12.3
Faces	435	9.7	11.9
Guitars	800	7.6	8.3
Houses	800	19.0	21.1
Leopards	200	12.0	15.0
Motorbikes	900	2.7	4.0

based and complete recognition where localization performance is important, the UIUC Cars (Side) dataset [1] is used. In this case the evaluation in recognition involves localizing multiple instances of the object.

3.2   Comparison of HSM and Full Model

We compare the HSM directly with the fully connected model [8], seeing how the recognition performance drops when the configuration representation is simplified. The results are shown in Table 1. It is pleasing to see that the drop in performance is relatively small, only a few percent at most. The performance even increases slightly in cases where the shape model is unimportant. Figures 6-9 show star models for guitars, bottles and houses.

3.3   Heterogeneous Part Experiments

Here we fixed all models to use 6 parts and have 40 detections/feature-type/frame. Table 2 shows the different combinations of features which were tried, along with the best one picked by means of the training/validation set. We see a dramatic difference in performance between different feature types. It is interesting to note that several of the classes perform best with all three feature types present. Figure 6 shows a heterogenous star model for Cars (Rear).

Table 2. The effect of using a combination of feature types on test equal error rate. Key: KB = Kadir & Brady; MSH = Multi-scale Harris; C = Curves. All models had 6 parts and 40 detection/feature-type/image. Figure in bold is combination automatically chosen by training/validation set.

Dataset	KB	MSH	C	KB,MSH	KB,C	MSH,C	KB,MSH,C
Airplanes	**6.3**	22.5	27.5	11.3	13.5	18.3	12.5
Bottles	24.2	23.3	17.5	24.2	20.8	**15.0**	17.5
Camel	25.7	**20.6**	26.9	24.6	24.0	22.9	24.6
Cars (Rear)	11.8	6.0	5.0	2.8	4.0	5.3	**2.3**
Faces	10.6	16.6	17.1	12.0	13.8	12.9	**10.6**
Guitars	**6.3**	12.8	26.0	8.5	9.3	18.8	12.0
Houses	**17.0**	22.5	36.5	20.8	23.8	26.3	20.5
Leopards	14.0	18.0	45.0	**13.0**	23.0	23.0	18.0
Motorbikes	**3.3**	3.8	8.8	3.0	3.3	3.8	3.5

3.4 Number of Parts and Detections

Taking advantage of the efficient nature of the star model, we now investigate how the performance alters as the number of parts and the number of detections/ feature-type/frame is varied. The choice of features-types for each dataset is fixed for these experiments, using the optimal combination, as chosen in Table 2.

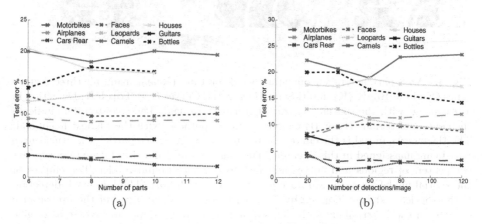

Fig. 5. (a) Test equal error rate versus number of parts, P, in the star model for 40 detections/feature-type/image. (b) Test equal error rate versus the number of detections/feature-type/image, N, for 8 part star models. In both cases the combinations of feature-types used was picked for each dataset from the results in Table 2 and fixed.

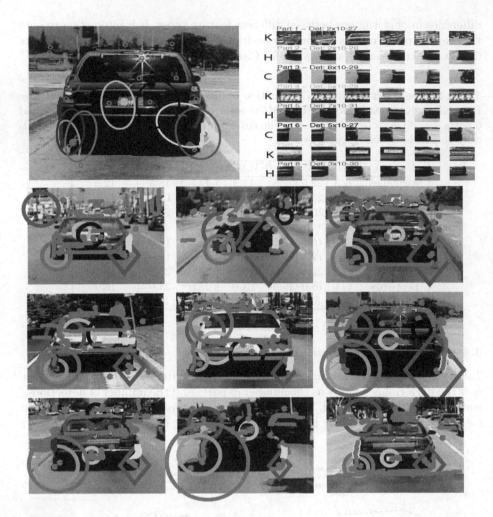

Fig. 6. An 8 part heterogeneous star model for Cars (Rear), using all three feature types (Kadir & Brady (K); multi-Scale Harris (H); Curves (C)) **Top left**: Detection in a test image with the spatial configuration model overlaid. The coloured dots indicate the centers of regions (K or H) chosen by the hypothesis with the highest likelihood. The thick curve in red is the curve selected by one of the curve parts – the other curve part being unassigned in this example. The magenta dots and thin magenta curves are the centers of regions and curves assigned to the background model. The ellipses of the spatial model show the variance in location of each part. The landmark detection is the top left red one. **Top right**: 7 patches closest to the mean of the appearance density for each part, along with the determinant of the variance matrix, so as to give an idea of the relative tightness of each distribution. The colour of the text corresponds to the colour of the dots in the other panels. The letter by each row indicates the type of each part. **Bottom panel**: More detection examples. Same as top left, but without the spatial model overlaid. The size of the coloured circles and diamonds indicate the scale of regions in the best hypothesis. The test error for this model is 4.5%.

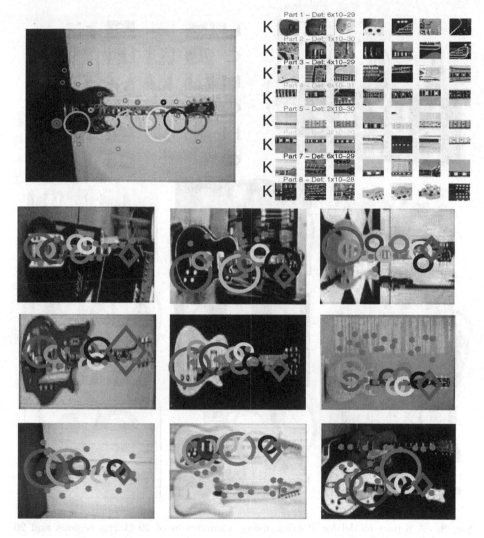

Fig. 7. An 8 part model for Guitars, using 40 Kadir & Brady features per image. 6.3% test error.

As the number of parts in the model is increased (for a fixed number of detections/frame) some of the categories show a slight change in performance but many remain constant. Examination of the models reveals that many of the additional parts do not find stable features on the object, suggesting that more features on the image are required. Increasing the number of detections/feature-type/image increases the error rate slightly in some cases such as camels, since many of the additional detections lie in the background of the image, so increasing the chances of a false positive. With a suitable combination of feature-types

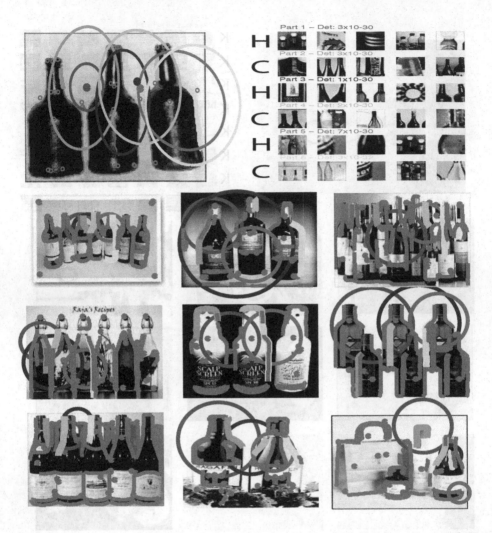

Fig. 8. A 6 part model for Bottles, using a maximum of 20 Harris regions and 20 Curves per image. 14.2% test error.

however, the increased number of parts and detections can give a more complete coverage of the object, improving performance (e.g. Cars (Rear) where the error drops from 4.5% at 8 parts to 1.8% with 12 parts, using 40 detections/image of all 3 feature types).

3.5 Complete Search Experiments

We now investigate the performance of feature-based recognition versus the complete approach. Taking the 8-part Cars (Rear) model shown in Figure 6, we apply it completely to the same test set resulting in the equal error rate dropping from

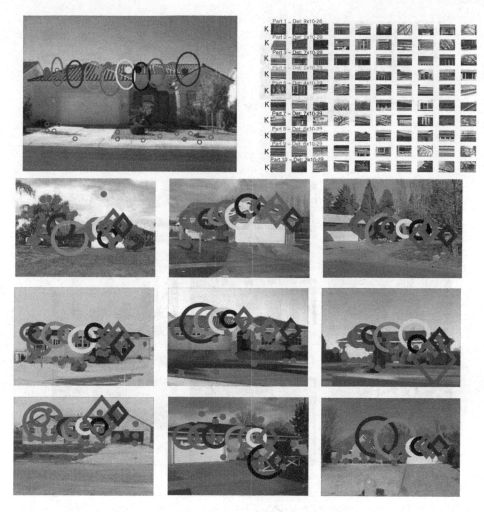

Fig. 9. A 10 part model for Houses, using 40 Kadir & Brady features per image. 16.5% test error.

4.5% to 1.8%. Detection examples for the complete approach are shown in Figure 11, with the ROC curves for the two approaches shown in Figure 11(b).

The localization ability of the complete approach is tested on the Cars (Side) dataset, shown in Figure 10. A fully connected model (Figures 10 (a) & (b)) was learnt and then decomposed into a star model and run completely over the test set. An error rate of 7.8% was achieved – a decrease from the 11.5% obtained with a fully connected model using feature-based detection in [8]. The performance gain shows the benefits of using the complete approach despite the use of a weaker shape model. Examples of the complete star model localizing multiple object instances can be seen in Figure 10(c).

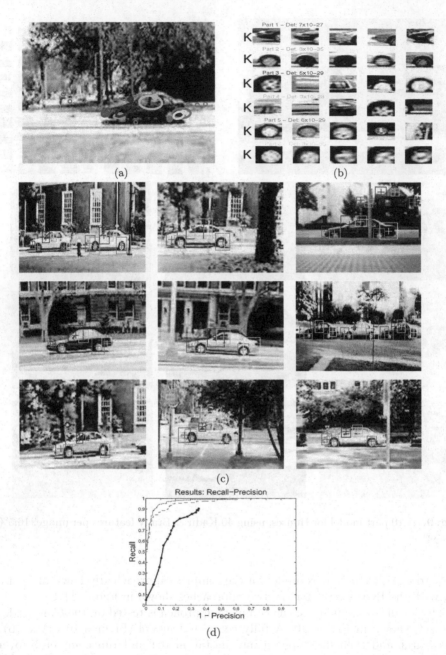

(a)

(b)

(c)

Results: Recall-Precision

(d)

Fig. 10. (a) & (b) A 6 part model Cars (Side), learnt using Kadir & Brady features.
(c) Examples of the model localizing multiple object instances by complete search.
(d) Comparison between feature-based and complete localization for Cars (Side). The
solid recall-precision curve is [1]; the dashed line is the fully connected shape model
with feature-based detection [8] and the dotted line is the complete-search approach
with star model, using the model shown in (a) & (b). The equal error rate of 11.5%
from [8] drops to 7.8% when using the complete search with the star model.

(a)

(b)

Fig. 11. (a) Detection examples of the 8 part Cars (Rear) model from Figure 6 being used completely. (b) ROC curves comparing feature-based (dashed) and complete detection (solid) for the 8 part Cars (Rear) model in Figure 6. Equal error improves from 4.5% for feature-based to 1.8% for complete.

4   Summary and Conclusions

We have presented a heterogeneous star model. This model retains the important capabilities of the constellation model [8,21], namely that it is able to learn from unsegmented and unnormalized training data; and in recognition on unseen images it is able to localize the detected model instance. The HSM outperforms the constellation model on almost all of the six datasets presented in [8]. It is also faster to learn, and faster to recognize (having $O(NP)$ complexity in recognition rather than the $O(N^P)$ of the constellation model). We have also demonstrated the model on many other object categories varying over compactness and shape. Note that while other models and methods have achieved superior performance to [8], for example [5,15,18,19], they are unable to both learn in a weakly-supervised manner and localize in recognition.

There are several aspects of the model that we wish to improve and investigate. Although we have restricted the model to a star topology, the approach is applicable to a trees and k-fans [4], and it will be interesting to determine which topologies are best suited to which type of object category.

Acknowledgments

We are very grateful for suggestions from and discussions with Michael Isard, Dan Huttenlocher and Alex Holub. Financial support was provided by: EC Project CogViSys; EC PASCAL Network of Excellence, IST-2002-506778; UK EPSRC; Caltech CNSE and the NSF.

References

1. S. Agarwal and D. Roth. Learning a sparse representation for object detection. In *Proceedings of the European Conference on Computer Vision*, pages 113–130, 2002.
2. E. Borenstein and S. Ullman. Class-specific, top-down segmentation. In *Proceedings of the European Conference on Computer Vision*, pages 109–124, 2002.
3. M. Burl, T. Leung, and P. Perona. Face localization via shape statistics. In *Int. Workshop on Automatic Face and Gesture Recognition*, 1995.
4. D. Crandall, P. Felzenszwalb, and D. Huttenlocher. Spatial priors for part-based recognition using statistical models. In *Proceedings of the IEEE Conference on Computer Vision and Pattern Recognition, San Diego*, volume 1, pages 10–17, 2005.
5. G. Csurka, C. Bray, C. Dance, and L. Fan. Visual categorization with bags of keypoints. In *Workshop on Statistical Learning in Computer Vision, ECCV*, pages 1–22, 2004.
6. P. Feltzenswalb and D. Huttenlocher. Pictorial structures for object recognition. *International Journal of Computer Vision*, 61:55–79, January 2005.
7. R. Fergus and P. Perona. Caltech Object Category datasets. http://www.vision.caltech.edu/html-files/archive.html, 2003.
8. R. Fergus, P. Perona, and A. Zisserman. Object class recognition by unsupervised scale-invariant learning. In *Proceedings of the IEEE Conference on Computer Vision and Pattern Recognition*, June 2003.
9. R. Fergus, P. Perona, and A. Zisserman. A visual category filter for Google images. In *Proceedings of the 8th European Conference on Computer Vision, Prague, Czech Republic*. Springer-Verlag, May 2004.
10. M. Fischler and R. Elschlager. The representation and matching of pictorial structures. *IEEE Transactions on Computer*, 22(1):67–92, Jan. 1973.

11. C. J. Harris and M. Stephens. A combined corner and edge detector. In *Proceedings of the 4th Alvey Vision Conference, Manchester*, pages 147–151, 1988.
12. F. Jurie and C. Schmid. Scale-invariant shape features for recognition of object categories. In *Proceedings of the IEEE Conference on Computer Vision and Pattern Recognition, Washington, DC*, pages 90–96, 2004.
13. T. Kadir and M. Brady. Scale, saliency and image description. *International Journal of Computer Vision*, 45(2):83–105, 2001.
14. Y. Ke and R. Sukthankar. PCA–SIFT: A more distinctive representation for local image descriptors. In *Proceedings of the IEEE Conference on Computer Vision and Pattern Recognition, Washington, DC*, June 2004.
15. B. Leibe, A. Leonardis, and B. Schiele. Combined object categorization and segmentation with an implicit shape model. In *Workshop on Statistical Learning in Computer Vision, ECCV*, 2004.
16. D. Lowe. Local feature view clustering for 3D object recognition. In *Proceedings of the IEEE Conference on Computer Vision and Pattern Recognition, Kauai, Hawaii*, pages 682–688. Springer, December 2001.
17. P. Moreels, M. Maire, and P. Perona. Recognition by probabilistic hypothesis construction. In *Proceedings of the 8th European Conference on Computer Vision, Prague, Czech Republic*, pages 55–68, 2004.
18. A. Opelt, A. Fussenegger, and P. Auer. Weak hypotheses and boosting for generic object detection and recognition. In *Proceedings of the 8th European Conference on Computer Vision, Prague, Czech Republic*, 2004.
19. J. Thureson and S. Carlsson. Appearance based qualitative image description for object class recognition. In *Proceedings of the 8th European Conference on Computer Vision, Prague, Czech Republic*, pages 518–529, 2004.
20. A. Torralba, K. P. Murphy, and W. T. Freeman. Sharing features: efficient boosting procedures for multiclass object detection. In *Proceedings of the IEEE Conference on Computer Vision and Pattern Recognition, Washington, DC*, pages 762–769, 2004.
21. M. Weber, M. Welling, and P. Perona. Unsupervised learning of models for recognition. In *Proceedings of the European Conference on Computer Vision*, pages 18–32, 2000.

Object Recognition by Combining Appearance and Geometry

David Crandall[1], Pedro Felzenszwalb[2], and Daniel Huttenlocher[1]

[1] Cornell University
Ithaca, NY 14850
{crandall,dph}@cs.cornell.edu
[2] The University of Chicago
Chicago, IL 60637
pff@cs.uchicago.edu

Abstract. We present a new class of statistical models for part-based object recognition. These models are explicitly parametrized according to the degree of spatial structure that they can represent. This provides a way of relating different spatial priors that have been used in the past such as joint Gaussian models and tree-structured models. By providing explicit control over the degree of spatial structure, our models make it possible to study questions such as the extent to which additional spatial constraints among parts are helpful in detection and localization, and the tradeoff between representational power and computational cost. We consider these questions for object classes that have substantial geometric structure, such as airplanes, faces and motorbikes, using datasets employed by other researchers to facilitate evaluation. We find that for these classes of objects, a relatively small amount of spatial structure in the model can provide statistically indistinguishable recognition performance from more powerful models, and at a substantially lower computational cost.

1 Introduction

Since the 1970's it has been observed that many objects can be represented in terms of a small number of parts arranged in a deformable configuration (e.g., [1,2,4,5,10,11,12,14,15,17]). In such models, the appearance of each part is usually captured by a template, and the spatial relationships between parts are represented by spring-like connections between pairs of parts. Recently there has been a considerable resurgence in the use of these models for object recognition – both for detection and localization – and in learning models from example images. Particular emphasis has been on the recognition of generic *classes* of objects using models that are learned from specific examples.

The models that have been used to capture geometric relationships between the parts of an object differ substantially in their representational power and computational complexity. On one hand, joint Gaussian models (e.g., [4,5,11]) have been used to explicitly capture spatial dependencies between all pairs of

J. Ponce et al. (Eds.): Toward Category-Level Object Recognition, LNCS 4170, pp. 462–482, 2006.

object parts, but the detection and localization algorithms that use these models rely on search heuristics in order to be computationally tractable. On the other hand, tree-structured graphical models (e.g., [10,14]) have been used to efficiently detect and localize certain kinds of objects such as humans and faces, but are only able to explicitly capture a small fraction of the spatial dependencies between the parts of an object. An important goal of this chapter is to improve our understanding of such tradeoffs between representational power and computational complexity for part-based recognition. We do this by introducing a family of spatial priors that provide explicit control over the degree of spatial structure that can be represented.

We use a problem formulation similar to the one in [10,12], where for detection or localization a single overall problem is solved that takes into account both how well individual parts match the image data at each location and also the global spatial arrangement of parts. This framework is different from most other object recognition approaches (e.g. [4,11]) that first perform feature detection to find possible locations for each part in an image and then use the detected feature locations to search for good object configurations. These methods have been popular because the explicit feature detection step reduces the number of object configurations that must be considered, but they have the disadvantage that false-negatives in the feature detection step can prevent parts from being properly localized. In [10] an efficient method was developed for tree-structured models that did not use feature detection, instead considering both part appearance and global spatial configuration at once. That method is able to provably compute the optimal object configuration in an image without explicitly searching the entire configuration space. A disadvantage to that method is that tree-structured models may not always be appropriate because of the relatively weak spatial structure that trees can capture.

In this chapter we extend the implicit search techniques of [10] in order to efficiently perform object recognition without feature detection using a class of spatial priors defined by graphs that we call k-fans. Models defined by k-fans provide a natural family of priors for part-based recognition. The parameter k controls both the representational power of the models and the computational cost of doing inference with them. When $k = 0$, the locations of the object parts are independent. As k increases the spatial prior captures more information. When $k = 1$ the graphical structure of the prior is a star graph. For $k = n - 1$ (where n is the number of parts in the model) there are no conditional independencies among the part locations as in the case of a joint Gaussian model. This family of models gives us a natural way of investigating the degree to which additional spatial constraints improve recognition and affect computational cost. Using more powerful (higher-k) models does not necessarily improve classification, as it can lead to over-fitting during learning.

Besides providing an explicit balance between representational power and computational cost, k-fan models have a strong geometrical foundation. In a k-fan model the locations of k distinguished parts can be used to define the pose of an object. With this view recognition using k-fans is related to geometric alignment [13]. From a different perspective k-fans can be used to define constraints on sets of $k + 1$ parts in the model. With this view recognition using k-fans is related to geometric invariants [6]. In both cases k-fan models generalize the geometric methods by explicitly modeling uncertainty and replacing hard constraints with soft constraints based on statistical models.

As our experimental results demonstrate, for certain object classes that have been used recently in the literature, such as motorbikes, faces and airplanes, a relatively small amount of spatial structure provides almost the same recognition accuracy that is obtained using more powerful models. For small values of k, recognition with k-fans is highly practical without relying on search heuristics or feature detection.

2   Part-Based Statistical Models

The central principle underlying part-based modeling is the observation that many objects can be represented by a small number of parts arranged in a characteristic configuration. The spatial relationships between parts in such a model are captured by a set of parameters S, while the appearance of each part is characterized by a set of parameters A. The model for an object is defined by the pair $M = (S, A)$.

Consider an object model with n parts $V = (v_1, \ldots, v_n)$. The location of the object in an image is given by a configuration of its parts $L = (l_1, \ldots, l_n)$, where l_i is the location of the ith part. Throughout this chapter we assume that the location of a part is given by a point in the image, $l_i = (x_i, y_i)$. Using Bayes' law, the probability that the object is at a particular location given an image and a fixed set of model parameters can be written as,

$$p_M(L|I) \propto p_M(I|L)p_M(L). \tag{1}$$

Here, $p_M(I|L)$ is the likelihood of observing image I given that a particular configuration of the object occurs in the scene, and $p_M(L)$ is the prior probability that the object configuration is L. In this chapter we consider three fundamental problems that can be formulated in terms of these distributions:

1. **Detection.** The detection problem is to decide if the image has an instance of the object (hypothesis w_1) or if the image is background-only (hypothesis w_0). It is natural to consider the ratio of the two likelihoods,

$$q = \frac{p_M(I|w_1)}{p_M(I|w_0)}, \tag{2}$$

   and compare it to a threshold to make the classification decision. The numerator is usually computed by summing over all possible configurations L as described in Section 3.4.

2. **Localization.** Assuming the object is present in the scene, the configuration that most likely corresponds to its true position is one with maximum posterior probability,

$$L^* = \arg\max_L p_M(L|I).$$

3. **Supervised learning.** The maximum-likelihood estimate of the model parameters given a set of labeled training images $\{(I_1, L_1), \ldots, (I_T, L_T)\}$ is,

$$S^* = \arg\max_S \prod_i p_M(L_i),$$

$$A^* = \arg\max_A \prod_i p_M(I_i|L_i).$$

The algorithmic complexity of solving these three problems is highly dependent on the form of the likelihood model $p_M(I|L)$ and the spatial prior $p_M(L)$. In the next section we discuss a particular likelihood model which has important structural properties, while the focus of the rest of the chapter is primarily on the form of the spatial prior.

2.1 Appearance

For computational purposes, the most important property of the appearance model is that $p_M(I|L)$ factors into two parts: a term which does not depend on the object configuration, and a product of functions each of which depends on the location of a single part. Because of this factorization, any independence assumption that is present in the spatial prior will also be present in the posterior. The majority of the recent work on part-based recognition has used a similar factorization. A notable exception is the patchwork of parts model in [2] which does not make this assumption in order to better capture overlapping parts.

In our work we use a simple template-based appearance model that operates on oriented edge maps in order to be relatively invariant to changes in image intensity. Let I be the output of an oriented edge detector, so that for each pixel p, $I(p)$ is either 0 indicating that there is no edge at p or a value in $\{1, \ldots, r\}$ indicating that there is an edge in one of r possible quantized orientations at p. We assume that the values of each pixel in the image are independent given the object configuration. The appearance of the ith part is given by a template $\mathcal{T}_i$. The probability that a pixel $p \in \mathcal{T}_i$ has value u is defined by a foreground model for that part, $f_i(p)[u]$. We further assume that each pixel in the background has value u with probability $b[u]$. The model parameters $A = ((\mathcal{T}_i, f_i), ..., (\mathcal{T}_n, f_n), b)$ encode the foreground model for each part and the background model.

Let w_0 be the hypothesis that the object is not present in the image. By our independence assumption we have,

$$p_M(I|w_0) = \prod_p b[I(p)].$$

We say that parts i and j do not overlap if $(\mathcal{T}_i \oplus l_i) \cap (\mathcal{T}_j \oplus l_j) = \emptyset$. Here $\oplus$ denotes Minkowsky addition, which is used to translate the templates according the locations of the parts. For a configuration L without overlap we have,

$$p_M(I|L) = p_M(I|w_0) \prod_{v_i \in V} g_i(I, l_i), \qquad (3)$$

where

$$g_i(I, l_i) = \prod_{p \in \mathcal{T}} \frac{f_i(p)[I(p + l_i)]}{b[I(p + l_i)]}. \tag{4}$$

Each term in g_i is the ratio of the foreground and background probabilities for a pixel that is covered by template $\mathcal{T}_i$. In equation (3) the denominator of g_i cancels out the contribution of $p_M(I|w_0)$ for those pixels that are under some part. As long as we only consider configurations L without overlapping parts the likelihood function defined above is a true probability distribution over images, in that it integrates to one. When parts overlap this is an approximation. Note that for many objects the spatial prior $p_M(L)$ strongly encourages parts in the model to not overlap, thus making this a reasonable appearance model.

2.2   Spatial Prior

The spatial prior $p_M(L)$ represents geometric relationships between the parts of an object. The simplest form of the prior assumes that there are no spatial dependencies between parts, so that the part locations are independent of one another (the naive Bayes assumption). Under this assumption, $p_M(L)$ can be written as:

$$p_M(L) = \prod_{v_i \in V} p_M(l_i).$$

The detection and localization problems are particularly easy with this spatial prior. For localization it is only necessary to maximize $g_i(I, l_i)p_M(l_i)$ independently for each l_i. This can be done in $O(nh)$ time for a model with n parts and h possible locations for each part. But while this model yields computationally tractable recognition and learning procedures, it is unable to accurately represent multi-part objects since it captures no relative spatial information.

Another option is to make no independence assumptions on the locations of different parts by, for example, using a joint Gaussian model for the spatial distribution $p_M(L)$ (e.g. as in [5]). Learning a maximum-likelihood distribution from labeled images in this case is easy, by simply computing the sample mean and covariance of the labeled part locations. However it is not known how to perform exact inference using this spatial prior efficiently. To make inference tractable, various heuristics have been employed to reduce the search space. For example, feature detection is normally used to constrain the possible locations of each part.

Spatial models between the two extremes just described can be defined by making certain conditional independence assumptions. These assumptions are commonly represented using an undirected graphical model (or Markov random field). Let $G = (V, E)$ be an undirected graph. The graph is used to define a distribution for the random variables $(l_1, \ldots, l_n)$ in the following way. The value for the location of v_i is independent of the values of all other nodes, conditioned on the values of the neighbors of v_i in the graph. The independence assumptions of the naive Bayes model are represented by a graph with no edges while a model with no independence assumptions such as the joint Gaussian corresponds to a complete graph.

Efficient learning and inference procedures for models with tree-structured spatial priors are known. The detection and localization problems can be solved in $O(nh^2)$ time using dynamic programming. Moreover, in many cases one can solve these problems in $O(nh)$ time – the same asymptotic time as the naive Bayes case where there are no dependencies between part locations (see [10]).

To summarize, we can imagine a spectrum of spatial priors, arranged according to the degree of spatial independence assumptions they make. On one end of the spectrum, we assume that all parts are spatially independent, so that the location of a given part does not constrain the location of *any* other part. Inference in this case is efficient but the object model is weak. At the other end are models that make no independence assumptions. This form of spatial prior can capture arbitrarily complex spatial relationships between part locations, but even for restricted cases it is not known how to perform exact inference efficiently. Tree-structured spatial priors fall in between the two extremes. In the following section, we introduce a family of spatial priors, called k-fans, which are explicitly parametrized according to where they fall along this spectrum.

3 k-Fans

Now we consider a class of spatial priors that lie between the two extremes of the naive Bayes assumption and a fully-connected spatial model. Our goal is to find models with recognition performance comparable to a fully-connected model but that support fast procedures for exact (discrete) inference and learning. We start by considering a restricted form of tree model, the star graph, and then extend that model. A star graph is a tree with a central node that is connected to all other nodes. Let $G = (V, E)$ be a star graph with central node v_r. Undirected graphical models with a star structure have a particularly simple interpretation in terms of conditional distributions. The values of random variables associated with nodes $v_i \neq v_r$ are independent when conditioned on the value of v_r. This leads to the following factorization of the prior distribution,

$$p_M(L) = p_M(l_r) \prod_{v_i \neq v_r} p_M(l_i | l_r).$$

We can think of the central node v_r as a *reference* part. The position of other parts in the model are evaluated relative to the position of this reference part.

k-fans extend the star graph model to include more than one reference part. Let $R \subseteq V$ be a set of reference parts, and $\overline{R} = V - R$ be the remaining parts in a model. Then a graph can be constructed which consists of a complete subgraph over the nodes in R, while each node in $\overline{R}$ is connected to every node in R (but to no other nodes). We call this graph a k-fan for $k = |R|$. Some examples of k-fans on six nodes are shown in Figure 1.

A *clique* in an undirected graph is a set of vertices for which there is an edge connecting every pair of nodes in the set. A k-fan can be seen as a collection of cliques of size $k+1$ connected together along a common clique of size k. The k nodes in the common clique are the reference parts R.

A k-fan can be constructed by starting with a k-clique corresponding to the reference nodes and sequentially adding new nodes by connecting each of them to the reference nodes and nothing else. With this view it is clear that k-fans are a special class of k-trees [16]. In particular k-fans are decomposable (also known as triangulated or chordal) graphs. Because k-fans are k-trees there are standard algorithms that can perform inference with these models in time that is polynomial in n and exponential in k, where n is the number of nodes in the graph [3]. An important difference between k-fans and arbitrary k-trees is that k-fan models can be learned in time polynomial in n and exponential in k while learning a k-tree is NP-hard even for small k.

As k grows from 0 to $n-1$ we get a set of graphs which intuitively interpolate between the empty graph and the complete graph on n nodes. Thus k-fans define a class of graphical models of increasing expressive power.

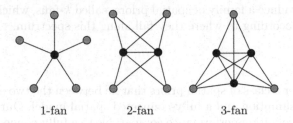

1-fan   2-fan   3-fan

Fig. 1. Some k-fans on six nodes. The reference nodes are shown in black while the regular nodes are shown in gray.

We claim that k-fans form an important class of graphical models for part-based recognition. These are exactly the models where the locations of the non-reference parts are conditionally independent given the locations of the reference parts. Let $R = \{v_1, \ldots, v_k\}$ be the reference parts in a k-fan. We denote by $l_R = (l_1, \ldots, l_k)$ a particular configuration of the reference parts. The spatial prior defined by a k-fan can be written in conditional form as,

$$p_M(L) = p_M(l_R) \prod_{v_i \in \overline{R}} p_M(l_i | l_R). \tag{5}$$

In general both the localization and detection problems for models with spatial priors based on k-fans can be solved in $O(nh^{k+1})$ time, where n is the number of parts in the model and h is the number of locations in the image. Thus k controls the computational complexity of inference with these models. With the additional assumption that $p_M(L)$ is Gaussian we can use distance transforms and convolutions to solve the inference problems in $O(nh^k)$, as described below. In practice the running time can be further improved using conservative pruning heuristics that eliminate low-probability configurations.

For learning k-fan models it will be useful to write the spatial prior in terms of marginal distributions,

$$p_M(L) = \frac{\prod_{v_i \in \overline{R}} p_M(l_i, l_R)}{p_M(l_R)^{n-(k+1)}}. \qquad (6)$$

The numerator is the product of marginal probabilities for the $n - k$ maximal cliques and the denominator involves the marginal probability for the nodes shared by all maximal cliques (the so-called separator set which in this case is R). This is a special form of the factorization for a triangulated graph, which is the ratio of a product over maximal cliques and a product over separators [7].

3.1   Geometric Interpretation

As mentioned in the introduction there is a natural connection between k-fan models and geometric alignment [13]. In a k-fan model the locations of the reference parts can be used to compute a global transformation aligning a geometrical model and the image. This alignment defines an ideal location for each non-reference part, and deviations from these ideal locations can be measured by the conditional distributions $p_M(l_i|l_R)$.

There is a also a close connection between k-fan models and object recognition using geometric invariants. Each maximal clique in a k-fan consists of exactly $k+1$ parts, and the location of these parts can be used to define shape constraints that are invariant to certain geometric transformations (see [6]). The number of reference parts controls the type of geometric invariants that can be represented.

In a k-fan the location of a non-reference part can be described in a reference frame defined by the locations of the k reference parts. For example, when $k = 1$ the location of a non-reference part can be described relative to the location of the single reference part. The values $l'_i = l_i - l_r$ are invariant under translations, so 1-fans can be used to define translation invariant models. For the case of $k = 2$ the two reference parts can be used to define models that are invariant to rigid motions and global scaling. When $k = 3$ we can use the three reference parts to define an affine basis in the image plane; if the location of every non-reference part is described in this basis we obtain affine invariant models. These models are important because they capture arbitrary views of planar objects under orthographic projection.

To enforce geometric invariants over $k + 1$ parts one could define $p_M(l_i|l_R)$ to be one if the $k + 1$ locations satisfy a geometric constraint and zero otherwise. In general our models capture soft geometric constraints, giving preference to configurations that satisfy relationships on $k + 1$ features as much as possible. The distribution over the reference part locations $p_M(l_R)$ could be uniform in the case where all geometric constrains are defined in terms of $k + 1$ parts. Non-uniform distributions can be used to represent interesting classes of non-rigid objects.

3.2   Gaussian k-Fans

We now consider k-fan models with the additional constraint that $p_M(L)$ is a Gaussian distribution. For a Gaussian model the marginal distribution of any subset of variables is itself Gaussian. Let μ_R and Σ_R be the mean and covariance for the locations of the reference parts. The marginal distribution of the reference parts together with one non-reference part is given by a Gaussian with mean and covariance,

$$\mu_{i,R} = \begin{bmatrix} \mu_i \\ \mu_R \end{bmatrix}, \quad \Sigma_{i,R} = \begin{bmatrix} \Sigma_i & \Sigma_{iR} \\ \Sigma_{Ri} & \Sigma_R \end{bmatrix}. \tag{7}$$

These can be used to define the spatial prior in terms of equation (6). We will use this for learning Gaussian k-fans. For inference we use the conditional form of the prior in equation (5). For a Gaussian distribution, conditioning on a set of variables preserves the Gaussian property. In particular, the conditional distribution of a non-reference part location given particular locations for the reference parts $p_M(l_i|l_R)$ has mean and covariance,

$$\mu_{i|R}(l_R) = \mu_i + \Sigma_{iR}\Sigma_R^{-1}(l_R - \mu_R), \tag{8}$$

$$\Sigma_{i|R} = \Sigma_i - \Sigma_{iR}\Sigma_R^{-1}\Sigma_{Ri}, \tag{9}$$

Note how the covariance $\Sigma_{i|R}$ is independent of the location of the reference parts. This is a non-trivial property that enables the use of distance transforms and convolutions to obtain faster inference algorithms than is possible with non-Gaussian models, as we will show in Sections 3.4 and 3.5.

3.3   Learning

We can learn the spatial prior for Gaussian k-fan models from labeled images using a maximum likelihood criterion. For a fixed set of reference parts, estimating the maximum likelihood parameters S^* involves estimating the mean and covariances in (7). These can be obtained from the sample mean and covariance of the labeled configurations.

The more interesting case is when the reference parts are not fixed. In this situation all possible reference sets of size k can be considered to find the set R that yields the best possible model. There are $\binom{n}{k}$ possible reference sets, which is not very large for small values of k. For each reference set we compute the maximum likelihood model parameters using the sample mean and covariance, as described above. We select the best reference set by choosing the set R that maximizes the likelihood of observing the training data given the model.

Learning the appearance parameters A^* for the models described in Section 2.1 using labeled training data is also simple. To estimate f_i, the position of the ith part in each training example is used to align the training images. The maximum likelihood estimate for $f_i(p)[v]$ is simply the frequency that pixel p has value v on the aligned data. The only parameter that is not learned from the data is the size and shape of the template $\mathcal{T}_i$. For the experiments shown in this chapter we used square windows of a fixed size.

3.4 Detection

For detection we consider the likelihood ratio in (2). The numerator of this ratio, which is the probability of an image given that it contains the object, can be expressed as a sum over all possible object configurations,

$$p_M(I|w_1) = \sum_L p_M(L)p_M(I|L).$$

Using the likelihood function (3) we see that

$$\frac{p_M(I|w_1)}{p_M(I|w_0)} = \sum_L p_M(L) \prod_{v_i \in V} g_i(I, l_i).$$

For a k-fan model the sum over all configurations L can be factored using the conditional form of the spatial prior in (5). For each $v_i \in \overline{R}$ we define

$$\alpha_i(l_R) = \sum_{l_i} p_M(l_i|l_R)g_i(I, l_i).$$

Now the likelihood ratio can be computed as,

$$\frac{p_M(I|w_1)}{p_M(I|w_0)} = \sum_{l_R} p_M(l_R) \prod_{v_i \in R} g_i(I, l_i) \prod_{v_i \in \overline{R}} \alpha_i(l_R).$$

Note that each α_i can be computed by brute force in $O(h^{k+1})$ time, while the likelihood ratio can be computed using the α_i in $O(nh^k)$ time. This procedure gives an $O(nh^{k+1})$ algorithm for computing the likelihood ratio.

For the case of a Gaussian k-fan we can compute the likelihood ratio even faster, using convolutions. For each non-reference part v_i we have,

$$p_M(l_i|l_R) = \mathcal{N}(l_i, \mu_{i|R}(l_R), \Sigma_{i|R}),$$

a Gaussian distribution with mean and covariance given by equations (8) and (9). Let $\alpha_i'(l_i)$ be the convolution of $g_i(I, l_i)$ with a Gaussian kernel of covariance $\Sigma_{i|R}$. It is not hard to see that,

$$\alpha_i(l_R) = \alpha_i'(\mu_{i|R}(l_R)).$$

So each α_i can be implicitly computed by a convolution in the space of possible part locations. This can be done in $O(h \log h)$ time instead of $O(h^{k+1})$.

The overall running time of the likelihood ratio computation for the case of a Gaussian k-fan model is $O(nh^k + nh \log h)$. Note that for a 1-fan model this is almost the same as $O(nh)$, the time that it would take to compute the likelihood ratio if the locations of the parts were completely independent. The $\log h$ dependency can be removed by using linear time methods that approximate Gaussian convolutions, such as the box-filter technique in [18].

3.5   Localization

For localization we look for an object configuration L^* with maximum posterior probability. Using Bayes law the posterior distribution for a k-fan model can be written in terms of the likelihood function (3) and the spatial prior (5). By manipulating the terms we get,

$$p_M(L|I) \propto p_M(l_R) \prod_{v_i \in R} g_i(I, l_i) \prod_{v_i \in \overline{R}} p_M(l_i|l_R) g_i(I, l_i).$$

For any $v_i \in \overline{R}$ the quality of an optimal location for the ith part can be expressed as a function of the reference locations,

$$\alpha_i^*(l_R) = \max_{l_i} p_M(l_i|l_R) g_i(I, l_i). \tag{10}$$

Using the α_i^* we can express the posterior probability of an optimal configuration for the object with particular reference locations l_R as,

$$\beta^*(l_R) = p_M(l_R) \prod_{v_i \in R} g_i(I, l_i) \prod_{v_i \in \overline{R}} \alpha_i^*(l_R). \tag{11}$$

These functions can be used to compute an optimal configuration for the object in time polynomial in the number of parts n and the number of locations for each part h (but exponential in k). Each α_i^* can be computed by brute force in $O(h^{k+1})$ time, while β^* can be computed in $O(nh^k)$ time. An optimal configuration for the reference parts l_R^* is one maximizing β^*. Finally, for each non-reference part we select l_i^* maximizing $p_M(l_i|l_R^*) g_i(I, l_i)$. This can be done in $O(h)$ time. The overall running time of this procedure is $O(nh^{k+1})$, which is reasonable for very small k.

As in the case of detection we can speed up the localization procedure for Gaussian k-fans. For localization the role of convolutions is played by generalized distance transforms [9]. In this case the running time is reduced to $O(nh^k)$.

4   Inference with Gaussian k-Fans

We have shown that in theory it is possible to perform exact inference (detection and localization) with Gaussian k-fan models efficiently without relying on feature detection. It turns out that the inference algorithms are also intuitive and straightforward to implement. In this section we describe how the localization algorithm works using generalized distance transforms, with a running example to illustrate each step of the process.

Figure 2(a) shows a diagram of a 1-fan model with six parts for detecting motorbikes. A simplified representation of the appearance model template of each part is shown, giving the probability of an edge at each location (disregarding orientation). Bright spots in the templates correspond to locations with higher edge probabilities. In this model the reference part is the back wheel and each non-reference part is positioned according to its mean location $\mu_{i|R}$ with respect to the reference. The figure also shows the conditional covariance $\Sigma_{i|R}$ of each non-reference part location, represented by an ellipse plotted at two standard deviations away from the mean. We will describe how the localization procedure works using this motorbike model on the sample input image shown in Figure 2(b). There are three steps to the procedure which are outlined below.

(a)   (b)

Fig. 2. A six part 1-fan model for motorbikes, with the back wheel as the reference part and a sample input image

4.1   Step 1: Apply Part Appearance Operators

The first step in performing localization is to evaluate $g_i(I, l_i)$ as defined in equation (4) for each part at each possible location. This produces a quality map for each part, indicating how well the part appearance model matches the local image information at each location. In practice we compute

$$C_i(l_i) = -\log g_i(I, l_i)$$

and think of $C_i(l_i)$ as the cost of placing part i at location l_i. While these costs have a particular form defined by the statistical model one can think of this step as essentially doing template matching with an edge template for each part. We can use the fact that edge images are sparse to compute the quality maps quickly.

Figure 3(a) shows the quality maps that were generated by the motorbike model on the sample input image, with good locations (low costs) represented by brighter intensities. Note that the individual quality maps are quite noisy, so that simply choosing the best location for each part without taking into account their relative positions (as in the naive Bayes method) would generate poor localization results. For example, the front and back wheel appearance models are similar and there are peaks at the location of the front wheel in the back wheel quality map, and vice-versa.

4.2   Step 2: Apply Distance Transforms

The next step takes into account the spatial dependencies in the model as encoded by the conditional covariances of each non-reference part with respect to

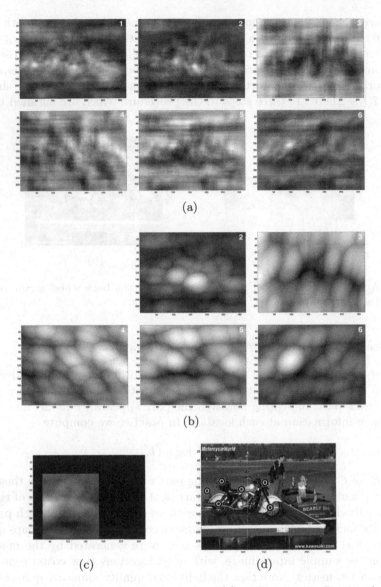

Fig. 3. Illustration of the localization procedure: (a) quality maps indicating the cost of placing each part at each location, with brighter intensity indicating better locations, (b) result of the distance transform applied to the quality maps of the non-reference parts, (c) final quality map showing the cost of placing the reference part at each location, and (d) final result, showing the localized part locations

the references. This is done by computing the generalized distance transform of the quality map for each non-reference part to allow for variations in its position relative to the references. The output is a new quality map $\mathcal{D}_i(l_i)$ for each non-reference part. The results of this step on the running example are shown in Figure 3(b). The transformation "spreads" the quality maps produced by the appearance models. Intuitively the resulting cost $\mathcal{D}_i(l_i)$ is low near locations where the original cost is low. The size and shape of this spreading operation is controlled by the conditional covariances $\Sigma_{i|R}$ for each part.

The new costs are defined by,

$$\mathcal{D}_i(x) = \min_y \; C_i(y) + \frac{(x-y)^T \Sigma_{i|R}^{-1}(x-y)}{2}.$$

The algorithm in [9] can be used to compute these distance transforms in time linear in the number of possible locations for each part.

4.3   Step 3: Combine Evidence

The last step in the localization procedure is to combine the distance transformed quality maps for the non-reference parts with the quality maps of the reference parts. The result is a cost for every configuration of the reference parts that takes into account the placement of the whole model. More specifically the cost for each placement of the reference parts encorporates the cost of the best placements of all the other parts. This is preciselly the negative logarithms of $\beta^*(l_R)$ in equation (11), up to an additive constant.

The procedure is particularly simple for the case of a translation invariant 1-fan model. In this case the computation of $-\log(\beta^*(l_R))$ up to an additive constant can be done as follows. We shift the distance transformed quality maps $\mathcal{D}_i(l_i)$ by the ideal position of part i relative to the reference part and sum these shifted quality maps together with the quality map for the reference part $C_r(l_r)$. The resulting map for the sample input image is shown in Figure 3(c). An optimal location for the reference part (the back wheel) l_r^* is determined by picking a lowest cost location in this map. After that the locations of the other parts can be found by selecting l_i^* for each non-reference part so as to maximize $p_M(l_i|l_r^*)g_i(I, l_i)$. The final localization results in the sample image are shown in Figure 3(f).

Performing localization using a k-fan model with $k > 1$ can be done in a similar way. In general equation (11) can be rewritten as

$$-\log(\beta^*(l_R)) = -\log(p_M(l_R)) + \sum_{v_i \in R} C_i(l_i) + \sum_{v_i \in \overline{R}} \mathcal{D}_i(\mu_{i|R}(l_R)) + Z.$$

For a 1-fan $-\log(\beta^*(l_R))$ is a two-dimensional quality map but for general k it is a $2k$ dimensional map. To compute $-\log(\beta^*(l_R))$ we iterate over all possible reference locations and evaluate the sum above.

5   Experiments

This section presents results from experiments we have conducted to characterize the detection and localization performance of k-fans as k is varied. Since the running time varies exponentially with k, it is clear that in practice it is best to choose the lowest value of k that still provides adequate detection and localization performance. We also compare our results to those of Fergus et al [11] who used full multivariate Gaussians (i.e. $n - 1$-fans, where n is the number of parts) as the spatial priors. However, since inference with this spatial model is intractable, they performed approximate inference using feature detection and various search heuristics. One of the goals of our experiments was to compare the performance of the *exact* (discrete) inference method for k-fans with small k to their *approximate* inference method for full Gaussian prior models.

To facilitate comparison of results with previous work we used some of the datasets from [11]: airplanes (800 images), faces (435 images), motorbikes (800 images), and background scenes (800 images). To further facilitate evaluation, we considered only the case of Gaussian k-fans (that is, we did not use the reference parts to define a geometric basis as described in Section 3.1). We tried to reproduce the experimental protocol of [11] as closely as possible, including using the same partitioning of the data into training and test images. We also pre-scaled all images so that object width was roughly uniform, using the same ground truth bounding boxes used in their experiments. To prevent biases related to image size, we padded out all images to a large, uniform size.

5.1 Learning the Models

As in [11], six parts were used to model each object. For airplanes we used the front and back landing gear, nose, wing tip, tail, and vertical stabilizer. For faces we used the two eyes, nose, two corners of the mouth, and chin. For motorbikes, the front and back wheel, headlight and tail light, and the front and back of the seat were used. Ground truth was collected by hand-labeling the training images. Note that [11] used an unsupervised training method but we should not expect supervised learning to necessarily give better results than unsupervised learning – a supervised approach is limited by the quality of the parts chosen and the accuracy of the hand-labeled ground truth.

The models were learned from labeled examples using the procedure described in Section 3.3. To learn the appearance model for a given part, a fixed-size patch surrounding the labeled part location was extracted from each training image. Canny edge detection was used to generate edge maps. Edge orientation was quantized into four directions (north/south, east/west, northeast/southwest, northwest/southeast) and represented as four separate binary edge maps. Note that opposing directions were quantized into the same bin. This prevents edge directions from changing when an object is moved from a light background to a dark background or vice-versa. Morphological dilation was applied on each map independently. Finally, foreground model probabilities were estimated by computing the frequency of each of the 16 possible combinations of edge orientations at each position in the template across all training images. The background model probabilities were estimated from the observed density of edges in background images.

Figure 4 illustrates some of the models we learned. Note that in each case the configuration of parts is readily recognizable as a prototype of the object. It is particularly interesting to compare the 1-fan and 2-fan models for the airplanes. Note that as k increases, the variability in the non-reference part locations (as

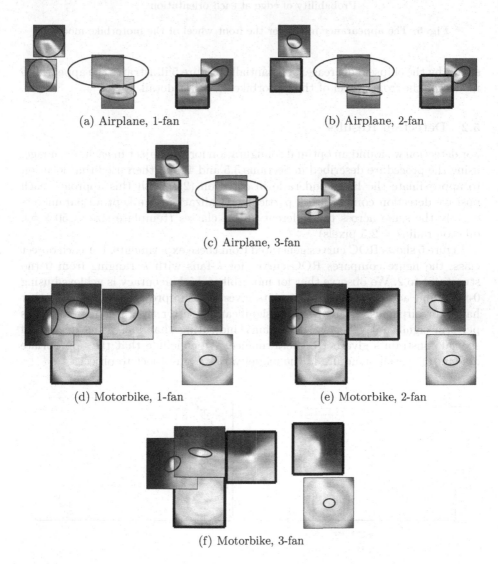

(a) Airplane, 1-fan   (b) Airplane, 2-fan

(c) Airplane, 3-fan

(d) Motorbike, 1-fan   (e) Motorbike, 2-fan

(f) Motorbike, 3-fan

Fig. 4. Illustration of some of the learned models. Images (a) through (f) show part appearance models positioned at their mean configuration. The reference parts have a black border around them. The ellipses illustrate the conditional covariances for a non-reference part given the locations of the references. High intensity pixels represent high edge probabilities. For clarity, just the probability of an edge is shown, although the actual models capture probabilities of each individual edge orientation. Note how the locations of parts are more constrained as k increases.

Vertical   Horizontal 45 degrees 135 degrees
Probability of edge at each orientation

Fig. 5. The appearance model for the front wheel of the motorbike model

shown by the ellipses) decreases substantially. Figure 5 illustrates the appearance model for the front wheel of the motorbike model in detail.

5.2   Detection Results

For detection we found an optimal configuration for the object in each test image, using the procedure described in Sections 3.5 and 4, and then used that location to approximate the likelihood ratio in equation (2). With this approach each positive detection comes with a particular localization. We kept all parameters exactly the same across the different object classes (template size $= 50 \times 50$, dilation radius $= 2.5$ pixels).

Figure 6 shows ROC curves generated from these experiments. For each object class, the figure compares ROC curves for k-fans with k ranging from 0 (no structure) to 2. We observe that for motorbikes, high accuracy is achieved using 0-fans, and adding spatial constraints gives little improvement. On the other hand, for airplanes, 1-fans perform significantly better than 0-fans, and 2-fans perform significantly better than 1-fans, indicating that increasing degrees of spatial constraints give better performance. We conclude that the appropriate amount of spatial structure in the model varies from object to object.

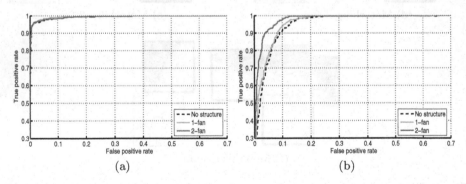

Fig. 6. Detection results for (a) motorbiks and (b) airplanes. Note that the ROC curves are truncated at a false positive rate of 0.7 and a true positive rate of 0.3.

Table 1 summarizes the recognition accuracy at the equal ROC points (point at which the true positive rate equals one minus the false positive rate). We note that our equal ROC results compare favorably with those obtained using

Table 1. Equal ROC performance for the detection experiments. A boldface number for a k-fan indicates a statistically significant difference between the areas under the ROC curves of the $k-1$ and k-fan models (with 95% confidence).

	Planes	Bikes	Faces
0-fans	90.5%	96.5%	98.2%
1-fans	**91.3%**	**97.0%**	98.2%
2-fans	**93.3%**	97.0%	98.2%

Table 2. Confusion matrices for the multi-class detection experiments. Rows correspond to actual classes, while columns correspond to predicted classes.

	0-fan			
	Planes	Bikes	Faces	BG
Planes	357	10	0	33
Bikes	4	382	0	14
Faces	3	9	205	0
Background	72	28	0	700

	1-fan				2-fan			
	Planes	Bikes	Faces	BG	Planes	Bikes	Faces	BG
Planes	362	5	0	33	370	8	0	22
Bikes	4	384	0	12	4	384	0	12
Faces	3	8	206	0	1	9	207	0
Background	68	24	0	708	53	23	0	724

full multivariate Gaussian structural models (with heuristics that make inference sub-optimal but computationally tractable) in [11]. They report 90.2%, 92.5% and 96.4% for airplanes, motorbikes and faces respectively, under the same experimental conditions.

We applied the statistical test in [8] to judge the differences in areas under the ROC curves of the various models. These results are also shown in Table 1. For each object class we computed the probability that the area under the ROC curve for the k-fan model is significantly different from the area under the ROC curve for the model with one less reference part. Differences significant at a greater than 95% confidence level are shown in boldface.

We also conducted multi-class detection experiments to test the ability of the models to differentiate between the three different object classes and the background images. For each test image, the three object detectors were applied, and the object class with the highest likelihood was chosen. That likelihood was compared to the threshold at the equal ROC point to decide between that object class and the background class. The results are shown in Table 2. The performance of multi-class recognition is similar to the single class case. The use of relatively accurate probabilistic models allows for direct comparison between the scores of each object class without tuning weighting parameters.

As in [11], we also tested the detectors in a setting where the object scale was not known (i.e. images were not pre-scaled to a uniform object width). The object widths varied between about 200 and 700 pixels for the motorbike and plane categories, while the face dataset had very little scale variation. We applied the detectors at four different scales to each image and chose the scale having the highest-likelihood detection. Recognition performance in this experiment was comparable to the case of pre-scaled images.

The average running time per image of the detection algorithm on these datasets on a 3GHz Pentium 4 is approximately 0.1 seconds for a 1-fan model, 3.3 seconds for a 2-fan model, and 37.6 seconds for a 3-fan model.

5.3   Localization Accuracy

Figure 7 illustrates some localization results produced by our system on the motorbike dataset, showing precise localization of the parts despite substantial variability in their appearances and configurations. Recent work has generally focused on evaluating detection performance but we believe it is also important to evaluate the accuracy of localization. For example, some applications may benefit from knowing the exact locations of each part individually. Also, examining localization performance helps to reveal the evidence that the detection algorithm is using to perform its classification decisions, and to ensure that it is not exploiting "unfair" biases in the image data, such as image size or patterns in the image backgrounds. For each object class, for the subset of images that were correctly classified during the detection task at the equal ROC point, the part

Fig. 7. Some localization results. In each of these cases all parts were localized correctly.

Table 3. Part localization errors for the correctly detected motorbike images, showing 75% and 90% trimmed means of Euclidean distance between estimated part locations and ground truth

Model	rear wheel		front wheel	
	75%	90%	75%	90%
No structure	15.6	34.4	1.9	2.3
1-fan	2.1	12.5	1.9	2.3
2-fan	1.9	2.4	1.9	2.3

Model	headlight		tail light		back of seat		front of seat	
	75%	90%	75%	90%	75%	90%	75%	90%
No structure	10.9	18.8	12.0	19.3	21.6	33.9	6.3	12.2
1-fan	10.9	18.6	11.4	18.7	20.6	32.9	6.3	12.0
2-fan	10.1	16.6	11.0	18.3	17.2	28.5	5.4	9.3

locations produced by our system were compared to hand-labeled ground truth. We computed the trimmed means (at 75% and 90%) of the Euclidean distances (in pixels) between estimated locations and the ground truth. For the motorbike models the localization errors are reasonably small (less than 10 pixels) for most parts when $k > 0$, while the errors for faces are less than 2 pixels. Table 3 summarizes the results for the motorbikes models. In this case the localization accuracy is high for most parts when using a model without spatial structure. The accuracy increases as we add spatial constraints even when recognition performance does not increase.

Acknowledgements

This material is based upon work supported under a National Science Foundation Graduate Research Fellowship.

References

1. Y. Amit. *2D Object Detection and Recognition, Models, Algorithms, and Networks.* MIT Press, 2002.
2. Y. Amit and A. Trouvé. Pop: Patchwork of parts models for object recognition. 2005.
3. U. Bertele and F. Brioschi. *Nonserial Dynamic Programming.* Academic Press, 1972.
4. M.C. Burl and P. Perona. Recognition of planar object classes. In *IEEE Conference on Computer Vision and Pattern Recognition*, 1996.
5. M.C. Burl, M. Weber, and P. Perona. A probabilistic approach to object recognition using local photometry and global geometry. In *European Conference on Computer Vision*, 1998.
6. S. Carlsson. Geometric structure and view invariant recognition. *Phil. Trans. R. Soc. Lond. A*, 359(1740), 1998.

7. R. F. Cowell, A. P. Dawid, S. L. Lauritzen, and D. J. Spiegelhalter. *Probabilistic Networks and Expert Systems*. Springer, 1999.
8. E.R. DeLong, D.M. DeLong, and D.L. Clarke-Pearson. Comparing the areas under two or more correlated roc curves: a non-parametric approach. *Biometrics*, 44(3), 1998.
9. P.F. Felzenszwalb and D.P. Huttenlocher. Distance transforms of sampled functions. September 2004. Cornell Computing and Information Science Technical Report TR2004-1963.
10. P.F. Felzenszwalb and D.P. Huttenlocher. Pictorial structures for object recognition. *International Journal of Computer Vision*, 61(1), 2005.
11. R. Fergus, P. Perona, and A. Zisserman. Object class recognition by unsupervised scale-invariant learning. In *IEEE Conference on Computer Vision and Pattern Recognition*, 2003.
12. M.A. Fischler and R.A. Elschlager. The representation and matching of pictorial structures. *IEEE Transactions on Computer*, 22(1), 1973.
13. D.P. Huttenlocher and S. Ullman. Recognizing solid objects by alignment with an image. *International Journal of Computer Vision*, 5(2):195–212, November 1990.
14. S. Ioffe and D.A. Forsyth. Probabilistic methods for finding people. *International Journal of Computer Vision*, 43(1), 2001.
15. P. Lipson, E. Grimson, and P. Sinha. Configuration based scene classification and image indexing. In *IEEE Conference on Computer Vision and Pattern Recognition*, 1997.
16. D. J. Rose. On simple characterizations of k-trees. *Discrete Mathematics*, 7(3-4):317–322, 1974.
17. H. Schneiderman and T. Kanade. Probabilistic formulation for object recognition. In *IEEE Conference on Computer Vision and Pattern Recognition*, 1998.
18. W.M. Wells, III. Efficient synthesis of Gaussian filters by cascaded uniform filters. *IEEE Transactions on Pattern Analysis and Machine Intelligence*, 8(2), 1986.

Shape Matching and Object Recognition

Alexander C. Berg and Jitendra Malik

U.C. Berkeley
{aberg,malik}@cs.berkeley.edu
http://www.cs.berkeley.edu/Research/Projects/vision

Abstract. We approach recognition in the framework of deformable shape matching, relying on a new algorithm for finding correspondences between feature points. This algorithm sets up correspondence as an integer quadratic programming problem, where the cost function has terms based on similarity of corresponding geometric blur point descriptors as well as the geometric distortion between pairs of corresponding feature points. The algorithm handles outliers, and thus enables matching of exemplars to query images in the presence of occlusion and clutter. Given the correspondences, we estimate an aligning transform, typically a regularized thin plate spline, resulting in a dense correspondence between the two shapes. Object recognition is handled in a nearest neighbor framework where the distance between exemplar and query is the matching cost between corresponding points. We show results on two datasets. One is the Caltech 101 dataset (Li, Fergus and Perona), a challenging dataset with large intraclass variation. Our approach yields a 45% correct classification rate in addition to localization. We also show results for localizing frontal and profile faces that are comparable to special purpose approaches tuned to faces.

1 Introduction

The problem of visual object recognition is really a family of inter-related problems. If we consider spatial extent, the notion of "object" extends downwards to parts (faces, eyes, propellers, wings), and upwards to scenes (kitchens, cityscapes, beaches). On the generalization dimension, we have categorization at varying levels all the way to identification of individuals (mammals,primates, humans, "Fred"). Sometimes, even the term "object" is questionable, when we consider visual recognition of materials such as sand or cornflakes.

What computational architecture would support a solution to all these problems in a common framework? In addition to the functional requirements above, processing must be fast, a large number of categories need to be handled, and the approach should be trainable with very few examples.

We propose a three stage architecture:

- *Initial Retrieval:* Retrieving a shortlist of potentially matching models for a query image based on feature descriptors. At this stage the spatial configuration of the feature locations can be ignored in order to facilitate rapid indexing.

J. Ponce et al. (Eds.): Toward Category-Level Object Recognition, LNCS 4170, pp. 483–507, 2006.

– *Shape Matching:* Aligning template views of stored exemplars to the support
  of an unknown object in the query image. In face recognition this would be
  the stage where the corners of eyes, nose, lips and other landmarks would
  be "lined up".
– *Discriminative Classification:* Given alignments of models to images we can
  now compare corresponding features as well as their configurations. Discriminative classifiers can give more weight to the characteristics that best
  distinguish examples of one category from other related categories.

This chapter outlines a solution to the second of these stages, shape matching.
Since we wish to deal with intra-category variability, all shape matching is for us
necessarily deformable shape matching. Back in the 1970s, at least three different
research groups working in different communities initiated such an approach:
in computer vision, Fischler and Elschlager [12], in statistical image analysis,
Grenander ([14]and earlier), and in neural networks, von der Malsburg ([17] and
earlier). The core idea that related but not identical shapes can be deformed
into alignment using simple coordinate transformations dates even further back,
at least to D'Arcy Thompson, in the 1910's with *On Growth and Form* [34].

The basic subroutine in deformable matching takes as input an image with
an unknown object (shape) and compares it to a model by first aligning the two
and then computing a *similarity* based on both the aligning *transform* and the
residual difference after applying the aligning transformation. Searching for an
alignment can be quite difficult. We show that the search can be approximated
by an easier discrete matching problem, *the correspondence problem*, between
key points on a model and a novel object.

Practically speaking, the basic difficult question for the correspondence problem is, "How do we algorithmically determine which points on two shapes correspond?" The correspondence problem in this setting is more difficult than in
the setting of binocular stereopsis, for a number of reasons:

1. Intra-category variation: the aligning transform between instances of a category is not a simple parameterized transform. It is reasonable to assume that
   the mapping is smooth, but it may be difficult to characterize by a small
   number of parameters as in a rigid or affine transform.
2. Occlusion and clutter: while we may assume that the stored prototype shapes
   are present in a clean, isolated version, the shape that we have to recognize
   in an image is in the context of multiple other objects, possibly occluding
   each other.
3. 3D pose changes: since the stored exemplars represent multiple 2D views of
   a 3D object, we could have variation in image appearance which is purely
   pose-related, the 3D shapes could be identical

The principal contribution of this work is a novel algorithm for solving the
correspondence problem for shape matching.

We represent shape by a set of points sampled from contours on the shape.
Typically 50-100 pixel locations sampled from the output of an edge detector are
used; as we use more samples we get better approximations. Note that there is

nothing special about these points – they are *not* required to be keypoints such as those found using a Harris/Forstner type of operator or scale-space extrema of a Laplacian of Gaussian operator, such as used by Lowe [21].

We exploit three kinds of constraints to solve the correspondence problem between shapes:

1. Corresponding points on the two shapes should have similar local appearance. For this purpose we develop geometric blur to measure rough shape similarity.
2. Minimizing geometric distortion: If i and j are points on the model corresponding to i' and j' respectively, then the vector from i to j, r_{ij} should be consistent with the vector from i' to j', $r_{i'j'}$. As examples: If the transformation from one shape to another is a translation accompanied by pure scaling, then these vectors must be scalar multiples. If the transformation is a pure Euclidean motion, then the lengths must be preserved. etc.
3. Smoothness of the transformation from one shape to the other. This enables us to interpolate the transformation to the entire shape, given just the knowledge of the correspondences for a subset of the sample points. We use regularized thin plate splines to characterize the transformations.

The similarity of point descriptors and the geometric distortion is encoded in a cost function defined over the space of correspondences. We purposely construct this to be an integer quadratic programming problem (cf. Maciel and Costeira [22]) and solve it using fast-approximate techniques.[1]

We address two object recognition problems, multi-class recognition and face detection. In the multiple object class recognition problem, given an image of an object we must identify the class of the object and find a correspondence with an exemplar. We use the Caltech 101 object class dataset consisting of images from 101 classes of objects: from accordion to kangaroo to yin-yang, available at [7]. This dataset includes significant intra class variation, a wide variety of classes, and clutter. On average we achieve **45%** accuracy on object classification with quite good localization on the correctly classified objects.

It is important to point out that these results are achieved with a simple generative model based solely on coarse shape. Better recognition can be achieved by building class specific discriminative models combining shape with other cues such as color and texture. The point here is experimental evidence of simple generative shape models proving useful for both localization and recognition.

We also consider face detection for large faces, suitable for face recognition experiments. Here the task is to detect and localize a number of faces in an image. The face dataset we use is sampled from the very large dataset used in [6] consisting of news photographs. With only 20 exemplar faces our generic system provides a ROC curve with slightly better generalization, and slightly worse false detection rate than the quite effective specialized face detector of Mikolajczyk [24] used in [6].

---

[1] It is worth noting that this formulation is amenable to various probabilistic models, maximum likelihood estimation for a product of Gaussians among others, but we do not address this further here.

2   Shape Descriptor

A simple descriptor based on blurred edge maps is used to compare shapes locally. These descriptors do not cover an entire object and so we refer to them as local shape descriptors, nevertheless they have a broader spatial support than typical local descriptors. The consequence of broad spatial support is variation between views of similar local structures. We use a spatially varying *geometric blur* over the positions of edges to provide the necessary robustness.

Descriptors are computed using geometric blur on edge maps. Oriented edge maps are computed and then blurred. Keypoints are then located along edges and sample points are drawn from the blurred edge maps. The vector of these samples is the descriptor as shown in Figure 8.

Geometric blur is an average over geometric transformations of a signal representing the spatial distribution of features in an image. The objective of the averaging is to make comparison of signals robust to typical geometric distortions within a bounded range. We will use a descriptor based on geometric blur to evaluate similarity between shapes.

First we motivate basing local shape descriptors on edge maps and the need for spatial uncertainty. This is followed by the mathematical definition of geometric blur. Two motivations for using a simple family of blurs — linearly increasing blur with distance from the center feature point — are presented, and a relatively low dimensional descriptor based on geometric blur is defined. A brief comparison to alternate descriptors concludes this section.

2.1   Motivation

The two helicopters shown in Figure 1 are easily recognizable as helicopters and a young child could indicate positions for the nose and tail of each. The crops below indicate the difficulty faced by a computer. Analogous structures in the images are only very roughly similar. In order to find a correspondence and then an alignment between the two objects it is necessary to find some way to get at this rough similarity. We approach this problem by first representing the rough spatial pattern of edges.

2.2   Simple Example

Before beginning the formal development of geometric blur a simple example of comparing distorted signals is presented to make concrete some of the mathematics to follow. Here we begin to show how geometric blur can provide robustness to spatial variation.

In Figure 2, which signal, A or C, is most similar to the signal B? The question is ambiguous, and we need to take into consideration some type of accepted variation, say small affine transformations. Note that here we mean spatial affine transformations, not transforms in intensity. Making robust comparison of signals with variation in intensity is rather better studied than the variation in signals due to distortions in geometry. Even with this added information, the

Fig. 1. In the **top row** are two images showing similar objects, helicopters. The **bottom row** shows that the local structure of the objects is only very roughly similar. Geometric blur is motivated by the goal of identifying rough similarity between bits of shapes.

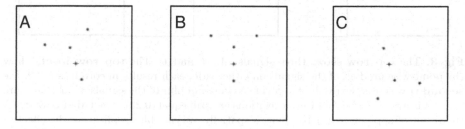

Fig. 2. Three similar signals composed of impulses. They represent the spatial location of features in an image. The goal is to recognize that a small transformation brings **A** and **B** into alignment, but not so for **B** and **C**.

correlation between either the left (*A* & *B*) or right (*B* & *C*) pair of signals is low and quite similar, providing no information about which are more similar. This can be seen in the first row of Figure 3 where the insets show the point-wise products of the signals on either side. Note that smoothing the signals with a uniform Gaussian does not quite solve the problem, as can be seen in the second row of the Figure 3. After blurring the signals with a uniform Gaussian the correlation between either pair of signals is similar, missing the clear differences. The basic idea of geometric blur is to blur or average the signals over the range of acceptable transformations (small affine transformations in this case), as shown in the third row of Figure 3. This will turn out to be mathematically equivalent to convolving the signal with a spatially varying kernel. Roughly speaking,

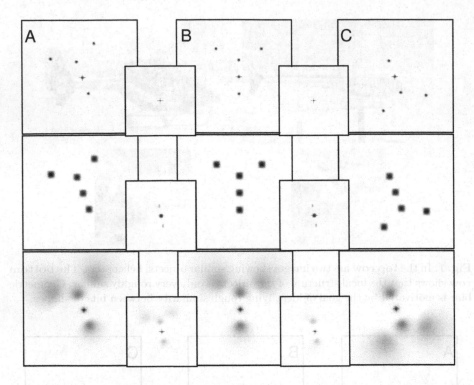

Fig. 3. The **top row** shows three signals, A, B, and C. The **top row insets** show the point-wise product of the signals on either side, each results in correlation 0.2. the **second row** shows the result of applying a Gaussian blur to the signals. Note that more context is now included, but the correlations are still equal (0.22). The **third row** shows the result of applying geometric blur, a spatially varying blur replicating the effect of averaging over small affine transforms of the signal. Now the insets indicate a difference between the correlations: 0.63 for the correct match versus 0.4 for the incorrect match.

parts of the signal farther from the center are blurred more because they have the opportunity to move more. After this type of blur, correlation can correctly identify the more similar pair, as can be seen on the bottom row of Figure 3.

2.3   Definition

We define geometric blur and show that it can be written as a spatially varying convolution.

The geometric blur $GB_I(x)$ of a signal $I(x)$ over coordinate x is the integral over a range of distorted versions of the signal:

$$GB_I(x) = \int_T I(T(x))d\mu \tag{1}$$

Where T are spatial transforms and μ is a measure on the space of transforms. Under appropriate conditions[2] there is a density ρ such that:

$$GB_I(x) = \int_P I(T_p(x))\rho(T_p)\,dp \qquad (2)$$

Where T_p is a transform specified by parameters p in $\mathbb{R}^k$ and the integral is computed with respect to the Lebesgue measure on $\mathbb{R}^k$. The density ρ is determined by the measure on transforms. In order to reduce notational clutter we will usually drop the subscript p and assume that the transform T is parameterized by p.

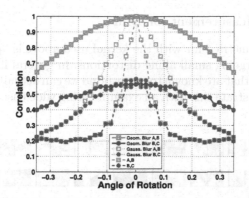

Fig. 4. Correlation of signal B and rotated (A) or rotated and flipped (C) versions of itself with no blur, uniform blur, or geometric blur. The far right end of the graph, rotation by 0.34 radians, corresponds to the signals shown in Figure 3.

Equation 1 is an integration over warped versions of the signal. We rewrite this to integrate over the range (spatial coordinates of I) of the transforms and change variables:

$$GB_I(x) = \int_z I(z) \int_{T:T(x)==z} \rho(T)\,d\tilde{p}\,dz \qquad (3)$$

$$= \int_y I(x-y) \int_{T:(x-T(x))==y} \rho(T)\,d\tilde{p}\,dy \qquad (4)$$

$$= \int_y I(x-y)K_x(y)\,dy \qquad (5)$$

The geometric blur is then a convolution with a spatially varying kernel, $K_x(y) = \int_{T:(x-T(x))==y} \rho(T)\,d\tilde{p}$.[3]

---

[2] Additional details and derivations concerning geometric blur, including motivation as an approximation to Bayesian estimation, can be found in [4].

[3] In Equations 3 and 4 $d\tilde{p}$ indicates integration with respect to the measure on the "slice", $\{T : T(x) == z\}$ and $\{T : x - T(x) == y\}$ respectively.

An Example: Returning to the example signals in Figures 2 and 3. We now consider comparing signal **B** to rotations of itself, and rotations of its vertical mirror image. The green dashed lines in Figure 4 show the correlation between **B** and rotated versions of itself, and the red dashed line shows correlations between **B** and rotated versions of its vertical mirror image. As a reference, the signals shown in Figure 2 would correspond to the signals used for a rotation of 0.35 radians as shown on the far right of Figure 4.

In this and all other examples in this section the kernel function is $K_x(y) = f(\alpha|x| + \beta)G_{\alpha|x|+\beta}(y)$, where G is a Gaussian with the specified standard deviation, and f is a normalization factor so that the K_x is L^2 normalized.

2.4   Empirical Measurement for Blur

By construction geometric blur with the kernel used above is appropriate in the case of signals undergoing small affine distortions. In general if we have enough examples of patches that are known to correspond we can actually find an optimal blur pattern. We illustrate this with an example using wide base-line stereo pairs.

Fig. 5. Rectified paired patches found by the Harris-Affine detector. Note that the centers of the patches are usually on edges or at corners, and that the orientations and scales of matched patches are often slightly different.

We use images from different camera positions looking at the same object or scene[4]. The correspondence between images is known. A region of interest operator is applied, and where it works correctly, producing corresponding regions on images, the corresponding patches are used. Figure 5 shows pairs of corresponding patches. The raw patches are replaced by edge maps and the covariance between corresponding patches of edge maps is shown in Figure 6. Each

---

[4] Images are from work by Mikolajczyk and Schmid [25] on region of interest operators and descriptors for wide-baseline matching.

small block in the figure represents the covariance of all the pixels in one patch of edge map with respect to a particular pixel in the corresponding patch of edge map. The general structure shows a more concentrated covariance near the center, and a more diffuse covariance near the periphery. Plotting this shows the nearly linear pattern in Figure 7. While these examples support the linearly increasing blur kernel, they are restricted to images of the same object or scene. Replicating this study on images of categories of objects it is necessary to find correspondences in the face of intra-category variation.

2.5 Descriptor

Creating a descriptor using geometric blur involves design choices for the region of interest operator, underlying features, blur kernel, and subsampling.

Region of Interest Operator. Descriptors and region of interest operators are the head and tail respectively of a thorny beast indeed. The two are coupled

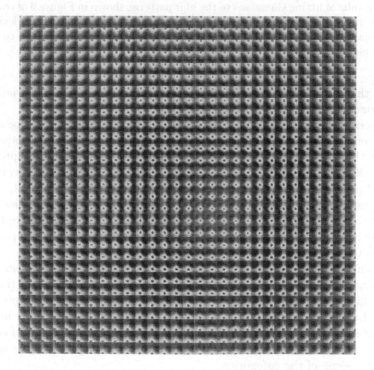

Fig. 6. Covariance of edge response between corresponding patches using a Harris-Affine detector. These have been reshaped so that each small block represents the covariance of all the pixels in one patch of edge map with respect to a particular pixel in the corresponding patch of edge map. The location of the small block specifies the pixel in the corresponding patch of edge map. For example the block at the lower right of the image shows the covariance of the all the pixels in a patch of edge map with the pixel in the lower right of the corresponding patch of edge map.

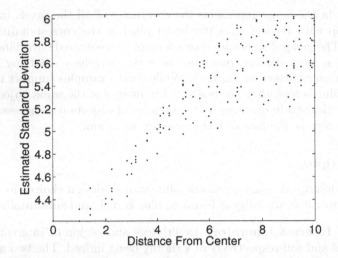

Fig. 7. Results of fitting Gaussians to the blur patterns shown in Figure 6 of covariance of edge response between corresponding patches. The estimated standard deviation is plotted against the distance from the center. The amount of blur in the covariance increases almost linearly.

because the choice of interest point operator effects the type of variation the descriptor must tolerate [4].

One benefit of the spatially varying blur is that geometric blur can be used for localization. The work by Berg & Malik [5] concentrates mainly on this aspect of geometric blur. This is quite different from other contemporary descriptors such as SIFT [20] that rely on an interest point operator to select similar locations for potential matches. As a result a somewhat promiscuous interest point operator can be used in conjunction with geometric blur, and the localization of the best match can be left up to the descriptor itself. We will place interest points anywhere in an image where there is a strong edge response, using sampling with repulsion to spread interest points throughout the image.

Choosing the scale for the descriptor can also be a complex problem. In this case we duck the issue by tying the scale of the descriptor to the scale of the object model. This means that if the object scale varies, multiple sets of descriptors must be used. Luckily geometric blur is designed to handle affine distortion including scale, and tolerates scale variation relatively well. For instance the multi-category recognition results shown later use a single scale of descriptor despite variation in scale for some of the categories.

Feature Channels. Motivated by wide ranges of appearance we base the feature channels on a coarse scale edge detector. The best results are obtained using the boundary detector of [23]. This boundary detector is constructed not to respond to texture, and produces relatively consistent boundary maps. In addition a simple and computationally less expensive edge detector based on elongated

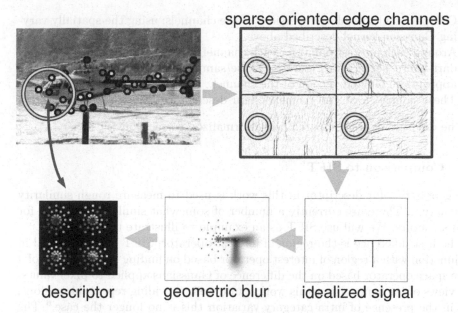

Fig. 8. The steps to compute a geometric blur descriptor. Starting with a feature point on an image (eg the point at the center of the circle in the **upper left**) and a region of interest (the circle). The sparse feature channels are cropped out as shown in the **upper right**. Geometric blur is applied to each channel (shown here with an idealized signal for clarity) and the signal is sub-sampled. The final descriptor is the vector of values indicated by dots with differing intensity at **lower left**.

derivative of Gaussian filters is used for comparison [27]. In both cases edge detection results are split up by orientation and oriented non-max suppression is applied producing multiple sparse channels as shown in Figure 8.

Blur Kernel. As before we use a simple blur kernel based on a Gaussian. If $G_a(x)$ is a Gaussian with standard deviation a then:

$$K_x(y) = G_{\alpha|x|+\beta}(y)$$

is our blur kernel. The kernel is normalized with respect to the L^2 norm.

Sub-sampling. The geometric blur of a signal should be sub-sampled using a pattern that matches the amount of blur introduced. In particular in the periphery fewer samples are required. For the kernel we consider above this implies a density of samples decreasing linearly with distance from the origin. The sampling pattern used in these experiments is shown in Figure 8.

A quick summary of steps for computing geometric blur descriptors for an image follows:

1. Detect feature locations: oriented edge detectors.
2. Choose interest points: random sampling with repulsion on points with high edge energy.

3. Compute multiple blurred versions of the channels: using the spatially varying Gaussian kernel described above.
4. Around each interest point, for each channel, sample points according to the
   dart-board pattern in Figure 8. These samples should be drawn from the
   appropriate blurred version of the channel.
5. These samples form the geometric blur descriptors.

The descriptors are compared using normalized correlation.

2.6   Comparison to SIFT

The geometric blur descriptor in this work is used to measure rough similarity
in structure. There are currently a number of somewhat similar descriptors for
local structure. We will use SIFT as an example to illustrate the differences.[5]

The first difference is the region of interest operator. SIFT is usually used in
conjunction with a region of interest operator based on finding local maxima of a
scale space operator based on the difference of Gaussians applied to pixel values.
For views of the same object this works quite well, providing repeatable regions,
but in the presence of intra-category variation this is no longer the case.[6] The
region of interest operator we use is based simply on edge response, which is
more repeatable across intra-category variation. The scale of the descriptor is
tied to the object scale as described section 2.5. It is worth noting that in general
the scale relative to the edge features is much *larger* that commonly found with
the SIFT region of interest operator. This larger scale allows more context to be
used.

The relatively large context of the geometric blur based descriptors requires
more tolerance of change in the signal, which is accomplished by the radially
increasing blur. One way to think of the SIFT descriptor is as constant blur
with a grid subsampling pattern (4x4) instead of the dart-board pattern used
for the geometric blur descriptor. As the relative size of the patch considered
increases the difference between constant blur and geometric blur increasing
linearly with distance becomes larger.

Finally the underlying features for the geometric blur based descriptor described in this chapter and SIFT are both based on oriented edge maps, with
slightly different details in engineering. In particular the number of orientations,
non-max suppression, and sometimes use of the *pb* detector from Martin *et al*[23].

---

[5] Shape contexts [3] are also quite similar in spirit to geometric blur based descriptors.
    The main differences are the hard decision about feature presence and location with
    shape contexts vs soft decision for both using geometric blur. Work on geometric
    blur introduced the connection between blur increasing linearly with distance and
    robustness to affine distortion, which was later used to justify the sampling pattern
    in shape contexts.

[6] It is important to note that some features will be reliably found even in the presence
    of intra-category variation, in order to find good alignment we require more matches,
    and so must tolerate more variation. The trick is to maintain discriminative infor-
    mation while being tolerant of more variation.

It is the smoothing and subsampling of the edge maps along with the region of interest operator where most differences arise.

Generally the SIFT type descriptors are suited to identifying parts of the same object from multiple views, while the geometric blur based descriptor described here is designed to evaluate potential similarity under intra-class variation exploiting larger support and spatially varying blur. There are many choices for descriptors, the experiments later in the chapter indicate that a generic geometric blur based descriptor fares well as part of a correspondence algorithm for a wide variety of object categories.

3   Geometric Distortion

Local shape similarity measurements are not sufficient to identify similar shapes. In order to combine local shape similarity measurements using geometric blur descriptors we need some way of measuring changes in the entire shape. This is accomplished be measuring the distortion in the configuration of feature points induced by a correspondence.

We consider correspondences between feature points $\{p_i\}$ in model image P and $\{q_j\}$ in image Q. A correspondence is a mapping σ indicating that p_i corresponds to $q_{\sigma(i)}$. To reduce notational clutter we will sometimes abbreviate $\sigma(i)$ as i', so σ maps p_i to $q_{i'}$.

The quality of a correspondence is measured in two ways: how similar feature points are to their corresponding feature points, and how much the spatial arrangement of the feature points is changed. We refer to the former as the match quality, and the later as the distortion of a correspondence.

We express the problem of finding a good correspondence as minimization of a cost function defined over correspondences. This cost function has a term for the match quality and for the geometric distortion of a correspondence: $\text{cost}(\sigma) = \omega_{\text{m}} C_{\text{match}}(\sigma) + \omega_{\text{d}} C_{\text{distortion}}(\sigma)$

Where constants ω_{m} and ω_{d} weigh the two terms. The match cost for a correspondence is:

$$C_{\text{match}}(\sigma) = \sum_i c(i, i') \tag{6}$$

Where $c(i, j)$ is the cost of matching i to j in a correspondence. We use the negative of the correlation between the feature descriptors at i and j as $c(i, j)$.

We use a distortion measure computed over pairs of model points in an image. This will allow the cost minimization to be expressed as an integer quadratic programming problem.

$$C_{\text{distortion}}(\sigma) = \sum_{ij} H(i, i', j, j') \tag{7}$$

Where $H(i, j, k, l)$ is the distortion cost of mapping model points i and j to k to l respectively. While there are a wide variety of possible distortion measures, including the possibility of using point descriptors and other features, in addition to location, we concentrate on geometric distortion and restrict ourselves to measures based on the two offset vectors $r_{ij} = p_j - p_i$ and $s_{i'j'} = q_{j'} - q_{i'}$.

$$C_{\text{distortion}}(\sigma) = \sum_{ij} \text{distortion}(r_{ij}, s_{i'j'}) \tag{8}$$

Our distortion cost is made up of two components:

$$C_{\text{distortion}}(\sigma) = \sum_{ij} \gamma d_a(\sigma) + (1 - \gamma) d_l(\sigma) \tag{9}$$

$$d_a(\sigma) = \left(\frac{\alpha_d}{|r_{ij}| + \beta_d} \right) \left| \arcsin \left(\frac{s_{i'j'} \times r_{ij}}{|s_{i'j'}||r_{ij}|} \right) \right| \tag{10}$$

$$d_l(\sigma) = \frac{||s_{i'j'}| - |r_{ij}||}{|r_{ij}| + \mu_d} \tag{11}$$

where d_a penalizes the change in direction, and d_l penalizes change in length.[7] A correspondence σ resulting from pure scale and translation will result in $d_a(\sigma) = 0$, while σ resulting from pure translation and rotation will result in $d_l(\sigma) = 0$. The constants α_d, β_d, μ_d, are all terms allowing slightly more flexibility for nearby points in order to deal with local "noise" factors such as sampling, localization, etc. They should be set relative to the scale of these local phenomena. The constant γ weighs the angle distortion term against the length distortion term.

Outliers. Each point p_i, in P, is mapped to a $q_{\sigma(i)}$, in Q. This mapping automatically allows outliers in Q as it is not necessarily surjective – points q_j may not be the image any point p_i under σ. We introduce an additional point q_{null} and use $\sigma(i) = \text{null}$ to allow a point p_i to be an outlier. We limit the number of points p_i which can be assigned to q_{null}, thus allowing for outliers in both P and Q.

4   Correspondence Algorithm

Finding an assignment to minimize a cost function described by the terms in Equations 7 and 6 above can be written as an Integer Quadratic Programming (IQP) problem.

$$\text{cost}(x) = \sum_{a,b} H(a,b)x_a x_b + \sum_a c(a)x_a \tag{12}$$

Where the binary indicator variable x has entries x_a, that if 1, indicate $\sigma(a_i) = a_j$. We then have $H(a,b) = H(a_i, a_j, b_i, b_j)$, and $c(a) = c(a_i, a_j)$ from Equations 7 and 6.

---

[7] It is possible to construct a pairwise distortion measure based on bending energy which is compatible with the thin plate spline we use alter for interpolation [29], however we are interested in more structured transformations such as rotation and scaling, resulting in the simple distortion measure presented here.

Fig. 9. An exemplar with a subset of feature points marked (**left**), the novel "probe" image with all feature points in white, and the feature points found to correspond with the exemplar feature points marked in corresponding colors (**left center**), the exemplar with all its feature points marked in color, coded by location in the image (**right center**), and the probe with the exemplar feature points mapped by a thin plate spline transform based on the correspondences, again colored by position in the exemplar (**far right**). See Figure 10 for more examples.

We constrain x to represent an assignment. Write x_{ij} in place of $x_{a_i a_j}$. We require $\sum_j x_{ij} = 1$ for each i. Furthermore if we allow outliers as discussed in Section 3, then we require $\sum_i x_{i\text{null}} \leq k$, where k is the maximum number of outliers allowed. Using outliers does not increase the cost in our problems, so this is equivalent to $\sum_i x_{i\text{null}} = k$. Each of these linear constraints are encoded in a row of A and an entry of b. Replacing H with a matrix having entries $H_{ab} = H(a, b)$ and c with a vector having entries $c_a = c(a)$. We can now write the IQP in matrix form:

$$\min \text{cost}(x) = x'Hx + c'x \text{ subject to,} \tag{13}$$
$$Ax = b, \quad x \in \{0, 1\}^n$$

4.1 Approximation

Integer Quadratic Programming is NP-hard, however specific instances may be easy to solve. We follow a two step process that results in good solutions to our problem. We first find the minimum of a linear bounding problem, an approximation to the quadratic problem, then follow local gradient descent to find a locally minimal assignment. Although we do not necessarily find global minima of the cost function in practice the results are quite good.

We define a linear objective function over assignments that is a lower bound for our cost function in two steps. First compute $q_a = \min \sum_b H_{ab} x_b$. Note that from here on we will omit writing the constraints $Ax = b$ and $x \in \{0, 1\}^n$ for brevity.

If x_a represents $\sigma(i) = j$ then q_a is a lower bound for the cost contributed to any assignment by using $\sigma(i) = j$. Now we have $L(x) = \sum_a (q_a + c_a) x_a$ as a lower bound for $cost(x)$ from Equation 13. This construction follows [22], and is a standard bound for a quadratic program. Of note is the operational similarity to geometric hashing.

The equations for q_a and L are both integer linear programming problems, but since the vertices of the constraint polytopes lie only on integer coordinates, they can be relaxed to linear programming problems without changing the optima, and solved easily. In fact due to the structure of the problems in our setup they can be solved explicitly by construction. If n is the length of x, each problem takes $O(n)$ operations with a very small constant. Computing q_a for $a = 1 \ldots n$ requires $O(n^2)$ time.

We then perform gradient descent changing up to two elements of the assignment at each step. This takes $O(n^2)$ operations per step, and usually requires a very small number of steps (we put an upper bound on the number of steps). In practice we can solve problems with $m = 50$ and $n = 2550$, 50 possible matches for each of 50 model points with outliers, in less than 5 seconds.

4.2   Example Correspondences

Given a model image P of an object, and a target image Q, possibly containing an instance of a similar object we find a correspondence between the images as follows:

1. Extract sparse oriented edge maps from each image.
2. Compute features based on geometric blur descriptors at locations with high edge energy.
3. Allow each of m feature points from P to potentially match any of the k most similar points in Q based on feature similarity and or proximity.
4. Construct cost matrices H and c as in Section 3.
5. Approximate the resulting Binary Quadratic Optimization to obtain a correspondence. Store the cost of the correspondence as well.
6. Extend the correspondence on m points to a smooth map using a regularized thin plate spline [28].

See Figures 9 and 10 for a number of examples. In the leftmost column of the figures is the image, P, shown with m points marked in color. In the middle left column is the target image Q with the corresponding points found using our algorithm. A regularized thin plate spline is fit to this correspondence to map the full set of feature points on the object in P, shown in the middle right column, to the target, as shown on the far right column. Corresponding points are colored the same and points are colored based on their position (or corresponding position) in P – in P colors are assigned in uniform diagonal stripes, the distortion of these striped in the far right column of the figure gives some idea of the distortion in the correspondence.

5   Object Recognition

The Caltech 101 [10] dataset consists of images from 101 categories of objects: from accordion to kangaroo to yin-yang[8]. Example images from 100 of the categories can be seen in Figure 13. There are a wide variety of image categories: man-made objects, animals, indoor images and outdoor images, drawings, etc.

---

[8] Available from http://www.vision.caltech.edu/Image_Datasets/Caltech101/Caltech101.html

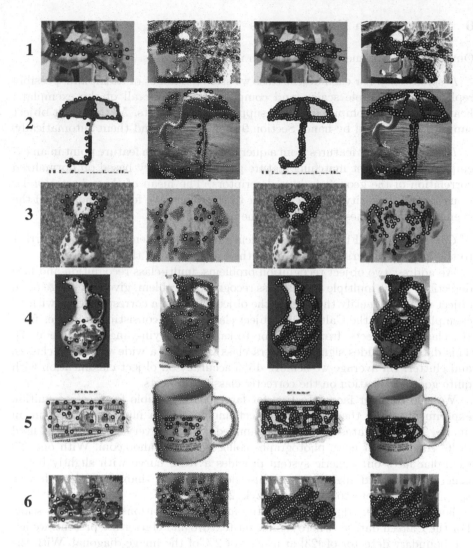

Fig. 10. Each row shows an alignment found using our technique described in section 4. Leftmost is an exemplar with some feature points marked. Left center is a probe image with the correspondences found indicated by matching colors (all possible feature matches are shown with white dots). All of the feature points on the exemplar are shown center right, and their image using a thin plate spline warp based on the correspondence are shown in the right most image of the probe. Note the ability to deal with clutter (1,6), scale variation(3), intraclass variation (all), also the whimsical shape matching (2), and the semiotic difficulty of matching a bank note to the image of a bank note painted on another object (5).

In addition many of the images have background clutter. There are up to 800 images in a category, although many categories contain 50 or fewer images. Some categories offer more variation and clutter than others.

6   Recognition Experiments

Our recognition framework is based on nearest neighbors.

Preprocessing: For each object class we store a number of exemplars, possibly replicated at multiple scales, and compute features for all of the exemplars. Features are only computed on the support of the objects. At this point object supports are marked by hand. Section 9 shows how to find them automatically.

Indexing: Extract features from a query image. For each feature point in an exemplar, find the best matching feature point in the query based on normalized correlation of the geometric blur descriptors. The mean of these best correlations[9] is the similarity of the exemplar to the query. We form a shortlist of the exemplars with highest similarity to the query image.

Correspondence: Find a correspondence from each exemplar in the shortlist to the query as described above. Pick the exemplar with the least cost.

We address two object recognition problems, multi-class recognition and face detection. In the multiple object class recognition problem, given an image of an object we must identify the class of the object and find a correspondence with an exemplar. We use the Caltech 101 object class dataset consisting of images from 101 classes of objects: from accordion to kangaroo to yin-yang, available at [7]. This dataset includes significant intra class variation, a wide variety of classes, and clutter. On average we achieve **45%** accuracy on object classification with quite good localization on the correctly classified objects.

We also consider face detection for large faces, suitable for face recognition experiments. Here the task is to detect and localize a number of faces in an image. The face dataset we use is sampled from the very large dataset used in [6] consisting of news photographs collected from yahoo.com. With only 20 exemplar faces our generic system provides a ROC curve with slightly better generalization, and slightly worse false detection rate than the quite effective specialized face detector of Mikolajczyk [24] used in [6].

For each image, edges are extracted at four orientations and a fixed scale. For the Caltech dataset where significant texture and clutter are present, we use the boundary detector of [23] at a scale of 2% of the image diagonal. With the face dataset, a quadrature pair of even and odd symmetric Gaussian derivatives suffices. We use a scale of $\sigma = 2$ pixels and elongate the filter by a factor of 4 in the direction of the putative edge orientation.

Geometric blur features are computed at 400 points sampled randomly on the image with the blur pattern shown in Figure 8. We use a maximum radius of 50 pixels (40 for faces), and blur parameters $\alpha = 0.5$ and $\beta = 1$.

For correspondence we use 50 (40 for faces) points, sampled randomly on edge points, in the correspondence problem. Each point is allowed to match to any of the most similar 40 points on the query image based on feature similarity. In addition for the Caltech 101 dataset we use $\gamma = 0.9$ allowing correspondences

---

[9] Some normalization is necessary to deal with relatively smaller or larger objects with fewer or more descriptors.

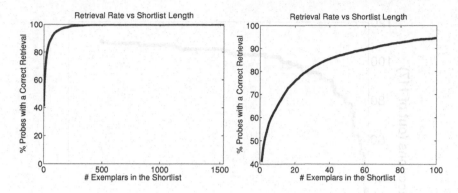

Fig. 11. For a probe or query image exemplars are ranked according to feature similarity. We plot the percentage of probes for which an exemplar of the correct class was found in the shortlist. Here the first exemplar is correct 41% of the time. **Left** Full curve. **Right** Curve up to shortlist length 100 for detail.

with significant variation in scale, while for the faces dataset we handle scale variation partly by repeating exemplars at multiple scales and use $\gamma = 0.5$.

7   Caltech 101 Results

Basic Setup: Fifteen exemplars were chosen randomly from each of the 101 object classes and the background class, yielding a total 1530 exemplars. For each class, we select up to 50 testing images, or "probes" excluding those used as exemplars. Results for each class are weighted evenly so there is no bias toward classes with more images.

The spatial support of the objects in exemplars is acquired from human labeling. The top entry in the shortlist is correct 41% of the time. One of the top 20 entries is correct 75% of the time. (Figure 11).

Recognition and Localization. Using each of the top ten exemplars from the shortlist we find a good correspondence in the probe image. We do this by first sampling 50 locations on the exemplar object and allowing each to be matched to its 50 best matching possibilities in the probe with up to 15% outliers. This results in a quadratic programming problem of dimension 2550. We use a distortion cost based mainly on the change in angle of edges between vertices ($\gamma = 0.9$). This allows matches with relatively different scales (Figure 10 line 3). The exemplar with the lowest distortion correspondence gives **45%** correct classification, at the same time providing localization. Note that this is using a simple nearest neighbor classifier and generative models. A baseline experiment comparing gray scale images using SSD and 1-nearest neighbor classification gives 16%. At press, the best results from the Caltech group are 40% using discriminative methods [15]. No other techniques have addressed correspondence at the level of detail presented here.

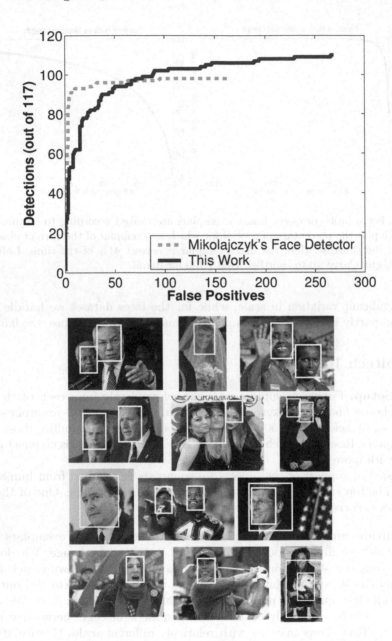

Fig. 12. Top ROC curves for our face detector using 20 exemplar images of faces (split between frontal and profile) and the detector of Mikolajczyk. Mikolajczyk's detector has proven to be effective on this dataset. simply finding sets of feature points in an image that have a good correspondence, based on distortion cost, to an exemplar. Good correspondences allow detection and localization of faces using a simple generative model, no negative examples were used. **bottom** Detections from our face detector marked with rectangles.

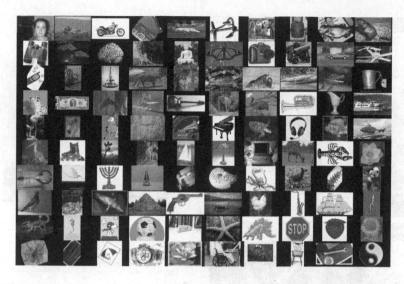

Fig. 13. Example images from 100 of the categories in the Caltech 101 dataset

Multiscale. We compute exemplar edge responses and features at a second scale for each exemplar resulting in twice as many exemplars. This improves shortlist performance by 1% or less, and does not change recognition performance. This illustrates the general lack of scale variation in Caltech 101. The face dataset exhibits a large range of scale variation.

8   Face Detection Results

We apply the same technique to detecting medium to large scale faces for use in face recognition experiments. The face dataset is sampled from the very large dataset in [6] consisting of A.P. news photographs. A set of 20 exemplar faces split between front, left, and right facing, was chosen from the database by hand, but without care. The test set was selected randomly from the remaining images on which the face detector of [24] found at least one 86×86 pixels or larger face. We use the generic object recognition framework described above, but after finding the lowest cost correspondence we continue to look for others. A comparison of the ROC curves for our detector and that of [24] is found in Figure 12. Our detector has an advantage in generalization, while producing more false positives. While not up the the level of specialized face detectors, these are remarkably good results for a face detector using 20 exemplars and a generative model for classification, without any negative training examples.

9   Automatic Segmentation

In the recognition experiments above, exemplar objects were hand segmented from their backgrounds. This can be automated by finding the repetitive aspects

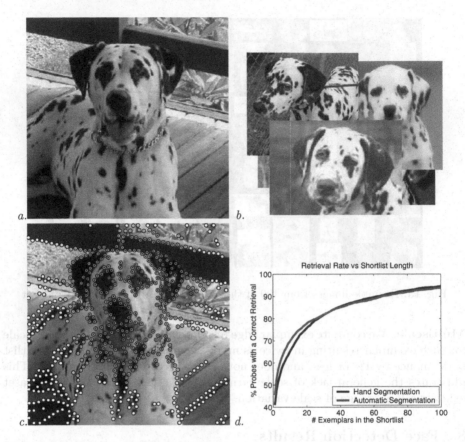

Fig. 14. Illustrating automatic model segmentation: One training image (**a.**) the remaining 14 training images (**b.**) darkness of the central circle for each feature indicates how well on average the area around the feature point matched after aligning transforms to each of the other training images (**c.**) At lower right, the percentage of probes for which an exemplar of the correct class was found in the shortlist. The **darker** curve shows performance with hand segmented exemplars, the **lighter** curve shows performance with *automatically* segmented exemplars. For hand segmented exemplars the first exemplar is correct 41% of the time, for automatically segmented exemplars 45%. (**d.**)

of objects in the example images. Starting with a set of example images $\{I_i\}$ from an object class find the support of the object in an image I_{i_0} as follows. For each image I_j where $j \neq i_0$:

1. Find a correspondence from I_{i_0} to I_j.[10]
2. Use a regularized thin plate spline to map all of the feature points in I_{i_0} to I_j.
3. For each mapped feature from I_{i_0}, the quality of the match is the similarity to the best matching nearby feature in I_j.

---

[10] Here we allow 40% outliers instead of 15% as used in the recognition experiments.

The median quality of match for a feature is the measure of how common that feature is in the training images.

Feature points with median quality within 90% of the best for that image are considered part of the object. Repeating the recognition experiments in Section 7, the shortlist accuracy improves by 1-4% (Fig. 14). While the estimated support is usually not perfect, recognition performance is similar to that using hand segmented images, 45%.

The learned models of support reflect a region of the image that is consistent across training images, as opposed to individual discriminative features. For instance the cheek on a face is not by itself discriminative for faces, but when considering faces transformed into alignment the cheek is usually consistent.

References

1. Y. Amit, D. Geman, and K. Wilder. Joint induction of shape features and tree classifiers. *IEEE Trans. PAMI*, 19(11):1300–1305, November 1997.
2. S. Belongie, J. Malik, and J. Puzicha. Matching shapes. In *Proc. 8th Int. Conf. Computer Vision*, pages I.454–461, 2001.
3. S. Belongie, J. Malik, and J. Puzicha. Shape matching and object recognition using shape contexts. *IEEE Trans. PAMI*, 24(4):509–522, April 2002.
4. A. C. Berg. *Shape Matching and Object Recognition*. PhD thesis, U.C. Berkeley, December 2005.
5. A. C. Berg and J. Malik. Geometric blur for template matching. In *Proc. IEEE Comput. Soc. Conf. Comput. Vision and Pattern Recogn.*, pages 607–614, 2001.
6. T. L. Berg, A. C. Berg, J. Edwards, M. Maire, R. White, Y. W. Teh, E. Learned-Miller, and D. A. Forsyth. Names and faces in the news. In *Proc. IEEE Comput. Soc. Conf. Comput. Vision and Pattern Recogn.*, pages 848–854, 2004.
7. Caltech 101 dataset
   www.vision.caltech.edu/feifeili/101_ObjectCategories .
8. H. Chui and A. Rangarajan. A new point matching algorithm for non-rigid registration. *Comp. Vision and Image Underst.*, 89:114–141, 2003.
9. L. Fei-Fei, R. Fergus, and P. Perona. A bayesian approach to unsupervised one-shot learning of object categories. In *Proc. 9th Int. Conf. Computer Vision*, pages 1134–1141, 2003.
10. L. Fei-Fei, R. Fergus, and P. Perona. Learning generative visual models from few training examples: an incremental bayesian approach tested on 101 object categories. In *Workshop on Generative-Model Based Vision*, 2004.
11. R. Fergus, P. Perona, and A Zisserman. Object class recognition by unsupervised scale-invariant learning. In *Proc. IEEE Comput. Soc. Conf. Comput. Vision and Pattern Recogn.*, pages 264–271, 2003.
12. M. Fischler and R. Elschlager. The representation and matching of pictorial structures. *IEEE Trans. Computers*, C-22(1):67–92, 1973.
13. D. Gavrila and V. Philomin. Real-time object detection for smart vehicles. In *Proc. 7th Int. Conf. Computer Vision*, pages 87–93, 1999.
14. U. Grenander, Y. Chow, and D.M. Keenan. *HANDS: A Pattern Theoretic Study Of Biological Shapes*. Springer, 1991.
15. A. Holub, M. Welling, and P. Perona. Combining generative models and fisher kernels for object recognition. In *Proc. 10th Int. Conf. Computer Vision*, pages 136– 143, 2005.

16. D.P. Huttenlocher, G. Klanderman, and W. Rucklidge. Comparing images using the Hausdorff distance. *IEEE Trans. PAMI*, 15(9):850–863, Sept. 1993.
17. M. Lades, C.C. Vorbrüggen, J. Buhmann, J. Lange, C. von der Malsburg, R.P. Wurtz, and W. Konen. Distortion invariant object recognition in the dynamic link architecture. *IEEE Trans. Computers*, 42(3):300–311, March 1993.
18. Y. Lamdan, J.T. Schwartz, and H.J. Wolfson. Affine invariant model-based object recognition. *IEEE Trans. Robotics and Automation*, 6:578–589, 1990.
19. T.K. Leung, M.C. Burl, and P. Perona. Finding faces in cluttered scenes using random labeled graph matching. In *Proc. 5th Int. Conf. Computer Vision*, pages 637–644, 1995.
20. D. G. Lowe. Object recognition from local scale-invariant features. In *Proc. 7th Int. Conf. Computer Vision*, pages 1150–1157, 1999.
21. D. G. Lowe. Distinctive image features from scale-invariant keypoints. *Int. Journal of Computer Vision*, 60(2):91–110, 2004.
22. J. Maciel and J Costeira. A global solution to sparse correspondence problems. *IEEE Trans. PAMI*, 25(2):187–199, 2003.
23. D. Martin, C. Fowlkes, and J. Malik. Learning to detect natural image boundaries using local brightness, color, and texture cues. *IEEE Trans. PAMI*, 26(5):530–549, 2004.
24. K. Mikolajczyk. *Detection of local features invariant to affines transformations*. PhD thesis, INPG, 2002.
25. K. Mikolajczyk and C. Schmid. A performance evaluation of local descriptors. In *Proc. IEEE Comput. Soc. Conf. Comput. Vision and Pattern Recogn.*, pages 257–263, 2003.
26. G. Mori, S. Belongie, and J. Malik. Shape contexts enable efficient retrieval of similar shapes. In *Proc. IEEE Comput. Soc. Conf. Comput. Vision and Pattern Recogn.*, volume 1, pages 723–730, 2001.
27. M. Morrone and D. Burr. Feature detection in human vision: A phase dependent energy model. *Proc. Royal Soc. of London B*, 235:221–245, 1988.
28. M. J. D. Powell. A thin plate spline method for mapping curves into curves in two dimensions. In *CTAC*, Melbourne, Australia, 1995.
29. A. Rangarajan, H. Chui, and E. Mjolsness. A relationship between spline-based deformable models and weighted graphs in non-rigid matching. In *Proc. IEEE Comput. Soc. Conf. Comput. Vision and Pattern Recogn.*, volume 1, pages 897–904, December 2001.
30. F. Rothganger, S. Lazebnik, C Schmid, and J Ponce. 3d object modeling and recognition using affine-invariant patches and multi-view spatial constraints. In *Proc. IEEE Comput. Soc. Conf. Comput. Vision and Pattern Recogn.*, pages II:272–275, 2003.
31. H. Schneiderman and T. Kanade. A statistical method for 3d object detection applied to faces and cars. In *Proc. IEEE Comput. Soc. Conf. Comput. Vision and Pattern Recogn.*, pages 746–751, 2000.
32. H. Schneiderman. Feature-centric evaluation for efficient cascaded object detection. In *Proc. IEEE Comput. Soc. Conf. Comput. Vision and Pattern Recogn.*, pages 29–36, 2004.
33. C. Schmid and R. Mohr. Local grayvalue invariants for image retrieval. *IEEE Trans. PAMI*, 19(5):530–535, May 1997.
34. D'Arcy Wentworth Thompson. *On Growth and Form*. Dover, 1917.

35. A. Torralba, K. P. Murphy, and W. T. Freeman. Sharing features: efficient boosting procedures for multiclass object detection. In *Proc. IEEE Comput. Soc. Conf. Comput. Vision and Pattern Recogn.*, pages 762–769, 2004.
36. S. Ullman, M. Vidal-Naquet, and E Sali. Visual features of intermediate complexity and their use in classification. *Nat. Neur.*, 13:682–687, 2002.
37. P. Viola and M. Jones. Robust real-time object detection. *2nd Intl. Workshop on Statistical and Computational Theories of Vision*, 2001.

An Implicit Shape Model for Combined Object Categorization and Segmentation

Bastian Leibe[1], Ales Leonardis[2], and Bernt Schiele[3]

[1] Computer Vision Lab,
ETH Zurich, Switzerland
leibe@vision.ee.ethz.ch
[2] Faculty of Computer and Information Science,
University of Ljubljana, Slovenia
alesl@fri.uni-lj.si
[3] Department of Computer Science,
TU Darmstadt, Germany
schiele@informatik.tu-darmstadt.de

Abstract. We present a method for object categorization in real-world scenes. Following a common consensus in the field, we do not assume that a figure-ground segmentation is available prior to recognition. However, in contrast to most standard approaches for object class recognition, our approach automatically segments the object as a result of the categorization.

This combination of recognition and segmentation into one process is made possible by our use of an Implicit Shape Model, which integrates both capabilities into a common probabilistic framework. This model can be thought of as a non-parametric approach which can easily handle configurations of large numbers of object parts. In addition to the recognition and segmentation result, it also generates a per-pixel confidence measure specifying the area that supports a hypothesis and how much it can be trusted. We use this confidence to derive a natural extension of the approach to handle multiple objects in a scene and resolve ambiguities between overlapping hypotheses with an MDL-based criterion.

In addition, we present an extensive evaluation of our method on a standard dataset for car detection and compare its performance to existing methods from the literature. Our results show that the proposed method outperforms previously published methods while needing one order of magnitude less training examples. Finally, we present results for articulated objects, which show that the proposed method can categorize and segment unfamiliar objects in different articulations and with widely varying texture patterns, even under significant partial occlusion.

1   Introduction

The goal of our work is object categorization in real-world scenes. That is, given some training examples of an object category, we want to recognize a-priori unknown instances of that category, assign the correct category label, and localize

J. Ponce et al. (Eds.): Toward Category-Level Object Recognition, LNCS 4170, pp. 508–524, 2006.

them in novel images. In order to transfer this capability to new domains, it is especially important that class characteristics be learned instead of hard-coded into the system. Therefore, we aim to learn solely from example images.

In order to learn an object category, we pursue a two-staged approach. In the first step, we learn a *Codebook of Local Appearance* that contains information which local structures may appear on objects of the target category. Next, we learn an *Implicit Shape Model* that specifies where on the object the codebook entries may occur. As the name already suggests, we do not try to define an explicit model for all possible shapes a class object may take, but instead define "allowed" shapes implicitly in terms of which local appearances are consistent with each other. The advantages of this approach are its greater flexibility and the smaller number of training examples it needs to see in order to learn possible object shapes. For example, when learning to categorize articulated objects such as cows, our method does not need to see every possible articulation in the training set. It can combine the information of a front leg seen on one training cow with the information of a rear leg from a different cow to recognize a test image with a novel articulation, since both leg positions are consistent with the same object hypothesis.

This idea is similar in spirit to approaches that represent novel objects by a combination of class prototypes [11], or of familiar object views [23]. However, the main difference of our approach is that here the combination does not occur between entire exemplar objects, but through the use of local image patches, which again allows a greater flexibility. Also, the Implicit Shape Model is formulated in a probabilistic framework that allows us to obtain a category-specific segmentation as a result of the recognition process. This segmentation can then in turn be used to improve the recognition results. In particular, we obtain a per-pixel confidence measure specifying how much both the recognition and the segmentation result can be trusted.

In addition, we extend the method to handle multiple objects in a scene and effectively resolve ambiguities between overlapping hypotheses by a novel criterion based on the MDL principle. We also extensively evaluate the method on two large data sets and compare its performance to existing methods from the literature. Our results show a significant improvement over previously published methods. Finally, we present results for articulated objects, which show that the proposed method can categorize and segment unfamiliar objects in different articulations, with widely varying texture patterns, and under significant partial occlusion.

The chapter is structured as follows. The next section discusses related work. After that, we describe the recognition approach and its extension to generate category-specific segmentations. Section 4 then presents an evaluation on a car detection task. Using the segmentation obtained in the previous step, Section 5 extends the approach to resolve ambiguities between multiple object hypotheses with an MDL-based criterion and compares our performance to existing methods. Finally, Section 6 shows experimental results for the recognition and segmentation of articulated objects. A final discussion concludes our work.

2   Related Work

Various shape models have been used for the recognition of object classes. When regularly textured objects are used, the shape can be modelled by spatial frequency statistics of texture descriptors [21]. For detection and recognition of more general object classes, many current methods learn global or local features in fixed configurations [22,20,24]. Since they treat the object as a whole, such approaches need a large number of training examples. Others learn the assembly of hand-selected object parts using configuration classifiers [19] or by modelling the joint spatial probability distribution [4]. Weber & Perona [25] also learn the local parts and explicitly compute their joint distribution. Fergus et al. [8] extend this approach to scale-invariant object parts and estimate their joint spatial and appearance distribution. However, the complexity of this combined estimation step restricts their methods to a small number of parts. Agarwal & Roth [1] keep a larger number of object parts and apply a feature-efficient classifier for learning spatial configurations between pairs of parts. However, their learning approach relies on the repeated observation of cooccurrences between the same parts in similar spatial relations, which again requires a large number of training examples.

The idea to use top-down knowledge to drive the segmentation process has recently developed into an area of active research. Approaches, such as Deformable Templates [27], or Active Appearance Models [7], are typically used when the object of interest is known to be present in the image and an initial estimate of its size and location can be obtained. Borenstein & Ullman [3] generate class-specific segmentations by combining object fragments in a jigsaw-puzzle fashion. However, their approach assumes only a single object to be present in the scene. Yu & Shi [26] present a parallel segmentation and recognition system in a graph theoretic framework, but only for a set of known objects.

Our approach integrates the two processes of recognition and segmentation in a common probabilistic framework. Given a set of training examples from an object class, it is able to automatically learn a category representation and recognize and segment a-priori unknown objects of this class in novel settings. By representing allowed part configurations in terms of an implicit model, it retains high flexibility while making efficient use of the available training data. The following sections describe this combination in detail.

3   Approach

In order to represent the appearance variability of an object category C, we introduce an Implicit Shape Model $ISM(C) = (I_C, P_{I,C})$, which consists of a class-specific alphabet I_C (in the following termed a *codebook*) of local appearances that are prototypical for the object category, and of a spatial probability distribution $P_{I,C}$ which specifies where each codebook entry may be found on the object.

We make two explicit design choices for the probability distribution $P_{I,C}$. The first is that the distribution is defined independently for each codebook entry.

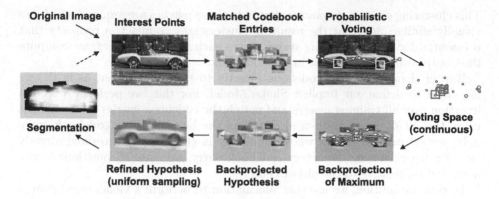

Fig. 1. The recognition procedure. Image patches are extracted around interest points and compared to the codebook. Matching patches then cast probabilistic votes, which lead to object hypotheses that can later be refined. Based on the refined hypotheses, we compute a category-specific segmentation.

This makes the approach flexible, since it allows to combine object parts during recognition that were initially observed on different training examples. In addition, it enables us to learn recognition models from relatively small training sets, as our experiments in Sections 4 and 6 demonstrate. The second constraint is that the spatial probability distribution for each codebook entry is estimated in a non-parametric manner. The method is thus able to model the true distribution in as much detail as the training data permits instead of making an oversimplifying Gaussian assumption.

The rest of this section explains how this learning and modeling step is implemented and how the resulting implicit model is used for recognition.

3.1   A Codebook of Local Appearance

In order to generate a codebook of local appearances of a particular object category, we use an approach inspired by the work of Agarwal and Roth [1]. From a variety of images, patches of size 25×25 pixels are extracted with the Harris interest point detector [10]. Starting with each patch as a separate cluster, agglomerative clustering is performed: the two most similar clusters C_1 and C_2 are merged as long as the average similarity between their constituent patches (and thus the cluster compactness) stays above a certain threshold t:

$$similarity(C_1, C_2) = \frac{\sum_{p \in C_1, q \in C_2} N\dot{G}C(p, q)}{|C_1| \times |C_2|} > t, \qquad (1)$$

where the similarity between two patches is measured by Normalized Greyscale Correlation (NGC):

$$NGC(p, q) = \frac{\sum_i (p_i - \overline{p_i})(q_i - \overline{q_i})}{\sqrt{\sum_i (p_i - \overline{p_i})^2 \sum_i (q_i - \overline{q_i})^2}} \qquad (2)$$

This clustering scheme guarantees that only those patches are grouped which are visually similar, and that the resulting clusters stay compact, a property that is essential for later processing stages. From each resulting cluster, we compute the cluster center and store it in the codebook.

Rather than to use this codebook directly to train a classifier, as in [1], we use them to define our Implicit Shape Model. For this, we perform a second iteration over all training images and match the codebook entries to the images using the NGC measure. Instead of taking the best-matching codebook entry only, we activate all entries whose similarity is above t, the threshold already used during clustering. For every codebook entry, we store all positions it was activated in, relative to the object center.

During recognition, we use this information to perform a Generalized Hough Transform [2,17]. Given a test image, we extract image patches and match them to the codebook to activate codebook entries. Each activated entry then casts votes for possible positions of the object center. Figure 1 illustrates this procedure. It is important to emphasize that we use a continuous voting space in order to avoid discretization artefacts. We search for hypotheses as maxima in the voting space using Mean-Shift Mode Estimation [5,6]. For promising hypotheses, all contributing patches are collected (Fig. 1(bottom)), therefore visualizing what the system reacts to. Moreover, we can refine the hypothesis by sampling all the image patches in its surroundings, not just those locations returned by the interest point detector. As a result, we get a representation of the object including a certain border area.

3.2   Probabilistic Formulation

In the following, we cast this recognition procedure into a probabilistic framework [13,12]. Let $\mathbf{e}$ be our evidence, an extracted image patch observed at location ℓ. By matching it to our codebook, we obtain a set of valid interpretations I_i. Each interpretation is weighted with the probability $p(I_i|\mathbf{e}, \ell)$. If a codebook cluster matches, it can cast its votes for different object positions. That is, for every I_i, we can obtain votes for several object identities o_n and positions x according to its spatial probability distribution $P(o_n, x|I_i, \ell)$. Formally, this can be expressed by the following marginalization:

$$p(o_n, x|\mathbf{e}, \ell) = \sum_i P(o_n, x|\mathbf{e}, I_i, \ell)p(I_i|\mathbf{e}, \ell). \tag{3}$$

Since we have replaced the unknown image patch by a known interpretation, the first term can be treated as independent from $\mathbf{e}$. In addition, we match patches to the codebook independent of their location. The equation thus reduces to

$$p(o_n, x|\mathbf{e}, \ell) = \sum_i P(o_n, x|I_i, \ell)p(I_i|\mathbf{e}). \tag{4}$$

$$= \sum_i P(x|o_n, I_i, \ell)p(o_n|I_i, \ell)p(I_i|\mathbf{e}). \tag{5}$$

The first term is the probabilistic Hough vote for an object position given its identity and the patch interpretation. The second term specifies a confidence that the codebook cluster is really matched on the object as opposed to the background. This can be used to include negative examples in the training. Finally, the third term reflects the quality of the match between image patch and codebook cluster.

By basing the decision on single-patch votes, assuming a uniform prior for the patches, and collecting contributing votes over a tolerance window $W(x)$, we obtain

$$score(o_n, x) = \sum_k \sum_{x_j \in W(x)} p(o_n, x_j | \mathbf{e}_k, \ell_k). \tag{6}$$

From this probabilistic framework, it immediately follows that the $p(I_i | \mathbf{e})$ and $p(x | o_n, I_i, \ell)$ should both sum to one. In our experiments, we spread the weight $p(I_i | \mathbf{e})$ uniformly over all valid patch interpretations (setting $p(I_i | \mathbf{e}) = \frac{1}{|I|}$, with $|I|$ the number of matching codebook entries), but it would also be possible to let the $p(I_i | \mathbf{e})$ distribution reflect the relative matching scores.

By this derivation, we have embedded the Hough voting strategy in a probabilistic framework. In this context, the Mean-Shift search over the voting space can be interpreted as a Parzen window probability density estimation for the correct object location. The power of this approach lies in its non-parametric nature. Instead of making Gaussian assumptions for the codebook cluster distribution on the object, our approach is able to model the true distribution in as much detail as is possible from the observed training examples.

3.3   Object Segmentation

In this section, we describe a probabilistic formulation for the segmentation problem (as derived in [13]). As a starting point, we take a refined object hypothesis $h = (o_n, x)$ obtained by the algorithm from the previous section. Based on this hypothesis, we want to segment the object from the background.

Up to now, we have only dealt with image patches. For the segmentation, we now want to know whether a certain image pixel $\mathbf{p}$ is *figure* or *ground*, given the object hypothesis. More precisely, we are interested in the probability $p(\mathbf{p} = figure | o_n, x)$. The influence of a given patch $\mathbf{e}$ on the object hypothesis can be expressed as

$$p(\mathbf{e}, \ell | o_n, x) = \frac{p(o_n, x | \mathbf{e}, \ell)p(\mathbf{e}, \ell)}{p(o_n, x)} = \frac{\sum_I P(o_n, x | I, \ell)p(I | \mathbf{e})p(\mathbf{e}, \ell)}{p(o_n, x)} \tag{7}$$

where the patch votes $p(o_n, x | \mathbf{e}, \ell)$ are obtained from the codebook, as described in the previous section. Given these probabilities, we can obtain information about a specific pixel by marginalizing over all patches that contain this pixel:

$$p(\mathbf{p} = figure | o_n, x) = \sum_{\mathbf{p} \in (\mathbf{e}, \ell)} p(\mathbf{p} = figure | o_n, x, \mathbf{e}, \ell)p(\mathbf{e}, \ell | o_n, x) \tag{8}$$

with $p(\mathbf{p} = figure | o_n, x, \mathbf{e}, \ell)$ denoting patch-specific segmentation information, which is weighted by the influence $p(\mathbf{e}, \ell | o_n, x)$ the patch has on the object hypothesis. Again, we can resolve patches by resorting to learned patch interpretations I stored in the codebook:

$$p(\mathbf{p} = \mathit{figure}|o_n, x) = \sum_{\mathbf{p} \in (\mathbf{e}, \ell)} \sum_{I} p(\mathbf{p} = \mathit{fig}.|o_n, x, \mathbf{e}, I, \ell) p(\mathbf{e}, I, \ell|o_n, x) \qquad (9)$$

$$= \sum_{\mathbf{p} \in (\mathbf{e}, \ell)} \sum_{I} p(\mathbf{p} = \mathit{fig}.|o_n, x, I, \ell) \frac{P(o_n, x|I, \ell) p(I|\mathbf{e}) p(\mathbf{e}, \ell)}{p(o_n, x)} \qquad (10)$$

This means that for every pixel, we build a weighted average over all segmentations stemming from patches containing that pixel. The weights correspond to the patches' respective contributions to the object hypothesis. For the *ground* probability, the result is obtained in an analogue fashion.

The most important part in this formulation is the per-pixel segmentation information $p(\mathbf{p} = \mathit{figure}|o_n, x, I, \ell)$, which is only dependent on the matched codebook entry, no longer on the image patch. In our approach, we implement this probability by keeping a separate segmentation mask for every stored *occurrence position* of each codebook entry. These patch figure-ground masks are extracted from a reference segmentation given for each training image. Further, we assume uniform priors for $p(\mathbf{e}, \ell)$ and $p(o_n, x)$, so that these elements can be factored out of the equations. In order to obtain a segmentation of the whole image from the figure and ground probabilities, we build the likelihood ratio for every pixel:

$$L = \frac{p(\mathbf{p} = \mathit{figure}|o_n, x)}{p(\mathbf{p} = \mathit{ground}|o_n, x)}. \qquad (11)$$

Figure 7 shows example segmentations of cars, together with $p(\mathbf{p} = \mathit{figure}|o_n, x)$, the system's confidence in the segmentation result. The darker a pixel, the higher its probability of being *figure*. The lighter it is, the higher its probability of being *ground*. The uniform gray region in the background of the segmentation image does not contribute to the object hypothesis and is therefore considered neutral. The estimate of how much the obtained segmentation can be trusted is especially important when the results shall later be combined with other cues for recognition or segmentation. It is also the basis for our MDL-based hypothesis selection criterion described in Section 5.

4 Results

In order to compare our method's performance to state-of-the-art approaches, we applied it to the UIUC car database [1]. This test set consists of 170 images containing a total of 200 sideviews of cars. The images include instances of partially occluded cars, cars that have low contrast with the background, and images with highly textured backgrounds. In the dataset, all cars are approximately the same size.

Together with the test set, Agarwal & Roth provide a training set of 550 car and 500 non-car images. In our experiments, we do not use this training set, but instead train on a much smaller set of only 50 hand-segmented images (mirrored to represent both car directions) that were originally prepared for a different experiment. In particular, our training set contains both European and American

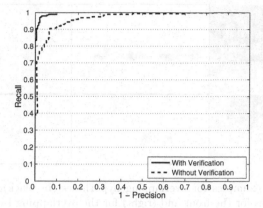

Fig. 2. Results on the UIUC car database with and without the MDL hypothesis verification stage

cars, whereas the test set mainly consists of American-style sedans and limousines. Thus, our detector remains more general and is not tuned to the specific test conditions. The original data set is at a relatively low resolution (with cars of size 100*40 pixels). Since our detector is learned at a higher resolution, we rescaled all images by a constant factor prior to recognition (Note that this step does not increase the images' information content). All experiments were done using the evaluation scheme and detection tolerances from [1].

Figure 2 shows a recall-precision curve (RPC) of our method's performance. As can be seen from the figure, our method succeeds to generalize from the small training set and achieves good detection results with an Equal Error Rate (EER) of 91%. Analyzing the results on the test set, we observed that a large percentage of the remaining false positives are due to *secondary hypotheses*, which contain only one of the car's wheels, e.g. the rear wheel, but hypothesize it to be the front wheel of an adjoining car (see Figure 3 for an example). This problem is particularly prominent in scenes that contain multiple objects. The following section derives a hypothesis verification criterion which resolves these ambiguities in a natural fashion and thus improves the recognition results.

5 Multiple-Object Scene Analysis

As already mentioned in the previous section, a large number of the initial false positives are due to secondary hypotheses which overlap part of the object. This is a common problem in object detection. Generating such hypotheses is a desired property of a recognition algorithm, since it allows the method to cope with partial occlusions. However, if enough support is present in the image, the secondary detections should be sacrificed in favor of other hypotheses that better explain the image. Usually, this problem is solved by introducing a bounding box criterion and rejecting weaker hypotheses based on their overlap. However, such an approach may lead to missed detections, as the example in Figure 3 shows.

516   B. Leibe, A. Leonardis, and B. Schiele

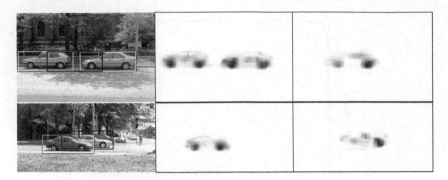

Fig. 3. (left) Two examples for overlapping hypotheses (in black); (middle) $p(\mathbf{p} = figure|h)$ probabilities for the front and (right) for the overlapping hypotheses. As can be seen, the overlapping hypothesis in the above example is fully explained by the two correct detections, while the one in the lower example obtains additional support from a different region in the image.

Here the overlapping hypothesis really corresponds to a second car, which would be rejected by the simple bounding box criterion. However, since our algorithm provides us with an object segmentation together with the hypotheses, we can improve on this. In the following, we derive a criterion based on the principle of Minimal Description Length (MDL), inspired by the approach pursued in [16].

The MDL principle is an information theoretic formalization of the general notion to prefer simple explanations to more complicated ones. In our context, a pixel can be described either by its grayvalue or by its membership to a scene object. If it is explained as part of an object, we also need to encode the presence of the object ("model cost"), as well as the error that is made by this representation. The MDL principle states that the best encoding is the one that minimizes the total description length for image, model, and error.

In accordance with the notion of description length, we can define the *savings* [16] in the encoding that can be obtained by explaining part of an image by the hypothesis h:

$$S_h = K_0 S_{area} - K_1 S_{model} - K_2 S_{error} \tag{12}$$

In this formulation, S_{area} corresponds to the number N of pixels that can be explained by h; S_{error} denotes the cost for describing the error made by this explanation; and S_{model} describes the model complexity. In our implementation, we assume a fixed cost $S_{model} = 1$ for each additional scene object. As an estimate for the error we use

$$S_{error} = \sum_{\mathbf{p} \in Seg(h)} (1 - p(\mathbf{p} = figure|h)) \tag{13}$$

that is, over all pixels that are hypothesized to belong to the segmentation of h, we sum the probabilities that these pixels are not *figure*.

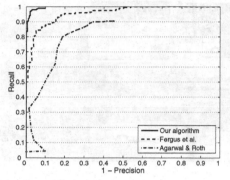

Method	Equal Error Rate
Agarwal & Roth [1]	~79%
Garg et al. [9]	~88%
Fergus et al. [8]	88.5%
Our algorithm	97.5%

Fig. 4. Comparison of our results on the UIUC car database with others reported in the literature

The constants K_0, K_1, and K_2 are related to the average cost of specifying the segmented object area, the model, and the error, respectively. They can be determined on a purely information-theoretical basis (in terms of bits), or they can be adjusted in order to express the preference for a particular type of description. In practice, we only need to consider the relative savings between different combinations of hypotheses. Thus, we can divide Eq(12) by K_0 and, after some simplification steps, we obtain

$$S_h = -\frac{K_1}{K_0} + (1 - \frac{K_2}{K_0})N + \frac{K_2}{K_0} \sum_{\mathbf{p} \in Seg(h)} p(\mathbf{p} = \textit{figure}|h). \qquad (14)$$

This leaves us with two parameters: $\frac{K_2}{K_0}$, which encodes the relative importance that is assigned to the support of a hypothesis, as opposed to the area it explains; and $\frac{K_1}{K_0}$, which specifies the total weight a hypothesis must accumulate in order to provide any savings. Good values for these parameters can be found by considering some limiting cases, such as the minimum support a hypothesis must have in the image, before it should be accepted.

Using this framework, we can now resolve conflicts between overlapping hypotheses. Given two hypotheses h_1 and h_2, we can derive the savings of the *combined hypothesis* $(h_1 \cup h_2)$:

$$S_{h_1 \cup h_2} = S_{h_1} + S_{h_2} - S_{area}(h_1 \cap h_2) + S_{error}(h_1 \cap h_2) \qquad (15)$$

Both the overlapping area and the error can be computed from the segmentations obtained in Section 3.3. Let h_1 be the stronger hypothesis of the two. Under the assumption that h_1 opaquely occludes h_2, we can set $p(\mathbf{p} = \textit{figure}|h_2) = 0$ wherever $p(\mathbf{p} = \textit{figure}|h_1) > p(\mathbf{p} = \textit{ground}|h_1)$, that is for all pixels that belong to the segmentation of h_1. Rather than to search for the globally optimal solution, which may become untractable, it is sufficient for our application to consider only pairwise combinations, as argued in [16].

Fig. 5. Example detections on difficult images from the test set

5.1   Experimental Results

Figure 2 shows the results on the UIUC car database when the MDL criterion is applied as a verification stage. As can be seen from the figure, the results are significantly improved, and the EER performance increases from 91% to 97.5%. Without the verification stage, our algorithm could reach this recall rate only at the price of a reduced precision of only 74.1%. This means that for the same recall rate, the verification stage manages to reject 64 additional false positives while keeping all correct detections. In addition, the results become far more stable over a wider parameter range than before. This can be illustrated by the fact that even when the initial acceptance threshold is lowered to 0, the MDL criterion does not return more than 20 false positives. This property, together with the criterion's good theoretical foundation and its ability to correctly solve cases like the one in Figure 3, makes it an important contribution.

Figure 4 shows a comparison of our method's performance with other results reported in the literature. The adjacent table contains a comparison of the equal error rates (EER) with three other approaches. With an EER of 97.5%, our method presents a significant improvement over previous results. Some example detections in difficult settings can be seen in Figure 5. The images show that our method still works in the presence of occlusion, low contrast, and cluttered backgrounds. At the EER point, our method correctly finds 195 of the 200 test cases with only 5 false positives. All of these error cases are displayed in Figure 6. The main reasons for missing detections are combinations of several factors, such as low contrast, occlusion, and image plane rotations, that push the object hypothesis below the acceptance threshold. The false positives are due to richly textured backgrounds on which a large number of spurious object parts are found.

In addition to the recognition results, our method automatically generates object segmentations from the test images. Figure 7 shows some example segmentations that can be achieved with this method. Even though the quality of the original images is rather low, the segmentations are reliable and can serve as

Fig. 6. All missing detections (above) and false positives (below) our algorithm returned on the car test set. The last picture contains both a false positive and a missing detection.

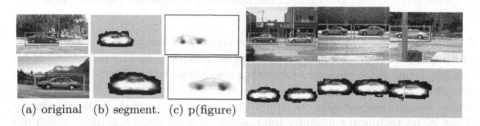

(a) original   (b) segment.   (c) p(figure)

Fig. 7. (left) Example object detections, segmentations, and *figure* probabilities automatically generated by our method; (right) Some more detections and segmentations (white: *figure*, black: *ground*, gray: *not sampled*)

a basis for later processing stages, e.g. to further improve the recognition results using global methods.

6   Recognition of Articulated Objects

Up to now, we have only considered static objects in our experiments. Even though environmental conditions can vary greatly, cars are still rather restricted in their possible shapes. This changes when we consider articulated objects, such as walking animals. In order to fully demonstrate our method's capabilities, we therefore apply it to a database of video sequences of walking cows originally used for detecting lameness in livestock [18]. Each sequence shows one or more cows walking from right to left in front of different, static backgrounds.

For training, we took out all sequences corresponding to three backgrounds and extracted 112 randomly chosen frames, for which we manually created a reference segmentation. We then tested on 14 different video sequences showing a total of 18 unseen cows in front of novel backgrounds and with varying lighting conditions. Some test sequences contain severe interlacing and MPEG-compression artefacts and significant noise. Altogether, the test suite consists of a total of 2217 frames, in which 1682 instances of cows are visible by at least

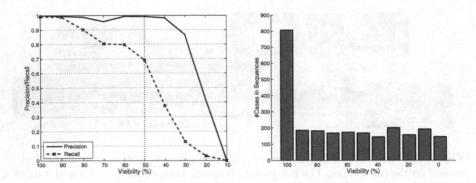

Fig. 8. (left) Precision/Recall curves for the cow sequences when x% of the cow's length is visible. (right) Absolute number of test images for the different visibility cases.

50%. This provides us with a significant number of test cases to quantify both our method's ability to deal with different articulations and its robustness to occlusion. Using video sequences for testing also allows to avoid any bias caused by selecting only certain frames. However, since we are still interested in a single-frame recognition scenario, we apply our algorithm to each frame separately. That is, no temporal continuity information is used for recognition, which one would obviously add for a tracking scenario.

We applied our method to this test set using exactly the same detector settings as before to obtain equal error rate for the car experiments. The only change we made was to slightly adjust the sensibility of the interest point detector in order to compensate for the lower image contrast. Using these settings, our detector correctly finds 1535 out of the 1682 cows, corresponding to a recall of 91.2%. With only 30 false positives over all 2217 frames, the overall precision is at 98.0%. Figure 8 shows the precision and recall values as a function of the visible object area. As can be seen from this plot, the method has no difficulties in recognizing cows that are fully visible (99.1% recall at 99.5% precision). Moreover, it can cope with significant partial occlusion. When only 60% of the object is visible, recall only drops to 79.8%. Even when half the object is occluded, the recognition rate is still at 69.0%. In some rare cases, even a very small object portion of about 20 − 30% is already enough for recognition (such as in the leftmost image in Figure 10). Precision constantly stays at a high level.

False positives mainly occur when only one pair of legs is fully visible and the system generates a competing hypothesis interpreting the front legs as rear legs, or vice versa. Usually, such secondary hypotheses are filtered out by the MDL stage, but if the correct hypothesis does not have enough support in the image due to partial visibility, the secondary hypothesis sometimes wins.

Figures 9 and 10 show example detection and segmentation results for two sequences[1]. As can be seen from these images, the system not only manages to

---

[1] The full result sequences are available at
http://www.mis.informatik.tu-darmstadt.de/projects/interleaved

Fig. 9. Example detections and automatically generated segmentations from one cow sequence. (middle row) segmentations obtained from the intial hypotheses; (bottom row) segmentations from refined hypotheses.

recognize unseen-before cows with novel texture patterns, but it also provides good segmentations for them. Again, we want to emphasize that no tracking information is used to generate these results. On the contrary, the capability to generate object segmentations from single frames could make our method a valuable supplement to many current tracking algorithms, allowing to (re-) initialize them through shape cues that are orthogonal to those gained from motion estimates.

7 Discussion and Conclusion

The probabilities $p(\mathbf{p} = figure|h)$ in Figs. 3 and 7 demonstrate why our approach is successful. These probabilities correspond to the per-pixel confidence the system has in its recognition and segmentation result. As can be seen from the figure, the cars' wheels are found as the most important single feature. However, the rest of the chassis and even the windows are represented as well. Together, they provide additional support for the hypothesis. This is possible because we do not perform any feature selection during the training stage, but store all local parts that are repeatedly encountered on the training objects. The resulting complete representation allows our approach to compensate for missing detections and partial occlusions.

Another factor to the method's success is the flexibility of representation that is made possible by the Implicit Shape Model. Using this framework, it can interpolate between local parts seen on different training objects. As a result, the method only needs a relatively small number of training examples to recognize and segment categorical objects in different articulations and with widely varying texture patterns.

Fig. 10. Example detections and automatically generated segmentations from another sequence. Note in particular the leftmost image, where the cow is correctly recognized and segmented despite a high degree of occlusion.

The price we have to pay for this flexibility is that local parts could also be matched to potentially illegal configurations, such as a cow with 6 legs. Since each hypothesized leg is locally consistent with the common object center, there would be nothing to prevent such configurations. An example where this happens can be seen in Fig. 9. In the experiments presented here, this effect did not hurt recognition performance, but it may become a problem in heavily crowded scenes. A recent extension of our method resolves this problem by adding a global, explicit shape model on top of the current implicit model [15].

Another restriction of the approach, as it is described in this chapter, is its reliance on single-scale interest points, which only tolerate relatively small scale changes of about $10 - 15\%$. In more recent work [14], we have however extended it also to scale-invariant detection. The key idea in this extension is to replace the single-scale Harris detector by scale-invariant interest points and let matched features vote not only for the object position, but also for its scale using a 3D voting space (see [14] for details).

Quite interestingly, the current model is purely representational. Although equation (5) allows for the inclusion of negative training examples, we do not yet use any such discriminative information, nor do we model the background explicitly. For the data sets used in this evaluation, this was not necessary, but we expect that the performance and robustness of our method can be further improved by incorporating these steps. In addition, future work will explore how the method scales to larger object sets and how multi-view objects should best be treated.

In conclusion, we have presented a method that combines the capabilities of object categorization and segmentation in a common probabilistic framework. The resulting approach is able to recognize previously unseen objects of a learned category, localize them in cluttered real-world images, and automatically segment them from the background. In order to resolve the ambiguities between overlapping hypotheses, we have introduced a further hypothesis verification criterion based on the MDL principle. This criterion significantly improves the method's results and allows it to handle scenes containing multiple objects in a principled manner. Finally, we have presented an extensive evaluation on two large data sets for cars and cows. Our results show that the method achieves excellent recognition and segmentation results, even under adverse viewing conditions and with significant occlusion. At the same time, its flexible representation enables it to generalize already from small training sets. These capabilities make it an interesting contribution with potential applications in object detection, categorization, segmentation and tracking.

Acknowledgments

This work has been funded, in part, by the EU projects CogVis (IST-2000-29375) and CoSy (IST-2002-004250), and the Swiss Federal Office for Education and Science (BBW 00.0617).

References

1. S. Agarwal and D. Roth. Learning a sparse representation for object detection. In *ECCV'02*, pages 113–130, 2002.
2. D.H. Ballard. Generalizing the hough transform to detect arbitrary shapes. *Pattern Recognition*, 13(2):111–122, 1981.
3. E. Borenstein and S. Ullman. Class-specific, top-down segmentation. In *ECCV'02*, LNCS 2353, pages 109–122, 2002.
4. M.C. Burl, M. Weber, and P. Perona. A probabilistic approach to object recognition using local photometry and global geometry. In *ECCV'98*, 1998.
5. Y. Cheng. Mean shift mode seeking and clustering. *Trans. PAMI*, 17(8):790–799, Aug. 1995.
6. D. Comaniciu and P. Meer. Distribution free decomposition of multivariate data. *Pattern Analysis and Applications*, 2(1):22–30, 1999.
7. T.F. Cootes, G.J. Edwards, and C.J. Taylor. Active appearance models. In *ECCV'98*, 1998.
8. R. Fergus, A. Zisserman, and P. Perona. Object class recognition by unsupervised scale-invariant learning. In *CVPR'03*, 2003.
9. A. Garg, S. Agarwal, and T. Huang. Fusion of global and local information for object detection. In *ICPR'02*, pages 723–726, 2002.
10. C. Harris and M. Stephens. A combined corner and edge detector. In *Alvey Vision Conference*, pages 147–151, 1988.
11. M. Jones and T. Poggio. Model-based matching by linear combinations of prototypes. MIT AI Memo 1583, MIT, 1996.
12. B. Leibe, A. Leonardis, and B. Schiele. Combined object categorization and segmentation with an implicit shape model. In *ECCV'04 Workshop on Stat. Learn. in Comp. Vis.*, pages 17–32, Prague, Czech Republic, May 2004.
13. B. Leibe and B. Schiele. Interleaved object categorization and segmentation. In *BMVC'03*, pages 759–768, Norwich, UK, Sept. 2003.

14. B. Leibe and B. Schiele. Scale invariant object categorization using a scale-adaptive mean-shift search. In *DAGM'04*, Springer LNCS, Vol. 3175, pages 145–153, Tuebingen, Germany, Aug. 2004.
15. B. Leibe, E. Seemann, and B. Schiele. Pedestrian detection in crowded scenes. In *CVPR'05*, 2005.
16. A. Leonardis, A. Gupta, and R. Bajcsy. Segmentation of range images as the search for geometric parametric models. *IJCV*, 14:253–277, 1995.
17. D.G. Lowe. Object recognition from local scale invariant features. In *ICCV'99*, 1999.
18. D. Magee and R. Boyle. Detecting lameness using 're-sampling condensation' and 'multi-stream cyclic hidden markov models'. *Image and Vision Computing*, 20(8):581–594, 2002.
19. A. Mohan, C. Papageorgiou, and T. Poggio. Example-based object detection in images by components. *Trans. PAMI*, 23(4):349–361, 2001.
20. C. Papageorgiou and T. Poggio. A trainable system for object detection. *IJCV*, 38(1):15–33, 2000.
21. C. Schmid. Constructing models for content-based image retrieval. In *CVPR'01*, 2001.
22. H. Schneiderman and T. Kanade. A statistical method of 3d object detection applied to faces and cars. In *CVPR'00*, pages 746–751, 2000.
23. S. Ullman. Three-dimensional object recognition based on the combination of views. *Cognition*, 67(1):21–44, 1998.
24. P. Viola and M. Jones. Rapid object detection using a boosted cascade of simple features. In *CVPR'01*, pages 511–518, 2001.
25. M. Weber, M. Welling, and P. Perona. Unsupervised learning of object models for recognition. In *ECCV'00*, 2000.
26. S.X. Yu and J. Shi. Object-specific figure-ground segregation. In *CVPR'03*, 2003.
27. A.L. Yuille, D.S. Cohen, and P.W. Hallinan. Feature extraction from faces using deformable templates. In *CVPR'89*, 1989.

Statistical Models of Shape and Texture for Face Recognition

Timothy F. Cootes, David Cristinacce, and Vladimir Petrović

Imaging Science and Biomedical Engineering,
University of Manchester, UK
{t.cootes,d.cristinacce,v.petrovic}@manchester.ac.uk
http://www.isbe.man.ac.uk

Abstract. Human faces are an example of a class of objects in which each example exhibits significant variation in shape and appearance, but which is composed of a fixed number of sub-parts which have a similar configuration in every case. For such objects we can define landmark points on each example which imply a correspondence between different examples. We can then build statistical models of the shape by considering the relative positions of landmarks, and can model the pattern of intensities across the object by warping them into a common reference frame. Such combined models of shape and appearance have been found to be powerful tools for image interpretation. They are generative models, capable of synthesizing new examples similar to those in the training set. The formulation of such models is described, and their application to face location and recognition investigated. Particular attention is paid to methods of matching such models to new images in a multi-stage process.

1 Introduction

When interpretting images of general scenes (eg images from photograph albums or newspaper archives) we commonly come across human faces. In some cases it is sufficient to know that a particular region contains a human face, but more commonly we wish to know more about that face. Typically we are interested in who the person is, and perhaps what their expression is. In an object recognition framework, we must sub-divide the class of "Human Faces" into multiple sub-classes, one for each individual, or alternatively, one class for each facial expression.

In order to interpret images of faces, it is important to have a model of how the face can appear. Faces can vary widely, but the changes can be broken down into two parts – changes in shape and changes in the texture (patterns of pixel values) across the face. Both shape and texture can vary because of differences between individuals, and due to changes in expression, viewpoint and lighting conditions. In this chapter we will describe a powerful method of generating compact models of shape and texture variation, and describe how such models can be used to interpret images of faces. This involves locating the faces in an image, and matching the models in a multi-stage process.

J. Ponce et al. (Eds.): Toward Category-Level Object Recognition, LNCS 4170, pp. 525–542, 2006.
© Springer-Verlag Berlin Heidelberg 2006

2   Statistical Models of Appearance

We wish to build models of facial appearance and variation. We adopt a statistical approach, learning the ways in which the shape and texture of the face vary across a range of images. This relies on obtaining a suitably large and representative training set of images of faces, each of which is annotated with a set of feature points defining correspondences across the images. The positions of the feature points are used to define the shape of the face, and are analysed to learn the ways in which the shape can vary. The patterns of intensities are then analysed to learn the ways in which the texture can vary. The result is a model which is capable of synthesizing any of the training images and generalising from them, but is specific enough that only face-like images are generated.

2.1   Statistical Shape Models

To build a statistical model, we require a set of training images. The set should be chosen so as to cover the types of variation we wish the model to represent. For instance, if we are only interested in faces with neutral expressions, we should only include neutral expressions in the model. If, however, we wish to be able to synthesize and recognise a range of expressions, the training set should include images of people smiling, frowning, winking and so on. The faces in the training set should be of at least as high a resolution as those in the images we wish to synthesize or interpret.

Each face must then be annotated with a set of points defining the key facial features. These points are used to define the correspondences across the training set, and to represent the shape of the face in the image. Thus the same number of points should be placed on each image, each with the same set of labels. Figure 1 shows a set of 68 points used to annotate frontal faces. The more points that are used, the more subtle the variations in shape that can be represented. Typically one would place points around the main facial features (eyes, nose, mouth, eyebrows) together with points around the outline to define the boundary of the face.

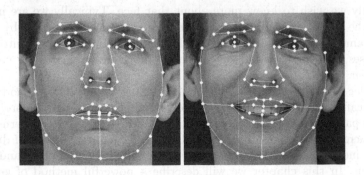

Fig. 1. Example of 68 points defining facial features

Shape is usually defined as that quality of a configuration of points which is invariant under some transformation. In two or three dimensions we usually consider either the similarity transformation (translation, rotation and scaling) or the affine transformation.

Let $S_t(\mathbf{x})$ apply a transformation defined by parameters $\mathbf{t}$. In 2D, similarity transformations have 4 parameters, affine transformations are defined by 6 parameters. The configurations of points defined by $\mathbf{x}$ and $S_t(\mathbf{x})$ are considered to have the same *shape*. Shape differences are those changes that cannot be explained by application of such a global transformation. If we use n points, $\{(x_j, y_j)\}$, to describe the face shape, then we can represent the shape as the $2n$ element vector, $\mathbf{x}$, where

$$\mathbf{x} = (x_1, \ldots, x_n, y_1, \ldots, y_n)^T \tag{1}$$

Given s training examples, we generate s such vectors $\mathbf{x}_i$ ($i = 1..s$). Before we can perform statistical analysis on these vectors it is important that the shapes represented are in the same co-ordinate frame. This can be achieved by using Procrustes Analysis [12]. This transforms each shape in a set, $\mathbf{x}_i$, so that the sum of squared distances of the shape to the mean ($D = \sum |S(\mathbf{x}_j) - \bar{\mathbf{x}}|^2$) is minimised.

Statistical Models of Variation. Let the vector $\mathbf{x}_i$ contain the n coordinates of the ith shape. These vectors form a distribution in $2n$ dimensional space. If we can model this distribution, we can generate new examples, similar to those in the original training set, and we can examine new shapes to decide whether they are plausible examples.

To simplify the problem, we first wish to reduce the dimensionality of the data from nd to something more manageable. An effective approach is to apply Principal Component Analysis (PCA) to the data [4]. The data form a cloud of points in the $2n$-D space. PCA computes the main axes of this cloud, allowing one to approximate any of the original points using a model with fewer than $2n$ parameters. The result is a linear model of the form

$$\mathbf{x} = \bar{\mathbf{x}} + \mathbf{P}_s \mathbf{b}_s \tag{2}$$

where $\bar{\mathbf{x}}$ is the mean of the data, $\mathbf{P}_s = (\phi_1|\phi_2|\ldots|\phi_t)$ contains the t eigenvectors of the covariance of the training set, corresponding to the largest eigenvalues, and $\mathbf{b}_s$ is a t dimensional parameter vector. The best choice of parameters for a given shape $\mathbf{x}$ is given by

$$\mathbf{b}_s = \mathbf{P}_s^T(\mathbf{x} - \bar{\mathbf{x}}) \tag{3}$$

($\mathbf{P}^T\mathbf{P} = \mathbf{I}$ since the eigenvectors are orthonormal.)

The vector $\mathbf{b}_s$ defines a set of parameters of a deformable model. By varying the elements of $\mathbf{b}_s$ we can vary the shape, $\mathbf{x}$, using Equation 2. The variance of the ith parameter, b_i, across the training set is given by λ_i. By applying suitable limits to the model parameters we ensure that the shape generated is similar to those in the original training set.

If the original data, $\{\mathbf{x}_i\}$, is distributed as a multivariate Gaussian, then the parameters $\mathbf{b}$ are distributed as an axis-aligned Gaussian, $p(\mathbf{b}) = N(\mathbf{0}, \Lambda)$ where $\Lambda = diag(\lambda_1, \ldots, \lambda_t)$. Our experiments on 2D images suggest that the Gaussian assumption is a good approximation to the face shape distribution, as long as the training set only contains modest viewpoint variation. Large viewpoint variation tends to introduce non-linear changes into the shape [3].

A shape in the image frame, $\mathbf{X}$, can be generated by applying a suitable transformation to the points, $\mathbf{x} : \mathbf{X} = S_t(\mathbf{x})$. Typically S_t will be a similarity transformation described by a scaling, s, an in-plane rotation, θ, and a translation (t_x, t_y).

Face Shape Variation. Figure 2 shows the first two most significant modes of face shape variation of a model built from examples of a single individual with different viewpoints and expressions. The model has learnt that the 2D shape change caused by 3D head rotation causes the largest shape change.

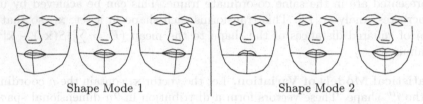

| Shape Mode 1 | Shape Mode 2 |

Fig. 2. Two modes of a face shape model (Parameters varied by ±2 s.d. from the mean)

2.2   Statistical Models of Texture

To build a statistical model of the texture (intensity or colour over an image patch) we warp each example image so that its feature points match a reference shape (typically the mean shape). The warping is usually achieved through a piece-wise affine transformation using a triangulation of the region. Warping to a reference shape removes spurious texture variation due to shape differences which would occur if we simply performed eigenvector decomposition on the un-normalised face patches (as in the eigen-face approach [16,20]). The intensity

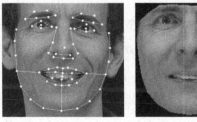

| Original Image | Warped to mean shape |

Fig. 3. Example of face warped to mean shape

information is sampled from the *shape-normalised* image over the region covered by the mean shape to form a texture vector, $\mathbf{g}_{im}$. Texture is sampled at N_t points on a regular grid. For example, Figure 3 shows a labelled face image and the face patch warped into the mean shape. Although the main shape changes due to smiling have been removed, there is considerable texture difference from a purely neutral face.

The texture sample is then normalised to remove global lighting effects. A simple approach is to apply a linear transformation

$$\mathbf{g} = (\mathbf{g}_{im} - \beta\mathbf{1})/\alpha \tag{4}$$

The values of α and β can be chosen so that the sum of elements is zero and the variance of elements is unity,

By applying PCA to the normalised data we obtain a linear model:

$$\mathbf{g} = \bar{\mathbf{g}} + \mathbf{P}_g\mathbf{b}_g \tag{5}$$

where $\bar{\mathbf{g}}$ is the mean normalised grey-level vector, $\mathbf{P}_g$ is a set of orthogonal *modes of variation* and $\mathbf{b}_g$ is a set of grey-level parameters.

The texture in the image frame can be generated from the texture parameters, $\mathbf{b}_g$, and the normalisation parameters α, β, by:

$$\mathbf{g}_{im} = \alpha(\bar{\mathbf{g}} + \mathbf{P}_g\mathbf{b}_g) + \beta\mathbf{1} \tag{6}$$

By varying the elements of the texture parameter vector $\mathbf{b}_g$ within limits learnt from the training set, we can generate a variety of plausible shape-normalised face textures. For instance Figure 4 shows the first four modes of a

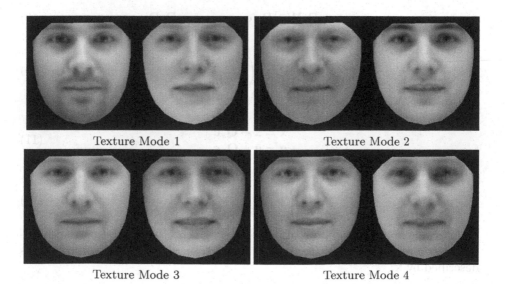

Texture Mode 1   Texture Mode 2

Texture Mode 3   Texture Mode 4

Fig. 4. Four modes of a face texture model (Parameters varied by ± 2 s.d. from the mean)

texture model built from 400 images of 100 different individuals (including neutral, smiling, frowning and surprised expressions of each). The model represents about $N_t = 20,000$ pixels.

2.3 Combined Models of Appearance

The shape and texture of any example can thus be summarised by the parameter vectors $\mathbf{b}_s$ and $\mathbf{b}_g$. Since there may be correlations between the shape and texture variations, we apply a further PCA to the data as follows. For each example we generate the concatenated vector

$$\mathbf{b} = \begin{pmatrix} \mathbf{W}_s \mathbf{b}_s \\ \mathbf{b}_g \end{pmatrix} = \begin{pmatrix} \mathbf{W}_s \mathbf{P}_s^T (\mathbf{x} - \bar{\mathbf{x}}) \\ \mathbf{P}_g^T (\mathbf{g} - \bar{\mathbf{g}}) \end{pmatrix} \tag{7}$$

where $\mathbf{W}_s$ is a diagonal matrix of weights for each shape parameter, allowing for the difference in units between the shape and grey models. We apply a PCA on these vectors, giving a further model

$$\mathbf{b} = \mathbf{P}_c \mathbf{c} \tag{8}$$

where $\mathbf{P}_c$ are the eigenvectors and $\mathbf{c}$ is a vector of *appearance* parameters controlling both the shape and grey-levels of the model. By the nature of its construction, $\mathbf{c}$ has zero mean across the training set.

Note that the linear nature of the model allows us to express the shape and grey-levels directly as functions of $\mathbf{c}$

$$\mathbf{x} = \bar{\mathbf{x}} + \mathbf{P}_s \mathbf{W}_s^{-1} \mathbf{P}_{cs} \mathbf{c} \ , \ \ \mathbf{g} = \bar{\mathbf{g}} + \mathbf{P}_g \mathbf{P}_{cg} \mathbf{c} \tag{9}$$

where

$$\mathbf{P}_c = \begin{pmatrix} \mathbf{P}_{cs} \\ \mathbf{P}_{cg} \end{pmatrix} \tag{10}$$

This can be summarized as

$$\begin{aligned} \mathbf{x} &= \bar{\mathbf{x}} + \mathbf{Q}_s \mathbf{c} \\ \mathbf{g} &= \bar{\mathbf{g}} + \mathbf{Q}_g \mathbf{c} \end{aligned} \tag{11}$$

where

$$\begin{aligned} \mathbf{Q}_s &= \mathbf{P}_s \mathbf{W}_s^{-1} \mathbf{P}_{cs} \\ \mathbf{Q}_g &= \mathbf{P}_g \mathbf{P}_{cg} \end{aligned} \tag{12}$$

An example image can be synthesised for a given $\mathbf{c}$ by generating the shape-free grey-level image from the vector $\mathbf{g}$ and warping it using the control points described by $\mathbf{x}$.

Example: A Facial Appearance Model. Figure 5 shows the first four modes of a combined appearance model built from the same 400 face images as described above. The modes combine the variation due to lighting, identity and expression.

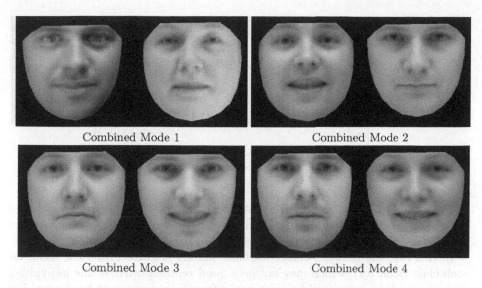

Combined Mode 1   Combined Mode 2

Combined Mode 3   Combined Mode 4

Fig. 5. Four modes of combined shape and texture model (Parameters varied by ± 2 s.d. from mean)

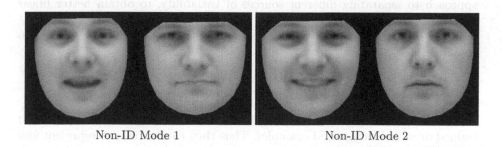

Non-ID Mode 1   Non-ID Mode 2

Fig. 6. Two modes of individual face variation (non-identity modes)

Separating Sources of Variability. Since we know the identity of the person in each training image, we can compute within-identity and between-identity covariance matricies for the parameters associated with each image. The eigenvectors, $\mathbf{P}_w$, of the within-identity covariance matrix give us a (linear) way of manipulating the face of an individual:

$$\mathbf{c} = \mathbf{P}_w \mathbf{c}_w \tag{13}$$

Varying the elements of the vector $\mathbf{c}_w$ varies the appearance parameters $\mathbf{c}$, and thus the appearance of the face in ways that an individual's face can change. Figure 6 shows the first two such modes for the data described above. These are predominantly expression changes.

Similarly those of the between-identity matrix, $\mathbf{P}_b$, allow us to examine the differences between individuals with fewer confounding effects from individual

ID Mode 1   ID Mode 2

Fig. 7. Two modes of variation between individuals (identity modes)

face variation. Figure 7 shows the first two such modes for the data described above. These modes should cause minimal apparent expression change, but describe the differences in face shape and texture between people.

In this case the between-class covariance matrix is formed from the mean for each class (identity), which may not be a good representative of the individual, and may itself be corrupted by some non-reference expression or head pose. For instance, the first ID mode in Figure 7 includes a small amount of expression change, so isn't a pure identity variation. Costen et al.[5] describe an iterative approach to separating different sources of variability, to obtain better linear models of facial variation.

In the following sections we describe an approach to matching the models to new images.

3   Model Matching

The models described above are capable of synthesizing almost any face, if trained on sufficiently varied examples. Thus they can be used to represent and interpret faces in new images. If we can find the model parameters which synthesize a face which is very similar to that in the target image, the parameters of the model then encode that face, and can be analysed in order to determine the identity or expression of the person.

However, in order to interpret a new image containing one or more faces, the first step is to locate the position of any faces in the image. Then a more local search is required to match the detailed appearance model. We have found that good results can be obtained by splitting the localisation stage into two steps. We first locate the approximate position of the facial features using combinations of templates, and use these to initialise an Active Appearance Model [10,2] which matches the full statistical appearance model to the face in the image.

In the following we will summarise the steps of the matching process.

3.1   Face Detection

The face is detected in the image by applying the Boosted Cascade Face Detector due to Viola and Jones [18]. This algorithm utilises a boosting method known as AdaBoost [11] to select and combine a set of features, which can discriminate between face and non-face image regions. The detector is run over a test image and the image window with the highest face score[1] deemed to be the location of the face in the image.

3.2 Feature Detectors

Detectors are built for 17 facial features using a manually labelled training set consisting of 1055 images collected in our lab. An example marked up face is shown in Figure 8(a). Images patches are extracted around each manually labelled point (excluding the chin and temples) and used to train a Boosted Cascade Detector for each individual feature. Example training patches are shown in Figure 8(b). The patches are sampled 5 times with small random rotations and scale changes, to provide 5275 positive training examples for each feature detector.

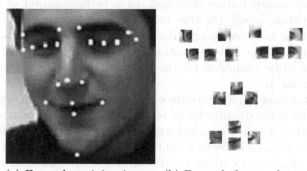

(a) Example training image   (b) Example feature detector
training patches

Fig. 8. Example of feature patch training set

During training a bounding box is computed on the range of each feature location within the region found by the face detector (for successful searches). Given the region computed by the face detector, feature detection can then proceed by merely searching within the bounded regions and the best match taken as the location of each feature. However, it has been shown that without further constraints such an approach does not work well [6]. Search accuracy can only be improved by employing a shape constraint to force the configuration of points returned by the feature detectors to form a valid face shape [6,7]. Typically this is achieved using a statistical shape model [9]. Good results can be achieved by learning pairwise relationships between feature locations and using these to combine feature responses using a voting strategy. Such an approach has been dubbed Pairwise Reinforcement of Feature Responses (PRFR) [8], and is summarised below.

---

[1] Calculated by summing the classifier scores from each level of the cascade.

3.3 PRFR Model

The method does not use an explicit shape model, rather it models shape implicitly by learning the pairwise distribution of all true feature locations relative to the best match of each individual feature detector. When searching, the location of each feature is predicted by multiple detectors. The combination of multiple predictions makes the final prediction of each feature point more robust compared to searching for each feature independently.

The pairwise distribution $P_{ij}(\mathbf{x}_i|\mathbf{x}_j)$ is defined as the distribution of the true location of feature i given the best match for feature detector j in the reference frame defined by the whole face region. In practice we use histograms of the form $H_{ij}(\mathbf{x}_i - \mathbf{x}_j)$ as an approximation to $P_{ij}(\mathbf{x}_i|\mathbf{x}_j)$. These distributions must be learnt for all possible pairs of feature detector and true feature locations. There are 17 feature detectors, trained to search for 17 feature locations, therefore 289 (=17x17) pairwise histograms are required.

Learning of histograms is achieved by applying the global face detector, followed by unconstrained feature detection, to a verification set of face images. For each verification image, the true location of all features within the global candidate frame is recorded along with the best match of each feature detector. The ensemble of true feature locations and detector matches allows relative histograms H_{ij} to be computed for the distribution of true feature location i relative to detector j.

Relative histograms H_{ij} for the right eye pupil location, are shown in Figure 9. Each diagram plots the distribution of true feature locations relative to the best match of a feature detector (marked with a cross). For example, the spread of true right eye locations relative to a right eye detection are shown in Figure 9(a). The spread of right eye locations relative to a left eye detection are shown in Figure 9(b).

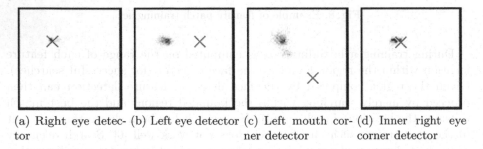

(a) Right eye detector (b) Left eye detector (c) Left mouth corner detector (d) Inner right eye corner detector

Fig. 9. Right eye pupil location histograms relative to the best match of four different feature detectors (black pixels indicate peaks in each histogram)

Using histograms allows realistic pairwise statistics to be modelled and makes no prior assumptions as to the distribution of any feature location relative to any particular feature detector. For example Figures 9(c) and 9(d) show multi-modal histograms which encode variation in the right eye pupil location relative to the more noisy left mouth corner and inner right eye corner feature detectors. This information may have been lost if simpler single Gaussian modelling had been used.

One disadvantage of using histograms is that a reasonably large amount of training data is required to obtain a representative sample of feature location/feature detection pairs. The number of samples required increases with the number of histogram bins. In our experiments, 100x100 bins were used for the whole candidate frame region, trained with 500 verification faces. It may be possible to approximate the distribution histograms using a Gaussian Mixture Model, if insufficient verification data is available. This would also produce a more compact model.

3.4   PRFR Search

Given an order list of detections for each feature detector we wish to predict the location $\hat{\mathbf{x}}_i$ of feature i by combining feature responses with the pairwise distributions $P_{ij}(\mathbf{x}_i|\mathbf{x}_j)$ as follows:-

$$\hat{\mathbf{x}}_i = \arg\max \sum_{j=1}^{n} \sum_{t=1}^{k} P_{ij}(\mathbf{x}_i|\mathbf{q}_{jt}) \tag{14}$$

Here $\mathbf{q}_{jt}$ is the position of the tth maxima in the response image for feature detector j. We sum the probabilities (effectively voting) rather than multiplying, as this generally gives more robust results. Multiplication would be appropriate if all features were independent, but in this case they are not. Note that the prior distribution $P(\mathbf{q}_{jt})$ of each feature detector is ignored here and only raw matches to the current face region are used to predict the final feature locations $(\hat{\mathbf{x}}_i)$.

The first k matches of each feature detector j are used instead of just the best match. This helps to protect against spurious false matches and provides more robust results. By empirical testing a suitable value of k is found to be 3. Similar results are obtained, using any value of k in the range $(3, 10)$. However taking more detections into account increases the time taken to perform PRFR.

In practice the pairwise distributions $P_{ij}(\mathbf{x}_i|\mathbf{x}_j)$ are represented by relative histograms $H_{ij}(\mathbf{x}_i - \mathbf{x}_j)$. When searching, the PRFR algorithm projects the top k feature locations from the jth detector into the histogram frame. Given the feature locations $\mathbf{q}_{jt}$ the relative histogram H_{ij} can be used to predict distributions D_{ijt} of likely locations for feature i. The most likely location $\hat{\mathbf{x}}_i$ is determined by simply summing over all predicted distributions D_{ijt} and selecting the highest ranking pixel in the histogram frame. The predicted feature locations $\hat{\mathbf{x}}_i$ in the histogram frame can then be mapped back to the corresponding location in the image being searched.

3.5   AAM Refinement

The Active Appearance Model (AAM) algorithm [1] can also be used to predict feature locations. The method attempts to match a shape and texture model to an unseen face by adapting the parameters of a linear appearance model (described above) so that it synthesizes an image as close as possible to the face in the target image. The basic search algorithm is described by Cootes et al. [2].

It has been found that using an objective function which minimises difference between raw intensity values is less robust than one which minimises differences between local features (such as normalised edge strength and cornerness) across the face region (see experiments below).

For instance, Scott et al. [19] computes four values for each pixel; g_x, the normalised gradient in the x direction, g_y the normalised gradient in the y direction, e a measure of "edgeness" and c a measure of "cornerness". A method based on the Harris corner detector [13] is used to compute the edge e and corner values c.

Such an approach is particularly useful when dealing with images with unconstrained lighting conditions, as the chosen features are less sensitive to such variation than raw intensities.

Although the AAM could be initialised directly from the results of the global face detector, it is demonstrated below that better accuracy is obtained if it is started from the point positions defined by the PRFR algorithm. This is because the AAM has only a relatively small bowl of convergence.

3.6   Examples of Facial Feature Location

Test Data. The accuracy of feature search is assessed by applying search algorithms to a publicly available test set known as the BIOID database[2] (which is completely independent of the training set). This data set was first used by Jesorsky et al. [14], to evaluate face detection and eye finding algorithms, but is now available with a set of 20 manually labelled feature points. The BIOID images consist of 1521 images of frontal faces taken in uncontrolled conditions using a web camera within an office environment. The face is reasonably large in each image, but there is background clutter and unconstrained lighting. Example images from the BIOID data set are shown in Figure 10.

Fig. 10. Examples from the BIOID test set

Some faces lie very close to the edge of the image in the BIOID data set, which prevents detection using the Boosted Cascade Face Detector. To avoid such edge effects, each BIOID image was extended by replicating edge pixels to create an artificial border around each image.

[2] http://www.humanscan.de/support/downloads/facedb.php

Proximity Measure. To assess the accuracy of feature detection the predicted feature locations are compared with manually labelled feature points. The average point to point error (m_e) is calculated as follows.

$$m_e = \frac{1}{ns} \sum_{i=1}^{i=n} d_i \tag{15}$$

Where d_i are the point to point errors for each individual feature location and s is the known inter-ocular distance between the left and right eye pupils. Here n is the number of feature points modelled. The search error m_e computed over the 17 features shown in Figure 8 is referred to as m_{e17}.

Results of Search. Figure 11a) plots the cumulative distribution of m_{e17} over the BIOID test set and shows that the PRFR algorithm outperforms both unconstrained search and average point prediction. For example, using a proximity threshold of $m_{e17} < 0.15$ the PRFR algorithm is successful in 96% of cases,

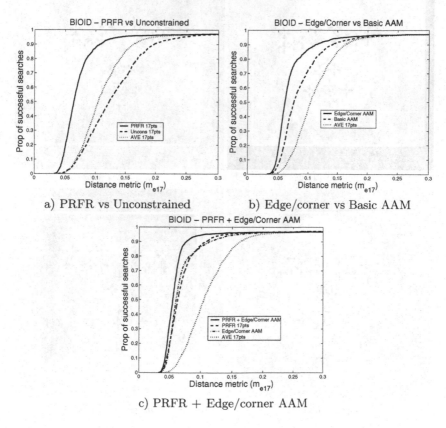

a) PRFR vs Unconstrained   b) Edge/corner vs Basic AAM

c) PRFR + Edge/corner AAM

Fig. 11. Search accuracy (m_{e17}) of various methods when applied to the BIOID test set

compared to 85% using average point prediction. Unconstrained feature detection performs very poorly achieving a success rate of only 68%.

Figure 11b) compares the edge/corner texture sampling AAM (described in section 3.5) with the basic AAM texture sampling method, initialised with the average points. The graph shows that with $m_{e17} = 0.15$ the edge/corner AAM achieves as success rate of 95%, compared to a success rate of 90% using the basic AAM. The edge/corner AAM is more successful than the basic AAM at all values of m_{e17}, so is clearly superior. Both AAM approaches improve on the search accuracy of average point prediction.

Figure 11c) compares the search accuracy of the edge/corner AAM, the PRFR method and PRFR followed by edge/corner AAM refinement. Figure 11c) shows that the PRFR followed by edge/corner AAM search is far superior to any other

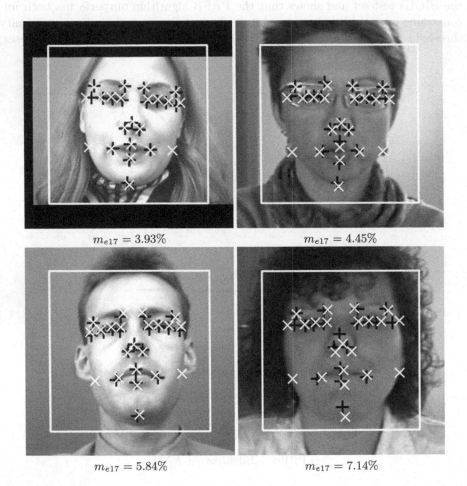

$$m_{e17} = 3.93\% \qquad\qquad m_{e17} = 4.45\%$$

$$m_{e17} = 5.84\% \qquad\qquad m_{e17} = 7.14\%$$

Fig. 12. Example searches and search errors (m_{e17}), using PRFR+edge/corner AAM on the BIOID data set. Here "+"= manually labelled ground truth and "x"= points predicted using PRFR+edge/corner AAM search.

method. For example with $m_{e17} = 0.1$, the PRFR+AAM search is successful for 96% of the BIOID images, whilst at the same accuracy threshold, both the PRFR method alone and the edge/corner AAM initialised with average points achieve only 87% success rate.

Some example search results and associated search errors using the PRFR +AAM method are shown in Figure 12.

The edge/corner AAM approach is shown to outperform the original AAM approach when searching the BIOID data set, initialised using average feature points predicted from the Boosted Cascade Face Detector (see Figure 11b). However, it is also shown that far superior results can be obtained by initialising the edge/corner AAM with points predicted by PRFR (see Figure 11c). This indicates that the AAM needs a very good initialisation to avoid inaccurate matching due to false minima. PRFR point prediction is much more accurate than average point prediction, so more false minima can be avoided and the overall search performance improved when using PRFR+AAM.

4   Face Recognition Using Combined Appearance Models

Given a face image, we can estimate the model parameters, c, which best match the model to the target face. If the model is sufficiently complex then the parameters should summarise almost all the important information required to describe the face, and can thus be used for face interpretation.

In particular, it is possible to use the parameters for face verification or recognition. By comparing the vectors representing two face images, c_1 and c_2, we can measure how similar they are. Experiments suggest that an effective measure of difference is the normalised dot product,

$$d = 1 - \frac{c_1}{|c_1|} \cdot \frac{c_2}{|c_2|} \tag{16}$$

This is zero for a perfect match. This out-performs other simple metrics such as the euclidean distance or the un-normalised dot product [15].

As mentioned above, the model parameters encode a range of variations, both those due to differences between people and those due to changes in an individual face. The changes of one individual's face can be larger than those between two different people, and can confound simple verification algorithms.

An effective method of dealing with these is to explicitly model the changes of an individual (see Section 2.3 above). The eigenvectors, P_w, of the within-individual covariance matrix describe the most significant facial changes (see Figure 6).

Given a set of face parameters, c, we can estimate the within-individual variation as $c_w = P_w^T c$ and remove it to give a set of parameters which represent the face without pose, expression or lighting variation.

$$c_n = c - P_w c_w = c - P_w P_w^T c \tag{17}$$

If we then compare these corrected vectors from different images, we obtain much better discrimination between individuals. This approach has been found to perform better than using Linear Discriminant Analysis to select a suitable subspace for face verification [15].

Recent experiments applying this technique to the XM2VTS data set [17] suggest that this approach can achieve equal error rates [3] of 0.8% when using hand annotations of the data set. This result was obtained using a face model trained on a completely separate data set of 1800 images. The within-individual variation models were estimated from 600 images in the XM2VTS registration set and tested on the 960 images from the XM2VTS test set. The result is sensitive to the number of modes used in the model of within-identity variation, and the choice points used to align the shape model (using only points from the eyes, nose and mouth during shape alignment gives better performance than using all the points, perhaps because they tend to be more stable). Note that if we do not correct for within-individual variations (using Eq.17), the performance is 7.1%, a considerable degradation.

It should be noted that the above results were performed with hand annotation of 68 points on each image, and thus give some measure of the upper limit of the technique. When the fully automatic search described above is used, the performance degrades significantly, from 0.8% to 4.1%. This is because the search algorithm introduces extra errors (and sometimes completely fails to converge). When used for recognition (rather than verification) we find the first choice of identity is correct 93% of the time. Note that without using the PRFR algorithm to initialise the AAM, the equal error rate more than doubles, demonstrating the importance of accurate feature location.

The inclusion of combined shape and texture variation allows for additional flexibility which makes the models more specific and more compact than rigid approaches such as 'eigen-face' approaches [16,20]. However, the resulting models require more parameters to be estimated during search, potentially leading to more frequent search failures. In cases in which the faces tend to be well constrained, for instance frontal images with neutral expressions (such as the XM2VTS database), the inclusion of shape variation can roughly halve the equal error rate (we obtained a rate of about 2% when repeating the experiment reported above with a rigid shape model on the manually labelled data). However, it is possible that the increased uncertainty in the matching a flexible model due to the larger number of parameters may lead to worse results overall for a full system. This is less likely to be the case for faces exhibiting larger pose or expression changes, for which rigid models are inappropriate.

5   Discussion and Conclusions

We have described statistical models of the shape and texture of faces capable of synthesizing convincing face images. They can represent a wide range of variations exhibited by faces, and can be used to separate the sources of variation

---

[3] Equal error rate (EER) - the error at the operating point of the system where the proportion of expected false positives is equal to that of false negatives.

(such as those due to differences between individuals from those due to changes of expression, head pose or lighting).

To accurately locate and classify a face in an image it is necessary to use multiple stages. In the first stage candidate faces are found using a global search with a face/non-face classifier. Each candidate location can then be explored more carefully by first locating facial features using combinations of feature detectors, then using their positions to initialise an Active Appearance Model. The resulting appearance model parameters can then be used for further analysis, such as recognising or verifying the identity of the person located.

Though described for application to faces, the techniques are applicable to modelling any other structures whose variability can be effectively described using a deformable template. However, it should be noted that the approach relies on establishing correspondences across a training set, and between models and new images.

The results demonstrate that the key to achieving reliable recognition or verification is accurate model matching. Even modest mis-alignment can lead to significant degradation in recognition performance. Though effective methods have been demonstrated, there is still considerable room for improvement.

Acknowledgements

The authors would like to thank their numerous colleagues who have contributed to the research summarised in this chapter, including C.Beeston, F.Bettinger, D.Cooper, N.Costen, G.Edwards, A.Hill, J.Graham, H.Kang, P.Kittipanya-ngam and C.J. Taylor.

References

1. T. F. Cootes, G. J. Edwards, and C. J. Taylor. Active appearance models. In H.Burkhardt and B. Neumann, editors, 5th European Conference on Computer Vision, volume 2, pages 484–498. Springer, Berlin, 1998.
2. T. F. Cootes, G. J. Edwards, and C. J. Taylor. Active appearance models. IEEE Transactions on Pattern Analysis and Machine Intelligence, 23(6):681–685, 2001.
3. T. F. Cootes, G.V.Wheeler, K.N.Walker, and C. J. Taylor. View-based active appearance models. Image and Vision Computing, 20:657–664, 2002.
4. T. F. Cootes, C. J. Taylor, D. Cooper, and J. Graham. Active shape models - their training and application. Computer Vision and Image Understanding, 61(1):38–59, Jan. 1995.
5. N. Costen, T. F. Cootes, and C. J. Taylor. Compensating for ensemble-specificity effects when building facial models. Image and Vision Computing, 20:673–682, 2002.
6. D. Cristinacce and T. Cootes. Facial feature detection using ADABOOST with shape constraints. In 14th British Machine Vision Conference, volume 1, pages 231–240, 2003.
7. D. Cristinacce and T. Cootes. A comparison of shape constrained facial feature detectors. In 6th International Conference on Automatic Face and Gesture Recognition 2004, Seoul, Korea, pages 375–380, 2004.

8. D. Cristinacce, T. Cootes, and I. Scott. A multi-stage approach to facial feature detection. In *15th British Machine Vision Conference*, volume 1, pages 277–286, 2004.
9. I. Dryden and K. V. Mardia. *The Statistical Analysis of Shape*. Wiley, London, 1998.
10. G. Edwards, C. J. Taylor, and T. F. Cootes. Interpreting face images using active appearance models. In 3rd *International Conference on Automatic Face and Gesture Recognition 1998*, pages 300–305, Japan, 1998.
11. Y. Freund and R. Schapire. A decision-theoretic generalization of on-line learning and an application to boosting. In *2nd European Conference on Computational Learning Theory*, 1995.
12. C. Goodall. Procrustes methods in the statistical analysis of shape. *Journal of the Royal Statistical Society B*, 53(2):285–339, 1991.
13. C. Harris and M. Stephens. A combined edge and corner detector. In *Alvey Vision Conference*, pages 147–151, 1988.
14. O. Jesorsky, K. J. Kirchberg, and R. W. Frischholz. Robust face detection using the hausdorff distance. In 3rd *International Conference on Audio- and Video-Based Biometric Person Authentication 2001*, 2001.
15. H. Kang, T. Cootes, and C. Taylor. A comparison of face verification algorithms using appearance models. In P.L.Rosin and D. Marshall, editors, 13th *British Machine Vison Conference*, volume 2, pages 477–486. BMVA Press, Sept. 2002.
16. M. Kirby and L. Sirovich. Application of the Karhumen-Loeve procedure for the characterization of human faces. *IEEE Transactions on Pattern Analysis and Machine Intelligence*, 12(1):103–108, 1990.
17. K. Messer, J. Matas, J. Kittler, J. Luettin, and G. Maitre. XM2VTSdb: The extended m2vts database. In *Proc. 2nd Conf. on Audio and Video-based Biometric Personal Verification*, pages 72–77. Springer Verlag, 1999.
18. P.Viola and M.Jones. Rapid object detection using a boosted cascade of simple features. In *Computer Vision and Pattern Recognition Conference 2001*, volume 1, pages 511–518, 2001.
19. I. Scott, T. Cootes, and C. Taylor. Improving active appearance model matching using local image structure. In *18th Conference on Information Processing in Medical Imaging*, pages 258–269, 2003.
20. M. Turk and A. Pentland. Eigenfaces for recognition. *Journal of Cognitive Neuroscience*, 3(1):71–86, 1991.

Part V

Joint Recognition and Segmentation

Image Parsing: Unifying Segmentation, Detection, and Recognition

Zhuowen Tu, Xiangrong Chen, Alan Yuille, and Song Chun Zhu

Department of Statistics, UCLA. Los Angeles, CA 90095. USA
{ztu,xrchen,yuille,sczhu}@stat.ucla.edu

Abstract. In this chapter we present a Bayesian framework for parsing images into their constituent visual patterns. The parsing algorithm optimizes the posterior probability and outputs a scene representation as a "parsing graph", in a spirit similar to parsing sentences in speech and natural language. The algorithm *constructs* the parsing graph and *re-configures* it dynamically using a set of moves, which are mostly reversible Markov chain jumps. This computational framework integrates two popular inference approaches – *generative* (top-down) methods and *discriminative* (bottom-up) methods. The former formulates the posterior probability in terms of generative models for images defined by likelihood functions and priors. The latter computes discriminative probabilities based on a sequence (cascade) of bottom-up tests/filters. In our Markov chain algorithm design, the posterior probability, defined by the generative models, is the invariant (target) probability for the Markov chain, and the discriminative probabilities are used to construct proposal probabilities to drive the Markov chain. Intuitively, the bottom-up discriminative probabilities activate top-down generative models. In this chapter, we focus on two types of visual patterns – generic visual patterns, such as texture and shading, and object patterns including human faces and text. These types of patterns compete and cooperate to explain the image and so image parsing unifies image segmentation, object detection, and recognition (if we use generic visual patterns only then image parsing will correspond to image segmentation [48].). We illustrate our algorithm on natural images of complex city scenes and show examples where image segmentation can be improved by allowing object specific knowledge to disambiguate low-level segmentation cues, and conversely where object detection can be improved by using generic visual patterns to explain away shadows and occlusions.

1 Introduction

1.1 Objectives of Image Parsing

We define image parsing to be the task of decomposing an image $\mathbf{I}$ into its constituent visual patterns. The output is represented by a hierarchical graph W — called the "parsing graph". The goal is to optimize the Bayesian posterior probability $p(W|\mathbf{I})$. Figure 1 illustrates a typical example where a football scene

J. Ponce et al. (Eds.): Toward Category-Level Object Recognition, LNCS 4170, pp. 545–576, 2006.
© Springer-Verlag Berlin Heidelberg 2006

is first divided into three parts at a coarse level: a person in the foreground, a sports field, and the spectators. These three parts are further decomposed into nine visual patterns in the second level: a face, three texture regions, some text, a point process (the band on the field), a curve process (the markings on the field), a color region, and a region for nearby people. In principle, we can continue decomposing these parts until we reach a resolution limit (e.g. there is not sufficient resolution to detect the blades of grass on the sports field). The parsing graph is similar in spirit to the parsing trees used in speech and natural language processing [33] except that it can include horizontal connections (see the dashed curves in Figure 1) for specifying spatial relationships and boundary sharing between different visual patterns.

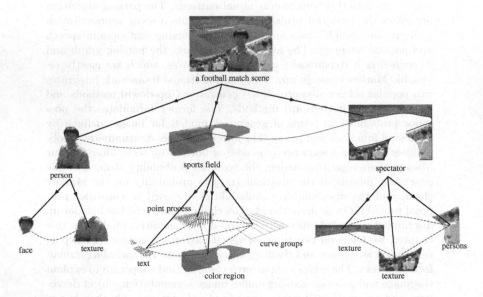

Fig. 1. Image parsing example. The parsing graph is hierarchical and combines generative models (downward arrows) with horizontal connections (dashed lines), which specify spatial relationships between the visual patterns. See Figure 4 for a more abstract representation including variables for the node attributes.

As in natural language processing, the parsing graph is not fixed and depends on the input image(s). An image parsing algorithm must *construct* the parsing graph on the fly[1]. Our image parsing algorithm consists of a set of reversible Markov chain jumps [21] with each type of jump corresponding to an operator for *reconfiguring* the parsing graph (i.e. creating or deleting nodes or changing the values of node attributes). These jumps combine to form an ergodic and reversible Markov chain in the space of possible parsing graphs. The Markov chain probability is guaranteed to converges to the invariant probability $p(W|\mathbf{I})$

---

[1] Unlike most graphical inference algorithms in the literature which assume fixed graphs, such as belief propagation [58].

and the Markov chain will simulate fair samples from this probability[2]. Our approach is built on previous work on Data-Driven Markov Chain Monte Carlo (DDMCMC) for recognition [61], segmentation [48], grouping [49] and graph partitioning [1,2].

Image parsing seeks a full generative explanation of the input image in terms of generative models, $p(\mathbf{I}|W)$ and $p(W)$, for the diverse visual patterns which occur in natural images, see Figure 1. This differs from standard approaches to computer vision tasks — such as segmentation, grouping, and recognition – which usually involve isolated vision modules which only explain different parts (or aspects) of the image. The image parsing approach enables these different modules to cooperate and compete to give a consistent interpretation of the entire image.

The integration of visual modules is of increasing importance as progress on the individual modules starts approaching performance ceilings. In particular, work on segmentation [45,48,17] and edge detection [26,8] has reached performance levels where there seems little room for improvement when only low-level cues are used. For example, the segmentation failures in Figure 2 can only be resolved by combining segmentation with object detection and recognition. Combining these cues is made easier because of recent successful work on the detection and recognition of objects [30,56,42,4,55,57] and the classification of natural scenes [3,39] using, broadly speaking, discriminative methods based on local bottom-up tests.

But combining different visual modules requires a common framework which ensures consistency. Despite the effectiveness of discriminative methods for computing scene components, such as object labels and categories, they can also generate redundant and conflicting results. Mathematicians have argued [6] that discriminative methods must be followed by more sophisticated processes to (i) remove false alarms, (ii) amend missing objects by global context information, and (iii) reconcile conflicting (overlapping) explanations through model comparison. In this chapter, we impose such processes by using generative models for the entire image.

As we will show, our image parsing algorithm is able to integrate discriminative and generative methods so as to take advantage of their complementary strengths. Moreover, we can couple modules such as segmentation and object detection by our choice of the set of visual patterns used to parse the image. In this chapter, we focus on two types of patterns: – generic visual patterns for low/middle level vision, such as texture and shading, and object patterns for high level vision, such as frontal human faces and text.

These two types of patterns illustrate different ways in which the parsing graph can be constructed (see Figure 16 and the related discussion). The object patterns (face and text) have comparatively little variability so they can often be effectively detected as a whole by bottom-up tests and their parts can be

---

[2] For many natural images the posterior probabilities $P(W|\mathbf{I})$ are strongly peaked and so fair samples are close to the posterior maximum $\arg\max_W P(W|\mathbf{I})$. So in this chapter we do not distinguish between sampling and inference (optimization).

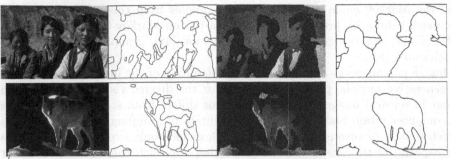

a. Input image   b. Segmentation c. Synthesized image d. Manual segmentation

Fig. 2. Examples of image segmentation failure by an algorithm [48] which uses only generic visual patterns (i.e. only low-level visual cues). The results (b) show that low-level visual cues are not sufficient to obtain good intuitive segmentations. The limitations of using only generic visual patterns are also clear in the synthesized images (c) which are obtained by stochastic sampling from the generative models after the parameters have been estimated by DDMCMC. The right panels (d) show the segmentations obtained by human subjects who, by contrast to the algorithm, appear to use object specific knowledge when doing the segmentation (though they were not instructed to) [35]. We conclude that to achieve good segmentation on these types of images requires combining segmentation with object detection and recognition.

located subsequentially. Thus their parsing sub-graphs can be constructed in a "decompositional" manner from whole to parts. By contrast, a generic texture region has arbitrary shape and its intensity pattern has high entropy. Detecting such a region by bottom-up tests will require an enormous number of tests to deal with all this variability, and so will be computationally impractical. Instead, the parsing subgraphs should be built by grouping small elements in a "compositional" manner [5].

We illustrate our algorithm on natural images of complex city scenes and give examples where image segmentation can be improved by allowing object specific knowledge to disambiguate low-level cues, and conversely object detection can be improved by using generic visual patterns to explain away shadows and occlusions.

This chapter is structured as follows. In Section (2), we give an overview of the image parsing framework and discuss its theoretical background. Then in Section (3), we describe the parsing graph and the generative models used for generic visual patterns, text, and faces. In Section (4) we give the control structure of the image parsing algorithm. Section (5) gives details of the components of the algorithm and show how AdaBoost can be used to get proposals for detecting objects such as text and faces. In Section (6) we present experimental results. Section (7) addresses some open problems in further developing the image parser as a general inference engine. We summarize the chapter in Section (8).

2   Overview of Image Parsing Framework

2.1   Bottom-Up and Top-Down Processing

A major element of our work is to integrate discriminative and generative methods for inference. In the recent computer vision literature, top-down and bottom-up procedures can be broadly categorized into two popular inference paradigms – *generative* methods for "top-down" and *discriminative* methods for "bottom-up", illustrated in Figure 3. From this perspective, integrating generative and discriminative models is equivalent to combining bottom-up and top-down processing[3].

The role of bottom-up and top-down processing in vision has been often discussed. There is growing experimental evidence (see [46,28]) that humans can perform high level scene and object categorization tasks as fast as low level texture discrimination and other so-called pre-attentive vision tasks. This suggests that humans can detect both low and high level visual patterns at early stages in visual processing. It contrasts with traditional bottom-up feedforward architectures [34] which start with edge detection, followed by segmentation/grouping, before proceeding to object recognition and other high-level vision tasks. These experiments also relate to long standing conjectures about the role of the bottom-up/top-down loops in the visual cortical areas [38,54], visual routines and pathways [53], the binding of visual cues [47], and neural network models such as the Helmholtz machine [14]. But although combining bottom-up and top-down processing is clearly important, there has not yet been a rigorous mathematical framework for how to achieve it.

In this chapter, we combine generative and discriminative approaches to design an DDMCMC algorithm which uses discriminative methods to perform rapid inference of the parameters of generative models. From a computer vision perspective, DDMCMC combines bottom-up processing, implemented by the discriminative models, together with top-down processing by the generative models. The rest of this section gives an overview of our approach.

2.2   Generative and Discriminative Methods

Generative methods specify how the image $\mathbf{I}$ is generated from the scene representation $W \in \Omega$. It combines a prior $p(W)$ and a likelihood function $p(\mathbf{I}|W)$ to give a joint posterior probability $p(W|\mathbf{I})$. These can be expressed as probabilities on graphs, where the input image $\mathbf{I}$ is represented on the leaf nodes and W denotes the remaining nodes and node attributes of the graph. The structure of the graph, and in particular the number of nodes, is unknown and must be estimated for each input image.

To perform inference using generative methods requires estimating $W^* = \arg\max P(W|\mathbf{I})$. This is often computationally demanding because there are

---

[3] Recently the term "discriminative model" has been extended to cover almost any approximation to the posterior distribution $P(W|\mathbf{I})$, e.g. Kumar and Hebert [27]. We will use "discriminative model" in its traditional sense of categorization.

usually no known efficient inference algorithms (certainly not for the class of $P(W|\mathbf{I})$ studied in this chapter).

In this chapter, we will perform inference by stochastic sampling W from the posterior:

$$W \sim p(W|\mathbf{I}) \propto p(\mathbf{I}|W)p(W). \tag{1}$$

This enables us to estimate $W^* = \arg\max P(W|\mathbf{I})$. Stochastic sampling is attractive because it is a general technique that can be applied to any inference problem. Moreover, it generate samples that can be used to validate the model assumptions. But the dimension of the sample space Ω for image parsing is very high and so standard sampling techniques are computationally expensive.

By contrast, discriminative methods are very fast to compute. They do not specify models for how the image is generated. Instead they give discriminative (conditional) probabilities $q(w_j|\mathrm{Tst}_j(\mathbf{I}))$ for components $\{w_j\}$ of W based on a sequence of bottom-up tests $\mathrm{Tst}_j(\mathbf{I})$ performed on the image. The tests are based on local image features $\{F_{j,n}(\mathbf{I})\}$ which can be computed from the image in a cascade manner (e.g. AdaBoost filters, see Section (5.2)),

$$\mathrm{Tst}_j(\mathbf{I}) = (F_{j,1}(\mathbf{I}), F_{j,2}(\mathbf{I}), ..., F_{j,n}(\mathbf{I})), \quad j = 1, 2, ..., K. \tag{2}$$

The following theorem (proved in [51]) shows that the KL-divergence between the true marginal posterior $p(w_j|\mathbf{I})$ and the optimal discriminant approximation $q(w_j|\mathrm{Tst}(\mathbf{I}))$ using test $\mathrm{Tst}(\mathbf{I})$ will decrease monotonically as new tests are added[4].

Theorem 1. *The information gained for a variable w by a new test $\mathrm{Tst}_+(\mathbf{I})$ is the decrease of Kullback-Leibler divergence between $p(w|\mathbf{I})$ and its best discriminative estimate $q(w|\mathrm{Tst}_t(\mathbf{I}))$ or the increase of mutual information between w and the tests.*

$$E_\mathbf{I}[KL(p(w|\mathbf{I}) \parallel q(w|\mathrm{Tst}(\mathbf{I})))] - E_\mathbf{I}[KL(p(w|\mathbf{I}) \parallel q(w|\mathrm{Tst}(\mathbf{I}), \mathrm{Tst}_+(\mathbf{I})))]$$
$$= MI(w \parallel \mathrm{Tst}, \mathrm{Tst}_+) - MI(w \parallel \mathrm{Tst})$$
$$= E_{\mathrm{Tst},\mathrm{Tst}_+}KL(q(w \mid \mathrm{Tst}_t, \mathrm{Tst}_+) \parallel q(w \mid \mathrm{Tst}_t)) \geq 0,$$

where $E_\mathbf{I}$ is the expectation with respect to $P(\mathbf{I})$, and $E_{\mathrm{Tst},\mathrm{Tst}_+}$ is the expectation with respect to the probability on the test responses $(\mathrm{Tst}, \mathrm{Tst}_+)$ induced by $P(\mathbf{I})$.

The decrease of the Kullback-Leibler divergence equals zero if and only if $\mathrm{Tst}(\mathbf{I})$ are sufficient statistics with respect to w.

In practice discriminative methods, particularly standard computer vision algorithms – see subsection (4.1), will typically only use a small number of features for computational practicality. Also their discriminative probabilities $q(w_j|\mathrm{Tst}(\mathbf{I}))$ will often not be optimal. Fortunately the image parsing algorithm in this chapter only requires the discriminative probabilities $q(w_j|\mathrm{Tst}(\mathbf{I}))$ to be rough approximations to $p(w_j|\mathbf{I})$.

---

[4] The optimal approximation occurs when $q(w_j|\mathrm{Tst}(\mathbf{I}))$ equals the probability $p(w_j|\mathrm{Tst}(\mathbf{I}))$ induced by $P(\mathbf{I}|W)P(W)$.

Generative methods   Discriminative methods

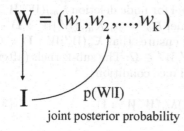

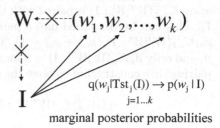

joint posterior probability   marginal posterior probabilities

Fig. 3. Comparison of two inference paradigms: Top-down *generative* methods versus bottom-up *discriminative* methods. The generative method specifies how the image **I** can be synthesized from the scene representation W. By contrast, the discriminative methods are based by performing tests $Tst_j(\mathbf{I})$ and are not guaranteed to yield consistent solutions, see crosses explained in the text.

The difference between discriminative and generative models is illustrated in Figure 3. Discriminative models are fast to compute and can be run in parallel because different components are computed independently (see arrows in Figure 3). But the components $\{w_i\}$ may not yield a consistent solution W and, moreover, W may not specify a consistent model for generating the observed image **I**. These inconsistencies are indicated by the crosses in Figure 3. Generative models ensure consistency but require solving a difficult inference problem.

It is an open problem whether discriminative methods can be designed to infer the entire state W for the complicated generative models that we are dealing with. Recent work [27] is a step in this direction. But mathematicians [6] have argued that this will not be practical and that discriminative models will always require additional post-processing.

2.3 Markov Chain Kernels and Sub-kernels

Formally, our DDMCMC image parsing algorithm simulates a Markov chain $\mathcal{MC} =< \Omega, \nu, \mathcal{K} >$ with kernel $\mathcal{K}$ in space Ω and with probability ν for the starting state. An element $W \in \Omega$ is a parsing graph. We let the set of parsing graphs Ω be finite as images have finite pixels and grey levels.

We proceed by defining a set of moves for reconfiguring the graph. These include moves to: (i) create nodes, (ii) delete nodes, and (iii) change node attributes. We specify stochastic dynamics for these moves in terms of transition kernels[5].

For each move we define a Markov Chain sub-kernel by a transition matrix $\mathcal{K}_a(W'|W : \mathbf{I})$ with $a \in \mathcal{A}$ being an index. This represents the probability that the system makes a transition from state W to state W' when sub-kernel a is

---

[5] We choose stochastic dynamics because the Markov chain probability is guaranteed to converge to the posterior $P(W|\mathbf{I})$. The complexity of the problem means that deterministic algorithms for implementing these moves risk getting stuck in local minima.

applied (i.e. $\sum_{W'} \mathcal{K}_a(W'|W : \mathbf{I}) = 1, \forall W$). Kernels which alter the graph struc-
ture are grouped into reversible pairs. For example, the sub-kernel for node cre-
ation $\mathcal{K}_{a,r}(W'|W : \mathbf{I})$ is paired with the sub-kernel for node deletion $\mathcal{K}_{a,l}(W'|W : \mathbf{I})$. This can be combined into a paired sub-kernel $\mathcal{K}_a = \rho_{ar}\mathcal{K}_{a,r}(W'|W : \mathbf{I}) + \rho_{al}\mathcal{K}_{a,l}(W'|W : \mathbf{I})$ $(\rho_{ar} + \rho_{al} = 1)$. This pairing ensures that $\mathcal{K}_a(W'|W : \mathbf{I}) = 0$ if, and only if, $\mathcal{K}_a(W|W' : \mathbf{I}) = 0$ for all states $W, W' \in \Omega$. The sub-kernels (after pairing) are constructed to obey the detailed balance condition:

$$p(W|\mathbf{I})\mathcal{K}_a(W'|W : \mathbf{I}) = p(W'|\mathbf{I})\mathcal{K}_a(W|W' : \mathbf{I}). \tag{3}$$

The full transition kernel is expressed as:

$$\mathcal{K}(W'|W : \mathbf{I}) = \sum_a \rho(a : \mathbf{I})\mathcal{K}_a(W'|W : \mathbf{I}), \quad \sum_a \rho(a : \mathbf{I}) = 1, \quad \rho(a : \mathbf{I}) > 0. \tag{4}$$

To implement this kernel, at each time step the algorithm selects the choice
of move with probability $\rho(a : \mathbf{I})$ for move a, and then uses kernel $\mathcal{K}_a(W'|W; \mathbf{I})$
to select the transition from state W to state W'. Note that both probabilities
$\rho(a : \mathbf{I})$ and $\mathcal{K}_a(W'|W; \mathbf{I})$ depend on the input image $\mathbf{I}$. This distinguishes our
DDMCMC methods from conventional MCMC computing [29,7].
    The full kernel obeys detailed balance, equation (3), because all the sub-
kernels do. It will also be ergodic, provided the set of moves is sufficient (i.e. so
that we can transition between any two states $W, W' \in \Omega$ using these moves).
These two conditions ensure that $p(W|\mathbf{I})$ is the invariant (target) probability of
the Markov Chain [7] in the finite space Ω.
    Applying the kernel $\mathcal{K}_{a(t)}$ updates the Markov chain state probability $\mu_t(W)$
at step t to $\mu_{t+1}(W')$ at $t + 1$, [6]:

$$\mu_{t+1}(W') = \sum_W \mathcal{K}_{a(t)}(W'|W : \mathbf{I})\mu_t(W). \tag{5}$$

In summary, the DDMCMC image parser simulates a Markov chain $\mathcal{MC}$ with
a unique invariant probability $p(W|\mathbf{I})$. At time t, the Markov chain state (i.e. the
parse graph) W follows a probability μ_t which is the product of the sub-kernels
selected up to time t,

$$W \sim \mu_t(W) = \nu(W_o) \cdot [\mathcal{K}_{a(1)} \circ \mathcal{K}_{a(2)} \circ \cdots \circ \mathcal{K}_{a(t)}](W_o, W) \longrightarrow p(W|\mathbf{I}). \tag{6}$$

where $a(t)$ indexes the sub-kernel selected at time t. As the time t increases,
$\mu_t(W)$ approaches the posterior $p(W|\mathbf{I})$ monotonically [7] at a geometric rate [15]
independent of the starting configuration. The following convergence theorem is
useful for image parsing because it helps quantify the effectiveness of the different
sub-kernels.

---

[6] Algorithms like belief propagation [58] can be derived as approximations to this
update equation by using a Gibbs sampler and making independence assumptions
[43].

Theorem 2. *The Kullback-Leibler divergence between the posterior $p(W|\mathbf{I})$ and the Markov chain state probability decreases monotonically when a sub-kernel $\mathcal{K}_{a(t)}, \forall\, a(t) \in \mathcal{A}$ is applied,*

$$KL(p(W|\mathbf{I}) \,\|\, \mu_t(W)) - KL(p(W|\mathbf{I}) \,\|\, \mu_{t+1}(W)) \geq 0 \qquad (7)$$

The decrease of KL-divergence is strictly positive and is equal to zero only after the Markov chain becomes stationary, i.e. $\mu = p$.

[Proof] See [51].

The theorem is related to the second law of thermodynamics [13], and its proof makes use of the detailed balance equation (3). This KL divergence gives a measure of the "power" of each sub-kernel $\mathcal{K}_{a(t)}$ and so it suggests an efficient mechanism for selecting the sub-kernels at each time step, see Section (7). By contrast, classic convergence analysis (c.f. [51]) show that the convergence of the Markov Chain is exponentially fast, but does not give measures of power of sub-kernels.

2.4   DDMCMC and Proposal Probabilities

We now describe how to design the sub-kernels using proposal probabilities and discriminative models. This is at the heart of DDMCMC.

Each sub-kernel[7] is designed to be of Metropolis-Hastings form [36,24]:

$$\mathcal{K}_a(W'|W : \mathbf{I}) = Q_a(W'|W : \mathrm{Tst}_a(\mathbf{I})) \min\{1, \frac{p(W'|\mathbf{I})Q_a(W|W' : \mathrm{Tst}_a(\mathbf{I}))}{p(W|\mathbf{I})Q_a(W'|W : \mathrm{Tst}_a(\mathbf{I}))}\},$$
$$(8)$$

where a transition from W to W' is proposed (stochastically) by the proposal probability $Q_a(W'|W : \mathrm{Tst}_a(\mathbf{I}))$ and accepted (stochastically) by the acceptance probability:

$$\alpha(W'|W : \mathbf{I}) = \min\{1, \frac{p(W'|\mathbf{I})Q_a(W|W' : \mathrm{Tst}_a(\mathbf{I}))}{p(W|\mathbf{I})Q_a(W'|W : \mathrm{Tst}_a(\mathbf{I}))}\}. \qquad (9)$$

The Metropolis-Hastings form ensures that the sub-kernels obey detailed balance (after pairing) [7].

The proposal probabilities $Q_a(W'|W : \mathrm{Tst}_a(\mathbf{I}))$ will be built from discriminative probabilities using tests $\mathrm{Tst}_a(\mathbf{I})$ performed on the image. The design of the proposal probabilities is a trade-off. Ideally the proposals would be sampled from the posterior $p(W'|\mathbf{I})$, but this is impractical. Instead the trade-off requires: (i) it is possible to make large moves in Ω at each time step, (ii) the proposals should encourage moves to states with high posterior probability, and (iii) the proposals must be fast to compute.

More formally, we define the scope $\Omega_a(W) = \{W' \in \Omega : \mathcal{K}_a(W'|W : \mathbf{I}) > 0\}$ to be the set of states which can be reached from W in one time step using

---

[7] Except for one that evolves region boundaries.

sub-kernel a. We want the scope $S_a(W)$ to be large so that we can make large moves in the space Ω at each time step (i.e. jump towards the solution and not crawl). The scope should also, if possible, include states W' with high posterior $p(W'|\mathbf{I})$ (i.e. it is not enough for the scope to be large, it should also be in the right part of Ω).

The proposals $Q_a(W'|W : \text{Tst}_a(\mathbf{I}))$ should be chosen so as to approximate

$$\frac{p(W'|\mathbf{I})}{\sum_{W'' \in \Omega_a(W)} p(W''|\mathbf{I})} \text{ if } W' \in \Omega_a(W), \ = 0, \text{ otherwise.} \tag{10}$$

The proposals will be functions of the discriminative models for the components of W' and of the generative models for the current state W (because it is computationally cheap to evaluate the generative models for the current state). The details of the model $p(W|\mathbf{I})$ will determine the form of the proposals and how large we can make the scope while keeping the proposals easy to compute and able to approximate equation (10). See the detailed examples given in Section (5).

This description gives the bare bones of DDMCMC. We refer to [49] for further details of these issues from an MCMC perspective. In the discussion section, we describe strategies to improve DDMCMX. Preliminary theoretical results for the convergence of DDMCMC are encouraging for a special case, see [51]. We refer to [51] for the important practical issue of how to maintain detailed balance when there are multiple routes to transition between two state W and W'. We describe two ways to do this and the trade-offs involved.

3   Generative Models and Bayesian Formulation

This section describes the graph structure and the generative models used for our image parsing algorithm in this chapter.

Figure 1 illustrates the general structure of a parsing graph. In this chapter, we use a two-layer-graph illustrated in Figure 4. The top node ("root") of the graph represents the whole scene (with a label). It has K *intermediate nodes* for the visual patterns (face, text, texture, and shading). Each visual pattern has a number of pixels at the bottom ("leaves"). In this graph no horizontal connections are considered between the visual patterns except the constraint that they share boundaries and form a partition of the image lattice (see [49] for an example of image parsing where horizontal connections are used, but without object patterns).

The number K of intermediate nodes is a random variable, and each node $i = 1, ..., K$ has a set of attributes (L_i, ζ_i, Θ_i) defined as follows. L_i is the shape descriptor and determines the region $R_i = R(L_i)$ of the image pixels covered by the visual pattern of the intermediate node. Conceptually, the pixels within R_i are child nodes of the intermediate node i. (Regions may contain holes, in which case the shape descriptor will have internal and external boundaries). The remaining attribute variables (ζ_i, Θ_i) specify the probability models

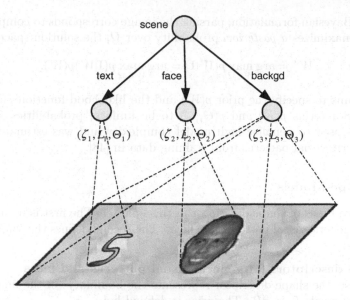

Fig. 4. Abstract representation of the parsing graph used in this chapter. The intermediate nodes represent the visual patterns. Their child nodes correspond to the pixels in the image.

$p(\mathbf{I}_{R(L_i)}|\zeta_i, L_i, \Theta_i)$ for generating the sub-image $\mathbf{I}_{R(L_i)}$ in region $R(L_i)$. The variables $\zeta_i \in \{1, ..., 66\}$ indicate the visual pattern type (3 types of generic visual patterns, 1 face pattern, and 62 text character patterns), and Θ_i denotes the model parameters for the corresponding visual pattern (details are given in the following subsections). The complete scene description can be summarized by:

$$W = (K, \{(\zeta_i, L_i, \Theta_i) : i = 1, 2, ..., K\}).$$

The shape descriptors $\{L_i : i = 1, ..., K\}$ are required to be consistent so that each pixel in the image is a child of one, and only one, of the intermediate nodes. The shape descriptors must provide a partition of the image lattice $\Lambda = \{(m, n) : 1 \leq m \leq Height(\mathbf{I}), 1 \leq n \leq Width(\mathbf{I})\}$ and hence satisfy the condition

$$\Lambda = \cup_{i=1}^{K} R(L_i), \quad R(L_i) \cap R(L_j) = \emptyset, \quad \forall i \neq j.$$

The generation process from the scene description W to $\mathbf{I}$ is governed by the likelihood function:

$$p(\mathbf{I}|W) = \prod_{i=1}^{K} p(\mathbf{I}_{R(L_i)}|\zeta_i, L_i, \Theta_i).$$

The prior probability $p(W)$ is defined by

$$p(W) = p(K) \prod_{i=1}^{K} p(L_i)p(\zeta_i|L_i)p(\Theta_i|\zeta_i).$$

In our Bayesian formulation, parsing the image corresponds to computing the W^* that maximizes *a posteriori* probability over Ω, the solution space of W,

$$W^* = \arg \max_{W \in \Omega} p(W|\mathbf{I}) = \arg \max_{W \in \Omega} p(\mathbf{I}|W)p(W). \qquad (11)$$

It remains to specify the prior $p(W)$ and the likelihood function $p(\mathbf{I}|W)$. We set the prior terms $p(K)$ and $p(\Theta_i|\zeta_i)$ to be uniform probabilities. The term $p(\zeta_i|L_i)$ is used to penalize high model complexity and was estimated for the three generic visual patterns from training data in [48].

3.1   Shape Models

We use two types of shape descriptor in this chapter. The first is used to define shapes of generic visual patterns and faces. The second defines the shapes of text characters.

1. Shape descriptors for generic visual patterns and faces
In this case, the shape descriptor represents the boundary[8] of the image region by a list of pixels $L_i = \partial R_i$. The prior is defined by:

$$p(L_i) \propto exp\{-\gamma |R(L_i)|^\alpha - \lambda |L_i|\}. \qquad (12)$$

In this chapter, we set $\alpha = 0.9$. For computational reasons, we use this prior for face shapes though more complicated priors [11] can be applied.

2. Shape descriptors for text characters
We model text characters by 62 deformable templates corresponding to the ten digits and the twenty six letters in both upper and lower cases. These deformable templates are defined by 62 prototype characters and a set of deformations.

Fig. 5. Random samples drawn from the shape descriptors for text characters

The prototypes are represented by an outer boundary and, at most, two inner boundaries. Each boundary is modeled by a B-spline using twenty five control

---

[8] The boundary can include an "internal boundary" if there is a hole inside the image region explained by a different visual pattern.

points. The prototype characters are indexed by $c_i \in \{1, ..., 62\}$ and their control points are represented by a matrix $TP(c_i)$.

We now define two types of deformations on the templates. One is a global affine transformation, and the other is a local elastic deformation. First we allow the letters to be deformed by an affine transform M_i. We put a prior $p(M_i)$ to penalize severe rotation and distortion. This is obtained by decomposing M_i as:

$$M_i = \begin{pmatrix} \sigma_x & 0 \\ 0 & \sigma_y \end{pmatrix} \begin{pmatrix} cos\theta & -sin\theta \\ sin\theta & cos\theta \end{pmatrix} \begin{pmatrix} 1 & h \\ 0 & 1 \end{pmatrix}.$$

where θ is the rotation angle, σ_x and σ_y denote scaling, and h is for shearing. The prior on M_i is

$$p(M_i) \propto \exp\{-a|\theta|^2 - b(\frac{\sigma_x}{\sigma_y} + \frac{\sigma_y}{\sigma_x})^2 - ch^2\},$$

where a, b, c are parameters.

Next, we allow local deformations by adjusting the positions of the B-spline control points. For a digit/letter c_i and affine transform M_i, the contour points of the template are given by $G_{TP}(M_i, c_i) = U \times M_s \times M_i \times TP(c_i)$. Similarly the contour points on the shape with control points S_i are given by $G_S(M_i, c_i) = U \times M_s \times S_i$ (U and M_s are the B-Spline matrices). We define a probability distribution $p(S_i|M_i, c_i)$ for the elastic deformation given by S_i,

$$p(S_i|M_i, c_i) \propto exp\{-\gamma|R(L_i)|^\alpha - D(G_S(M_i, c_i)||G_{TP}(M_i, c_i))\},$$

where $D(G_S(M_i, c_i)||G_{TP}(M_i, c_i))$ is the overall distance between contour template and the deformed contour (these deformations are small so the correspondence between points on the curves can be obtained by nearest neighbor matches, see [50] for how we can refine this). Figure 5 shows some samples drawn from the above model.

In summary, each deformable template is indexed by $c_i \in \{1..62\}$ and has a shape descriptor:

$$L_i = (c_i, M_i, S_i),$$

The prior distribution on L_i is specified by:

$$p(L_i) = p(c_i)p(M_i)p(S_i|M_i, c_i).$$

Here $p(c_i)$ is a uniform distribution on all the digits and letters (we do not place a prior distribution on text strings, though it is possible to do so [25]).

3.2   Generative Intensity Models

We use four families of generative intensity models for describing intensity patterns of (approximately) constant intensity, clutter/texture, shading, and face. The first three are similar to those defined in [48].

1. Constant intensity model $\zeta = 1$:
This assumes that pixel intensities in a region R are subject to independently and identically distributed (iid) Gaussian distribution,

$$p_1(\mathbf{I}_{R(L)}|\zeta = 1, L, \Theta) = \prod_{v \in R(L)} G(\mathbf{I}_v - \mu; \sigma^2), \quad \Theta = (\mu, \sigma)$$

2. Clutter/texture model $\zeta = 2$:
This is a non-parametric intensity histogram $h()$ discretized to take G values (i.e. is expressed as a vector $(h_1, h_2, ..., h_G)$). Let n_j be the number of pixels in $R(L)$ with intensity value j.

$$p_2(\mathbf{I}_{R(L)}|\zeta = 2, L, \Theta) = \prod_{v \in R(L)} h(\mathbf{I}_v) = \prod_{j=1}^{G} h_j^{n_j}, \quad \Theta = (h_1, h_2, ..., h_G).$$

3. Shading model $\zeta = 3$ and $\zeta = 5, ..., 66$:
This family of models are used to describe generic shading patterns, and text characters. We use a quadratic form

$$J(x, y; \Theta) = ax^2 + bxy + cy^2 + dx + ey + f,$$

with parameters $\Theta = (a, b, c, d, e, f, \sigma)$. Therefore, the generative model for pixel (x, y) is

$$p_3(\mathbf{I}_R(L)|\zeta \in \{3, (5, ..., 66)\}, L, \Theta) = \prod_{v \in R(L)} G(\mathbf{I}_v - J_v; \sigma^2), \quad \Theta = (a, b, c, d, e, f, \sigma).$$

4. The PCA face model $\zeta = 4$:
The generative model for faces is simpler and uses Principal Component Analysis (PCA) to obtain representations of the faces in terms of principal components $\{B_i\}$ and covariances Σ. Lower level features, also modeled by PCA, can be added [37]. We also add other features such as the occlusion process, as described in Hallinan et al [22].

$$p_4(\mathbf{I}_R(L)|\zeta = 4, L, \Theta) = G(\mathbf{I}_{R(L)} - \sum_i \lambda_i B_i; \Sigma), \quad \Theta = (\lambda_1, .., \lambda_n, \Sigma).$$

4   Overview of the Algorithm

This section gives the control structure of an image parsing algorithm based on the strategy described in section (2), see the diagram in Figure 7. Our algorithm must construct the parse graph on the fly and estimate the scene interpretation W.

Figure 6 illustrates how the algorithm selects the Markov chain moves (dynamics or sub-kernels) to search through the space of possible parse graphs of

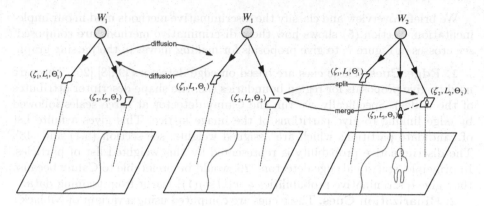

Fig. 6. Examples of Markov chain dynamics that change the graph structure or the node attributes of the graph giving rise to different ways to parse the image

the image by altering the graph structure (by deleting or adding nodes) and by changing the node attributes. An equivalent way of visualizing the algorithm is in terms of a search through the solution space Ω, see [48,49] for more details of this viewpoint.

We first define the set of moves to reconfigure the graph. These are: (i) birth or death of face nodes, (ii) birth or death of text characters, (iii) splitting or merging of regions, (iv) switching node attributes (region type ζ_i and model parameters Θ_i), (v) boundary evolution (altering the shape descriptors L_i of nodes with adjacent regions). These moves are implemented by sub-kernels. The first four moves are reversible jumps [21], and will be implemented by the Metropolis-Hastings equation (8). The fifth move, boundary evolution, is implemented by a stochastic partial differential equation.

The sub-kernels for these moves require proposal probabilities driven by elementary discriminative methods, which we review in the next subsection. The proposal probabilities are designed using the criteria in subsection (2.4), and full details are given in Section (5).

The control structure of the algorithm is described in Section (4.2). The full transition kernel for the image parser is built by combining the sub-kernels, as described in subsection (2.3) and Figure 7. The algorithm proceeds (stochastically) by selecting a sub-kernel, selecting where in the graph to apply it, and then deciding whether or not to accept the operation.

4.1 The Discriminative Methods

The discriminative methods give approximate posterior probabilities $q(w_j|\mathrm{Tst}_j(\mathbf{I}))$ for the elementary components w_j of W. For computational efficiency, these probabilities are based only on a small number of simple tests $\mathrm{Tst}_j(\mathbf{I})$.

We briefly overview and classify the discriminative methods used in our implementation. Section (5) shows how these discriminative methods are composed, see crosses in Figure 7, to give proposals for making moves in the parsing graph.

1. Edge Cues. These cues are based on edge detectors [9],[8],[26]. They are used to give proposals for region boundaries (i.e. the shape descriptor attributes of the nodes). Specifically, we run the Canny detector at three scales followed by edge linking to give partitions of the image lattice. This gives a finite list of candidate partitions which are assigned weights, see section (5.1) and [48]. The discriminative probability is represented by this weighted list of particles. In principle, statistical edge detectors [26] would be preferable to Canny because they give discriminative probabilities $q(w_j|\text{Tst}_j(\mathbf{I}))$ learnt from training data.

2. Binarization Cues. These cues are computed using a variant of Niblack's algorithm [40]. They are used to propose boundaries for text characters (i.e. shape descriptors for text nodes), and will be used in conjunction with proposals for text detection. The binarization algorithm, and an example of its output, are given in Section (5.2). Like edge cues, the algorithm is run at different parameters settings and represents the discriminative probability by a weighted list of particles indicating candidate boundary locations.

3. Face Region Cues. These cues are learnt by a variant of AdaBoost [44],[55] which outputs discriminative probabilities [19], see Section (5.2). They propose the presence of faces in sub-regions of the image. These cues are combined with edge detection to propose the localization of faces in an image.

4. Text Region Cues. These cues are also learnt by a probabilistic version of AdaBoost, see Section (5.2). The algorithm is applied to image windows (at a range of scales). It outputs a discriminative probability for the presence of text in each window. Text region cues are combined with binarization to propose boundaries for text characters.

5. Shape Affinity Cues. These act on shape boundaries, produced by binarization, to propose text characters. They use shape context cues [4] and information features [50] to propose matches between the shape boundaries and the deformable template models of text characters.

6. Region Affinity Cues. These are used to estimate whether two regions R_i, R_j are likely to have been generated by the same visual pattern family and model parameters. They use an affinity similarity measure [45] of the intensity properties $\mathbf{I}_{R_i}, \mathbf{I}_{R_j}$.

7. Model Parameter and Visual Pattern Family cues. These are used to propose model parameters and visual pattern family identity. They are based on clustering algorithms, such as mean-shift [12]. The clustering algorithms depend on the model types and are described in [48].

In our current implementation, we conduct all the bottom-up tests $\text{Tst}_j(\mathbf{I})$, $j = 1, 2, ..., K$ at an early stage for all the discriminative models $q_j(w_j|\text{Tst}_j(\mathbf{I}))$, and they are then combined to form composite tests $\text{Tst}_a(\mathbf{I})$ for each subkernel $\mathcal{K}_a$ in equations (8,9). It may be more efficient to perform these test as required, see discussion in section (7).

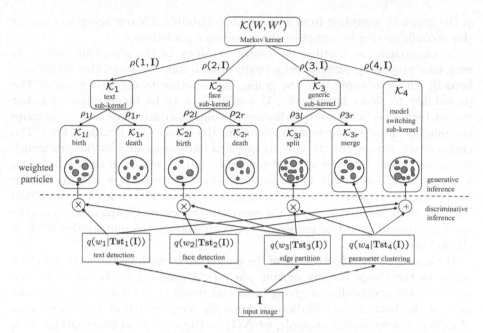

Fig. 7. Integrating generative (top-down) and discriminative (bottom-up) methods for image parsing. This diagram illustrates the main points of the image parser. The dynamics are implemented by an ergodic Markov chain $\mathcal{K}$, whose invariant probability is the posterior $p(W|\mathbf{I})$, and which is composed of reversible sub-kernels $\mathcal{K}_a$ for making different types of moves in the parse graph (e.g. giving birth to new nodes or merging nodes). At each time step the algorithm selects a sub-kernel stochastically. The selected sub-kernel proposes a specific move (e.g. to create or delete specific nodes) and this move is then evaluated and accepted stochastically, see equation (8). The proposals are based on both bottom-up (discriminative) and top-down (generative) processes, see subsection (2.4). The bottom-up processes compute discriminative probabilities $q(w_j|\mathrm{Tst}_j(\mathbf{I})), j = 1, 2, 3, 4$ from the input image $\mathbf{I}$ based on feature tests $\mathrm{Tst}_j(\mathbf{I})$. An additional sub-kernel for boundary evolution uses a stochastic partial differential equation will be described later.

4.2   Control Structure of the Algorithm

The control strategy used by our image parser is illustrated in Figure 7. The image parser explores the space of parsing graphs by a Markov Chain Monte Carlo sampling algorithm. This algorithm uses a transition kernel $\mathcal{K}$ which is composed of sub-kernels $\mathcal{K}_a$ corresponding to different ways to reconfigure the parsing graph. These sub-kernels come in reversible pairs[9] (e.g. birth and death) and are designed so that the target probability distribution of the kernel is the generative posterior $p(W|\mathbf{I})$. At each time step, a sub-kernel is selected stochastically. The sub-kernels use the Metropolis-Hasting sampling algorithm, see equation (8), which proceeds in two stages. First, it proposes a reconfiguration

---

[9] Except for the boundary evolution sub-kernel which will be described separately.

of the graph by sampling from a proposal probability. Then it accepts or rejects this reconfiguration by sampling the acceptance probability.

To summarize, we outline the control strategy of the algorithm below. At each time step, it specifies (stochastically) which move to select (i.e. which sub-kernel), where to apply it in the graph, and whether to accept the move. The probability to select moves $\rho(a : \mathbf{I})$ was first set to be independent of $\mathbf{I}$, but we got better performance by adapting it using discriminative cues to estimate the number of faces and text characters in the image (see details below). The choice of where to apply the move is specified (stochastically) by the sub-kernel. For some sub-kernels it is selected randomly and for others is chosen based on a *fitness factor* (see details in section (5)), which measures how well the current model fits the image data. Some annealing is required to start the algorithm because of the limited scope of the moves in the current implementation (the need for annealing will be reduced if the compositional techniques described in [1]) are used).

We improved the effectiveness of the algorithm by making the move selection adapt to the image (i.e. by making $\rho(a : \mathbf{I})$ depend on $\mathbf{I}$). In particular, we increased the probability of giving birth and death of faces and text, $\rho(1)$ and $\rho(2)$, if the bottom-up (AdaBoost) proposals suggested that there are many objects in the scene. For example, let $N(\mathbf{I})$ be the number of proposals for faces or text above a threshold T_a. Then we modify the probabilities in the table by $\rho(a_1) \mapsto \{\rho(a_1) + kg(N(\mathbf{I}))\}/Z$, $\rho(a_2) \mapsto \{\rho(a_2) + kg(N)\}/Z$, $\rho(a_3) \mapsto \rho(a_3)/Z$, $\rho(a_4) \mapsto \rho(a_4)/Z$, where $g(x) = x$, $x \leq T_b$ $g(x) = T_b$, $x \geq T_b$ and $Z = 1 + 2k$ is chosen to normalize the probability.

The basic control strategy of the image parsing algorithm is summarized as follows:

1. Initialize W (e.g. by dividing the image into four regions), setting their shape descriptors, and assigning the remaining node attributes at random.
2. Set the temperature to be T_{init}.
3. Select the type a of move by sampling from a probability $\rho(a)$, with $\rho(1) = 0.2$ for faces, $\rho(2) = 0.2$ for text, $\rho(3) = 0.4$ for splitting and merging, $\rho(4) = 0.15$ for switching region model (type or model parameters), and $\rho(5) = 0.05$ for boundary evolution. This was modified slightly adaptively, see caption and text.
4. If the selected move is boundary evolution, then select adjacent regions (nodes) at random and apply stochastic steepest descent.
5. If the jump moves are selected, then a new solution W' is randomly sampled as follows:
   - For the birth or death of a face, we propose to create or delete a face. This includes a proposal for where in the image to do this.
   - For the birth of death of text, we propose to create a text character or delete an existing one. This includes a proposal for where to do this.
   - For region splitting, a region (node) is randomly chosen biased by its fitness factor. There are proposals for where to split it and for the attributes of the resulting two nodes.

- For region merging, two neighboring regions (nodes) are selected based on a proposal probability. There are proposals for the attributes of the resulting node.
- For switching, a region is selected randomly according to its fitness factor and a new region type and/or model parameters is proposed.

- The full proposal probabilities, $Q(W|W : \mathbf{I})$ and $Q(W'|W : \mathbf{I})$ are computed.
- The Metropolis-Hastings algorithm, equation (8), is applied to accept or reject the proposed move.

6. Reduce the temperature $T = 1 + T_{init} \times exp(-t \times c|R|)$, where t is the current iteration step, c is a constant and $|R|$ is the size of the image.
7. Repeat the above steps and until the convergence criterion is satisfied (by reaching the maximum number of allowed steps or by lack of decrease of the negative log posterior).

5   The Markov Chain Kernels

This section gives an example of the Markov Chain kernels, the proposal probabilities, and their fitness factors.

We first need boundary evolution, see Figure (8). This evolves the positions of the region boundaries but preserve the graph structure. It is implemented by a stochastic partial differential equation (Langevin equation) driven by Brownian noise and can be derived from a Markov Chain [20]. The deterministic component of the PDE is obtained by performing steepest descent on the negative log-posterior, as derived in [60].

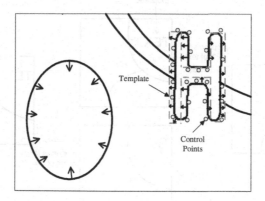

Fig. 8. The evolution of the region boundaries is implemented by stochastic partial differential equations which are driven by models competing for ownership of the regions

The other sub-kernels alter the graph structure. See Figure (9) for an example where regions are split or merged. We will describe below the sub-kernel for the birth and death of text. We refer to [51] for the other subkernels.

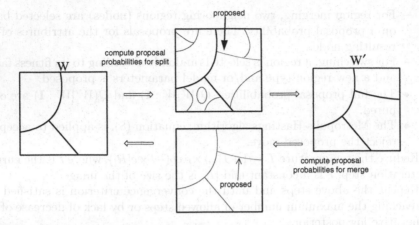

Fig. 9. An example of the split-merge sub-kernel. State W consists of three regions and proposals are computed for 7 candidate splits. One is selected, see arrow, which changes the state to W'. Conversely, there are 5 candidate merges in state W' and the one selected, see arrow, returns the system to state W.

5.1   Markov Chain Sub-kernel for the Birth and Death of Text

This pair of jumps is used to create or delete text characters. We start with a parse graph W and transition into parse graph W' by creating a character. Conversely, we transition from W' back to W by deleting a character.

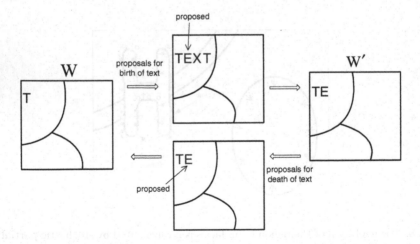

Fig. 10. An example of the birth-death of text. State W consists of three generic regions and a character "T". Proposals are computed for 3 candidate characters, "E", "X", and "T", obtained by AdaBoost and binarization methods (see section (5.2)). One is selected, see arrow, which changes the state to W'. Conversely, there are 2 candidate in state W' and the one selected, see arrow, returns the system to state W.

The proposals for creating and deleting text characters are designed to approximate the terms in equation (10). We obtain a list of candidate text character shapes by using AdaBoost to detect text regions followed by binarization to detect candidate text character boundaries within text regions (see section (5.2)). This list is represented by a set of particles which are weighted by the similarity to the deformable templates for text characters (see below):

$$S_{1r}(W) = \{ (z_{1r}^{(\mu)}, \omega_{1r}^{(\mu)}) : \mu = 1, 2, ..., N_{1r} \}.$$

Similarly, we specify another set of weighted particles for removing text characters:

$$S_{1l}(W') = \{ (z_{1l}^{(\nu)}, \omega_{1l}^{(\nu)}) : \nu = 1, 2, ..., N_{1l} \}.$$

$\{z_{1r}^{(\mu)}\}$ and $\{z_{1l}^{(\nu)}\}$ represent the possible (discretized) shape positions and text character deformable templates for creating or removing text, and $\{\omega_{1r}^{(\mu)}\}$ and $\{\omega_{1l}^{(\nu)}\}$ are their corresponding weights. The particles are then used to compute proposal probabilities

$$\mathbf{Q}_{1r}(W'|W : \mathbf{I}) = \frac{\omega_{1r}(W')}{\sum_{\mu=1}^{N_{1r}} \omega_{1r}^{(\mu)}}, \quad \mathbf{Q}_{1l}(W|W', \mathbf{I}) = \frac{\omega_{1l}(W)}{\sum_{\nu=1}^{N_{1l}} \omega_{1l}^{(\nu)}}.$$

The weights $\omega_{1r}^{(\mu)}$ and $\omega_{1l}^{(\nu)}$ for creating new text characters are specified by shape affinity measures, such as shape contexts [4] and informative features [50]. For deleting text characters we calculate $\omega_{1l}^{(\nu)}$ directly from the likelihood and prior on the text character. Ideally these weights will approximate the ratios $\frac{p(W'|\mathbf{I})}{p(W|\mathbf{I})}$ and $\frac{p(W|\mathbf{I})}{p(W'|\mathbf{I})}$.

5.2   AdaBoost for Discriminative Probabilities for Face and Text

This section describes how we use AdaBoost techniques to compute discriminative probabilities for detecting faces and text (strings of letters). We also describe the binarization algorithm used to detect the boundaries of text characters.

The standard AdaBoost algorithm, for example for distinguishing faces from non-faces [55], learns a binary-valued *strong classifier* H_{Ada} by combining a set of n binary-valued "weak classifiers" or feature tests $Tst_{Ada}(\mathbf{I}) = (h_1(\mathbf{I}), ..., h_n(\mathbf{I}))$ using a set of weights $\boldsymbol{\alpha}_{Ada} = (\alpha_1, ..., \alpha_n)[18]$,

$$H_{Ada}(Tst_{Ada}(\mathbf{I})) = \text{sign}(\sum_{i=1}^{n} \alpha_i h_i(\mathbf{I})) = \text{sign} < \boldsymbol{\alpha}_{Ada}, Tst_{Ada}(\mathbf{I}) > . \qquad (13)$$

The features are selected from a pre-designed dictionary Δ_{Ada}. The selection of features and the tuning of weights are posed as a supervised learning problem. Given a set of labeled examples, $\{(\mathbf{I}_i, \ell_i) : i = 1, 2, ..., M\}$ ($\ell_i = \pm 1$), AdaBoost learning can be formulated as greedily optimizing the following function [44]

$$(\boldsymbol{\alpha}_{Ada}^*, Tst_{Ada}^*) = \arg \min_{Tst_{Ada} \subset \Delta_{Ada}} \arg \min_{\boldsymbol{\alpha}_{Ada}} \sum_{i=1}^{M} \exp^{-\ell_i < \boldsymbol{\alpha}_{Ada}, Tst_{Ada}(\mathbf{I}_i) >} . \qquad (14)$$

To obtain discriminative probabilities we use a theorem [19] which states that the features and test learnt by AdaBoost give (asymptotically) posterior probabilities for the object labels (e.g. face or non-face). The AdaBoost strong classifier can be rederived as the log posterior ratio test.

Theorem 3. (Friedman et al 1998) *With sufficient training samples M and features n, AdaBoost learning selects the weights α^*_{Ada} and tests $\text{Tst}^*_{\text{Ada}}$ to satisfy*

$$q(\ell = +1|\mathbf{I}) = \frac{e^{<\alpha_{\text{Ada}},\text{Tst}_{\text{Ada}}(\mathbf{I}_i)>}}{e^{<\alpha_{\text{Ada}},\text{Tst}_{\text{Ada}}(\mathbf{I}_i)>} + e^{-<\alpha_{\text{Ada}},\text{Tst}_{\text{Ada}}(\mathbf{I}_i)>}}.$$

Moreover, the strong classifier converges asymptotically to the posterior probability ratio test

$$H_{\text{Ada}}(\text{Tst}_{\text{Ada}}(\mathbf{I})) = \text{sign}(<\alpha_{\text{Ada}}, \text{Tst}_{\text{Ada}}(\mathbf{I})>) = \text{sign}(\frac{q(\ell = +1|\mathbf{I})}{q(\ell = -1|\mathbf{I})}).$$

In practice, the AdaBoost classifier is applied to windows in the image at different scales. Each window is evaluated as being face or non-face (or text versus non-text). For most images the posterior probabilities for faces or text are negligible for almost all parts of an image. So we use a cascade of tests [55,57] which enables us to rapidly reject many windows by setting their marginal probabilities to be zero.

Of course, AdaBoost will only converge to approximations to the true posterior probabilities $p(\ell|\mathbf{I})$ because only a limited number of tests can be used (and there is only a limited amount of training data).

Note that AdaBoost is only one way to learn a posterior probability, see theorem (1). It has been found to be very effective for object patterns which have relatively rigid structures, such as faces and text (the shapes of letters are variable but the patterns of a sequence are fairly structured [10]).

We refer to Viola and Jones [55] and Chen and Yuille [10] for details of how AdaBoost learning [18,19] can be performed to detect face and text.

In both cases, we evaluated the log posterior ratio test on testing datasets using a number of different thresholds (see [55]). In agreement with previous work on faces [55], AdaBoost gave very high performance with very few false positives and false negatives, see table (1). But these low error rates are slightly misleading because of the enormous number of windows in each image, see table (1). A small false positive rate may imply a large number of false positives for any regular image. By varying the threshold, we can either eliminate the false positives or the false negatives but not both at the same time. We illustrate this by showing the face regions and text regions proposed by AdaBoost in Figure 11. If we attempt classification by putting a threshold then we can only correctly detect all the faces and the text at the expense of false positives.

When Adaboost is integrated with the generic region models in the image parser, the generic region proposals can remove false positives and find text that AdaBoost misses. For example, the '9' in the right panel of Figure 11 is not detected because our AdaBoost algorithm was trained on text segments and can fail to detect isolated letters. Instead it is detected as a generic shading region

Table 1. Performance of AdaBoost at different thresholds

Object	False Positive	False Negative	Images	Subwindows
Face	65	26	162	355,960,040
Face	918	14	162	355,960,040
Face	7542	1	162	355,960,040
Text	118	27	35	20,183,316
Text	1879	5	35	20,183,316

Fig. 11. The boxes show faces and text as detected by the AdaBoost log posterior ratio test with fixed threshold. Observe the false positives due to vegetation, tree structure, and random image patterns. It is impossible to select a threshold which has no false positives and false negatives for this image. As it is shown in our experiments later, the generative models will remove the false positives and also recover the missing text.

and later recognized as a letter '9', see Figure 13. Some false positive text and faces in Figure 11 are removed in Figures 13 and 15.

The AdaBoost algorithm for text needs to be supplemented with a binarization algorithm, described below, to determine text character location. This is followed by appling shape contexts [4] and informative features [50] to the binarization results to make proposals for the presence of specific letters and digits.

In many cases, see Figure 12, the results of binarization are so good that the letters and digits can be detected immediately (i.e. the proposals made by the binarization stage are automatically accepted). But this will not always be the case. We note that binarization gives far better results than alternatives such as edge detection [9].

The binarization algorithm is a variant of one proposed by Niblack [40]. We binarize the image intensity using an adaptive thresholding based on a adaptive window size. Adaptive methods are needed because image windows containing text often have shading, shadow, and occlusion. Our binarization method determines the threshold $T_b(v)$ for each pixel v by the intensity distribution of its local window $r(v)$ (centered on v).

$$T_b(v) = \mu(\mathbf{I}_{r(v)}) + k \cdot std(\mathbf{I}_{r(v)}),$$

where $\mu(\mathbf{I}_{r(v)})$ and $std(\mathbf{I}_{r(v)})$ are the intensity mean and standard deviation within the local window. The size of the local window is selected to be the smallest possible window whose intensity variance is above a fixed threshold. The parameter $k = \pm 0.2$, where the $\pm$ allows for cases where the foreground is brighter or darker than the background.

Fig. 12. Example of binarization on the detected text

6   Experiments

The image parsing algorithm was applied to a number of outdoor/indoor images. The speed in PCs (Pentium IV) is comparable to segmentation methods such as normalized cuts [32] or the DDMCMC algorithm in [48]. It typically runs around 10-20 minutes. The main portion of the computing time is spent in segmenting the generic patterns and by boundary diffusion [60].

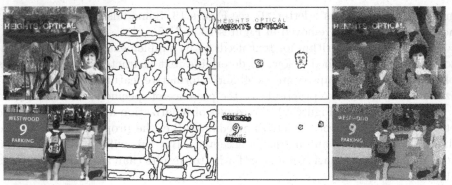

a. Input image   b. Segmentation c. Object recognition d. Synthesized image

Fig. 13. Results of segmentation and recognition on two images. The results are improved compare to the purely bottom-up (AdaBoost) results displayed in Figure 11.

a. Input image   b. Synthesis 1   c. Synthesis 2

Fig. 14. A close-up look of an image in Figure 13. The dark glasses are explained by the generic shading model and so the face model does not have to fit this part of the data. Otherwise the face model would have difficulty because it would try to fit the glasses to eyes. Standard AdaBoost only correctly classifies these faces at the expense of false positives, see Figure 11. We show two examples of synthesized faces, one (Synthesis 1) with the dark glasses (modelled by shading regions) and the other (Synthesis 2) with the dark glasses removed (i.e. using the generative face model to sample parts of the face (e.g. eyes) obscured by the dark glasses.

Figures 13, 14, and 15 show some challenging examples which have heavy clutter and shading effects. We present the results in two parts. One shows the segmentation boundaries for generic regions and objects, and the other shows the text and faces detected with text symbols to indicate text recognition, i.e. the letters are correctly read by the algorithm. Then we synthesize images sampled from the likelihood model $p(\mathbf{I}|W^*)$ where W^* is the parsing graph (the faces, text, regions parameters and boundaries) obtained by the parsing algorithm. The synthesized images are used to visualize the parsing graph W^*, i.e. the image content that the computer "understand".

In the experiments, we observed that the face and text models improved the image segmentation results by comparison to our previous work [48] which only used generic region models. Conversely, the generic region models improve object detection by removing some false alarms and recovering objects which were not initially detected. We now discuss specific examples.

In Figure 11, we showed two images where the text and faces were detected purely bottom-up using AdaBoost. It is was impossible to select a threshold so that our AdaBoost algorithm had no false positives or false negatives. To ensure no false negatives, apart from the '9', we had to lower the threshold and admit false positives due to vegetation and heavy shadows (e.g. the shadow in the sign "HEIGHTS OPTICAL").

The letter '9' was not detected at any threshold. This is because our AdaBoost algorithm was trained to detect text segments, and so did not respond to a single digit.

By comparison, Figure 13 shows the image parsing results for these two images. We see that the false alarms proposed by AdaBoost are removed because they are better explained by the generic region models. The generic shading models help object detection by explaining away the heavy shading on the text "HEIGHTS OPTICAL" and the dark glasses on the women, see Figure 14. Moreover, the missing digit '9' is now correctly detected. The algorithm first detected

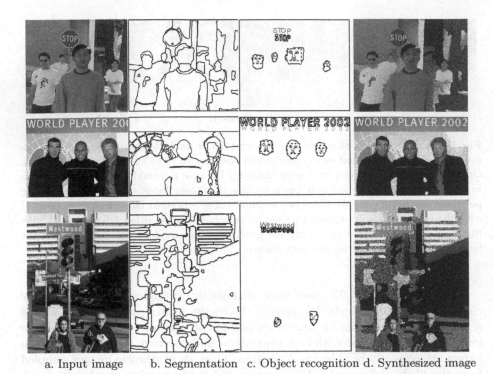

a. Input image   b. Segmentation   c. Object recognition   d. Synthesized image

Fig. 15. Results of segmentation and recognition on outdoor images. Observe the ability to detect faces and text at multiple scale.

it as a generic shading region and then reclassified as a digit using the sub-kernel that switches node attributes.

The ability to synthesize the image from the parsing graph W^* is an advantage of the Bayesian approach. The synthesis helps illustrate the successes, and sometimes the weaknesses, of the generative models. Moreover, the synthesized images show how much information about the image has been captured by the models. In table (2), we give the number of variables used in our representation W^* and show that they are roughly proportional to the jpeg bytes. Most of the variables in W^* are used to represent points on the segmentation boundary, and at present they are counted independently. We could reduce the coding length of W^* substantially by encoding the boundary points effectively, for example, using spatial proximity. Image encoding is not the goal of our current work, however, and more sophisticated generative models would be needed to synthesize very realistic images.

Table 2. The number of variables in W^* for each image compared to the JPG bytes

Image	Stop	Soccer	Parking	Street	Westwood
jpg bytes	23,998	19,563	23,311	26,170	27,790
$|W^*|$	4,886	3,971	5,013	6,346	9,687

7   Discussion

In this section, we describe two challenging technical problems for image parsing. Our current work addresses these issues.

1. Two mechanisms for constructing the parsing graph

In the introduction to this chapter we stated that the parsing graph can be constructed in compositional and decompositional modes. The compositional mode proceeds by grouping small elements while the decompositional approach involves detecting an object as a whole and then locating its parts, see Figure 16.

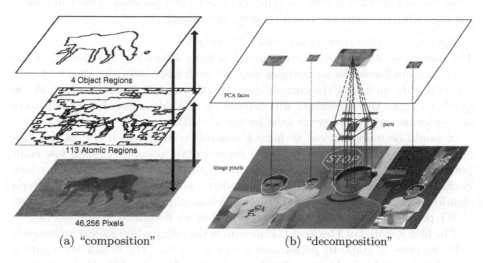

(a) "composition"   (b) "decomposition"

Fig. 16. Two mechanisms for constructing the parsing graph. See text for explanation.

The compositional mode appears most effective for Figure 16(a). Detecting the cheetah by bottom-up tests, such as those learnt by AdaBoost, seems difficult owing to the large variability of shape and photometric properties of cheetahs. By contrast, it is quite practical using Swendsen-Wang Cuts [2] to segment the image and obtain the boundary of the cheetah using a bottom-up compositional approach and a parsing tree with multiple levels. The parsing graph is constructed starting with the pixels as leaves (there are $46,256$ pixels in Figure 16(a)). The next level of the graph is obtained using local image texture similarities to construct graph nodes (113 of them) corresponding to "atomic regions" of the image. Then the algorithm constructs nodes (4 of them) for "texture regions" at the next level by grouping the atomic regions (i.e. each atomic region node will be the child of a texture region node). At each level, we compute a discriminative (proposal) probability for how likely adjacent nodes (e.g. pixels or atomic regions) belong to the same object or pattern. We then apply a transition kernel implementing split and merge dynamics (using the proposals). We refer to [2] for more detailed discussion.

For objects with little variability, such as the faces shown in Figure 16(b), we can use bottom-up proposals (e.g. AdaBoost) to activate a node that represents the entire face. The parsing graph can then be constructed downwards (i.e. in the decompositional mode) by expanding the face node to create child nodes for the parts of the face. These child nodes could, in turn, be expanded to grandchild nodes representing finer scale parts. The amount of node expansion can be made adaptive to depend on the resolution of the image. For example, the largest face in Figure 16(b) is expanded into child nodes but there is not sufficient resolution to expand the face nodes corresponding to the three smaller faces.

The major technical problem is to develop a mathematical criterion for which mode is most effective for which types of objects and patterns. This will enable the algorithm to adapt its search strategy accordingly.

2. Optimal ordering strategy for tests and kernels
The control strategy of our current image parsing algorithm does not select the tests and sub-kernels in an optimal way. At each time step, the choice of sub-kernel is independent of the current state W (though the choice of where in the graph to apply the sub-kernel will depend on W). Moreover, bottom-up tests are performed which are never used by the algorithm.

It would be more efficient to have a control strategy which selects the sub-kernels and tests adaptively, provided the selection process requires low computational cost. We seek to find an optimal control strategy for selection which is effective for a large set of images and visual patterns. The selection criteria should select those tests and sub-kernels which maximize the gain in information.

We propose the two information criteria that we described in Section (2).

The first is stated in Theorem 1. It measures the information gained for variable w in the parsing graph by performing a new test Tst_+. The information gain is $\delta(w||\text{Tst}_+) = KL(p(w|\mathbf{I}) \,||\, q(w|\text{Tst}(\mathbf{I}))) - KL(p(w|\mathbf{I}) \,||\, q(w|\text{Tst}_t(\mathbf{I}), F_+))$, where $\text{Tst}(\mathbf{I})$ denotes the previous tests (and KL is the Kullback-Leibler divergence).

The second is stated in Theorem 2. It measures the power of a sub-kernel $\mathcal{K}_a$ by the decrease of the KL-divergence $\delta(\mathcal{K}_a) = KL(p \,||\, \mu_t) - KL(p \,||\, \mu_t \mathcal{K}_a)$. The amount of decrease δ_a gives a measure of the power of the sub-kernel $\mathcal{K}_a$ when informed by $\text{Tst}_t(\mathbf{I})$.

We need also take into account the computational cost of the selection procedures. See [6] for a case study for how to optimally select tests taking into account their computational costs.

8   Summary and Future Work

This chapter introduces a computational framework for parsing images into basic visual patterns. We formulated the problem using Bayesian probability theory and designed a stochastic DDMCMC algorithm to perform inference. Our framework gives a rigorous way to combine segmentation with object detection and recognition. We give proof of concept by implementing a model whose visual patterns include generic regions (texture and shading) and objects (text and faces). Our approach enables these different visual patterns to compete and cooperate to explain the input images.

This chapter also provides a way to integrate discriminative and generative methods of inference. Both methods are extensively used by the vision and machine learning communities and correspond to the distinction between bottom-up and top-down processing. Discriminative methods are typically fast but can give sub-optimal and inconsistent results, see Figure 3. By contrast, generative methods are optimal (in the sense of Bayesian Decision Theory) but can be slow because they require extensive search. Our DDMCMC algorithm integrates both methods, as illustrated in Figure 7, by using discriminative methods to propose generative solutions.

The goal of our algorithm is to construct a parse graph representing the image. The structure of the graph is not fixed and will depend on the input image. The algorithm proceeds by constructing Markov Chain dynamics, implemented by sub-kernels, for different moves to configure the parsing graph – such as creating or deleting nodes, or altering node attributes. Our approach can be scaled-up by adding new sub-kernels, corresponding to different vision models. This is similar in spirit to Ullman's concept of "visual routines" [54]. Overall, the ideas in this chapter can be applied to any other inference problem that can be formulated as probabilistic inference on graphs.

Other work by our group deals with a related series of visual inference tasks using a similar framework. This includes image segmentation [48], curve grouping [49], shape detection [50], motion analysis [2], and 3D scene reconstruction [23]. In the future, we plan to integrate these visual modules and develop a general purpose vision system.

Finally, we are working on ways to improve the speed of the image parsing algorithm as discussed in Section (7). In particular, we expect the use of the Swendsen-Wang cut algorithms [1,2] to drastically accelerate the search. We anticipate that this, and other improvements, will reduce the running time of DDMCMC algorithms from 10-20 minutes [48] to well under a minute.

Acknowledgments

This work was supported by an NIH (NEI) grant RO1-EY 012691-04, an NSF SGER grant IIS-0240148, an NSF grant IIS-0244763 and an ONR grant N00014-02-1-0952. The authors thank the Smith-Kettlewell research institute for providing us with text training images. We thank Yingnian Wu for stimulating discussions on the Markov chain convergence theorems.

References

1. A. Barbu and S.C. Zhu, "Graph partition by Swendsen-Wang cut", *Proc. of Int'l Conf. on Computer Vision*, Nice, France, October, 2003.
2. A. Barbu and S.C. Zhu, "Multi-grid and multi-level Swendsen-Wang cuts for hierarchic graph partition", *Proc. of IEEE Conf. on Computer Vision and Pattern Recognition*, Washington DC, June, 2004.

3. K. Barnard and D.A. Forsyth, "Learning the semantics of words and pictures", *ICCV*, 2001.
4. S. Belongie, J. Malik, and J. Puzicha. "Shape matching and object recognition using shape contexts", *IEEE Trans. on Pattern Analysis and Machine Intelligence*, 24:509–522, 2002.
5. E. Bienenstock, S. Geman, and D. Potter, "Compositionality, MDL Priors, and Object Recognition", NIPS, 1997.
6. G. Blanchard and D. Geman, "Hierarchical testing designs for pattern recognition," Technical report, Math. Science, Johns Hopkins University, 2003.
7. P. Bremaud, "Markov Chains: Gibbs Fields, Monte Carlo Simulation and Queues," Springer, 1999. (Chapter 6).
8. K.W. Bowyer, C. Kranenburg, and S. Dougherty, "Edge detector evaluation using empirical ROC curves", *Computer Vision and Image Understanding*, 84, no. 1, pp.77-103, Oct. 2001.
9. J. Canny, "A computational approach to edge detection", *IEEE Trans. on PAMI*, vol.8, no.6, nov. 1986.
10. X. Chen and A.L. Yuille. "AdaBoost Learning for Detecting and Reading Text in City Scenes". *Proc. of IEEE Conf. on Computer Vision and Pattern Recognition*. Washington DC, June, 2004.
11. T. F. Cootes, G. J. Edwards, and C. J. Taylor, "Active appearance models", *IEEE Trans. on PAMI* no. 23, vol. 6, 2001.
12. D. Comaniciu and P. Meer, "Mean Shift Analysis and Applications," *Proc. of ICCV*, 1999.
13. T. M. Cover and J. A. Thomas, *Elements of Information Theory*, (pp 33-36) John Wiley and Sons, Inc, NY, 1991.
14. P. Dayan, G. Hinton, R. Neal and R. Zemel. "The Helmholtz Machine". *Neural Computation*, 7, pp 889-904. 1995.
15. P. Diaconis and P. Hanlon, "Eigenanalysis for some examples of the Metropolis algorithms", *Contemporary Mathematics*, vol. 138, pp 99-117, 1992.
16. H. Drucker, R. Schapire, and P. Simard, "Boosting performance in neural networks," *Intl J. Pattern Rec. and Artificial Intelligence*, vol. 7, no. 4, 1993.
17. C. Fowlkes and J. Malik, "How Much Does Globalization Help Segmentation?", *CVPR 2004*.
18. Y. Freund and R. Schapire, "Experiments with a new boosting algorithm", *Proc. of 13th Int'l Conference on Machine Learning*, 1996.
19. J. Friedman, T. Hastie and R. Tibshirani, "Additive logistic regression: a statistical view of boosting", Dept. of Statistics, Stanford Univ. Technical Report. 1998.
20. S. Geman and C.R. Huang, "Diffusion for global optimization", *SIAM J. on Control and Optimization*, vol. 24, no. 5, 1986.
21. P. J. Green, "Reversible Jump Markov Chain Monte Carlo Computation and Bayesian Model Determination," *Biometrika*, vol. 82, no. 4, pp. 711-732, 1995.
22. P. Hallinan, G. Gordon, A. Yuille, P. Giblin, and D. Mumford, *Two and Three Dimensional Patterns of the Face*, A.K. Peters, 1999.
23. F. Han and S.C. Zhu, "Bayesian reconstruction of 3D shapes and scenes from a single image", *Proc. Int'l Workshop on High Level Knowledge in 3D Modeling and Motion*, Nice France, October, 2003.
24. W.K. Hastings, "Monte Carlo sampling methods using Markov chains and their applications", *Biometrika*, 57, 97-109, 1970.
25. D. Klein and C. D. Manning, "A generative constituent-context model for improved grammar induction", *Porc. of 40th Annual Meeting of the Assoc. for Computational Linguistics*, July 2002.

26. S. Konishi, J. M. Coughlan, A. L. Yuille, and S. C. Zhu, "Statistical edge detection: learning and evaluating edge cues", *IEEE Trans. on Pattern Analysis and Machine Intelligence*, vol. 25, no.1, pp 57-74, 2003.

27. S. Kumar and M. Hebert. "Discriminative Random Fields". *Proc. of Int'l Conf. on Computer Vision*, Nice, France, October, 2003.

28. F.F. Li R. VanRullen, C. Koch, and P. Perona, "Rapid natural scene categorization in the near absence of attention", *Proc. of National Academy of Sciences*, vol.99, no.14, 2003.

29. J.S. Liu, "Monte Carlo Strategies in Scientific Computing", Springer, 2001

30. L.D. Lowe, "Distinctive image features from scale-invariant keypoints", *IJCV*, 2003.

31. R. Maciuca and S.C. Zhu, "How Do Heuristics Expedite Markov Chain Search," *Proc. of 3rd Workshop on Statistical and Computational Theory for Vision*, 2003.

32. J. Malik, S. Belongie, T. Leung and J. Shi, "Contour and texture analysis for image segmentation", *Int'l Journal of Computer Vision*, vol.43, no.1, 2001.

33. C.D. Manning and H. Schütze. *Foundations of Statistical Natural Language Processing*. MIT Press. 2003.

34. D. Marr. *Vision*. W.H. Freeman and Co. San Francisco, 1982.

35. D. Martin, C. Fowlkes, D. Tal and J. Malik, "A database of human segmented natural images and its application to evaluating segmentation algorithms and measuring ecological statistics", *Proc. of 8th Int'l Conference on Computer Vision*, 2001.

36. N. Metropolis, M.N. Rosenbluth, A.W. Rosenbluth, A.H. Teller, and E. Teller, "Equations of State Calculations by Fast Computing Machines", *J. Chem. Phys.* 21, 1087-92, 1953.

37. B. Moghaddam and A. Pentland, "Probabilistic visual learning for object representation", *IEEE Trans. PAMI*, vol.19, no.7, 1997.

38. D.B. Mumford. "Neuronal Architectures for Pattern-theoretic Problems". In *Large-Scale Neuronal Theories of the Brain*. Eds. C. Koch and J. L. Davis. MIT Press. A Bradford Book. 1995.

39. K. Murphy, A. Torralba, and W.T. Freeman, "Using the forest to see the tree: a graphical model relating features, objects and the scenes", *NIPS*, 2003.

40. W. Niblack. *An Introduction to Digital Image Processing*. pp. 115-116, Prentice Hall, 1986.

41. P. J. Phillips, H. Wechsler, J. Huang, and P. Rauss, "The FERET database and evaluation procedure for face recognition algorithms", *Image and Vision Computing Journal*, vol. 16, no. 5, 1998.

42. J. Ponce, S. Lazebnik, F. Rothganger, and C. Schmid, "Toward true 3D object recognition", *Reconnaissance de Formes et Intelligence Artificielle*, Toulous, FR. 2004.

43. M. Rosen-Zvi, M. Jordan, and A.L. Yuille. "The DLR Hierarchy of Approximate Inference". *In Proceedings Uncertainty in Artificial Intelligence*. pp 493-500. 2005.

44. R. E. Schapire, "The boosting approach to machine learning: an overview", *MSRI Workshop on Nonlinear Estimation and Classification*, 2002.

45. J. Shi and J. Malik, "Normalized Cuts and Image Segmentation," *IEEE Trans. PAMI*, vol. 22, no. 8, Aug. 2000.

46. S. Thorpe, D. Fize, and C. Marlot, "Speed of processing in the human visual system", *Nature*, vol. 381 (6582), 520-522, Janue, 1996.

47. A. Treisman, "Features and objects in visual processing", *Scientific American*, November, 1986.

48. Z. Tu and S.C. Zhu, "Image segmentation by Data-driven Markov chain Monte Carlo", *IEEE Trans. PAMI*, vol. 24, no.5, pp. 657-673, 2002.
49. Z.W. Tu and S.C. Zhu, "Parsing images into regions, curves and curve groups", *Int'l Journal of Computer Vision*, (Under review), A short version appeared in the *Proc. of ECCV*, 2002.
50. Z.W. Tu and A.L. Yuille. "Shape Matching and Recognition: Using Generative Models and Informative Features". In *Proceedings European Conference on Computer Vision*. ECCV'04. Prague. 2004.
51. Z.W. Tu, Z. Chen, A.L. Yuille, and S.C. Zhu. "Image Parsing: Unifying Segmentation, Detection, and Recognition." *Int. Journal of Computer Vision*. (63) 2 pp 113-140. 2005.
52. M. Turk and A. Pentland, "Eigenfaces for recognition," *J. of Cognitive Neurosciences*, vol.3, no.1, pp. 71-86, 1991.
53. S. Ullman, "Visual routines", *Cognition*, vol.18, pp.97-159, 1984.
54. S. Ullman, "Sequence Seeking and Counterstreams: A Model for Bidirectional Information Flow in the Cortex". In *Large-Scale Neuronal Theories of the Brain*. Eds. C. Koch and J. L. Davis. MIT Press. A Bradford Book. 1995.
55. P. Viola and M. Jones, "Fast and robust classification using asymmetric Adaboost and a detector cascade", In *Proc. of NIPS01*, 2001.
56. M. Weber, M. Welling and P. Perona, "Towards Automatic Discovery of Object Categories", *Proc. of CVPR*, 2000.
57. J. Wu, J.M. Regh, and M.D. Mullin, "Learning a rare event detection cascade by direct feature selection", NIPS, 2004.
58. J.S. Yedidia, W.T. Freeman, and Y. Weiss, "Generalized belief propagation". In *Advances in Neural Information Processing Systems 13*, pp 689-695. 2001.
59. A.L. Yuille. "Belief Propagation and Gibbs Sampling". Submitted to *Neural Computation*. 2004.
60. S. C. Zhu and A. L. Yuille, "Region competition: unifying snakes, region growing, and Bayes/MDL for multiband image segmentation," *IEEE Trans. PAMI*, vol. 18, no. 9, 1996.
61. S.C. Zhu, R. Zhang, and Z.W. Tu, "Integrating top-down/bottom-up for object recognition by data-driven Markov chain Monte Carlo", *Proc. of IEEE Conf. on Computer Vision and Pattern Recognition*, Hilton Head, SC. 2000.

Sequential Learning of Layered Models from Video

Michalis K. Titsias and Christopher K.I. Williams

School of Informatics, University of Edinburgh,
Edinburgh EH1 2QL, UK
M.Titsias@sms.ed.ac.uk, c.k.i.williams@ed.ac.uk
http://www.anc.ed.ac.uk/

Abstract. A popular framework for the interpretation of image sequences is the layers or sprite model, see e.g. [15], [6]. Jojic and Frey [8] provide a generative probabilistic model framework for this task, but their algorithm is slow as it needs to search over discretized transformations (e.g. translations, or affines) for each layer simultaneously. Exact computation with this model scales exponentially with the number of objects, so Jojic and Frey used an approximate variational algorithm to speed up inference. Williams and Titsias [16] proposed an alternative sequential algorithm for the extraction of objects one at a time using a robust statistical method, thus avoiding the combinatorial explosion.

In this chapter we elaborate on our sequential algorithm in the following ways: Firstly, we describe a method to speed up the computation of the transformations based on approximate tracking of the multiple objects in the scene. Secondly, for sequences where the motion of an object is large so that different views (or aspects) of the object are visible at different times in the sequence, we learn appearance models of the different aspects. We demonstrate our method on four video sequences, including a sequence where we learn articulated parts of a human body.

1 Introduction

A powerful framework for modelling video sequences is the layer-based approach which models an image as a composite of 2D layers, each one representing an object in terms of its appearance and region of support or mask, see e.g. Wang and Adelson [15] and Irani et al. [6]. A layered representation explicitly accounts for occlusion between the objects, permits motion segmentation in a general multiple-frame setting rather than in pairs of frames, and provides appearance models for the underlying objects. These properties can allow layered models to be useful for a number of different purposes such as video compression, video summarization, background substitution (e.g. alpha matting applications), object recognition (e.g. learning an object recognition system from video clips without needing human annotation) and others.

Jojic and Frey [8] provided a principled generative probabilistic framework for learning a layered model allowing transparency between the layers. Williams and Titsias [16] developed a similar model where layers strictly combine by occlusion.

J. Ponce et al. (Eds.): Toward Category-Level Object Recognition, LNCS 4170, pp. 577–595, 2006.

Learning these models using an exact EM algorithm faces the problem that as the number of objects increases, there is a combinatorial explosion of the number of configurations that need to be considered. If there are L possible objects, and there are J transformations that any one object can undergo, then we will need to consider $O(J^L)$ combinations to explain any image. Jojic and Frey [8] tackled this problem by using a variational inference scheme searching over all transformations simultaneously, while Williams and Titsias [16] developed a *sequential* approach using robust statistics which searches over the transformations of one object at each time. Both these methods do not require a video sequence and can work on unordered sets of images. In this case, training can be very slow as it is necessary to search over all possible transformations of at least a single object on every image. However, for video sequences we could considerably speed up the training by first localizing each object based on a recursive processing of the consecutive frames. Recursive localization can approximate the underlying sequence of transformations of an object in the frames and thus learning can be carried out with a very focused search over the neighbourhood of these transformations or without search at all when the approximation is accurate. We refer to the recursive localization procedure as object tracking.

In this chapter we describe two developments of the above model. Firstly, assuming video data and based on tracking we speed up the method of Williams and Titsias [16]. First, the moving background is tracked and then its appearance is learned, while moving foreground objects are found at later stages. The tracking algorithm itself recursively updates an appearance model of the tracked object and approximates the transformations by matching this model to the frames through the sequence.

Secondly, in order to account for variation in object appearance due to changes in the 3D pose of the object and self occlusion, we model different visual aspects or views of each foreground object. This is achieved by introducing a set of mask and appearance pairs, each one associated with a different view of the object. To learn different viewpoint object models we use approximate tracking, so that we first estimate the 2D or planar transformations of each foreground object in all frames and then given these transformations we stabilize the video and learn the viewpoint models for that object using a mixture modelling approach.

The structure of the remainder of the chapter is as follows: In section 2 we describe the layered generative model which assumes multiple views for each foreground object. Section 3 describes learning the model from a video sequence, while section 4 discusses related work. Section 5 gives experimental results and we conclude with a discussion in section 6.

2   Generative Layered Model

For simplicity we will present the generative model assuming that there are two layers, i.e. a foreground object and a static background. Later in this section we will discuss the case of arbitrary number of foreground layers and a moving background.

Let $\mathbf{b}$ denote the appearance image of the background arranged as a vector. Assuming that the background is static, $\mathbf{b}$ will have the same size as the data image size (although note that for moving backgrounds, $\mathbf{b}$ will need to be larger than the image size). Each entry b_i stores the ith pixel value which can either be a grayscale intensity value or a colour value. In our implementation we allow coloured images where b_i is a three-dimensional vector in the RGB space. However, for notational convenience below we assume that b_i is a scalar representing a grayscale value.

In contrast to the background, the foreground object occupies some region of the image and thus to describe this layer we need both an appearance $\mathbf{f}$ and mask $\boldsymbol{\pi}$. The foreground is allowed to move so there is an underlying transformation with index j that e.g. corresponds to translational or affine motion and a corresponding transformation matrix so that $T_j\mathbf{f}$ and $T_j\boldsymbol{\pi}$ is the transformed foreground and mask, respectively. A pixel in an observed image is either foreground or background. This is expressed by a vector of binary latent variables $\mathbf{s}$, one for each pixel drawn from the distribution

$$P(\mathbf{s}|j) = \prod_{i=1}^{P}(T_j\boldsymbol{\pi})_i^{s_i}(1 - T_j\boldsymbol{\pi})_i^{1-s_i}, \tag{1}$$

where $\mathbf{1}$ denotes the vector of ones. Each variable s_i is drawn independently so that for pixel i, if $(T_j\boldsymbol{\pi})_i \simeq 0$, then the pixel will be ascribed to the background with high probability, and if $(T_j\boldsymbol{\pi})_i \simeq 1$, it will be ascribed to the foreground with high probability. Note that $\mathbf{s}$ is the binary mask of the foreground object in an example image, while $\boldsymbol{\pi}$ is the prior untransformed mask that captures roughly the shape of the object stored in $\mathbf{f}$.

Selecting a transformation index j, using prior P_j over J possible values with $\sum_{j=1}^{J} P_j = 1$, and a binary mask $\mathbf{s}$, an image $\mathbf{x}$ is drawn from the Gaussian

$$p(\mathbf{x}|j,\mathbf{s}) = \prod_{i=1}^{P} N(x_i; (T_j\mathbf{f})_i, \sigma_f^2)^{s_i} N(x_i; b_i, \sigma_b^2)^{1-s_i}, \tag{2}$$

where each pixel is drawn independently from the above conditional density. To express the likelihood of an observed image $p(\mathbf{x})$ we marginalise out the latent variables, which are the transformation j and the binary mask $\mathbf{s}$. Particularly, we first sum out $\mathbf{s}$ using (1) and (2) and obtain

$$p(\mathbf{x}|j) = \prod_{i=1}^{P}(T_j\boldsymbol{\pi})_i N(x_i; (T_j\mathbf{f})_i, \sigma_f^2) + (1 - T_j\boldsymbol{\pi})_i N(x_i; b_i, \sigma_b^2). \tag{3}$$

Using now the prior P_j over the transformation j, the probability of an observed image $\mathbf{x}$ is $p(\mathbf{x}) = \sum_{j=1}^{J} P_j p(\mathbf{x}|j)$. Given a set of images $\{\mathbf{x}^1, \ldots, \mathbf{x}^N\}$ we can adapt the parameters $\theta = \{\mathbf{b}, \mathbf{f}, \boldsymbol{\pi}, \sigma_f^2, \sigma_b^2\}$ to maximize the log likelihood using the EM algorithm.

The above model can be extended so as to have a moving background and L foreground objects [16]. For example, for two foreground layers with parameters $(\mathbf{f}_1, \boldsymbol{\pi}_1, \sigma_1^2)$ and $(\mathbf{f}_2, \boldsymbol{\pi}_2, \sigma_2^2)$ and also a moving background, the analogue of equation (3) is

$$p(\mathbf{x}|j_1, j_2, j_b) = \prod_{i=1}^{P} (T_{j_1}\boldsymbol{\pi}_1)_i N(x_i; (T_{j_1}\mathbf{f}_1)_i, \sigma_1^2) + (1 - T_{j_1}\boldsymbol{\pi}_1)_i \times$$

$$[(T_{j_2}\boldsymbol{\pi}_2)_i N(x_i; (T_{j_2}\mathbf{f}_2)_i, \sigma_2^2) + (1 - T_{j_2}\boldsymbol{\pi}_2)_i N(x_i; (T_b\mathbf{b})_i, \sigma_b^2)], \quad (4)$$

where j_1, j_2 and j_b denote the transformation of the first foreground object, the second foreground object and the background, respectively.

Furthermore, we can allow for an arbitrary occlusion ordering between the foreground objects, so that it can vary in different images, by introducing an additional hidden variable that takes as values all $L!$ possible permutations of the foreground layers.

2.1   Incorporating Multiple Viewpoints

The layered model presented above assumes that the foreground object varies due to a 2D (or planar) transformation. However, in many video sequences this assumption will not be true e.g. a foreground object can undergo 3D rotation so that at different times we may see different views (or aspects) of the object. For example, Figure 3 shows three frames of a sequence capturing a man walking; clearly the man's pose changes substantially during time. Next we generalize the layered model so that the appearance of a foreground object can be chosen from a set of possible appearances associated with different viewpoints.

Assume again that there are two layers: one static background and one moving foreground object. We introduce a discrete latent variable v, that can obtain V possible values indexed by integers from 1 to V. For each value v we introduce a separate pair of appearance $\mathbf{f}^v$ and mask $\boldsymbol{\pi}^v$ defined as in section 2. Each pair $(\mathbf{f}^v, \boldsymbol{\pi}^v)$ models a particular view of the object.

To generate an image $\mathbf{x}$ we first select a transformation j and a view v using prior probabilities P_j and P_v, respectively. Then we select a binary mask $\mathbf{s}$ from the distribution $P(\mathbf{s}|j, v) = \prod_{i=1}^{P} (T_j\boldsymbol{\pi}^v)_i^{s_i} (1 - T_j\boldsymbol{\pi}^v)_i^{1-s_i}$, and draw an image $\mathbf{x}$ from the Gausssian $p(\mathbf{x}|j, v, s) = \prod_{i=1}^{P} N(x_i; (T_j\mathbf{f}^v)_i, \sigma_f^2)^{s_i} N(x_i; b_i, \sigma_b^2)^{1-s_i}$. Note the similarity of the above expressions with equations (1) and (2). The only difference is that now the appearance $\mathbf{f}$ and mask $\boldsymbol{\pi}$ are indexed by v to reflect the fact that we have also chosen a view for the foreground object.

To express the probability distribution according to which an image is generated given the transformation, we sum out the binary mask and the view variable and obtain

$$p(\mathbf{x}|j) = \sum_{v=1}^{V} P_v p(\mathbf{x}|j, v), \quad (5)$$

where $p(\mathbf{x}|j, v)$ is given as in (3) with $\mathbf{f}$ and $\boldsymbol{\pi}$ indexed by v. Notice how the equation (5) relates to equation (3). Clearly now $p(\mathbf{x}|j)$ is a mixture model of the type of model given in (3) so that each mixture component is associated with a visual aspect. For example, if we choose to have a single view the latter expression reduces to the former one.

It is straightforward to extend the above model to the case of L foreground layers with varying viewpoints. In this case we need a separate view variable v_ℓ for each foreground object and a set of appearance and mask pairs: $(\mathbf{f}_\ell^{v_\ell}, \boldsymbol{\pi}_\ell^{v_\ell})$, $v_\ell = 1, \ldots, V_\ell$. For example, when we have two foreground objects and a moving background the conditional $p(\mathbf{x}|j_1, j_2, j_b, v_1, v_2)$ is given exactly as in (4) by introducing suitable indexes to the foreground appearances and masks that indicate the choices made for the viewpoint variables.

3   Learning

Given the set of possibly unordered images $\{\mathbf{x}^1, \ldots, \mathbf{x}^N\}$ a principled way to learn the parameters $\theta = (\{\mathbf{f}_1^{v_1}, \boldsymbol{\pi}_1^{v_1}, \sigma_{1,v_1}^2\}_{v_1=1}^{V_1}, \ldots, \{\mathbf{f}_L^{v_L}, \boldsymbol{\pi}_L^{v_L}, \sigma_{L,v_L}^2\}_{v_L=1}^{V_L}, \mathbf{b}, \sigma_b^2)$ is by maximizing the log likelihood $L(\theta) = \sum_{n=1}^{N} \log p(\mathbf{x}^n|\theta)$ using the EM algorithm. However, an exact EM algorithm is intractable. If the foreground objects and the background can undergo J transformations and assuming V views for each foreground object, the time needed to carry out the E-step for a training image is $O(J^{L+1} V^L L!)$. Clearly, this computation is infeasible as it grows exponentially with L. A variational EM algorithm can be used to simultaneously infer the parameters, the transformations and the viewpoint variables in all images in time linear with L. However such algorithm can face two problems: (i) it will be very slow as the number of all transformations J can be very large (e.g. for translations and rotations can be of order of hundred of thousands) and (ii) simultaneous search over all the unknown quantities can be prone to severe local maxima, e.g. there is a clear danger of confusion the aspects of one object and the corresponding aspects of a different object.

Our learning algorithm works for video data and proceeds in stages so that, roughly speaking, each stage deals with a different set of unknown variables. Table 1 illustrates all the different steps of the algorithm. At **Stage 1**, we ignore the search needed to compute the occlusion ordering of the foreground objects and we focus on approximating the transformations $\{j_1^n, j_2^n, \ldots, j_L^n, j_b^n\}_{n=1}^N$ and inferring the viewpoint variables $\{v_1^n, \ldots, v_L^n\}_{n=1}^N$ for all training images. In this stage also we obtain good initial estimates for the parameters of all objects. At **Stage 2** we compute the occlusion orderings and we jointly refine all the parameters by optimizing the complete likelihood of the model where all the transformations, view variables and occlusion orderings have been "filled in" using their approximate values.

Stage 1 is the intensive part of the learning process and is divided in sub-stages. Particularly, the object parameters and their associated transformations are estimated in a greedy fashion so as to deal with one object at a time. Particularly, we first track the background in order to approximate the transformations $(j_b^1, \ldots, j_b^N)$ and then given these transformations we learn the background appearance. Then for each foreground object sequentially we track it and learn all of its different views.

Table 1. The steps of the learning algorithm

- **Stage 1**:
  1. Track the background to compute the transformations $(j_b^1, \ldots, j_b^N)$. Then learn the background parameters $(\mathbf{b}, \sigma_b^2)$.
  2. Suppress all the pixels that have been classified as part of the background in each training image, so that $\mathbf{w}_1^n$ indicates the remaining non-background pixels in the image $\mathbf{x}^n$.
  3. for $\ell = 1$ to L
     (a) Using the $\mathbf{w}_\ell^n$ vectors track the ℓth object to compute the transformations $(j_\ell^1, \ldots, j_\ell^N)$. Then learn the parameters $\{\mathbf{f}_\ell^{v_\ell}, \boldsymbol{\pi}_\ell^{v_\ell}, \sigma_{\ell,v_\ell}^2\}_{v_\ell=1}^{V_\ell}$.
     (b) If $\ell = L$ go to **Stage** 2. Otherwise, construct the vectors $\mathbf{w}_{\ell+1}^n$ from $\mathbf{w}_\ell^n$ so that all the pixels classified as part of the ℓth object in all images are additionally suppressed.
- **Stage 2**: Using the inferred values of the parameters θ from **Stage** 1, the transformations, and the view variables, compute the occlusion ordering of the foreground layers in each image. Then using these occlusion orderings refine the parameters of the objects.

The next three sections explain in detail all the steps of the learning algorithm. Particularly, section 3.1 discusses learning the background (step 1 in **Stage** 1), section 3.2 describes learning the foreground objects (steps 2 and 3 in **Stage** 1) and section 3.3 discusses computation of the occlusion ordering of the foreground objects and refinement of the parameters (**Stage** 2). A preliminary version of this algorithm was presented in [12].

3.1   Learning the Background

Assume that we have approximated the transformations $\{j_b^1, \ldots, j_b^N\}$ of the background in each frame of the video. We will discuss shortly how to obtain such approximation using tracking. Using these transformations we wish to learn the background appearance.

At this stage we consider images that contain a background and many foreground objects. However, we concentrate on learning only the background. This goal can be achieved by introducing a likelihood model for the images that only accounts for the background while the presence of the foreground objects will be explained by an outlier process. For a background pixel, the foreground objects are interposed between the camera and the background, thus perturbing the pixel value. This can be modelled with a mixture distribution as $p_b(x_i; b_i) = \alpha_b N(x_i; b_i, \sigma_b^2) + (1 - \alpha_b)U(x_i)$, where α_b is the fraction of times a background pixel is not occluded, and the robustifying component $U(x_i)$ is a uniform distribution common for all image pixels. When the background pixel is occluded it should be explained by the uniform component. Such robust models have been used for image matching tasks by a number of authors, notably Black and colleagues [2].

The background can be learned by maximizing the log likelihood $L_b = \sum_{n=1}^{N} \log p(\mathbf{x}^n | j_b^n)$ where

$$p(\mathbf{x}|j_b) = \prod_{i=1}^{P} \alpha_b N(x_i; (T_{j_b}\mathbf{b})_i, \sigma_b^2) + (1 - \alpha_b)U(x_i). \tag{6}$$

The maximization of the likelihood over $(\mathbf{b}, \sigma_b^2)$ can be achieved by using the EM algorithm to deal with the pixel outlier process. For example, the update equation of the background $\mathbf{b}$ is

$$\mathbf{b} \leftarrow \sum_{n=1}^{N} [T_{j_b^n}^T (\mathbf{r}^n(j_b^n) * \mathbf{x}^n)]./ \sum_{n=1}^{N} [T_{j_b^n}^T \mathbf{r}^n(j_b^n)], \tag{7}$$

where $\mathbf{y} * \mathbf{z}$ and $\mathbf{y}./\mathbf{z}$ denote the element-wise product and element-wise division between two vectors $\mathbf{y}$ and $\mathbf{z}$, respectively. In (7) the vector $\mathbf{r}(j_b)$ stores the value

$$r_i(j_b) = \frac{\alpha_b N(x_i; (T_{j_b}\mathbf{b})_i, \sigma_b^2)}{\alpha_b N(x_i; (T_{j_b}\mathbf{b})_i, \sigma_b^2) + (1 - \alpha_b)U(x_i)} \tag{8}$$

for each image pixel i, which is the probability that the ith image pixel is part of the background (and not some outlier due to occlusion) given j_b.

The update for the background appearance $\mathbf{b}$ is very intuitive. For each image $\mathbf{x}^n$, the pixels which are ascribed to non-occluded background (i.e. $r_i^n(j_b^n) \simeq 1$) are transformed by $T_{j_b^n}^T$, which reverses the effect of the transformation by mapping the image $\mathbf{x}^n$ into the larger and stabilized background image $\mathbf{b}$ so that $\mathbf{x}^n$ is located within $\mathbf{b}$ in the position specified by j_b^n. Thus, the non-occluded pixels found in each training image are located properly into the big panorama image and averaged to produce $\mathbf{b}$.

Tracking the Background. We now discuss how we can quickly approximate the transformations $\{j_b^1, \ldots, j_b^N\}$ using tracking. To introduce the idea of our tracking algorithm assume that we know the appearance of the background $\mathbf{b}$ as well as the transformation j_b^1 that associates $\mathbf{b}$ with the first frame. Since motion between successive frames is expected to be relatively small we can determine the transformation j_b^2 for the second frame by searching over a small discrete set of neighbouring transformations centered at j_b^1 and inferring the most probable one (i.e. the one giving the highest likelihood given by equation (6), assuming a uniform prior). This procedure can be applied recursively to determine the sequence of transformations in the entire video.

However, the background $\mathbf{b}$ is not known in advance, but we can still apply roughly the same tracking algorithm by suitably initializing and updating the background $\mathbf{b}$ as we process the frames. More specifically, we initialize $\mathbf{b}$ so that the centered part of it will be the first frame $\mathbf{x}^1$ in the sequence. The remaining values of $\mathbf{b}$ take zero values and are considered as yet not-initialized which is indicated by a mask $\mathbf{m}$ of the same size as $\mathbf{b}$ that takes the value 1 for initialized pixels and 0 otherwise. The transformation of the first frame j_b^1 is the identity, which means that the first frame is untransformed. The transformation of the second frame and in general any frame $n+1$, $n \geq 1$, is determined by evaluating the posterior probability

$$R(j_b) \propto \exp\left\{ \frac{\sum_{i=1}^{P}(T_{j_b}\mathbf{m}^n)_i \log p_b(x_i^{n+1};(T_{j_b}\mathbf{b}^n)_i)}{\sum_{i=1}^{P}(T_{j_b}\mathbf{m}^n)_i} \right\}, \tag{9}$$

over the set of possible j_b values around the neighbourhood of j_b^n. The approximate transformation j_b^{n+1} for the frame is chosen to be $j_b^{n+1} = j_b^*$, where j_b^* maximizes the above posterior probability. Note that (9) is similar to the likelihood (6), with the only difference being that pixels of the background that are not initialized yet are removed from consideration and the score is normalized (by $\sum_{i=1}^{P}(T_{j_b}\mathbf{m}^n)_i$) so that the number of not-yet-initialized pixels (which can vary with j_b) does not affect the total score. Once we know j_b^{n+1}, we use all the frames up to the frame $\mathbf{x}^{n+1}$ (i.e. $\{\mathbf{x}^1,\ldots,\mathbf{x}^{n+1}\}$) to update $\mathbf{b}$ according to equation (7) where the vectors $\mathbf{r}^t(j_b^t)$ with $t = 1,\ldots,n+1$ have been have been updated according to equation (8) for the old value $\mathbf{b}^n$ of the background. The mask $\mathbf{m}$ is also updated so that it always indicates the pixels of $\mathbf{b}$ that are explored so far.

The effect of these updates is that as we process the frames the background model $\mathbf{b}$ is adjusted so that any occluding foreground object is blurred out, revealing the background behind. Having tracked the background, we can then learn its full structure as described earlier in this section.

3.2   Learning the Foreground Objects

Imagine that the background $\mathbf{b}$ and its most probable transformations in all training images have been approximated. What we wish to do next is to learn the foreground objects. We are going to learn the foreground objects one at each time. Particularly, we assume again that we have approximated the transformations $\{j_\ell^1,\ldots,j_\ell^N\}$ of the ℓth foreground object in all frames. This approximation can be obtained quickly using a tracking algorithm (see later in this section), that is repeatedly applied to the video sequence and each time outputs the transformations associated with a different object.

Learning of the ℓth foreground object will be based on a likelihood model for the images that only accounts for that foreground object and the background, while the presence of the other foreground objects is explained by an outlier process. Particularly, the other foreground objects can occlude both the ℓth foreground object and the background. Thus, we robustify the foreground and background pixel densities so that the Gaussians in equation (2) are replaced by $p_f(x_i; f_i) = \alpha_f N(x_i; f_i, \sigma_f^2) + (1 - \alpha_f)U(x_i)$ and $p_b(x_i; b_i) = \alpha_b N(x_i; b_i, \sigma_b^2) + (1 - \alpha_b)U(x_i)$ respectively, where $U(x_i)$ is an uniform distribution in the range of all possible pixel values and α_f and α_b express prior probabilities that a foreground (resp. background) pixel is not occluded. Any time a foreground or background pixel is occluded this can be explained by the uniform component $U(x_i)$.

Based on this robustification, we can learn the parameters associated with all different aspects of the object by maximizing the log likelihood

$$L_\ell = \sum_{n=1}^{N} \log \sum_{v_\ell=1}^{V_\ell} P_{v_\ell} \prod_{i=1}^{P} \left\{ (T_{j_\ell^n} \boldsymbol{\pi}_\ell^{v_\ell})_i p_f(x_i^n; (T_{j_\ell^n} \mathbf{f}_\ell^{v_\ell})_i) + (1 - T_{j_\ell^n} \boldsymbol{\pi}_\ell^{v_\ell})_i p_b(x_i^n; (T_{j_b^n} \mathbf{b})_i) \right\},$$

$$(10)$$

where $p_f(x_i^n; (T_{j_\ell^n} \mathbf{f}_\ell^{v_\ell})_i)$ and $p_b(x_i^n; (T_{j_b^n} \mathbf{b})_i)$ have been robustified as explained above. This maximization is carried out by EM where in the E-step the quantities, $Q^n(v_\ell)$, $\mathbf{r}^n(j_\ell)$ and $\mathbf{s}^n(j_\ell)$ are computed as follows. $Q^n(v_\ell)$ denotes the probability $p(v_\ell | x^n, j_b^n, j_\ell^n)$ and is obtained by

$$Q^n(v_\ell) = \frac{P_{v_\ell} p(\mathbf{x}^n | j_b^n, j_\ell^n, v_\ell)}{\sum_{v_\ell=1}^{V_\ell} P_{v_\ell} p(\mathbf{x}^n | j_b^n, j_\ell^n, v_\ell)}, \qquad (11)$$

while the vectors $\bar{\mathbf{s}}^n(j_\ell)$ and $\mathbf{r}_i^n(j_1^n)$ store the values

$$\bar{s}_i^n(v_\ell) = \frac{(T_{j_\ell^n} \boldsymbol{\pi}_\ell^{v_\ell})_i p_{f_\ell}(x_i^n; (T_{j_\ell^n} \mathbf{f}_\ell^{v_\ell})_i)}{(T_{j_\ell^n} \boldsymbol{\pi}_\ell^{v_\ell})_i p_{f_\ell}(x_i^n; (T_{j_\ell^n} \mathbf{f}_\ell^{v_\ell})_i) + (1 - T_{j_\ell^n} \boldsymbol{\pi}_\ell^{v_\ell})_i p_b(x_i^n; (T_{j_b^n} \mathbf{b})_i)}, \qquad (12)$$

and

$$r_i^n(v_\ell) = \frac{\alpha_f N(x_i^n; (T_{j_1^n} \mathbf{f}_\ell^{v_\ell})_i, \sigma_1^2)}{\alpha_f N(x_i^n; (T_{j_1^n} \mathbf{f}_\ell^{v_\ell})_i, \sigma_1^2) + (1 - \alpha_f) U(x_i^n)}, \qquad (13)$$

for each image pixel i. In the M-step we update the parameters $\{\mathbf{f}_\ell^{v_\ell}, \boldsymbol{\pi}_\ell^{v_\ell}, \sigma_{\ell,v_\ell}^2\}_{v_\ell=1}^{V_\ell}$. For example the updates of $\boldsymbol{\pi}_\ell^{v_\ell}$ and $\mathbf{f}_\ell^{v_\ell}$ are

$$\boldsymbol{\pi}_\ell^{v_\ell} \leftarrow \sum_{n=1}^{N} Q^n(v_\ell) T_{j_\ell^n}^T [\bar{\mathbf{s}}^n(v_\ell)]. / \sum_{n=1}^{N} Q^n(v_\ell) [T_{j_\ell^n}^T \mathbf{1}], \qquad (14)$$

$$\mathbf{f}_\ell^{v_\ell} \leftarrow \sum_{n=1}^{N} Q^n(v_\ell) T_{j_\ell^n}^T [\bar{\mathbf{s}}^n(v_\ell) * \mathbf{r}^n(v_\ell) * \mathbf{x}^n]. / \sum_{n=1}^{N} Q^n(v_\ell) T_{j_\ell^n}^T [\bar{\mathbf{s}}^n(v_\ell) * \mathbf{r}^n(v_\ell)]. \quad (15)$$

The above updates are very intuitive. Consider, for example, the appearance $\mathbf{f}_\ell^{v_\ell}$. For pixels which are ascribed to the ℓth foreground and are not occluded (i.e. $(\mathbf{s}^n(v_\ell) * \mathbf{r}^n(v_\ell))_i \simeq 1$), the values in $\mathbf{x}^n$ are transformed by $T_{j_\ell^n}^T$ which reverses the effect of the transformation. This allows the foreground pixels found in each training image to be mapped in a stabilized frame and then be averaged (weighted by the viewpoint posterior probabilities $Q^n(v_\ell)$) to produce $\mathbf{f}_\ell^{v_\ell}$.

Tracking the Foreground Objects. The appearance of each foreground object can vary significantly through the video due to large pose changes. Thus, our algorithm should be able to cope with such variation. Below we describe a tracking algorithm that each time matches a mask π_ℓ and appearance $\mathbf{f}_\ell$ to the current frame. Large viewpoint variation is handled by on-line updating π_ℓ and $\mathbf{f}_\ell$ so that each time they will fit the shape and appearance of the object in the current frame.

We first discuss how to track the first foreground object, so we assume that $\ell = 1$. The pixels which are explained by the background in each image $\mathbf{x}^n$ are flagged by the background responsibilities $\mathbf{r}^n(j_b^n)$ computed according to equation (8). Clearly, the mask $\bar{\mathbf{r}}^n(j_b^n) = 1 - \mathbf{r}^n(j_b^n)$ roughly indicates all the pixels of frame $\mathbf{x}^n$ that belong to the foreground objects. By focusing only on these pixels, we wish to start tracking one of the foreground objects through the entire video sequence and ignore for the moment the rest foreground objects.

Our algorithm tracks the first object by matching to the current frame and then updating in an on-line fashion a mask π_1 and appearance $\mathbf{f}_1$ of that object. The mask and the appearance are initialized so that $\pi_1^1 = 0.5 * \bar{\mathbf{r}}^1(j_b^1)$ and $\mathbf{f}_1^1 = \mathbf{x}^1$, where 0.5 denotes the vector with 0.5 values[1]. Due to this initialization we know that the first frame is untransformed, i.e. j_1^1 is the identity transformation. To determine the transformation of the second frame and in general the transformation j_1^{n+1}, with $n \geq 1$, of the frame $\mathbf{x}^{n+1}$ we evaluate the posterior probability

$$R(j_1) \propto \exp\left\{ \sum_{i=1}^{P} (\mathbf{w}_1^{n+1})_i \log\Big((T_{j_1}\pi_1^n)_i \times \right.$$
$$\left. p_f(x_i^{n+1}; (T_{j_1}\mathbf{f}_1^n)_i) + (1 - T_{j_1}\pi_1^n)_i(1 - \alpha_b)U(x_i^{n+1}) \Big) \right\}, \quad (16)$$

where $p_f(x_i^{n+1}; (T_{j_1^{n+1}}\mathbf{f}_1^n)_i)$ is robustified as explained earlier, j_1 takes values around the neighbourhood of j_1^n and $\mathbf{w}_1^{n+1} = \bar{\mathbf{r}}^{n+1}(j_b^{n+1})$. $R(j_1)$ measures the goodness of the match at those pixels of frame $\mathbf{x}^{n+1}$ which are not explained by the background. Note that as the objects will, in general, be of different sizes, the probability $R(j_1)$ over the transformation variable will have greater mass on transformations relating to the largest object. The transformation j_1^{n+1} is set to be equal to j_1^*, where j_1^* maximizes the above posterior probability. Once we determine j_1^{n+1} we update both the mask π_1 and appearance $\mathbf{f}_1$. The mask is updated according to

$$\pi_1^{n+1} = \left(\beta\pi_1^n + T_{j_1^{n+1}}^T[\bar{\mathbf{s}}^{n+1}] \right) ./ \left(\beta + T_{j_1^{n+1}}^T[\mathbf{1}] \right), \quad (17)$$

where β is a positive number. The vector $\bar{\mathbf{s}}^{n+1}$ expresses a soft segmentation of the object in the frame $\mathbf{x}^{n+1}$ and is computed similarly to equation (12). The update (17) defines the new mask as a weighted average of the stabilized segmentation in the current frame (i.e. $T_{j_1^{n+1}}^T[\bar{\mathbf{s}}^{n+1}(j_1^{n+1})]$) and the current value of the mask. β determines the relative weight between these two terms. In all

---

[1] The value of 0.5 is chosen to express our uncertainty about whether these pixels will ultimately be in the foreground mask or not.

our experiments we have set $\beta = 0.5$. Similarly, the update for the foreground appearance $\mathbf{f}_1$ is given by

$$\mathbf{f}_1^{n+1} = \left(\beta \mathbf{f}_1^n + T_{j_1^{n+1}}^T [\bar{\mathbf{s}}^{n+1} * \mathbf{r}^{n+1} * \mathbf{x}^{n+1}] \right) ./ \left(\beta + T_{j_1^{n+1}}^T [\bar{\mathbf{s}}^{n+1} * \mathbf{r}^{n+1}] \right). \quad (18)$$

The vector $\mathbf{r}^{n+1}$ is defined similarly to equation (13). Again the above update is very intuitive. For pixels which are ascribed to the foreground (i.e. $\bar{\mathbf{s}}^{n+1} * \mathbf{r}^{n+1} \simeq 1$), the values in $\mathbf{x}^{n+1}$ are transformed by $T_{j_1^{n+1}}^T$ into the stabilized frame which allows the foreground pixels found in the current frame to be averaged with the old value $\mathbf{f}^n$ in order to produce $\mathbf{f}^{n+1}$. Note that the updates given by (17) and (18) are on-line versions of the respective batch updates of the EM algorithm for maximizing the log likelihood (6) assuming that $V_1 = 1$.

The above tracking algorithm is a modification of the method presented in [12] with the difference that the batch updates of $(\mathbf{f}_1, \boldsymbol{\pi}_1)$ used there have been replaced by on-line counterparts that allow tracking the object when the appearance can significantly change from frame to frame.

Once the first object has been tracked we learn the different viewpoint models for that object by maximizing (10). When these models has been learned we can go through the images to find which pixels are explained by this object. Then we can remove these pixels from consideration by properly updating each $\mathbf{w}^n$ vector which allows tracking a different object on the next stage. Particularly, we compute the vector $\boldsymbol{\rho}_1^n = \sum_{v_1=1}^{V_1} Q^n(v_1)(T_{j_1^n}\boldsymbol{\pi}_1^{v_1}) * \mathbf{r}^n(v_1^n)$. $\boldsymbol{\rho}_1^n$ will give values close to 1 only for the non-occluded object pixels of image $\mathbf{x}^n$, and these are the pixels that we wish to remove from consideration. We can now run the same tracking algorithm again by updating $\mathbf{w}_{\ell+1}^n$ ($\ell \geq 1$) as by $\mathbf{w}_{\ell+1}^n = (1 - \boldsymbol{\rho}_\ell^n) * \mathbf{w}_\ell^n$ which allows tracking a different object on the $\ell+1$th iteration. Note also that the new mask $\boldsymbol{\pi}_{\ell+1}$ is initialized to $0.5 * \mathbf{w}_{\ell+1}^n$ while the appearance $\mathbf{f}_{\ell+1}$ is always initialized to the first frame $\mathbf{x}^1$.

3.3 Specification of the Occlusion Ordering and Refinement of the Object Models

Once we run the greedy algorithm (Stage 1 in Table 1), we obtain an estimate of all model parameters, an approximation of the object transformation in each training image as well as the probabilities $Q^n(v_\ell)$ which express our posterior belief that image $\mathbf{x}^n$ was generated by the view v_ℓ of model ℓ. Using now these quantities we wish to compute the occlusion ordering of the foreground objects in each training image. This is necessary since even when the occlusion ordering remains fixed across all video frames, the algorithm might not extract the objects in accordance with this ordering, i.e. discovering first the nearest object to the camera, then the second nearest object etc. The order the objects are found is determined by the tracking algorithm and typically the largest objects that occupy more pixels than others are more likely to be tracked first.

A way to infer the occlusion ordering of the foreground objects or layers in an image $\mathbf{x}^n$ is to consider all possible permutations of these layers and choose the permutation that gives the maximum likelihood. The simplest case is to have two foreground objects with parameters $\{\boldsymbol{\pi}_1^{v_1}, \mathbf{f}_1^{v_1}, \sigma_{1,v_1}^2\}_{v_1=1}^{V_1}$ and $\{\boldsymbol{\pi}_2^{v_2}, \mathbf{f}_2^{v_2}, \sigma_{2,v_2}^2\}_{v_2=1}^{V_2}$, respectively. From the posterior probabilities $Q^n(v_1)$ and $Q^n(v_2)$ corresponding to image $\mathbf{x}^n$ we choose the most probable views v_1^n and v_2^n. Conditioned on these estimated views as well as the transformations, the log likelihood values of the two possible orderings are

$$
L_{kl}^n = \sum_{i=1}^P \log\Big\{ (T_{j_k^n} \boldsymbol{\pi}_k^{v_k^n})_i p_{f_k}(x_i^n; (T_{j_k^n} \mathbf{f}_k^{v_k^n})_i) + (1 - T_{j_k^n} \boldsymbol{\pi}_k^{v_k^n})_i \times
$$
$$
[(T_{j_l^n} \boldsymbol{\pi}_l^{v_l^n})_i p_{f_l}(x_i^n; (T_{j_l^n} \mathbf{f}_l^{v_l^n})_i) + (1 - T_{j_l^n} \boldsymbol{\pi}_l^{v_l^n})_i p_b(x_i^n; (T_{j_b^n} \mathbf{b})_i)] \Big\}, \quad (19)
$$

where $k = 1$, $l = 2$ or $k = 2$, $l = 1$. The selected occlusion ordering for the image $\mathbf{x}^n$ is the one with the largest log likelihood. When we have L foreground objects we work exactly analogously as above by expressing all $L!$ permutations of the foreground layers and selecting the one with the largest likelihood.

The above computation of the occlusion ordering takes $L!$ time and it can be used only when we have few foreground objects. However, in most of the cases we can further speed up this computation and estimate the occlusion ordering for large number of objects. The idea is that an object ℓ usually does not overlap (either occludes or is occluded) with all the other $L - 1$ objects, but only with some of them. Thus, if for each object we identify the overlapping objects, the complexity in the worse case will be $O(G!)$ where G is the largest number of objects that simultaneously overlap with each other. Details of this algorithm together with illustrative examples are given in section B.3 in [13].

Once the occlusion ordering has been specified for each training image, we can maximize the complete log likelihood for the model described in section 2 (using the approximated transformations, viewpoints and the occlusion orderings) and refine the appearances and masks of the objects. Note that for this maximization we need the EM algorithm in order to deal with the fact that each pixel follows a $L + 1$-component mixture distribution (for $L = 2$ see equation (4)). However, this EM runs quickly since all the transformations, viewpoints and occlusion orderings have been "filled in" with the approximated values provided at previous stages of the learning process.

4   Related Work

There is a huge literature on motion analysis and tracking in computer vision, and there is indeed much relevant prior work. Particularly, Wang and Adelson [15] estimate object motions in successive frames and track them through the sequence by computing optical flow vectors, fit affine motion models to these vectors, and then cluster the motion parameters into a number of objects using k-means. Darrell and Pentland [3], and Sawhney and Ayer [10] used similar approaches based on optical flow estimation between successive frames and apply the MDL principle for selecting the number of objects. Note that a major limitation of optical-flow based methods concerns regions of low texture where flow information can be sparse, and when there is large inter-frame motion. The method of Irani et al. [6] is much more relevant to ours. They do motion estimation using optical flow by matching the current frame against an accumulative appearance image of the tracked object. The appearance of a tracked object develops though time, although they do not take into account issues of occlusion, so that if a tracked object becomes occluded for some frames, it may be lost.

The work of Tao et al. [11] is also relevant in that it deals with a background model and object models defined in terms of masks and appearances. However, note that in their work the mask is assumed to be of elliptical shape (parameterised as a Gaussian) rather than a general mask. The mask and appearance models are dynamically updated. However, the initialization of each model is handled by a "separate module", and is not obtained automatically. For the aerial surveillance example given in the paper initialization of the objects can be obtained by simple background subtraction, but that is not sufficient for the examples we consider. Later work by Jepson et al. [7] uses a *polybone* model for the mask instead of the Gaussian, but this still has limited representational capacity in comparison to our general mask. Jepson et al. also use more complex tracking methods which include the birth and death of polybones in time, as well as temporal tracking proposals.

The idea of focusing search when carrying our transformation-invariant clustering has also been used before, e.g. by Fitzgibbon and Zisserman [4] in their work on automatic cast listing of movies. However, in that case prior knowledge that faces were being searched for meant that a face detector could be run on the images to produce candidate locations, while this is not possible in our case as we do not know what objects we are looking for apriori.

As well as methods based on masks and appearances, there are also feature-based methods for tracking objects in image sequences, see e.g. [14], [17]. These attempt to track features through a sequence and cluster these tracks using different motion models. Allan et al. [1] describe a feature-based algorithm for computing the transformations of multiple objects in a video by simultaneously clustering features of all frames into objects. The obtained transformations are then used to learn a layered generative model for the video.

Currently in our method we ignore the spatial continuity in the segmentation labels of the pixels. This might result in noisy segmentations at some cases. A method for learning layers that incorporates spatial continuity has been recently considered by [17] and [9]. They use a layered model with a MRF prior for the pixel labels and make use of the graph cuts algorithm for efficient updating of the masks. Note that within our framework we could also incorporate a MRF for the pixel labels at the cost of increased computation.

Finally, the mechanism for dealing with multiple viewpoints using mixture models has been considered before in [5]. However, in this work they consider one object present in the images against a cluttered background, and only the appearance images of different poses of the object are learned (not masks). Also they do not apply tracking and they consider a global search over transformations. In contrast, our method can be applied to images with multiple objects and learns the background as well as different poses for the foreground objects. An important aspect of our method is the use of tracking (applied prior to learning) which stabilizes an object and then efficiently learns its views.

5 Experiments

We consider four video sequences: the Frey-Jojic (FJ) sequence (Figure 1) available from http://www.psi.toronto.edu/layers.html, the arms-torso video sequence showing a moving human upper body (Figure 2), the man-walking sequence (Figure 3) and the Groundhog day van sequence[2] (Figure 4). We will also assume that the number of different views that we wish to learn for each foreground object is known.

The FJ sequence consists of 44 118×248 images (excluding the black border). This sequence can be well modelled by assuming a single view for each of the foreground objects, thus we set $V = 1$ for both objects. During tracking we used a 15×15 window of translations in units of one pixel during the tracking stage. The learning stage requires EM which converged in about 30 iterations. Figure 1a shows the evolution of the initial mask and appearance ($t = 1$) through frames 10 and 20 as we track the first object (Frey). Notice that as we process the frames the mask focuses on only one of the two objects and the appearance remains sharp only for this object. The real running time of our MATLAB implementation for processing the whole sequence was 3 minutes. The computer used for all the experiments reported here was a 3GHz Pentium. Figure 1b shows the results after **Stage 1** of the algorithm is completed. Figure 1c shows the final appearances of the foreground objects after the computation of the occlusion ordering and the joint refinement of all the parameters. Comparing Figure 1b with Figure 1c, we can visually inspect the improvement over the appearances of the objects, e.g. the ghosts in the masks of Figure 1b have disappeared in Figure 1c.

When we carry out the refinement step, we always initialize the background and the foreground appearances and masks using the values provided by the greedy algorithm. The variances are reinitialized to a large value to help escape from local maxima. Note also that for this maximization we maintain the robustification of the background and foreground pixel densities (α_b and α_f are set to 0.9) in order to deal with possible variability of the objects, e.g. local clothing deformation, or changes of the lighting conditions. The EM algorithm used for the above maximization converges in few iterations (e.g. less than 20). This is because the objects' appearances obtained from the greedy algorithm are already close to their final values, and all the transformations of the objects have been "filled in" with the approximated values provided by the greedy algorithm.

We demonstrate our method for learning parts of human body using the arms-torso sequence that consists of 79 76×151 images. Three frames of this

---

[2] We thank the Visual Geometry Group at Oxford for providing the Groundhog day van data.

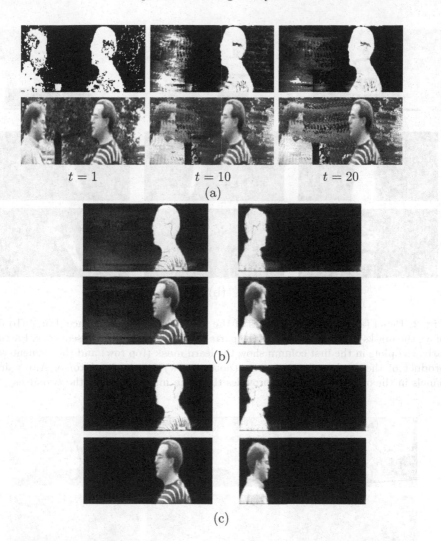

$t = 1$ $t = 10$ $t = 20$

(a)

(b)

(c)

Fig. 1. Panel (a) shows the evolution of the mask π_1 (top row) and the appearance f_1 (bottom row) at times 1, 10 and 20 as we track the first object (Frey). Again notice how the mask becomes focused on one of the objects (Frey) and how the appearance remains clear and sharp only for Frey. Panel (b) shows the mask and the element-wise product of the mask and appearance model ($\pi * f$) learned for Frey (first column from the left) and Jojic (second column) using the greedy algorithm (after **Stage 1**; see Table 1). Panel (c) displays the corresponding masks and appearances of the objects after the refinement step.

sequence are shown in Figure 2a. To learn the articulated parts we use translations and rotations so that the transformation matrix T_{j_ℓ} that applies to π_ℓ and f_ℓ implements an combination of translation and rotation. We implemented this using the MATLAB function *tformarray.m* and nearest neighbour interpolation. Note that we set the number of views $V_\ell = 1$ for all foreground objects. The

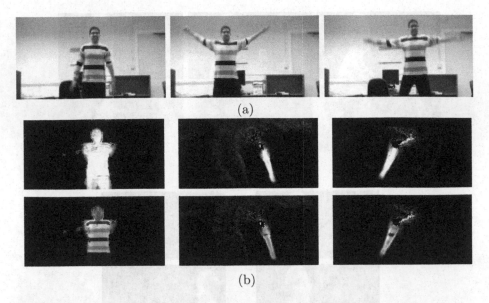

Fig. 2. Panel (a) shows three frames of the arms-torso video sequence. Panel (b) displays the masks and appearances of the parts of the arms-torso video sequence. Particularly, the plots in the first column show the learn mask (top row) and the element-wise product of the mask and appearance (bottom row) for the head/torso. Any pair of panels in the other two columns provides the same information for the two arms.

Fig. 3. The panels in the first row show three frames of the man-walking sequence. The panels in the last two rows show the element-wise product of the mask (thresholded to 0.5) and appearance (showing against a grey background) for all six viewpoint models.

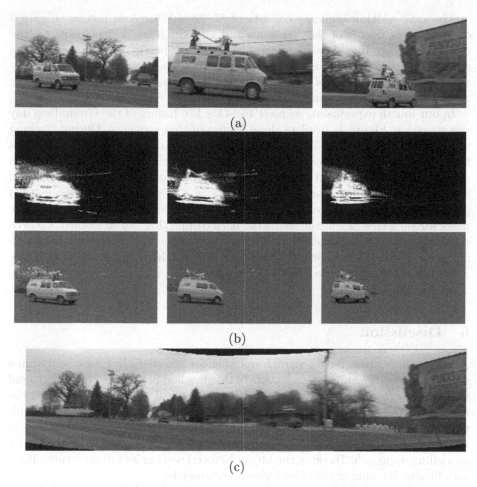

Fig. 4. Panel (a) shows three frames of the van sequence. Panel (b) shows the pairs of mask and the element-wise product of the mask and appearance (showing against a grey background) for all different viewpoints. Note that the element-wise products are produced by making the masks binary (thresholded to 0.5). Panel (c) displays the background.

tracking method searches over a window of 10×10 translations and 15 rotations (at 2° spacing) so that it searches over 1500 transformations in total. Figures 2b shows the three parts discovered by the algorithm i.e. the head/torso and the two arms. Note that the ambiguity of the masks and appearances around the joints of the two arms with the torso which is due to the deformability of the clothing in these areas. The total real running time for learning this sequence was roughly one hour. Note that when we learn object parts we should also learn a joint distribution over the parts; a method for computing such a distribution is described in [13].

The man-walking sequence consists of 85 72×176 colour images. Figure 3 displays three frames of that sequence and also the learned visual aspects (the element-wise product of each appearance and mask pair). We assumed that the number of different views is six, i.e. $V_1 = 6$. When we applied the tracking algorithm we used a window of 15×15 translations in units of one pixel. Processing the whole video took 5 minutes.

In our fourth experiment, we used 46 144×176 frames of the Groundhog day van sequence. Figure 4a displays three frames of that sequence. During tracking we assumed a window of 15×15 translations in units of one pixel, plus 5 scalings for each of the two axes spaced at a 1% change in the image size, and 5 rotations at 2° spacing. We assumed that the number of different views of the foreground object that we wish to learn is three, i.e. $V_1 = 3$. Figure 4b shows the learned prior mask ($\pi_1^{v_1}$) and the element-wise product of the appearance ($\mathbf{f}_1^{v_1}$) and the mask for each view. Figure 4c shows the background that is also learned. Clearly, each appearance has modelled a different view of the van. However, the masks are a bit noisy; we believe this could be improved by using spatial continuity constraints. Processing the whole video took 6 hours, where the most of the time was spent during tracking.

6   Discussion

Above we have presented a general framework for learning a layered model from a video sequence. The important feature of this method is tracking the background and the foreground objects sequentially so as to deal with one object and the associated transformations at each time. Additionally, we have combined this tracking method with allowing multiple views for each foreground object so as to deal with large viewpoint variation. These models are learned using a mixture modelling approach. Tracking the object before knowing its full structure allows for efficient learning of the object viewpoint models.

Some issues for the future are to automatically identify how many views are needed to efficiently model the appearance of each object, to determine the number of objects, and to deal with objects/parts that have internal variability. Another issue is to automatically identify when a detected model is a part or an independent object. This might be achieved by using a mutual information measure, since we expect parts of the same object to have significant statistical dependence.

Acknowledgements

This work was supported in part by the IST Programme of the European Community, under the PASCAL Network of Excellence, IST-2002-506778. This publication only reflects the authors' views.

References

1. M. Allan, M. K. Titsias, and C. K. I. Williams. Fast Learning of Sprites using Invariant Features. In *Proceedings of the British Machine Vision Conference 2005*, pages 40–49. 2005.
2. M.J. Black and A.D. Jepson. EigenTracking: Robust Matching and Tracking of Articulated Objects Using a View-Based Representation. *Proc. ECCV*, pages 329–342, 1996.
3. T. Darrell and A. P. Pentland. Cooperative Robust Estimation Using Layers of Support. *IEEE Transactions on Pattern Analysis and Machine Intelligence*, 17(5):474–487, 1995.
4. A. Fitzgibbon and A. Zisserman. On Affine Invariant Clustering and Automatic Cast Listing in Movies. In *Proceedings of the Seventh European Conference on Computer Vision, ECCV 2002*, pages III 304–320. Springer, 2002. LNCS2353.
5. B. J. Frey and N. Jojic. Transformation Invariant Clustering Using the EM Algorithm. *IEEE Trans Pattern Analysis and Machine Intelligence*, 25(1):1–17, 2003.
6. M. Irani, B. Rousso, and S. Peleg. Computing Occluding and Transparent Motions. *International Journal of Computer Vision*, 12(1):5–16, 1994.
7. A. D. Jepson, D. J. Fleet, and M. J. Black. A Layered Motion Representation with Occlusion and Compact Spatial Support. In *Proceedings of the Seventh European Conference on Computer Vision, ECCV 2002*, pages I 692–706. Springer, 2002. LNCS 2353.
8. N. Jojic and B. J. Frey. Learning Flexible Sprites in Video Layers. In *Proceedings of the IEEE Conference on Computer Vision and Pattern Recognition 2001*. IEEE Computer Society Press, 2001. Kauai, Hawaii.
9. M. P. Kumar, P. H. S. Torr, and A. Zisserman. Learning layered pictorial structures from video. In *Proceedings of the Indian Conference on Computer Vision, Graphics and Image Processing*, pages 158–163, 2004.
10. H. S. Sawhney and S Ayer. Compact Representations of Videos Through Dominant and Multiple Motion Estimation. *IEEE Transactions on Pattern Analysis and Machine Intelligence*, 18(8):814–830, 1996.
11. H. Tao, H. S. Sawhney, and R. Kumar. Dynamic Layer Representation with Applications to Tracking. In *Proceedings of the IEEE Conference on Computer Vision and Pattern Recognition*, pages II:134–141, 2000.
12. M. K. Titsias and C. K. I. Williams. Fast unsupervised greedy learning of multiple objects and parts from video. In *Proc. Generative-Model Based Vision Workshop*, 2004.
13. M. K. Titsias. Unsupervised Learning of Multiple Objects in Images. PhD thesis, School of Informatics, University of Edinburgh, 2005.
14. P. H. S. Torr. Geometric motion segmentation and model selection. *Phil. Trans. Roy. Soc. Lond. A*, 356:1321–1340, 1998.
15. J. Y. A. Wang and E. H. Adelson. Representing Moving Images with Layers. *IEEE Transactions on Image Processing*, 3(5):625–638, 1994.
16. C. K. I. Williams and M. K. Titsias. Greedy Learning of Multiple Objects in Images using Robust Statistics and Factorial Learning. *Neural Computation*, 16(5):1039–1062, 2004.
17. J. Wills, S. Agarwal, and S. Belongie. What Went Where. In *Proceedings of the IEEE Conference on Computer Vision and Pattern Recognition, CVPR 2003*, pages I:37–44, 2003.

An Object Category Specific MRF for Segmentation

M. Pawan Kumar[1], Philip H.S. Torr[1], and Andrew Zisserman[2]

[1] Department of Computing,
Oxford Brookes University,
Oxford, OX33 1HX
{pkmudigonda,philiptorr}@brookes.ac.uk
http://cms.brookes.ac.uk/computervision
[2] Department of Engineering Science,
University of Oxford,
Oxford, OX1 3PJ
az@robots.ox.ac.uk
http://www.robots.ox.ac.uk/~vgg

Abstract. In this chapter we present a principled Bayesian method for detecting and segmenting instances of a particular object category within an image, providing a coherent methodology for combining top down and bottom up cues. The work draws together two powerful formulations: pictorial structures (PS) and Markov random fields (MRFs) both of which have efficient algorithms for their solution. The resulting combination, which we call the object category specific MRF, suggests a solution to the problem that has long dogged MRFs namely that they provide a poor prior for specific shapes. In contrast, our model provides a prior that is global across the image plane using the PS. We develop an efficient method, OBJCUT, to obtain segmentations using this model. Novel aspects of this method include an efficient algorithm for sampling the PS model, and the observation that the expected log likelihood of the model can be increased by a single graph cut. Results are presented on two object categories, cows and horses. We compare our methods to the state of the art in object category specific image segmentation and demonstrate significant improvements.

1 Introduction

Image segmentation has seen renewed interest in the field of computer vision, in part due the arrival of new efficient algorithms to perform the segmentation [5], and in part due to the resurgence of interest in object category recognition [2,8,17]. Segmentation fell from favour partly due to an excess of papers attempting to solve ill posed problems with no means of judging the result. Interleaved object recognition and segmentation [4,17] is both well posed and of practical use. Well posed in that the result of the segmentation can be quantitatively judged e.g. how many pixels have been correctly and incorrectly assigned to the object. Of practical use because (a) the more accurately the image can be

J. Ponce et al. (Eds.): Toward Category-Level Object Recognition, LNCS 4170, pp. 596–616, 2006.

segmented the more certain the recognition results will be, and (b) image editing tools can be designed that provide a "power assist" to cut out applications like 'Magic Wand', e.g. "I know this is a horse, please segment it for me, without the pain of having to manually delineate the boundary."

Markov Random Fields (MRFs) provide a useful model of images for segmentation and their prominence has been increased by the availability of efficient publically available code for their solution. Boykov and Jolly [5], and more recently Rother et al. [21], strikingly demonstrate that with a minimum of user assistance objects can be rapidly segmented. However samples from the Gibbs distribution defined by the MRF very rarely give rise to realistic shapes and on their own MRFs are ill suited to segmenting objects. What is required is a way to inject prior knowledge of object shape into the MRF. Within this chapter we derive a Bayesian way of doing this in which the prior knowledge is provided by a Pictorial Structure (PS). Pictorial Structures [6] and the related Constellation of Parts model [8] have proven to be very successful for the task of object recognition. In addition, PS have been highly effective in localizing object parts, e.g. human limbs. We cast the problem of object category specific segmentation as that of estimating an MRF (representing bottom up information) which is influenced by a set of latent variables, the PS (representing top down information), encouraging the MRF to resemble the object. Unlike MRFs, which model the prior using pairwise potentials, the PS model provides a prior over the shape of the segmentation that is global across the image plane.

Many different approaches for segmentation using a global shape prior have been reported in the literature. Huang et al. [13] describe an iterative algorithm which alternates between fitting an active contour to an image and segmenting it on the basis of the shape of the active contour. However, the computational inefficiency of the algorithm restricts the application of this method. Freedman et al. [9] describe an efficient algorithm based on MINCUT which uses a shape prior for segmentation. Both these methods, however, require manual initialization.

Borenstein and Ullman [4] describe an automatic algorithm for segmenting instances of a particular object category from images using a patch-based approach. Leibe and Schiele [17] provide a probabilistic formulation for this while incorporating spatial information of the relative location of the patches. However, in order to deal with intra-class shape and appearance variation, as well as large deformations of articulated objects, these methods have to resort to the computational inefficiency of hundreds of exemplars.

In this chapter, we propose a novel probabilistic MRF model which overcomes the above problems. We develop an efficient method, OBJCUT, to obtain segmentations using this model. The basis of our method are two new theoretical/algorithmic contributions: (1) we make the (not obvious) observation that the expectation of the log likelihood of an MRF with respect to some latent variables can be efficiently optimized with respect to the labels of the MRF by a single graph cut optimization; (2) we provide a highly efficient algorithm for marginalizing or optimizing the latent variables when they are a PS following a Potts model.

The chapter is organized as follows. In Section 2 the probabilistic MRF model of the image is described in broad terms. Section 3 gives an overview of an efficient method for solving this model for figure-ground labellings. In section 4 the layered pictorial structures (LPS) model is described, which extends the PS model so that it handles partial self occlusion. The important issue of automatic initialization of the LPS is addressed in section 5. The OBJCUT algorithm is described in section 6. Results are shown for two object categories, namely cows and horses, and a comparison with other methods is given in section 7.

2   Object Category Specific MRF

In this section we describe the model that forms the basis of our work. We formally specify and build upon previous work on segmentation, providing a Bayesian graphical model for work that has previously been specified in terms of energy functions [5]. Notably there are three issues to be addressed in this section: (i) how to make the segmentation conform to object and background appearance models, (ii) how to encourage the segmentation to follow edges within the image, (iii) how to encourage the segmentation to look like an object.

Given an image $\mathbf{D}$ containing an instance of a known object category, e.g. cows, we wish to segment the image into *figure*, i.e. pixels belonging to the object, and *ground*, i.e. the background. Taking a Bayesian perspective, we define a set of binary labels, $\mathbf{m}$, one label m_x for each pixel x, that optimizes the posterior probability given by the Gibbs distribution

$$p(\mathbf{m}|\mathbf{D}) = \frac{p(\mathbf{D}|\mathbf{m})p(\mathbf{m})}{p(\mathbf{D})} = \frac{1}{Z_1} \exp(-\Psi_1(\mathbf{m})). \tag{1}$$

Here Z_1 is the normalizing constant (or partition function), i.e.

$$Z_1 = \int p(\mathbf{D}|\mathbf{m})p(\mathbf{m})d\mathbf{m}, \tag{2}$$

which ensures that the probabilities sum up to one. The energy is defined by the summation of clique potentials and has the form:

$$\Psi_1(\mathbf{m}) = \sum_x \left(\phi(\mathbf{D}|m_x) + \sum_y \psi(m_x, m_y) \right), \tag{3}$$

where y is a neighbouring pixel of x. The likelihood term $\phi(\mathbf{D}|m_x)$ is the emission model for one or more pixels and is given by

$$\phi(\mathbf{D}|m_x) = \begin{cases} -\log(p(x \in \text{figure}|\mathcal{H}_{obj})) & \text{if } m_x = 1 \\ -\log(p(x \in \text{ground}|\mathcal{H}_{bkg})) & \text{if } m_x = 0, \end{cases}$$

where $\mathcal{H}_{obj}$ and $\mathcal{H}_{bkg}$ are the RGB distributions for foreground and background respectively. The prior $\psi(m_x, m_y)$ takes the form of an Ising model:

$$\psi(m_x, m_y) = \begin{cases} P & \text{if } m_x \neq m_y, \\ 0 & \text{if } m_x = m_y. \end{cases}$$

which (equally) favours any two neighbouring pixels having the same label, thus ensuring smoothness.

In the MRFs used for image segmentation, a contrast term is used to favour pixels with similar colour having the same label [3,5], thereby pushing the boundary to lie on image edges. This is done by reducing the cost within the Ising model for two labels being different in proportion to the difference in intensities of their corresponding pixels e.g. by subtracting an energy term $\gamma(x,y) = \lambda(1 - \exp\left(\frac{-g^2(x,y)}{2\sigma^2}\right)\frac{1}{dist(x,y)})$, where $g^2(x,y)$ measures the difference in the RGB values of pixels x and y, and $dist(x,y)$ gives the spatial distance between x and y [3,5]. In our experiments, we use $P = \lambda = 0.1$ and $\sigma = 5$. Together with the prior, this makes the pairwise terms discontinuity preserving [14]. However, this has previously not been given a proper Bayesian formulation which we now address. It can not be included in the prior, for the prior term cannot include the data. Rather it leads to a pair wise linkage between neighbouring labels and their pixels as shown in the graphical model given in Figure 1. The posterior probability is now given by $p(\mathbf{m}|\mathbf{D}) = \frac{1}{Z_2}\exp(-\Psi_2(\mathbf{m}))$ where

$$\Psi_2(\mathbf{m}) = \sum_x \left(\phi(\mathbf{D}|m_x) + \sum_y (\phi(\mathbf{D}|m_x, m_y) + \psi(m_x, m_y)) \right) \qquad (4)$$

and $Z_2 = \int p(\mathbf{D}|\mathbf{m})p(\mathbf{m})d\mathbf{m}$. The contrast term of the energy function is given by:

$$\phi(\mathbf{D}|m_x, m_y) = \begin{cases} -\gamma(x,y) & \text{if } m_x \neq m_y, \\ 0 & \text{if } m_x = m_y. \end{cases}$$

MRF-based segmentation techniques which use MINCUT [14] have achieved excellent results [3,5] with manual initialization. However, due to the lack of a shape model, these methods do not work so well for automatic segmentation of instances of specific object categories. We would like to use the power of the MINCUT algorithm for interleaved object recognition and segmentation. In some sense the result of the recognition will replace the user interventions. In order to achieve this we introduce a stronger shape model to the MRF. This shape model will supply a set of latent variables, Θ, which will favour segmentations of a specific shape, as shown in the graphical model depicted in Figure 1. We call this new MRF model the object category specific MRF, which has the following energy function:

$$\Psi_3(\mathbf{m}, \Theta) = \sum_x \left(\phi(\mathbf{D}|m_x) + \phi(m_x|\Theta) + \sum_y (\phi(\mathbf{D}|m_x, m_y) + \psi(m_x, m_y)) \right) (5)$$

with posterior $p(\mathbf{m}, \Theta|\mathbf{D}) = \frac{1}{Z_3}\exp(-\Psi_3(\mathbf{m}, \Theta))$, where

$$Z_3 = \int p(\mathbf{D}|\mathbf{m}, \Theta)p(\mathbf{m}, \Theta)d\mathbf{m}d\Theta, \qquad (6)$$

is the partition function. The function $\phi(m_x|\Theta)$ is chosen so that if we were given an estimate of the location and shape of the object, then pixels falling

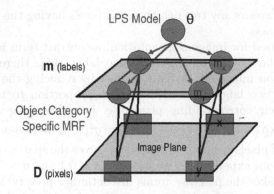

Fig. 1. Graphical model representation of the object category specific MRF. The connections introducing the contrast term are shown in blue. Note that some of these connections (going diagonally) are not shown for the sake of clarity of the image. The labels **m** lie in a plane. Together with the pixels shown below this plane, these form the contrast-dependent MRF used for segmentation. In addition to these, the object category specific MRF makes use of an underlying shape parameter in the form of an LPS model (shown lying above the plane). The LPS model guides the segmentation towards a realistic shape closely resembling the object of interest.

near to that shape would be more likely to have object label than pixels falling far from the shape. It has the form:

$$\phi(m_x|\Theta) = -\log p(m_x|\Theta). \tag{7}$$

In this work, we choose to define $p(m_x|\Theta)$ as

$$p(m_x = \text{figure}|\Theta) = \frac{1}{1 + \exp(\mu * dist(x, \Theta))} \tag{8}$$

and $p(m_x = \text{ground}|\Theta) = 1 - p(m_x = \text{figure}|\Theta)$, where $dist(x, \Theta)$ is the spatial distance of a pixel x from the shape defined by Θ (being negative if inside the shape). The parameter μ determines how much the points outside the shape are penalized compared to the points inside the shape. We use $\mu = 0.2$ in our experiments. Note energy function $\Psi_3(\mathbf{m}, \Theta)$ can still be minimized via MINCUT [14].

We combine the Contrast Dependent MRF with the layered pictorial structures (LPS) model (see section 4). However we observe that the methodology below is completely general and could be combined with any sort of latent shape model.

The optimal figure-ground labelling should be obtained by integrating out the latent variable Θ. The surprising result of this work is that this rather intractable looking integral can in fact be optimized by a simple and computationally efficient set of operations. In order to do this, we need to demonstrate two things: (i) Given an estimate of **m** we can sample efficiently for Θ. This we shall demonstrate for the case of LPS, and in §5.1 we describe a new algorithm for efficient calculation of the marginal distribution for a non regular Potts model (i.e. when the labels are not specified by an underlying grid of parameters, complementing the result of Felzenszwalb and Huttenlocher [7]). (ii) Given the distribution of Θ we can efficiently optimize $\mathbf{m}$ so as to increase the posterior. For a MRF this is not immediately obvious. However we shall demonstrate this in the next section.

3   Roadmap of the Solution

For the problem of segmentation the parameters $\mathbf{m}$ are of immediate interest and the EM framework provides a natural way to deal with the latent parameters Θ [11] by treating them as missing data. We are interested in maximizing the log posterior density of $\mathbf{m}$ is given by

$$\log p(\mathbf{m}|\mathbf{D}) = \log p(\Theta, \mathbf{m}|\mathbf{D}) - \log p(\Theta|\mathbf{m}, \mathbf{D}), \tag{9}$$

where $p(\Theta, \mathbf{m}|\mathbf{D}) = \frac{1}{Z_3} \exp(-\Psi_3(\mathbf{m}, \Theta))$. The EM framework iteratively refines the estimate of $\mathbf{m}$ by marginalizing the latent parameters Θ. Given the current guess of the labelling $\mathbf{m}'$, we treat Θ as a random variable with the distribution $p(\Theta|\mathbf{m}', \mathbf{D})$. Averaging over Θ yields

$$\log p(\mathbf{m}|\mathbf{D}) = \mathcal{E}(\log p(\Theta, \mathbf{m}|\mathbf{D})) - \mathcal{E}(\log p(\Theta|\mathbf{m}, \mathbf{D})), \tag{10}$$

where $\mathcal{E}$ is the averaging over Θ under the distribution $p(\Theta|\mathbf{m}', \mathbf{D})$.

The key result of EM is that the second term on the right side of equation (10), i.e.

$$\mathcal{E}(\log p(\Theta|\mathbf{m}, \mathbf{D})) = \int (\log p(\Theta|\mathbf{m}, \mathbf{D})) p(\Theta|\mathbf{m}', \mathbf{D}) d\Theta \tag{11}$$

is maximized when $\mathbf{m} = \mathbf{m}'$. Our goal then is to choose a labelling $\mathbf{m}''$ (different from $\mathbf{m}'$) which maximizes

$$\mathcal{E}(\log p(\Theta, \mathbf{m}|\mathbf{D})) = \int (\log p(\Theta, \mathbf{m}|\mathbf{D})) p(\Theta|\mathbf{m}', \mathbf{D}) d\Theta. \tag{12}$$

This labelling increases $\mathcal{E}(\log p(\Theta, \mathbf{m}|\mathbf{D})$ (the first term of equation (10)) and decreases $\mathcal{E}(\log p(\Theta|\mathbf{m}, \mathbf{D}))$ (the second term of equation (10) which is maximized when $\mathbf{m} = \mathbf{m}'$). Thus, it increases the posterior $p(\mathbf{m}|\mathbf{D})$. The expression in equation (12) is called $Q(\mathbf{m}|\mathbf{m}')$, the expected complete-data log-likelihood, in the EM literature.

In §5.1 it will be shown that we can efficiently sample from a PS which suggests a sampling based solution to maximizing (12). Let the set of s samples be $\Theta_1 \ldots \Theta_s$, with weights $p(\Theta_i|\mathbf{m}', \mathbf{D}) = w_i$, then the minimization corresponding to equation (12) can be written as

$$\hat{\mathbf{m}} = \arg\min_{\mathbf{m}} \sum_{i=1}^{i=s} w_i \Psi_3(\mathbf{m}, \Theta_i) - C. \tag{13}$$

Here $C = \sum_i w_i \log Z_3$ is a constant which can be ignored during minimization. This is the key equation of our approach. Section 6 describes an efficient method for minimizing the energy function (13). We observe that this energy function is a weighted linear sum of the energies $\Psi_3(\mathbf{m}, \Theta)$ which, being a linear combination, can also be optimized using MINCUT [14]. This demonstrates the interesting result that for Markov random fields, with latent variables, it is computationally feasible to optimize $Q(\mathbf{m}|\mathbf{m}')$.

The EM algorithm often converges to a local minima of the energy function and its success depends on the initial labelling $\mathbf{m}^0$ (i.e. the labelling $\mathbf{m}'$ at the first iteration). In the last section a generative graphical model for pixel by pixel segmentation was set up. However, it would be computationally extravagant to attempt to minimize this straight off. Rather an initialization stage is adopted in which we get a rough estimate of the object's posterior extracted from a set of image features $\mathbf{Z}$, defined in § 4.1. Image features (such as textons and edges) can provide high discrimination at low computational cost. We approximate the initial distribution $p_0(\Theta|\mathbf{m}, \mathbf{D})$, as $g(\Theta|\mathbf{Z})$, where $\mathbf{Z}$ are some image features chosen to localize the object in a computationally efficient manner. Thus, the weights w_i required to evaluate equation (13) on the first EM iteration are obtained by sampling from the distribution $g(\Theta|\mathbf{Z})$, defined in Section 4.

The next section describes the LPS model in detail. In the remainder of the chapter, we describe an efficient method to obtain the samples from the posterior of a PS model required for the marginalization in equation (13), and the OBJCUT algorithm which re-estimates the labelling $\mathbf{m}$ by minimizing equation (13). These methods are applicable to any articulated object category which can be modelled using an LPS. We demonstrate the results on two quadrupeds, namely cows and horses.

4   Layered Pictorial Structures

Pictorial structures (PS) are compositions of 2D patterns, termed *parts*, under a probabilistic model for their shape, appearance and the spatial layout. When calculating the likelihood of model parameters, a typical assumption under the PS model is that the parts do not (partially) occlude each other [15]. Thus, the estimated poses of similar parts of the PS model tend to overlap. For example, the two forelegs of a cow tend to be explain the same pixels in the image as this provides a high likelihood.

In the layered pictorial structures (LPS) model introduced in [16] (and in a similar model described in [1]), in addition to shape and appearance, each part p_i is also assigned a layer number l_i which determines its relative depth. Several parts can have the same layer number if they are at the same depth. A part p_i can partially or completely occlude part p_j if and only if $l_i > l_j$. The parts of an LPS are defined as rigidly moving components of the object. In the case of side views of quadrupeds, this results in 2 layers containing a total of 10 parts: head, torso and 8 half limbs (see Figure 2). The parts are obtained as described in § 4.2.

An LPS can also be viewed as an MRF with the sites of the MRF corresponding to parts. Each site takes one of n_L part labels which encode the putative poses of

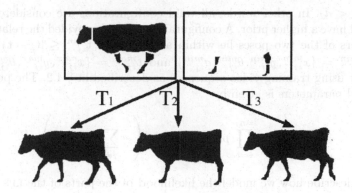

Fig. 2. Layered pictorial structure of a cow. The various parts belonging to layers 2 and 1 are shown in the top left and right image respectively. Pairwise potentials defined for every pair of parts as shown in equation (16) only allow valid configurations of a cow. Three such configurations are shown in the bottom row.

the part. The pose of the ith site is defined by $\mathbf{t}_i = (x_i, y_i, \theta_i, \sigma_i)$, where (x_i, y_i) is the location, θ_i is the orientation, σ_i is the scale.

For a given part label $\mathbf{t}_i$ and image $\mathbf{D}$, the ith part corresponds to the set of pixels $\mathbf{D}_i \subset \mathbf{D}$ which are used to calculate features $\mathbf{z}_i = (z_1, z_2)$. Let n_P be the number of parts. The shape and appearance parameters for part p_i, represented as $\mathbf{s}_i$ and $\mathbf{a}_i$, are used to compute z_1 and z_2 respectively. The feature $z_2(\mathbf{D}_i)$ is initially obtained using texture exemplars as described in § 4.1. Once an initial estimate of the model is obtained, the location of the object is used to estimate the RGB histograms for object and background as described in § 5.2 (and texture exemplars are no longer used). Assuming that $\mathbf{D}_i$ does not include pixels accounted for by p_j, $l_j > l_i$, we get

$$p(\mathbf{Z}|\Theta) = \prod_{i=1}^{i=n_P} p(\mathbf{z}_i|\mathbf{a}_i, \mathbf{s}_i), \tag{14}$$

where $\mathbf{Z} = \{\mathbf{z}_1 \ldots \mathbf{z}_{n_P}\}$ are the image features.

LPS, like PS, are characterized by pairwise only dependencies between the sites. These are modelled as a prior on the relative poses of parts:

$$p(\Theta) \propto \exp\left(-\sum_{i=1}^{i=n_P} \sum_{j=1, j\neq i}^{j=n_P} \alpha(\mathbf{t}_i, \mathbf{t}_j)\right). \tag{15}$$

Note that we use a completely connected MRF. In our approach, the pairwise potentials $\alpha(\mathbf{t}_i, \mathbf{t}_j)$ are given by a Potts model, i.e.

$$\alpha(\mathbf{t}_i, \mathbf{t}_j) = \begin{cases} d_1 & \text{if valid configuration} \\ d_2 & \text{otherwise,} \end{cases}$$

where $d_1 < d_2$. In other words, all valid configurations are considered equally likely and have a higher prior. A configuration is valid provided the relative shape parameters of the two poses lie within a box, i.e. if $\mathbf{t}_{ij}^{min} \leq |\mathbf{t}_i - \mathbf{t}_j| \leq \mathbf{t}_{ij}^{max}$, where $\mathbf{t}_{ij}^{min} = \{x_{ij}^{min}, y_{ij}^{min}, \theta_{ij}^{min}, \sigma_{ij}^{min}\}$ and $\mathbf{t}_{ij}^{max} = \{x_{ij}^{max}, y_{ij}^{max}, \theta_{ij}^{max}, \sigma_{ij}^{max}\}$ are learnt using training video sequences as described in § 4.2. The posterior of the model parameters is given by

$$g(\mathbf{\Theta}|\mathbf{Z}) \propto \prod_{i=1}^{i=n_P} p(\mathbf{z}_i|\mathbf{a}_i, \mathbf{s}_i) \exp\left(-\sum_{j \neq i} \alpha(\mathbf{t}_i, \mathbf{t}_j)\right) \qquad (16)$$

We now describe how we model the likelihood of the parts of the LPS.

4.1 Feature Likelihood for Parts

We define the features $\mathbf{Z}$ extracted from the pixels $\mathbf{D}$. As described earlier, we use two types of features $\mathbf{z}_i(\mathbf{D}_i) = (z_1(\mathbf{D}_i), z_2(\mathbf{D}_i))$ for the shape and appearance of the part respectively. Assuming independence of the two features, the likelihood based on the whole data is approximated as

$$p(\mathbf{z}_i|\mathbf{a}_i, \mathbf{s}_i) = p(z_1|\mathbf{s}_i)p(z_2|\mathbf{a}_i) \qquad (17)$$

where $p(z_1|\mathbf{s}_i) = \exp(-z_1)$ and $p(z_2|\mathbf{a}_i) = \exp(-z_2)$.

Outline $(z_1(\mathbf{D}_i))$: In order to handle the variability in shape among members of an object class (e.g. horses), it is necessary to represent the part outline by a set of exemplar curves. Chamfer distances are computed for each exemplar for each pose $\mathbf{t}_i$. The first feature $z_1(\mathbf{D}_i)$ is the minimum of the truncated chamfer distances over all the exemplars of p_i at pose $\mathbf{t}_i$. Truncated chamfer distance measures the similarity between two shapes $\mathcal{U} = (u_1, u_2, ... u_n)$ and $\mathcal{V} = (v_1, v_2, ... v_m)$. It is the mean of the distances between each point $u_i \in \mathcal{U}$ and its closest point in $\mathcal{V}$:

$$d_{cham} = \frac{1}{n} \sum_i \min\{\min_j ||u_i - v_j||, \tau_1\}, \qquad (18)$$

where τ_1 is a threshold for truncation which reduces the effect of outliers and missing edges. Edge orientation is included by computing the chamfer score only for edges with similar orientation, in order to make the distance function more robust [10]. We use 8 orientation groups for edges.

Texture $(z_2(\mathbf{D}_i))$: Similar to the outline of a part, we represent the texture of an object by a set of exemplars. We use the VZ classifier [23] which obtains a texton dictionary by clustering the vectorized raw intensities of $N \times N$ neighbourhood of each pixel in the exemplars. We use $N = 3$. The exemplars are then modelled as a histogram of pixel texton labellings [18]. The feature $z_2(\mathbf{D}_i)$ is defined as the minimum χ^2 distance of the histogram of texton labellings for $\mathbf{D}_i$ with the histogram modelling the exemplars. We now describe how the LPS parameters are learnt so as to handle intra-class variability in shape and appearance.

4.2   Learning the LPS

The various parameters of the LPS model are learnt using the method described in [16] which divides a scene in a video into rigidly moving components and provides the segmentation of each frame. We use this approach on 20 cow videos of 45 frames each[1]. Correspondence between parts learnt from two different videos is established using shape context with continuity constraints [22]. This gives us the multiple shape exemplars for each part required to compute the feature z_1 and multiple texture exemplars for calculating z_2 along with the layer numbers of all parts (see Figure 3). Furthermore, this provides us with an estimate of $|\mathbf{t}_i - \mathbf{t}_j|$ (after normalizing the size of all cows to 230×130), for each frame and for all pairs of parts p_i and p_j. This is used to compute the parameters $\mathbf{t}_{ij}^{min}$ and $\mathbf{t}_{ij}^{max}$ that define valid configurations.

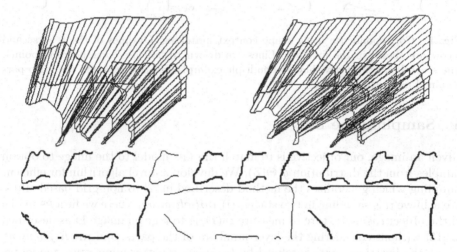

Fig. 3. Correspondence using shape context matching. Outlines of the two cows are shown in the first row. Lines are drawn to indicate corresponding points. The second and third row show the multiple exemplars of the head and the torso part obtained using this method.

To obtain the shape exemplars and texture examples for horses, we use 20 segmented images of horses[2]. A point to point correspondence is established over the outline of a cow from a training video to the outlines of the horses using shape context with continuity constraints [22]. Using this correspondence and the learnt parts of the cow, the parts of the horse are determined (see Figure 4). The part correspondence thus obtained maps the parameters $\mathbf{t}_{ij}^{min}$ and $\mathbf{t}_{ij}^{max}$ that were learnt for cows to horses. In the next section, we describe an efficient algorithm for matching the LPS model in the image.

---

[1] Courtesy Derek Magee, University of Leeds.
[2] Courtesy Eran Borenstein, Weizmann Institute of Science.

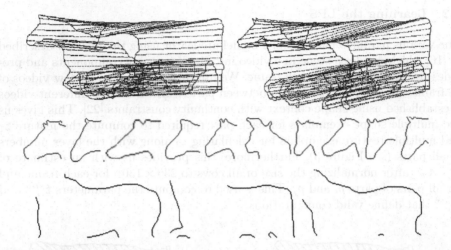

Fig. 4. Correspondence using shape context matching. Outlines of the a horse and a cow are shown in the first row. Lines are drawn to indicate corresponding points. The second and third row show the multiple exemplars of the head and the torso part obtained using this method.

5 Sampling the LPS

Given an image, our objective is to match the LPS model to the image to obtain samples from the distribution $g(\Theta|\mathbf{Z})$. We develop a novel algorithm for efficient sampling which generalizes the method described in [7] to non-grid based MRFs. We achieve this sampling in two stages: (i) *Initialization*, where we fit a PS model of the object (using texture to measure $z_2(\mathbf{D}_i)$) to a given image $\mathbf{D}$ as described in [15] without considering the layer numbers of the parts, and (ii) *Refinement*, where the initial estimate is refined by (a) using a better appearance model i.e. the RGB distribution for the object and background and (b) using the layering of the LPS parts.

5.1 Initial Estimation of Poses

We find the initial estimate of the poses of the PS for an image $\mathbf{D}$ in two stages: (i) *part detection*, or finding putative poses for each part along with the corresponding likelihoods and, (ii) *estimating posteriors* of the putative poses.

Part detection: The putative poses of the parts are found using a *tree cascade of classifiers* as described in [15]. In our experiments, we constructed a 3-level tree by clustering the templates using a cost function based on chamfer distance. We use 20 exemplars per part and search over discrete rotations between $-\pi/4$ and $\pi/4$ in intervals of 0.1 radians and scales between 0.7 and 1.3 in intervals of 0.1. The edge image of $\mathbf{D}$ is found using edge detection with embedded confidence [19]. The feature $z_1(\mathbf{D}_i)$ (truncated chamfer distance) is computed efficiently by using a distance transform of the edge image. The feature $z_2(\mathbf{D}_i)$ is computed only at level 3 of the tree cascade by efficiently determining the nearest neighbour of the histogram of texton labelling of $\mathbf{D}_i$ among the histogram of texture examples using the method described in [12] (modified for χ^2 distance instead of Euclidean distance).

Associated with each node of the cascade is a threhold used to reject bad poses. The putative poses $\mathbf{t}_i$ of parts p_i are found by traversing through the tree cascade starting from the root node. The likelihoods $p(\mathbf{D}_i|\mathbf{a}_i, \mathbf{s}_i)$ are approximated by feature likelihoods $p(\mathbf{z}_i|\mathbf{a}_i, \mathbf{s}_i)$ as shown in equation (17).

Next, an initial estimate of the model is obtained by commputing the posteriors of the putative poses. The pose of each part in the initial estimate is given by the putative pose which has the highest posterior.

Estimating posteriors: We use loopy belief propagation (LBP) to find the posterior probability of p_i having a part label $\mathbf{t}_i$. LBP is a message passing algorithm proposed by Pearl [20]. It is a Viterbi-like algorithm for graphical models with loops.

The message that p_i passes to its neighbour p_j at iteration t is a vector of length equal to the number of discrete part labels n_L of p_j and is given by:

$$m_{ij}^t(\mathbf{t}_j) \leftarrow \sum_{\mathbf{t}_i} p(\mathbf{z}_i|\mathbf{a}_i, \mathbf{s}_i) \exp(-\alpha(\mathbf{t}_i, \mathbf{t}_j)) \prod_{s\neq i, s\neq j} m_{si}^{t-1}(\mathbf{t}_i). \tag{19}$$

The beliefs (posteriors) after T iterations are calculated as:

$$b_i^T(\mathbf{t}_i) = p(\mathbf{z}_i|\mathbf{a}_i, \mathbf{s}_i) \prod_{s\neq i} m_{si}^T(\mathbf{t}_i), \tag{20}$$

and

$$b_{ij}^T(\mathbf{t}_i, \mathbf{t}_j) = p(\mathbf{z}_i|\mathbf{a}_i, \mathbf{s}_i) p(\mathbf{z}_i|\mathbf{a}_i, \mathbf{s}_i) \prod_{s\neq i, s\neq j} m_{si}^T(\mathbf{t}_i) m_{sj}^T(\mathbf{t}_j). \tag{21}$$

All messages are initialized to 1. The algorithm is said to have converged when the rate of change of all beliefs falls below a certain threshold. The time complexity of this algorithm is $O(n_P n_L^2)$ where n_P is the number of parts in the LPS and n_L is the number of putative poses per part. This makes sampling infeasible for large n_L which is the case with smaller parts of the LPS model such as the half-limbs. Thus, we develop an efficient novel algorithm for LBP for the case where the pairwise potentials are given by a Potts model as shown in equation (16). The algorithm exploits the fact that the number of pairs of part labels n_L', one for each of the two parts p_i and p_j, which form a valid configuration is much smaller than the total number of such pairs, n_L^2, i.e. $n_L' \ll n_L^2$. Note that a similar method is described in [7] which takes advantage of fast convolutions using FFT. However, it is restricted to MRFs with regularly discretized labels, i.e. the labels lie on a grid, which is not true for putative poses of parts of the LPS.

Let $\mathcal{C}_i(\mathbf{t}_j)$ be the set of part labels of p_i which form a valid pairwise configuration with $\mathbf{t}_j$. The part labels $\mathcal{C}_i(\mathbf{t}_j)$ are computed just once before running LBP.

We define

$$T(i,j) = \sum_{\mathbf{t}_i} p(\mathbf{z}_i|\mathbf{a}_i, \mathbf{s}_i) \prod_{s \neq i, s \neq j} m_{si}^{t-1}(\mathbf{t}_i), \qquad (22)$$

which is independent of the part label $\mathbf{t}_j$ of p_j and needs to be calculated only once before p_i passes a message to p_j. It is clear from equation (19) that if no part label $\mathbf{t}_i$ forms a valid configuration with $\mathbf{t}_j$, then the message $m_{ij}(\mathbf{t}_j)$ is simply $\exp(-d_2)T(i,j)$. To compute the contribution of the labels $\mathbf{t}_i \in \mathcal{C}_i(\mathbf{t}_j)$ in computing $m_{ij}(\mathbf{t}_j)$ we define

$$S(i, \mathbf{t}_j) = \sum_{\mathbf{t}_i \in \mathcal{C}_i(\mathbf{t}_j)} p(\mathbf{z}_i|\mathbf{a}_i, \mathbf{s}_i) \prod_{s \neq i, s \neq j} m_{si}^{t-1}(\mathbf{t}_i), \qquad (23)$$

which is computationally inexpensive to calculate since $\mathcal{C}_i(\mathbf{t}_j)$ consists of very few part labels. The message $m_{ij}^t(\mathbf{t}_j)$ is calculated as

$$m_{ij}^t(\mathbf{t}_j) \leftarrow \exp(-d_1)S(i, \mathbf{t}_j) + \exp(-d_2)(T(i,j) - S(i, \mathbf{t}_j)). \qquad (24)$$

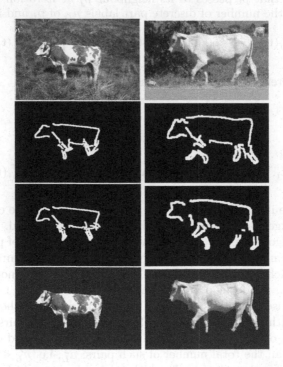

Fig. 5. Two example cow images are shown in the first row. The second row shows the initial estimate obtained for poses of parts (see § 5.1). The half-limbs tend to overlap since layer numbers are not used. Refined estimates of the poses obtained using the RGB distribution of foreground and background together with the LPS model are shown in the third row (see § 5.2). The fourth row shows the segmentation obtained using the OBJCUT algorithm (see § 6).

Our method speeds up LBP by a factor of nearly n_L. Extension to Generalized Potts model is trivial. The beliefs computed using LBP allow us to determine the MAP estimate which provides the initial estimate of the poses of the parts. Figure 5 (row 2) shows the initial estimate obtained for two cow images. The initial estimate is refined using the LPS model as described below.

5.2   Layerwise Refinement

Once the initial estimate of the parts is obtained using texture, we refine it by using the colour of the object and background together with the LPS model. The colour of the object and background are represented as histograms $\mathcal{H}_{obj}$ and $\mathcal{H}_{bkg}$ of RGB values learnt using the initial estimate. The feature $z_2(\mathbf{D}_i)$ is now redefined such that

$$p(z_2|\mathbf{a}_i) = \prod_{x \in \mathbf{D}_i} \frac{p(x|\mathcal{H}_{obj})}{p(x|\mathcal{H}_{bkg})}, \tag{25}$$

i.e. no longer using texture exemplars.

The refined estimate of the poses are obtained by compositing the parts of the LPS in descending order of their layer numbers as follows. When considering layer l_i, putative poses of the parts p_j belonging to l_i are found using the tree cascade of classifiers around the initial estimate of p_j. In our experiments, we consider locations which are at most at a distance of 15% of the size of the object as given by the initial estimate. When computing the likelihood of the part at a given pose, pixels which have already been accounted for by a previous layer are not considered. The posteriors over the putative poses is computed using the efficient LBP algorithm.

5.3   Sampling the LPS

One might argue that if the MAP estimate of the poses has a very high posterior compared to other configuration of poses, then equation (13) can be approximated using only the MAP estimate $\boldsymbol{\Theta}^*$ instead of the samples $\boldsymbol{\Theta}_1 \ldots \boldsymbol{\Theta}_s$. However, we found that this is not the case especially when the RGB distribution of the background is similar to that of the object. Figure 5 (row 3) shows the MAP estimate of the refined poses of the parts using the initial estimate shown in Figure 5 (row 2). Note that the legs of the first cow in Figure 5 (row 3) are detected incorrectly since the parts of the background have roughly the same colour as the cow. Thus, it is necessary to use multiple samples of the LPS model.

We describe the method for sampling for 2 layers. The extension to an arbitrary number of layers is trivial. To obtain a sample $\boldsymbol{\Theta}_i$, parts belonging to layer 2 are considered first. The posterior for sample $\boldsymbol{\Theta}_i$ is approximated using LBP as

$$g(\boldsymbol{\Theta}_i|\mathbf{Z}) = \frac{\prod_{ij} b_{ij}(\mathbf{t}_i, \mathbf{t}_j)}{\prod_i b_i(\mathbf{t}_i)^{q_i-1}}, \tag{26}$$

where q_i is the number of neighbouring parts of part i. Note that the posterior is exact only for a singly connected graph. However, using this approximation LBP has been shown to converge to stationary points of the Bethe free energy [24]. The posterior is then sampled for poses of parts, one part at a time (i.e. Gibbs sampling), such that the pose of the part being sampled forms a valid configuration with the poses of the parts previously sampled. The process is repeated to obtain multiple samples Θ_i which do not include the poses of parts belonging to layer 1. This method of sampling is efficient since $C_i(j)$ are pre-computed and contain very few part labels. The best n_S samples, with the highest belief, are chosen.

To obtain the poses of parts in layer 1 for sample Θ_i, we fix the poses of parts belonging to layer 2 as given by Θ_i and calculate the posterior over the poses of parts in layer 1 using LBP. We sample this posterior for poses of parts such that they form a valid configuration with the poses of the parts in layer 2 and with those previously sampled. As in the case of layer 2, multiple samples are obtained and the best n_S samples are chosen. The process is repeated for all samples Θ_i for layer 2, resulting in a total of n_S^2 samples.

However, since computing the likelihood of the parts in layer 1 for each Θ is inefficient, we approximate by using only those poses whose overlap with layer 2 is below a threshold τ. Figure 6 shows some of the samples obtained using the above method for cows shown in Figure 5. These samples are the input for the OBJCUT algorithm.

Fig. 6. Posteriors over the putative poses of parts are calculated using LBP. The posterior is then sampled to obtain instances of the object (see § 5.3) . The half-limbs are detected correctly in some samples.

6   Estimation – The OBJCUT Algorithm

Given an image **D** containing an instance of a known object category, and the samples $\Theta_1 \ldots \Theta_s$ of the LPS parameters, we wish to obtain the segmentation of the object, i.e. infer labels **m**. We now present the OBJCUT algorithm which provides reliable segmentation using both (a) modelled and (b) unmodelled deformations of articulated object categories.

Modelled deformations. These are taken into account by the LPS model which uses multiple shape exemplars for each part and allows for all valid configurations of the object category using pairwise potentials $\alpha(\mathbf{t}_i, \mathbf{t}_j)$. The various samples Θ_i localize the parts of the object in the image. They also provide us with refined estimates of the histograms $\mathcal{H}_{obj}$ and $\mathcal{H}_{bkg}$ which model the appearance of the figure and ground.

Unmodelled deformations. These are accounted for by merging pixels surrounding the object which are similar in appearance to the object. Only those pixels which lie in a 'band' surrounding the outline of the object are considered. The width of the band is 10% of the size of the object as specified by the sample of the LPS. Points lying inside the object are given preference over the points surrounding the object. As is the case with MRF-based segmentations, boundaries are preferred around image edges (using the contrast term $\phi(bfD|m_x, m_y)$).

The segmentation is obtained by minimizing equation (13) using the MINCUT algorithm. The various terms in equation (13) are defined as follows. The weights w_i are approximated as $w_i \approx g(\Theta_i|\mathbf{Z})$. The data likelihood term $\phi(\mathbf{D}|m_x)$ is computed using equation (4). The contrast term is given by equations (4) and (5). The function $\phi(m_x|\Theta_i)$ is defined by equation (7). Table 1 summarizes the main steps of obtaining the segmentation using the OBJCUT algorithm.

The figure-ground labelling $\mathbf{m}$ obtained as described above can be used iteratively to refine the segmentation using the EM algorithm. However, we found that this does not result in a significant improvement over the initial segmentations as the samples $\Theta_1 \ldots \Theta_s$ do not change much from one iteration to the other.

Table 1. The OBJCUT algorithm

---

1. Given an image $\mathbf{D}$, an object category is chosen, e.g. cows or horses.
2. Initial estimate of the pose of the pictorial structure (PS) using edges and texture:
   (a) A set of candidate poses $(t_j = (x_i, y_i, \theta_i, \sigma_j))$ for each part is identified using a tree cascade of classifiers [15].
   (b) An initial estimate of the PS is found using the efficient LBP algorithm described in §5.1.
3. Improved estimation of the pose of the layered pictorial structure (LPS) taking in to account occlusion and colour:
   (a) Update the appearance model of both foreground and background as described in §5.2.
   (b) Generate a new set of candidate poses for each part by densely sampling pose space around the estimate found in step 2 above.
   (c) Estimate the pose of the (LPS) using efficient LBP and layering as described in §5.2.
4. Obtain the samples $\Theta_1, \cdots, \Theta_S$ from the posterior $g(\Theta|\mathbf{Z})$ of the LPS (§5.3).
5. OBJCUT
   (a) Compute the weights $w_i = g(\Theta_i|\mathbf{Z})$.
   (b) Minimize the energy in equation (13) using a single MINCUT operation to obtain the segmentation $\mathbf{m}$.

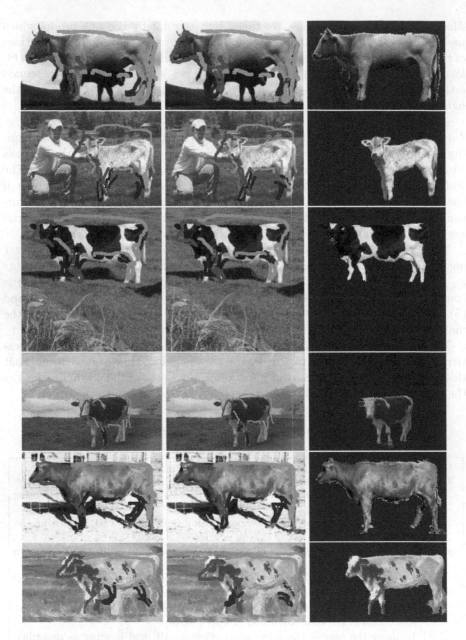

Fig. 7. Segmentation results I. The first two images in each row show some of the samples of the LPS model. The segmentation obtained using the object category specific MRF is shown in the last column. Most of the errors were caused by the tail (which was not a part of the LPS model) and parts of the background which were close and similar in colour to the object.

7 Results

We present several results of the OBJCUT algorithm for two object categories, namely cows and horses, and compare it with a state-of-the-art method and ground truth. In all our experiments, we used the same values of the parameters. Figure 5 (row 4) shows the results of the OBJCUT algorithm for two cow images. Figures 7 and 8 show the segmentation of various images of cows and horses respectively. To obtain a comparison with ground truth, all 8 cow images and 5 horse images were manually segmented. For the cow images, out of the

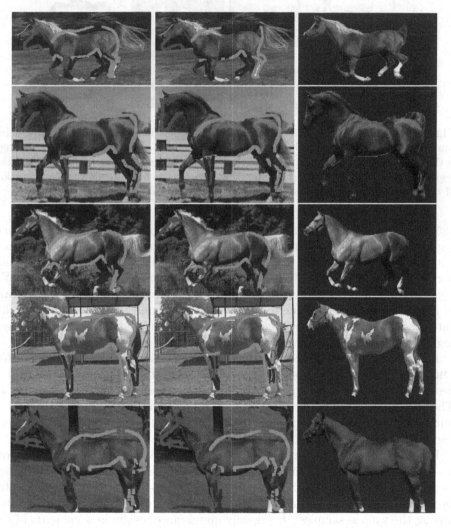

Fig. 8. Segmentation results II. The LPS model for the horse learnt using segmented horse images was used to segment previously unseen images. Most of the errors were caused by unmodelled parts i.e. the mane and the tail.

Fig. 9. Comparison with Leibe and Schiele. The first two images of each row show some of the samples obtained by matching the LPS model to the image. The third image is the segmentation obtained using the OBJCUT algorithm and the fourth image is the segmentation obtained using [17]. Note that OBJCUT provides a better segmentation of the torso and head without detecting extra half limbs.

125,362 foreground pixels and 472,670 background pixels present in the ground truth, 120,127 (95.82%) and 466,611 (98.72%) were present in the segmentations obtained. Similarly, for the horses images, out of the 79,860 foreground pixels and 151,908 background pixels present in the ground truth, 71,397 (89.39%) and 151,185 (99.52%) were present in the segmentations obtained. In the case of horses, most errors are due to unmodelled mane and tail parts. Results indicate that, by considering both modelled and unmodelled deformations, excellent segmentations are obtained by OBJCUT.

Figure 9 shows a comparison of the segmentation results obtained when using OBJCUT with a state-of-the-art method for object category specific segmentation described in Leibe and Schiele [17]. A similar approach was described in [4]. The OBJCUT algorithm provides better segmentations using significantly smaller number of exemplars by exploiting the ability of MINCUT for providing excellent segmentations using a good initialization obtained by LPS.

Figure 10 shows the effects of using only the shape or only appearance information by discarding the other completely. Shape alone undersegments the image as different samples assign different poses to the half-limbs. Thus, the segmentation mainly includes the head and the torso (which do not change considerably among the various samples). Using only appearance results in some parts of the background, which have a similar colour to the object, being pulled into the segmentation. Results indicate that good segmentations depend on combining both shape and appearance, as is the case with the OBJCUT algorithm.

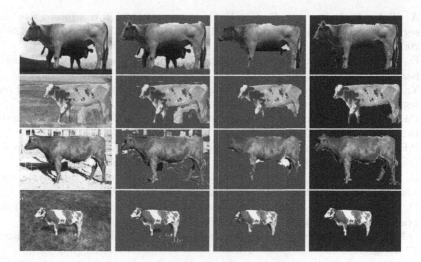

Fig. 10. Effects of shape and appearance information. The first column shows an image containing a cow. The segmentation results obtained by using only the RGB histograms for the object and the background provided by the LPS model are shown in the second column. The results obtained by using only the shape prior provided by the LPS model is shown in the third column. The fourth column shows the segmentations we get using the OBJCUT algorithm. Results indicate that good segmentation is obtained only when both shape and appearance information are used.

8   Summary and Conclusions

We presented a new model, called the object category specific MRF, which combines the LPS and the MRF model to perform object category specific segmentation. The method needs to be extended to handle multiple visual aspects of an object category and to deal with partial occlusion by other objects.

Acknowledgments

We thank Dan Huttenlocher for fruitful discussions on efficient LBP. This work was supported in part by the IST Programme of the European Community, under the PASCAL Network of Excellence, IST-2002-506778. This publication only reflects the authors' views.

References

1. A. Agarwal and B. Triggs. Tracking articulated motion using a mixture of autoregressive models. In *ECCV*, pages III:54–65, 2004.
2. S. Agarwal and D. Roth. Learning a sparse representation for object detection. In *ECCV*, page IV: 113 ff., 2002.

3. A. Blake, C. Rother, M. Brown, P. Perez, and P.H.S. Torr. Interactive image segmentation using an adaptive GMMRF model. In *ECCV*, pages Vol I: 428–441, 2004.
4. E. Borenstein and S. Ullman. Class-specific, top-down segmentation. In *ECCV*, page II: 109 ff., 2002.
5. Y. Boykov and M.P. Jolly. Interactive graph cuts for optimal boundary and region segmentation of objects in N-D images. In *ICCV*, pages I: 105–112, 2001.
6. P.F. Felzenszwalb and D.P. Huttenlocher. Efficient matching of pictorial structures. In *CVPR*, pages II: 66–73, 2000.
7. P.F. Felzenszwalb and D.P. Huttenlocher. Fast algorithms for large state space HMMs with applications to web usage analysis. In *NIPS*, 2003.
8. R. Fergus, P. Perona, and A. Zisserman. Object class recognition by unsupervised scale-invariant learning. In *CVPR*, pages II: 264–271, 2003.
9. D. Freedman and T. Zhang. Interactive graph cut based segmentation with shape priors. In *CVPR*, pages I: 755–762, 2005.
10. D.M. Gavrilla. Pedestrian detection from a moving vehicle. In *ECCV*, pages II: 37–49, 2000.
11. A. Gelman, J. Carlin, H. Stern, and D. Rubin. *Bayesian Data Analysis*. Chapman and Hall, 1995.
12. J. Goldstein, J. Platt, and C. Burges. Indexing high-dimensional rectangles for fast multimedia identification. Technical Report MSR-TR-2003-38, Microsoft Research, 2003.
13. R. Huang, V. Pavlovic, and D.N. Metaxas. A graphical model framework for coupling MRFs and deformable models. In *CVPR*, pages II: 739–746, 2004.
14. V. Kolmogorov and R. Zabih. What energy functions can be minimized via graph cuts. *IEEE PAMI*, 26(2):147–159, 2004.
15. M. P. Kumar, P. H. S. Torr, and A. Zisserman. Extending pictorial structures for object recognition. In *BMVC*, pages II: 789–798, 2004.
16. M. P. Kumar, P. H. S. Torr, and A. Zisserman. Learning layered pictorial structures from video. In *ICVGIP*, pages 148–153, 2004.
17. B. Leibe and B. Schiele. Interleaved object categorization and segmentation. In *BMVC*, pages II: 264–271, 2003.
18. T. Leung and J. Malik. Recognizing surfaces using three-dimensional textons. In *ICCV*, pages 1010–1017, 1999.
19. P. Meer and B. Georgescu. Edge detection with embedded confidence. *PAMI*, 23:1351–1365, December 2001.
20. J. Pearl. *Probabilistic Reasoning in Intelligent Systems: Networks of Plausible Inference*. Morgan Kauffman, 1998.
21. C. Rother, V. Kolmogorov, and A. Blake. Grabcut: interactive foreground extraction using iterated graph cuts. In *SIGGRAPH*, pages 309–314, 2004.
22. A. Thayananthan, B. Stenger, P.H.S. Torr, and R. Cipolla. Shape context and chamfer matching in cluttered scenes. In *CVPR*, pages I: 127–133, 2003.
23. M. Varma and A. Zisserman. Texture classification: Are filter banks necessary? In *CVPR*, pages II:691–698, 2003.
24. J. Yedidia, W. Freeman, and Y. Weiss. Bethe free energy, Kikuchi approximations, and belief propagation algorithms. Technical Report TR2001-16, MERL, 2001.

Author Index

Vol. 4287: C. Mao, T. Yokomori (Eds.), DNA Computing. XII, 440 pages. 2006.

Vol. 4286: P. Spirakis, M. Mavronicolas, S. Kontogiannis (Eds.), Internet and Network Economics. XI, 401 pages. 2006.

Vol. 4285: Y. Matsumoto, R. Sproat, K.-F. Wong, M. Zhang (Eds.), Computer Processing of Oriental Languages. XVII, 544 pages. 2006. (Sublibrary LNAI).

Vol. 4284: X. Lai, K. Chen (Eds.), Advances in Cryptology – ASIACRYPT 2006. XIV, 468 pages. 2006.

Vol. 4283: Y.Q. Shi, B. Jeon (Eds.), Digital Watermarking. XII, 474 pages. 2006.

Vol. 4282: Z. Pan, A.D. Cheok, M. Haller, R.W.H. Lau, H. Saito, R. Liang (Eds.), Advances in Artificial Reality and Tele-Existence. XXIII, 1347 pages. 2006.

Vol. 4281: K. Barkaoui, A. Cavalcanti, A. Cerone (Eds.), Theoretical Aspects of Computing - ICTAC 2006. XV, 371 pages. 2006.

Vol. 4280: A.K. Datta, M. Gradinariu (Eds.), Stabilization, Safety, and Security of Distributed Systems. XVII, 590 pages. 2006.

Vol. 4279: N. Kobayashi (Ed.), Programming Languages and Systems. XI, 423 pages. 2006.

Vol. 4278: R. Meersman, Z. Tari, P. Herrero (Eds.), On the Move to Meaningful Internet Systems 2006: OTM 2006 Workshops, Part II. XLV, 1004 pages. 2006.

Vol. 4277: R. Meersman, Z. Tari, P. Herrero (Eds.), On the Move to Meaningful Internet Systems 2006: OTM 2006 Workshops, Part I. XLV, 1009 pages. 2006.

Vol. 4276: R. Meersman, Z. Tari (Eds.), On the Move to Meaningful Internet Systems 2006: CoopIS, DOA, GADA, and ODBASE, Part II. XXXII, 752 pages. 2006.

Vol. 4275: R. Meersman, Z. Tari (Eds.), On the Move to Meaningful Internet Systems 2006: CoopIS, DOA, GADA, and ODBASE, Part I. XXXI, 1115 pages. 2006.

Vol. 4274: Q. Huo, B. Ma, E.-S. Chng, H. Li (Eds.), Chinese Spoken Language Processing. XXIV, 805 pages. 2006. (Sublibrary LNAI).

Vol. 4273: I. Cruz, S. Decker, D. Allemang, C. Preist, D. Schwabe, P. Mika, M. Uschold, L. Aroyo (Eds.), The Semantic Web - ISWC 2006. XXIV, 1001 pages. 2006.

Vol. 4272: P. Havinga, M. Lijding, N. Meratnia, M. Wegdam (Eds.), Smart Sensing and Context. XI, 267 pages. 2006.

Vol. 4271: F.V. Fomin (Ed.), Graph-Theoretic Concepts in Computer Science. XIII, 358 pages. 2006.

Vol. 4270: H. Zha, Z. Pan, H. Thwaites, A.C. Addison, M. Forte (Eds.), Interactive Technologies and Sociotechnical Systems. XVI, 547 pages. 2006.

Vol. 4269: R. State, S. van der Meer, D. O'Sullivan, T. Pfeifer (Eds.), Large Scale Management of Distributed Systems. XIII, 282 pages. 2006.

Vol. 4268: G. Parr, D. Malone, M. Ó Foghlú (Eds.), Autonomic Principles of IP Operations and Management. XIII, 237 pages. 2006.

Vol. 4267: A. Helmy, B. Jennings, L. Murphy, T. Pfeifer (Eds.), Autonomic Management of Mobile Multimedia Services. XIII, 257 pages. 2006.

Vol. 4266: H. Yoshiura, K. Sakurai, K. Rannenberg, Y. Murayama, S. Kawamura (Eds.), Advances in Information and Computer Security. XIII, 438 pages. 2006.

Vol. 4265: L. Todorovski, N. Lavrač, K.P. Jantke (Eds.), Discovery Science. XIV, 384 pages. 2006. (Sublibrary LNAI).

Vol. 4264: J.L. Balcázar, P.M. Long, F. Stephan (Eds.), Algorithmic Learning Theory. XIII, 393 pages. 2006. (Sublibrary LNAI).

Vol. 4263: A. Levi, E. Savaş, H. Yenigün, S. Balcısoy, Y. Saygın (Eds.), Computer and Information Sciences – ISCIS 2006. XXIII, 1084 pages. 2006.

Vol. 4262: K. Havelund, M. Núñez, G. Roşu, B. Wolff (Eds.), Formal Approaches to Software Testing and Runtime Verification. VIII, 255 pages. 2006.

Vol. 4261: Y. Zhuang, S. Yang, Y. Rui, Q. He (Eds.), Advances in Multimedia Information Processing - PCM 2006. XXII, 1040 pages. 2006.

Vol. 4260: Z. Liu, J. He (Eds.), Formal Methods and Software Engineering. XII, 778 pages. 2006.

Vol. 4259: S. Greco, Y. Hata, S. Hirano, M. Inuiguchi, S. Miyamoto, H.S. Nguyen, R. Słowiński (Eds.), Rough Sets and Current Trends in Computing. XXII, 951 pages. 2006. (Sublibrary LNAI).

Vol. 4257: I. Richardson, P. Runeson, R. Messnarz (Eds.), Software Process Improvement. XI, 219 pages. 2006.

Vol. 4256: L. Feng, G. Wang, C. Zeng, R. Huang (Eds.), Web Information Systems – WISE 2006 Workshops. XIV, 320 pages. 2006.

Vol. 4255: K. Aberer, Z. Peng, E.A. Rundensteiner, Y. Zhang, X. Li (Eds.), Web Information Systems – WISE 2006. XIV, 563 pages. 2006.

Vol. 4254: T. Grust, H. Höpfner, A. Illarramendi, S. Jablonski, M. Mesiti, S. Müller, P.-L. Patranjan, K.-U. Sattler, M. Spiliopoulou, J. Wijsen (Eds.), Current Trends in Database Technology – EDBT 2006. XXXI, 932 pages. 2006.

Vol. 4253: B. Gabrys, R.J. Howlett, L.C. Jain (Eds.), Knowledge-Based Intelligent Information and Engineering Systems, Part III. XXXII, 1301 pages. 2006. (Sublibrary LNAI).

Vol. 4252: B. Gabrys, R.J. Howlett, L.C. Jain (Eds.), Knowledge-Based Intelligent Information and Engineering Systems, Part II. XXXIII, 1335 pages. 2006. (Sublibrary LNAI).

Vol. 4251: B. Gabrys, R.J. Howlett, L.C. Jain (Eds.), Knowledge-Based Intelligent Information and Engineering Systems, Part I. LXVI, 1297 pages. 2006. (Sublibrary LNAI).

Vol. 4250: H.J. van den Herik, S.-C. Hsu, T.-s. Hsu, H.H.L.M. Donkers (Eds.), Advances in Computer Games. XIV, 273 pages. 2006.

Vol. 4249: L. Goubin, M. Matsui (Eds.), Cryptographic Hardware and Embedded Systems - CHES 2006. XII, 462 pages. 2006.

Vol. 4248: S. Staab, V. Svátek (Eds.), Managing Knowledge in a World of Networks. XIV, 400 pages. 2006. (Sublibrary LNAI).

Lecture Notes in Computer Science

For information about Vols. 1–4247

please contact your bookseller or Springer